VA Research, 1925 – 1980

Toward better medical care for those who have borne the battle

Marguerite T. Hays, M.D.

With chapters by :
Timothy Takaro, M.D., John Farrar, M.D.
Richard Wedeen, M.D. and Thomas Benedek, M.D.

AuthorHouse™
1663 Liberty Drive
Bloomington, IN 47403
www.authorhouse.com
Phone: 1-800-839-8640

First published by AuthorHouse 4/29/2010

ISBN: 978-1-4490-6726-7 (e)
ISBN: 978-1-4490-6725-0 (sc)

Printed in the United States of America
Bloomington, Indiana

This book is printed on acid-free paper.

Table of Contents												i

Appendices (available on request: ritahays19@yahoo.com)

Preface

In 1988, I was having lunch with Ralph Peterson, M.D., a prominent endocrinologist who was then the Director of the VA's Medical Research Service, a position I had held during the 1970s. As I told him about events from before he joined the VA, he was struck how little information had been written about earlier times in the VA research program. A few days later, he called to ask me to give a talk on the history of the VA research program.

Challenged by this opportunity, I began to interview some of the earlier participants in the program and found their stories fascinating. I explored the VA Central Office library in Washington, DC and discovered another side to the dark memories of the early Veterans' Bureau, evidence that the early veterans' doctors strived for excellence and looked for ways to improve their care of sick veterans.

As opportunities arose, I interviewed people associated with the VA research program. I collected the materials they gave me, some of it lovingly stored in their garages for years. Many in the VA, in Central Office and in the medical centers, participated in this effort — there is no way I can thank them individually here, but I am grateful to each of them.

This work continued to be encouraged and supported by those who came after Ralph Peterson in leading the VA research program. In particular, I should mention Martin Albert, M.D., Ph.D., who, as Director, Medical Research Service, 1992-1996, was especially helpful. John Feussner, M.D., Chief Research and Development Officer, 1996-2002, supported this effort with his usual enthusiasm. He contracted with me to bring the work to fruition after I retired from my VA clinical position. Philip Lavori, Ph.D., Chief of the Palo Alto VA Cooperative Studies Program Coordinating Center, provided space and facilities for the project and has been of great personal support.

The actual writing and much of the research for the book began during a VA sabbatical spent at the Johns Hopkins Medical School's Welsh library. Members of the library staff were most helpful and supportive. I thank them and especially their Director, Gert Brieger, for their hospitality and kindness.

Anne Knight, Barbara Klein and Robert Putnam, editors, have improved the quality of the text in many ways, and Dorothy Shoemaker has provided important bibliographic assistance. Many colleagues were kind enough to review individual chapters. Joel Braslow, M.D., Ph.D., made important contributions to the chapter describing VA psychopharmacology trials. I owe particular thanks to the late Clark Sawin, M.D., for a careful and helpful review of the entire manuscript. Of course, the responsibility for the final product rests with me.

Marguerite T. Hays, M.D.
Palo Alto, CA

Introduction

Tracing the path of progress in VA medical research does not involve drawing a straight line. It requires, rather, sketching a jagged streak forward—the many high points marked by significant findings and the development of medical advances, the few downticks indicating an occasional disappointment—the trend always upward toward promise and hope for improved health care and a better quality of life.

The focus of this history is the innovation produced in this remarkable program; to cite just a few examples:

- The first decisive trials of effective treatments for tuberculosis;
- Demonstration of the lifesaving value of treating hypertension;
- Development of the concept of CT scanning;
- Discovery and development of radioimmunoassay, facilitating measurements of previously impossible precision;
- Cooperative studies proving the efficacy of psychoactive drugs in stabilizing psychiatric disorders;
- Demonstration of the relationship between smoking and lung cancer, leading to initial warnings in the Report of the Surgeon General; and
- Development of a practical, implantable cardiac pacemaker.

Although this research program produced more than enough accomplishments to completely occupy its text, this history also attempts to depict the pioneers who carved that path of progress. In large measure, the history of VA medical research is their story.

In several instances, personal comments are included from the men and women—investigators, managers and administrators—who brought VA research alive. Some of their accounts are truly fascinating, sounding more like adventure stories than what might appear in scientific journals. For example, Ludwig Gross, M.D., a war refugee who escaped Poland just ahead of the Nazis, came to America and became a U.S. Army doctor. Even while in the Army, he carried out research, keeping his special mice in cages in the trunk of his car. In 1944, the Army assigned him to the clinical staff of the Bronx (NY) VA Hospital, and he remained there for a long productive career. At first, he did his research in an old bathroom after hours, breeding his own mice for his experiments. His work led to the proof of the viral cause of mammalian leukemia.

And, when Dr. William Oldendorf was working as a VA neurologist at the Los Angeles VA Hospital, he was looking for a way to avoid suffering by his patients who needed brain imaging, rather than doing painful pneumoencephalography. He reasoned that composite pictures of the brain area from x-ray images taken at many angles would serve the purpose. Using simple equipment—including an old model-railroad track—he personally built the prototype for CT scanning—which has since benefited millions of patients worldwide.

Some few of these researchers achieved a degree of celebrity, gaining eminence in their field, and perhaps even becoming perceived in the general medical community as having extraordinary genius and exceptional vision. There are many more stories of researchers whose careers reflect little of celebrity, but much of imagination, competence, and intense excitement about their work.

The personal stories reveal another important characteristic of these investigators: the patience with which they approached the mundane tasks along the way to achieving results. Records clearly indicate that "payoffs" in scientific knowledge often emerged only after extensive, long-term follow-through study. The keys to success were determination to proceed, to persist, to prevail. As one VA research leader said, "there were more 'wear-throughs' than breakthroughs."

A word about the scope of this book is in order: The recording of history is a never-ending process, but preparation for publication must have an organized, terminal point. In covering the more distant history of VA medical research—extending back to the era of the Veterans' Bureau in the late 1920s—through the year 1980, it was the intention of this work to record and, in some sense, safeguard that period of history most at risk of being lost to posterity.

Unlike this text, VA research did not conclude in 1980. Together with Health Services Research and Development, and Rehabilitation Research and Development, the VA Medical Research Service continued to evolve and to engage in vitally important studies. Investigation of primary clinical issues continued, and new special studies were launched in areas of special interest to the veteran patient, such as post-traumatic stress disorder, "The Gulf War Syndrome," prostate cancer and AIDS. Between records developed since 1980, the personal knowledge of the current VA staff, and the recollections of those who have departed in recent years, the story of this continued history exists in rich detail. It can only be hoped that this next chapter of the story of VA research will be recorded and told.

That, however, is a matter for future exploration. For now, the story of the beginnings of VA medical research, and its truly remarkable accomplishments over the span of its first half-century, should be adventure enough.

Commonly used acronyms

The organization responsible for veterans' health care
VA (1930-1989)   Veterans Administration
DVA, also VA (1989 to present)   Department of Veterans Affairs
VACO   VA Central Office

The Office in VACO specifically responsible for the veterans' medical care program
DM&S (1946-1989)   Department of Medicine and Surgery
VHA (1989 to present)   Veterans' Health Administration

Head of the VACO office responsible for veterans' medical care
CMD (1946-1989)   Chief Medical Director
USH (1989 to present)   Undersecretary for Health

Head of the VACO office overseeing the VA research program
ACMD/R&E (1945 to 1972)   Assistant Chief Medical Director for Research and
Education
ACMD/R&D (1972 to 1989)   Assistant Chief Medical Director for Research and
Development
AsCMD/R&D (1989 to 1996)   Associate Chief Medical Director for Research and
Development
CRADO (1996 to present)   Chief Research and Development Officer

Person at a VA medical facility responsible for the research program
ADPSR (1947 to1961)   Assistant Director of Professional Services for
Research
ACOS/R&E (1961 to1972)   Associate Chief of Staff for Research and
Education
ACOS/R&D (1972 to present)   Associate Chief of Staff for Research and
Development

Services within Research and Development in VACO (after 1972)
MRS   Medical Research Service
HSR&D   Health Services Research and Development
Service
RER&D, later RR&D   Rehabilitation (Engineering) Res. and Dev. Service

Advisory and review groups
Local:
R&E Committee (1948 to 1972)   Research and Education Committee
R&D Committee (1972 to present)   Research and Development Committee

Central
CVMP   Committee on Veterans' Medical Problems
                                   (NAS/NRC)

RAC	Research Advisory Committee
RRAG, later RAG	(Regional) Research Advisory Group
CSEC	Cooperative Studies Evaluation Committee
MRB	Merit Review Board

Other VA acronyms

R&D	Research and Development
CRIP	Central Research Instrumentation Pool
CSP	Cooperative Studies Program
CSPCC	Cooperative Studies Program Coordinating Center
CNPRL	Central Neuropsychiatry Research Laboratory

Other Washington area groups influencing the VA research program

CMR	Committee on Medical Research (WWII)
NAS	National Academy of Sciences
NRC	National Research Council of the NAS
OMB	Office of Management and Budget
NIH	National Institutes of Health
NCI	National Cancer Institute

Not abbreviated: Veterans' Bureau (1922-1930), Medical Service (1922-1946), Medical Director (1922-1946), Chief, Research Subdivision (1925-1938), Chief, Postdoctoral Training and Research Division (1938-1945).

Persons interviewed

William Adams, M.D.
Ernest Allen, Ph.D.
Herbert Allen, M.D.
Hal O. Anger
Joan Armer, R.N.
Oscar Auerbach, M.D.
Clifford Bachrach, M.D.
John Bailar, M.D.
Maureen S. Baltay
Marion Barry
Claude Baxter, Ph.D.
Chester Bazel, R.Ph.
Gilbert Beebe, Ph.D.
Howard Berman
Leon Bernstein, M.D.
Lionel Bernstein, M.D.
William Best, M.D.
Robert Birch, M.D.
William Blahd, M.D.
Dorothy Bluestein
Hollis Boren, M.D.
Linda Boxer, M.D., Ph.D.
Marion Brault
Norman Q. Brill, M.D.
Ernest Burgess, M.D.
Belton Burrows, M.D.
Allen B. Cady, M.D.
Eugene Caffey, M.D.
Arthur Cain, M.D.
Chu Carr
Jules Cass, D.V.M.
Ralph Casteel
Thomas Chalmers, M.D.
Sonny Chang, Ph.D.
John D. Chase, M.D.
Robert A. Chase, M.D.
Howard H. Chauncey, Ph.D., D.M.D.
Lawrence G. Christianson, M.D.
Sidney E. Cleveland, Ph.D.
Betty Cobbs
Marvin Cohen, M.D.
David Cohn, Ph.D.
Frank Coombs
John A.D. Cooper, M.D.
Gregory Crowe
Lawrence Crowley, M.D.
Martin Cummings, M.D.
David N. Daniels, M.D.
Carolyn Davidson
Kenneth Davis, M.D.
Michael DeBakey, M.D.

Chester DeLong, Ph.D.
Walter Dempsey, Ph.D.
Gerald DeNardo, M.D.
Paul Densen, Ph.D.
Nicholas D'Esopo, M.D.
Vincent DeVita, M.D.
Daniel Deykin, M.D.
Harold (Jack) Divers
Abraham Dury, Ph.D.
Richard V. Ebert, M.D.
E.E. Eddleman, M.D.
Robert Efron, M.D.
Roger Egeberg, M.D.
Seymour Eisenberg, M.D.
Frederick Eldridge, M.D.
James Elliott, M.D.
Robert Ellsworth, Ph.D.
Lawrence Eng, Ph.D.
H. Martin Engel, M.D.
Carleton Evans, M.D.
George Fairweather, Ph.D.
Robert Farese, M.D.
Lori Fertel
William Figueroa, M.D.
Richard Filer, Ph.D.
James Finklestein, M.D.
Robert Fitzgerald, Ph.D.
Robert Fleming
Lysia Forno, M.D.
Irene Forrest, Ph.D.
William H. Forrest, M.D.
Laurence Foye, M.D.
James Fozard, Ph.D.
Earl Freed, Ph.D.
Edward Freis, M.D.
Andrew Gage, M.D.
Al Gavazzi
Samuel Gershon, M.D.
Bruno Gerstl, M.D.
Margaret Giannini, M.D.
Gerald Goldstein, Ph.D.
Richard Goode, M.D.
Harold Goodglass, Ph.D.
Clo Gooding
Gregory Goodrich, Ph.D.
David Goodwin, M.D.
Earl Gordon, M.D.
Abraham Gottlieb, M.D.
Mark Graeber, M.D.
Howard W. Green, M.D.
Richard Greene, M.D., Ph.D.

Ludwig Gross, M.D.
George Gulevich, M.D.
Lee Gurel, Ph.D.
Paul Haber, M.D.
Francis Haddy, M.D., Ph.D.
James Hagans, M.D., Ph.D.
Charles Hall, M.D.
Charles H. Halsted, M.D., son of James Halsted, M.D.
Paul Heller, M.D.
Victor Herbert, M.D.
George Higgins, M.D.
Richardson Hill, M.D.
Gladys L. Hobby, Ph.D.
Esther Hodges
William Hofman, M.D.
Leo Hollister, M.D.
David S. Howell, M.D.
Herbert N. Hultgren, M.D.
Seymour Jablon
Henry Jones, M.D.
Samuel C. Kaim, M.D.
Martin S. Kalser, M.D., Ph.D.
Eugene Kanabrocki, Ph.D.
Ervin Kaplan, M.D.
Abba Kastin, M.D.
Laurence H. Kedes, M.D.
Paul Kennedy
Robert Kevan
C. James Klett, Ph.D.
Leonard Knott
Shoichi Kohatsu, M.D.
Bert Kopell, M.D.
Ross Kory, M.D.
Jon C. Kosek, M.D.
Leonard Krasner, Ph.D.
Jeannette Landis
Milton Landowne, M.D.
Alfred Lawton, M.D.
Lyndon Lee, M.D.
Larry Leifer, Ph.D.
Gerald Libman
Charles Lieber, M.D.
Clyde J. Lindley
Armand Littman, M.D.
Richard Lolley, Ph.D.
Leon Lombroso, Ph.D.
Theodore Lorei, M.S.W.
Maurice Lorr, Ph.D.
Sanford Mabel, Ph.D.
Roy Maffley, M.D.
Joseph Mason
Jack Matoole, M.D.
James H. Matthews, M.D.
Richard Mazze, M.D.
Willa McBride
Donna McCartney

Burley McCraw
Dennis McGinty, Ph.D.
Paul W. McReynolds, Ph.D.
Jeffrey Meade, M.D., son of Robert Meade, M.D.
Shirley Meehan, Ph.D., M.B.A.
Sherman Mellinkoff, M.D.
Thomas Merigan, M.D.
Joe Meyer, Ph.D.
Ralph Meyerson, M.D.
James Grier Miller, M.D., Ph.D.
Anne Moore
Rudolph Moos, Ph.D.
James Moses, Ph.D.
Eugene F. Murphy, Ph.D.
Wendell Musser, M.D.
Boyce Nall
Thomas Newcomb, M.D.
Vernon Nickel, M.D.
John C. Nunemaker, M.D.
Charles P. O'Brien, M.D., Ph.D.
William H. Oldendorf, M.D.
John Overall, Ph.D.
William Page, Ph.D.
William Pare, Ph.D.
Cecil Peck, Ph.D.
Inder Perkash, M.D.
John Peters
Jon Peters, P.T.
Adolph Pfefferbaum, M.D.
Lajos Piko, Ph.D.
James A. Pittman, M.D.
Robert Prien, Ph.D.
John Prusmak, M.D.
Jose Rabinowitz, Ph.D.
Malcolm J. Randall
Gerald Reaven, M.D.
Paul Rogers, Esq.
Charles A. Rosenberg, M.D.
Joseph Ross, M.D.
Bernard Roswit, M.D.
Dennis Roth
Walton Thomas Roth, M.D.
Marcus Rothschild, M.D.
Robert Rynearson
Mohinder Sambhi, M.D.
Andrew Schally, Ph.D.
Harold Schnaper, M.D.
Robert Schneiter
Harold Schoolman, M.D.
Robert Schrek, M.D.
Ruth Schrek
Leonard Seeff, M.D., Ch.B.
Robert Shamaskin
Lawrence Shaw
Austin Shug, Ph.D.
Jay Shurley, M.D.

David G. Simons, M.D.
Orin T. Skouge, M.D.
James J. Smith, M.D.
Marion Smith, Ph.D.
David H. Solomon, M.D.
George F. Solomon, M.D.
Harold Sox, M.D.
Herta Spencer, M.D.
Jerry Spenney, M.D.
Leonard Spolter, Ph.D.
Norton Spritz, M.D.
Paul Srere, Ph.D.
Barry Sterman, Ph.D.
Robert E. Stewart, D.D.S.
Richard Streiff, M.D.
Leon Swell, Ph.D.
Robert Swenson, M.D.
Keith Taylor, M.D.
David D. Thomas
William C. Thomas, M.D.
Samuel Threefoot, M.D.
Jereld R. Tinklenberg, M.D.
Leonard Ullman, Ph.D.
Roger H. Unger, M.D.
Kosaku Uyeda, Ph.D.
William Valentine, M.D.
Hugh Vickerstaff
Harry E. Walkup, M.D.
John Weakland
James Wear, Ph.D.
Fred Weibell, Ph.D.
Louis Jolyon West, M.D.
Walter Whicomb, M.D.
Darlene Whorley
Clyde Williams, M.D., Ph.D.
John Willoughby
Marjorie T. Wilson, M.D.
Mark Walcott, M.D.
Julius Wolf, M.D.
Stewart G. Wolf, M.D.
Rosalyn S. Yalow, Ph.D.
Jerome Yesavage, M.D.
Larry Yuen
Vincent P. Zarcone, M.D.
Leslie Zieve, M.D.
Hyman Zimmerman, M.D.
Eugene Zukowsky, Ph.D.

Part 1. Ancestral roots 1925-1945

Chapter 1. Origins of the VA Research Program, 1917 - 1925

America's tradition of providing medical care to the nation's servicemembers and veterans is a well-documented subject, with origins reaching back to Colonial times. The Federal government has frequently modified and clarified its role during the course of over two centuries of our democracy, acting through legislation and executive orders to form the institutions and programs that identified the recipients and established the mechanisms to provide medical service. History also records the gradual distinction that exists today between systems of care for active-duty personnel and those whose service is completed— our veterans.

While the evolution of Federal programs for the delivery of post-service care to veterans is well charted, the point at which medical research became an important consideration is less defined. No direct act of the legislative or executive branches of government dictated that veterans health care could be enhanced with a research component. The association of research and clinical care grew mainly from the wisdom and foresight of medical practitioners themselves. Records from the earliest meetings of advisors and consultants charged with addressing large-scale medical needs among veterans after World War I reveal gathering convictions that research could and should be integrated into veterans' health care. Beyond the positive benefit of relating that research to the unique medical circumstances of veterans, the move was seen as key to reinforcing an evolving system of care. Many of these advisors felt that making the system attractive to physicians with research interests and cultivating relationships with medical education institutions would ensure the highest quality of care to veterans.

In the era well before 1946 when the Veterans Administration (VA) established formal partnerships with medical schools, the Veterans' Bureau and its successor, the Veterans Administration, sponsored a modest program of intramural research by its own clinical staff. This early VA research program almost completely disappeared during the Second World War. After World War II, a rejuvenated VA medical care system emerged as a result of postwar reforms that included affiliation of VA hospitals with medical schools. Relatively few links between the research program of the 1920s and 1930s and the later emergence of medical research in the VA after World War II survived the enormous societal upheavals that affected not only VA but medicine in general. Nonetheless, these early efforts did provide a valuable and noteworthy prologue for what would come later.

The foremost goals of early Veterans' Bureau advisors forming an intramural agency research program was to "mine" rich clinical data to gain knowledge through follow-up studies and population statistics of a large system with many patients of similar backgrounds. The administrators were especially interested in problems caused directly by wartime service, such as long-term effects of poison gasses encountered on the battlefield. And clinicians in the veterans' hospitals were deeply concerned about helping these patients by studying their most prevalent medical problems regardless of whether they were the direct result of military service.

The early research program of the veterans' hospital system emerged from the combined influence of a reform-minded lay bureau Director, a chief medical officer considered to be ambitious and politically knowledgeable, an influential group of advisors with strong bonds to academia, and a cadre of medical officers in the veterans' hospitals who used the means at their disposal to seek better ways to treat their patients. They are at the heart of events that identified the need for reform, the efforts made by and the influence of academically oriented advisors in shaping that reform.

Beginnings of systematic health care for disabled veterans

In 1917 and 1918, upon America's entry into World War I, no hospitals for veterans existed, but over five million men were in military service.[1] By the end of 1925, 51 hospitals for veterans had been established and some 30,000 veterans were hospitalized at government expense.[2] The Congress that had provided benefits for war veterans did not appear inclined to create a separate veterans' hospital system, much less to launch a program of medical research. Indeed, although some veterans had been treated under government auspices in the past, the very concept that the Federal Government should handle the medical needs of *all* war-disabled veterans was a one new in 1917.[3]

In 1923, a committee of consultants appointed by the Secretary of the Treasury described the 1917 provision for hospitalization of World War veterans as "a task which had never been attempted by any government prior to that time, and there had been no experience in all history which could serve as a guide."[4] While the United States had long provided pensions for its disabled war veterans, until after World War I there were no systematic arrangements for their later medical care. Sick merchant seamen had been cared for in Marine Hospitals since 1799.[5] A few thousand indigent Civil War and Spanish-American War veterans lived in national or state-supported domiciliaries or Soldiers' Homes.[3] Otherwise, before 1917, disabled veterans did not receive medical care from their government. Those injured or ill from military service received monetary compensation in the form of pensions. Their families, aided by the medical and hospital systems available to all citizens, were expected to meet their needs for medical care and rehabilitation.

The pension system for Civil War veterans had been very costly and was subject to intense and continuing political pressures.[6] In 1917, Secretary of the Treasury William McAdoo, President Wilson's son-in-law,[7] appointed a Council on National Defense, which had a subcommittee charged with drafting a plan to meet the needs of the men about to go to war. Judge Julian W. Mack, a distinguished jurist and advocate for the disadvantaged, chaired this subcommittee. Other members included Dr. Leo S. Rowe, Assistant Secretary of the Treasury; Captain H.S. Wolfe, a prominent accountant and actuary; Julia C. Lathrop, of the Children's Bureau; V. Everit Macy, president of the National Civic Federation; Professors Henry R. Seager and Thomas Parkinson of Columbia University; and the staff of the Legislative Drafting Research Fund of Columbia University.

Under Judge Mack's leadership, this group recommended a radically new concept of government responsibility and sent a draft for review to interested persons, including President Wilson and former President Theodore Roosevelt, who both enthusiastically endorsed it.[8] The concept entailed government aid to former soldiers and sailors based on their needs and the impact of military service on their lives. Unlike the Civil War pensions, this aid was not seen to be a dole provided simply because of military service. This plan was introduced as a Treasury Department bill and passed into law October 6, 1917. Although the new law completely omitted pensions for World War veterans and their families, it provided for:

1. Allotments to dependents while their breadwinner was on military duty, paid partly from pay deductions.

2. A voluntary death and disability insurance program, with premiums set at peacetime rates, funded by pay deductions. These two deductions often took up most of the soldier's pay, and could leave him less than $10 a month.[9]

3. Compensation for injuries sustained while on active service and compensation to the families of those who died.

4. Vocational rehabilitation of the injured.

5. Perhaps most importantly, for the first time it provided for the medical and surgical treatment and prosthetic appliances for all service men and women who were injured or became ill in the line of duty. [8, 10]

This massive new program became the responsibility of the Bureau of War Risk Insurance, an agency separate from the old Pension Bureau, which continued to handle pension claims of veterans of earlier wars and their dependents. In October 1917, the Bureau of War Risk Insurance, which had been established in 1914 to insure merchant ships against wartime aggression, was a modest operation with only 20 employees occupying four rooms.[8] Despite wartime shortages of personnel and space, the Bureau expanded rapidly to meet its new challenges. Until the armistice of November 11, 1918, most of the Bureau's new work involved selling insurance policies to servicemen, processing insurance claims and paying allotments to families and compensation payments for injury and death. Until the end of the war, medical care and rehabilitation were handled by military hospitals,[11, 12] but discharged veterans still needing care were dependent on the Bureau.

It seems unlikely that the members of Congress who voted for this sweeping restructuring of veterans' benefits fully realized that a separate veterans' hospital system was being created. In fact, Congress did not appropriate any money to build new hospitals for veterans until 1921. Nevertheless, this bill was the seed from which grew today's massive system of veterans' health care.

World War I was the first U.S. war during the modern era of hospital care. In the 19th century, hospitals were considered charitable institutions for the impoverished. Other sick and injured persons were treated in their own homes. Military hospitals during the Civil War treated huge numbers of the sick and injured, but after discharge veterans did not expect or receive hospitalization. Early in the 20th century, with the introduction of improved surgical techniques, increased medical specialization, and the use of clinical laboratories and radiology, hospitals became places for all the sick, the rich as well as the poor.[13] So it was that a nation that in the past expected families and communities to care for the war-disabled, as long as pensions spared them from penury, suddenly expected veterans' care in government hospitals.

At the end of the war, many patients being treated in military hospitals demanded to be released from active duty. Of those discharged, about 2,500 were tuberculosis cases and 50,000 were classified with nervous and mental disorders.[14] Suddenly, the many sick and injured became the medical responsibility of, and expected medical care from, the Bureau of War Risk Insurance, which was not prepared to handle them. Since the Bureau had no hospitals or doctors of its own, it turned to the Public Health Service for use of its Marine Hospitals. In 1919, the Marine Hospital system had a capacity of only 1,548 beds but was expected to handle 20,000 applications for hospitalization.[14]

A disabled veteran applying to the Bureau of War Risk Insurance for medical care would first be subject to a determination of eligibility that would place him in the hands of the Public Health Service. Care at a Marine Hospital with room would then be provided. But in the early stages of this program many Marine Hospitals were full, so the patient ended up at a Soldiers' Home infirmary or in a private or state hospital. Often these also were full, and some were not considered suitable for providing an acceptable level of care for deserving veterans.

In 1919, Congress tried to correct the shortage of veterans' hospital beds by authorizing transfer of a group of military hospitals to the Public Health Service and the purchase or construction of others. But transferred hospitals were mostly of temporary construction, and many were unusable. Powerful members of Congress believed that the huge Army hospitals built during the war, even though intended to be temporary, should be used to serve veterans' needs. As a result, the Congress did not appropriate the funds needed to carry out the authorized construction.[15] By 1921, no new veterans' hospitals had yet been constructed.[16] Even with the hospitals that had been transferred to the Public Health Service, there wasn't enough room for the disabled veterans. Public attention to the problem was growing as newspapers carried pictures of sick veterans lying on the floors of jails and almshouses.[17]

Finally, in 1921, Congress acted. On March 4, 1921, on his last day in office, President Wilson signed Public Law 384, later referred to as the first Langley bill. It provided $18.6 million for construction of new veterans' hospitals and remodeling and extending existing plants.[16] This construction program was one of the first responsibilities of President Harding's new Secretary of the Treasury, A. W. Mellon, whose department included both the Public Health Service and the Bureau of War Risk Insurance. To assist him in this task, he appointed a Committee of Consultants, generally known as the White Committee after its chairman, William C. White, M.D. (Appendix IIa)

The Consultants, together with their advisory committee, traveled widely, visiting the institutions caring for ex-service men. They gathered an extensive body of data, including the distributions of general and veteran population, existing government and nongovernment hospitals, access to transportation and predictions of future needs. They also corresponded extensively and held hearings of "interested groups." As noted in their report:

"In addition to the task of assembling available data, there were requests for hearings from over 100 groups - Senators, Representatives, State and municipal committees, chambers of commerce, etc. - representing those interested in the location of hospitals in their particular districts. These scarcely provided the data on which to build a rational Federal program, but all were heard."[18]

Members of the White Committee were from academic settings, suggesting that the Committee would favor placing new veterans' hospitals near medical schools. But this did not happen, and the final report sheds light on how they came to a critical turning point in their work:

"What would secure for the beneficiaries of the Government the best type of medical service? Should they be confined solely to isolated Government institutions, or should they have available such consultant and expert advice as surrounds the best type of teaching institutions? Which would secure the most rapid recovery and return to active participation in the duty of life? Here again, the tendency was all for centralization in Government institutions, in spite of the fact that there had been gathered from all over the United States the willingness and desire on the part of those institutions which had devoted themselves to the care of the public to assist in this work. This tendency to centralize had grown so rapidly and the change in administration had come about so quickly that it was impossible to wield any influence in securing special care by physicians who had become highly expert in special technique for the benefit of these men, and, although in the location of these hospitals the consultants had constantly in mind that they should be as near as possible to centers of medical education and assistance of this character, it was felt that the effort was largely wasted.

"There was an opinion frequently expressed that our soldiers were not to be submitted to experiment and student teaching, and yet the very best type of medical care given is in those institutions that come under the critical eye of students and in which teaching is carried on - to wit, Johns Hopkins, Harvard, Columbia, Chicago, and elsewhere - and it is a duty of our Government, where possible, to accept its share in opening the doors of these institutions for instruction of oncoming doctors and nurses who will in the future have to deal with those who are sick.

"In an attempt to solve these questions the consultants found great difficulty, because of the variation of expert opinion. Men of equal prominence and success in life at times presented diametrically opposite views, and the only conclusion that could be drawn was that in fields involving human activity, where positive knowledge was not available, no standards could be set, and any attempt to standardize human organization could only be met with failure. Each institution in its administration is a separate institution, modified and it is impossible to lay down standards that will universally apply. To overcome this difficulty a request was made that the medical director for each institution be chosen during the process of construction, so that the Supervising Architect's Office should have his advice continuously in securing an institution which would fill his administrative point of view."[19]

While in some cases Committee members undoubtedly succumbed to pressures for their decisions, the White Committee also actively sought out suitable locations for veterans' hospitals. In May 1921, the month after the Committee originally received its charge, member Frank Billings sent the following telegram to Ray Lyman Wilbur, M.D., who was then president of Stanford University:

"Will local people buy and present to government 100 or more acres to afford additional ground space to existing federal owned property to insure location of permanent government hospital at Palo Alto? Letter follows. Wire or write reply to Dr. W.C. White, C/O Bureau of War Risk Insurance, Arlington Building, Washington."[20]

One week later, Dr. Wilbur answered:
"Very appreciative of telegram and letter of Dr. Billings regarding Federal Hospital Palo Alto. Have consulted with Palo Alto Chamber of Commerce and feel that if your committee decides upon this as a permanent site Palo Alto Chamber of Commerce will raise sufficient subscription to pay differences so that fifty to one hundred acres adjoining present site can be purchased at cost to Government of $600 per acre. Community small but fully sympathetic with hospital and will do their best. Would appreciate opportunity to do anything further if I can."[21]

In due time, one of the White Committee's new hospitals was placed in Palo Alto, a hospital that continued to be of great interest to Dr. Wilbur.

Figure 1.1: Ray Lyman Wilbur, M.D., President of Stanford University and chairman of the Veteran's Bureau Medical Council

Among the first issues facing the White Committee was the poor service received by veterans. Three separate agencies, the Bureau of War Risk Insurance, the Public Health Service and the Rehabilitation Division of the Federal Board for Vocational Education, were involved, and often a single veteran needed service from all of them. To address this problem, as their first task they prepared a proposed organizational chart that would put the three agencies under a single Bureau of Soldier Rehabilitation.[22]

Meanwhile, the American Legion, distressed with the problems faced by its members, had been campaigning for unification of the three separate veterans' agencies. The lobbying effort seemingly had its effect on newly elected President Warren G. Harding who, shortly after taking office, appointed a committee of prominent citizens chaired by Gen. Charles E. Dawes to formulate a unification proposal. Members included Theodore Roosevelt, Jr., and representatives of the American Legion, the Red Cross, and labor, women's and government groups.[23] This committee accepted the White Committee's proposal almost without change. Its recommendations to President Harding became law in August 1921 with establishment of the Veterans' Bureau.[24, 25]

The Veterans' Bureau

While the new agency assumed all the responsibilities of the Bureau of War Risk Insurance and the Rehabilitation Division, at first it didn't have responsibility for sick and injured veterans. This was resolved about 8 months later, in April 1922, when President Harding issued an executive order that turned over to the Veterans' Bureau all 57 Public Health Service hospitals which by then were primarily serving veterans. Later, new Public Health Service hospitals funded under the first Langley Act were also transferred to the Veterans' Bureau.[26]

Figure 1.2: Charles R. Forbes, first Director, Veteran's Bureau (1921-1923)

The high hopes for these reforms were quickly steered off course as the new Veterans' Bureau became plagued with problems. Waste, fraud and mismanagement during its first 2 years were brought to light in extensive 1923 Congressional hearings[27] that raised charges against the Bureau's first director, Charles R. Forbes, a personal friend of President Harding.

In September 1921, Forbes had "summarily dismissed" the Bureau's first Medical Director, Dr. Haven Emerson, a distinguished physician detailed from the Public Health Service to the Veterans' Bureau, which had no doctors on its staff.

Figure 1.3: Haven Emerson, M.D., first Medical Director, Veteran's Bureau (1921)

Emerson publicly stated that the Bureau was "being made the football of politics" and that "plumbers and policemen" were "being substituted for scientific medical men."[28] In a talk in Columbus, OH, Emerson charged that $500,000 was being used for political patronage. Forbes maintained that this charge was false. He told Emerson that "his services were no longer desired," and replaced him with Col. R.U. Patterson.[29]

Figure 1.4: Robert U. Patterson, M.D., Medical Director (1921-1923), later a member of the Medical Council

In February 1923, at the request of President Harding, Forbes was forced to resign after he was found to be selling government property to a business associate.[30] Congressional hearings in October and November of that year brought out evidence against Forbes so serious that the Justice Department later took up the case, resulting in prison terms for Forbes and one of his business associates.

With this tumultuous beginning, the new agency sorely needed a leader who was above reproach. Harding's choice was Gen. Frank T. Hines, a veteran of the Spanish-American War and World War I. Hines, whose first job was to investigate and clean up the scandals, worked rapidly to improve service and lessen political control over the Bureau.[31] He set in place systems of controls and supervision that, in some cases, persist to the present.

Compensation vs. Care

Of the benefits to veterans provided by the 1917 law, the two that fell to the new medical department of the Veterans' Bureau were establishing ratings for monetary compensation for disability and death, and providing medical care. Both compensation and care were complex new assignments, and, in the immediate postwar years, compensation received the most attention. Compensation was most familiar to the Congressional overseers of the new Bureau because, like the old pension system, compensation decisions could be sensitive to political influence. Under Forbes, such influence had been a major problem. Although the 1923 Congressional hearings sought ways to improve Bureau performance in all regards,[32] more attention was paid to issues of compensation than to quality of medical care. While hospitals and dispensaries were finally in place, testimony at the hearings made clear that determining a veteran's degree of compensable disability was their primary focus.

**Figure 1.5: General Frank T. Hines, Director, Veteran's Bureau (1923-1930)
and Administrator, Veterans Administration (1930-1945)**

Dr. Lester Rogers, who had become the Bureau's Medical Director in May 1923 when Patterson was recalled to the Army, expressed concern in his testimony about medical care in the veterans' hospitals. Nevertheless, the Senators and their staff interrogated Rogers at length, and with considerable criticism, about his compensation decisions. There was little

Figure 1.6: Lester B. Rogers, M.D., Medical Director 1923-1924

11

apparent interest in his complaints that he had insufficient authority to inspect the hospitals, or that many of the beds available could not be used because of the location or poor condition of some hospitals.[33] In January 1924, soon after the hearings concluded, the frustrated Rogers requested, and received, transfer to the New Haven (CT) Veterans' Hospital.

Other testimony during the hearings cited instances of hospitals crowded with patients who could have been discharged except for their disability status. Because hospitalization itself was considered evidence of disability, a veteran's compensation payment often decreased upon discharge, so the motivation to recover was not great.[34] Yet despite pressures on physicians and staff at the hospitals to place emphasis on administrative efficiency, good medical care was also expected.

Advisors to the medical department

Even with the emphasis on compensation issues, one of Gen. Hines's main interests, once he had cleaned up the scandals and increased efficiency, was to improve the quality of medical care in the hospital system inherited from the Public Health Service. One of his first needs was for a new Medical Director to replace Dr. Rogers. In seeking a new permanent Medical Director for the Bureau, Hines sought advice from prominent physicians, including Dr. Wilbur, president of Stanford University, as previously mentioned, who also was president of the American Medical Association.[35] In April 1924,

Figure 1.7: Edgar O. Crossman, M.D., Medical Director, 1924-1926, 1928-1929

as a result of his search, Hines chose Edgar O. Crossman, M.D., a New Hampshire psychiatrist and professor of psychiatry at the University of Vermont, who had also been active in politics. Dr. Crossman had served in both houses of the New Hampshire legislature and as Federal Collector of Internal Revenue for northern New England. He had been president of the New Hampshire Medical Society and, more recently, New England District Manager for the Veterans' Bureau.[36] It is likely, judging by rapid progress in upgrading medical care after his appointment, that his recruitment included agreements about increased authority for the medical department and measures to increase quality.

Hines had laid the groundwork for Crossman's mission in earlier contacts with Wilbur that included requests to nominate appropriate physicians to serve as "Special Consultants" to the Veterans' Bureau[37] and asking Wilbur himself to "act in an advisory capacity to the Veterans' Bureau when called upon on medical matters pertaining to your specialty". Hines' targets were specific:

> "It will be desired from time to time to obtain from you and from other members of the Consultant Board in General Medicine and Surgery, recommendations and advice concerning plans for construction and operation of general medical and surgical hospitals; the application of clinical methods of examination and treatment in hospitals, dispensaries and out-patient services; the question of medical follow-up care; and the questions of rating, for compensation and insurance purposes and for vocational training, of disabilities arising from general medical and surgical disabilities."

Hines further explained that the Government was restricted in its ability to compensate adequately for expert advice, but that "it is confidently hoped that your deep and scientific interest in the problems of veterans' relief, will prevail upon you to accept this request of the Bureau." Payment of railroad and Pullman fares and incidental travel expenses, plus a $20 daily fee, were offered.[37]

The Medical Council

Other advisors were also recruited, and, on July 22-24, 1924, 18 of the 22 members appointed to the "Council on Medical and Hospital Affairs," assembled for their first meeting in the Veterans' Bureau Central Office at the Arlington Building in Washington, DC,[38] which had originally been built to house the Bureau of War Risk Insurance. (It has been continuously occupied by Federal veterans' agencies and today is the headquarters of the Department of Veterans Affairs.) At its first meeting, the group modified its name to the "Medical Council of the Veterans' Bureau," and asked that its members be called "Councillors." The Council suggested additional members with needed expertise and formed committees for Tuberculosis, Neuro-psychiatry, General Medicine and Surgery and for "Hospitals, Dispensaries and General Medical Welfare." On the second day of their meeting, they met with President Coolidge.[39]

The Medical Council members were distinguished in their spheres of professional activity and leaders in organized, academic, public and private medicine (Appendix IIb). Most of them were listed in *Who's Who in America* and held important positions in organized medicine, including the American Medical Association, American Hospital Association, American Public Health Association, American College of Surgeons, American Psychiatric Association, National Tuberculosis Association and the American Heart Association. They held prominent university and government appointments and edited important journals. While no record exists describing how the original members were selected, a number of them had previously been advisors to the Veterans' Bureau or the Public Health Service. Appointments were permanent and subsequent Council members were recommended by the Council itself to add balance or replace those who had resigned or become inactive.

Although not present for the first meeting, Dr. Wilbur was elected to be Permanent Chairman. Wilbur had been one of the first professors of medicine and later dean of the Cooper Medical College of Stanford University. In 1929, Wilbur became Secretary of the Interior in the Hoover administration, but he continued on the Medical Council while Dr. Lewellys F. Barker from Johns Hopkins University assumed the chair. Barker was William Osler's successor as Chairman of Medicine at Johns Hopkins, a position he held from 1905 to 1913. He established research laboratories as integral parts of the university's Department of Medicine, an unprecedented marrying of research and clinical practice.[40] Barker later played an active role in the Washington, DC Diagnostic Center (Chapter 2).

Figure 1.8: Lewellys F. Barker, M.D.

At the first meeting of the Medical Council,[41] a major concern expressed by the Bureau's Central Office medical staff and Council members was placed on the agenda, labeled "Medical Personnel - Status as to Rank and Pay." The subject was summarized for the record as follows:

> "As the Bureaus' medical activities will last for 60 to 75 years for world war veterans alone, should the medical officers have a permanent status offering continuous service, automatic and regular promotion which will assure young men a future, in which independent professional opinion and action can be exercised, or have a Civil Service status with lower pay, fewer allowances, and be subject to alterations of pay and the exclusive control of political superiors with each change of administration or oftener; average age of applicants for Civil Service jobs, 54 years."[42]

At the time, the fact was that Bureau physicians received less pay and had lower status than their colleagues in the Public Health Service or the armed services. At its first meeting, the Medical Council recommended the legal establishment of a Medical Corps for the Veterans' Bureau, that would be comparable to those in the other Federal medical services. In the years that followed that first discussion, the Council spent considerable effort trying to get such a law passed,[43] but to no avail. Only after World War II was a VA Medical Corps created when Public Law 293 of 1946 established the Department of Medicine and Surgery.[44]

Other ways of improving the Veterans' Bureau hospitals as places for doctors to practice were suggested by staff and endorsed by the Council: systematic programs of instruction, such as the neuropsychiatric and tuberculosis schools already started on a pilot basis, and establishing medical reference libraries in all hospitals and clinics. The Medical Council endorsed these concepts at its first meeting and came up with its own, more ambitious ideas to improve the quality of the professional staff and medical services. These included:

- Establishing a system of diagnostic beds for the evaluation of problem cases.
- Publishing a journal.
- Initiating a research program.

Hines and Crossman quickly accepted these innovative concepts in principle. And by the time the Council met for the second time 4 months later, planning for them was well under way.

At its second meeting, in November 1924, which became known as the "The Cure-better-than-Compensation Conference," the Medical Council addressed a major philosophical question that had been problematic in providing Federal veterans programs. Wilbur addressed the group with this challenge:

"If there is anything in this Medical Council, it seems to me it should come from the direction of the application of modern medicine to the problems of these men considered from a standpoint of curative medicine.... It seems to me that we must shift from compensation, and think in terms of repair and cure instead of in terms of how much damage has been done ... Let us see what we can do from the medical standpoint of harmonizing the out-patient with the hospital service to get the whole thing going as a medical concern, which will have the point of view of cure and attention instead of compensation and disability."[45]

The Council's Committee on Investigation and Research expressed the same concept, stating that a research program is "all the more called for by the recent shift in emphasis from administration to treatment as the primary objective of the Bureau."

Making the transition from a hospital system that primarily "warehoused" the disabled to one that focused on "cure" was to be a gradual and incomplete process. But along the way there were signs that the movement had taken hold. For example, Wilbur wrote in a 1924 site visit report that the Palo Alto Veterans' Hospital appeared to be a well-run neuropsychiatric hospital with the latest equipment, advanced clinical laboratory and radiology facilities. Wilbur described the wards as "cheerful" and said that "The whole aspect of the hospital is one of cheer and hopefulness as compared with the ordinary institution of the sort." He also commented that the chief of the laboratory "has an instinct for research."[46] On the other hand, there undoubtedly existed less favored veterans' hospitals that never reached excellence during this early period. Nevertheless, the most important contribution of the Medical Council was to help the Veterans' Bureau leaders focus on curative medicine as an important and laudable goal.

Dr. Michael Davis, a Medical Council member who was an authority on outpatient care, described the transition from "compensation" to "cure" after his 1926 inspection of some Veterans' Bureau outpatient facilities:

> "The work of the bureau physician for ambulatory cases was originally conceived chiefly as an aid in determining the compensation to be allowed the veteran. The importance of thorough medical treatment has come forward more recently as the important element in bureau policy."[47]

Also in 1926, Dr. Winthrop Adams of the Bureau's Central Office Medical Service described this change of focus to readers of the *Medical Bulletin*:

> "Regardless of the fact that all of us who have been connected with this work...have realized that more could be done in the way of applying medical knowledge to the cure or relief of veterans' disabilities, it has, nevertheless, been apparent to all of us that the compensation feature was the paramount issue.... However, it is extremely gratifying to note that a decided change has taken place in this respect during the past year or two ...."

Adams credited the Medical Council for this change, saying:

> "The Bureau has had for the past two years recourse to the advice of a body of eminent physicians, which is known as the Medical Council... The Council has at each of its conferences insisted that the Bureau must accomplish more than it has in the past from the curative or therapeutic side."[48]

Introduction of a research concept for the Veterans' Bureau

At its first meeting in July 1924, the Medical Council appointed ad hoc committees to review member-proposed resolutions. Dr. H. Kennon Dunham, a tuberculosis expert from Cincinnati, recommended that the Veterans' Bureau establish a medical research effort. An ad hoc committee was appointed to review and formulate such a resolution. The committee chair, Louis Dublin, Ph.D., vice-president of the Metropolitan Life Insurance Company and a pioneer in the development of population statistics, commented that "The statistical equipment of this Bureau, excepting that of the Census Bureau, is probably the largest in the Government."

Dublin's committee proposed an ambitious resolution, which the Council discussed at length. Members were divided about whether they should add a new formal Group on Investigation and Research to their committee structure. Some were uncertain about the proposed research mission of the Bureau. The Group on Tuberculosis recommended that "adequate research should be planned in connection with tuberculosis." All members saw the need for "statistical investigation," but some members questioned what could be done in clinical research. Eventually, the Council established a permanent Group on Investigation and Research and passed the following resolution to be forwarded to Gen. Hines:

Figure 1.9: Louis I. Dublin, Ph.D.

"The Committee unanimously agrees that the Veterans' Bureau should emphasize at every point the opportunity for investigation and research. This, because of the magnitude and importance of the work of the Bureau, and especially because of the field in which the work of the Bureau lies. Medical science is preeminently one in which investigation and research are called for. It therefore recommends:

"1. That an office for investigation and research be established around the existent Division of Costs and Statistics.

2. That a permanent committee of the Council be appointed to formulate lines of investigation and research and which shall act as liaison for such work between the Bureau on the one hand and the medical profession on the other.

3. That problems of investigation and research shall cover:
   a. Those that arise directly from the administrative needs of the Bureau
   b. Those that arise through the clinical and laboratory care of patients
   c. Those that will add definite contributions to medical knowledge

4. The Committee further recommends that it should be the policy of the Bureau, with the guidance of the Council Committee, to develop active relations and exchanges of material with various accredited research agencies throughout the country.

5. It further recommends that the results of such investigations as the Bureau may undertake, either under its own auspices or through the cooperation of outside agencies, be published in a bulletin of the Bureau, which may be issued either monthly or quarterly.

6. It recommends that the medical staff of the Bureau should be encouraged in every way to participate in the field of investigation insofar as immediate duties will permit of such participation.

7. The Committee urges that the Bureau make every effort to obtain autopsy records through cooperating with local hospitals in order to improve its record of deceased cases in its files.

8. The Committee will further examine the work of the Division of Costs and Statistics, and will make, later, a report specifying the most pressing investigations which should be undertaken at once.

"The Committee recognizes the enormous scope of the field of investigation and research which the Bureau might properly undertake. On the other hand, it is felt that many difficulties will be encountered of a legal and financial character which might put great difficulties in the path of the entire program unless the field of investigation were narrowed somewhat to include, at the beginning, only those items of investigation which directly bear on the welfare of the men for whom the Bureau is responsible."[49]

A second resolution put forward by the Medical Council at this first meeting recommended establishing "regional diagnostic groups, consisting of the best available Bureau and local medical personnel, utilizing so far as possible, as consultants, members of this Council ..." The Council recommended that patients with doubtful diagnoses be referred to these groups and that the consultants be adequately compensated.[50] This resolution led to the establishment of several Diagnostic Centers (discussed below) that contributed to the research program through the 1920s and 1930s.

The resolution about Diagnostic Centers also obliquely recommended affiliation with medical schools: "It is further suggested that where teaching institutions are available their use for this purpose will furnish excellent opportunity for the development of the attached Bureau officers as expert diagnosticians." Another committee of the Council, the Neuropsychiatric Committee, also favored affiliation with teaching institutions: "It is recommended that in the planning of future neuropsychiatric hospitals of the Veterans' Bureau, that are to be located in or near medical teaching centers or areas of large population, that certain of these be constructed and operated so that they may serve as teaching centers or schools for the medical personnel of the Veterans' Bureau."[51] Despite these recommendations, no formal affiliations between veterans' hospitals and medical schools occurred until after World War II.[52] The early VA research program had little or no formal input from academia except through the members of the Medical Council.

Before the second meeting of the Medical Council in November 1924, its membership was expanded by nine new members, four of whom, Drs. Albert E. Cohn, Allen K. Krause, Horatio M. Pollack and Joseph W. Schereschewsky, joined Drs. Louis Dublin and Michael Davis to form the Group on Investigation and Research. Davis left the Council in 1927, but the other five men continued as active advisors to the research program through the life of the Council. This enrichment of the Council's research expertise by adding four new members with research interests was consistent with Dr. Dublin's professed enthusiasm and the support of research attributed to Dr. Crossman and his staff.[53]

At this second meeting, the newly formed Group on Investigation and Research met and prepared an extensive report in which they referred to "enthusiasm for scientific work...from the Medical Director down...." They made the following recommendations:

"1. The establishment of a Section on Investigation and Research in the Medical Service.
 2. The appointment of a Director of Research ... This Committee shall act as advisor to the Research Director.

3. The Director of Research shall survey the present condition of the records kept both in the Bureau and in the field to determine their adequacy for the purposes of investigation....

4. The Director of Research shall investigate the standards and definitions for the clinical routine in hospitals, clinics and laboratories, and shall investigate the standards of diagnosis and treatment in the various establishments.

5. He shall have authority to study the work of all hospitals and other establishments of the Bureau.

6. He shall make plans for revision of the rating schedule.

7. He shall institute a study of the future hospital needs of the Bureau in cooperation with the Federal Board of Hospitalization.

8. He shall be responsible for the study of the clinical material available in the hospitals, clinics and out-patient departments of the Bureau, and emphasis shall be placed on the results of various methods of treatment.

9. . . . The Research Director shall hold conferences with the medical officers at regular intervals to discuss medical problems and the results of the investigations conducted at the several hospitals. The staffs shall be encouraged to engage in research work in so far as their duties will permit, and favorable notation shall be made on the record of such medical officers as produce useful research work.

10. The Bureau shall arrange for the publication of a Monthly Bulletin, which shall be the medium for the publication of the studies made by the medical staff and the Research Director."[54]

The duties described for the Research Director represented an ambitious agenda for a single individual. The committee appears to have included functions they were sure the Bureau leadership wanted in order to persuade them that they needed a Director of Research. Nevertheless, it spells out what the committee, influenced by its two statistician members, thought of when they referred to research. Statistical studies of Bureau activities, systematically performed so that useful conclusions could be drawn, were related directly to Dublin's positions and expertise at Metropolitan Life. Adequate patient records were seen as essential to such studies, as well as to clinical research. Furthermore, standardized procedures were important not only to assuring quality control in patient care but also to acquiring usable data for clinical outcome studies.

The provision for research by clinical staff contained in the recommendations suggests that not much was expected of them. There was no provision for freeing clinicians' time to allow them to conduct the suggested research, and this limitation undoubtedly limited the growth of such endeavors.[55] Nevertheless, research projects in the hospitals and dispensaries did materialize.

By the time of the third meeting of the Medical Council on February 27-28, 1925, a section on Medical Research in the Bureau's central office had been formally established and recruitment for a Director of Research was under way. The Group on Investigation and Research advised the following qualifications for this Director:

"1. He should be a physician familiar with Bureau procedure, and preferably one of the medical officers of the Veterans' Bureau.

2. He should have a good general and medical education.

3. He should have shown unusual interest in study and research and given some evidence of this interest in published work.

4. He should be a man in vigorous health and preferably under 45.

5. He should have unquestioned administrative ability.

6. He should be a man of personality, having the respect of the medical personnel of the Bureau."[56]

Other related progress was also under way in early 1925. A Diagnostic Center had been established in Cincinnati and one was in preparation for Washington, DC. The first issue of the Veterans' Bureau *Medical Bulletin* was published in July 1925. Considering the many impediments to change that were evident then, the speed of these events testify to the energetic efforts by Dr. Crossman and his staff, as well as Gen. Hines's decisiveness.

References

1. Jones, R.S., *The History of the American Legion.* Indianapolis and New York: The Bobbs-Merrill Company, 1946, 123.

2. Crossman, E.O., "U.S. Veterans' Bureau Hospitals." *Mod Hosp,* 1926. **26**: 30-32.

3. Griffith, C.M., "The Medical and Hospital Service of the Veterans' Administration." *Military Surgeon,* 1936. **79**: 251-267.

4. White, W.C., Billings, F., Bowman, J.G. and Kirby, G.H., *Report of the Consultants on Hospitalization Appointed by the Secretary of the Treasury to Provide Additional Hospital Facilities under Public Act 384 (Approved March 4, 1921).* Washington, DC: U.S.Government Printing Office, 1923, 1.

5. Furman, B., *A Profile of the United States Public Health Service, DHEW Publication No. (NIH) 73-369.* Washington, DC: U.S. Government Printing Office, 1973, 20.

6. Skocpol, T., *Protecting Soldiers and Mothers.* Cambridge, MA and London, England: The Belknap Press of the Harvard University Press, 1992, 107-130.

7. Leigh, R.D., *Federal Health Administration in the United States.* New York and London: Harper & Brothers Publishers, 1927, 314.

8. Adkins, R.E., *Medical Care of Veterans.* Washington, DC: U.S. Government Printing Office, 1967, 92-93.

9. Jones, *History of American Legion.* 1946, 125-126.

10. Leigh, *Federal Health Administration.* 1927, 168-169.

11. Adkins, *Medical Care of Veterans.* 1967, 102-103.

12. Leigh, *Federal Health Administration.* 1927, 172-174.

13. Rosen, G., *The Structure of American Medical Practice, 1875-1941,* Philadephia: University of Pennsylvania Press, 1983, 43-48.

14. Lewis, B.J., *VA Medical Program in Relation to Medical Schools.* Washington, DC: U.S. Government Printing Office, 1970, 65.

15. Leigh, *Federal Health Administration.* 1927, 181-191.

16. White, *Report of Consultants on Hospitalization.* 1923, iii, 1-2, and 63-64.

17. Adkins, *Medical Care of Veterans.* 1967, 65.

18. White, *Report of Consultants on Hospitalization.* 1923, 7.

19. White, *Report of Consultants on Hospitalization.* 1923, 15-16.

20. Telegram from Frank Billings, M.D. to Ray Lyman Wilbur, M.D., written at Chicago, IL, May 27, 1921.

21. Telegram from Ray Lyman Wilbur, M.D. to William C. White, M.D., written at Palo Alto, CA, June 3, 1921.

22. White, *Report of Consultants on Hospitalization.* 1923, 9.

23. Jones, *History of American Legion.* 1946, 132.

24. Adkins, *Medical Care of Veterans.* 1967, 110-112.

25. Leigh, *Federal Health Administration.* 1927, 200-203.

26. White, *Report of Consultants on Hospitalization.* 1923, 61.

27. *Investigation of the Veterans' Bureau: Hearings before the Select Committee on Investigation of the Veterans' Bureau, United States Senate, Sixty-Seventh Congress, October 22 to November 7, 1923.* Washington, DC: Government Printing Office, 1923

28. Leigh, *Federal Health Administration.* 1927, 207.

29. *New York Times,* New York, September 14, 1921. 19.

30. Smith, F.C., M.D., witness. "Testimony of Doctor Frederick Charles Smith." *Hearings Before the Select Committee on Investigation of Veterans' Bureau, United States Senate.* Washington, D.C.: Government Printing Office, 1923, **1**: 651-664.

31. *Investigation of the Veterans' Bureau.* 1923, 755.

32. *Investigation of the Veterans' Bureau.* 1923, 10-150.

33. *Investigation of the Veterans' Bureau.* 1923, 790-791.

34. "Minutes of the Second Conference of the Medical Council with the Director and the Medical Director of the United States Veterans' Bureau." Washington, DC: U.S. Veterans' Bureau, 1924, 8.

35. Letter from Ray Lyman Wilbur, M.D. to Frank T. Hines, written at Palo Alto, CA, February 12, 1924.

36. Anonymous obituary, "Doctor Crossman." *US Veterans' Bureau Medical Bulletin,* 1929. **5**: 647-648.

37. Letter from General Frank T. Hines to Ray Lyman Wilbur, M.D., written at Washington, DC, February 19, 1924.

38. "Minutes of First Conference, Medical Council, U.S. Veterans' Bureau, 22-24 July, 1924." Washington, DC: U.S. Veterans' Bureau, 1924, 16.

39. "Minutes of First Medical Council Meeting, 22-24 July, 1924." 1924, 34.

40. Harvey, A.M., *Science at the Bedside: Clinical Research in American Medicine, 1905-1945.* Baltimore and London: John Hopkins University Press, 1981, 64-70.

41. "Agenda of First Conference, Medical Council , U.S. Veterans' Bureau." Washington, DC: U.S. Veterans' Bureau, 1924, 14.

42. "Agenda of First Medical Council Meeting." 1924, 5.

43. Adkins, *Medical Care of Veterans.* 1967, 138-139.

44. Adkins, *Medical Care of Veterans*. 1967, 180 and pp. 209-211.

45. "Minutes of Second Medical Council Meeting, 10-11 November, 1924." 1924, 12.

46. Letter from Ray Lyman Wilbur, M.D. to E.O. Crossman, M.D., written at Palo Alto, CA, October 7, 1924.

47. Davis, M.M., "Improvement in out-patient service, with special reference to medical records." *US Veterans' Bureau Medical Bulletin*, 1926. **2**: 108-112.

48. Adams, W., "The organization and administration of the medical divisions of regional offices." *US Veterans' Bureau Medical Bulletin*, 1926. **2**: 113-117.

49. "Minutes of First Medical Council Meeting, 22-24 July, 1924." 1924, 23.

50. "Minutes of First Medical Council Meeting, 22-24 July, 1924." 1924, 14-15.

51. "Minutes of First Medical Council Meeting, 22-24 July, 1924." 1924, 21.

52. Adkins, *Medical Care of Veterans*. 1967, 215-218.

53. "Minutes of Second Medical Council Meeting, 10-11 November, 1924." 1924, 28.

54. "Minutes of Second Medical Council Meeting, 10-11 November, 1924." 1924, 29-30.

55. Ziegler, E.E., "Some properties of pneumocholin, a biochemical analysis." *J Lab Clin Med*, 1933. **18**: 695-704.

56. "Minutes of the Third Conference of the Medical Council with the Director and the Medical Director of the United States Veterans' Bureau at Washington, D.C., 27-28 February, 1925." Washington, DC: U.S. Veterans' Bureau, 1925, 28.

Chapter 2. The VA Research Program before 1946

The year 1925 marked the effective transition from recommendation to action. The Veterans' Bureau leadership quickly grasped key initiatives that the Medical Council viewed as vital to strengthening this Federal agency that had been thrust into the role of delivering health-care services. A system of diagnostic centers with links to outside consultants was established, and the *Veterans' Bureau Medical Bulletin* began publication as an important medium for sharing information. The formal establishment of a research component within the Veterans' Bureau that year was also a major milestone.

The advent of clearly identified medical research activity meant the marriage of projects and practitioners that had been informally at work with the type of hospital-based clinical research envisioned by the Medical Council. The Bureau's first research chief, Philip B. Matz, M.D., was an advocate of that philosophy and steered the agency's efforts primarily toward hospital-based inquiry directly related to the clinical conditions of a veteran patient population.

In 1930, the most significant reorganization of Federal veterans programs to date occurred when President Hoover ordered a merger of three agencies to create the Veterans Administration (VA). The Veterans' Bureau, the Treasury Department's Bureau of Pensions, and the domiciliary system of National Homes were now under one umbrella that would endure as the government's largest independent agency for the next half century.

By 1932, as the Nation's economy worsened, pressures were brought to bear on many government programs, including those serving veterans. Provisions within the Economy Act of 1933 limited access to veterans' hospitals for a time with revised eligibility criteria. Even though many restrictions were lifted as a result of public pressure, the VA still was burdened by the need to conserve funds. Some of Dr. Matz's initiatives toward centrally directed research bogged down. With mounting demands for medical care, the Depression also forced some research-related programs such as the diagnostic clinics to provide direct forms of treatment. The monthly *Medical Bulletin* was reduced to a quarterly. Even the influential and highly regarded Medical Council was placed on an eight-year hiatus from 1931 to 1939.

The medical research climate of the 1920s and 1930s

What did the Medical Council members have in mind when they urged the Veterans' Bureau to launch a hospital-based clinical research program? Clearly, they were not thinking of what we now call "basic" medical research. Research facilities as we know them today did not exist in Veterans' Bureau hospitals, nor, for that matter, in most hospitals, even most of those affiliated with medical schools.[1] Erwin Chargaff later described the general climate of medical research in the United States in 1928 as "dominated by an unhurried, good-natured, second-rateness."[2]

Alfred Cohn, a member of the Research Group of the Medical Council, was the first editor of the *Journal of Clinical Investigation*. In its 1924 first issue, he wrote an introductory editorial on the purposes of medical research. He urged the mastery of the methodologies of physics, physiology, nosology and chemistry and asserted that the business of medical research "involves a legitimate interest in learning as well as a means for furthering the methods which lead to the cure of disease."[3] While many authors in his journal focused primarily on the first aim, the basic understanding of medical problems, most of the early Veterans' Bureau authors, whether they published in the *Medical Bulletin* or in other journals, focused primarily on the second aim, seeking methods to cure them.

As late as 1941, Alan Gregg, Rockefeller Foundation Director for the Medical Sciences, discussed his view of what constituted medical research.[4] He defined "research" as having "a flavor of dissatisfaction with the search made hereto, or with the hereto accepted explanations," and stated that "scientific research attains in its successful moments a constantly closer approximation to the truth." Like Cohn, he divided research into two forms, observational and experimental. In his view, observational research (which covers most of the early VA research to be discussed in this chapter) requires that the investigator "bring so fresh and sensitive a mind to reexploration that the discoveries of exploration are possible." He admitted, however, that medical research is "often shot through with irregularities (and) intuitive guesses."

Support of medical research in the 1920s and 1930s came from researchers themselves and from foundations, universities, industry and, lastly, the government. Each of these sectors was represented on the Medical Council's Group on Research.

Foundations were the most important funders. From 1937 to 1940, American foundations' annual support of medicine and public health was estimated to be in the range of $12.2[5] to $13.5 millions. Foremost of the foundations was the Rockefeller Institute, founded in 1902. The Institute was the site of basic and clinical research in infectious diseases, cardiology and other prevalent medical problems.

The most prominent industrial support of medical research came from the life insurance industry, which was represented on the Medical Council and the Group on Research by Louis Dublin of Metropolitan Life Insurance Company, a major player in the public health movement. Dublin undoubtedly influenced the direction of the early Veterans' Bureau research toward demographic studies of a type that might be hard to reconcile with Gregg's definition of "true" research.

Probably the foremost medical school in support of research at the time was Johns Hopkins. Allen K. Krause, who directed a privately endowed laboratory there to study tuberculosis, was active in the Medical Council and its Group on Research.

A prominent player in governmental psychiatric research was St. Elizabeth's Hospital, the large Federal psychiatric hospital in Washington, DC, led by William Alanson White, also an active member of the Medical Council. The Public Health Service, with its tradition for control of infectious diseases, continued a program of intramural research in its Hygienic Laboratory.[6] The former Assistant Surgeon General for research, Joseph W. Schereschewsky, was an active member of the Medical Council and its Group on Research.

With regard to governmental support, Gregg warned that: "The usual reservation regarding research under governmental control is that political preferment or unenlightened parsimony may spoil the quality of the work."[7] And while these factors may have kept the VA research program small before 1946, the VA was not alone in receiving little governmental funding. As late as 1945, the National Institute of Health (as it was then known) spent only three million dollars on medical research, while foundations contributed some $16 millions.[8]

Before World War II, VA hospitals were not affiliated with medical schools, but this probably was not the key factor keeping the research program small. Only a few of the most prominent medical schools, especially those with full-time clinical faculty, had significant clinical research programs. The dilemma of most medical school faculty, likely shared by VA physicians, is described by Marks:

" Clinical investigators working in medical schools had to meet the demands of department chairmen to place service obligations before their research. As physicians, they faced competition from their medical colleagues for income, for patients to study, and for the allegiance of their students." In addition, "Outside of a few isolated research centers, few clinical specialists controlled the resources called for by their research programs."[9]

Important basic research, funded mostly by foundations, was being done at a few places, such as the Rockefeller Institute, the Mayo Clinic and a few medical schools,[10] but such studies were not expected of the Veterans' Bureau. Rather, the clinical research the Medical Council urged was closely associated with the patient. It endeavored to bring systematic observation and scientific method to bedside treatment.[11]

What did the VA mean by "Research"?

The Medical Council's view of research appropriate to the Veterans' Bureau emphasized standardization of practice and records and statistical studies. Members also emphasized the importance to the Veterans' Bureau of clinical research, particularly that which studied outcomes. As Chairman Wilbur said in a 1926 address:

"If we can get the best medical brains of this country concerned with the neuropsychiatric veteran, not only to study him but to get him back 'on the job,' and also trace through over a period of years just what actually does happen, keeping alive a constant scientific interest in the problem, we will have done a real service in the advance of medicine."[12]

In 1926, Dr. Matz, chief of research at Bureau headquarters, described his view of that component of the agency's mission:

"It must be clearly understood at the outset that research work in our service must show that upon consummation it will result in the betterment of the treatment of the beneficiary. It is not within the province of the Veterans' Bureau to carry on research work of a purely academic character; there are other governmental agencies for this line of endeavor; ours must be research based on practicability - something akin to the research work carried on by the large commercial corporations of the country. Our research work must eventually result in larger percentages of recoveries and reduced mortality rates of the beneficiaries of the United States Veterans' Bureau. One of the functions of the research subdivision of central office is to guide and advise those research workers who are in need of help. The research group of the Medical Council has kindly volunteered to cooperate with the bureau in this important work and it is strongly urged that the personnel in the field avail themselves of this privilege and ask for advice when in need of it."[13]

Review of clinical research in 1926

An overview of American clinical research in 1926 can be drawn from the published medical literature for that year. An examination of such journals as *American Journal of Psychiatry, American Review of Tuberculosis* and *American Journal of Syphilis*, as well as general medical journals, *Journal of the American Medical Association, American Journal of the Medical Sciences* and the Veterans' Bureau's own *Medical Bulletin* reveals the types of studies that were attracting attention. Included in the review for comparison was the *Journal of Clinical Investigation*.

Most of the authors who published in these journals were practicing physicians. There were many papers from the more prestigious medical schools and private hospitals, especially in the *Journal of Clinical Investigation*. Nevertheless, a substantial number of authors reported research conducted in their private practices or in hospitals and public institutions without academic affiliations.

Table 2.1 displays the types of reports published in these journals in 1926. These varied considerably among the journals. Of the journals reviewed, only the *Journal of Clinical*

Table 2.1. Comparison of articles published in medical journals, July-December, 1926

Subject matter covered	Percent of pages in original articles						
	Med Bull	JAMA	AJMS	JCI	AJSyph	AJPsy	AmRevTbc
Diagnostic methods	7	6	10	9	14	0	14
Population statistics	7	1	2	0	0	0	30
Descriptive studies	39	30	57	12	39	31	10
Therapeutic interventions	15	19	6	8	7	44	4
Interpretation and synthesis	32	37	18	0	33	25	18
Preclinical and pathophysiology	0	7	6	71	7	0	25
Total	100	100	100	100	100	100	100

Investigation, then a quarterly journal in its second year, published a substantial amount of work on the pathophysiology of human disease, studies such as the effect of hypothyroidism on plasma volume in patients, with repeat studies as the patients improved serving as the controls.[14] "Preclinical" studies, experimental studies on normal animals or human subjects, appeared in most of the journals reviewed but were in substantial proportion only in *Journal of Clinical Investigation* and the *American Review of Tuberculosis*. All of the journals reviewed, except the *Journal of Clinical Investigation*, published "interpretation and synthesis" papers presenting generalizations from personal experience or from review of the literature, with little or no new objective data.

Therapeutic interventions were emphasized in the *American Journal of Psychiatry* more than in the other journals, but some appeared in all. However, there were no reports of the prospective, randomized, placebo-controlled studies commonly seen today. Any studies that employed untreated controls were sequential, either comparing the patient's condition before and after treatment or showing the outcome in a series of untreated patients from previous years compared with the treated series. Randomized studies with untreated controls were rare at the time. Even the later work of the prestigious Cooperative Clinical Group[15] did not meet this standard. In searching for the best treatment for syphilis, the Group presented standardized clinical statistics rather than controlled comparisons, despite a commitment to rigorous therapeutic investigation.

Population statistics were prominent in the *American Review of Tuberculosis* and the *Medical Bulletin*.

Most prominent in the journals reviewed were careful descriptions of the authors' clinical experience with their own patients. Case reports of one or a few patients presenting with unusual conditions or unusual manifestations of disease were frequently published, as they are today. There also were frequent clinical series, generally presenting one practitioner's or one clinic's experience with a certain disease condition. Such reports reflect a carryover, that still exists in some areas, of the situation Marks describes: "Physicians accumulated knowledge of disease over the course of a long career, making age synonymous with expertise." [16]

When diagnostic methods were presented, they were generally descriptions or standardizations of methods and there was little evidence of any attempts to objectively validate the diagnostic usefulness of these methods.

This research climate supported investigations by Veterans' Bureau practitioners. In a sense, each patient successfully diagnosed and treated was himself a research project. The major skills needed to contribute to the medical literature were careful observation of patients and systematic recording of findings. These were within the reach of whoever was motivated to apply them. In the early days, many in the Veterans' Bureau were so motivated.

Even before the Central Office's formal research initiative began, doctors in the Veterans' Bureau hospitals were already doing this type of research. The first survey of ongoing research in 1926 revealed a wide variety of projects of the types that could be done in a patient care setting (Table 2.2).[13]

Table 2.2. Problems under investigation in Veterans' Bureau hospitals in 1926.

1. Penetration of aniline dyes into the central nervous system of experimental animals.
2. Study of immunity by injecting iodine and feeding thyroid extract to guinea pigs.
3. Basal metabolic estimation in tuberculosis.
4. Influence of nasal conditions on neuritis, chronic bronchitis and pleurisy. Use of plumbi acetatis in acute edematous conditions.
5. Malingering test by radio for deafness.
6. Relation of malaria to paresis.
7. Use of x-ray in treating tonsils.
8. The sputum in cases of pulmonary spirochetosis.
9. Study of the treatment of encephalitis lethargica.
10. Empyema and its relation to tuberculosis.
11. Psychoneurosis as evidence of organic pathology.
12. Production of a serum for treatment of tuberculosis.
13. Constitutional effect of exercise on nontuberculous and tuberculous patients.
14. Pulmonary tuberculosis and gastrointestinal symptomatology.
15. Electrocardiographic studies of neurocirculatory asthenia, mitral stenosis and myocarditis.
16. Electrocardiographic studies of pulmonary tuberculosis.
17. Efficiency of stovarsol in treatment of amoebic dysentery.
18. Gastric secretion in cases of colitis.
19. Comparison of McLean's kidney function test with phenolsulphonephthalien.
20. The bacteriology of osteomyelitis.
21. Laboratory investigation of phenoltetrachlorphthalein test for hepatic function.
22. Comparison of Kahn precipitation with the complement fixation test of syphilis.
23. Statistics on patients showing positive serological findings but negative clinical histories and no manifestations of syphilis.
24. X-ray abnormalities of the sella turcica and their relations to sugar tolerance and basal metabolic findings.
25. Investigation of leukocytosis following epileptic seizures.
26. Treatment of neurosyphilis with tryparsamide and bismuth, sulpharsphenamine and bismuth, and malarial blood inoculation.
27. Therapeutic study of effect of intramuscular and intravenous inoculation of bacillus typhosus vaccine in encephalitis lethargica.
28. Effect of intravenous administration of hypertonic dextrose solutions in cases of encephalitis lethargica.
29. Method for correcting colloidal gold solutions.
30. Study of the etiological factors in the production of inadequate behavior through neuropsychiatric symptoms.
31. Use of mercurochrome and gentian violet in cases of encephalitis lethargica.
32. Tuberculosis urinary antigens and the production of specific immunity.
33. Calcium content in the blood of tuberculosis patients.
34. The effect upon the blood sugar of potassium oxalate when used as an anti-coagulant.
35. Index of x-ray films, showing the rate of incidence of tuberculosis in pneumonoconiosis.
36. Study of positive Wasserman cases to determine what per cent show parenchymal infiltrations of lungs which simulate tuberculosis but are negative clinically.
37. Relation of atrophy of testicle to mumps.
38. Influence of intercurrent attacks of pneumonia on the course and prognosis of tuberculosis.

Initiatives to implement the Medical Council's recommendations

Following the July 1924 Medical Council recommendations, the staff of the Central Office Medical Service of the Veterans' Bureau quickly started three key initiatives: a system of diagnostic beds where problem cases could be evaluated, an internal journal to communicate findings and information, and a formal research program. These three mutually important steps were accomplished within the next year.

Efforts to bolster veterans' health care: the Diagnostic Centers

The new Diagnostic Centers, centers of excellence within the hospital system charged with analyzing difficult diagnostic problems, were started in Cincinnati (OH) and Washington (DC) in 1925 and in Palo Alto (CA) (Figure 2.1) in 1928. Each of these units had in-house medical staff and a "board of consultants" that included local leaders in various fields of medical practice. Some members of the Medical Council also participated in these Diagnostic Centers. Dr. Roy D. Adams was the chief consultant at the Washington Center, which had 250 beds,[17] and Drs. Llewellys D. Barker, Allen K. Krause and William A. White were on the consultant staff.[18] Dr. H. Kennon Dunham directed the Cincinnati Center.[19] The Council Chairman, Dr. Ray Lyman Wilbur played an active role in acquiring the Center for Palo Alto[20] and supervised the recruiting of its consultant staff.[21]

Figure 2.1: The Diagnostic Center at the Palo Alto Veterans' Hospital, 1928

In 1929, the Palo Alto Diagnostic Center had 50 beds. In addition there were 50 beds in the same building for discharged Diagnostic Center patients who needed further treatment and another 50 beds for patients with other medical and surgical problems. The hospital also had several other buildings containing 860 beds for neuropsychiatric patients. The Diagnostic Center was equipped with a surgical operating suite, ENT department, radiology department, laboratory, dental clinic and pharmacy. Its physician staff consisted of four generalists, four internists, a general surgeon, two neuropsychiatrists, an ENT specialist, a radiologist and a pathologist. In addition, 17 part-time specialists and nine consultants came from Stanford University and the University of California medical schools' faculties. Patients were examined by a number of physicians, given a spectrum of diagnostic procedures, and then had their cases reviewed in a conference. For example, a patient with gastrointestinal complaints would have gastric analysis, fluoroscopic x-ray series, barium enema, gall bladder x-ray, and multiple stool exams and blood tests.[22]

All physicians throughout the system were urged to transfer patients with complex problems to the Diagnostic Centers for workup and therapy recommendations. These centers were credited with upgrading medical care in the Veterans' Bureau, and in 1929 the American Legion urged that new centers be started in Boston and at the Mayo Clinic.[23] A fourth Diagnostic Center was established in Chicago in 1930 with Dr. Charles A. Elliott of the Medical Council as "Dean of Consultants."[24]

As originally conceived, the Diagnostic Centers were not intended to carry out continuing treatment but to limit their role to diagnosis and specialized procedures. In the 1930s, the demand for treatment beds eroded this distinction. By 1931, many of the beds in the Palo Alto Diagnostic Center were used for routine treatment[25] even though there was continued demand for more diagnostic beds. In late 1934, the west coast Diagnostic Center was moved from Palo Alto to the new VA hospital in San Francisco.[26] Ten doctors, 11 nurses, 30 other employees and 81 patients moved from Palo Alto to the new Diagnostic Center in San Francisco.[27] The Cincinnati Center, which was not connected to a VA hospital, closed some time after the opening of the large Diagnostic Center at the Hines VA Hospital in Chicago.[19]

Diagnostic Center staff were encouraged to do research, and they contributed to the general medical literature as well as to the *Medical Bulletin*. The Centers were well set up for case reports and record analyses as described in 1928 for the Washington, DC Veterans' Bureau Hospital:

"A final copy of the final report on each case is forwarded to the records and research section, where all diagnoses and other pertinent data are indexed according to the scheme outlined in the August, 1928, issue of the *Bulletin*. The monthly and annual medical statistical reports are compiled and written up from the data assembled in this section. This section further serves as an aid in furnishing valuable data for the writing of medical papers."[28]

The *Medical Bulletin*

A key early recommendation of the Medical Council was that the Veterans Bureau establish a journal. This publication, called the *United States Veterans' Bureau Medical Bulletin*, and later the *United States Veterans Administration Medical Bulletin*, was issued continuously from 1925 through 1944.

In the 1925 preface to the first issue, Dr. Edgar O. Crossman, the Medical Director said:

"*The United States Veterans' Bureau Medical Bulletin* is issued for the purpose of maintaining the high standard of medical service rendered claimants and beneficiaries of the bureau, by the collection and correlation of the experience of its medical officers in the diagnosis and treatment of their patients, and in the solution of their medical and administrative problems. It is also expected to promote research along practical lines and to present the results of study of the wealth of medical statistics contained in the records of the bureau. It is evident that the field for investigation is unlimited and that the opportunity to make helpful application of the conclusions is unprecedented."[29]

Especially as a monthly publication (until 1932), the *Medical Bulletin* was full of news of the veterans' medical service, articles reflecting clinical experience, review articles and statistical studies. It included reports of original research by staff physicians. Even controversy and divergent opinions were encouraged.[30] It primarily published clinical papers, including many interesting case reports. There also were reports of carefully observed large patient populations and epidemiological reports using the database set up by the Research Subdivision. Every physician hired by the Veterans' Bureau was asked to submit at least one article for the *Bulletin* each year. At first, about half of them did, and the editors chose from many submitted articles. In 1926 about 75 papers were submitted monthly for editorial review.[31] Many of the articles, particularly reports of unusual or difficult cases, were written by staff of the Diagnostic Centers.

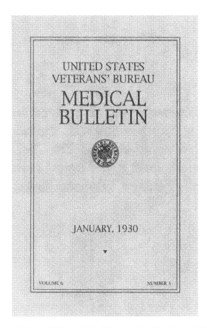

Figure 2.2: The *Medical Bulletin*, 1925 - 1944

The *Bulletin* served the Veterans' Bureau and Veterans' Administration in much the same way as its *Journal* served the American Medical Association. Both journals allocated a large fraction of space to administrative matters, reviews, letters, editorials and meeting reports. Most of the original articles were based on authors' clinical experiences, either case reports, case series, or teaching articles based on extensive experience. Some epidemiological and methodological articles appeared in both journals. Preclinical science played a very small role.

The scientific and medical subject matter of the *Bulletin* was closely aligned with veterans' health care needs. Table 2.3 shows the distribution of topics in 1926, 1927, 1931 and

33

1935. There were many articles on treatment of patients with tuberculosis, unusual forms of tuberculosis, syphilis, both tuberculosis and syphilis, and psychiatric disorders as well as reports of favorable results from innovative psychiatric treatments.

Table 2.3. Subjects of Articles in the *Medical Bulletin*, July-December, 1926, 1927, 1931 and 1935

	(% of total pages)			
	1926	1927	1931	1935
Tuberculosis	23.8	16.2	16.7	13.9
Neurosyphilis	1.9	4.1	6.8	5.6
Nonsyphilitic psychoses	8.0	12.8	8.0	5.6
Other psychiatric disorders	13.6	9.5	3.1	0.0
Neurologic (nonsyphilitic) disorders	8.3	0.9	2.7	3.0
Infectious diseases (other than neurosyphilis)	5.9	6.8	11.4	15.2
Neoplasms	8.0	2.5	20.1	11.4
Cardiovascular and arteriosclerotic disorders	11.5	9.7	6.3	6.1
Gastrointestinal disorders	2.9	7.2	2.7	2.5
Endocrine, renal, GU and arthritic disorders	8.8	5.2	9.0	11.6
Sequelae of trauma	2.4	3.2	2.5	4.0
Other	4.8	2.1	10.9	21.2

Physicians in the Veterans' Bureau were not the only contributors to the *Bulletin*. For example, librarians ("book therapy" for patients with mental illness), physical therapists, nurses and hospital managers also wrote articles. The *Bulletin* carried a news section, reporting activities of the Medical Council, items from Central Office and field hospitals, conferences at the hospitals, and Veterans' Bureau physicians' participation in other organizations' medical meetings.

The Central Office Research Subsection

The Medical Research Subdivision that had been recommended by the Medical Council became a reality when Philip B. Matz, M.D. (Figure 2.3), a pathologist, joined the Central Office as its Chief in September 1925.[32] He met with an enthusiastic Medical Council Group on Investigation and Research at the fourth Council meeting in October. They noted that Matz, who had been Chief of Laboratory Service at the Legion, TX, Veterans' Hospital, was selected from field hospital staff recommendations of people who had the desired qualifications.

Administrative details of his appointment to Central Office were incomplete, so he was temporarily assigned to the Washington, DC, Veterans' Hospital. He had already:

"a.   Made a survey of the pathological laboratory of U.S. Veterans' Hospital #32, where he has been temporarily assigned.
b.   Installed a cross-index filing system for that hospital.

c. Investigated apparently irregular blood findings of employees in the X-ray laboratory of the hospital and prepared a report on this study for publication in the *Bulletin*.

d. Undertaken a survey of the facilities and personnel for investigation, and all research work now in progress in all Bureau hospitals.

e. Got under way the standardization of the Wasserman test for all Bureau hospitals.

f. Prepared and submitted to our Group a tentative working program for the Medical Research Division."[33]

Figure 2.3: Philip B. Matz, M.D., Chief, Research Subsection, 1925-1938.

The Medical Council Group recommended that the Division of Medical Research should concentrate its first efforts on completing the survey of research facilities and on standardization of methods for diagnosis and treatment. Nevertheless, "in anticipation of future work," they recommended that:

"a. While the Chief of the Research Subdivision should foster and encourage all evidences of originality in the pursuit of research work, as a matter of policy, all projected studies should be submitted to him for approval. He should also recommend, at his discretion, to qualified stations in the field, problems for medical research.

b. The Group is of the opinion that the Chief of the Division of Medical Research should install a system of regular progress reports on research work being carried out in the field.

c. The Group believes it advisable for the Chief of Medical Research to keep in touch with selected medical schools and laboratories, so as to be in a position to locate suitably qualified research personnel, with a view to cooperating with the Civil Service Commission in filling existing vacancies in this line of work, or for acquiring new personnel for such activities."[34]

<u>Philip Matz, M.D., Chief of the Research Subdivision</u>

Dr. Matz was a 40-year-old pathologist from Baltimore, a 1908 graduate of the Long Island College of Medicine in Brooklyn. In 1909 he joined the staff of the Leavenworth (KS) National Military Home, where he was chief of the laboratory until 1914. From 1914 to 1917, he was in private practice, conducting laboratories in Leavenworth and Kansas City and serving as consultant serologist to the Federal penitentiary at Leavenworth.

During World War I, Matz was chief of the Laboratory Service at the Base Hospital, Camp Travis, TX. In 1919, he published an extensive paper about the bacteriology of pneumonia in influenza victims. He reported that, on throat culture, Pfeiffer's bacillus (believed at the time to cause influenza) was present in 39% and pneumococcus in 10% of 868 patients with uncomplicated influenza. None of the blood cultures from patients with uncomplicated influenza was positive. In influenza patients with complicating pneumonia, on the other hand, pneumococcus was present in the sputum in 68% of 1,505 sputum cultures and Pfeiffer's bacillus in none of them. Of 178 blood cultures from pneumonia cases, 11% were positive, all with pneumococcus. Spinal fluid cultures in 16 cases of meningitis also all revealed pneumococcus of various types. He found acidosis and urea retention in the pneumonia patients, with acute parenchymous inflammation in the kidneys at autopsy.[35]

After the war, Matz joined the Public Health Service and was assigned as Chief, Laboratory Service, to a series of five Public Health (later Veterans' Bureau) Hospitals. During this period, he wrote an extensive clinical research paper on the calcium content of the blood in normal and tuberculous subjects. He established the normal range of fasting serum calcium in 50 normal subjects and showed that it was no different in 72 patients with tuberculosis. In both normal and tuberculous subjects, he demonstrated a modest increase in serum calcium after a high calcium meal or ingestion of inorganic calcium salts, an effect that increased when cod liver oil was given. He presented a few studies in both normal and tuberculous subjects showing an inverse relationship between serum calcium and the coagulation time.[36]

He had also taken postgraduate work at the University of Kansas, St. Louis University, Rush Medical School and the Rockefeller Institute for Medical Research.[37]

After Matz moved to the Central Office, he and his small staff continued to follow the guidance of the Medical Council's Group on Research. The staff concentrated on setting up a statistical system for tracking patients, which was necessary to understand the Bureau's medical care responsibilities better. Early publications were primarily statistical descriptions of the Bureau's patient population and used information gathered by the Evaluation Division in Central Office.

A 1926 study of cardiovascular disease among veterans[38] currently hospitalized showed that 59% of the 537 such cases reported had valvular heart disease. Another 21% had myocarditis, a surprising finding that Matz attributed in part to the high incidence of tuberculous myocarditis. In a later report of 330 deaths due to cardiovascular disease during 1923-1925,[39] valvular disease was responsible in 47% and myocarditis in 28% of the fatalities. Average age at death was 34 years. "Angina pectoris" was listed as the cause of death in four cases, but "myocardial infarction" or its equivalent was not included as a cause of death.

Similar reports described the Bureau's patient populations having tuberculosis (6,715 inpatients),[40] degenerative diseases of the heart, blood vessels and kidney,[41, 42] and neuropsychiatric diseases.[43] The tuberculosis study reported a preponderance of moderately advanced cases(48%) and far advanced cases (44%). It demonstrated a poorer response to treatment among "colored" than among white patients, even when the stage of their disease was taken into account. The study of 4,020 cases of "degenerative diseases" included 306 patients with arteriosclerosis (local, cerebral, general or unclassified), 435 with cardiac hypertrophy and 3,279 with some form of nephritis. The study of neuropsychiatric diseases reported that 65% of 12,220 such veteran patients suffered from dementia praecox (schizophrenia), 6.4% from general paresis (tertiary syphilis of the brain). Comparing 4,313 Veterans' Bureau psychiatric admissions with 71,676 admissions to civilian mental hospitals, he found similar incidences of dementia praecox and general paresis, but that more patients with manic-depressive psychosis were admitted to civilian hospitals and more patients with nonpsychotic conditions were admitted to veterans' hospitals. A 1927 article reports the distribution of compensable disabilities among World War I veterans.[44] Matz also published demographic reports on the Veterans' Bureau hospital activities monthly from October 1926 through March 1927.[45-49]

Dr. Matz's writings in the *Medical Bulletin*, as well as articles from field hospitals encouraged by him, were sprinkled with information about fever therapies for general paresis, a form of tertiary syphilis. In 1926, he reviewed recent publications about the procedure.[50] There followed in 1927 a report of early experience with malarial treatment at the Hines, Bronx, Augusta, Gulfport and North Little Rock Veterans' Hospitals. Of 112 patients treated, 65% showed short-term improvement. Spinal fluid Wasserman became negative in only 28%, while the blood Wasserman became negative in 62%. This report concludes "It is believed that the results obtained following this form of treatment justify its continuation and further development. While no rational explanation can be given of its mode of action . . . the effect may be attributable to certain indefinable alterations or reactions of the body."[51] A follow-up article reported on 179 cases, including 67 new cases. By that time, patients had been under observation for as long as 18 months, and the results were "highly satisfactory": 72% were "improved" or "greatly improved" and 66% and 28%, respectively, had negative blood and spinal fluid Wasserman tests.[52]

In 1926, Matz also published in the *Medical Bulletin* review summaries of articles reporting autopsy findings in paretics treated with malaria. There was reversion of histology toward normal, compared with untreated patients, and a lack of spirochetes in the brain tissues.[53] He published practical information about the procedure: a note about how to transport blood containing malaria plasmodia through the mail for use in patients at other hospitals.[54]

In 1928, Matz published an updated report of Veterans' Bureau experience, now reporting 346 patients treated with "inoculation malaria." This time, instead of the in-house *Medical Bulletin*, he published the Veterans' Bureau results in the *Journal of Nervous and Mental Diseases*. This report included a review of the current status of the treatment, quoting the experience of civilian authors extensively, comparing Veterans' Bureau experience with that of others. The Veterans' Bureau hospitals reported no mortality due to treatment, in contrast to about 5% mortality in other series. This was thought to derive from excluding poor-risk patients and the relatively young age of veteran patients. Among treated patients, 24 % were greatly improved and 23% were improved, results comparable to other series. For comparison, Matz quoted the published incidence of spontaneous remissions from general paresis to be in the range of 3% to 10%.[55]

Other articles by Matz reported experience in treatment of paretic patients with ratbite fever (sodoku, due to spirochaeta morsus-muris, an organism that causes a malaria-like fever), with an early suggestion of improvement with less reported mortality than with malaria or relapsing fever.[56] Other reports reviewed clinical conditions and standardization of clinical and laboratory tests.[57-63]

In 1926, Dr. Matz and Dr. H.L. Gilchrist, Medical Director of the Army's Chemical Warfare Service, advised by Drs. Allen K. Krause and H. Kennon Dunham of the Medical Council, began to locate and study veterans who had been victims of poison gasses during World War I. In 1928, they presented a preliminary report,[64] in which they described the study and its difficulties. While the group wanted to study each of the gasses separately, often several types of gas had been used together. There were a total of 70,742 U.S. gas exposure casualties in World War I. In only 37,025 of these was the type of gas known: chlorine, 1,843; mustard, 27,771; phosgene, 6,834; arsenicals, 577. Frequently, men who were gassed had other injuries, which could interact with gas effects. Of the 70,742 total gas casualties, 200 died on the battlefield and 1,221 died in field hospitals, a 2.01% early-death rate.

In 1921, the Army had reviewed the status of a sample of the casualties who had lived to be discharged from the field hospitals. Of the 3431 cases reviewed, 353 (10.3%) were thought to have a gas-related disability in 1921. The long-term effects of gassing were unknown.

In a survey of the problem, Matz and Gilchrist contacted U.S. and international physicians who had wide experience in treatment of gas victims, asking for their opinions about late (8-10 years) effects. The results were not helpful: "An analysis of the opinion of the civilian clinicians as well as the army officers of this and of foreign countries was so at variance and so conflicting that a summarization would result in no definite conclusions. It was felt, therefore, that this difference of opinions was sufficiently great to justify the present study of the residual effects of wartime gassing."[65]

The Veterans' Bureau study, carried out from 1926 to 1928, included a review of all deaths in the men reviewed by the Army in 1921, and a thorough clinical follow-up of those in the Army study believed in 1921 to have a possible gas-related disability. About ten years after the initial gassing, they called the veterans in for a complete reexamination and review of their complete case histories.

The authors acknowledged that the selection method made impossible an overall statistical analysis of the late effects of wartime gassing, since those who showed no evidence of effects in 1921 were not studied in the 1926-1928 review. Rather, they sought to establish

Table 2.5. Summary of results of the 1926-1928 Veterans' Bureau - Army
   study of the late effects of wartime gassing

Incidence of gas - related death or residual disability in 1926 - 1928 (8 - 10 years after gas exposure)
   among those surviving to leave the field hospital:

	Chlorine	Mustard	Phosgene	Arsenicals
Total number examined	96	89	79	43
Death	0.24%	1.48%	0.40%	0.87%
Residua	2.00%	4.41%	1.58%	0.73%
Death or residua	2.24%	5.89%	1.98%	1.60%

(Note that these incidence figures omit any casualties who had no evidence of gas - related disability
   in 1921 but who may have developed a disability after 1921.)

Gas - related clinical findings in 1926 - 1928

	Chlorine	Mustard	Phosgene	Arsenicals
Chronic bronchitis	x	x	x	x
Emphysema	x	x	x	
Pulmonary tuberculosis	x		x	
Bronchial asthma		x	x	
Pulmonary fibrosis			x	
Pleurisy				x
Bronchopneumonia				x
Chronic conjunctivitis		x		
Corneal opacities		x		

as unequivocally as possible in a select group those conditions that might be due to gassing. They found in some of the men infrequent but definite anatomic and clinical residua of the gassing, apart from other considerations. The most frequent effect was a chronic bronchitis with asthma-like features. Gassing did not appear to predispose to tuberculosis, but it did aggravate existing tuberculosis.[65-68] The results of this study are summarized in Table 2.5.

Matz also published a follow-up study of veterans who had developed mental illnesses while in the military.[69] This was of special importance because of the Veterans' Bureau's heavy psychiatric workload (Table 2.6). This study and its sequelae enriched the practical experience with psychiatric disease of VA doctors, who, by the middle 1930s, found that more than half of their patients suffered from neuropsychiatric diseases.[70] These doctors played an active role in setting up methods for psychiatric screening of inductees at the beginning of World War II.[71]

Table 2.6. Analysis of veterans who were service connected for neuropsychiatric disease

Military discharges for neuropsychiatric disease, 1917-1919: 78,930

Veterans hospitalized for neuropsychiatric disease

Year	Veterans' hospitals	Other hospitals	Total
1920	4,926	3,556	8,482
1928	13,057	1,620	14,677

Follow-up of selected patients admitted in the first half of 1922

1922 diagnosis	1928 status (%)			
	Improved	Unimproved	Died	Unknown
General paresis (neurosyphilis) (n=246)	15	1	72	0
Dementia praecox (schizophrenia) (n=843)	38	37	10	14
Nonpsychotic (n=609)	40	56	1	5

The Medical Research Division expanded modestly during the late 1920s. In his 1929 address to the Medical Council, Dr. Crossman said:

"You will recall that the matter of research was discussed at the last meeting and we have, as a result of the recommendations which were made, authority to employ a cardio-vascular specialist to head up this part of the research department....

A medical statistician has been authorized, and we have in view, I think, a very good candidate for that particular position. However, we do need your assistance in securing the type of man we are looking for to handle the cardio-vascular work...."[72]

This expansion was transient, however. A 1934 report names only Dr. Matz and two assistants in the Research Subdivision.[73] In 1930, Dr. Matz reported of his own work that:

"The following studies have been conducted by the Research Subdivision and papers have been prepared and published in various medical journals during the fiscal year:

1. A study of intestinal tuberculosis among ex-service men.[74]
2. The future incidence of nervous and mental disease among ex-service men.[75]
3. The Gerson-Sauerbruch regimen in tuberculosis.[76]

"The following studies are now being conducted and will shortly be completed:

1. A clinical and statistical study of diabetes mellitus.
2. A study of malignancy among ex-service men.

40

3. A study of manic-depressive psychosis - to be presented at the Association for Research in Nervous and Mental Disease, December, 1930.
4. A study of the arthritides."

These studies were all later published,[77-85] as were studies of habit-forming drugs,[86] food poisoning,[87, 88] the coincidence of malignancy and tuberculosis,[89] the outcome of surgical treatment of tuberculosis[90] and the incidence of bronchogenic carcinoma.[91] In a 1932 report on dispensary care in the VA, he compared the outcome of VA clinics with those of other hospitals, showing that the VA outcome compared favorably. Of the patients discharged from VA clinics, 82% were considered to be cured or improved.[92]

In 1935, Matz published in the *New England Journal of Medicine* a series of five articles about heart disease in veterans.[93-97] In 1937 and 1938, he published a series of articles about silicosis.[98-101] Altogether, 89 publications from his time as Chief, Research Subdivision were listed in the *Index Medicus*.

Figure 2.4. Philip Matz, M.D., relaxing

On June 1, 1938, Dr. Matz undertook a two-month tour of VA hospitals that were active in research. On June 28, he was in Los Angeles, where he held a conference on studies of tuberculosis. After the meetings, he and a group of VA colleagues went to the beach in Santa Monica, where he suffered a heart attack and dropped dead at the age of 53.[37, 102]

Matz had been an active and creative leader. His assistant, Anne Bambery, wrote to his sister after his death:

"I worked with Dr. Matz for about thirteen years and in that time I learned to know him as a very sincere counselor and friend. He was so kind and considerate of every one."[103]

Horatio Pollack, statistician for the New York Department of Mental Hygiene, who was in the Group on Research of the Medical Council, wrote:

"In connection with my work on the Medical Council of the Veterans' Administration, Dr. Matz and I became intimate friends. I had the highest regard for him as a man, as a physician, and as a research worker."[104]

Arthur Vorwald of the Trudeau Foundation, Saranac Lake, wrote:

"I shall remember Dr. Matz for his keen enthusiasm and vision so well displayed at the various round table discussions held in connection with the National Tuberculosis Foundation."[105]

After Matz died, there were no major new VA research initiatives until after World War II. The independent Research Subdivision in VA Central Office was merged with a section on postdoctoral training to form the "Postdoctoral Training and Research Division," headed by Hugo Mella, M.D. Mella was a neuropsychiatrist who, during his postdoctoral fellowship at Harvard had published basic and clinical neurological studies.[106-114] He had entered the Veterans' Bureau about 1926 and had held a variety of administrative positions. While he was Clinical Director at the Palo Alto VA Hospital and Manager of the VA hospital at St. Cloud, Minnesota, he had published a variety of clinically oriented and philosophical papers.[115-123] After he became chief of the "Postdoctoral Training and Research Division", he published only the results of a follow-up study on neurosyphilis that Dr. Matz had not had time to complete,[124] and a report of results of sulfapyradine treatment of 92 cases of lobar pneumonia.[125] Otherwise, his research activities were primarily supervisory, consisting of receiving monthly reports from the three designated research laboratories and arranging for their budgets and personnel. The vigorous leadership Dr. Matz had provided, reflected in acknowledgements in publications by VA doctors, had been lost. Pressures of funding, short staffing, and, later, wartime conscriptions took their toll. The small but vigorous research effort reflected in the *Medical Bulletin* dwindled.

Research in the hospitals

From the beginning, research was encouraged in the Veterans' Bureau hospitals, though until 1932 there seems to have been no organized effort to establish centrally funded laboratories specifically dedicated to full-time research. Earlier, the policy encouraging research led to many small investigations by hospital staff members.

Most of these are studies that could be done without specific funding. For others, the source of the money is unknown. Most likely, in the tradition of the time, the investigators funded their own research or used their ingenuity to adapt existing resources to research use.

An interesting series of studies on the effect of using bile salts to treat pneumococcal pneumonia were reported in the early 1930s by Edwin E. Ziegler, M.D., a graduate of the George Washington University School of Medicine, who entered the VA's Associate Physician program in 1929. This was a program in which about twenty young doctors per month were recruited straight out of internship and given a six-week training course before being assigned to a VA hospital.[126]   Ziegler was assigned to the Laboratory at Northport VA Hospital, where he probably worked under the guidance of Linneaus H. Prince, M.D., a pathologist whose name is connected with a variety of innovative research projects. Ziegler attended VA postdoctoral courses in pathology and later cited the VA as the source of his pathology training.[127]

In his first paper on the subject of bile acids and the pneumococcus,[128] Ziegler stated:

> "Since pneumococci are soluble in solutions of bile salts, my coworkers and I thought of using the bile salts themselves in the treatment of pneumonia. This paper deals with the treatment of pneumonia with the bile salts sodium taurocholate and sodium glycocholate, with some laboratory experiments on the salts and their properties."

Using in vitro studies, he showed that concentrations of bile salts that lyse pneumococci did not damage erythrocytes. He reported results in three patients, including one with meningitis, whose pneumococcal pneumonia improved after intravenous bile salts. However, the injections led to a sclerosing phlebitis.

Ziegler went on to study sodium dehydrocholate, which was less toxic to the veins and "can be given intravenously in quite large doses and in convenient concentrations without injury."[129, 130] He extended these studies when he was visiting the Army Medical School Department of Bacteriology, while taking a postgraduate course in pathology and bacteriology given by the Veterans' Bureau in affiliation with the Army Medical School.[129] His findings demonstrated an antipneumococcal action of the dehydrocholate, both in vitro and in animals, with minimal toxicity. He extended these studies to demonstrate immunity to pneumococcus in rabbits injected with a mixture of sodium dehydrocholate and pneumococci.

As seems to have been frequent in the early VA, Ziegler was reassigned several times during his VA tenure. He continued to study the sodium dehydrocholate-pneumococcus mixture, "pneumocholin", while working as a pathologist at the Coatesville, PA, and Boise, ID, VA Hospitals over the next few years. In 1933, he reported that pneumocholin caused no deleterious effects when injected intravenously and that it "induces a very effective immunity for between three and four days,"[131, 132] an effect that he felt would be useful in clinical practice because of the extended clinical time course in pneumococcal pneumonia.

Ziegler also devised a method for measuring the "oxygen absorbing power" from the ratio of oxygen consumption to respired volume, as measured with a basal metabolism device.[133, 134]

Another young physician, Justin J. Stein, from Texas via the Mayo Clinic, joined the tumor clinic at the Hines VA Hospital in 1935 as a member of the "X-ray, Radium Therapy and Surgery" section. He became certified in radiology in 1937. Publishing a series of clinical papers on the importance of early diagnosis and treatment of cancer[135] and on unusual tumors of the intestine,[136-138] Stein reported extensively on aspects of lung carcinoma, particularly cancers of the apex of the lung.[139-144] Even after he joined the Navy, he reported in the *Medical Bulletin* about his combat experiences[145, 146]. After the war, Stein moved to Los Angeles, where he became a faculty member at UCLA, a consultant at the

West Los Angeles VA hospital and chief of radiation therapy at the Long Beach, CA, VA hospital.[147]

A series of intriguing reports in early issues of the *Medical Bulletin* deal with the use of Mercurochrome intravenously in the treatment of bacterial infections. This approach had been started at the Brady Urological Institute at Johns Hopkins in 1922, when it was used to cure a man believed to be moribund from septicemia. In July, 1925, C. D. Allen, from the Memphis Veterans Bureau Hospital, published his experience with 100 cases in the first issue of the *Medical Bulletin*,[148] and added another 51 cases the following year.[149] He found the best results to be in infections of the genitourinary tract and in arthritis. Albert Martin from the San Fernando Veterans' Hospital (a southern California hospital later important in the VA tuberculosis trials) reported a case of hemolytic streptococcus bacteremia following empyema cured by intravenous Mercurochrome,[150] and R.L. Harris from the Augusta (GA) VA Hospital reported similar success in a case of bacteremia due to streptococcus viridans.[151] H.E. Foster from the Sheridan (WY) VA Hospital reviewed the literature on this treatment in the *Medical Bulletin*, concluding that "In from 50 to 75 per cent of the cases treated it has been highly efficacious in single or repeated doses."[152] Mercurochrome was perhaps the most successful of the external disinfectants used internally, but its use was eventually abandoned.[153]

A major follow-up study of fractures of the long bones in World War I by J.B. Walker, a consultant to the Veterans' Bureau Regional Office in New York City, appeared in the *Medical Bulletin* in 1929.[154-157] Of 16,339 soldiers with one or more battle fractures of a long bone, 2019 (16.6%) died. Of 39,569 soldiers with nonbattle fractures, 1,346 (3.4%) died. Of the soldiers with long bone fractures, 4,178 (7.5%) had amputations, and 187 of those soldiers died. Osteomyelitis was a major cause of death and disability. This report details various types of fractures, treatments and outcomes.

While a large part of VA research during this pre-World War II period was carried out in coordination with the Central Office research unit or by the three designated Research Laboratories (below), VA professional staff continued to publish in the *Medical Bulletin* from its inception in 1925 until the beginning of the war. Table 2.7 presents a sampling of titles from the *Medical Bulletin* through these years, reflecting areas of interest of VA staff whose primary responsibility was patient care rather than research.

Table 2.7. Sampling of titles from the *Medical Bulletin*, articles written by clinicians in the hospitals, not in designated research units

1925:

Resume of treatment of 25 cases of diabetes mellitus with insulin.[158]

Residuals of encephalitis lethargica.[159]

The blood vessels in tuberculosis: some aspects of the part played by the blood vessels in the dissemination of tuberculosis.[160]

Treatment of Raynaud's Disease by negative pressure.[161]

1926:

A study of Larson's ring test applied to 315 cases of tuberculosis.[162]

Adenocarcinoma - primary in the renal tubules.[163]

A preliminary report on attempts at active immunization of guinea pigs by urinary antigens from cases of tuberculosis.[164]

Correlation of clinical and laboratory procedures in tuberculosis: 1. The complement fixation test.[165]

1927:

Studies on the bacteriocidal properties in vitro of certain fatty acids irradiated with the quartz-mercury-vapor spectrum.[166]

Report of cases of leprosy with unusual manifestations.[167]

Notes on amnesia.[168]

1928:

Thoracotomy for empyema complicating pneumonia - end results in 100 consecutive cases.[169]

Multiple sclerosis.[170]

Ancient Greek, Etruscan and Roman dentistry.[171]

A study of the emotions in psychotic patients (A report of the examination of 100 psychotic patients with the Pressey test).[172]

A comparative study of the Kahn and complement fixation tests of spinal fluid.[173]

1929:

Tetany from overbreathing.[174]

The Gregerson test.[175]

Julius Caesar, epileptic.[176]

1930:

Preliminary report of fifteen cases of Sodoku treatment of general paresis.[177]

Typhoid vaccine in the treatment of general paralysis of the insane.[178]

Narcolepsy.[179]

Value of media containing certain iron compounds in differentiating typhoid-colon organisms.[180]

An improved method for staining tubercle bacilli in tissues cut by the frozen-section technique.[181]

Carbon dioxide - oxygen inhalations in catatonic dementia praecox.[182]

45

1931:

Experiments on bacteriophage adsorption by vulnerable bacteria.[183]

Medical science in the thirteenth century.[184]

The use of subarachnoid lavage and ethylhydrocupeine in meningitis.[185]

Stramonium in encephalitis.[186]

1932:

Bronchial spirochetosis, with report of a case.[187]

A world's record for the transportation of entamoeba histolytica.[188]

Elliptical human erythrocytes: report of two cases.[189, 190]

Observations of heart action under vagus stimulation.[191]

The incidence of syphilis in 5,000 Negro ex-service men.[192]

1933:

Intravenous administration of sodium amytal in acute psychotic episodes.[120]

Psychosis with alcoholic pellagra.[193]

1934:

An unusual case of hysteria with a retrocursive gait.[194]

1935:

Super-diathermy in the treatment of dementia paralytica.[195]

Nineteen cases of pneumonia in members of the Civilian Conservation Corps with no deaths.[196]
Brain abscess consequent to latent head trauma.[197]

Sulphur (colloidal) therapy in the treatment of arthritis.[198]

1936:

Effects of long hospitalization on psychotic patients.[199]

1937:
Use of benzedrine sulphate in catatonic stupors.[200]
Molokai and its leper colony.[201]

1938:

Hypoglycemic shock therapy in schizophrenia: results of treatment of six cases.[202]

Experience with the insulin shock therapy of schizophrenia.[203]

Bacteriological examination of eating utensils.[204]

1940:

Herpes zoster in early syphilis.[205]

1941:

The treatment of schizophrenia with desoxycorticosterone acetate.[206]

The status of thyroid ablation for intractable heart disease.[207]

Physicians in Veterans' Bureau hospitals received some recognition outside the agency and its *Medical Bulletin*. In 1927, seven Veterans' Bureau scientific and medical exhibits were included in the national meeting of the American Medical Association, in Washington, D.C. Included were exhibits on treatment of neurosyphilis with malaria or rat-bite fever, on laboratory findings in various psychoses and in syphilis, and on the effects of bran on gastrointestinal x-rays.

In 1930, progress reports from the Bronx (NY) and Perry Point (MD) VA Hospitals were reported in the *Medical Bulletin*.

"From the Bronx Veterans Administration Hospital:

1. "Sodoku treatment" for general paralysis given 19 patients between April 1929 and April 1930. Results: Some improvement, no deaths.
2. 12 paretics inoculated with tertian malaria blood. The malarial paroxysms were terminated by quinine. This treatment was followed by sulpharsphenamine. The patients were gaining weight and strength, and there had been no deaths.
3. During March, seven patients with chronic encephalitis lethargica were given Rosenow serum subcutaneously. It was planned to treat another seven with the same dose by nasal spray. Five others have received 500 milliamperes current by diathermy for 20 minutes to the brain, and have reported subjective improvement.
4. Experiments on use of autocondensation current in multiple sclerosis.

"From Perry Point:

1. One hundred paretics have been given malaria treatment.
2. Two paretics were treated with sulfosin. The reaction was so severe that the study was stopped.
3. Twenty–nine epileptics were treated with a meat-free diet. They had no weight loss, and appear to be well. The severity but not the number of their convulsions has improved.
4. In accordance with instructions from the Research Subdivision, Central Office, the results of liver feeding in patients with neurological symptoms are being studied."[208]

Later in 1930, in a more complete report of research activities in field hospitals coordinated by his office, Dr. Matz listed four projects "recently assigned" to field hospitals and 19 projects from field hospitals for which final reports had been received (Table 2.8).[209]

Table 2.8. Research problems at Veterans Administration hospitals (*Medical Bulletin*, 1930).

Recently assigned
1. The use of the Gerson-Sauerbruch regimen in the treatment of pulmonary as well as surgical tuberculosis.
2. A study of 1001 autopsy protocols for the purpose of correlating clinical and anatomic findings.
3. The application of the Shaw-MacKensie test for malignancy, for the purpose of ascertaining whether or not this precipitation test will yield information in the diagnosis of malignant disease.
4. Therapeutic use of liver in the degenerative diseases of the spinal cord.

Recently completed
1. The use of typhoid vaccine in the treatment of general paresis of the insane.
2. Study of 100 cases of dementia praecox and manic-depressive psychosis.
3. Two modifications of the Benedict quantitative determination of dextrose in the urine.
4. Standardization of cholesterinized alcoholic beef heart antigen for use in complement fixation procedures.
5. Evaluation of results obtained by the use of liver, liver extract, and insulin in the reduction of blood sugar in diabetes mellitus.
6. Comparison of results with Meinicke and Kline tests.
7. Improved method of staining tubercle bacilli in tissue cut by frozen section method.
8. A study of the Gregerson test for the detection of occult blood.
9. The ketogenic diet in the treatment of epilepsy.
10. A resume of 250 electrocardiographs.
11. The use of lipiodol in the treatment of bronchiectesis.
12. The use of sodium ricinoleate in the treatment of intestinal tuberculosis.
13. A study of intestinal tuberculosis.
14. Pernicious anemia in the Negro.
15. Liver feeding in organic neurological conditions.
16. Rapid precipitation test for syphilis.
17. The 'Zoning' phenomenon in complement fixation with cholesterinized alcohol beef heart extract.
18. Studies in venous pressure - its clinical application.
19. Buffered diluent as preservative for diphtheria toxin for the Schick test.

A new approach in the 1930s: Centrally funded research laboratories

When the Veterans Administration was formed in 1930, the Medical Department found itself two layers down in the bureaucracy. Despite this, the activities of the Research Subdivision continued active through the mid-1930s. In 1931, Mr. Ijams, director of the Veterans' Bureau, now a section of the Veterans Administration, said in his address to the Medical Council:

"I am very glad to advise you gentlemen of a little meeting held here in Washington just a few weeks ago, and attended by some members of your body who were good enough to come over here and assist us. At that meeting was brought up a matter that has been close to my heart for some time - the matter of research. I do not claim any authorship for this, as this was sold to me many years ago by a former medical director. He impressed upon me the fact that we have a vast reservoir of material that we were not using for the advancement of medical science. Dr. Griffith and I talked this over

48

and we decided to do what we could towards securing funds for the employment of men who were qualified to do this work. We wanted these men to do research work only, and not be called upon every five minutes to make a physical examination or to consider Mary Jones's efficiency report, etc. Following the conference with members of this council, the recommendation was made to General Hines that this work be started in the bureau. We appreciated the fact that we could not hope to secure a great deal of money for this purpose. We felt it would be much better to start in a modest sort of way and sell the idea by producing results. I am quite confident that if we can show results in the start of this work we will then have no difficulty in the future in securing whatever funds may be needed to carry on.

"General Hines has approved this idea in principle, and I think that funds will be made available during the next fiscal year, beginning July 1, to enable us to start this most important work."[210]

Figure 2.5. Col. George E. Ijams

Despite this promising start, the outcome of that decision at that time seems to have been the establishment of a single funded research laboratory in 1933, at the Hines VA Hospital in Chicago. This laboratory was primarily responsible for research, but it was also closely integrated with the patient care program of the hospital.

In 1935, the VA's Medical Director, Dr. Charles Griffith, called a second meeting about research, also involving members of the Medical Council, Drs. Barker, Adams, Barrett, Cohn, William F. Lorenz and White, as well as other experts.[211] Apparently feeling that their efforts at the Hines hospital took care of the cancer problem, the Medical Department decided that the VA's major research needs were in neuropsychiatry and cardiac disease and had set aside $15,000 in their annual budget for each of these new initiatives, the same sum already being allotted to the Hines laboratory. Some of the conferees felt that this amount of money was so ridiculously small that there was no point in even planning a program. Dr. Lorenz told the group that New York State was spending $50,000 on research in neuropsychiatry alone. After considerable general discussion, the conferees split into two groups, one for neuropsychiatry and one for cardiology. Each group recommended that a laboratory in its field be established, and that the available monies be used for hiring two professional leaders. The review of this meeting published in the *Medical Bulletin* placed the cardiovascular research unit at the Washington, DC, VA Hospital and the neuropsychiatric research unit at the North Chicago VA Facility.[212] However, on the same page in the *Medical Bulletin* is the announcement of a new neuropsychiatric research unit at the Northport, NY, VA facility.[213] It appears that the unit proposed for North Chicago was cancelled in favor of Northport, but the cardiovascular research unit at the Washington, DC, hospital did indeed open in late 1935.

The Tumor Research Unit at the Hines VA Hospital

In 1932, the Tumor Research Laboratory at the Hines VA Hospital, the first research laboratory to receive funds from VA Central Office specifically for research work, was established to collaborate with the Hines Cancer Treatment Center. This special cancer treatment unit, a referral center modeled after Memorial Hospital in New York, had been established at Hines in 1930 in association with the new Diagnostic Center at Hines. Surgeons, radiologists, and organ-systems specialists worked together. A Tumor Board met daily to examine and discuss patients. There was an active teaching program with local and national conferences and an arrangement for training visiting physicians. It had the latest cancer therapy equipment, most notably a gram of radium and all necessary machinery for preparation and implantation of radon beads into cancer patients.[214] The research laboratory complemented this effort.

Seward E. Owen, Ph.D., a biochemist, initially led the Hines Tumor Research Laboratory. His early work was directed to assays of "prolans." (The term "prolan" was used at that time to define the substances excreted in the urine that cause positive pregnancy tests in animals; the effect is that of chorionic gonadotropin.) These substances were interesting to the Hines Tumor Clinic because they observed that prolans were increased in most malignant testicular tumors, particularly the less well-differentiated tumors. The term "teratoma testis" was used to include a spectrum of testicular tumors, including chorionepithelioma, embryonal adenocarcinoma, without and with lymphoid stroma, seminoma and mixed or adult type of testicular cancer. Prolan concentration in the urine varied by type of teratoma testis, the highest concentration seen with chorionepithelioma and the least with the adult type. Owen developed a quantitative bioassay for prolans,[215] first in the rabbit and then in the mouse, for which he reported an innovative, inexpensive metabolic cage.[216] Collaborating with Max Cutler, M.D., chief of the Tumor Clinic, he did extensive clinical correlations of this method in patients with testicular tumors.[217, 218] The method was used for follow-up of treated patients who lived at a distance from the hospital; they sent in their urine specimens by mail and were recalled for further treatment only when the results suggested recurrence. The method was applied to diagnose and follow two cases of chorionepithelioma[219] and five cases of malignant tumors in undescended testes.[220] In 1936, Owen reported results of prolan assays in 71 patients who were later proven to have "teratoma testis," compared with 29 in whom it was suspected who later proved to have other diagnoses. From this study, he defined the diagnostic level of urinary prolans. Follow-up studies showed reduction in prolans after surgery and radiation with increase on recurrence of the tumor. False positives were found in 3 patients who had received orchiectomy for other conditions.[221] Owen and Cutler studied patients with prostatic hypertrophy and prostate cancer, measuring prolans and estrogenic substances by mouse bioassay. They found no abnormalities in those patients.[222]

This method of bioassay was very laborious and used many animals. Owen searched for a more economical method. He studied bitterling fish, into whose water the assay substances were placed.[223] The male bitterling fish develops a typical mating coloration when sexually stimulated; the female develops an extension of the ovipostor. After the responses of the fish to urine from pregnant women had been confirmed, urine extracts from patients with testicular tumors were tested. Female fish responded only to extremely high concentrations. The male fish generally responded to the concentrations of clinical interest, but their response was too erratic to make fish a practical substitute for rabbits and mice in this bioassay. Owen also tested these fish for a testosterone bioassay but concluded that a better understanding of their color responses was needed before a practical test was possible.[224] He also developed a chemical assay for the prolans,[225] which correlated fairly well with the bioassay and which he concluded would be a useful "qualitative" tool.

Owen also searched for agents that might cause malignant growth. In a series of articles in the journal *Growth*, he explored the role of the sulphydryl amino acids cystine and cysteine on wound healing in mice[226] and on extracts of insect larvae,[227] and he studied the release of sulphydryl groups from protein substances when they were exposed to carcinogens.[228] He published review articles about carcinogenesis.[229, 230] Collaborating with H.A. Weiss and L.H. Prince, he reported in *Science* and the *American Journal of Cancer* that various carcinogens stimulate regeneration and reproduction in the planarian, an aquatic worm that regenerates both head and tail segments when cut in half.[231, 232] He also studied radiation effects in bred females of a high breast cancer strain of mice. Irradiation reduced the incidence of later spontaneous breast cancer compared with similarly bred control mice, but not to the low incidence seen in randomly bred mice. He speculated that the irradiation may have reduced ovarian function and estrogen secretion, but noted that even nonsterilizing doses of radiation had a protective effect.[233] Following up on the likelihood that estrogens increase susceptibility to breast cancer, he and G. R. Allaben of the Tumor Clinic published a case report of a woman with breast cancer which they believed was caused by prolonged estrogen therapy.[234]

When Owens left to join the military in 1938, Dr. Cutler, though still a consultant, became nominal head of the Tumor Research Laboratory. In fact, the laboratory seems to have lain dormant. Robert Schrek, M.D., was recruited from St. Cloud, MN, VA Hospital to Hines, his transfer orders instructing him "to work in the Tumor Research Laboratory." However, when he arrived, Dr. Schrek found that he was needed full-time in clinical service, and he was not able to start working in the research laboratory until 1940 or 1941.[235]

Dr. Schrek was a pathologist who had done basic oncologic research while at Vanderbilt.[236-244] When his Vanderbilt fellowship ended, he went to work as a pathologist at the Pondville Hospital in Wrentham, Massachusetts. While there, he did clinical research studies on cutaneous carcinoma that eventually led to three publications.[245-247] He entered the VA at St. Cloud and immediately began looking for an opportunity to do research.

Schrek's earliest publications from Hines presented statistical methodology.[248-250] These seem to have resulted from work done on his own, before the research laboratory could reopen. He also wrote a descriptive and statistical review of the Hines Tumor Clinic's 1941 activities.[251] Early in his days at Hines, Schrek formed a club with members from all Chicago area medical schools interested in cancer. During the war, Dr. Schrek became a Major in the U.S. Army, but his assignment was to continue work in the Tumor Research Laboratory.[235]

Figure 2.6. Robert Schrek, M.D.

At first, the laboratory consisted of Schrek and two technical people. They set up a method that he had devised while at Vanderbilt to distinguish viable white blood cells from dead cells using the fact that only dead cells take up eosin in solution.[243] They used this method to assess factors affecting leukocyte life span. These studies were very laborious, since cell counts were done by hand-counting cells in a hemacytometer. He obtained reasonably pure preparations of lymphocytes from rabbit thymus and spleen, and of polymorphonuclear leukocytes from rabbit bone marrow and from peritoneal exudate after intraperitoneal injection of an albumin-lecithin mixture. In short-term (2-4 hours) experiments, he found that lymphocytes are much more sensitive to the toxic effects of heat and of moccasin venom than are polymorphonuclear leukocytes.[252] He found that oxygen was not necessary for cell survival, and that polymorphonuclear leukocytes survived equally well with or without glucose in the medium. Glycolysis occurred under both aerobic and anaerobic conditions. The major factor affecting cell survival was the type of cell. In studies of human leukocytes, he found that those from patients with lymphatic and myelogenous leukemias had the same metabolic characteristics as did normal leukocytes.[253] In other studies, he showed that leukocytes are quite resistant to osmotic challenge[254] and that the response of other tissues varies.[255]

Schrek's most noteworthy studies from the pre-1946 period were of the effects of radiation on leukocytes. Using his in vitro leukocyte preparation and a statistical method he devised to estimate 50% and 10% survival times, he clearly demonstrated marked radiosensitivity of lymphocytes, with considerable radioresistance of the polymorphonuclear leukocytes.

This was equally true of preparations from the rabbit, from normal human blood and from the blood of patients with lymphocytic and myelogenous leukemia. The cytocidal effect of radiation on lymphocytes was seen only in the presence of oxygen. Schrek recalled that when the paper reporting these findings was in press in *Radiology* one of the editors visited him and suggested that he contact Austen Brues of the metallurgy department at the University of Chicago (predecessor of Argonne National Laboratory). Schrek did not follow up on this suggestion, which he later realized would have resulted in his being reassigned to atomic bomb research in the Manhattan Project.[256]

Meanwhile, Schrek continued to study the patients in the Hines Tumor Clinic and to develop new methods.[257] He published a summary of 1,943 admissions in *Cancer Research*, pointing out that relatively more patients from the South presented with cancers of the exposed skin and relatively fewer with cancers of the stomach and testis.[258] He reported on a series of 20 black patients with skin cancers.[259] Five of these occurred at the site of a previous injury. While the incidence of carcinomas in sun-exposed areas of the skin was dramatically decreased in blacks, the incidence in covered areas of the body was similar in blacks and in whites. He also studied the racial distribution of other cancers, using data from Hines and also from a U.S. Public Health Service survey and from national mortality statistics. He reported that carcinoma of the male breast was much higher in blacks than in whites, while the incidence of breast cancer in black women was only slightly greater than in whites.[260] Cancer of the penis and scrotum was increased in blacks.[261]

In the early postwar period, in collaboration with clinicians of the Tumor Clinic, he reviewed the smoking histories of patients with cancers of the lung, larynx and pharynx, compared with those of the total population of cancer patients at Hines. They concluded that: "There is strong circumstantial evidence that cigarette smoking was an etiological factor in cancer of the respiratory tract."[262] This paper was later cited in the Surgeon General's report on the dangers of cigarette smoking.[263]

In his later work, Schrek continued to develop new techniques, one of the most useful of which was a time-lapse photography method using an inverted phase microscope.[264] Using this method, he showed that the in vitro radiosensitivity of the lymphocytes of a patient with lymphocytic leukemia was predictive of the patient's prognosis. In 61 patients with radiosensitive lymphocytes, median survival was 22 months, while it was only 4 months in the 19 patients with radioresistant lymphocytes. This was not due to a change with time in radiosensitivity, since the patients with radiosensitivity continued to have radiosensitive lymphocytes throughout their clinical course.[265] He also described and characterized the "hairy cell," a previously unrecognized form of malignant white blood cell, and the course of hairy cell leukemia.[266]

Schrek seems to be unique among the pre-WWII VA research investigators in that he made a smooth transition to the postwar, very different, VA. At the end of the war, the Tumor Research Laboratory at Hines was transferred to local administration. The Hines hospital, as a referral center, already had many consultants from nearby medical schools. The atmosphere in the Tumor Clinic was academic, so the introduction of a formal medical school affiliation made less difference than it might have otherwise. Schrek remained at the Hines VA Hospital, in charge of the Tumor Research Laboratory, until he retired in 1977. He continued to analyze data and publish long after his retirement. After the war, he became a member of the pathology department of the Northwestern, and later the Loyola, Universities' Schools of Medicine, as they became affiliated with Hines. He collaborated widely, presented at national and international meetings and published 144 papers.

The Neuropsychiatric Research Units at the Northport VA Hospital

The neuropsychiatric research laboratory recommended by the 1935 conference was located at the Northport VA Hospital on Long Island in New York. In fact, two officially designated Neuropsychiatric Research Units were based at Northport, with a three-year lapse between them and apparently little or no overlap in staff. The first of these units, called the "Neuro-Psychiatric Research Unit for the Study of the Influence of Heterophile Antigen in Nervous and Mental Disease," was established October 1, 1935 and closed in October 1938. The announcement of its opening was published in the *Medical Bulletin*:

> "Upon authority received from the Administrator, a research unit was established in October at Veterans' Administration Facility, Northport, Long Island, N.Y., of which Dr. E.W. Lazell of the staff was placed in charge. The purpose of this unit is to investigate the nature of heterophile antigens and their significance in the diagnosis and treatment of certain diseases, particularly epilepsy. The personnel of this unit consists of Dr. E.W. Lazell, physician in charge; James E. Stanley, laboratorian in bacteriology; Mabel M. Blomberg, assistant laboratorian in bacteriology; Margaret Hickey, research clerk."[213]

In 1919 and 1920, Edward W. Lazell, M.D., had been a psychotherapist working for William A. White, M.D. at St. Elizabeth's Hospital (DC), where attempts were being made to treat psychotic patients by psychoanalytic methods. In 1930, he published an innovative method to apply psychoanalytic concepts to group treatment of psychotic patients.[267] He developed a concept of the unity of the mind and the body,[268, 269] which led him to try to identify a physical cause for neuropsychiatric disease. In 1929, he and Linneaus H. Prince reported a search for a transmissible substance in the serum of patients with dementia praecox (schizophrenia).[270] This study was done while both Lazell and Prince had full-time clinical duties, but Prince, as a pathologist, had a laboratory at his disposal. They exposed bullfrog tadpoles to serum from normal and schizophrenic subjects and found that a 1:1000 dilution of normal serum was compatible with normal development of the tadpoles. On the other hand, a 1:1000 dilution of serum of schizophrenic subjects uniformly killed the tadpoles within three days. They seem not to have pursued this fascinating finding, but Lazell quoted it in later work as seminal in his studies:

> " While trying to explain the phenomena shown in the pollywog experiment, our attention was casually directed to the existence of heterophile antigen. In this manner

the toxic or lethal factor in the blood of epileptics and heterophile antigen became associated in our minds."[271]

Lazell then undertook a study of the general field of immunology, searching for an immune cause for neuropsychiatric disease. In 1932, he published a general review,[272] focusing on the Forssman heterophile antibody, a type of antibody which has an affinity for the receptors of a species other than those in response to which it developed. Extrapolating from the observations that heterophile antibodies can be induced by feeding products from certain animals and could lead to allergic reactions, Lazell speculated that such a reaction might also cause such conditions as epilepsy and dementia praecox.

In the spring of 1935, Lazell studied a group of 14 veterans, all committed as insane to Northport, who also were epileptic. He found that certain patients had convulsions after eating certain foods. By injecting rabbits with the suspect foods, he found that they developed a heterophile antibody, thus identifying the foods as heterophile antigens. He confirmed the food allergies by scratch and intracutaneous skin tests. Sera from 29 epileptic patients at a different hospital confirmed the presence of the heterophile antibody in those with idiopathic epilepsy, but not in those whose convulsions were due to syphilis or encephalitis. He concluded that the patients with idiopathic epilepsy and dementia praecox were sensitized to heterophile antigen, that these diseases are allergic in nature, and that the pathology followed ingestion of excessive amounts of heterophile antigen-containing foods.

Lazell presented these findings to the American Psychiatric Society on May 13, 1935.[273] From October 1935 to the end of 1936, the laboratory pursued this lead. On a research ward, they studied intensively 36 patients with idiopathic epilepsy, 4 of them also with dementia praecox. Finding that skin tests were unreliable and also sometimes triggered convulsions, they sought better ways to identify the allergens responsible for a patient's problem. They made extensive use of an observed leukopenic response to suspect foods. They tried elimination diets to prevent convulsions but concluded that so many foods had to be eliminated that such diets were impractical - the patients would starve. They concluded that "The greatest hope is offered by the search for a general desensitizer."[274]

One of the intriguing findings in this research was the "epileptic cycle." Lazell and his colleagues observed that, after a seizure, the evidence of allergy (response to allergens in skin tests, circulating precipitins and leukocyte reduction) was reduced. It was a logical jump, given the assumption that "there is a close connection between dementia praecox and idiopathic epilepsy," to hypothesize that induction of seizures might alleviate the symptoms of dementia praecox. This hypothesis directed their attention to insulin shock therapy, which was just coming into use in the United States.[274]

In early 1937, Dr. Lazell attended a training course at the Harlem Valley State Hospital on the treatment of schizophrenia with insulin coma, directed by Dr. Manfred Sokol of Vienna, originator of this treatment.[275] On his return to Northport, Lazell began to treat patients with insulin. Soon, Northport was set up as a training site, and, between March 1937 and August 1938, 17 physicians from other VA hospitals were trained in this technique. As Lazell stated: "The work entailed by this training fell to the research personnel; and the laboratory studies necessary for the treatment and for these courses were done by them."[274]

The patients referred for insulin therapy were studied by the same methods as had been the epileptic patients. Lazell found that skin sensitization in dementia praecox patients was less marked in general and directed to different substances than was the case with patients with epilepsy. On the other hand, the leukopenic response to ingestion of certain foods was as marked in dementia praecox as in epilepsy, though the more frequent food allergens were different. Patients with dementia praecox and with epilepsy showed similar heterophile antibodies.

Following up on their observation that dementia praecox patients seemed to improve when seizures occurred during their insulin treatments, Lazell and his colleagues began adding metrazol to the treatment regimen. The logic of the combined treatment seems to have been that metrazol was more effective than insulin alone in inducing seizures, but that patients already in insulin coma developed seizures after a much smaller dose of metrazol than was otherwise needed.

Lazell and his colleagues attempted to desensitize patients with epilepsy and dementia praecox against the heterophile antigen. One substance that they found to be promising was intravenous sodium oleate, but those studies had not been completed when the laboratory was closed.[274] However, they did demonstrate that sodium oleate, when applied directly to tissues, counteracted the effects of allergic dermatitis and hay fever.[276] In the report of this treatment, Lazell commented that,

> "One of the author's sons, overhearing the discussion about sodium oleate as a cure for ivy poisoning, went into the woods and deliberately squeezed a mass of poison ivy in both hands and rubbed it on his face, arms and legs. When seen the next day, they were very red; but the immediate use of sodium oleate as a wet dressing justified this youngster's confidence."

In 1937, Lazell was joined at Northport by Emanuel Messinger, M.D., a psychiatrist,[277] who had been at the St. Cloud (MN) VA Hospital and earlier at the VA in Lyons (NJ). Despite the fact that he was a psychiatrist, he had published about cardiac function.[278] After he moved to Northport, he undertook the study of the cardiovascular changes associated with insulin shock treatment, which he reported in the *Annals of Internal Medicine*. He showed that, during insulin coma, the heart, aorta and pulmonary artery dilate markedly.[279] Collaborating with N. Moros, he published an article on the cardiovascular effects of metrazol, written in early 1938 but published in 1940, that reported transient tachycardia and cardiac arrhythmias.[280]

This laboratory was officially closed in October 1938, a few months after Dr. Matz died. Lazell published his final report of the laboratory's work in 1940.[274] Some 45 reports were issued from this laboratory.

A new Neuropsychiatric Research Unit of a different character was set up at Northport in 1941. James A. Huddleston, M.D., was the director and William J. Turner, M.D., was in charge of laboratory activities. Other staff included a biochemist, a statistician, a laboratorian, a laboratory assistant and a secretary-stenographer. This new laboratory was under the immediate supervision of Dr. Hugo Mella, the central office research chief. It had multiple responsibilities: In addition to "conduct of clinical and laboratory research in neuropsychiatric disorders," it was responsible for "standardization of diagnostic and treatment methods in neuropsychiatry," and for "teaching modern concepts and methods in neurology, psychiatry and neuropathology to physicians of the VA detailed for courses of instruction."[281]

An early product of this new laboratory was a review by its statistician, Charles S. Roberts, of the long-term results of the pharmacologic (insulin and metrazol) shock therapies that Drs. Lazell and Messinger and their trainees conducted in 1937 and 1938. They matched cases with untreated hospitalized control patients of like time of admission, age, sex (all males), race, diagnosis and prior length of psychiatric illness. They followed 74 treated-control pairs for at least two years after the shock therapy, 60 pairs for at least three years. Using a standardized scale of clinical status, they rated the pairs of patients at 30 to 90 days after completion of the treated patient's series of treatments, after one year, after two years and after three years. Two of the treated patients died during the treatment. Twenty-one (28%) of the treated patients and ten (14%) of the controls showed some improvement at some time. No treated patients, and only one control, were considered "cured" at follow-up. At evaluation 30 to 90 days after completion of the treatment series, 21% of the treated patients were "improved" or "much improved," while only 8% of the controls were so classified. This difference gradually eroded with longer follow-up: Early in the second year, improvement was 19% and 7%, respectively; in the third year, 8% and 8%; and in the fourth year, also 8% and 8%. Roberts concluded that the main effect of pharmacologic shock therapy "appears to be that of facilitating improvement of a transient nature."[282]

A series of papers reporting systematic clinical observations of important neuropsychiatric conditions emerged from the staff of this new laboratory: "The alcoholic personality: a statistical study"[283]; "Some dynamic aspects of alcoholic psychoses"[284]; "Factors in the development of general paralysis"[285]; "Note on psychoses and psychoneuroses with malaria."[286] They also reported on their early work on electroencephalography.[287, 288]

This group also carried out biochemical tests. They studied trioses in the blood and devised an improved method for measuring blood hydroxyacetone, published in the *Journal of Biological Chemistry*.[289] Results of clinical application of this method were negative. They studied blood glucose and diastase in a group of depressed patients with manic-depressive psychosis, comparing results with a standardized-scaled psychiatric examination. They found that "voice loudness," "speech rate" and "facial expression of sadness" were all positively correlated with glucose levels, while "voice loudness" correlated negatively and "apathy" positively with diastase levels. The report of this study, of which Roberts was first author, reflects a sophisticated approach to probability and statistics.[290]

Publications from this group about electric shock therapy, which appeared in 1945 and 1946, included articles about prediction of outcome,[291] method,[292] and complications.[293-295]

No post-1946 record of this laboratory has been found.

The Cardiovascular Research Unit at the Washington, D.C., VA Hospital

The third prewar official VA research laboratory was the Cardiovascular Research Unit at the Washington, DC, VA Hospital. As was the Northport laboratory, it was established shortly after the 1935 Central Office conference about research.[211] The earliest of its published reports is a 1937 review in *Annals of Internal Medicine* by John Reisinger, M.D., the unit's chief, presenting observations about the hospital's hypertensive patients from October 1, 1935 to April 1, 1936.[296]

In 1938, Blanche Wilcox, Ph.D., a statistician, and Reisinger collaborated on a study of the prediction of heart weight (confirmed at autopsy) from the x-ray.[297] Dr. Wilcox remained with the unit until it closed in 1949.

Publications from this laboratory were primarily statistical analyses and reports of advances in clinical cardiology and systematic observation of cardiology patients. The statistical analyses followed incidence of heart disease at the Washington VA hospital and also presented comparative data from midwestern and western VA hospitals.[298-300]

Reisinger wrote on the uses of the Masters' exercise test[301] and the cold-pressor test.[302] An article in the *Archives of Internal Medicine* reported four cases of dissecting aneurysm proved at autopsy, including two observed for three and fourteen months before death.[303, 304]

Reisinger also reported a case of primary tumor of the inferior vena cava.[305] He and Basil Blumenthal, who was probably a consultant to the Unit rather than a staff member, published their observations about the pain of coronary artery disease and myocardial infarction.[306-309]

In 1943, Reisinger published on "neurocirculatory asthenia," with data from a review of 50 World War I veterans with this diagnosis. Neurocirculatory asthenia was the term used for the condition known in the Civil War as "irritable heart of soldiers" and by the British in World War I as "soldier's heart"[310] or "effort syndrome." Patients "manifested physical unfitness which could not be accounted for by auscultation of the heart or by any other methods of examination." He recorded good experience of others with gradually increasing physical training for these patients and recommended that such a program be established for the large number of such patients expected to emerge from service in World War II.[311]

Milton Mazer, M.D., joined the Unit about 1941 and remained for a year or two after Reisinger joined the Navy in 1942. He and Reisinger published a review of thiocyanate treatment of hypertension, with a report of nine cases.[312] Mazer published technical papers on the heart x-ray and electrocardiogram,[313-316] and he wrote an article on "Palindromic rheumatism."[317] He and Albert Kistin, who was active in the Unit after the war, wrote a pair of articles for the *Medical Bulletin* on "Current practice in cardiovascular diseases."[318, 319]

Aaron H. Traum, M.D., was the chief of the Unit at the end of World War II. He and Blanche Wilcox reviewed extensive records from the experience of the Unit. They also reviewed thousands of records of service members being discharged from the military. They published in the *New England Journal of Medicine* a survey of 19,870 cases of cardiovascular disease from the pension rolls of World War II veterans.[320] Of these cases, 44% had valvular or rheumatic heart disease; 15% were hypertensive; 9% were arteriosclerotic; 13% had peripheral vascular disease; 6% had neurocirculatory asthenia; and 13% had other conditions. Seeking better ways to screen out persons with heart disease before induction into the military, Traum and Wilcox performed a complete record review of 150 of these veterans, whose heart conditions had the same distribution as found in the larger series. They reviewed the Selective Service questionnaires and examination records, as well as all subsequent records and found that in many cases the veteran had known of his condition before induction and that some of them had mentioned it on the questionnaire. In a number of cases ultimately discharged for hypertension, no blood pressure had been recorded at induction.[321]

Traum reviewed the 10,500 patients who had received electrocardiograms at the Washington, DC, VA Hospital between 1936 and 1944 and found 259 with right axis deviation. From these, he identified 26 patients with definite diagnoses of arteriosclerotic (22 patients) or hypertensive (4 patients) heart disease. Comparing them with the much larger numbers of patients without right axis deviation, he found that only 9% of the arteriosclerotics with right axis deviation had died, compared with 20% of 573 other patients with arteriosclerosis. On the other hand, 3 of the 4 hypertensives had died compared with a 32% death rate among 737 other hypertensives, suggesting that right axis deviation might be a poor prognostic sign in hypertensives but a good one in arteriosclerotic heart disease.[322] He also published a case history uncovered in his record review of a 47-year-old World War I veteran with Lutembacher's Syndrome, a congenital condition which usually caused death before age 40. This condition had not been detected during military service or, indeed, until the patient was about 40 years old.[323]

In terms of its wide recognition and lasting significance, the most important product of the Washington VA Hospital Cardiovascular Research Unit was a 1948 study of coronary artery disease in men under age 40, in which Traum and Wilcox collaborated with members of the Armed Forces Institute of Pathology.[324] This study reviewed 450 Army men under age 40 who had died of coronary disease and were studied at autopsy, as well as 416 Army men under age 40 who had survived well-documented episodes of myocardial infarction. From an extensive review of the literature, they found previous reports of a total of 744 deaths from coronary artery disease in persons under age 40, with a 27:1 male: female ratio. In their study, they collected demographic information and medical histories from interviews of survivors and questionnaires sent to relatives of those who had died. They used a variety of control groups: amputees, those with gunshot wounds and, where appropriate, the Army as a whole. They found increasing incidence of coronary disease with age within the age groups studied. Compared with controls, the men with coronary artery disease were more likely to be hypertensive and to have a family history of heart conditions. The authors could not demonstrate a relationship with smoking, alcohol intake or obesity. Incidence in Negroes was about two thirds that in whites. The clinical and pathological features of the heart attacks and subsequent course in these young men were similar to those observed in coronary artery disease in older persons.

In September 1948, Milton Landowne, M.D., arrived at the Washington, DC, VA Cardiovascular Research Unit as its new chief. He had trained extensively in cardiology and had joined the faculty of the University of Chicago. During the War, he had studied the pneumoconioses while assigned to the Public Health Service.

When he arrived, Albert Kistin, M.D., and Blanche Wilcox, the statistician, were on the staff of the unit. The physical plant of the unit, as Landowne recalled, was quite large, occupying most of a wing of the hospital. The Cardiovascular Research Unit performed the electrocardiograms and angiograms for the hospital. They had a chemistry laboratory and facilities for housing and studying dogs. Office space was plentiful. Support staff included two electrocardiograph technicians, an animal technician and secretaries, and recruitment of a chemist was authorized.

The research under way was centered on angiography and electrocardiography. Kistin was very much interested in angiography and had invented an improved cassette changer.[325] George Robb, a cardiologist from Johns Hopkins who was interested in angiography, had influenced the VA to do advanced angiography in its Cardiovascular Research Unit, and he had arranged for a prototype fluorescent image amplifier from General Electric to be placed there. This had not yet arrived when the Unit was closed in late 1949, but, meanwhile, Robb collaborated with Kistin in electrocardiology. They published an analysis of the normal esophageal and gastric electrocardiogram [326] and a case report of the effects of Wolff-Parkinson-White Syndrome on the electrocardiogram in myocardial infarction.[327]

Kistin published on the anatomy of the bundle of His[328] and on optimal placement of electrocardiography electrodes.[329] With other clinicians, he published about two cases of paralysis of the recurrent laryngeal nerve in rheumatic heart disease[330] and a case of an anomalous pulmonary vein proven by angiography.[331]

After Landowne arrived, he and Kistin worked together trying to understand the cause of premature ventricular contraction (PVC) of the heart. They recorded esophageal electrocardiograms on 33 patients whose traditional electrocardiogram showed frequent PVCs. Fifteen of them, including 6 with normal hearts, showed evidence of retrograde conduction from the ventricle to the auricle.[332, 333] They also reported on the diagnostic signs of ventricular aneurysm, based on 8 cases which they had demonstrated angiographically.[334] They did a comparative study of electrocardiography machines with Solomon Gilford, an engineer at the National Bureau of Standards.

In July 1949, just ten months after he arrived, Landowne, without warning, received word that the Unit was to be closed. He and Dr. Kistin were offered the opportunity to continue their research at some other VA Hospital, but both preferred to leave the organization. Kistin went into private practice and later worked with miners in West Virginia suffering from pneumoconioses. Landowne joined the NIH Aging Study Unit (under Nathan Shock) in Baltimore. The Cardiovascular Research Unit officially closed in November 1949.[335]

Decline in the research program

There seems to be little question that the enthusiasm for excellence in the veterans' hospital system of the 1920s had waned by the middle of the 1930s. This happened despite the fact that medical progress in the VA was occurring, as reflected in the *Medical Bulletin*. Much of this decline can be attributed to aging: of the agency leadership, of the patients being served, and of the physicians serving them.

General Hines continued as Administrator of the Veterans Administration until after World War II. The tight controls he had established in 1923, when he came in to reform a corrupt and wasteful agency, were now stifling. It is said that he personally approved every staff promotion in the VA, even of secretaries and janitors, and that he never spent all of the budget allocated to the agency. Dr. Griffith, his Medical Director from 1931 through the war, is described as an amiable person who subordinated himself to Hines's direction.

The patient population changed as the World War I veteran aged (Figure 2.8). Many of the tuberculous patients who filled the hospitals in the early 1920s had either died or improved. The acute illnesses and injuries of the young had mostly resolved or no longer required hospital care. Now, more VA patients suffered from the diseases of middle age, especially heart disease and cancer. The syphilitics left in the hospitals were the hopeless cases with tertiary disease, especially neurosyphilis. The population of patients with psychoses continued to increase, as there was no effective way to control these dread diseases even though the patients generally lived an almost normal life span. By 1941, nearly 60% of VA patients suffered from neuropsychiatric diseases. These were patients who did not appeal to many physicians; the rewards of caring for them were small.

At the same time, the mechanics of recruiting and retaining quality physicians for the veterans' hospitals under the Civil Service system was a constant problem. The attempts to set up a medical corps for the VA had been unsuccessful, and the energy behind such attempts waned over time. Veteran preference under Civil Service laws generally meant that only physicians who were World War I veterans were hired,[126] and they, too, were aging.

Final Meeting of the Medical Council

After 1931, the Medical Council did not meet for eight years, a constraint attributed to tightened federal spending during and after the Depression. When they were called together once more in 1939, the members were not pleased with what had been happening in their absence. They noted that the character of the Diagnostic Clinics had changed. These centers no longer confined their activities to diagnosis. Now their efforts were diluted with treatment activities.[336]

The Research Group, in a report read by Dr. Louis Dublin, was particularly unhappy with the way things were going:

"Your Research Committee has, from the very beginning of the Council, repeatedly stressed the importance of research as an essential activity in the Medical Service of the Veterans Administration. It has been our opinion that a research unit would pay for itself many times over in the better administration of the Medical Service, as well as in an advancement of medical knowledge. Yet, in spite of such recommendations, often reiterated, the Administration has not developed such a research organization....

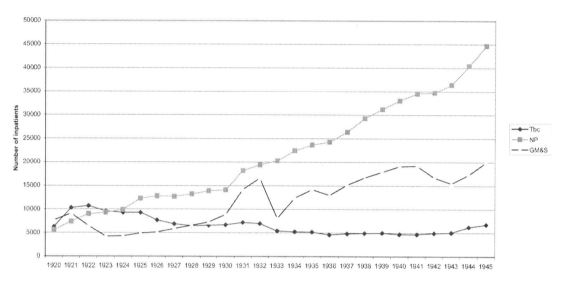

Figure 2.7 Patient care load in the VA before the end of WWII

"To be sure, Dr. Matz did organize a very simple but effective unit of statistical investigation. Some research activities have also been conducted in individual hospitals, with commendable results. Here and there, individual physicians have taken advantage of their opportunity to record their experiences; but all these efforts, in our judgment, do not constitute an adequate approach to the research problem of the Veterans Administration."

". . . Any organization which is concerned with the hospitalization of tens of thousands of patients annually, and which spends many millions of dollars, must in the very nature of the case, organize itself for effective self-criticism, and for the analysis and solution of problems which arise out of its varied operations. To do that, the first consideration is a leader, who by training and aptitude would be competent to carry on the work in a manner equal to the opportunity. At no time in the past has there been available this essential of a research organization. We believe that little progress will be made in this direction until this first step is taken. With such a step there would be a possibility of a development commensurate with the richness of the material which is available."

". . . Finally, the Research Committee believes that the development of a research organization, with the Medical Service, should not be carried on without consultation with it. It is impossible to advise the Administration with any effectiveness if appointments of heads of divisions are made without consultation, and the Research Committee finds itself confronted with accomplished facts, which in its judgment stand in the way of a development such as it has in mind."

They presented a plan for a research organization with a Central Office staff who would work with all of the major divisions of the Medical Service, addressing the most pressing problems of each. Research "would not be limited to statistical investigations alone. The statistical method lends itself, of course, to the conduct of research in administration, therapeutics, the natural history of disease and analysis of disease processes. All of these fields should be the subject of investigation."[337]

They also recommended establishing separate research units in some of the larger hospitals, citing the Tumor Research Unit at Hines, attached to the Tumor Clinic at Hines and the Cardiovascular Research Unit, attached to the cardiac clinic at the Washington, D.C. hospital as a beginning in this direction.

The Council as a whole showed their displeasure that their advice was not being sought as much as in the past. They urged that they be called together annually.[338] As Dr. Barker commented, "I think this meeting has shown that the Councillors have a deep interest in the welfare of the Veterans Administration and that they have many suggestions that will be helpful."[339]

Although there were occasional later meetings of the Executive Committee and individual members were called on to inspect hospitals, there were no further meetings of the full Medical Council after this October 1939 meeting. The advice about research and other activities proffered in October 1939, unlike the advice of the 1924 Medical Council, went unheeded.

In 1944, Hines appointed a new advisory group, with Drs. Piersol and Adams as chairman and secretary and including Drs. Lorenz and MacEachern. Joining these members of the old Medical Council were 12 other physicians, each representing a medical specialty. This Special Medical Advisory Group was short-lived. It met three times during early 1945, appears to have effected no changes, and disbanded when Hines left in August 1945.[340] It was replaced by a new Special Medical Advisory Group mandated in the 1946 law that established the Department of Medicine and Surgery (Chapter 3).

Wartime changes

No recorded changes in the VA research program occurred as a result of the Medical Council advice, and soon wartime stresses took their toll. During World War II, many of the younger VA physicians left for the military. Not until 1943 was the VA declared a national priority. In a move to preserve a coherent medical staff, Administrator Hines arranged for VA's remaining physicians to be commissioned military officers, with the same salaries, benefits and recognition as their colleagues in the camps and war fronts. But, by this time, the physician ranks in the VA were so depleted that supervision of patient care became very difficult.

As Dr. Paul Magnuson described his 1946 visit to the Palo Alto VA Hospital in his autobiography:

"I didn't expect much, but the place gave me a shock. They had five doctors there, taking care - question mark in a very large way - of one thousand patients. The outside of the facility was very nice, with well tended shrubs and flowerbeds, but what went on inside was just beyond description."[341]

His account contrasts sharply with the upbeat institution described by Dr. Wilbur in 1924, when he wrote of the Palo Alto Veterans Hospital that "the whole aspect of the hospital is one of cheer and hopefulness as compared with the ordinary institution of the sort."[342]

There were, of course, exceptions. An occasional clinician still conducted research, as we will see when we examine the work of Ludwig Gross in Chapter 3. However, judging by the papers published in the Medical Bulletin during its last ten years of publication, 1935 through 1944, original research seems almost to have disappeared in the hospitals except in the formal centralized research laboratories.

In November 1944, in response to an inquiry from Albert Q. Maisel, a reporter who later wrote a scathing article in the *Reader's Digest*[343] about the VA, Ray Lyman Wilbur wrote:

". . . In my judgment the principal difficulty has been that the whole problem of medical service was gauged on too low a financial level and that priorities were given to veterans throughout the whole organization sometimes regardless of their skills and training.

"The Medical Council was desirous of developing research and putting in superior men in the hospitals to carry it on, so that the work of the hospitals would not become largely custodial but would provide a series of research studies on a gradually aging group with the ailments that come with the years. . . . If some diagnostic and research centers could be established under the complete control of some of the best medical men developed by the war I believe that it would be worth while financially and in every other way."[344]

Wilbur went on to urge salary increases for VA professional staff, pointing out that "in the Indian Health Service and in the Veterans Hospital service, generally speaking, the salaries paid and the conditions of service have not attracted the best trained and the best qualified doctors and nurses."

Wilbur sent a copy of this letter to General Hines, whose response did not acknowledge these problems. With regard to research, Hines wrote:

"I know that you will be glad to know that there are three research units now being operated by the Veterans Administration. The unit at Hines, Illinois, conducts extensive research on tumors and enjoys an enviable reputation with research workers throughout the country interested in this field. The unit at Washington, D.C. is utilized for research covering the field of cardiology, while the more recently established unit at Northport, Long Island, devotes its time to research problems in the neuropsychiatric field.

"The established research units are not only working on basic projects in medicine but are concentrating on problems concerned with disabled veterans. The units are staffed by outstanding medical officers and superior auxiliary personnel who have been carefully selected for the specific type of work to which they are assigned. Each unit has made contributions to scientific literature. In addition, many medical officers throughout the Service are also working on research problems."[345]

Despite what Hines portrayed, there is very little evidence of research being done during the war in the VA hospitals, except in the research units.

By the time a new VA medical research effort began in 1946, it was indeed a new beginning. Eventually, today's strongly academic VA research program grew in conjunction with the agency's postwar collaboration with medical schools. However, this was a gradual and incomplete transition; some research continued in hospitals with weak affiliations or even without medical school affiliations. This post-World War II research retained some of the post-World War I tradition of clinical research on the health problems of veterans, carried out by individual physicians looking for better ways to treat their patients.

References

1. Rothstein, W., *American Medical Schools and the Practice of Medicine*. New York and Oxford: Oxford University Press, 1987, 235-236.

2. Chargaff, E., "In praise of smallness - how can we return to small science?" *Perspectives in Biology and Medicine*, 1980. **23**: 374.

3. Cohn, A.E., "Purposes in medical research. An introduction to the Journal of Clinical Investigation." *J Clin Invest*, 1924. **1**: 1-11.

4. Gregg, A., *The Furtherance of Medical Research*. London: Oxford University Press, 1941, 1-14.

5. Shryock, R.H., *American Medical Research, Past and Present*. New York: The Commonwealth Fund, 1947, 101.

6. Furman, B., *A Profile of the United States Public Health Service, 1798-1948*. Washington, DC: US Department of Health, Education and Welfare, 1973

7. Gregg, *The Furtherance of Medical Research*. 1941, 33.

8. Shryock, *American Medical Research*. 1947, 136.

9. Marks, H.M., *The Progress of Experiment: Science and Therapeutic Reform in the United States, 1900-1990*. Cambridge, New York and Melbourne: Cambridge University Press, 1997, 30-31.

10. Harvey, A.M., *Science at the Bedside. Clinical Research in American Medicine, 1905-1945*. Baltimore and London: Johns Hopkins University Press, 1981

11. Kohler, R.E., *From medical chemistry to biochemistry; the making of a biomedical discipline*. Cambridge, London, New York, New Rochelle, Melbourne, Sydney: Cambridge University Press, 1982

12. Wilbur, R.L., "Address to the Medical Council." *US Veterans' Bureau Medical Bulletin*, 1926. **2**: 5-6.

13. Matz, P., "Research work in the United States Veterans' Bureau." *US Veterans' Bureau Medical Bulletin*, 1926. **2**: 188-192.

14. Thompson, W.O., "Studies in blood volume: I. The blood volume in myxedema, with a comparison of plasma volume changes in myxedema and cardiac edema." *J Clin Invest*, 1926. **2**: 477-520.

15.   Marks, *The Progress of Experiment*. 1997, 53-60.

16.   Marks, *The Progress of Experiment*. 1997, 43.

17.   "Minutes of the Fourth Conference of the Medical Council." October 22-24, 1925, 1925, 40.

18.   "The Establishment of Diagnostic Centers." *United States Veterans' Bureau Medical Bulletin*, 1925. **1**: 58-59.

19.   "Death of Dr. Kennon Dunham." *US Veterans Administration Medical Bulletin*, 1944. **21**: 120.

20.   Black, B.W., "Address of Medical Director B.W. Black to the Medical Council." *US Veterans' Bureau Medical Bulletin*, 1928. **4**: 584-586.

21.   "Establishment of a new Diagnostic Center." *US Veterans' Bureau Medical Bulletin*, 1928. **4**: 287.

22.   Swackhamer, W.B., "Organization and procedure in United States Veterans' Diagnostic Center." *US Veterans' Bureau Medical Bulletin*, 1929. **5**: 947-950.

23.   "American Legion urges more Diagnostic Centers." *The Live Oak (US Veterans' Hospital, Palo Alto, CA)*, Menlo Park, CA, November 18, 1929.

24.   "Death of Dr. Charles A. Elliott." *US Veterans Administration Medical Bulletin*, 1939. **16**: 191.

25.   "Palo Alto Center expansion to wait." *The Live Oak (US Veterans' Hospital, Palo Alto. CA)*, Menlo Park, CA, October 18, 1931.

26.   "Opening of facility at San Francisco." *US Veterans Administration Medical Bulletin*, 1935. **11**: 274.

27.   "Ten doctors and 11 nurses move to San Francisco facility." *The Live Oak (US Veterans' Hospital, Palo Alto, CA)*, Menlo Park, CA, October 3, 1934.

28.   Beardsley, L.G., "Procedure of medical study in United States Veterans' Diagnostic Center, Washington, DC." *US Veterans' Bureau Medical Bulletin*, 1928. **4**: 901-905.

29.   Crossman, E.O., "Preface - United States Veterans' Bureau Medical Bulletin (introduction)." *US Veterans' Bureau Medical Bulletin*, 1925. **1**: vi.

30.   "Notes and discussion." *US Veterans' Bureau Medical Bulletin*, 1926. **2**: 734-735.

31.   "Special articles received for the Bulletin from the hospitals." *US Veterans' Bureau Medical Bulletin*, 1926. **2**: 301-303.

32.   "Notes and discussion." *United States Veterans' Bureau Medical Bulletin*, 1925. **1**: 63-64.

33.   "Minutes of the Fourth Conference of the Medical Council with the Director and the Medical Director of the United States Veterans' Bureau." October 22-24, 1925. Washington, DC, 1925, 25-26.

34.   "Minutes of the Fourth Conference of the Medical Council." 1925, 26-27.

35.   Matz, P.B., "Laboratory studies in influenza at Camp Travis, Texas." *Am J Med Sci*, 1919. **158**: 723 - 730.

36.   Matz, P.B., "Studies on the calcium content of blood of normal and tuberculous subjects." *Am Rev Tuberculosis*, 1925. **II**: 250 -274.

37.   Griffith, C.M., "Dr. Philip B. Matz." *Ann Int Med*, 1938. **12**: 280-282.

38.   Matz, P.B., "Statistical studies on cardiovascular diseases in the United States Veterans' Bureau." *US Veterans Bureau Medical Bulletin*, 1926. **2**: 304-307.

39.   Matz, P.B., "Statistical studies of the mortality of heart diseases in the United States Veterans' Bureau." *US Veterans Bureau Medical Bulletin*, 1926. **2**: 399-401.

40.   Matz, P.B., "Statistical studies on tuberculosis in the United States Veterans' Bureau." *US Veterans Bureau Medical Bulletin*, 1926. **2**: 793-794, 977-978, 1087-1090.

41.   Matz, P.B., "Statistical studies on degenerative diseases in the United States Veterans' Bureau." *US Veterans Bureau Medical Bulletin*, 1926. **2**: 1182-1189.

42.   Matz, P.B., "Statistical studies on degenerative diseases in the United States Veterans' Bureau." *US Veterans Bureau Medical Bulletin*, 1927. **3**: 72-77.

43.   Matz, P.B., "Statistical studies on neuropsychiatric disabilities in the United States Veterans' Bureau." *US Veterans Bureau Medical Bulletin*, 1927. **3**: 156-160, 253-259.

44.   Matz, P.B., "Statistical studies on compensation in the United States Veterans' Bureau." *US Veterans Bureau Medical Bulletin*, 1927. **3**: 376-389.

45. Matz, P.B., "Hospital statistics for November, 1926." *US Veterans Bureau Medical Bulletin*, 1927. **3**: 611-617.

46. Matz, P.B., "Analysis of United States Veterans' Bureau Hospital statistics for December, 1926." *US Veterans Bureau Medical Bulletin*, 1927. **3**: 728-736.

47. Matz, P.B., "Analysis of United States Veterans' Bureau Hospital statistics for January, 1927." *US Veterans Bureau Medical Bulletin*, 1927. **3**: 818-824.

48. Matz, P.B., "Analysis of United States Veterans' Bureau Hospital statistics for February, 1927." *US Veterans Bureau Medical Bulletin*, 1927. **3**: 931-944.

49. Matz, P.B., "Analysis of United States Veterans' Bureau Hospital statistics for March, 1927." *US Veterans Bureau Medical Bulletin*, 1927. **3**: 1051-1060.

50. Matz, P.B., "Malaria treatment of general paralysis of the insane." *US Veterans Bureau Medical Bulletin*, 1926. **2**: 712.

51. Matz, P.B., "The treatment of neurosyphilis by means of "inoculation malaria"." *US Veterans Bureau Medical Bulletin*, 1927. **3**: 42-46.

52. Matz, P.B., "Report on the treatment of 179 cases of neurosyphilis by means of "inoculation malaria"." *US Veterans Bureau Medical Bulletin*, 1927. **3**: 387-389.

53. Matz, P.B., "Histopathology of the brain in paresis following malaria treatment." *US Veterans Bureau Medical Bulletin*, 1927. **3**: 619-621.

54. Matz, P.B., "The preparation for transmission through the mail of malarial blood suitable for the treatment of paresis." *US Veterans Bureau Medical Bulletin*, 1927. **3**: 944.

55. Matz, P.B., "The treatment of neurosyphilis by "inoculation malaria" in the United States Veterans Bureau." *J Nerv and Ment Dis*, 1928. **68**: 113 - 133.

56. Teitelbaum, A.D., "Preliminary Report of Fifteen Cases of Sodoku Treatment of General Paralysis." *US Veterans' Bureau Medical Bulletin*, 1930. **6**: 263-270.

57. Matz, P.B., "Standardization of clinical laboratory work in hospitals and regional offices: examination of sputum." *US Veterans Bureau Medical Bulletin*, 1928. **4**: 46-55.

58. Matz, P.B., "Standardization of clinical laboratory work in hospitals and regional offices: the spinal fluid." *US Veterans Bureau Medical Bulletin*, 1928. **4**: 149-158, 265-277, 365-383, 463-474.

59.   Matz, P.B., "Standardization of clinical laboratory work in hospitals and regional offices: examination of gastric contents." *US Veterans Bureau Medical Bulletin*, 1928. **4**: 551-561.

60.   Matz, P.B., "Standardization of clinical laboratory work in hospitals and regional offices: examination of feces (Clinical Bulletin #23)." *US Veterans Bureau Medical Bulletin*, 1928. **4**: 711-716, 802-810.

61.   Matz, P.B., "Standardization of clinical laboratory work in hospitals and regional offices: blood chemistry." *US Veterans Bureau Medical Bulletin*, 1928. **4**: 871-880, 958-971, 1050-1060.

62.   Matz, P.B., "Standardization of clinical laboratory work in hospitals and regional offices: blood chemistry - the dietetic management of various diseases." *US Veterans Bureau Medical Bulletin*, 1929. **5**: 61-67.

63.   Matz, P.B., "Standardization of clinical laboratory work in hospitals and regional offices: examination of transudates and exudates." *US Veterans Bureau Medical Bulletin*, 1929. **5**: 136-141.

64.   Matz, P.B., "Preliminary report of board of medical officers on residual effects of warfare gassing." *US Veterans' Bureau Medical Bulletin*, 1928. **4**: 681-683.

65.   Gilchrist, H.L. and Matz, P.B., "The residual effects of warfare gases: the use of chlorine gas, with report of cases." *US Veterans Administration Medical Bulletin*, 1933. **9**: 229-270.

66.   Gilchrist, H.L. and Matz, P.B., "The residual effects of warfare gases: the use of phosgene gas, with report of cases." *US Veterans Administration Medical Bulletin*, 1933. **10**: 1-36.

67.   Gilchrist, H.L. and Matz, P.B., "The residual effects of warfare gases: the use of arsenical compounds, with report of cases." *US Veterans Administration Medical Bulletin*, 1933. **10**: 79-98.

68.   Gilchrist, H.L. and Matz, P.B., "The residual effects of warfare gases: the use of mustard gas, with report of cases." *US Veterans Administration Medical Bulletin*, 1933. **9**: 339-390.

69.   Matz, P.B., "Outcome of hospital treatment of ex-service patients with nervous and mental diseases in the U.S. Veterans Bureau." *Psy Quar*, 1929. **3**: 550 -568.

70.   "Increase of 6,264 in Veterans' Hospitals." *JAMA*, 1935: 1348.

71.   Adkins, R.E., *Medical Care of Veterans*. 1967, 161.

72.   Crossman, E.O., "Address to the Medical Council." *United States Veterans' Bureau Medical Bulletin*, 1929. **5**: 569-570.

73.   Weber, G.A. and Schmeckebier, L.F., *The Veterans' Administration: its history, activities and organization*. Washington: The Brookings Institution, 1934, 319.

74.   Matz, P.B., "A study of intestinal tuberculosis among exservice men." *Am J Med Sci*, 1930. **179**: 532-546.

75.   Matz, P.B., "Future incidence of nervous and mental disease among ex-service men." *Am J Psychiatry*, 1930. **9**: 1043-1060.

76.   Matz, P.B., "The Gerson-Sauerbruch dietetic regimen in tuberculosis." *US Veterans' Bureau Medical Bulletin*, 1930. **6**: 27-32.

77.   Matz, P.B., "Study of diabetes mellitus among ex-service men." *Military Surgeon*, 1931. **68**: 591-635.

78.   Matz, P.B., "The treatment of diabetes mellitus." *US Veterans Administration Medical Bulletin*, 1932. **8**: 331-350.

79.   Matz, P.H., "A study of diabetes mellitus among ex-service men." *JAMA*, 1936. **106**: 2214 - 2221.

80.   Matz, P.H., "A study of diabetes mellitus among ex-service men." *Military Surgeon*, 1937. **80**: 122 - 131.

81.   Matz, P.B., "A study of diabetes mellitus in ex-service men." *US Veterans Administration Medical Bulletin*, 1931. **7**: 533-549, 625-642.

82.   Matz, P.B., "A study of cancer in ex-service men." *US Veterans Administration Medical Bulletin*, 1931. **7**: 1010-1031, 1128-1149.

83.   Matz, P.B., "The coincidence of malignancy and tuberculosis." *US Veterans' Bureau Medical Bulletin*, 1930. **6**: 939-942.

84.   Matz, P.B., "A study of manic depressive psychosis in ex-service men." *US Veterans Administration Medical Bulletin*, 1932. **8**: 1-19.

85.   Matz, P.B., "Clinical and economic features of arthritis in ex-members of the military service." *N Eng J Med*, 1933. **209**: 639.

86.   Matz, P.B., "Habit-forming drugs." *US Veterans Administration Medical Bulletin*, 1934. **11**: 198-209.

87. Matz, P.H., "Food poisoning--its cause and Its control." *Mod Hosp*, 1935. **45**: 90 - 94.

88. Matz, P.B., "Food poisoning in hospitals and domiciliary institutions." *US Veterans Administration Medical Bulletin*, 1935. **11**: 159-165.

89. Matz, P.B., "Malignancy and tuberculosis." *Mil Surg*, 1935. **77**: 207.

90. Matz, P.H., "The end-results of the surgical treatment of pulmonary tuberculosis." *Am Rev Tuberc*, 1936. **33**: 533 - 548.

91. Matz, P., "The incidence of primary bronchiogenic carcinoma." *JAMA*, 1938. **111**: 2086-2092.

92. Matz, P.B., "The dispensary care of disabled ex-service men." *US Veterans Administration Medical Bulletin*, 1932. **8**: 186-194.

93. Matz, P.B., "A study of heart disease among veterans: I. Clinical classification of five hundred cases." *N Eng J Med*, 1935. **212**: 868 - 874.

94. Matz, P.H., "A study of heart disease among veterans: II. Analysis of a group of cases as to age at onset and duration of heart disability." *N Eng J Med*, 1935. **212**: 929-932.

95. Matz, P.H., "A study of heart disease among veterans: III. Hereditary and famillial factors in the causation of cardiovascular disease." *N Eng J Med*, 1935. **212**: 977-978.

96. Matz, P.H., "A study of heart disease among veterans: IV. An analysis of the more frequent types of anatomic heart disease." *N Eng J Med*, 1935. **212**: 1042-1048.

97. Matz, P.H., "A study of heart disease among veterans: V. Syphilitic heart disease." *N Eng J Med*, 1935. **212**: 1087 - 1089.

98. Matz, P.B., "Pathology of the lungs and other organs In silicosis." *Military Surgeon*, 1937. **81**: 88.

99. Matz, P., "Roentgenologic classification and diagnosis of silicosis." *Am J Roentgenol*, 1938. **40**: 848-858.

100. Matz, P.B., "A study of silicosis." *Am J Med Sci*, 1938. **196**: 548-559.

101. Matz, P.B., "Pathology of the lungs and other organs in silicosis." *Am J Clin Path*, 1938. **8**: 345-365.

102. "Dr. P.B. Matz, Research Unit Chief, expires: famed pathologist was on tour inspecting Veterans' Hospitals." *Unknown (provided by Oscar Schabb, nephew).*

103. Letter from Anne Bambery to Mrs. Joseph Rudolph, Baltimore, MD (letter provided by Oscar Schabb), written at Washington, DC, November 1, 1938.

104. Letter from Horatio M. Pollack to Medical and Hospital Service, VACO, written at Albany, NY, 1938.

105. Letter from Arthur J. Vorwald to Medical and Hospital Service, VACO, written at Saranac lake, NY, 1938.

106. Mella, H., "The circulation of phenol sulphothalein in the cerebrospinal fluid." *J Nerv Ment Dis*, 1922. **56**: 599-601.

107. Mella, H., "Thrombotic cortical amaurosis: report of a case of bilateral calcarine softening." *J Nerv Ment Dis*, 1922. **56**: 563-566.

108. Mella, H., "The cerebrospinal fluid in jaundice." *Arch Neur Psychiatr*, 1922. **8**: 329-330.

109. Mella, H., "Irradiation of the thymus in myasthenia gravis." *Med Clin N America*, 1923. **7**: 939-949.

110. Mella, H., "The diencephalic centers controlling associated locomotor movements." *Arch Neur Psychiatr*, 1923. **10**: 141-153.

111. Mella, H., "Neurosyphilis as an etiological factor in the Parkinsonian syndrome." *J Nerv Ment Dis*, 1924. **59**: 225-230.

112. Mella, H., "The experimental production of basal ganglion sympathectomy in Macacus Rhesus." *Arch Neur Psychiatr*, 1924. **11**: 405-417.

113. Mella, H., "Bulbocapnin: its use in the treatment of tremor and in experimental production of basal ganglion symptomatology." *Arch Neur Psychiatr*, 1926. **15**: 325-329.

114. Ebaugh, F.G. and Mella, H., "The use of Lipiodol in the localization of spinal lesions." *Am J Med Sci*, 1926. **172**: 117-123.

115. Mella, H., "Improving our contact with relatives of patients." *US Veterans' Bureau Medical Bulletin*, 1927. **3**: 801-802.

116.   Mella, H., "Panniculitis." *US Veterans' Bureau Medical Bulletin*, 1930. **6**: 697-698.

117.   Mella, H., "The use of subarachnoid lavage and ethylhydrocupreine in meningitis." *US Veterans' Bureau Medical Bulletin*, 1931. **7**: 77-78.

118.   Mella, H., "Loss of associated locomotor movements in diencephalic lesions." *US Veterans Administration Medical Bulletin*, 1931. **7**: 762-763.

119.   Mella, H. and O'Neill, R.T., "Ultraviolet irradiation in general paresis." *US Veterans Administration Medical Bulletin*, 1932. **9**: 29-32.

120.   Mella, H. and O'Neill, R.T., "Intravenous administration of sodium amytal in acute psychotic episodes." *US Veterans Administration Medical Bulletin*, 1933. **9**: 271-275.

121.   Mella, H. and Blomberg, M.M., "A study of the absorption spectra of cerebrospinal fluid in the visible part of the spectrum." *J Nerv Ment Dis*, 1936. **83**: 685-688.

122.   Mella, H., "Treatment of 43 cases of lobar pneumonia." *US Veterans Administration Medical Bulletin*, 1937. **13**: 247-250.

123.   Mella, H., "Senescence and rejuvenation." *US Veterans Administration Medical Bulletin*, 1938. **14**: 322-328.

124.   Mella, H., "A study of results of the treatment of neurosyphilis." *US Veterans Administration Medical Bulletin*, 1939. **16**: 106-119.

125.   Mella, H., "Report of 92 cases of pneumonia treated with sulfapyridine." *US Veterans Administration Medical Bulletin*, 1940. **16**: 197-209.

126.   Interview with Abraham Gottlieb, M.D., December 18, 1991 at Palo Alto, CA. VAMC

127.   *Directory of Medical Specialists holding certification by American Boards, Volume VI, published for the Advisory Board for Medical Specialties.* Chicago: A.N. Marquis Company, 1953, 1022.

128.   Ziegler, E.E., "The specific effect of bile salts on pneumococci and on pneumococcus pneumonia." *Ach Int Med*, 1930. **46**: 644-656.

129.   Ziegler, E.E., "The effects on pneumococci of sodium dehydrocholate, a bile salt derivative III." *J Lab Clin Med*, 1931. **17**: 317-324.

130.   Ziegler, E.E., "The effects on pneumococci of sodium dehydrocholate, a bile salt derivative." *US Veterans Administration Medical Bulletin*, 1932. **8**: 105-112.

131.   Ziegler, E.E., "Pneumocholin; a new biochemical antigen." *US Veterans Administration Medical Bulletin*, 1933. **9**: 276-286.

132.   Ziegler, E.E., "Some properties of pneumocholin, a biochemical antigen." *J Lab Clin Med*, 1933. **18**: 695-704.

133.   Ziegler, E.E., "A new measurement of oxygen absorbing power." *Med Ann District of Columbia*, 1933. **2**: 225-230.

134.   Ziegler, E.E., "A new measurement of oxygen absorbing power (preliminary report)." *J Aviation Medicine*, 1933. **4**: 119-129.

135.   Stein, J.J., "The early diagnosis and treatment of cancer." *US Veterans Administration Medical Bulletin*, 1936. **12**: 412-421.

136.   Stein, J.J. and Hantsch, F.K., "Adenocarcinoma of the rectum with unusual sites of metastases." *JAMA*, 1937. **108**: 1776-1779.

137.   Stein, J.J., "Tumors of the small intestine: a review of the literature and report of eight additional cases." *Am J Digestive Diseases and Nutrition*, 1938. **4**: 517-522.

138.   Stein, J.J., "Metastases to bone from carcinoma of the gastro-intestinal tract." *Radiology*, 1940. **35**: 486-488.

139.   Stein, J.J., "The clinical and pathological features of tumors occurring in the region of the apex of the lung." *Texas State J Med*, 1937. **33**: 293-299.

140.   Stein, J.J., "Apical lung tumors: further observations with report of seven additional cases." *JAMA*, 1938. **111**: 1612-1617.

141.   Stein, J.J. and Joslin, H.L., "Carcinoma of the bronchus: a clinical and pathological study of 164 cases." *Surg Gyn and Obst*, 1938. **66**: 902-911.

142.   Stein, J.J., "Bone metastases from primary carcinoma of the lung. Report of an unusual case." *J Bone and Joint Surg*, 1939. **21**: 992-996.

143.   Stein, J.J., "Carcinoma of the lung: a clinical study." *US Naval Med Bull*, 1940. **38**: 329-334.

144.   Stein, J.J., "Tumors occurring in the region of the pulmonary apex: further observations with report of twelve additional cases." *Illinois Med J*, 1942. **81**: 21-29.

145.   Stein, J.J., "Sudden compression injuries of the abdomen." *US Veterans Administration Medical Bulletin*, 1943. **20**: 6-7.

146.   Stein, J.J., "Combat experiences in the Pacific areas." *US Veterans Administration Medical Bulletin*, 1944. **21**: 177-187.

147.   "Justin John Stein", in *Who's Who in America*. 1980, Marquis Who's Who: Chicago. **2** 3160.

148.   Allen, C.D., "Report of results obtained in 100 cases by intravenous injection of Mercurochrome." *US Veterans' Bureau Medical Bulletin*, 1925. **1**: 27-33.

149.   Allen, C.D., "A further report on the use of Mercurochrome intravenously, with a review of its action in 151 cases." *US Veterans' Bureau Medical Bulletin*, 1926. **2**: 443-446.

150.   Martin, A., "Hemolytic streptococcus bacteremia following empyema, with recovery." *US Veterans' Bureau Medical Bulletin*, 1929. **5**: 541-543.

151.   Harris, R.L., "Mercurochrome treatment of a case of streptococcus viridans septicemia with recovery." *US Veterans' Bureau Medical Bulletin*, 1930. **6**: 413-415.

152.   Foster, H.E., "Facts and fancies regarding Mercurochrome-220 Soluble." *US Veterans' Bureau Medical Bulletin*, 1930. **6**: 300-308.

153.   Dowling, H.F., *Fighting infection: conquests of the Twentieth Century*. Cambridge, MA and London: Harvard University Press, 1977, 106.

154.   Walker, J.B., "Late results of fractures of the long bones - a statistical study of World War cases - I." *US Veterans' Bureau Medical Bulletin*, 1927. **3**: 293-314.

155.   Walker, J.B., "Late results of fractures of the long bones - a statistical study of World War cases - II." *US Veterans' Bureau Medical Bulletin*, 1927. **3**: 409-427.

156.   Walker, J.B., "Late results of fractures of the long bones - a statistical study of World War cases - III." *US Veterans' Bureau Medical Bulletin*, 1927. **3**: 525-543.

157.   Walker, J.B., "Late results of fractures of the long bones - a statistical study of World War cases - IV." *US Veterans' Bureau Medical Bulletin*, 1927. **3**: 651-657.

158. Caldwell, H., "Resume of treatment of 25 cases of diabetes mellitus with insulin." *US Veterans' Bureau Medical Bulletin*, 1925. **1**: 1-6.

159. Rogers, J.C., "Residuals of encephalitis lethargica." *US Veterans' Bureau Medical Bulletin*, 1925. **1**: 20-23.

160. Prince, L.H., "The blood vessels in tuberculosis: some aspects of the part played by the blood vessels in the dissemination of tuberculosis." *US Veterans' Bureau Medical Bulletin*, 1925. **1**: 11-18.

161. Crichlow, R.S., "Treatment of Raynaud's Disease by negative pressure." *US Veterans' Bureau Medical Bulletin*, 1925. **1**: 14-17.

162. Bacon, H.P., "A study of Larson's Ring Test applied to 315 cases of pulmonary tuberculosis." *US Veterans' Bureau Medical Bulletin*, 1926. **2**: 56-60.

163. Prince, L.H. and Wight, T.H.T., "Adenocarcinoma - primary in the renal tubule." *US Veterans' Bureau Medical Bulletin*, 1926. **2**: 987-991, 1095-?

164. Enright, J.J., "A preliminary report on attempts at active immunization of guinea pigs by urinary antigens from cases of tuberculosis." *US Veterans' Bureau Medical Bulletin*, 1926. **2**: 357-361.

165. Josewich, A. and Grave, F., "Correlation of clinical and laboratory procedures in tuberculosis. I. The complement fixation test." *US Veterans' Bureau Medical Bulletin*, 1926. **2**: 346-356.

166. Wrenn, H.T., "Studies on the bactericidal properties in vitro of certain fatty oils irradiated with the quartz-mercury-vapor spectrum." *US Veterans' Bureau Medical Bulletin*, 1927. **3**: 898-910.

167. Armstrong, C.L., "Report of cases of leprosy with unusual manifestations." *US Veterans Bureau Medical Bulletin*, 1927. **3**: 1248-1254.

168. Covey, C.B., "Notes on amnesia." *United States Veterans' Bureau Medical Bulletin*, 1927. **3**: 356-362.

169. Freed, H., Haley, S.W. and Stephenson, W.O., "Thoracotomy for empyema complicating pneumonia - analysis of end results in 100 consecutive cases." *US Veterans' Bureau Medical Bulletin*, 1928. **4**: 22-26.

170. Crouch, E.L., "Multiple sclerosis." *US Veterans' Bureau Medical Bulletin*, 1928. **4**: 839-845.

171. Denson, R.L., "Ancient Grecian, Etruscan and Roman dentistry." *US Veterans' Bureau Medical Bulletin*, 1928. **4**: 251-258.

172.   Flowers, H.L., "A study of the emotions in psychotic patients (a report of the examination of 100 psychotic patients with the Pressey test)." *US Veterans' Bureau Medical Bulletin*, 1928. **4**: 309-321.

173.   Rabinovitch, A. and Roberts, C.G., "A compartative study of the Kahn and complement fixation tests of spinal fluid." *US Veterans' Bureau Medical Bulletin*, 1928. **4**: 692-696.

174.   Read, J.M., "Tetany from overbreathing." *US Veterans' Bureau Medical Bulletin*, 1929. **5**: 491-493.

175.   Alvarez, R.S. and Wight, T.H.T., "The Gregerson Test." *US Veterans' Bureau Medical Bulletin*, 1929. **5**: 888-890.

176.   Seymour, W.Y., "Julius Caesar, epileptic." *US Veterans' Bureau Medical Bulletin*, 1929. **5**: 266-272.

177.   Teitelbaum, A.D., "Preliminary Report of Fifteen Cases of Sodoku Treatment of General Paralysis." *US Veterans' Bureau Medical Bulletin*, 1930a. **6**: 263-270.

178.   Schelm, G.W., "Typhoid vaccine in the treatment of general paralysis of the insane." *US Veterans' Bureau Medical Bulletin*, 1930. **6**: 544-548.

179.   Crouch, E.L., "Narcolepsy." *US Veterans' Bureau Medical Bulletin*, 1930. **6**: 371-377.

180.   Wight, T.H.T. and Meehan, W., "Value of media containing certain iron compounds in differentiating the typhoid-colon group of organisms." *United States Veterans' Bureau Medical Bulletin*, 1930. **6**: 493-495.

181.   Moss, E.S., "An improved method for staining tubercle bacilli in tissues cut by the frozen section method." *US Veterans' Bureau Medical Bulletin*, 1930. **6**: 590-595.

182.   Lasche, P.G. and Rubin, H., "Carbon dioxide-oxygen inhalations in catatonic dementia praecox." *US Veterans' Bureau Medical Bulletin*, 1930. **6**: 1037-1041.

183.   Brown, C.P. and Gemar, F., "Experiments on bacteriophage adsorption by vulnerable bacteria." *US Veterans Administration Medical Bulletin*, 1931. **7**: 224-229.

184.   Rothrock, A.M., "Medical science in the thirteenth century." *US Veterans Administration Medical Bulletin*, 1931. **7**: 1005-1009.

185.   Mella, H., "The Use of Subarachnoid Lavage and Ethylhydrocupreine in Meningitis." *United States Veterans' Bureau Medical Bulletin*, 1931a. **7**: 77-78.

186. Fisher, S.G., "Stramonium in encephalitis." *US Veterans Administration Medical Bulletin*, 1931. **7**: 379-382.

187. Burkett, J.A., "Bronchial spirochetosis, with report of a case." *US Veterans Administration Medical Bulletin*, 1932. **8**: 26-37.

188. Wight, T.W.T., "A world's record for the transportation of Entamoeba Histolytica." *US Veterans Administration Medical Bulletin*, 1932. **8**: 306-307.

189. Terry, M.C. and Hollingsworth, E.W., "Elliptical human erythrocytes: report of two cases." *US Veterans Administration Medical Bulletin*, 1932. **9**: 7-17.

190. Terry, M.C., Hollingsworth, E.W. and Eugenio, V., "Elliptical human erythrocytes: report of two cases." *Arch Path*, 1932. **13**: 193-206.

191. Sanders, A.O., "Observations of heart action under vagus stimulation." *US Veterans Administration Medical Bulletin*, 1931. **7**: 212-217.

192. Garrett, G.H., "Pulmonary tuberculosis complicated by syphilis." *US Veterans' Bureau Medical Journal*, 1925. **1**: 1-9.

193. Kennedy, J.A., "Psychosis with alcoholic pellagra." *US Veterans Administration Medical Bulletin*, 1933. **10**: 155-158.

194. Monat, H.A., "An unusual case of hysteria with a retrocursive gait." *US Veterans Administration Medical Bulletin*, 1934. **11**: 167-168.

195. Cullins, J.G., Morgan, H.P. and Seymour, W., "Super-diathermy in the treatment of dementia paralytica." *US Veterans Administration Medical Bulletin*, 1935. **11**: 217-222.

196. Broglum, F.L., "Nineteen cases of pneumonia in members of the Civilian Conservation Corps with no deaths." *US Veterans Administration Medical Bulletin*, 1935. **11**: 258-261.

197. Smith, A.P., "Brain abscess consequent to latent head trauma." *US Veterans Administration Medical Bulletin*, 1935. **11**: 337-339.

198. Woldenberg, S.C., "Sulphur (colloidal) therapy in the treatment of arthritis." *US Veterans Administration Medical Bulletin*, 1935. **12**: 10-26.

199. Bogen, E.F., "Effects of long hospitalization on psychotic patients." *US Veterans Administration Medical Bulletin*, 1936. **12**: 345-353.

200. Carlisle, C.L. and Hecjer, C.H., "Use of benzedrine sulphate in catatonic stupors: case reports." *US Veterans Administration Medical Bulletin*, 1937. **13**: 224-227.

201. Woodward, F.A., "Molokai and its leper colony." *US Veterans Administration Medical Bulletin*, 1937. **14**: 60-61.

202. Baganz, C.N. and Laxson, G.O., "Hypoglycemic shock therapy in schizophrenia: results of treatment of six patients." *US Veterans Administration Medical Bulletin*, 1938. **14**: 301-305.

203. McClintock, H.A., "Experience with the insulin therapy of schizophrenia." *US Veterans Administration Medical Bulletin*, 1939. **16**: 97-105.

204. Carlisle, C.L., "Bacteriological examination of eating utensils." *US Veterans Administration Medical Bulletin*, 1939. **15**: 294-296.

205. Lasche, P.G., "Herpes zoster in early syphilis." *US Veterans Administration Medical Bulletin*, 1940. **16**: 253-256.

206. Haynes, H.J., "The treatment of schizophrenia with desoxycorticosterone acetate." *US Veteran Administration Medical Bulletin*, 1941. **18**: 141-147.

207. Bernard, L.J., "The status of thyroid ablation for intractable heart disease." *US Veterans Administration Medical Bulletin*, 1941. **17**: 336-342.

208. Matz, P.B., "Research projects." *US Veterans' Bureau Medical Bulletin*, 1930. **6**: 622-623.

209. Matz, P.B., "Research." *US Veterans' Bureau Medical Bulletin*, 1930. **6**: 1005-1007.

210. Ijams, G.E., "Address of the director to the 12th conference of the Medical Council." *US Veterans' Bureau Medical Bulletin*, 1931. **7**: 701-703.

211. "Report of Conference on Establishment of Research Units in Cardiovascular and Neuropsychiatric Disease." Typewritten, 1935.

212. "Conference on Medical Research." *US Veterans Administration Medical Bulletin*, 1936. **13**: 326-327.

213. "Medical Research Unit at Northport." *US Veterans Administration Medical Bulletin*, 1936. **13**: 327.

214.   Scott, H., "Treatment of cancer at Edward Hines, Jr., Facility, Hines, Ill." *US Veterans Administration Medical Bulletin*, 1935. **12**: 1-9.

215.   Owen, S.E., "The biologic diagnosis of teratoma testis." *J Lab Clin Med*, 1934. **20**: 296-301.

216.   Owen, S.E., "Small animal metabolism cage." *J Lab Clin Med*, 1934. **19**: 1135-1137.

217.   Cutler, M. and Owen, S.E., "Clinical value of Prolan A determinations in teratoma testis." *Am J Cancer*, 1935. **24**: 318-325.

218.   Owen, S.E. and Cutler, M., "Diagnosis of teratoma testis by biologic assay of prolans." *US Veterans Administration Medical Bulletin*, 1937. **14**: 1-5.

219.   Fortner, H.C. and Owen, S.E., "Chorionepithelioma in the male." *Am J Cancer*, 1935. **25**: 89-97.

220.   Christoffersen, W.G. and Owen, S.E., "Neoplasms in cryptorchids." *Am J Cancer*, 1936. **26**: 259-268.

221.   Owen, S.E. and Cutler, M., "Comparison of prolan bioassays in teratoma and other conditions." *Am J Med Sci*, 1936. **192**: 61-67.

222.   Owen, S.E. and Cutler, M., "Sex hormones and prostatic pathology." *Am J Cancer*, 1936. **27**: 308-315.

223.   Owen, S.E., "The reaction of fish to sex hormones." *Endocrinol*, 1936. **20**: 214-218.

224.   Owen, S.E., "The Bitterling fish response to male sex hormones." *Endocrinol*, 1937. **21**: 689-690.

225.   Owen, S.E., Polanco, Q.G. and Prince, L.H., "Urine chemistry in the diagnosis of embryonal tumors." *Am J Cancer*, 1937. **31**: 613-617.

226.   Owen, S.E., "Sulphydryl and radon induced necrosis." *Growth*, 1937. **1**: 130-134.

227.   Owen, S.E., "Sulphur and growth stimulation (a consideration of larval preparations)." *Growth*, 1938. **2**: 355-361.

228.   Owen, S.E., "The action of growth stimulants on proteins." *Growth*, 1940. **4**: 135-137.

229.   Owen, S.E., "Sex hormones, carcinogenics and sterols." *Quarterly Rev Biology*, 1937. **12**: 340-347.

230.   Owen, S.E., "The genesis of cancer." *Mil Surg*, 1938. **82**: 218-225.

231.   Owen, S.E., Weiss, H.A. and Prince, L.H., "Carcinogens and growth stimulation." *Science*, 1938. **87**: 261-262.

232.   Owen, S.E., Weiss, H.A. and Prince, L.H., "Carcinogens and planarian tissue regeneration." *Am J Cancer*, 1939. **35**: 424-426.

233.   Owen, S.E. and Williams, A.E., "Irradiation and hereditary mammary cancer." *Radiology*, 1940. **34**: 541-544.

234.   Allaben, G.R. and Owen, S.E., "Adenocarcinoma of the breast coincidental with strenuous endocrine therapy." *JAMA*, 1939. **112**: 1933-1934.

235.   Telephone interview with Robert Schrek, M.D., May 8, 1988.

236.   Schrek, R., "Effect of pH on heat inactivation of tetanolysin." *J Immun*, 1933. **25**: 183-197.

237.   Schrek, R., "A quantitative study of the growth of the Walker rat tumor and the Flexner-Jobling rat carcinoma." *Am J Cancer*, 1935. **24**: 807-822.

238.   Schrek, R., "A comparison of the growth curves of malignant and normal (embryonic and post-embryonic) tissues of the rat." *Am J Path*, 1936. **12**: 515-530.

239.   Schrek, R., "A biological method for sterilizing contaminated transplantable tumors." *Am J Path*, 1936. **12**: 531-543.

240.   Schrek, R., "Further quantitative methods for the study of transplantable tumors. The growth of R39 sarcoma and Brown-Pearce carcinoma." *Am J Cancer*, 1936. **28**: 345-363.

241.   Schrek, R., "The effect of the size of inoculum on the growth of transplantable rat tumors." *Am J Cancer*, 1936. **28**: 364-371.

242.   Schrek, R., "Permanent and transient (fortuitous) variations of the growth components of transplantable rat tumors." *Am J Cancer*, 1936. **28**: 372-388.

243.   Schrek, R., "A method for counting the viable cells in normal and in malignant cell suspensions." *Am J Cancer*, 1936. **28**: 389-392.

244.   Schrek, R. and Avery, R.C., "Histologic observations on transplantable rat and rabbit tumors cultivated in the chorio-allantoic membrane of chick embryos, with special reference to the Walker rat tumor 256." *Am J Path*, 1937. **13**: 45-55.

245.   Schrek, R. and Gates, O., "Cutaneous carcinoma I. A statistical analysis with respect to the duration and site of the tumors and the age of the patients at onset and at biopsy of tumor." *Arch Pathology*, 1941. **31**: 411-421.

246.   Schrek, R., "Cutaneous carcinoma II. A statistical analysis with respect to measures of innate and clinical malignancy." *Arch Pathology*, 1941. **31**: 422-433.

247.   Schrek, R., "Cutaneous carcinoma III. A statistical analysis with respect to site, sex and preexisting scars." *Arch Pathology*, 1941. **31**: 434-448.

248.   Schrek, R., "A nomogram for determining the statistical significance and the probable error of differences of percentages." *J Lab Clin Med*, 1939. **25**: 180-184.

249.   Schrek, R., "Logarithmic frequency distributions." *Human Biology*, 1941. **13**: 1-22.

250.   Schrek, R., "Logarithmic correlation coefficients and regression equations." *Human Biology*, 1942. **14**: 95-103.

251.   Schrek, R., "Operation of the Tumor Clinic at Hines, Ill., during the calendar year 1941." *US Veterans Administration Medical Bulletin*, 1943. **20**: 181-186.

252.   Schrek, R., "Studies in vitro on the physiology of normal and cancerous cells I. The effect of high temperature and of moccasin venom on the viability of rabbit lymphocytes and polymorphonuclear leukocytes as determined by the method of unstained cell counts." *Arch Path*, 1943. **35**: 857-868.

253.   Schrek, R., "Studies in vitro on the physiology of normal and cancerous cells II. The survival and the glycolysis of cells under aerobic and under anaerobic conditions." *Arch Path*, 1944. **37**: 319-327.

254.   Schrek, R., "Studies in vitro on physiology of cells: effect of anisotonic solutions." *Proc Soc Exp Biol Med*, 1944. **57**: 348-351.

255.   Schrek, R., "Studies in vitro on physiology of cells: histologic reactions of living tissues to hypotonic solutions." *Am J Path*, 1945. **21**: 1101-1119.

256.   Schrek, R., "Radiosensitivity of lymphocytes and granulocytes In vitro according to the method of unstained cell counts." *Proc Soc Exp Biol Med*, 1945. **58**: 285-286.

257. Schrek, R., "A method for mounting gross pathologic specimens in Petri dishes." *J Lab Clin Med*, 1944. **29**: 91-96.

258. Schrek, R. and Allaben, G.R., "Statistical analysis of 2407 admissions to the Tumor Clinic of Veterans Hospital, Hines, Illinois, during 1943." *Cancer Res*, 1945. **5**: 539-546.

259. Schrek, R., "Cutaneous carcinoma IV. Analysis of 20 cases in Negroes." *Cancer Research*, 1944. **4**: 119-127.

260. Schrek, R., "The racial distribution of cancer I. Epithelial tumors of the skin, lip and breast." *Cancer Research*, 1944. **4**: 433-437.

261. Schrek, R., "The racial distribution of cancer II. Tumors of the kidney, bladder and male genital organs." *Ann Surg*, 1944. **120**: 809-812.

262. Schrek, R., Baker, L.A., Ballard, G.P. and Dolgoff, S., "Tobacco smoking as an etiologic factor in disease. I. Cancer." *Cancer Research*, 1950. **10**: 49-58.

263. Advisory Committee to the Surgeon General, *Smoking and Health*. Washington, DC: Public Health Service, 1964, 152 and p. 252.

264. Schrek, R., "Studies in vitro on physiology of cells: histologic reactions of living tissues to hypotonic solutions." *Am J Path*, 1945a. **21**: 1101-1119.

265. Schrek, R., "Studies in vitro on cellular physiology: the effect of X-rays on the survival of cells." *Radiology*, 1946. **46**: 395-410.

266. Schrek, R. and Donnelly, W.J., ""Hairy" cells in blood in lymphoreticular neoplastic disease and "flagellated" cells of normal lymph nodes." *Blood*, 1966. **27**: 199-211.

267. Lazell, E.W., "The group psychic treatment of dementia praecox by lectures in mental reeducation." *US Veterans Bureau Medical Bulletin*, 1930. **6**: 733-747.

268. Lazell, E.W., "The mechanism of psychic regression." *US Veterans Bureau Medical Bulletin*, 1927. **3**: 1089-1104.

269. Lazell, E.W., *The anatomy of emotion: man's two natures*. Vol. 3. New York and London: The Century Co., 1929, 267.

270. Lazell, E.W., "A study of the causative factors of dementia praecox: the influence of the blood and serum on embryological cells, a preliminary report." *United States Veterans' Bureau Medical Bulletin*, 1929. **5**: 40-41.

271.	Lazell, E.W., "Sensitization in the convulsive states with special reference to heterophile antigen: I. Heterophile hemolysis." *J Lab Clin Med*, 1938. **23**: 1160-1184.

272.	Lazell, E.W., "The Forssman or heterophile antigen." *US Veterans Bureau Medical Bulletin*, 1932. **8**: 477-485.

273.	Lazell, E.W., "Sensitization in the convulsive states with special reference to heterophile antigen: I. Heterophile hemolysis." *J Lab Clin Med*, 1938. **23**: 1161.

274.	Lazell, E.W., "The influence of heterophile antigen in nervous and mental disease." *US Veterans Bureau Medical Bulletin*, 1940. **16**: 235-252, 353-370.

275.	"Hypoglycemic treatment of schizophrenia." *US Veterans Bureau Medical Bulletin*, 1937. **14**: 94-96.

276.	Lazell, E.W., "The treatment of hay fever and ivy poisoning by local desensitization with sodium oleate and salts of other unsaturated fatty acids." *US Veterans Bureau Medical Bulletin*, 1938. **14**: 216-219.

277.	"Messinger, Emanuel", in *Directory of Medical Specialists, Volume 12*, Marquis - Who's Who: Chicago 1535.

278.	Messinger, E., "The estimation of cardiac function by simple clinical methods." *Ann Int Med*, 1937. **10**: 986-999.

279.	Messinger, E., "Cardiovascular changes associated with the insulin shock treatment." *Ann Int Med*, 1938. **12**: 853-865.

280.	Messinger, E. and Moros, N., "Cardiovascular effects of large doses of metrazol as employed in the treatment of schizophrenia." *Ann Int Med*, 1940. **13**: 1184-1204.

281.	"New Neuropsychiatric Research Unit at Northport." *US Veterans Administration Medical Bulletin*, 1941. **18**: 225.

282.	Roberts, C.S., "Follow-up report of 74 patients treated by pharmacologic shock compared with matched controls." *US Veterans Administration Medical Bulletin*, 1942. **19**: 49-59.

283.	Moros, N., "The Alcoholic personality: a statistical study." *Quarterly Journal of Studies on Alcohol*, 1942. **3**: 45-49.

284.	Turner, W.J., "Some dynamic aspects of alcoholic psychoses." *Am J Psychiatr*, 1942. **99**: 252-254.

285. Moros, N., "Factors in the development of general paralysis." *US Veterans Administration Medical Bulletin*, 1943. **20**: 196-201.

286. Huddleson, J.H., "Note on psychoses and psychoneuroses with malaria." *US Veterans Administration Medical Bulletin*, 1944. **21**: 1-4.

287. Turner, W.J., "A year's experience with electroencephalography." *US Veterans Administration Medical Bulletin*, 1944. **20**: 239-245.

288. Turner, W.J. and Roberts, C.S., "An adhesive nondrying electrode paste." *J Lab Clin Med*, 1944. **29**: 81.

289. Turner, W.J., Kress, B.H. and Harrison, N.B., "Determination of dihydroxyacetone in blood." *J Biol Chem*, 1943. **148**: 581-584.

290. Roberts, C.S., Turner, W.J. and Huddleson, J.H., "Variations of blood diastase and glucose in depression." *J Nerv Ment dis*, 1944. **99**: 250-255.

291. Turner, W.J., Lowinger, L. and Huddleson, J.H., "The correlation of pre-electroshock electroencephalogram and therapeutic result in schizophrenia." *Am J Psychiatr*, 1945. **102**: 299-300.

292. Huddleson, J.H. and Lowinger, L., "Note on initial and succeeding voltages to obtain grand mal in electroshock therapy." *J Nerv Ment Dis*, 1945. **102**: 191-193.

293. Turner, W.J., "A note on a mechanism of arterial rupture in cerebral arteriosclerosis." *J Neuropath and Exp Neurol*, 1946. **5**: 168.

294. Huddleson, J.H. and Gordon, H.L., "Fractures in electroshock therapy as related to roentgenographic spinal findings." *Military Surgeon*, 1946. **98**: 38-39.

295. Lowinger, L. and Huddleson, J.H., "Complications in electric shock therapy." *Am J Psychiatr*, 1946. **102**: 594-598.

296. Reisinger, J.A., "Study of hypertension in veterans." *Ann Int Med*, 1937. **10**: 1371 - 1389.

297. Reisinger, J.A. and Wilcox, B.B., "Heart weight and the measurement of the cardiac silhouette." *US Veterans Administration Medical Bulletin*, 1938. **15**: 108-117.

298. Reisinger, J.A., "Statistical study of heart diseases." *US Veterans Administration Medical Bulletin*, 1939. **16**: 33-44.

299.   Reisinger, J.A. and Wilcox, B.B., "Statistical study of heart diseases." *US Veterans Administration Medical Bulletin*, 1942. **18**: 351-362.

300.   Traum, A.H., "An etiologic study of 1036 cases of organic heart disease." *US Veterans Administration Medical Bulletin*, 1944. **20**: 377-388.

301.   Reisinger, J.A., "The determination of exercise tolerance by the two-step test." *Am Heart J*, 1938. **15**: 341-353.

302.   Reisinger, J.A., "The cold-pressor test." *Med Ann District of Columbia*, 1941. **10**: 381-386.

303.   Reisinger, J.A., "Dissecting aneurysm of the aorta." *Arch Int Med*, 1940. **65**: 1097-1115.

304.   "Article by John A. Reisinger." *US Veterans Administration Medical Bulletin*, 1940. **17**: 195.

305.   Reisinger, J.A., Pekin, T.J. and Blumenthal, B., "Primary tumor of the inferior vena cava and heart with hemopericardium and alternation of the ventricular complexes in the electrocardiogram." *Ann Int Med*, 1942. **17**: 995-1004.

306.   Blumenthal, B., "Nonclinical features of coronary arteriosclerotic heart disease." *US Veterans Administration Medical Bulletin*, 1939. **16**: 45-52.

307.   Blumenthal, B. and Reisinger, J.A., "Prodromal pain in coronary occlusion." *Am Heart J*, 1940. **20**: 141-159.

308.   Blumenthal, B. and Reisinger, J.A., "Pain in coronary arteriosclerotic disease of the heart." *US Veterans Administation Medical Bulletin*, 1941. **18**: 166-172.

309.   Reisinger, J.A., "Coronary arteriosclerosis and heart pain." *US Veterans Administration Medical Bulletin*, 1942. **19**: 127-133.

310.   Howell, J.D., ""Soldier's heart": the redefinition of heart disease and specialty formation in early twentieth century Great Britain." *Medical History*, 1985. **Supplement No. 5**: 34-52.

311.   Reisinger, J.A., "Neurocirculatory asthenia." *US Veterans Administration Medical Bulletin*, 1943. **20**: 8-20.

312.   Mazer, M. and Reisinger, J.A., "The thiocyanates in the treatment of hypertension." *US Veterans Administration Medical Bulletin*, 1942. **19**: 42-48.

313.   Mazer, M., "A simple method for measuring cardiac area from the orthodiagram." *Am Heart J*, 1942. **24**: 511-513.

314.   Mazer, M. and Reisinger, J.A., "An electrocardiographic study of cardiac aging based on records at rest and after exercise." *Ann Int Med*, 1944. **21**: 645-652.

315.   Mazer, M. and Reisinger, J.A., "Criteria for differentiating deep Q3 electrocardiograms from normal and cardiac subjects." *Am J Med Sci*, 1943. **206**: 48-53.

316.   Mazer, M. and Wilcox, B.B., "A simple graphic method for measuring the area of the orthodiagram." *Am J Roentgenol*, 1944. **51**: 444-446.

317.   Mazer, M., "Palindromic rheumatism." *JAMA*, 1942. **120**: 364-365.

318.   Kistin, A.D. and Mazer, M., "Current practice in cardiovascular diseases: I. The treatment of acute myocardial infarction." *US Veterans Administration Medical Bulletin*, 1943. **19**: 369-384.

319.   Mazer, M. and Kistin, A.D., "Current practice in cardiovascular diseases: I. The use of digitalis." *US Veterans Administration Medical Bulletin*, 1943. **19**: 247-264.

320.   Traum, A.H. and Wilcox, B.B., "Cardiovascular disease among veterans of World War II: a survey of 19,870 cases." *N Eng J Med*, 1946. **234**: 82-86.

321.   Traum, A.H. and Wilcox, B.B., "An analysis of one hundred and fifty cases of cardiovascular disease in World War II veterans." *Mil Surgeon*, 1945. **95**: 5-10.

322.   Traum, A.H., "Arteriosclerotic and hypertensive heart disease with right axis deviation." *Am J Med Sci*, 1944. **208**: 355-360.

323.   Traum, A.H., "Interauricular septal defect with mitral stenosis - Lutembacher's syndrome." *US Veterans Administration Medical Bulletin*, 1944. **20**: 274-276.

324.   Yater, W.M., Traum, A.H., Brown, W.G., Fitzgerald, R.P., Geisler, M.A. and Wilcox, B.B., "Coronary artery disease in men eighteen to thirty-nine years of age." *Am Heart J*, 1948. **36**: 334-372; 481-526; 683-722.

325.   Kistin, A.D., "Simple manual cassette changer for multiple exposures in angiocardiography." *Am J Roentgen*, 1951. **65**: 615-618.

326.   Kistin, A.D., Brill, W.D. and Robb, G.P., "Normal esophageal and gastric electrocardiograms: description, statistical analysis and bearing on theories of "electrocardiographic position"." *Circulation*, 1950. **2**: 578-597.

327. Kistin, A.D. and Robb, G.P., "Modification of the electrocardiogram of myocardial infarction by anomalous atrioventricular excitation (Wolff-Parkinson-White syndrome)." *Am Heart J*, 1949. **37**: 249-257.

328. Kistin, A.D., "Observations on the anatomy of the atrioventricular bundle (Bundle of His) and the question of other muscular atrioventricular connections in normal human hearts." *Am Heart J*, 1949. **37**: 849-867.

329. Kistin, A.D. and Brill, W.D., "Clinically significant differences between precordial electrocardiograms derived from V and CF leads." *Ann Int Med*, 1950. **33**: 636-647.

330. Thompson, J.L. and Kistin, A.D., "Hoarseness in heart disease." *Ann Int Med*, 1948. **29**: 259-273.

331. Cooke, F.N., Evans, J.M., Kistin, A.D. and Blades, B., "An anomaly of the pulmonary veins." *J Thor Surg*, 1951. **21**: 452-459.

332. Kistin, A.D. and Landowne, M., "Analysis of retrograde conduction to the aorta from premature ventricular contractions, a common occurrence in the human heart." *Fed Proc*, 1950. **9**: 71-72.

333. Kistin, A.D. and Landowne, M., "Retrograde conduction from premature ventricular contractions, a common occurrence in the human heart." *Circulation*, 1951. **3**: 738-751.

334. Landowne, M. and Kistin, A.D., "The diagnosis of ventricular aneurysm. A study of certain clinical and dynamic features." *J Lab Clin Med*, 1950. **36**: 847-848.

335. Telephone interview with Milton Landowne, M.D., June 25, 1997.

336. "Proceedings of the Thirteenth Conference of the Medical Council, Veterans Administration." October 12-13, 1939. Washington, DC, 1939, 37.

337. "Proceedings of the Thirteenth Conference of the Medical Council." October 12-13, 1939, 1939, 27-29.

338. "Proceedings of the Thirteenth Conference of the Medical Council." October 12-13, 1939, 1939, 43-44.

339. "Proceedings of the Thirteenth Conference of the Medical Council." October 12-13, 1939, 1939, 40.

340. Adkins, R.E., *Medical Care of Veterans*. 1967, 170-171.

341.   Magnuson, P.B., *Ring the Night Bell*. Birmingham, AL: Little, Brown&Company. reprinted by University of Alabama Press, 1986, 1960, 303.

342.   Letter from Ray Lyman Wilbur, M.D. to E.O. Crossman, M.D., written at Palo Alto, CA, October 7, 1924.

343.   Maisel, A.Q., "The veteran betrayed: how long will the Veterans' Administration continue to give third-rate medical care to first-rate men?" *The Reader's Digest*, April, 1945, 45-50.

344.   Letter from Ray Lyman Wilbur, M.D. to Albert Q. Maisel, written at Palo Alto, CA, November 21, 1944.

345.   Letter from Frank T. Hines to Ray Lyman Wilbur, M.D., written at Washington, DC, December 21, 1944.

Part II. Beginnings of the modern program, 1946-1953

Chapter 3: Postwar Progress: Modern VA Research Begins

From 1946 to 1953, the effects of World War II on medicine in general and the VA in particular were notable. The war's impact on literally millions of people, and the concerted response of the world medical community to unprecedented new challenges, brought sweeping changes to the health care landscape. In America, huge numbers of returning veterans already had pushed the VA to its limits and beyond. The era would mark the transformation of the entire VA system, including the rebirth of a near-dormant medical research program.

From the prewar, hospital-based research efforts—scattered randomly at sites where local interest and initiative provided the impetus—emerged a modest, new intramural VA research program. As it gradually took form, initial efforts were made to establish an infrastructure from which coordinated initiatives could be directed. These formative years were marked by limited funding, demands upon hospital space for clinical needs, and creating a new culture among practitioners striving to establish research as a formal part of the VA mission.

A key figure in the overall conversion of the agency was Gen. Omar N. Bradley, who had been appointed by President Truman in 1945 as Administrator of Veterans Affairs. Bradley's enormous public persona had been earned largely on the battlefield. He was viewed, especially among the rank-and-file, as a soldier's soldier—someone who, despite his four stars, understood the basic needs of his troops. Given the enormous task at hand, Bradley's great credibility would be indispensable in earning the political support needed to push through legislation that would enable the VA to measure up to public expectations.

Bradley immediately named Paul Hawley, M.D., to head the VA's Medical Department. Dr. Hawley had been Chief Surgeon of the European Theater of Operations, adding another dimension of direct familiarity with the medical needs of wounded and returning service personnel. Bradley and Hawley recruited more high-profile leadership with the naming of Paul Magnuson, M.D., as Assistant Chief Medical Director for Research and Education. A dynamic academic surgeon from Chicago, Dr. Magnuson was widely known among the leaders of the nation's medical schools, and became instrumental in associating VA medicine with these institutions.

The postwar restructuring of VA medicine

Between the two World Wars, VA medicine was a vigorous, ingrown, semi-military system, which published its own journal and had a modest in-house research program. However, budget cuts during the Great Depression and shortages during World War II took their toll in staffing. During the first year of the war alone, the VA lost 7000 employees.[1]

Until the 1930s, most VA physicians were veterans of World War I.[2] Most of the younger doctors hired after 1933 were drafted into World War II. As a result, the VA's small, aging physician staff was severely overworked. For these and other reasons, the VA had acquired a reputation for inferior medical care. During the war, Paul Magnuson, M.D., who later became the first Assistant Chief Medical Director for Research and Education, worried about the care of servicemen when the fighting was over:

"As every doctor knew, and as we from Chicago could see for ourselves at the Veterans Administration's big Hines General Hospital west of town with its 3,253 beds, the Veterans Administration Medical Department was in a sad state of decay. Medical treatment was so far below standard that the newspapers were beginning to notice the smell. I didn't know it then, but before the war was over this thing was going to blow up into a first-class nationwide scandal of bad treatment, costly blunders and administrative incompetence."[3]

At war's end, the VA was unable to cope with the huge numbers of returning ill and injured soldiers and sailors. Through 1945, some doctors assigned to the VA by the Army and Navy helped, but in January 1946, the VA had fewer than a thousand doctors to care for 100,000 patients.[4, 5] As Michael DeBakey, M.D., described the situation: "the VA, at the end of the War, was simply unable to take care of the wounded."[6] The same was true of those with illnesses resulting from their service in the war.

Establishment of the Department of Medicine and Surgery (DM&S)

In 1945 serious delays in appointing medical staff held back the rebuilding of the VA medical system. Young, qualified physicians being discharged from the military wanted to join the VA; at the same time the VA desperately needed them. As Magnuson said, "Doctors without patients, patients without doctors!"[7] A means was needed to free the hiring of doctors, dentists and nurses from Civil Service restrictions and delays.

From the beginning, VA staff and advisors had tried to establish a VA medical corps. Early on, Administrator Hines supported these efforts, but later he opposed them despite the many difficulties of using the Civil Service procedures to recruit physicians. Slow recruitment and laborious promotion procedures (in which Hines personally signed off on all promotion actions)[8] saved money, an important goal to him. Nevertheless, these delays prevented the VA from responding rapidly to new demands for medical care. Also, the Medical Department didn't report directly to the Administrator. In Hines's opinion, the Medical Department was better at a lower level in the organization, where doctors could concentrate on professional work and not worry about non-medical aspects of running the hospitals.

Magnuson, Hawley and Bradley worked together to push the medical corps concept through the Congress. With Public Law 293, the Department of Medicine and Surgery (DM&S) was born. In supporting this action, Hawley told the Senate:

"Unless (Public Law 293) is enacted into law at once, before the recess of Congress, the Medical Service of the Veterans Administration will suffer further grave consequences, which may be irreparable. In the interests of the thousands of disabled veterans who have by their sacrifices earned better medical care than they are now receiving, I urge immediate action on this bill."[9]

Not surprisingly, the Civil Service leaders opposed the bill and urged the President not to sign, which would amount to a "pocket veto." In his autobiography, *Ring the Night Bell*, Magnuson gives a dramatic portrayal of the last minute reprieve of Public Law 293, 79th Congress. According to Magnuson, Truman signed the bill only after the *Washington Post* reported that the Civil Service Commission and Bureau of the Budget urged a Presidential veto.[10]

Figure 3.1: Magnuson, Bradley and Hawley, the architects of Public Law 293

Armed with freedom to hire physicians, improved salaries, and partnership with the nation's medical schools, the new Department of Medicine and Surgery prospered. Within six months, the VA's full-time physician staff increased from 600 to 4,000,[11] not including the resident physicians assigned to the VA after medical school affiliations had begun.

Affiliation with medical schools—the concept

The nation's medical schools helped to remedy the crisis in VA medicine. Affiliations with medical schools grew rapidly under Magnuson's leadership, and he is generally credited for having the vision to establish these partnerships. Two years before he joined VA, Magnuson had made just such a proposal to Administrator Hines:

> "when the Veterans Administration built or leased or otherwise created new hospitals to meet the tremendous need that was coming, it ought to put them near the established medical schools and make them teaching hospitals like Presbyterian and Belleview . . . . I suggested that the Veterans Administration arrange to have the deans of the medical schools staff the hospitals, putting in chiefs of service, residents and interns."[12]

But the concept of VA-medical school partnership was not unique to Magnuson. Renowned heart surgeon Michael DeBakey recalled that others shared the concept:

"one of the ideas cropped up - I can't tell whose original idea it was because, you know, these things were talked back and forth, and I was participating in it - was to have the medical schools affiliated with the VA. One of the reasons we talked about this was because we had various general hospital units in the Army that were sponsored by medical schools. In fact, my own school had a unit, Tulane, but you had the Harvard Unit, you had the Hopkins Unit, and so on."[6]

Others had similar ideas. In 1944, Dr. Roy Kracke, Dean of the Medical College of Alabama, wrote General Hines suggesting that a VA hospital be built in Birmingham and serve as a teaching hospital for the medical college. Hines rejected this proposal as well as the concept of medical school affiliation.[13]

Medical school affiliations begin

Medical school affiliations began as soon as the legislation establishing DM&S came into effect. Under the new law, well-trained physicians leaving the military could now be hired as staff physicians in VA hospitals without delay. Dr. Magnuson, strongly supported by Generals Bradley and Hawley, worked feverishly to invigorate the VA medical program with the help of medical schools. By the beginning of 1947, VA hospitals, which had no resident physicians in training before 1946, now boasted some 1,000 residents.[14]

VA physicians hired as a part of a medical school affiliation expected to do research as an integral part of their academic roles. This required that research be carried out in VA hospitals. However, most VA hospitals had no laboratories suitable for basic research.[15] The original concept of Magnuson, Hawley and their co-workers was that VA research would be primarily clinical. The new VA doctors, however, wanted to be first-class academic physicians; for many, that meant doing bench research.

The barriers to research were many: Hospitals had no research space, no research equipment and no technical staff. Existing regulations forbade accepting research support from any person or agency other than the VA, which didn't even have a research budget.[8, 16] Hospital management was inexperienced in supporting research and didn't understand research and its benefits for their hospitals. There was little research tradition in many medical schools and none in most VA hospitals. On the other hand, the new Dean's Committees were very active in fostering research programs.

Keeping all VA doctors well informed: the *Technical Bulletins*

After the VA's *Medical Bulletin* stopped publication in 1944, the VA was without an official journal. However, the new leadership wanted to keep the medical staff up to date about medicine, science and administration. Toward this end, between 1946 and 1955, the new DM&S published a series of *Technical Bulletins* intended to inform VA physicians about the latest research and clinical care. Arthur Walker, the talented Tuberculosis Service research chief, became the editor. While some *Technical Bulletins* were administrative, others contained a great deal of new medical information. Many were written by highly respected authorities (Appendix III). For example, Jay Shurley, who later became a Senior Medical Investigator, wrote a *Technical Bulletin* on insulin shock therapy. At that time, he was running a unit that was a leader in insulin shock therapy. Louis Welt and Donald Seldin wrote on edema, and Welt also wrote about dehydration. J. H. Means wrote a *Technical Bulletin* advocating radioiodine therapy for hyperthyroidism in 1946, when peaceful use of atomic energy was just beginning (Chapter 6). Exciting results of the first streptomycin trial (Chapter 5) were shared with VA staff even before other publication. Richard Ebert wrote about measurement of cardiac output. Peter Florsheim and George Thorn wrote about adrenal cortical insufficiency in 1950, just when cortisone became available for treatment. Willem Kolff wrote about dialysis for renal failure, well before this was common practice. Also ahead of its time was a *Bulletin* written in 1950 on cardiac massage after operating room cardiac arrest.

American medical research in 1946

During WWII, the war effort stimulated medical research. At a national level, the Committee on Medical Research (CMR), an arm of the powerful Office of Science and Technology, the same governmental office that supervised atomic bomb development, coordinated wartime medical research. The CMR arranged for the National Research Council (NRC) of the National Academy of Sciences to manage peer review committees to help decide who should receive contracts for medical research. Military medicine made great strides, thanks both to CMR-coordinated research and to a modern system of medical records.[6, 17] As Shryock wrote in 1947, "The American people have been slow in realizing the significance of basic research. It has taken time to build up the interest prerequisite to public support in a democracy."[18]

At the end of World War II, American medical research was still limited to a few institutions and a few dedicated investigators, frequently working with their own resources or private support.[19] It was only in 1946 that the National Institute for Health (NIH) (soon to be expanded to the National Institutes of Health) began a grants program and established its Division of Research Grants. Previously, all NIH research support, except for a small National Cancer Institute grants program, was intramural or contractual.[20] The entire 1945 NIH budget was only $180,000, but by 1947 it had shot up to $8 million.[21] Only a few medical schools had large research programs. Most medical research, in medical schools and elsewhere, was clinical in nature.[22]

Research leaders in the early postwar VA

Magnuson, as the VA's first Assistant Chief Medical Director for Research and Education (ACMD/R&E), and several assistants established the Research and Education Service. Robert Kevan, a young officer who had planned to study hospital administration, became his executive officer in December 1945.[23, 24] In 1946, Magnuson recruited Edward Harvey Cushing, M.D., to be Chief of the Education Section.[25] and, in 1947, Louis Welt, M.D., to be Chief of the Research Section. When Magnuson was promoted to Chief Medical Director in 1948, Cushing moved up to his position as ACMD/R&E. Cushing resigned in 1951 and was replaced by George Lyon, M.D., who continued as ACMD/R&E until 1956.

Figure 3.2: Paul Magnuson, M.D.

Paul Magnuson, M.D., the first ACMD/R&E (1945-1948)

Dr. Magnuson is described by those who knew him as a "stormy petrel,"[8] a "whirling dervish,"[26] a "pistol," a brilliant man who did a tremendous amount of work.[27] Robert Kevan, who was Magnuson's Administrative Officer, described him as a great man who was very blunt, forceful, and driving. Magnuson knew what he wanted and would do almost anything to get it.

Figure 3.3: Robert Kevan

Kevan recalled that he was a wonderful man to work with. If you made the "right" decision, he would back you up. If you made the "wrong" decision, he would give you a hard time.[23, 24] Ralph Casteel, who succeeded Kevan in 1948, agreed. He recalled that Magnuson "preached that the best medicine was practiced by those who also taught and who explored new therapeutic modalities."

Magnuson believed that "the fight against bureaucracy and bureaucratic thinking is never won." By his own admission, he was insubordinate: "I have never in my life worked for anybody but a patient."[28] As ACMD/R&E and later as Chief Medical Director, he worked tirelessly to set up and protect the VA-medical school partnerships. Even after he left the VA in early 1951, he remained active. He was known to have contacted the White House when a new hospital was planned at a site other than what he had promised.[29] Martin Cummings, M.D., recalled that it was actually Magnuson who recruited him to come to

Central Office as Director, Research Service, in 1953. Cummings's new boss, Dr. George Lyon, was taken by surprise.[30]

Figure 3.4 Ralph Casteel

Magnuson was interested in all aspects of academic medicine, but most of his attention went to upgrading patient care and teaching programs. Cummings recalled that, when Magnuson and John Barnwell, M.D., visited his laboratory near the Atlanta VA Hospital in 1950, Barnwell stayed to discuss science while Magnuson went off to the hospital to look at the clinical service.[30]

Edward Harvey (Pat) Cushing, the second ACMD/R&E (1948-1951)

Figure 3.5: E.H. (Pat) Cushing, M.D.

Cushing (Figure 3.5) was energetic, intelligent and well-educated.[31] An internist from Harvard Medical School, he had been in private practice in Cleveland before the War. He was a nephew of Harvey Cushing, the famous neurosurgeon, and was the fifth physician in his family line. According to Dr. Alfred H. Lawton, who was Research Chief under him, he was a delightful person who "ran the office as a committee."[16]

Cushing was a disciple of Magnuson. He stayed on about a year after Administrator Carl Gray fired Magnuson. When Cushing resigned in February 1952, his departure was abrupt and without warning.[8] Why he left is unclear, but his obituary says that it was in protest.[32]

George Lyon, M.D., the third ACMD/R&E (1951-1956)

Cushing's successor as ACMD/R&E was George M. Lyon, M.D., who had been Special Assistant to the Chief Medical Director for Atomic Medicine and Chief of the Radioisotope Section (Chapter 6).

Dr. Lyon has been described as "an old maid about everything," who irritated people working for him. Instead of pushing for budget increases, he would ask for three budgets: Plan A/reduction, Plan B/hold-even and Plan C/slight increase. Lyon retained his loyalty to the radioisotope program, though he was obviously also very loyal to the VA research program.

Figure 3.6 George Lyon, M.D.

Early chiefs of the Research Section

Research program leadership fell first to Louis Welt, M.D., a young Instructor of Medicine at Yale, Chief of the Research Section from 1947 to 1948.[33] Welt was replaced by Alfred H. Lawton, dean of the two-year medical school in North Dakota. [16] After Lawton left in 1951, the position remained vacant for two years. During that time, John Nunemaker, M.D., who was later Director, Education Service, was Acting Chief for a few months, and he was followed by Arthur Abt, M.D.[34] Then the position was vacant until 1953 when Martin Cummings came to VACO (Chapter 7).

Louis Welt, M.D. (1947-1948)

Welt, as the first Chief of the Research Section (1947-1948), was active in starting collaborative programs with the National Academy of Sciences (NAS). He also arranged contracts with medical school faculty to carry out clinical research of importance to the veteran patient. Welt worked with the VA Construction Service to try to alter plans for new VA hospitals to include research laboratory space. He is remembered as bright, young and energetic. Magnuson hired him without concern for the VA's usual recruitment processes.[23, 24, 35] After staying only about a year, Welt returned to Yale as an NIH fellow and later Assistant Professor. He subsequently moved to the University of North Carolina, where he rose to become Chairman of Medicine, and then returned to Yale as Chairman of Medicine.[33] During the 1950s, he wrote two *VA Technical Bulletins* on fluid metabolism.[36, 37] At the time of his sudden death in 1973, he was assisting NAS in beginning a review of the VA patient care program (Chapter 16).[38]

Alfred Lawton, M.D. (1948-1951)

Lawton had been dean of the two-year medical school at the University of North Dakota. He recalled that he spent a large fraction of his Central Office time traveling about the country trying to start research laboratories. Two major problems were finding staff capable of doing research and finding appropriate space. As he recalled, money was not a problem; research funds were available for justifiable programs. He left the VA in 1951 to start a medical research program for the Air Force.[39]

Figure 3.7: Alfred Lawton, M.D., right, with Roger Egeberg, M.D., Chief of Medicine, West Los Angeles VA Hospital, 1949.

Struggle for research space

Dr. Welt and his successor VACO Chiefs of Research made a major effort to insert research space into plans for the new VA hospitals being rapidly built to correct the national shortage of beds for veterans. Most new hospital plans didn't include space for research or radioisotope laboratories. Sometimes plans could be changed before construction, but research space was generally inadequate. For years, hospitals had to be retrofitted for research. Given the limits of the VA construction system, research space was squeezed into places like renovated closets, garages, laundries and bathrooms. Since construction monies were hard to get, these laboratories were primarily built with operational monies, each project costing less than the $15,000 limit.[16] Despite these obstacles, Welt, Lawton, and their successors and counterparts at hospitals succeeded in making the intramural program flourish. By 1952, the VA had medical research programs at 66 hospitals, with 373 employees paid from money set aside for support of research.[40] In 1952, Harold F. Weiler joined the Central Office team, as Chief of the Research Laboratories Section, to spearhead the construction and furnishing of the needed laboratories.

Figure 3.8 Harold F. Weiler

A "Research Hospital" is built

An important exception to the neglect of research space construction was the opening in 1953 of the new Chicago VA Research Hospital, later called the Chicago Lakeside VA Medical Center. A Chicago consulting group, considered the best hospital architects in the business, designed it.[41] Unlike other new VA hospitals, it had an all-marble exterior. Magnuson worked on every aspect of design and construction and watched each step carefully. According to his executive assistant Ralph Casteel, Magnuson "knew every crack in the rails between Washington and Chicago" from his frequent overnight trips to see how the construction was going.[8] This hospital was designed for the most advanced patient care available, and an entire floor was devoted to research laboratories. Francis Haddy, M.D., one of the first three physicians to work there in 1953, recalled that while the hospital construction had been finished when he arrived, the hospital was empty. For the first few months, the three physicians who were there, together with a helpful supply officer, went through catalogs and ordered everything "from bedpans to the most sophisticated research equipment." Haddy remembers no budget restrictions; they could buy the best.[42]

Half of the research floor was devoted to the radioisotope laboratory. John A.D. Cooper, M.D., of the Northwestern University faculty, who had trained under Magnuson, worked with the architects to design this laboratory and later became its chief. Every facility needed to do cutting edge radioisotope research and clinical care was available when the hospital opened.[43]

Gifts for research get the green light

When the VA research program was reborn after World War II, VA scientists were not allowed to accept gifts for research. Dr. Cushing pushed a policy, announced January 18, 1952 that nongovernmental gifts could be received and placed in the General Post Fund after approval of the Chief Medical Director. Expenditures, however, must honor donor stipulations.[44]

When Dr. Lyon described the new policy to the Committee on Veteran's Medical Problems, he noted that interagency transfer of funds at the Central Office was possible, but the U.S. Public Health Service did not transfer funds appropriated for research grants to the VA. He also stated, "It is not the policy of the VA to encourage VA personnel to seek funds from agencies other than the VA for research."[45] The result was that there was no way that a VA person could get an NIH grant until that policy was changed in 1954 (Chapter 7).

Cortisone research initiative

In 1950, Lawton negotiated with Merck and Co. to make more than 2,000 grams - said to be their entire supply - of the newly synthesized hormone cortisone available to the VA for research. Twelve VA hospitals, including Bronx, Chamblee, Cleveland, Ft. Hamilton, Ft. Logan (Denver), Framingham, Hines, Los Angeles, Minneapolis, Mt. Alto (Washington, DC), New Orleans and San Francisco, participated in cortisone studies, both physiological and clinical. Their preliminary results were reported at a conference at Central Office in August 1950. Many of the leaders in VA research presented basic and clinical papers. Among the speakers were Solomon Papper, Marcus Krupp, Norman Shumway, Martin Cummings, Thaddeus Sears, William Adams, Ralph Goldman, James Halsted, Thomas Sternberg, William Merchant, Samuel Bassett, Louis Alpert, Hyman Zimmerman, Bernard Straus, Max Michael, James Hammarsten and Maurice Strauss.[46] This conference stimulated further research in this area, and two other conferences followed. This special program ended when the FDA approved cortisone for general clinical use.[16]

VA research funding, 1946-1952

During this formative period, the overall research budget grew only modestly (Figure 3.9). Early on, the contract program grew, but later it declined as the intramural program began to solve its early problems and to reach "critical mass".

Research sponsored by other units in DM&S

In addition to research leadership in the Research and Education Service, several other Services identified research chiefs within their disciplines. Dr. K.R. Pfeiffer was Chief, Dental Research between 1949 and 1952. Tuberculosis Service also had its Research Chief, Arthur Walker, who coordinated the early tuberculosis cooperative studies (Chapter 5).

Neuropsychiatry Service Research Chiefs for both Psychiatry and Psychology played key roles in launching the mental health research programs of the 1950s and 1960s. The VA early developed an active internship program for clinical psychology Ph.D. students, and these students were expected to produce research dissertations. Psychology leadership in

Central Office actively encouraged research, and the Chief of Psychology Research, Maurice Lorr, reviewed all the resulting dissertations.[47]

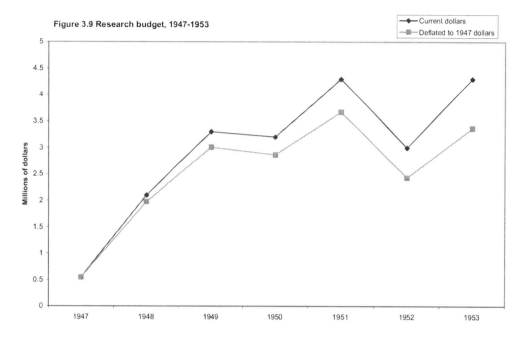

Figure 3.9 Research budget, 1947-1953

While informal interaction occurred between these programs and people in the Research Service, there seems to have been no effort at that time to centralize the various research programs. Each Service operated independently and found the money to pay for the research it sponsored.

Six important research programs began during this early period, apart from and in addition to the VA's formal intramural research program. Medical research contracts, the prosthetics research contracts and the Follow-up Agency, all of them carried out in collaboration with the National Academy of Sciences, are discussed in Chapter 4. Important research began within the Neuropsychiatry Service during this early period and led to vigorous psychopharmacology studies of the late 1950s and 1960s (Chapter 8). Chapters 5 and 6 describe the research sponsored by Tuberculosis Service and the Atomic Medicine Section of Research and Education Service.

VA research conferences

In January 1951, Cushing and Lawton held a Medical Research Conference in Chamblee, Georgia. This began a series of conferences of VA research investigators, which continued to be an important part of the research program until the late 1960s. In later years, these meetings became large and complex, with associated meetings of the radioisotope, tuberculosis and psychopharmacology groups.

Research in the hospitals

By 1948, a formal structure of local governance of the research programs in VA hospitals was in place.[48]   Each hospital had a Research and Education Committee, consisting of service chiefs and two Deans Committee representatives.   In a 1952 presentation to the Committee on Veterans Medical Problems, Dr. Lyon described the role of the Executive Secretary of the hospital Research Committee and announced he was attempting to formalize that position at the hospital level as the Chief, Investigational Service.[40] By the late 1950s, this position was called the Associate Director of Professional Services for Research (ADPSR).[49]   By 1961, the title of this research chief had been changed to Associate Chief of Staff for Research and Education (ACOS/R&E), and in 1972 it was once again changed to Associate Chief of Staff for Research and Development (ACOS/R&D).

Even in 1946, many more small clinical studies were probably under way than those known to Central Office. The average VA intramural researcher was entrepreneurial and resourceful. Except for reporting their publications, which had to be approved by Central Office, they were more accountable to their local superiors than to Central Office. A few examples follow.

Salt Lake City VA Hospital

When John Nunemaker began as Chief, Medical Service, at Salt Lake City VA Hospital in 1946, he used every means possible to start his research program. Most of the equipment he used belonged to the clinical laboratory. He established an animal facility in an old warehouse, raised rabbits on his farm and brought them in for experiments. For his bacteriological studies, he needed enriched serum and found that horse serum made a good medium. To obtain it, he would visit a slaughterhouse that prepared animal feed from horse meat. He would hold a bucket to collect the blood, which he anticoagulated to remove the red cells. He then let the serum clot, put it through a sausage grinder and then through a bacterial filter. The organisms grew well.[50] In the early 1950s, Nunemaker moved to VA Central Office, where he became Director, Education Service (Chapter 7).

Halloran VA Hospital (Staten Island) and East Orange, NJ VA Hospital

Pathologist Oscar Auerbach, who worked at the Halloran VA Hospital from 1947 to 1952, used clinical facilities for his research studies. Auerbach recalled that he worked full time as a routine hospital pathologist and did his research between 4 and 6 a.m. and during evenings and weekends.[51] He moved to the new VA hospital at East Orange, NJ, in 1952. In the late 1950s, he carried out the work for which he is best known, showing smoking to be an important cause of lung cancer (Chapter 10). During the early postwar years, Auerbach's studies were primarily on the pathology of tuberculosis, although he also wrote on the germinal epithelium in male paraplegics,[52] hepatocellular carcinoma[53] and osteogenic sarcoma.[54] He collaborated with Gladys Hobby, Ph.D., then at Pfizer but later at East Orange VA Hospital, on animal studies directed to develop an immunization method better than BCG for protection against tuberculosis.[55] He reported a huge series of observations from autopsies at Seaview Hospital, a tuberculosis hospital on Long Island where he had worked before the war. He brought the material with him when he joined the VA. From these records and slides, he extracted clinical information about rare complications of tuberculosis: 311 cases of tuberculous empyema,[56] 421 cases of tracheobronchial tuberculosis,[57] 108 cases of tuberculous meningitis[58, 59] and about 200 cases of serosal (pleural, peritoneal or pericardial) tuberculosis.[60] After streptomycin became available, he published on the ways treatment affects the pathology of the disease.[61-63]

Oakland VA Hospital

Figure 3.10 Bruno Gerstl, M.D., and
Hospital Manager at the Oakland VA Hospital

Bruno Gerstl, a pathologist, went to the Oakland VA Hospital in California (later moved to Martinez) in 1946 or 1947. The hospital, in a renovated hotel, was loosely affiliated with the University of California at San Francisco. He collaborated with members of the Medical Service on clinical studies of mitral insufficiency,[64] erythrocyte fragility[65] and cryptococcosis.[66] In 1953, he and other pathologists reported on water, sodium and potassium contents of the human, guinea pig and rabbit lung.[67] Gerstl became interested in the immunology of cancer, for which he needed an animal room to house his guinea pigs and eventually he obtained one. Gerstl also studied the immunology of tuberculosis, especially methods to measure tuberculosis antibodies.[68-70]

Bronx VA Hospital

Bernard Roswit, Rosalyn Yalow and Solomon Berson were active in setting up a radioisotope unit and doing research using radioisotopes at the Bronx VA Hospital during this period. Their work is described in Chapter 11.

Ludwig Gross, M.D., was also active in research at the Bronx, where he had transferred while still in uniform. During the time he could spare from his clinical duties, Gross was working in an old bathroom. There, he bred leukemia-prone mice and tried to prove his theory of the viral cause of mammalian leukemia by transmitting this tendency to develop leukemia to normal mice. In 1949, he finally succeeded.

Gross was a war refugee from Poland. In 1939, he had given a lecture at NIH in which he speculated that leukemia was caused by a virus and that some day we would have a vaccine for it. He was introduced at that time to the Surgeon General and to the nucleus of the NIH staff. He then returned to Europe and was in Poland when the Nazis invaded. He escaped just in front of the Nazi line.

Figure 3.11 Ludwig Gross, M.D., in 1975

When, after many difficulties, he managed to return to the United States, he applied for a commission in the U. S. Army. At first he was turned down because he was not a citizen. He went to the Polish Ambassador, who introduced him to the Surgeon General, who wrote a letter that supported his entry in the U.S. Army Reserve in Cincinnati.

While he was in Cincinnati, he studied neuroblastoma, a condition that may be found in the grandfather and in the grandson. Gross considered that this might be due to vertical transmission of disease from generation to generation through the genome. This led to the concept that the virus responsible for the cancer transmission became associated with the genome. Not everyone carrying the genome developed cancer, since there was some mutual benefit between the genome and the virus.

He wanted to continue his research even after he entered active Army service. He wrote to Bittner, the discoverer of a genetic line of mice that were very prone to breast cancer. He asked Bittner for a breeding pair of his mice and Bittner sent them. He had no laboratory, so he kept his mice in coffee cans covered with screens, in the trunk of his car and sometimes in his apartment.

In 1944, the Army transferred him to a station in North Carolina near Durham. While on leave, he went to Philadelphia, where he visited Dr. Baldwin Lucke, who was working on transmission of kidney cancer in frogs. They discussed the problem of viral transmission.

When Lucke went with him to his car, Gross opened the trunk and showed him his mice. Lucke was a consultant to the Surgeon General, and one week after this meeting, Gross received transfer orders to the Bronx VA Hospital.

When he arrived at the Bronx, they told him to look for a room where he could set up a lab. He found a room that was being used for storage of oxygen tanks, which contained two toilets. The hospital staff cleared it out, and the carpenters covered the toilets. There, he studied the hemolytic action of mouse mammary carcinoma filtrates and extracts on mouse erythrocytes[71, 72] and a similar effect of human cancer extracts on human erythrocytes.[73] He later continued his interest in breast cancer transmission, studying possibly oncogenic particles in mouse and human breast milk.[74]

But Gross's main interest was leukemia, and all he had when he arrived at the Bronx were his mice with a 90% chance of developing breast cancer. Jacob Furth at Cornell had a strain of leukemia-prone mice, the AK strain. When Gross asked Furth for a breeding pair, he gave him 11 of his AK mice.

Gross bred the mice himself. While there was no specific money for research, the hospital allowed him to spend some of his time conducting his studies. He spent five years, 1944-1949, trying to transmit the tendency to leukemia to non-leukemia-prone mice by injection of filtrates. The hospital was considering taking away his research time and space, as he seemed to be nonproductive.

Figure 3.12: the laboratory in which Ludwig Gross carried out his original work on mouse leukemia.

In 1949, Dr. Gilbert Dallborf gave a lecture at the hospital about the Coxsakie virus. He explained that it could be transmitted only in newborns. Before Dallborf even finished the lecture, Gross ran out to his laboratory where he had some newborn normal mice. He injected them with cells from AK mice, and they developed leukemia.[75, 76] Later he found that he could also transmit leukemia with just a filtrate,[77] and that the effect extended into the next generation.[78] He characterized transmission of other viruses as well during this early period[79-82] and evolved a theory about the viral transmission of malignancies.[83, 84]

After Gross's success in transmitting leukemia through the newborn mice, the Hospital Director, Ralph G. Devoe, a former general, became very supportive and gave him lots of space.

Gross had trained as a surgeon and had to learn experimental techniques from scratch. C. P. Rhodes at Memorial Hospital adopted him as a friend and taught him much that he needed to know to do research. The man who made the filters he was using also helped him to develop his techniques.[85]

While extreme, Gross's early experience at the Bronx VA Hospital exemplifies the determination and independence shown by many early VA researchers. They had little guidance and often were not well understood. Little or no research infrastructure was available. But a venturesome spirit that encouraged original thinking and inventiveness permeated the newly "academic" organization.

Washington, DC, VA Hospital

Hyman Zimmerman, M.D., joined the VA in 1949 at the old Mt. Alto (Washington, DC) Hospital and had started a research laboratory there. The question of getting money for research was not even raised. He simply carried out the research himself, using clinical equipment and supplies, as well as some of his own funds. It wasn't that he asked for money and was turned down, but rather that neither he nor anyone else even *thought* about asking for money to support his research. However, in 1951 he was recruited to the Omaha VA Hospital to be Chief of the Medical Service. In Omaha, no research laboratory awaited him, although he made the availability of a laboratory a condition of his recruitment. The Hospital Director contacted the Regional Director, and the Regional Director contacted Dr. Lawton. The princely sum of $25,000 was allocated to set up the new laboratory. There was no review of his research, and, as he recalled, the later support of his ongoing research came from the local hospital budget.[86]

West Los Angeles Wadsworth VA Hospital

Shortly after DM&S was established, the huge Wadsworth VA Hospital in Los Angeles formed a Dean's Committee that included leaders from both the University of Southern California (USC) and the College of Medical Evangelists, now Loma Linda School of Medicine. After faculty for the planned University of California at Los Angeles (UCLA) School of Medicine began to arrive, UCLA also sat on the Dean's Committee. B.O. Ralston, dean of the School of Medicine at USC, was the chairman. Ralston met Roger Egeberg, M.D., who had been General McArthur's personal physician during the war, in Washington, and recruited him to be Chief of Medicine at Wadsworth. Egeberg (Figure 3.7) arrived in July 1946 and began working with the "old guard" to try to upgrade the facility. Planning for the new UCLA School of Medicine was under way, and key faculty were being recruited. Until 1955, UCLA had no hospital, and many of the new faculty worked at Wadsworth.[87]

William Adams, M.D., arrived in Los Angeles in 1948 and joined the Wadsworth staff. Shortly thereafter, Adams and Ralph Goldman, M.D., began a multidisciplinary effort. Once they had acquired laboratory space, they still lacked staff and funds to hire staff. Adams made two trips to Washington, where he talked with Alfred Lawton. He presented Lawton with a proposed Table of Organization, and Lawton gave him funds to hire 14 or 15 technical staff. Adam's argument was that this was needed to attract senior people, and Lawton listened. After that, it still took over a year to get the lab set up.

Figure 3.13 Samuel Bassett, M.D.

Samuel Bassett, M.D., came to Wadsworth about 1950. Bassett was seen as instrumental in the discovery of potassium deficiency syndrome in corrected severe diabetic acidosis. Adams remembered a patient who had become paralyzed after treatment for diabetic acidosis. Bassett suggested that she might have a low blood potassium level. Adams ran the potassium measurement himself by a colorimetric method (flame photometry was not yet available). No one believed the results because they were so low. After the patient was given potassium, they were able to take her out of the respirator and she improved. The resident who wrote the paper received the credit for this important discovery.[88]

John Lawrence, M.D., the newly appointed Chairman of Medicine at UCLA, used money from Parke Davis Company to renovate four Quonset huts on the VA campus behind Building 114 for the use of the new UCLA faculty. These Quonset huts were empty and they had to put in everything, including the heating system. They got the bench work free from the old chemistry building at the University, when a new chemistry building was built. They put in a walk-in cold room at a cost of $2,500. A weighing room had to be specially constructed, because the Quonset hut shook. To stabilize the balances, they laid a concrete slab through the floor.[89]

Egeberg's effort as Chief of Medicine was primarily to build the Medical Service and, incidentally, to protect his staff during the McCarthy era.[87] He wrote clinical papers even before there was a research laboratory at Wadsworth.[90, 91] His personal research interest was coccidioidomycosis. In addition to clinical treatment trials,[92, 93] he worked to find out where the coccidioidomycosis organism was when it was not in the human body. Dr. Ann Leconnen, who was in charge of the Outpatient Department at the LA County General Hospital, collaborated on this project with Egeberg and his wife. They had collected just about everything they could find around the Lost Hills area, which is in a coccidioidomycosis endemic area. They were unable to culture the organism from any of the plants or soil or warm-blooded animals.

Thinking that a cold-blooded animal might be a possible vector, they decided to try to infect rattlesnakes with coccidioidomycosis organisms by having the snakes inhale the organisms. To obtain the snakes, Dr. Leconnen contracted with the owner of a small general store in the San Joaquin Valley. One evening after her children had gone to bed, the store owner came to her house carrying a gunny sack. He opened the gunny sack and dumped a dozen rattlesnakes on the floor.

In order to make the rattlesnakes inhale the suspension of coccidioidomycosis organisms, they found a resident who had been in the desert during his military service and had learned how to handle rattlesnakes. He would grasp the snake behind its head, causing it to expose its fangs. Venom would drop from the fangs. The snake would then hold its breath, often as long as five minutes. Holding a syringe full of the suspension of coccidioidomycosis organisms, Egeberg would wait in front of the snake, watching to see when it would take its first breath. When the snake finally breathed, he would empty the syringe into the snake's mouth, forcing it to inhale the organisms. Ultimately, the snakes failed to develop cocci, and the project was dropped.[94]

Figure 3.14 Ralph Goldman, M.D.

Ralph Goldman, M.D., who later entered the field of gerontology and headed the VA's nationwide Extended Care program, was a nephrologist. In addition to clinical reports on hereditary hemorrhagic telangiectasis,[95] unsuccessful attempts to treat Hodgkin's Disease with aureomycin,[96] and acute renal failure due to phenylbutazone,[97] he took advantage of the metabolic unit he had helped to establish. There, he studied the diurnal variation in excretion of water, and electrolytes and steroids in congestive heart failure and in hepatic cirrhosis.[98, 99] He also studied renal function in multiple myeloma, showing that reduction in glomerular, vascular and tubular function is parallel, consistent with destruction of entire nephron units.[100] With Bassett, he studied calcium and phosphorus excretion after calcium administration in patients with hypoparathyroidism and found a disproportionate increase in calcium excretion when serum calcium had normalized.[101] He also studied the mode of creatinine excretion in renal failure, excluding fecal excretion and increased creatine formation as alternative routes.[102]

Bassett collaborated widely, working in a metabolic unit at Wadsworth that Adams and Goldman established. Among his fellows was William Blahd, who later became a leader in Nuclear Medicine (Chapter 6). While working with Bassett, Blahd published an attempt to treat Hand-Schuller-Christian Syndrome with cortisone, apparently one of the cortisone studies begun by Lawton (above).[103] He demonstrated that prolonged epinephrine administration did not impair adrenal cortical function.[104] And Blahd carried out a study of potassium deficiency that was probably the trigger for his later extensive work on potassium metabolism.[105]

Seeking an alternative pathway for iron loss, William Adams performed an early study measuring iron excretion in sweat. He and his colleagues found that sweat itself contained no measurable iron, though the skin cells desquamated with the sweat were iron-rich.[106] He had a special interest in multiple myeloma patients, in whom he studied fibrin formation and the effects of plasmapheresis.[107, 108] With Bassett, he studied metabolic balance of calcium, phosphorus, electrolyes and nitrogen in multiple myeloma patients treated with ACTH, establishing the negative balances now recognized,[109] and the effect of cortisone and ACTH in leukemias of various types.[110]

With Melvin Levin and others, Bassett also studied metabolism in gout, showing little effect of an acute gouty attack on adrenal function and equivocal therapeutic benefit from ACTH, cortisone and testosterone. They found that therapeutic doses of colchicine were followed by sodium and chloride retention.[111, 112]

Atlanta VA Hospital

In Atlanta, Max Michael, an internist, studied the inflammatory response, with a special interest in sarcoidosis. His follow-up epidemiological study of 350 cases of sarcoidosis showed a predominance in persons who reside in the South and in rural areas.[113] He demonstrated delay in response to an inflammatory stimulus in rabbits treated with cortisone.[114]

In 1949, Martin Cummings, who had been Chief of the Tuberculosis Research Laboratory at the Communicable Disease Center in Atlanta, moved to the Atlanta VA Hospital as chief of a new special tuberculosis laboratory. He, Michael and Walter Bloom collaborated on studies comparing macrophage response in peritoneal exudates in rats and rabbits in an attempt to explain the greater resistance of rats to tuberculosis[115] and the influence of cortisone in reducing the rat's natural resistance to experimental tuberculosis.[116] In other collaborations, Cummings expanded on the latter finding, showing that cortisone-enhanced tuberculosis in rats responded to streptomycin,[117] and that induction of diabetes with alloxan also made rats susceptible to virulent tuberculosis.[118] He and his collaborators also showed that ACTH and cortisone do not suppress the tuberculin reaction in guinea pigs,[119] that centrifugation is not an effective way to concentrate tubercle bacilli in sputum,[120] and that certain amino acids may enhance resistance to tuberculosis in a variety of animals.[121] Cummings and his coworkers also published clinical articles on the hemagglutinen test for tuberculosis,[122] methods of culture for the tubercle bacillus[123] and treatment of tuberculous meningitis.[124] After he moved to Central Office, Cummings collaborated with statistician Dorothy Livings on a report of the incidence of streptomycin-resistant tubercle bacilli in VA patients.[125]

Minneapolis VA Hospital

Dr. Richard Ebert had been stationed in Europe during WWII as a part of a Harvard Medical School medical unit. There he met General Bradley. After the war, Ebert, who was looking for a job, was approached by Cecil Watson, Chairman of Medicine at the University of Minnesota. In February 1946, Ebert joined the Minneapolis VA Hospital as Chief of Medicine. At that time, the Dean's Committee was just beginning to be active. The hospital was generally very slow moving. The large Tuberculosis Service had many patients with long stays. In addition, demobilized service people demanded VA care.

With the backing of the Deans Committee and of Central Office, Ebert rapidly built up the Medical Service. Within six months, a program of resident and medical student training was thriving.

Not long after that, they began a research program. Watson and Morris Visscher, the Chairman of Physiology, were interested in the VA. Vischer arranged for Herbert Wells, who was in the Department of Physiology but who had an M.D. degree, to join the VA's patient care staff. They also recruited an equipment specialist to help them equip the research laboratories. The Minneapolis research program was becoming active, and they began to look for money. They contacted Central Office and were told to contact NIH, but then they learned that NIH policy was not to give grants to VA researchers. In about 1947, they were among the first to receive research money from the VA.[126]

In 1947, Dr. Craig Borden, later Chief of Medicine at the Chicago Lakeside VA Hospital, and Ebert set up the first cardiac catheterization laboratory west of the Mississippi. It was an opportunity for both advanced patient care and clinical research. With this laboratory, they made some of the first circulatory measurements, such as measurements of pressures in the pulmonary circulation.[127, 128] They studied pulmonary hypertension,[129, 130] the anoxia of myocardial infarction,[131] and ventilation[132, 133] and lung elasticity in various clinical conditions.[134] In 1949, Ebert and Abraham Falk reported in the *Journal of the American Medical Association* on 17 cases of tuberculous pericarditis treated with streptomycin in the cooperative clinical trial (Chapter 5) and found that circulatory failure was cured or much improved in eight of them.[135] With others, Ebert published in *Science* an article about erythrocyte disappearance kinetics in normal persons and in persons with hemolytic diseases.[136]

Figure 3.17 Number of VA publications

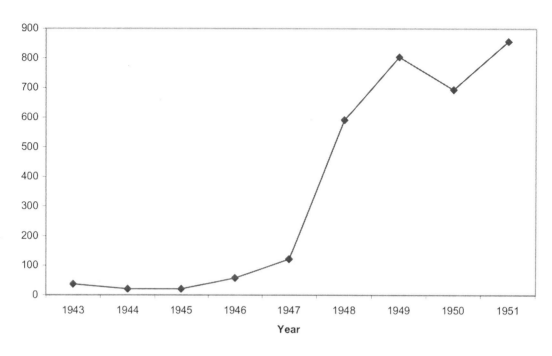

In late 1946, Ebert recruited William Tucker, M.D., from the University of Chicago to head the 200-bed Tuberculosis Service. Other key recruits were James Hammarsten, M.D., Benjamin Heller, M.D and Leslie Zieve, M.D. These physicians collaborated among themselves and with Ebert and others. Among their publications were studies of blood volume,[137, 138] reports on acceleration of liver disease in tuberculous patients treated with amithiozone,[139] the effects of cortisone in nephropathies[140] and adrenaline on renal function and electrolyte excretion.[141] Clinical reports included a 1949 compilation of the studies of streptomycin treatment methods up to that time[142] and case reports on acute myocarditis[143] and on transfusion reactions.[144]

VA research in the early 1950s

The intramural program quickly bore fruit. VA publications increased from fewer than 100 per year in 1945 and 1946 to more than 800 in 1951. Even without a mandate from the Congress (Chapter 7), more and more money was being spent on intramural research. The VA was on its way to leadership in medical research.

References

1. Adkins, R.E., *Medical Care of Veterans*. Washington, D.C.: U.S. Government Printing Office, 1967, 166.

2. Interview with Abraham Gottlieb, M.D., December 18, 1991 at Palo Alto, CA VA Medical Center.

3. Magnuson, P.B., M.D., *Ring the Night Bell*. Birmingham, Ala: Little Brown and Company, 1960, 268.

4. Magnuson, *Ring the Night Bell*. 1960, 278.

5. Adkins, *Medical Care of Veterans*. 1967

6. Interview with Michael DeBakey, M.D., January 28,1994 at Dr. DeBakey's office at Baylor Medical Center, Houston, TX.

7. Magnuson, *Ring the Night Bell*. 1960, 276.

8. Interview with Ralph Casteel, May 3, 1988 at a restaurant in Bethesda, MD.

9. Adkins, *Medical Care of Veterans*. 1967, 211.

10. Magnuson, *Ring the Night Bell*. 1960, 289-298.

11. Adkins, *Medical Care of Veterans*. 1967, 214.

12. Magnuson, *Ring the Night Bell*. 1960, 269.

13. Adkins, *Medical Care of Veterans*. 1967, 181.

14. National Academy of Sciences - National Research Council. "Minutes of First Meeting, Committee on Veterans Medical Problems." September 20, 1946. Washington, D.C.: National Research Council, 1946, 2.

15. NAS-NRC. "Minutes, First Meeting of the CVMP." September 20, 1946, 1946, 2-3.

16. Telephone interview with Alfred H. Lawton, M.D., April 26, 1988.

17. Shryock, R.H., *American Medical Research, Past and Present*. New York: The Commonwealth Fund, 1947

18. Shryock, *American Medical Research*. 1947, 321.

19. Harvey, A.M., *Science at the Bedside. Clinical Research in American Medicine, 1905-1945*. Baltimore and London: Johns Hopkins University Press, 1981, 554.

20. Telephone interview with Ernest Allen, Ph.D., April 11, 1988.

21. McCarthy, C.R. "Testimony before the U.S. House of Representatives Committee on Veterans' Affairs." *Hearing on Government Sponsored Research involving Radioactive Materials Conducted in VA Medical Centers*. February 8, 1994. Washington, D.C., 1994, 4.

22. Harvey, *Science at the Bedside*. 1981

23. Magnuson, *Ring the Night Bell*. 1960, 285-286.

24. Telephone interview with Robert Kevan, January 11, 1992.

25. Magnuson, *Ring the Night Bell*. 1960, 306.

26. Magnuson, *Ring the Night Bell*. 1960, 320.

27. Interview with Dorothy Bluestein, May 5, 1992 at Ms. Bluestein's home in Silver Spring, MD.

28. Magnuson, *Ring the Night Bell*. 1960, 344.

29. Magnuson, *Ring the Night Bell*. 1960, 349-350.

30. Interview with Martin M. Cummings, M.D., February 7, 1994 at Dr. Cummings's home in Florida.

31. Interview with Marjorie T. Wilson, M.D., April 29, 1988 at Dr. Wilson's office at ECFMG, in Washington, D.C.

32. "Edward Cushing, District Physician." *The Washington Post*, Washington, D.C., November 16, 1969.

33. Louis Welt, M.D. Curriculum Vitae, provided by Yale University

34. National Academy of Sciences - National Research Council. "Minutes, Twenty fifth Meeting of the CVMP." December 5, 1952. Washington, D.C.: National Research Council, 1952, 17.

35. Interview with Gilbert W. Beebe, Ph.D., June 1, 1994 at a hotel lobby in Washington, DC.

36. Welt, L. and Seldin, D., "The pathologic physiology and treatment of edema." *Veterans Administration Technical Bulletin*, 1951. **10-69**.

37. Welt, L., "The pathogenesis and management of dehydration." *Veterans Administration Technical Bulletin*, 1955. **10-105**.

38. Interview with Richard Greene, M.D., Ph.D, April 7, 1993 at Dr. Greene's home in Washington, D.C.

39. National Academy of Sciences - National Research Council. "Minutes, Twenty first Meeting of the CVMP." May 25, 1951. Washington, D.C.: National Research Council, 1951, 10.

40. NRC. "Minutes, Twenty fifth Meeting of the CVMP." 1952, Appendix 2, p. 546.

41. Magnuson, *Ring the night bell*. 1960, 315-316.

42. Telephone interview with Francis Haddy, M.D., Ph.D., April 6, 1988.

43. Telephone interview with John A.D. Cooper, M.D., March 24, 1988.

44. NAS-NRC. "Minutes, Twenty fifth Meeting of the CVMP." December 5, 1952. Washington, D.C.: National Research Council, 1952, Appendix 2, 547.

45. NAS-NRC. "Minutes, Twenty fifth Meeting of the CVMP." December 5, 1952. Washington, D.C.: National Research Council, 1952, 548.

46. Lawton, A.H. "Veterans Administration Conference on Cortisone Research." 1950.

47.   Interview with Maurice Lorr, Ph.D., April 28, 1994 at Dr. Lorr's office in Washington, D.C.

48.   "Veterans Administration Technical Bulletin 10A-152: Medical research program."

49.   Chapple, C., "Newsletter." *R and E Newsletter*, May, 1960, 2.

50.   Telephone interview with John C. Nunemaker, M.D., January 14, 1992.

51.   Interview with Oscar Auerbach, M.D., October 30, 1992 at Dr. Auerbach's office at the East Orange, NJ VA Medical Center.

52.   Stemmerman, G., Weiss, L., Auerbach, O. and Friedman, "A study of the germinal epithelium in male paraplegics." *Am J Clin Path*, 1950. **20**: 24-34.

53.   Auerbach, O. and Trubowitz, S., "Primary carcinoma of the liver with extensive skeletal metastasis and panmyelophthisis." *Cancer*, 1950. **3**: 837-843.

54.   Auerbach, O., Friedman, M., Weiss, L. and Amory, H., "Extraskeletal osteogenic sarcoma arising in irradiated tissue." *Cancer*, 1951. **4**: 1095-1106.

55.   Hobby, G., Lenert, T. and Auerbach, O., "The immunizing properties of an isoniazid-resistant mutant of the Vallee strain of M. Tuberculosis as compared with BCG." *Am Rev Tuberc*, 1954. **70**: 527-530.

56.   Auerbach, O., "Empyema as a complication of chronic pulmonary tuberculosis." *Am Rev Tuberc*, 1949. **59**: 601-618.

57.   Auerbach, O., "Tuberculosis of the trachea and major bronchi." *Am Rev Tuberc*, 1949. **60**: 604-620.

58.   Auerbach, O., "Tuberculous meningitis: Correlation of therapeutic results with the pathogenesis and pathologic changes. I. General considerations and pathogenesis." *Am Rev Tuberc*, 1951. **64**: 408-418.

59.   Auerbach, O., "Tuberculous meningitis: Correlation of therapeutic results with the pathogenesis and pathologic changes. II. Pathologic changes in treated and untreated cases." *Am Rev Tuberc*, 1951. **64**: 419-429.

60.   Auerbach, O., "Pleural, peritoneal and pericardial tuberculosis." *Am Rev Tuberc*, 1950. **61**: 845-861.

61.   Auerbach, O. and Stemmermann, G., "Anatomic change in tuberculosis following streptomycin therapy." *Am Rev Tuberc*, 1948. **58**: 449-462.

62.   Stemmermann, G. and Auerbach, O., "Massive pulmonary hemorrhage in tuberculosis. A report of two unusual cases." *Am Rev Tuberc*, 1950. **62**: 324-330.

63.   Auerbach, O., Katz, H. and Small, M., "The effect of streptomycin therapy on the broncho-cavitary junction and its relation to cavitary healing." *Am Rev Tuberc*, 1953. **67**: 173-200.

64.   Movitt, E. and Gerstl, B., "Pure mitral insufficiency of rheumatic origin in adults." *Ann Int Med*, 1953. **38**: 981-1001.

65.   Movitt, E., Gerstl, B. and McKinlay, E., "Osmotic erythrocyte fragility in patients with jaundice." *Am J Med Sci*, 1951. **222**: 535-537.

66.   Berk, M. and Gerstl, B., "Torulosis (cryptococcosis) producing a solitary pulmonary lesion. Report of a four year cure with lobectomy." *J Am Med Assn*, 1952. **149**: 1310-1312.

67. Mendenhall, R.M., Ramorino, P.M. and Gerstl, B., "Water, sodium, and potassium content of human, guinea pig, and rabbit lung." *Proc Soc Exper Biol and Med*, 1953. **82**: 318-322.

68. Gerstl, B., Kirsh, D., Andros, E., Winter, J. and Kidder, L., "Evaluation of hemolytic modification of Middlebrook-Dubos test for tuberculosis antibodies." *Am J Clin Path*, 1952. **22**: 337-344.

69. Gerstl, B., Kirsh, D., Davis, W. and Barbieri, M., "Absence of circulating antibodies in patients with pulmonary tuberculosis." *Science*, 1954. **120**: 853-854.

70. Gerstl, B., Kirsh, D., Winter, J., Weinstein, S., Hollander, A., Cova, P. and Barbieri, M., "Nonspecific reactions with the Middlebrook-Dubos Test for tuberculosis antibodies." *J Lab Clin Med*, 1954. **44**: 443-448.

71. Gross, L., "Hemolytic action of mouse mammary carcinoma filtrate on mouse erythrocytes in vitro." *Proc Soc Exper Biol and Med*, 1947. **65**: 292-293.

72. Gross, L., "Increased hemolytic potency of mouse mammary carcinoma extracts following incubation with tumor cells." *Proc Soc Exper Biol and Med*, 1948. **67**: 341-343.

73. Gross, L., "Destructive action of human cancer extracts on red cells in vitro." *Proc Soc Exper Biol and Med*, 1949. **70**: 656-662.

74. Gross, L., Gessler, A. and McCarthy, K., "Electron-microscopic examination of human milk particularly from women having family record of breast cancer." *Proc Soc Exper Biol and Med*, 1950. **75**: 270-276.

75. Gross, L., "Suseptibility of suckling-infant, and resistance of adult, mice of the C3H and of the C57 lines to inoculation with AK leukemia." *Cancer*, 1950. **3**: 1073-1087.

76. Gross, L., "Susceptibility of newborn mice of an otherwise apparently "resistant" strain to inoculation with leukemia." *Proc Soc Exper Biol and Med*, 1950. **73**: 246-249.

77. Gross, L., ""Spontaneous" leukemia developing in C3H mice following inoculation, in infancy, with AK-leukemic extracts, or AK-embryos." *Proc Soc Exper Biol and Med*, 1951. **76**: 27-32.

78. Gross, L., "Pathogenic properties, and "vertical" transmission of the mouse leukemia agent." *Proc Soc Exper Biol and Med*, 1951. **78**: 342-348.

79. Gross, L., "Presence of leukemic agent in normal testes and ovaries of young mice of AK line." *Acta Haemat*, 1953. **10**: 18-26.

80. Gross, L., "Neck tumors, or leukemia, developing in adult C3H mice following inoculation, in early infancy, with filtered (Berkefeld N), or centrifuged (144,000Xg), AK-leukemic extracts." *Cancer*, 1953. **6**: 948-957.

81. Gross, L., "Biological properties of the mouse leukemia agent." *Cancer*, 1953. **6**: 153-158.

82. Gross, L., "A filterable agent, recovered from AK leukemic extracts, causing salivary gland carcinomas in C3H mice." *Proc Soc Exper Biol and Med*, 1953. **83**: 414-421.

83. Gross, L., "The "vertical" transmission of mouse mammary carcinoma and chicken leukemia. Its possible implications for human pathology." *Cancer*, 1951. **4**: 626-633.

84. Gross, L., "Delayed effects of inoculation of AK-leukemic cells in mice of the C3H line. A working hypothesis on the etiology of mouse leukemia." *Cancer*, 1952. **5**: 620-624.

85.   Interview with Ludwig Gross, M.D., October 28, 1992 at Dr. Gross's office at the Bronx VAMC.

86.   Interview with Hyman Zimmerman, M.D., April 6, 1988 at Washington, DC VAMC.

87.   Interview with Roger Egeberg, M.D., February 25 and 26, 1992 at Dr. Egeberg's home in Washington, DC.

88.   Telephone interview with William Adams, M.D., February 17, 1992.

89.   Telephone interview with William Valentine, M.D., February 14, 1992.

90.   Coodley, E., Weiss, B. and Egeberg, R., "Reiter's Syndrome: Report of six cases." *Ann West Med Surg*, 1948. **2**: 500-505.

91.   Egeberg, R., "Treatment of chest emergencies: medical aspects." *Ann West Med Surg*, 1951. **5**: 133-137.

92.   Weir, R., Egeberg, R., Lack, A. and Leiby, G., "A clinical trial of prodigiosin in disseminated coccidioidomycosis." *Am J Med Sci*, 1952. **224**: 70-76.

93.   Egeberg, R., "Coccidioidomycosis: its clinical and climatological aspects with remarks on treatment." *Am J Med Sci*, 1954. **227**: 268-271.

94.   Telephone interview with Roger Egeberg, M.D., April 11, 1994.

95.   Goldman, R., Asher, L. and Ware, E., "Hereditary hemorrhagic telangiectasis." *Gastroenterol*, 1949. **12**: 495-501.

96.   Goldman, R., "The effect of aureomycin upon Hodgkin's Disease." *Am J Med Sci*, 1951. **221**: 195-198.

97.   Lipsett, M. and Goldman, R., "Phenylbutazone toxicity: Report of a case of acute renal failure." *Ann Int Med*, 1954. **41**: 1075-1079.

98.   Goldman, R., "Studies in diurnal variation of water and electrolyte excretion: Nocturnal diuresis of water and sodium in congestive cardiac failure and cirrhosis of the liver." *J Clin Invest*, 1951. **30**: 1191-1199.

99.   Goldman, R. and Bassett, S., "Diurnal variation in the urinary excretion of neutral lipid-soluble reducing steroids in congestive heart failure and cirrhosis of the liver with ascites." *J Clin Invest*, 1952. **31**: 253-258.

100.   Goldman, R., Adams, W. and Luchsinger, E., "Renal function in multiple myeloma." *J Lab Clin Med*, 1952. **40**: 519-522.

101.   Goldman, R. and Bassett, S., "Effect of intravenous calcium gluconate upon the excretion of calcium and phosphorus in patients with idiopathic hypoparathyroidism." *J Clin Endocrinol Metab*, 1954. **14**: 278-286.

102.   Goldman, R., "Creatinine excretion in renal failure." *Proc Soc Exper Biol and Med*, 1954. **85**: 446-448.

103.   Blahd, W., Levy, M. and Bassett, S., "A case of Hand-Schuller-Christian Syndrome treated with cortisone." *Ann Int Med*, 1951. **35**: 927-937.

104. Leslie, A., Blahd, W. and Adams, W., "The effect of prolonged administration of epinephrine on adrenal cortical function and epinephrine tolerance in chronic asthmatics." *J Lab Clin Med*, 1953. **41**: 865-870.

105. Blahd, W. and Bassett, S., "Potassium deficiency in man." *Metabolism*, 1953. **2**: 218-224.

106. Adams, W., Leslie, A. and Levin, M., "The dermal loss of iron." *Proc Soc Exper Biol and Med*, 1950. **74**: 46-48.

107. Craddock, C., Adams, W. and Figueroa, W., "Interference with fibrin formation in multiple myeloma by an unusual protein found in blood and urine." *J Lab Clin Med*, 1953. **42**: 847-859.

108. Adams, W., Blahd, W. and Bassett, S., "A method of human plasmaphoresis." *Proc Soc Exper Biol and Med*, 1952. **80**: 377-379.

109. Adams, W., Mason, E. and Bassett, S., "Metabolic balance investigation of three cases of multiple myeloma during ACTH administration; Exchanges of calcium, phosphorus, nitrogen and electrolytes." *J Clin Invest*, 1954. **33**: 103-121.

110. Adams, W., Valentine, W., Bassett, S. and Lawrence, J., "The effect of cortisone and ACTH in leukemia." *J Lab Clin Med*, 1952. **39**: 570-581.

111. Levin, M., Fred, L. and Bassett, S., "Metabolic studies in gout." *J Clin Endocrinol Metab*, 1952. **12**: 506-518.

112. Levin, M., Rivo, J. and Bassett, S., "Metabolic studies in gout with emphasis on the role of electrolytes in acute gouty arthritis." *Am J Med*, 1953. **15**: 525-534.

113. Michael, M., Jr., Cole, R., Beeson, P. and Olson, B., "Sarcoidosis: Preliminary report on study of 350 cases with special reference to epidemiology." *Natl Tuberc Assoc*, 1950. **46**: 208-212.

114. Michael, M. and Whorton, C., "Delay of the early inflammatory response by cortisone." *Proc Soc Exper Biol and Med*, 1951. **76**: 754-756.

115. Bloom, W., Cummings, M. and Michael, M., "Macrophage content of oil-induced peritoneal exudate in rats and rabbits." *Proc Soc Exper Biol and Med*, 1950. **75**: 171-172.

116. Michael, M., Cummings, M. and Bloom, W., "Course of experimental tuberculosis in the albino rat as influenced by cortisone." *Proc Soc Exper Biol and Med*, 1950. **75**: 613-616.

117. Cummings, M., Hudgens, P., Whorton, M. and Sheldon, W., "The influence of cortisone and streptomycin on experimental tuberculosis in the albino rat." *Am Rev Tuberc*, 1952. **65**: 596-602.

118. Roche, P., Cummings, M. and Hudgens, P., "Comparison of experimental tuberculosis in cortisone-treated and alloxan-diabetic albino rats." *Am Rev Tuberc*, 1952. **65**: 603-611.

119. Sheldon, W., Cummings, M. and Evans, L., "Failure of ACTH or cortisone to suppress tuberculin skin reactions in tuberculous guinea pigs." *Proc Soc Exper Biol and Med*, 1950. **75**: 616-618.

120. Klein, G., Maltz, M., Cummings, M. and Fish, C., "Efficacy of centrifugation as a method of concentrating tubercle bacilli." *Am J Clin Path*, 1952. **22**: 581-585.

121. Lewis, G., Hankey, L., Adair, F. and Cummings, M., "A study of certain amino acids as they may relate to the problem of host resistance to tuberculosis." *Am Rev Tuberc*, 1952. **66**: 378-380.

122. Fleming, J., Runyon, E. and Cummings, M., "An evaluation of the hemagglutination test for tuberculosis." *Am J Med*, 1951. **10**: 704-710.

123. Cummings, M., "Diagnostic methods in tuberculosis. II. Demonstration of M. tuberculosis by culture." *Am J Clin Path*, 1951. **21**: 684-690.

124. Atkins, E. and Cummings, M., "Tuberculous meningitis: Treatment of spinal block with intrathecal administration of tuberculin." *New England J Med*, 1952. **247**: 715-717.

125. Cummings, M. and Livings, D., "The prevalence of streptomycin resistant tubercle bacilli among 5,526 patients admitted consecutively to hospitals." *Am Rev Tuberc*, 1954. **70**: 637-640.

126. Telephone interview with Richard Ebert, M.D., December 22, 1993.

127. Ebert, R., Borden, C., Wells, H. and Wilson, R., "Studies of the pulmonary circulation. I. The circulation time from the pulmonary artery to the femoral artery and the quantity of blood in the lungs in normal individuals." *J Clin Invest*, 1949. **28**: 1134-1137.

128. Borden, C., Ebert, R., Wilson, R. and Wells, H., "Studies of the pulmonary circulation. II. The circulation time from the pulmonary artery to the femoral artery and the quantity of blood in the lungs in patients with left ventricular failure." *J Clin Invest*, 1949. **28**: 1138-1143.

129. Borden, C., Ebert, R., Wilson, R. and Wells, H., "Pulmonary hypertension in heart disease." *New England J Med*, 1950. **242**: 529-534.

130. Borden, C., Wilson, R., Ebert, R. and Wells, H., "Pulmonary hypertension in chronic pulmonary emphysema." *Am J Med*, 1950. **8**: 701-709.

131. Borden, C., Ebert, R. and Wilson, R., "Anoxia in myocardial infarction and indications for oxygen therapy." *J Am Med Assn*, 1952. **148**: 1370-1371.

132. Wilson, R., Borden, C., Ebert, R. and Wells, H., "A comparison of the effect of voluntary hyperventilation in normal persons, patients with pulmonary emphysema, and patients with cardiac disease." *J Lab Clin Med*, 1950. **36**: 119-126.

133. Brown, C., Fry, D. and Ebert, R., "The mechanics of pulmonary ventilation in patients with heart disease." *Am J Med*, 1954. **17**: 438-446.

134. Stead, W., Fry, D. and Ebert, R., "The elastic properties of the lung in normal men and in patients with chronic pulmonary emphysema." *J Lab Clin Med*, 1952. **40**: 674-681.

135. Falk, A. and Ebert, R., "Tuberculous pericarditis treated with streptomycin." *J Am Med Assn*, 1951. **145**: 310-314.

136. Evans, R., Amatuzio, D. and Ebert, R., "Red blood cell studies: Ashby curves." *Science*, 1952. **115**: 572-573.

137. Schultz, A., Hammarsten, J., Heller, B. and Ebert, R., "A critical comparison of the T-1824 dye and iodinated albumin methods for plasma volume measurement." *J Clin Invest*, 1953. **32**: 107-112.

138. Hammarsten, J., Heller, B. and Ebert, R., "The effects of dextran in normovolemic and oligemic subjects." *J Clin Invest*, 1953. **32**: 340-344.

139. Falk, A., Zieve, L., Tucker, W. and Hanson, M., "The hepatic toxicity of amithiozone." *Am Rev Tuberc*, 1951. **64**: 159-169.

140.   Heller, B., Jacobson, W. and Hammarsten, J., "The effect of cortisone in glomerulonephritis and the nephropathy of disseminated lupus erythematosis." *J Lab Clin Med*, 1951. **37**: 133-142.

141.   Jacobson, W., Hammarsten, J. and Heller, B., "The effects of adrenaline upon renal function and electrolyte excretion." *J Clin Invest*, 1951. **30**: 1503-1506.

142.   Tucker, W., "Evaluation of streptomycin regimens in the treatment of tuberculosis." *Am Rev Tuberc*, 1949. **60**: 715-754.

143.   Borden, C., "Acute myocarditis. Report of a case with observations on the etiologic factor." *Am Heart J*, 1950. **39**: 131-135.

144.   Borden, C. and Hall, W., "Fatal transfusion reactions from massive bacterial contamination of blood." *New England J Med*, 1951. **245**: 760-765.

Chapter 4. Research cooperation between the NAS and the VA

The National Academy of Sciences (NAS), through its National Research Council (NRC) and standing Committee on Veterans Medical Problems (CVMP), was prominent in the VA's early postwar research. In time, the VA's own intramural research program grew (Chapter 3), but the NRC continued to be influential. Until the CVMP disbanded in 1962, it advised the VA on research. An NRC committee continued to guide the VA's Prosthetic Research contracts program until 1975. The Medical Follow-up Agency, which was started in the NRC with VA funding, remains today, although now as part of the Institute of Medicine. In addition to these advisory functions, the NRC conducted comprehensive, objective reviews of the VA intramural research program in 1960, 1968 and 1977.

In 1945, as World War II drew to an end, Michael E. DeBakey, M.D. (Figure 4.4), was a colonel, the chief of the Surgical Consultants Division of the Army's Surgeon General Office. He recalled neurosurgeon Harvey Cushing's frustration at the lost opportunity to benefit from World War I medical experience with follow-up studies. DeBakey realized the important information to be gained from follow-up studies to learn the long-term outcome of war injuries and he worried that postwar interest in war-related medical research would wane.[1]

DeBakey wrote a memorandum to Surgeon General Kirk, recommending an NRC-coordinated joint effort of the VA and the military services to mine military records and use follow-up studies to learn about medical outcomes.[2] At Kirk's request,[3] the NRC called a meeting of the Surgeons General of the Army, Navy and Public Health Service, the Medical Director of the Veterans Administration and the NRC. To outline a program, they formed an ad hoc committee that held two meetings in May and June of 1946 (Appendix IIc.)

The group recommended that the Academy, through the NRC, establish a standing Committee on Veterans Medical Problems. The NRC assigned Dr. DeBakey and Gilbert Beebe, Ph.D., a statistician who later became Chief of the Follow-up Agency, to write an action plan. Approved by the ad hoc committee, its recommendations included formation of a standing Committee on Veterans Medical Problems to advise the NRC and the VA, and a Medical Follow-up Agency in the NRC to carry out studies of long-term outcomes of wartime injuries and illnesses.[4]

The Committee on Veterans Medical Problems (CVMP)

The standing Committee on Veterans Medical Problems (Appendix IIc) first met on September 20, 1946.[5] It became apparent that the originally proposed clinical follow-up research had to expand and include research by VA physicians. Chief Medical Director Hawley informed the CVMP that for a number of years the Veterans Administration would not be sufficiently staffed or equipped to undertake research in major clinical and biological problems and could support only small clinical studies. Nevertheless, as early as the June 13, 1946 meeting of the planning committee,

"Dr. (Perrin H.) Long called attention to the fact that investigative projects had already been planned or even set up, and that unless such work, costing a considerable amount of money, were supported, the younger men would not remain in the Veterans Administration."[6]

In fact, the intramural research program, research initiated by staff in the VA hospitals (Chapter 3), took root simultaneously with the programs sponsored by the NAS through the CVMP.

The contractual relations between the VA and the NRC that the CVMP reviewed fell into three categories:

1. <u>VA contracts to non-VA institutions</u>, primarily medical schools, for medical research. This program flourished through 1953, when it was almost entirely replaced by the VA intramural research program.

2. <u>Prosthetics research contracts</u> with academic and other non-VA institutions. The contract prosthetics research program continued until the late 1970s, when it was partially replaced by intramural VA rehabilitation research. Early on, the CVMP oversaw this program. Soon, NRC advice came directly to the VA from the NRC's Advisory Committee on Artificial Limbs (Chapter 20). The NRC role in reviewing prosthetics research contracts continued until 1976.

3. <u>The Medical Follow-up Agency</u>. In the early CVMP active period, the Follow-up Agency was funded entirely by the VA. This Agency remained in the NRC until 1988 and then moved organizationally to the Institute of Medicine. With funding from multiple sources, the Follow-up Agency continues to play an active role in medical research.

The CVMP originally oversaw the entire VA research program, though this oversight role later decreased as the intramural program expanded. To complete the necessary scientific reviews, especially of contract requests, the NRC reestablished a system of advisory committees similar to the wartime NRC medical advisory committees.[7]

Those committees had begun to form in 1940, when the Surgeon General's Office of the Army asked the NAS for advice on chemotherapy and transfusions. At that time, the NRC formed two advisory committees of civilian specialists. Additional requests led to the creation of more committees, so that by June 1941, eight major medical committees and 33 subcommittees were active. With the onset of the war, the President's Office of Science and Technology (that sponsored, among other projects, work on the atomic bomb) became active and well funded. Its sponsorship of the medical research needed for the war effort was carried out by its Committee on Medical Research (CMR), which requested advice from these NRC committees. By 1943, 52 NRC committees and subcommittees, with 221 members, were advising the CMR, and most research contracts funded by the CMR were funded in response to an NRC committee's recommendation. To finance this committee structure, the Office of Science and Technology provided contractual support to NAS. The Chairman of the NAS Division of Medical Sciences became vice chairman of the CMR.

At war's end, the CMR closed its contracts program. It, and the NRC committee structure supporting it, were abolished in 1946.[8] A postwar effort required a new start by the NRC, with new oversight and subject matter advisory groups.

By December 1946, the NRC had established advisory committees on Medicine (with subcommittees on venereal diseases, cardiovascular diseases and tuberculosis), and on Surgery, Neuropsychiatry, Chemotherapy, Sanitary Engineering, Growth, Prosthetic Devices and Sensory Devices. The latter two committees and their successor committees were important to the VA's early research in rehabilitation (Chapter 20).

CVMP's activity was funded by a separate VA contract to the National Academy of Sciences. It actively advised the VA research program, meeting 30 times from 1946 through 1953.

The VA's extramural contracts program

Until the end of 1953, the CVMP reviewed all VA general research contracts, as well as follow-up studies. The Committee depended on reviews by NRC's subject matter committees, but the CVMP itself also reviewed all contract applications. In addition, it established a roster of consultant statisticians,[9] a concept unusual for the time.

During the first year, many contracts (Appendix IV) were for follow-up studies and required access to VA records or examination of VA patients. Prominent in those begun in 1947 was the follow-up study on peripheral nerves, led by Barnes Woodhall, of Duke. This study became part of the Follow-up Agency work and eventually resulted in a monograph.[10]

In 1948, VA-supported contracts included a spectrum of veterans' medical care problems. One contract studied treatment of coccidioidomycosis, a problem among veterans stationed in endemic areas. Even though new cases of syphilis were well treated with penicillin, tertiary syphilis continued to be a problem for VA patients, and in 1948 contracts were awarded for study of paresis and of cardiovascular syphilis. A contract with a Yale scientist explored the physiology of prefrontal lobotomy.

While many contract-supported investigators applied through their VA affiliates, most were medical school faculty members, and the medical schools administered the contracts. It is likely that some of this contract research was performed in the affiliated VA hospital. Contract recipients included such luminaries as Norman Brill, Barnes Woodhall, George Burch, Michael DeBakey, Harold Wolff, Thomas Sternberg, Paul Beeson, Milton Winternitz, George Taplin, I.L. Chaikoff, Brian Blades, Harold Beecher, Cyril N.H. Long, Franz Ingelfinger, Leslie Zieve, and Marshall Urist.

University charges for overhead costs became a problem that Dr. Cushing discussed in a September 1951 report to the VA's Special Medical Advisory Group:

"One university . . . which proposed a contractual research project with the VA that was approved by the National Research Council has raised an issue on the overhead allowance proposed in the contract. The contract submitted by the VA to this university provided for twelve per cent of the total amount of the contract as overhead. The university came back and said that they could not accept the contract as the overhead was entirely too low. The overhead which this school desired was either 44 per cent of the salaries and wages mentioned in the contract, or 31 per cent of the total amount of the contract. VA thanked them very much and said that the contract was not sufficiently important to it to proceed on that basis. . . . How far is 'Uncle Sugar' going to go in supporting, by overhead, some of these grants?"[11]

Administering these contracts burdened the very small VACO research staff, and contracts were loosely supervised until Marjorie Wilson, M.D., joined the staff. Dr. Wilson recalled that she came to Washington, DC, in 1951 and found a job in the VA's Research and Education Service. When she arrived, she found three filing cabinets filled with 150-200 contracts that had not been organized in any way. She read all the contracts and systematized the files, establishing expense and result records and sending the progress reports to the NRC committees to help them in their annual reviews of renewal requests. VA contracts for prosthetics research (Chapter 18) were handled by the Prosthetics and Sensory Aids Service at that time.

Figure 4.1 VA expenditures for research contracts, 1947-1953

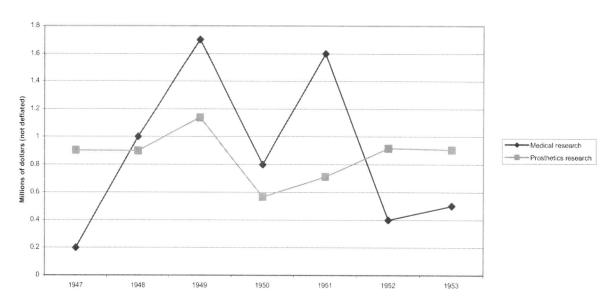

Dr. Wilson remembered the contract holders as the "giants" in academic medicine. Virtually all contracts were for clinical investigations.[12]

The Medical Follow-up Agency

The plan for follow-up studies devised by DeBakey and Beebe and debated by the 1946 ad hoc Committee on Veterans Medical Programs included a three-pronged approach:

1. A separate agency to be established to work with the VA and armed services to perform follow-up studies on WWII veterans.
2. A program of clinical follow-up research to be initiated by faculty of the affiliated schools on contract, and later included in an intramural research program, and
3. Large-scale epidemiologic studies.

At its first meeting in September 1946, the CVMP accepted the De Bakey-Beebe report and recommended that the NRC establish an independent Follow-up Agency, to be funded by a VA contract but administratively responsible to the NRC. The Medical Follow-up Agency was started, with Beebe as its statistical leader and John Ransmeier, M.D., as the medical leader. Over the next two years, Follow-up Agency staff worked closely with the VA to put the follow-up program in motion.

Figure 4.2: Gilbert Beebe, Ph.D.

The Follow-up Agency's initial task was records identification. Some dedicated military physicians had developed personal rosters of Service personnel with conditions that especially interested them, and these were collected.[13] However, these records, by and large, were not usable for large-scale studies. It soon became apparent that it was necessary to find a way to work with the existing records systems. In March 1948, the Follow-up Agency reported to its organizational superior in the NAS that:

"In December 1947 the Veterans Administration published Technical Bulletin 3-30, its 'Procedure for Following National Research Council Access to Information from Files of the Veterans Administration and Army Medical Records of World War II Veterans,' which made it possible to determine the present addresses of veterans and to assemble their Army records in either Washington or an appropriate study center. In order to locate subjects for the various study centers, approximately 22,000 National Research Council Locator Requests have been processed through the Veterans Administration. Providing service medical records to the centers has necessitated calling in approximately 700 medical records from the Veterans Administration, exclusive of those obtained from the Army and Navy directly. This phase of the work is only beginning, the effort thus far having been confined to giving each study center an initial group of cases with which to test its procedures and make a start in its work. Cooperation from all portions of the far-flung Veterans Administration organization has been complete, but an endeavor of this scope inevitably proceeds slowly until there is wide understanding of just what is required."

"The truly cooperative nature of the follow-up program is well illustrated by the full participation of both Army and Navy in the process of creating rosters and securing both personnel and medical records. Many tabulations have been made by the medical statistics divisions of both Army and Navy according to specifications established by the Committee, and listings and duplicate punch-cards have been furnished covering tens of thousands of admissions for many different conditions. Army personnel and medical records of World War II are housed in St. Louis, and it has been necessary to establish there a branch record office for the Committee in order to arrange necessary access to those records and to abstract or reproduce them as required by responsible investigators. Navy and Marine Corps records have been made available in similar fashion except that, until recently, they were concentrated in Washington, D.C. where personnel from the Committee's main record office could have access to them. The removal of non-current Navy records to Garden City will necessitate a small unit there unless the Navy can continue to call records back to Washington on request."[14]

Having Follow-up Agency staff work at the Armed Services' centralized records depots was successful, and good relations were maintained with the medical records departments of the Army and the Navy, as well as the VA.[15]

An early problem in conducting follow-up studies was the VA General Counsel's decision that follow-up examinations performed for research purposes could not be combined with required medical examinations when a veteran was applying for compensation. In those cases, the veteran needed to make a separate trip, generally to a university clinic, for the follow-up examination, thus removing the financial motivation that encouraged the veteran to cooperate in the compensation exam. To improve compliance in difficult cases, the Follow-up Agency worked with the Red Cross, which sent staff to intercede with the veterans and help them get to the centers for examination.[15] This is described in the report of the study of peripheral nerve injuries:

"At that point (when the man had not replied to repeated letters, including a certified letter) the center was considered to have exhausted its power of appeal and the man was referred to the American Red Cross, through its national headquarters, to help under a cooperative agreement worked out with the Follow-up Agency. Red Cross representatives were provided with a statement about the project and visited each center to learn something of the nature of the examination and of the essential medical interests of the investigators. . . . An immediate benefit of the Red Cross participation in the follow-up work was the information it provided about the apparent motivation of men who refused to participate and about the interaction between subjects and personnel of the follow-up center."[16]

128

Even before the Follow-up Agency became functional, proposals for studies poured in to the CVMP for review. As of December 1947, these included follow-ups of liver function following hepatitis, tuberculosis, schistosomiasis, peripheral nerve injuries, spinal cord injuries, aneurysms and fistulae, arterial injuries, psychoneuroses and epilepsy.[17] Some of these fell by the wayside, but a number became a part of the Follow-up Agency's long-term program.

By early 1949, the Follow-up Agency had planned a number of projects and pilot feasibility studies were under way.[18] At the same time, members of its statistical staff were increasingly called on for advice about other contracts under review by the CVMP. The Agency also assisted in planning and coordinating other VA contract follow-up studies at 30 centers, primarily universities. Most of these required actual reexamination of patients, rather than just records review. Mr. Seymour Jablon, a mathematical statistician who joined the Agency in 1948, worked closely with Dr. Beebe and eventually replaced him as Chief when Beebe retired in 1977.[19]

Figure 4.3: Seymour Jablon
Courtesy of National Academies Press

By late 1949, costs and the slow and uncertain return of results from follow-up studies were beginning to arouse the concern of the CMVP and the VA Research staff responsible for their funding. None of the studies had yet been published. Some of the contract follow-up studies were experiencing problems because they had been set up hastily. Faults in statistical design were surfacing. The CVMP ruled that any future proposals must be approved twice, once in concept and later, after input from the Follow-up Agency staff on the designs, before they were actually funded.[20]

In early 1951, the VA and the CVMP jointly appointed a subcommittee to review the Follow-up Agency's activities. The Agency's cumulative cost through FY 1951 was $1.752 million. The subcommittee reported enthusiastically about the following projects under way, with comments on the status of results as of 1951:

"Infectious Hepatitis. A follow-up of approximately 1,000 survivors of the original infection has revealed no residual of severe liver damage or evidence of progressive liver disease (Projects #22, #31, #49).

Psychoneurosis. It is expected that the complete analysis will produce information of value to the Armed Forces in setting policies for induction, assignment to combat duty, and the disposition of men who break down in service (Project #7).

Peripheral Nerve Injuries. Emphasis is placed on the value of specialized neurologic treatment, use of special neuropsychological techniques as an adjunct to surgery, and improvement in the management of peripheral nerve injuries (Project #13).

Arterial Injuries. The study has developed methods for objective study and information concerning improved handling of vascular injuries (Projects #14-17).

Schizophrenia. The average length of service prior to breakdown was two and a half years. The majority could have been detected by adequate study at time of induction (Project #18).

Tuberculosis. The incidence of more than 25% of positive tuberculin reactors among veterans is almost double that of non-veterans. The incidence of positive reactors increases with the length of service (Project #20). The final analysis should develop data on which constructive recommendations may be made to the Armed Forces for improved screening procedures for tuberculosis at admission and discharge (Project #89).

Tumors of the Testis. The result of this study of the largest known series of testicular tumors (approximately 1,000) indicates significant differences in the prognosis for certain types. Pure seminomas (comprising about 40% of this total) had a five-year mortality rate of 1%; other types and combinations had 5-year mortalities ranging from 40 to 75%.

Rheumatic Fever. The conclusions resulting from the final analysis should reveal significant information concerning future induction of men with history of rheumatic fever and the disposition of men having this disease while in service (Project #65)

Million-volt Irradiation. Among the late effects of million-volt irradiation are fibrosis of the lung, and severe damage to the gastrointestinal tract including ulceration, perforation and obstruction. Any dose above 2,000r may produce severe tissue damage; however some patients are able to withstand 4,000r. "

All of these were studies of World War II veterans, aimed at discovering the long-term effects of diseases and injuries incident to their service. By their very nature, these studies required time to accumulate data, but by this time the reviewers wanted to see at least intermediate results. Most of the studies in this list did have outcomes published shortly after this report. Results of the hepatitis studies have stood the test of time.[21] The psychoneurosis studies formed the basis for adjusting psychiatric standards for mobilization.[22] The irradiation studies led to methods of evaluating tolerance levels for the gastrointestinal tract.[23]

After reviewing this report, the CVMP enthusiastically endorsed the Follow-up Agency's activities.[24]

Figure 4.4. Meeting, about 1950, of the group working on the follow-up study of WWII vascular injuries. Dr. Beebe is second from left, second row, and Dr. DeBakey is at the far right, front row.

A year later, however, some concern remained about the effectiveness of the Follow-up Agency. Dr. Winternitz, chairman of the NAS Division of Medical Sciences, commented to the CVMP that the total cost, including all follow-up activities, over five years had been $2.4 million, with "relatively little harvest to date." None of the major projects had yet been completed. The CVMP again appointed an ad hoc committee to review the status of the follow-up studies.[25] This led to an in-depth review by Donald Mainland, Ph.D., Professor of Medical Statistics at New York University. In his report of March 22, 1953,

Dr. Mainland praised the statistical excellence of the Follow-up Agency staff but pointed to problems caused by early enthusiasm, large numbers of hastily planned studies and more recent lagging because of clinician investigators' competing responsibilities. He advised NRC to phase down the program and use its statistical staff to improve the quality of NRC-sponsored research.[26]

By 1953, of the 26 follow-up studies, 8 were completed, 14 targeted for completion over the next 18 months, 2 abandoned and 2 long term studies had no completion date. The NRC and the VA placed a moratorium on starting new follow-up studies.[27]

Until 1954, the VA provided the entire support for the Follow-up Agency. During late 1953, the VA found it necessary to reduce the Follow-up Agency annual budget abruptly from $228,000 to $163,000. The Agency had to drop 10 staff members. Dr. R. Keith Cannan described the situation to a meeting of the executive committee of the NRC Division of Medical Sciences:

"--- the future of the Follow-up Agency of the Division is in jeopardy. The Veterans Administration's 1954 budget request has been cut from 6.5 to 5.5 million dollars, while the number of their research laboratories has approximately tripled in three years. At the same time, there has been a shift in emphasis from extra-mural to intra-mural research. The question now before the Division is whether or not an effort should be made to maintain the Follow-up Agency."

After extensive discussion, the committee resolved that:

"The medical experience of the Armed Forces and of the veteran population provide a unique opportunity for medical follow-up studies of importance to clinical medicine and to the Armed Forces and the Veterans Administration. The Division of Medical Sciences provides a logical focus of leadership and organization for the many interests in such studies, and steps should be taken to re-establish, as a broad inter-agency program, a significant program of follow-up studies."[20]

The Follow-up Agency prepared a new plan, eventually adopted, in which they would seek support from the VA and other agencies as well. They would keep a small "core" staff, which would be temporarily enlarged when new projects were funded. VA support would come as a contribution to "core" and also to specific contracts.[28] By the end of 1954, the Follow-up Agency, still on shaky ground, continued to seek a stable funding base. By this time, only 4 of its original 26 projects were still current. Owing to the moratorium, no new projects had been added.[29]

Within a few months the situation improved: three projects continued under VA sponsorship, but now the Army and the USPHS were each sponsoring two new projects.[30] Multiple agency funding continued thereafter.

The multiple sclerosis studies

In 1954, the Follow-up Agency, working with a VA neurologist, John Kurtzke, M.D., undertook its first controlled clinical trial. This study resulted from the observation that isoniazid given to a patient with both tuberculosis and multiple sclerosis appeared to lead to improvement in his multiple sclerosis. Since the initial serendipitous observation, 30 patients with multiple sclerosis were treated and "ninety percent . . . showed striking improvement over a period of two years in comparison with controls from an earlier period."[31] With the encouragement of the CVMP, the Follow-up Agency coordinated a study of 186 multiple sclerosis patients in 11 VA hospitals, comparing 100 mg isoniazid thrice daily with placebo. The results were negative: "By all criteria, including laboratory findings and over-all clinical impressions, the differences between the isoniazid and placebo groups were insignificant. No beneficial effects that could be ascribed to isoniazid in multiple sclerosis were observed in nine months or more of follow-up."[32] In this, one of the earliest placebo-controlled clinical trials, this particular treatment was laid to rest. However, the collaborating group built on this study to conduct a five-year follow-up of the clinical course of these well-studied patients with this puzzling disease.[33] There were 52 deaths during the 5-year period. Eight patients improved, 35 were unchanged and, in the others, the disease worsened. Mortality was directly related to severity of the disease at the time of the original study. There was no long-term difference between patients treated with isoniazid during the controlled trial and those given placebo.

Surgical adjuvant studies

When, in 1957, the VA began collaborative studies with the National Cancer Institute on the value of adjunctive chemotherapy in surgical oncology (Chapter 13), the Follow-up Agency broadened its support of the VA research program by providing ongoing statistical support.

The twin registry

The leaders of the Follow-up Agency early recognized the value of follow-up studies in pairs of twins. From the mid-1950s, they explored the possibility of establishing a twin registry. In 1958, partially funded by the VA, the Agency staff began the long, complex process of assembling a roster of veteran twin pairs from World War II. They started with lists of male twins born between 1917 and 1927 in 29 states. Of the 45,000 male twin pairs identified, there were 8,000 where both were veterans. To determine zygosity (whether identical or fraternal) of these twin pairs, the Follow-up Agency asked the FBI for copies of their fingerprints that were made at induction into the military. The FBI found this to be difficult and provided only some of the fingerprints. In addition, all subjects answered a questionnaire that included the question "As children, were you and your twin as alike as two peas in a pod?" The answer to this question correlated 95 percent with the results of fingerprint matching, and it was used to classify zygosity when fingerprints were not available.

A special committee reviewed all requests to use the twin registry and used strict criteria in their review, turning down two of the first three requests. The concern was not to trouble the subjects unduly but to maintain the registry by contacting them periodically. Some studies conducted in subsequent years required the twins to appear for examination, but most have depended on records. Altogether, some 200 articles have been published that used this twin registry as a resource.

The Follow-up Agency later assisted the VA in setting up a registry of Vietnam-era veteran twins; this is now managed as a part of the VA's intramural epidemiologic program.[34]

Results of studies by the Follow-up Agency

All told, between 1949 and 1996, the Follow-up Agency played a key role in studies leading to some 500 publications.[35] Its bibliography has been described as "a chronicle of the history of epidemiology in military and veteran populations."[36]

Among the results of the early, VA-sponsored, Follow-up Agency studies were:

Infectious Hepatitis. A group of 367 men living in the Minneapolis area who had documented hepatitis during World War II, including 69 with multiple attacks, received thorough workups four to six years later. They were compared with 137 men who had been heavily exposed to hepatitis without a clinical episode and to 212 controls. There were no significant differences among the groups.[21] A separate study from Philadelphia showed similar results in 271 men who had suffered clinical hepatitis, 138 "heavily exposed" men and 242 controls.[37] A third study was a 10-year follow-up of 460 men with acute hepatitis who were subjects of controlled treatment trials during the Korean War. At follow-up, there was no difference between groups treated in different ways (bed rest, forced diet).[38]

Psychoneurosis. The psychiatric status of 955 former enlisted personnel diagnosed with psychoneurosis during their service was studied about five years after the original episode. Only 11 percent of these veterans had sought psychiatric care from the VA. Of the total, 62 percent came in for examination by a psychiatrist and information about all but 1.5 percent was available from some source such as VA records. The mortality pattern in the sample matched that of the general population except for an increase in suicides (six compared with an expected two). Only 1.8 percent were judged to be psychotic at follow-up, but 72 percent were judged to have some psychiatric disease. In general, the trend was judged to be toward improvement with the passage of time.[39, 40]

Peripheral Nerve Injuries. In this study, one of the first approved by the CVMP, late results in 3,656 World War II peripheral nerve injuries were assessed in five clinical centers. The study supported use of radical surgery for complete loss of nerve function but conservative treatment when nerve continuity has not been interrupted. It also demonstrated the value of physical therapy in recovery of function. The study showed an inverse relation between functional recovery and the distance from the lesion to its area of principal innervation.[41]

Tuberculosis. This study compared induction and discharge chest x-rays of about 3,000 men discharged from the military for tuberculosis and 3,000 matched controls. In about half of those discharged for tuberculosis, evidence of tuberculosis was present in the induction film. New tuberculosis was more frequent in nonwhites, in tall, thin men and in former prisoners of war.[42]

Rheumatic Fever. 135 men, selected randomly, with confirming records of diagnosis, were examined 3 to 8 years after Army hospitalization for acute rheumatic fever. At the follow-up examination, 32 of these men (23.7 percent) had rheumatic heart disease, a lower incidence than seen after rheumatic fever in children. Even in those with physical evidence of rheumatic heart disease, most were living normal lives with 95 percent employed or in school.[43]

Sarcoidosis. This was an epidemiological study of the 350 cases of sarcoidosis recognized among Armed Forces personnel during WW II. Residence in rural areas of the Southeast within regions of fine sandy soil appeared to favor development of sarcoidosis, and it was seen more frequently in Negroes.[44, 45]

Hand injuries. Follow-up of 104 patients with severe war wounds to the hand showed that adequate physical therapy is of great importance to functional recovery, more important than reconstructive surgery that might require immobilization of the hand. All but four of the men studied were employed at follow-up.[46]

Combat-related schizophrenia. Two physicians who had treated 341 patients with acute schizophrenia in New Guinea during World War II were able to make personal contact with 156 of them 5 to 8 years after the initial episode. They followed the remainder through VA records. Thirty control subjects, selected by the Follow-up Agency, were also examined. Although there was a trend toward improvement with time, 186 of the patients were still considered moderately or severely impaired five or more years after the initial episode. Neither the military nor the domestic experiences of the schizophrenic patients differed from controls. The authors concluded that there is little profit to be gained in attempting to screen out potential schizophrenics at induction.[47, 48]

Prisoners of War   The Follow-up Agency has carried out a series of studies of long-term morbidity and mortality of former prisoners of war (POWs). The first, published in 1955, showed that overall mortality was increased in World War II POWs from the Pacific, but not the European, theater. This excess mortality was almost entirely due to tuberculosis and accidents.[49] In the second study, which included Korean War veterans, POWs also had excess mortality.[50] However, by 1975 this excess in mortality rate had waned in both World War II and Korean War ex-POWs.[51] A 1975 study of morbidity in former POWs showed the most frequent illnesses to be psychiatric, with higher rates of hospitalization and VA disability. Excess morbidity correlated well with retrospective accounts of captivity weight loss, nutritional deficiencies and symptoms.[52]

Head injuries   This was a follow-up of 739 World War II veterans who had suffered penetrating wounds of the brain. Four centers examined their status extensively some ten years after their injuries. Epilepsy, found in 28 percent, was worse and more frequent when the wounds were larger and deeper. Impaired judgment and altered personality were also related to the size of the wound but not to its location.[53, 54]

Buerger's Disease Epidemiology and 10-year prognosis were studied in 936 Army males with Buerger's Disease documented from 1942 to 1948. Compared with Army men in general, they were older, more likely to be officers and more likely to be Jews. Incidence was estimated at about 3.5 per 100,000 Army men aged 20-44. Mortality was increased and related to severity of the disease. Amputations and sympathectomies also were related to disease severity at onset, and neither decreased in frequency with time.[55]

Hodgkin's Disease Epidemiology of and survival over 17 years from Hodgkin's Disease were studied in 388 documented cases, diagnosed during World War II. Patients with Hodgkin's Disease were better educated, of higher economic class and less likely to be married than Army men in general. The number of signs and symptoms of the disease at onset correlated with the histologic type and with survival. After 17 years, 8.4 percent of the men with granuloma and 28.6 percent of those with paragranuloma were alive. All five men with Hodgkin's sarcoma died within one year.[56]

Ulcerative colitis In a study of the epidemiology of ulcerative colitis among Army men in 1944, 525 patients were compared with matched controls. The incidence was seen to rise with age, and Jews were affected more than twice as frequently as non-Jews.[57] In a follow-up study of mortality from these samples, 10.7 percent of the patients with ulcerative colitis died in the first 17 years after the index hospitalization, compared to 5.0 percent in the controls. Half of this excess mortality was due to ulcerative colitis, generally within the early years after diagnosis. The other half was due to cancer of the colon, most frequently in later years. A bad prognosis correlated strongly with the extent of colon involvement in x-rays made in 1944.[58]

Missiles in the heart Forty men who survived missiles in the heart which had not been removed were studied 17 to 20 years after their injuries. Most had normal electrocardiograms and chest x-rays at follow-up. Pericarditis had occurred in 25 percent. Only one patient had had serious migration of the missile. However, all of those examined suffered a "formidable strain of living with a missile in the heart," and five were totally incapacitated by an anxiety neurosis.[59]

Lumbar disk disease The epidemiology of herniated nucleus pulposis (HNP) was studied in 1,095 first Army admissions, matched on age and period of World War II service with holders of Army National Life Insurance policies. HNP was found to be associated with mechanical factors related to body build (excess height, excess weight, good posture) and occupation (enlisted, ground combat, craftsman, rural residence). There was no difference from controls in prior service hospitalizations, including those for trauma.[60]

Retrospective on the role of the Follow-up Agency in VA research

There has been speculation that it might have been better if the Follow-up Agency had originally been made a part of the VA.[19] Among the reasons cited were that such an arrangement would have given needed stability, though it might have reduced the Agency's freedom of action. Also, participation in a strong in-house VA biostatistics and epidemiology program in the early days could have enriched the VA program and provided guidance and consistency. Feedback from the VA could have improved the early follow-up studies.

On the other hand, as an independent agency, the Follow-up Agency was later able to branch out to other sources of funding when the VA's attention turned toward other priorities. It could meet urgent non-VA needs, such as those of the Atomic Bomb Casualties Commission. And though the Agency grew away from its VA roots, relations between the Follow-up Agency and VA Research remained good through the years and continue to be mutually beneficial.

Closing of the Committee on Veterans Medical Problems

By 1954, CVMP activity was winding down. The Follow-up Agency was well established. As the VA intramural program reached firmer ground, the research program had turned away from supporting research contracts.[61] Review of the contracts program, a key role of the CVMP, was no longer necessary. The CVMP no longer oversaw the prosthetics research program. From 1954 to 1959, the CVMP met only about once a year to review the overall VA research program and oversee the Follow-up Agency. It formally disbanded at the end of 1962.[62]

References

1. Letter from Gilbert W. Beebe, Ph.D. to author, written at Bethesda, MD, July 5, 2002.

2. Letter from Michael DeBakey, M.D. to Norman T. Kirk, Surgeon General of the Army, written at the Pentagon, March 5, 1946.

3. Letter from Norman T. Kirk to Frank B. Jewitt, President of the National Academy of Sciences, written at Washington, D.C.,

4. National Research Council, *Report on the Value and Feasibility of a Long-Term Program of Follow-up Study and Clinical Research*. Washington, D.C.: National Academy of Sciences, 1946.

5. National Academy of Sciences - National Research Council. "Minutes of First Meeting, Committee on Veterans Medical Problems." September 20, 1946. Washington, D.C.: National Research Council,

6. National Research Council, *Report on Follow-up Study and Clinical Research.*

7. National Academy of Sciences - National Research Council. "Minutes, Second Meeting of the CVMP." December 9, 1946. Washington, D.C.: National Research Council.

8. Richards, A.N., "Foreword," in *Advances in Military Medicine Made by American Investigators Working under the Sponsorship of the Committee on Medical Research*, Andrus, E.C., Bronk, D.W., Carden, G.A., Keefer, C.S., Lockwood, J.S., Wearn, J.T., and Winternitz, M.C., Editors. 1948, Little, Brown and Company: Boston.

9. NAS-NRC. "Minutes, First Meeting of the CVMP." September 20, 1946, 29.

10. *Peripheral Nerve Regeneration: A Follow-up Study of 3,656 World War Ii Injuries*. Woodhall, B. and Beebe, G.W., eds.; Washington, D.C.: U.S. Government Printing Office, 1957.

11. Cushing, E.H. "Minutes, Special Medical Advisory Group." Washington, D.C., 9.

12. Interview with Marjorie T. Wilson, M.D., April 29, 1988 at Dr. Wilson's office at ECFMG, in Washington, D.C.

13. National Academy of Sciences - National Research Council. "Minutes, Third Meeting of the CVMP." March 14, 1947. Washington, D.C.: National Research Council, Appendix C.

14. Medical Follow-up Agency "Report to Chairman, Division of Medical Sciences, National Academy of Sciences." 1948. 3-4.

15. Interview with Gilbert W. Beebe, Ph.D. and Seymour Jablon, May 3, 1988 at Mr. Jablon's office at NIH.

16. *Peripheral Nerve Regeneration*. Woodhall and Beebe, eds.; 1957, 18-19.

17. National Academy of Sciences - National Research Council. "Minutes, Fifth Meeting of the CVMP." December 11, 1947. Washington, D.C.: National Research Council.

18. Medical Follow-up Agency "Report to Chairman, Division of Medical Sciences, National Academy of Sciences." 1949. 5.

19. Interview with Gilbert W. Beebe, Ph.D., June 1, 1994 at a hotel lobby in Washington, DC.

20. National Academy of Sciences - National Research Council. "Minutes, Fourteenth Meeting of the CVMP." November 18-19, 1949. Washington, D.C.: National Research Council.

21. Zieve, L., Hill, E., Nesbitt, S. and Zieve, B., "The Incidence of Residuals of Viral Hepatitis." *Gastroenterology*, 1953. **25**: 495-531.

22. Brill, N.Q. and Beebe, G., "Some Applications of a Follow-up Study to Psychiatric Standards for Mobilization." *Am J Psychiatry*, 1952. **109**: 401-420.

23. Amory, H. and Brick, I., "Irradiation Damage of the Intestines Following 1000-Kv Roentgen Therapy." *Radiology*, 1951. **56**: 49-57.

24. Medical Follow-up Agency "Report to Chairman, Division of Medical Sciences, National Academy of Sciences." 1951. 5.

25. National Academy of Sciences - National Research Council. "Minutes, Twenty Fifth Meeting of the CVMP." December 5, 1952. Washington, D.C.: National Research Council.

26. Mainland, D. "The VA-NRC Program of Follow-up Studies: Evaluation and Suggestions." 1953.

27. Follow-up Agency "Report, Division of Medical Sciences, NRC." 1953.

28. National Academy of Sciences - National Research Council. "Minutes, Twenty Eighth Meeting of the CVMP." December 7, 1953. Washington, D.C.: National Research Council.

29. National Academy of Sciences - National Research Council. "Minutes, Thirtieth Meeting of the CVMP." Washington, D.C.: National Research Council.

30. National Academy of Sciences - National Research Council. "Minutes, Thirty First Meeting of the CVMP." April 15, 1955. Washington, D.C.: National Research Council.

31. NAS-NRC. "Minutes, Thirtieth Meeting of the CVMP." November 2, 1954. Washington, D.C.: National Research Council.

32. Veterans Administration Multiple Sclerosis Study Group, "Isoniazid in treatment of multiple sclerosis: Report on Veterans Administration Cooperative Study." *JAMA*, 1957. **163**: 168-172.

33. Veterans Administration Multiple Sclerosis Study Group, "Five year follow-up on multiple sclerosis: Report on Veterans Administration Cooperative Study." *Archives of Neurology*, 1964. **11**: 583-592.

34. Berkowitz, E.D. and Santangelo, M.J., *The Medical Follow-up Agency: The First Fifty Years, 1946-1996*. Washington, D.C.: National Academy Press, 1999, 27-28, 31, 45, 65, 67.

35. Berkowitz and Santangelo, *Medical Follow-up Agency*. 87-124.

36. Remington, R. "Remarks by Chairman, Committee on Epidemiology and Veteran Follow-up Studies, Commission on Life Sciences, National Research Council." *Conference on Epidemiology in Military and Veteran Populations*, quoted in Report of an Ad Hoc Executive Committee charged to review the Medical Follow-up Agency, July 27, 1987.

37. Neefe, J., Gambescia, J., Kurtz, C., Smith, H., Beebe, G., Jablon, S., Reinhold, J. and Williams, S., "Prevalence and nature of hepatic disturbance following acute viral hepatitis with jaundice." *Ann Intern Med*, 1955. **43**: 1-32.

38.   Nefzger, M. and Chalmers, T., "The treatment of acute infectious hepatitis." *Am J Med*, 1963. **35**: 299-309.

39.   Brill, N.Q. and Beebe, G., "Follow-up study of psychoneuroses." *Am J Psychiatry*, 1951. **108**: 417-425.

40.   Brill, N.Q. and Beebe, G.W., *A Follow-up Study of War Neuroses*. VA Medical Monograph. Washington, D.C.: U.S. Government Printing Office, 1955.

41.   *Peripheral Nerve Regeneration*. Woodhall and Beebe, eds.; 1957.

42.   Long, E.R. and Jablon, S., *Tuberculosis in the Army of the United States in World War II*. VA Medical Monograph. Washington, D.C.: U.S. Government Printing Office, 1955.

43.   Engleman, E.P., Hollister, L.E. and Kolb, F.O., "Sequelae of rheumatic fever in men. Four to eight year follow-up study." *JAMA*, 1954. **155**: 1134-1140.

44.   Michael, M., Jr., Cole, R., Beeson, P. and Olson, B., "Sarcoidosis: Preliminary report on study of 350 cases with special reference to epidemiology." *Natl Tuberc Assoc*, 1950. **46**: 208-212.

45.   Gentry, J.T., Notowsky, H.M. and Michael, M., "Studies on the epidemiology of sarcoidosis in the United States: The relationship to soil areas and to urban-rural residence." *J Clin Invest*, 1955. **34**: 1839-1856.

46.   Freni, D.R. and Warren, R., "End-results of rehabilitation of war wounds of the hand." *Arch Surg*, 1951. **63**: 774-782.

47.   Ripley, H. and Wolf, S., "Long-term study of combat area schizophrenic reactions." *Am J Psychiatry*, 1951. **108**: 409-416.

48.   Ripley, H. and Wolf, S., "The course of wartime schizophrenia compared with a control group." *J Nerv Ment Dis*, 1954. **120**: 184-195.

49.   Cohen, M.B. and Cooper, M.Z., *A Follow-up Study of World War II Prisoners of War*. VA Medical Monograph. Washington, D.C.: U.S. Government Printing Office, 1955.

50.   Nefzger, M., "Follow-up studies of World War II and Korean War prisoners." *Am J Epidemiology*, 1970. **91**: 123-138.

51.   Keehn, R.J., "Follow-up studies of World War II and Korean Conflict prisoners: III. Mortality to January 1, 1976." *Am J Epidemiology*, 1980. **111**: 194-211.

52.   Beebe, G.W., "Follow-up studies of World War II and Korean War prisoners. II. Morbidity, disability, and maladjustments." *Am J Epidemiology*, 1975. **101**: 400-422.

53.   Walker, A. and Jablon, S., "A Follow-up of head-injured men of World War II." *J Neurosurg*, 1959. **16**: 600-610.

54.   Walker, A.E. and Jablon, S., *A Follow-up Study of Head Wounds in World War II*. VA Medical Monograph. Vol. 16. Washington, D.C.: U.S. Government Printing Office, 1961, 600-610.

55.   De Bakey, M.E. and Cohen, B.M., *Buerger's Disease: A Follow-up Study of World War II Army Cases*. Springfield, IL: Charles C. Thomas, 1963

56.   Cohen, B.M., Smetana, H.F. and Miller, R.W., "Hodgkin's Disease: Long survival in a study of 388 World War II Army Cases." *Cancer*, 1964. **17**: 856-866.

57.   Acheson, E.D. and Nefzger, M.D., "Ulcerative colitis in the United States Army in 1944. epidemiology: Comparisons between patients and controls." *Gastroenterology*, 1963. **44**: 7-19.

58.   Nefzger, M. and Acheson, E., "Ulcerative colitis in the United States Army in 1944. Follow-up with particular reference to mortality in cases and controls." *Gut*, 1963. **4**: 183-192.

59.   Bland, E. and Beebe, G., "Missiles in the heart. A twenty-year follow-up report of World War II cases." *New Eng J Med*, 1966. **274**: 1039-1046.

60.   Hrubek, Z. and Nashold, B.S., "Epidemiology of lumber disk lesions in the military in World War II." *Am J Epidemiology*, 1975. **102**: 366-376.

61.   National Academy of Sciences - National Research Council. "Minutes, Twenty Ninth Meeting of the CVMP." Washington, D.C.: National Research Council, 5.

62.   Letter from R. Keith Cannon to members of the Committee on Veterans' Medical Problems, written at Washington, D.C., September 19, 1962

Chapter 5. The tuberculosis treatment trials

Tuberculosis, the "White Plague," was a major public health problem in the nineteenth century and first half of the twentieth century. Thanks in part to public health action, especially isolation of active cases and the campaign against public spitting, the incidence of the disease generally decreased in the United States. Deaths from tuberculosis declined from 195 per year per 100,000 population in 1900, to 113 in 1920 and 46 in 1940.[1] However, military personnel during wartime were exposed to crowding, disease and poor nutrition. Many who served in the two World Wars contracted tuberculosis.

Tuberculosis in the World War I veteran

In 1917, when the United States was on the brink of World War I, a new law defining the nation's responsibility to provide for the health of those who served in its wars replaced the previously politically driven pensions system (Chapter 1). Under this new law, injured and ill former servicemen had the right to care in government hospitals.[2]

Patients with tuberculosis were prominent among those needing care in veterans' hospitals, and accounted for 12 percent of the 178,000 World War I service disability discharges.[3] During the early and mid-1920s, a network of veterans' hospitals devoted entirely to the care of the tuberculous grew up in the United States.

Before the Veterans' Bureau was established, World War I veterans stricken with tuberculosis were treated in U. S. Public Health Service hospitals, but the number of beds was inadequate and allowed care of only a small minority. Many were hospitalized in private hospitals under government contract. Many others stayed home, where they often infected their families and friends. As soon as available, new VA tuberculosis beds were filled. The number of hospitalized veterans with tuberculosis skyrocketed from 12,000 in 1920 to a 1922 peak of 44,951.[3] After that, the number of veterans' tuberculosis admissions decreased and stabilized at about 11,000 per year from 1929 through 1945.[4]

In this pre-antibiotic era, VA care for tuberculosis was considered to be the best in the nation. Following the advice of the American Tuberculosis Association,[5] hospitals were placed in locations considered best for controlling the disease. These were in areas away from cities, often in the mountains, where the clear air was thought to be beneficial. Even though a 1927 Veterans' Bureau study showed climate had no effect on outcome of tuberculosis,[6] the generally held medical opinion was that it did. Patients were kept in bed because bed rest was the mainstay of treatment. Increasingly, pneumothorax and thoracoplasty, operations to rest the diseased area of lung, became accepted treatment for tuberculosis and were added to bed rest.[7, 8]

The Medical Council, VA's advisory council in the 1920s and 1930s (Chapter 1), included a special group to consider treatment of tuberculosis. They advised on such matters as frequency of refills of pneumothorax, evaluation of "arrested" cases needing readmission and frequency of bacteriological studies.[9]

In 1926, the VA's new Research Subdivision's first published report was a statistical analysis of veterans hospitalized with tuberculosis who also had a second disability: 38,715 such veterans had been hospitalized since 1919.[10] Significantly more veterans with far advanced tuberculosis and a second disability were "colored" (62 percent) than white (42 percent). The following year, a systematic study of veterans examined the prevalent view that climate influences the outcome of tuberculosis treatment.[6] Treatment results at the 19 veterans' tuberculosis hospitals scattered throughout the country in a variety of climates and settings were correlated with their climatic conditions. The study concluded that "climate is not an important factor, and does not influence the end results."

During the period between the two World Wars, tuberculosis remained one of the most important problems of veterans' medical care, though the fraction of tuberculous patients in veterans' hospitals declined from 40 percent in 1922 to 8 percent in 1941.[11, 12] The VA's own medical journal, the *Medical Bulletin*, published articles by VA staff that generally reflected their thoughts about their attempts to improve patients' care. In the year 1927 alone, the *Medical Bulletin* published 10 clinical research articles about tuberculosis. Topics included treatment of bone tuberculosis by actinotherapy,[13] heliotherapy in laryngeal tuberculosis,[14] statistical analysis of tuberculosis in mental hospitals,[15] interaction between tuberculosis and intercurrent diseases,[16] an outcomes study of 500 cases of pulmonary tuberculosis,[17] a systematic (negative) study of the effect of climate on outcome of tuberculosis treatment[6] and an essay on the history of tuberculosis.[18] There were case reports of lupus vulgaris,[19] generalized tuberculous adenitis,[20] tuberculous pericarditis[21] and tuberculous duodenal ulcer.[22] Also published were various essays on the importance of early diagnosis of tuberculosis,[23] proper history taking[24] and advice about care of the tuberculous patient.[25]

Tuberculosis in the World War II veteran

As the United States mobilized for the Second World War, the Veterans Administration staff dwindled.[26] Doctors and nurses were needed in the military. When they left the VA, there were no replacements. Facilities deteriorated because of shortage of staff and materials for upkeep. At the end of the war, the sudden influx of demobilized soldiers, many with tuberculosis, created overcrowding and short staffing. In some cases, patient care was not good and the patriotic public was alerted through newspapers and magazines.[27] Eleanor Roosevelt learned of the situation and informed President Truman.[28] It was at that point that Truman called on General Omar Bradley to head the VA., with Bradley, in turn, naming General Paul Hawley to head the VA's medical department (Chapter 3).

One of the first problems Hawley tackled was the needs of the new veterans who had tuberculosis. At that time, some 12,000 veterans were hospitalized in VA hospitals for tuberculosis, and their number was growing steadily.

Hawley persuaded Dr. John Barnwell, a professor at the University of Michigan, to come to Washington to lead the VA fight against tuberculosis. Barnwell was a well-known authority on the disease, who himself had been treated for tuberculosis. Equally important, he was active in the American Trudeau Society (a non-government organization advocating tuberculosis research) and a personal friend of leaders in the field. His goal was to use every resource available to him to improve the care of the tuberculous veteran.

Figure 5.1 John Barnwell, M.D.

In 1946, the best medical centers and sanitoria continued to treat tuberculosis with rest therapy. Patients were confined to special hospitals or to special units in general hospitals. Complete bed rest was enforced, with patients not even getting up to use the bathroom. Pneumothorax and thoracoplasty, to "rest" the diseased area or to reduce the size of tuberculous cavities, were common. Typically, a tubercular patient would be hospitalized for a year or more. Given the danger of infection, sufferers were isolated from their normal worlds. Even if their disease was eventually arrested, the personal and social impact of the disease was significant. The possibility of death was very real; sometimes entire families were wiped out by tuberculosis.

Streptomycin comes on the scene

For half a century, since Robert Koch's discovery of the tubercle bacillus as the cause of tuberculosis, attempts at systemic treatment had been made. These treatment approaches began with Koch's own enthusiastic, but eventually disappointing, use of tuberculin, an inactivated product of the tubercle bacillus, and ranged through the use of sanocrysin, a gold compound, in the 1920s and 1930s. A study that may have been the first placebo-controlled clinical trial in the world proved sanocrysin to be disappointingly ineffective in curing tuberculosis.[29] Transient enthusiasms occurred for proposed cures, only to prove ineffective. An example is the use of turtle serum, thought to be effective because the turtle has antibodies to a type of mycobacterial disease.[30] One disappointment after another led to a pervading skepticism about any proposed new treatment for this persistent and resistant disease. When streptomycin appeared in the wake of penicillin's spectacular wartime success and showed promise in treatment of tuberculosis, it was greeted with suspicion by the older, more experienced, phthisiologists.[30]

Very little streptomycin was available at the beginning of 1946. Its distribution to civilians in the United States and England was controlled by central governmental agencies. In early 1946, the entire VA hospital system received only 2 kg per month. General Hawley appointed a "Streptomycin Committee," chaired by Dr. Barnwell, to distribute this scant supply to VA hospitals. Barnwell recruited Dr. Arthur Walker, who had worked on the clinical development of penicillin during the war, to serve as secretary to the committee and coordinate the streptomycin treatment program. At first, all of the streptomycin was used for nontuberculous conditions such as tularemia. Gradually, the manufacturers succeeded in increasing production. By April 1946, some streptomycin was available to explore treating selected tuberculosis patients.

Figure 5.2 Arthur Walker, M.D.

In preliminary clinical trials,[31] streptomycin, which had been discovered in 1944,[32] showed promise against tuberculosis. It was known to inhibit the tubercle bacillus in culture. But despite a few isolated cases successfully treated, no one really knew if clinical tuberculosis would be helped by streptomycin.

Tuberculosis is a very complex disease. The tubercle bacillus grows slowly and often attacks sites that are not very vascular, so the antibiotic might not reach the bacillus through the blood stream. It walls itself off in "tubercles," surrounded by fibrous tissue with little blood supply. It invades many parts of the body and shows itself in various ways.

The body fights tuberculosis through its immune system. The treatments that had been successful up to that time, such as bed rest, depended on the immune defensive resources of the patient's body. Patients frequently would improve without specific treatment. Permanent arrests of the disease often occurred, though it was generally felt that people were never completely "cured." Whether streptomycin would alter the course of this complex clinical picture and bring about true cures was doubtful. Barnwell and Walker set out to try to answer that question.[33]

Design of the VA-Armed Forces Streptomycin trial

Walker had been a part of the central group coordinating the wartime studies of penicillin treatment of syphilis. Those studies depended on systematic study of the patient before and during treatment, standardization of a prescribed regimen of treatment and adequate follow-up. Comparison with an untreated control series of patients, or with patients treated with the then-standard arsenical and bismuth regimens, was not a part of these studies.

Instead, the investigators drew on their significant personal clinical knowledge about the natural history of syphilis, knowledge believed sufficient to predict the course the disease would have without penicillin.[34]

The design for the first VA-Armed Forces study of streptomycin in tuberculosis, begun in 1946, followed the same pattern as that used for the study of penicillin in syphilis: carefully defined study of the patient before treatment, prediction of what the patient's clinical course would be without treatment, standardization of treatment to a single dosage schedule, observation for the effect of treatment on signs and symptoms of tuberculosis, repeated cultures to isolate the tubercle bacillus, observation for treatment complications, and post-treatment follow-up.

In their first report to the AMA Council on Pharmacy and Therapeutics, Barnwell and Walker cited the preliminary reports about streptomycin, especially those already published from the Mayo Clinic. The reports made clear that the widespread VA-Armed Forces clinical study was founded on good evidence that streptomycin was effective in at least some instances:

> "There was thus available to the federal agencies, at the time their investigation was designed, considerable information as to the effectiveness and dangers of streptomycin in the treatment of human tuberculosis. Without this information the investigation would not have been undertaken."[35]

This statement describes the prevailing attitude at the time in the United States. It was the physician's responsibility to do the best thing for his patient. The patient's responsibility was to adhere to the prescribed treatment, generally without participating actively in the therapeutic decision. "Informed consent," even with new medications, for an unestablished treatment was not the norm.

Barnwell and Walker chose seven VA and two military hospitals for their study of streptomycin in tuberculosis. Included were the VA hospitals at Bronx (NY), Hines (IL), Livermore (CA), Oteen (Asheville) (NC), and three hospitals that have since been closed: Rutland Heights (NJ), San Fernando (CA), and Sunmount (NY). Also included were Fitzsimons General Army Hospital in Denver, CO, and the Sampson, NY, Navy Hospital. Only patients selected for the study in these hospitals received the drug. Hospital selection for the first study was based on having doctors knowledgeable about tuberculosis who were eager to cooperate in a study to see what effect streptomycin had on moderately advanced tuberculous disease.

These hospitals were given an allotment of the precious streptomycin that was adequate to treat those patients who qualified for the protocol. Barnwell and Walker worked together with representatives of the Army and Navy to establish and follow a common protocol. Requirements of the protocol were:

> "a. That all cases would have been observed for a period of at least sixty days prior to initiation of treatment and that during this period the pulmonary lesion would

have become more extensive or, at best, remained stationary;

b. That tubercle bacilli would have been recently recovered from the sputum or gastric contents and that confirmation of their identity by inoculation into guinea pigs, or by culture, would have been started;

c. That moderately advanced disease would be preferred but that far advanced disease would be acceptable, provided the patient had an estimated life expectancy of at least twelve months without streptomycin therapy;

d. That the x-rays would disclose some exudative component, the more the better, in the pulmonary lesion;

e. That all patients would preferably have been on complete bed rest prior to therapy but, if this was not the case, that they would observe the same degree of physical activity during therapy as was in effect before treatment was started;

f. That pneumothorax would not be present on the side toward which the treatment was primarily directed;

g. That no collapse procedures would be initiated during treatment but, if pneumoperitoneum, phrenic paralysis, or contralateral pneumothorax was present prior to treatment, they would be maintained at the preexisting level."[35]

Since the first question to be answered was whether streptomycin really had any effect on the course of tuberculosis, Barnwell and Walker and their colleagues first decided to use a dosage schedule that could be expected to maintain blood streptomycin levels over the course of 24 hours. Based on previous experience with penicillin, patients in the first study received a daily dose of 1.8 grams of streptomycin, 0.3 grams intramuscularly every four hours. As they state in their early paper describing the study:

"These decisions concerning dosage and duration of treatment were admittedly arbitrary for there were no data on which to base an informed judgment but, in order that the study have any statistical significance, it was considered essential that this first group of patients be treated in accordance with a single regimen."[33]

Barnwell and Walker visited the study hospitals to review the patients chosen for the study and to assist in meeting the criteria. They soon found that the majority of patients in the VA tuberculosis wards had far-advanced disease, so a larger fraction than planned of these patients were included in the study.

The question of controls

From the beginning of this study, discussion and worry centered about the use of controls. Some felt that concurrent untreated controls were essential. However, withholding the drug raised ethical concerns, once clinicians became convinced that it worked, even though that hadn't been proven. Finding it impractical to include prospectively randomized controls in their study, Barnwell and Walker and their advisors then substituted two other types of controls:

a. Use of the patient as his own control, and

b. Use of untreated patients, similar clinically, from a time before streptomycin was available.

Not everyone, however, was satisfied with the decision to omit the use of concurrent randomized controls. Gilbert Beebe, Ph.D., a statistician who headed the National Research Council's Follow-up Agency (Chapter 4), met with Barnwell and urged the use of untreated controls.[36] Heated discussion of the issue of controls occurred at the third Streptomycin Conference in 1947, but the issue was not really resolved. The following exchange between Dr. Walker and Paul Densen, a distinguished statistician who had joined VA Central Office, is recorded in the minutes:

"Dr. Densen: From the statistical research end, it would be better to work only five cases in many different ways rather than to enlarge such a study to 50 cases. If you do five cases intensively, and do five cases without streptomycin, on which you get the same kind of laboratory observations, you will have a better series statistically than if you do all 10 cases on streptomycin."

"Dr. Walker: You and I have been arguing on opposite sides of the control question for the last few days."[37]

After this discussion with the statisticians, the clinicians met in executive session, without the statisticians, and decided not to include untreated controls.

The Streptomycin Conferences begin

In December 1946, the streptomycin trial participants met in Chicago for the first of what proved to be a 25-year series of conferences. In addition to the VA, Army and Navy participants, Dr. Corwin Hinshaw of the Mayo Clinic, the first physician to use streptomycin in patients, attended. Other participants included Dr. Esmond Long of the Phipps Institute in Philadelphia, who later led the USPHS study discussed below, and Dr. C.J. Van Slyke, Medical Director of the National Institute of Health.

At this first meeting, those participating in the study brought the records and biweekly chest x-ray films of the patients they had treated. As Dr. Walker described it, "34 individuals sat in a tight semicircle for three days gazing devotedly at x-ray view-boxes." The assembled group read the series of x-rays from each of 135 patients, and wrote down their opinions about changes in the tuberculous lesions. A statistician from the VA Central Office statistics group then tabulated the opinions.

The proceedings of this conference and of all of the later conferences were published by the VA and distributed widely.[38]

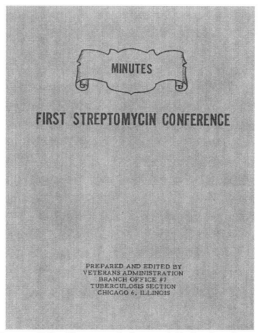

**Figure 5.3: Cover of the published minutes
of the First Streptomycin Conference**

Results of the first VA-Armed Forces streptomycin study

Since the organizers of the study had little idea about the expected outcome, the first patients were studied very thoroughly. They received chest x-rays, many of them stereoscopic, every two weeks during treatment. Auditory and vestibular function and screens for renal or hepatic toxicity were frequently assessed. Bacteriologic response was monitored, and blood streptomycin measured. Careful clinical records were kept.[33]

Clinically, the initial improvement in the first group of 223 patients was impressive. The investigators were enthusiastic about their patients' increased sense of well-being. Most patients (85 percent) had improved appetites and gained weight. Most (73 percent) who had fever became afebrile. Sputum production, cough and the number of tubercle bacilli in the sputum decreased. Of this first group of patients, 43 percent became bacteriologically negative during the 120 days of streptomycin treatment.

But there were also adverse effects. Most frequent and disturbing (92 percent) was vestibular (inner ear) damage, which disturbed the patient's balance, and this persisted after treatment, though many patients adapted to it. The caloric test for vestibular function was affected in 77 percent, but only 0.5 percent had objective hearing loss; 67 percent developed casts in their urine and 70 percent developed eosinophilia.

Encouraged by the results but suspicious of chest-film readings by those participating in the study, Barnwell and Walker sought a more objective assessment. For this, they recruited a jury of seven tuberculosis experts chosen by the President of the American Trudeau Society, the premier society for the study of tuberculosis. These seven men met together for six consecutive days in May 1947 to read and compare films. They were

150

presented with blinded film sets from patients with and without streptomycin treatment, each set containing three films. The first two films in each set were taken at a two-month interval, the third after a four-month interval. In the case of the treated patients, the first two-month interval was the pretreatment observation period. The first x-ray reviewed was taken two months before treatment began and the second immediately before treatment. The second, four-month, interval, was the period of streptomycin treatment in the treated group. The jury of experts evaluated interval changes in 222 lesions in 131 patients during the two months just prior to streptomycin treatment and during the 4 months of streptomycin administration.

The corresponding interval changes were also judged in 142 lesions in 88 "historical control" patients, patients at the same hospitals who met the criteria of the study but who had been treated before streptomycin became available.

Table 5.1. Chest film review by panel of experts. Review of 222 lesions in 131 patients treated with streptomycin and of 142 lesions in 88 historical control patients.

	Percent of exudative lesions	
Interval	Treated (n=222)	Untreated (n=142)
2 mo. before "treatment"		
Worse	36.9	7.0
No Change	34.2	57.1
Better	28.9	35.9
4 mo. during "treatment"		
Worse	0.5	4.2
No Change	14.5	65.6
Better	85.0	30.2

The results of their review were dramatic (Table 5.1). First of all, it looked as if the historical controls chosen from the participating hospitals were, on average, less ill than the treated patients. Fewer of their exudative lesions worsened over a two-month period than did those in the study patients during the two-month pretreatment observation period. Among the untreated patients, the natural history of the illness was predictably stable, with about as many lesions worsening or improving over the next four months as during the first two months. On the other hand, in the treated patients, exudative lesions were much more likely to improve during the four months of streptomycin than during the pretreatment period. Only one of the 222 lesions evaluated in the treated patients worsened during treatment.

A more extensive, but less objective, analysis included all of the biweekly films of all 223 patients (Table 5.2). In this study, physicians at the various participating hospitals read the films. Again, a dramatic improvement occurred during the period of streptomycin treatment.

Resistance to streptomycin

Eight percent of the patients in Table 5.2, after an initial improvement, began to do worse while still receiving streptomycin. This pattern would not have shown up on the "expert panel" readings, as that panel didn't review films taken during the treatment course. The pattern of improvement followed by worsening suggested that resistance of the organisms to streptomycin was developing. Bacteriological analysis confirmed that 44 percent of the patients' organisms had become moderately or markedly resistant to streptomycin by the end of two to three months' treatment at 1.8 grams/day and 65 percent were resistant at four months.[33] This finding, that the tubercle bacillus became resistant to streptomycin as treatment progressed, and that resistance was associated with a reduced clinical response to the drug, was a uniform finding in all three streptomycin studies described in this chapter.

Table 5.2. Chest Xray readings by physicians at the patients' hospitals (223 Patients)

	Percent of Patients		
	Before Rx	During Rx	After Rx
Progression	75.3	0.5	16.4
Stationary	17.1	6.5	44.1
Regression	7.6	84.7	39.5
Regression, then progression	NA	8.3	NA

Conclusion: Streptomycin is effective in treating pulmonary tuberculosis

In May 1947, the VA-Armed Forces group had completed treatment of 543 cases, all having received 1.8 or 2 grams of streptomycin per day. The investigators were convinced that the answer to their first question was "yes": Streptomycin does have a beneficial effect in treatment of tuberculosis. The expert panels convened at that time and in July 1947 confirmed this conclusion.

Results in other types of tuberculosis

In addition to the study of pulmonary tuberculosis, by far the most prevalent type of the disease, the group studied other forms, following a variety of protocols tailored to each condition. By the time of their first publication in November 1947, the group could clearly recommend streptomycin in tuberculous cutaneous sinuses, tuberculous lymphadenitis, tracheobroncial and laryngeal tuberculosis, and tuberculosis of the tongue, tonsils, intestine and peritoneum. In fact, the results were so favorable that they never were able to complete the protocols planned for those conditions—there were no longer enough patients. Other extrapulmonary tuberculosis, of the urinary system, bone, joints and pericardium, showed less clear-cut benefit. Even miliary or meningeal tuberculosis, previously a death sentence, sometimes yielded to streptomycin.

<u>Letting the practitioner know the results</u>

At the third VA-AF Streptomycin Conference, held in May 1947, participants discussed the best way to let others know about their early results. Dr. Walker felt strongly that participants from each hospital should publish their own results. Barnwell suggested a summary article, followed by articles from individual hospitals. This was the plan eventually followed. There was concern, however, that information dissemination shouldn't wait for the formal publication process. As Barnwell said:

> "There is one thing that we have been warned about repeatedly in all matters of this sort, and that is that we should get this thing to the profession before it gets to the layman. We have already put the profession in a position of having to keep strict silence on this program. Items have been appearing in lay magazines and the daily press. It is high time we got it to the profession through their own journals, instead of putting the profession in the position of having patients read about streptomycin in the newspapers."[39]

Dr. W. Van Winkle, who represented the American Medical Association, suggested that there be a brief statement in *JAMA*:

> "It seems to me that we have a twofold problem, one of acquainting the general profession, and the second of acquainting those who are treating tuberculosis patients, with the details of the results. The first thing is most important at the present time; that is, to acquaint the general profession with streptomycin. I would urge that some sort of statement be published . . . . The A.M.A. is receiving from 10 to 12 letters a week asking about streptomycin in tuberculosis, and we have no good reference to give them."[40]

The first of a series of such statements to the profession, officially authored by the chief medical officers of the VA, Army and Navy but presumably written by Walker and Barnwell, was published as a report to the AMA Council on Pharmacy and Chemistry in the November 8, 1947 issue of *JAMA*. It concluded that:

> " The findings of Hinshaw and his several collaborators have been confirmed. Streptomycin is a useful adjunct in the treatment of tuberculosis."[35]

The primary publication of this first VA-AF study of streptomycin in tuberculosis presenting results in the first 223 patients was published that same month in the *American Review of Tuberculosis.*[33]

<u>Later studies by the VA-Armed Forces group</u>

By the May 1947 meeting, it was clear that the side effects of streptomycin, especially the damage it caused to the vestibular system, were troubling. Also, a large fraction of the treated patients now harbored tubercle bacilli that were resistant to streptomycin. These patients and those who caught the disease from them could no longer benefit from streptomycin. The VA-Armed Forces collaborative group decided to branch out, to try different treatment schedules in a search for one that would have a therapeutic effect, but less toxicity and drug resistance.

Figure 5.4: Executive Committee Meeting, VA-Armed Forces Cooperative Study on the Chemotherapy of Tuberculosis, VA Hospital, Sunmount, N.Y., September 10, 1959. Clockwise: Dr. Wm. Harris, VA Hospital, Salt Lake City, UT; Dr. Wm. Hentel, VA Hospital, Albuquerque, NM; Dr. H.E. Walkup, VA Hospital, Oteen, NC; Dr. Patrick Storey, VA Hospital, Baltimore, MD; Dr. B. Ramin, Area Chief for Tuberculosis, VA Regional Office, Boston, MA; Dr. W. Spencer Schwartz, VA Hospital, Oteen, NC; Dr. R.H. Schmidt, Jr., Tuberculosis Service, VACO; Dr. Edward Dunner, Research Service, VACO; Mrs. Dorothy Livings, VACO statistician, Dr. N. D'Esopo, VA Hospital, West Haven, CT; Dr. A. Falk, Consultant, St. Paul, MN; Capt R.G. Streeter (MC) USNavy; Dr. Maurice Small, VA Hospital, East Orange, NJ; Dr. Wm. Feldman, Research Service, VACO.

They compared the 2-gram-per-day dose they had been using with 1-gram-per-day. Again, they did not use true randomization. Instead, the group divided itself for comparison, with some hospitals continuing the 2-gram/day regimen, others changing to 1-gram/day. They found the results comparable, but with less toxicity when 1-gram/day was administered. They provided this information in an addendum to their primary publication in November 1947.[33]

All the many subsequent VA-Armed Forces trials of treatment regimens for tuberculosis used comparison groups but always compared the current "best" treatment with the proposed new treatment. At first, the comparison was among hospitals that adopted different "arms" of the study. But in 1948, they introduced comparison groups within the hospitals, randomizing by the patient's hospital number (patients with odd numbers receiving one regimen, those with even numbers the other.) The consortium of investigators continued to work together, examining new opportunities for the treatment of tuberculosis and meeting annually until 1972. The group of investigators and their particular interests and areas of expertise expanded. Specialty committees met, and an Executive Committee determined the overall course of the studies.

The MRC streptomycin study

In 1946, the British National Health Service met an even more difficult challenge than did the VA. Streptomycin was in such short supply that in all of Great Britain there was only enough to treat 50 patients with pulmonary tuberculosis.[41] Taking this problem as an opportunity, A. Bradford Hill, an eminent statistician, and Phillip D'Arcy Hart, the director of the tuberculosis research unit of the Medical Research Council (MRC), persuaded the MRC to sponsor a truly randomized clinical trial of tuberculosis.

Study design

In the MRC study, patients who met very narrow criteria, as judged by a central committee, were referred to the cooperating hospitals. They were randomized either to a ward where they would receive streptomycin or to one where they would not. As is commonly done today in cooperative clinical trials, randomization was by a "statistical series based on random sampling numbers drawn up for each sex at each centre by Professor Bradford Hill."[42] Unlike present-day practice, however, none of the patients were told they were a part of a research protocol.

Patients in the streptomycin group received 2 grams/day, 0.5 gram intramuscularly every 6 hours, for four months, essentially the same dosage schedule used in the first VA-Armed Forces study described above. In all respects except administration of streptomycin, the care of the streptomycin group and the control group was the same. All patients in both groups were kept at bed rest for the six-month study period.

As in the VA-Armed Forces study, a panel of experts read the sequential x-ray films of the patients, blinded to their treatment group. The design of this review was somewhat simpler than in the VA-DOD study, but the outcome was very similar.

Results

Just as in the larger and "looser" VA study, the MRC group found that the early response to streptomycin was dramatic: at 6 months, only 7 percent of the streptomycin-treated patients had died, compared with 27 percent of the controls. Of those still living, only 18 percent of the streptomycin-treated patients had deteriorated clinically, compared with 46 percent of the controls. Radiological improvement had occurred in 69 percent of the streptomycin patients, but in only 33 percent of the controls. Of the streptomycin patients, 15 percent had no tubercle bacilli in their sputum or gastric washings; in only 4 percent of the control series was that the case. On the other hand, of those in the streptomycin-treated group who still harbored tubercle bacilli, 85 percent of those bacilli were resistant to streptomycin.[42]

The USPHS streptomycin study

In 1947, the U.S. Public Health Service (USPHS) began planning its own study of streptomycin in pulmonary tuberculosis. Heading this study was Carroll Palmer, a statistician who had argued unsuccessfully for the use of untreated controls in the original VA study.[43] Its senior physician was Esmond R. Long, M.D., who was also involved in the VA studies. Participants included Dr. Emil Bogen of Olive View Sanatorium in Southern California, who, as a consultant at the San Fernando VA Hospital, was also an active participant in the VA study. Other "crossover" participants included John Barnwell, Corwin Hinshaw, Walsh McDermott, Paul Bunn, Nicholas D'Esopo and William Tucker.[44]

Study design

At the 5th VA-Armed Forces Streptomycin Conference, held in April 1948, Shirley H. Ferebee, the USPHS statistician who coordinated the study, presented the protocol to the VA group.

The USPHS group planned five studies, the first of which asked: "How useful is streptomycin in the treatment of tuberculosis?" The plan for that study was to enroll 1,000 patients with pulmonary tuberculosis, half of whom would receive streptomycin in addition to other indicated treatment. The controls would "receive any therapy indicated other than streptomycin." In her presentation, Ferebee emphasized the following conditions: all cooperating investigators must agree to adhere to the protocol and make and record observations in the prescribed manner; a panel of experts would judge the suitability of patients for the study; the central study office would make assignment to treatment group by chance and would evaluate the results, using "quantitative" observations.[45]

Patients with all types of tuberculosis and treatments were included. Even prior treatment with streptomycin was permitted, but accounted for only a small number of patients. Streptomycin dosage (about 1.4 grams/day) was somewhat smaller than used in the original VA-Armed Forces and MRC studies but more than the 1 gram/day dose reported by the VA-Armed Forces group to reduce complications, compared with 2 grams/day, without affecting outcome. Unlike the original VA-Armed Forces and MRC studies, in which streptomycin was given for four months, it was given for three months in the USPHS study.

The idea behind this study design was to conduct a field study, assessing streptomycin effects under all sorts of tuberculous conditions, in contrast to the VA-Armed Forces and MRC studies, in which patients had been selected for suitability. The inclusion of randomly selected control patients who did not receive streptomycin was key to this study. This was by no means uncontroversial. Even the establishment of a central "Appeals Board" to approve deviations from the protocol didn't reassure those who questioned the use of untreated controls. J. Burns Amberson, who, ironically, had been leader of a placebo-controlled study of tuberculosis treatment in the 1920s, a study that proved sanocrystin to be useless in treatment of tuberculosis, opposed the use of a central group to control the physician's clinical judgment:

> "As a matter of fact I do not believe it is possible to give a definition (of life threatening disease) which would cover all the possibilities. Fundamentally, it rests on the judgment of the physician who is treating the case and who knows the patient best. He is in a far better position than anyone else to make the decision. If he is capable of undertaking a clinical investigation of therapy, he is certainly capable of assuming the responsibility for such judgment."[46]

In the end, a total of 23 of the 271 control patients received streptomycin, 12 of them with approval of the Appeals Board and 11 of them without such clearance. These were partly balanced by 7 of the 270 patients who were randomized to streptomycin but who refused the drug. The statisticians were able to deal with these small numbers of deviations from the protocol and to present a definitive result, assessing each patient at the end of a one-year observation period.

Results

Just as had the VA-Armed Forces and MRC study groups, the USPHS investigators found that improvement occurred more frequently in the streptomycin group than in the control group by all of the criteria they examined: mortality, temperature, body weight, conversion of sputum culture and x-ray appearance of the thorax. These results were statistically significant, and, it was believed, would convince the doubters about streptomycin's efficacy when they were published in 1950.[44]

The use of untreated control patients in these studies

The original VA-Armed Forces streptomycin study has been criticized for its lack of suitable controls. The planners of the study were aware that simultaneous, untreated, controls were desirable, but they decided against using them. In their primary report of their study, the VA-Armed Forces investigators explained:

> "It was the original decision of the Committee to have the Units select suitable cases and then divide them at random into two groups, the one to be treated with streptomycin, the other to provide controls. It seemed a feasible procedure at the time. The very scanty supplies of streptomycin, and the real ignorance of its effectiveness, made it reasonable to leave half the patients without treatment or, rather, to treat them by other methods than streptomycin. In retrospect, it would have been highly desirable to do this . . ."[33]

But, by the time the study had been launched, there was enough streptomycin to treat all eligible patients. The authors then went on to rationalize the approach they had taken:

> "The purpose of controls, in such a situation as this, is to compare the results of one form of therapy with another. In so far as a comparison of the effects of bed-rest upon

pulmonary tuberculosis is concerned, these cases may reasonably be said to serve as their own controls."[33]

Table 5.3. Characteristics of the three major trials of streptomycin efficacy in pulmonary tuberculosis

	VA-DOD	MRC	USPHS
Date planning begun	May 1946	Sept. 1946	July 1947
Date first patients entered	July 1946	Jan. 1947	Nov 1947
Date series completed	May 1947	April 1948	May 1950
Date of primary publication	Nov. 1947	Oct. 1948	Nov. 1950
Study design:			
Number of study sites	7	6	14
Type of institutions	VA&military	public	variable
Controls	Pre-rx obs of pt, historical conts	Prospective, randomized	Prospective, randomized
Screening of patients	Local	Central	Central
Chest x-ray evaluation	Impartial jury	Impartial jury	Impartial jury
Data analysis	Central	Central	Central
Patient characteristics:			
Number given streptomycin	223	55	270
Number of concurrent controls	None	52	271
Ages	97.3% < 46y	Under 30	81% <45y
Gender	98.2% male	40% male	53% male
Race	74.8% white	not stated	61% white
Restrictions on clinical type	Exudative lesions	New disease	Not minimal
	No collapse Rx	No collapse	Any assoc Rx
	Life expect.>1yr	Progressive	Not terminal
% with positive cultures on entry	100	100	100
% with fever on entry	72	70	66
% with elevated ESR on entry	83	95	not stated
Treatment protocol:			
Pre SM observation	60 days	1 week	Variable
Time on streptomycin	120 days	4 months	91 days
Minimum post-Rx observ.	120 days	2 months	9 months
Daily streptomycin dose	1.8 grams	2 grams	20mg/kg
Dosage schedule	0.3gq4h	0.5gq6h	3 daily doses
Surveillance:			
For complications			
Auditory	Yes	Not stated	Not stated
Vestibular	Yes	Variable	Not stated
Renal	Yes	No	Yes
Hepatic	Yes	No	No
Hematologic	Yes	No	Yes
For clinical response			
Chest xray	q2wk	Monthly (?)	q3mo(?)
TPR	q4h	yes	qd
ESR, wt	q2wk	Yes	Yes
Physical exam	q2wk	Yes	q3mo
Nude photos	Rx beg and end	No	No
For bacteriological response			
Culture	q2wk	variable	7 in 1 year
Sensitivity to SM	variable	variable	all positives
Blood SM concentration	variable	not done	not done

When the MRC group decided to include untreated control patients, they faced a simpler ethical situation: At that time, there really was a shortage of streptomycin, and only a few patients could be treated, whatever study design was adopted:

> "The selection of this type of disease constituted full justification for having a parallel series of patients treated only by bed-rest, since up to the present this would be considered the only form of suitable treatment in such cases. Additional justification lay in the fact that all the streptomycin available in the country was in any case being used, the rest of the supply being taken up for two rapidly fatal forms of the disease, military and meningeal tuberculosis."[42]

In addition, in the austere medical climate of postwar Britain, the patient selected for the study, even though randomized to the control group, still benefited:

> "When a patient had been accepted as suitable, request was made through the local authority for admission to one of the streptomycin centers; in spite of long waiting-lists these patients were given complete priority, and the majority were admitted within a week of approval."[42]

The rationale was different for using untreated controls in the USPHS study. Its planners and the Study Section that reviewed this very expensive project felt that a large, controlled study was necessary to establish once and for all whether streptomycin had a real effect:

> "Previous investigations had indicated a distinct and often dramatic improvement in many cases treated with streptomycin. However, further evidence was essential to distinguish the effect of the drug from the vagaries of the disease and the effect of other treatment. The Study Section agreed that the major portion of the funds specifically appropriated by the Congress for streptomycin research could best be employed in a rigorously planned investigation designed to determine, through the use of concurrent controls, the effect of adding streptomycin to other therapeutic measures."[44]

A central question about the USPHS study was the ethical justification for leaving a group of patients untreated with an antibiotic that was readily available and that might have helped them. The VA and MRC studies, each in its own way, had already shown that addition of streptomycin to standard treatment in pulmonary tuberculosis was superior to standard treatment alone. But the VA-Armed Forces study was statistically "loose," and the MRC study had a relatively small number of patients. Both of the earlier studies had been limited to patients with particular forms of a most variable disease. Perhaps the results of the VA-Armed Forces and MRC studies had not been widely accepted at the time the USPHS study was begun. In the past, there had been so many disappointments, so many "turtle serum" type enthusiasms, that academic leaders and responsible public officials may have felt the need to be sure of their ground before advocating the use of a treatment that was also toxic to many patients.

On the other hand, streptomycin was becoming widely used before the results of the USPHS study were published in 1950 and investigators were moving on to other treatments (Table 5.4). By the time the USPHS study had completed patient intake, combined therapy with streptomycin and paraaminosalycilate (PAS) was already under study by the VA-Armed Forces and MRC groups and was proving to be superior to streptomycin alone. Both groups published those results before publication of the USPHS study (which did not use the combined therapy). The USPHS study may have suffered the fate of other studies for which planning, funding and preparation take a long time: it may have become obsolete by the time its results were published.

One must assume that the investigators in the USPHS study, some of the leaders of academic phthisiology, still had sufficient doubt about the question of streptomycin's efficacy to justify staying with the study to its completion.

The use of untreated, or placebo treated, controls continues to be controversial in some situations and debate continues.[47]

"Informed consent" by patients in these studies

Even though the concept of informed consent by experimental subjects has its roots in the reaction to Nazi atrocities that claimed to be carried out in the name of science, it was not a widespread concept in the late 1940s. The organizers of the USPHS study faced the dilemma of withholding streptomycin from randomly assigned patients by making access to the study, and its funding, available only to investigators who were willing to study untreated control patients. They also provided an appeals mechanism for desperate cases. They dealt with the problem of pressure for treatment from patients in the control group by simply not informing the patients that they might benefit from streptomycin treatment.

The untreated patients in the MRC randomized controlled study also didn't know that they were a part of a randomized study: "Patients were not told before admission that they were to get special treatment."[42] They were placed on different wards from treated patients and were probably unaware of the possibility of streptomycin treatment. In the MRC study, it was easier to justify randomization of patients to the arms of the study, because the shortage of streptomycin in Britain at that time was so severe that patients who were not in the study did not have access to streptomycin treatment. Nevertheless, the planners of the study appear not to have felt the need to inform the patients about the goals and procedures of the study or to obtain their permission.

> "It was important for the success of the trial that the details of the control scheme should remain confidential," the study report states. "It is a matter of great credit to the many doctors concerned that this information was not made public throughout the 15 months of the trial, and the Committee is much indebted to them for their cooperation."[42]

The VA group was dealing with a patient population that was more aware of their options. Patients needed to be told about the drug and its risks as well as its benefits, though no formal consent process was required. At the January 1947 meeting of participants in the VA-Armed Forces study, Dr. Walker told the group:

> " It has seemed wise to have each patient who has received streptomycin, sign some general statement. A copy of something you might use for that purpose is enclosed in your folder."[48]

Dr. S.T. Allison, Chief of the Medical Service at the Rutland Heights (NJ) VA Tuberculosis Hospital, commented at the VA-Armed Forces study participants' meeting in May 1947: "This primarily is a research problem, but we in the field have to more or less sell this experiment to the patient." Allison went on to comment, in response to the suggestion that very small doses of streptomycin be tried:

> "If we are going to get patients to subject themselves to streptomycin treatment, we have to show some results or we won't get the patients. I know that in my hospital, where we have 500 patients under treatment for tuberculosis, it is one big family, and they are interested in results. If they see a group of patients putting on weight and getting better, they will be for streptomycin. On the other hand, if it is purely experimental, if we don't get results, one patient will say, 'So-and-so didn't get any benefit, so I won't take it. I won't subject myself to this treatment.' We have got to think not only of the research problem but of the clinical problem as well."[39]

Nevertheless, the use of a formal consent form appears to have been optional, and it is uncertain whether the VA patients realized that they were a part of a research protocol.

This issue of patient autonomy and its associated transfer of responsibility from the physician to the patient is one that still confronts clinical researchers and those who oversee their work.

Later studies of treatment of tuberculosis

A major difference between the original VA-Armed Forces study and those of the MRC and USPHS was that the original VA-Armed Forces investigation was planned by the investigators themselves, with little input from statisticians. As time went on and they gained more experience, the VA-Armed Forces group gradually came to accept statistical guidance, although they never carried out a placebo-controlled study.

Table 5.4. Reports involving antituberculosis chemotherapeutic agents
     cited under "Tuberculosis - therapy" in *Index Medicus*.
Entries are the number of citations mentioning the agent in their titles.

	1947	1948	1949	1950
Streptomycin	44	120	102	86
PAS	4	10	32	45
Combined agents	3	3	8	12
Thiosemicarbazones	0	2	8	42
Other antibiotics	2	13	12	10

Gradually, the VA studies and those of the MRC and USPHS grew more alike. In April 1948, the VA investigators began testing paraaminosalicylic acid (PAS) in combination with streptomycin, using the streptomycin-alone regimen for the control series. As soon as the streptomycin-PAS regimen was shown to be superior, it was taken as the control against which new treatments were tested. The MRC and USPHS groups used similar strategies, once the original question of efficacy of streptomycin was established. They no longer studied untreated control patients but instead compared patients receiving the new treatment with those receiving an established one.

After feeling their way along in the early days, learning as they gained experience with their studies, negotiating with the statisticians, and coping with the realities of human behavior, in 1960 the VA investigators established their concept of the essential principles of a clinical trial:

1. The design of the trial is of critical importance.
2. Ethical considerations are essential, particularly in the selection of regimens to be investigated.
3. The "experimental" regimen to be studied should be compared with a "control" series, usually the best known available form of therapy.
4. Such comparisons preferably should be concurrent, not retrospective.
5. Assignment to treatment should be by a method of random selection, as free from possible bias as the circumstances permit.
6. The number of patients studied should be sufficiently large to permit valid deductions to be drawn.
7. Every effort should be made to ensure that observations of results are as objective and uniform as possible.
8. Statistical guidance should be provided at all stages of the study, from design to rigid statistical evaluation of results.[49]

These principles form the basis for the extensive and productive VA Cooperative Studies Program of today.

References

1. Daniel, T.M., "An immunochemist's view of the epidemiology of tuberculosis." in *Prehistoric Tuberculosis in the Americas*, Buikstra, J.E., Editor. 1976, Department of Anthropology, Northwestern University: Evanston, IL 40-41.

2. Jones, R.S., *The History of the American Legion*. Indianapolis and New York: The Bobbs-Merrill Company, 1946, 125-126.

3. Hawley, P.R., "The tuberculosis problem of the Veterans' Administration." *Am Rev Tuberc*, 1947. **55**: 1-7.

4. *Tuberculosis Service*. Washington, D.C.: Veterans Administration, 1945

5. Edwards, H.R., "The National Tuberculosis Association and its interest in the tuberculous veteran." *Am Rev Tuberculosis*, 1947. **55**: 8-16.

6. Matz, P.B., "The effect of climate upon the treatment of pulmonary tuberculosis." *US Veterans' Bureau Medical Bulletin*, 1927. **3**: 1150-1159.

7. Matz, P.B., "The surgical treatment of pulmonary tuberculosis in the United States Veterans' Bureau." *Am Rev Tuberculosis*, 1929. **20**: 809-832.

8. Matz, P.B., "The end-results of The surgical treatment of pulmonary tuberculosis." *Am Rev Tubercul*. 1936. **33**: 533-548.

9. Veterans' Bureau Medical Council, "Report of Group of Tuberculosis." *US Veterans' Bureau Medical Bulletin*, 1927. **3**: 840-841.

10. Matz, P.B., "Statistical studies on tuberculosis in the United States Veterans' Bureau." *Medical Bulletin of the Veterans' Bureau*, 1926. **2**: 793-794.

11. Forbes, C.F., *Annual Report of the Director, United States Veterans' Bureau*. Washington, DC: Veterans Bureau, 1922, 31.

12. Hines, F.T., *Annual Report of the Administrator of Veterans' Affairs*. Veterans Administration, 1941, 7-8.

13. Carr, B.W., "Bone tuberculosis treated by actinotherapy." *US Veterans' Bureau Medical Bulletin*, 1927. **3**: 1003-1004.

14. Fisher, E., "Heliotherapy in the treatment of laryngeal tuberculosis." *US Veterans' Bureau Medical Bulletin*, 1927. **3**: 1066-1068.

15. Matz, P.B., "Tuberculosis in mental hospitals." *US Veterans' Bureau Medical Bulletin*, 1927. **3**: 490-491.

16. Matz, P.B., "The effect of intercurrent diseases on the clinical course and the hospitalization period of cases of pulmonary tuberculosis." *US Veterans' Bureau Medical Bulletin*, 1927. **3**: 998-1002.

17. Marcley, W.J., "End results of pulmonary tuberculosis-A study of 500 cases." *US Veterans' Bureau Medical Bulletin*, 1927. **3**: 128-133.

18. Park, W.E., "History of tuberculosis." *US Veterans' Bureau Medical Bulletin*, 1927. **3**: 692-699.

19. Carman, W.L., "Use of actiniotherapy with results of treatment in A case of lupus vulgaris." *US Veterans' Bureau Medical Bulletin*, 1927. **3**: 815-817.

20. McKnight, J.L., "Generalized tuberculous adenitis, with report of case." *US Veterans' Bureau Medical Bulletin*, 1927. **3**: 725-727.

21. Benedict, C.C., "Pericarditis complicating pulmonary tuberculosis with report of case." *US Veterans' Bureau Medical Bulletin*, 1927. **3**: 789-797.

22. Buckley, R.C., "Tuberculous ulcer of duodenum-Case report with postmortem findings." *US Veterans' Bureau Medical Bulletin*, 1927. **3**: 228-230.

23. Smith, R.W., "Paramount importance of early diagnosis in treatment of tuberculosis of spine." *US Veterans' Bureau Medical Bulletin*, 1927. **3**: 1226-1230.

24. Starns, C.E., "The importance of proper history taking in tuberculosis hospital." *US Veterans' Bureau Medical Bulletin*, 1927. **3**: 450-452.

25. "The tuberculous patient." *US Veterans' Bureau Medical Bulletin*, 1927. **3**: 505-507.

26. Hines, F.T., *Annual Report of VA Administrator*. 1941, 1-3.

27. Maisel, A.Q., "The veteran betrayed: How long will the Veterans' Administration continue to give third-rate medical care to first-rate men?" *The Reader's Digest*, April, 1945, 45-50.

28. Adkins, R.E., *Medical Care of Veterans*. Washington, DC: Government Printing Office, 1967, 174.

29. Amberson, J.B., McMahon, B.T. and Pinner, M., "A clinical trial of sanocrysin in pulmonary tuberculosis." *Am Rev Tuberculosis*, 1931. **24**: 401-435.

30. Interview with Nicholas D'Esopo, M.D., December 6,1995 at American Lung Association offices in Hamden, CT.

31. Hinshaw, H.C. and Feldman, W.H., "Evaluation of chemotherapeutic agents in clinical tuberculosis." *Am Rev Tuberculosis*, 1944. **50**: 202-213.

32. Schatz, A., Bugie, E. and Waksman, S.A., "Streptomycin, a substance exhibiting antibiotic activity against gram-positive and gram-negative bacteria." *Proc Soc Exp Biol Med*, 1944. **55**: 66-69.

33. Barnwell, J.B., Bunn, P.A. and Walker, A.M., "The effect of streptomycin upon pulmonary tuberculosis." *Am Rev Tuberc*, 1947. **56**: 485-507.

34. Hobby, G.L., *Penicillin: Meeting the Challenge*. New Haven and London: Yale University Press, 1985, 156-157.

35. Streptomycin Committee, "The effects of streptomycin on tuberculosis in man, report to the Council on Pharmacy and chemistry." *JAMA*, 1947. **135**: 634-641.

36. Interview with Gilbert Beebe, P.D., June 1, 1994 at a hotel lobby in Washington, DC.

37. "Minutes." *Third Streptomycin Conference*. May 1-3, 1947. St. Louis, Mo.: VA Branch Office, St. Louis. Mo, 1947, 125.

38. "Minutes." *First Streptomycin Conference*. December 12 -14, 1946. Chicago, IL: VA Branch Office #7, Chicago, IL, 1946,

39.   "Minutes." *Third Streptomycin Conference.* 5/1-3/47, 1947, 128.

40.   "Minutes." *Third Streptomycin Conference.* 5/1-3/47, 1947, 130-131.

41.   Hill, A.B., "Suspended Judgement: Memories of the British streptomycin trial in tuberculosis." *Controlled Clinical Trials*, 1990. **11**: 77-79.

42.   Marshall, G., Blacklock, J.W.S., Cameron, C., Capon, N.B., Cruickshank, R., Gaddum, J.H., Heaf, F.R.G., Hill, A.B., Houghton, L.E., Hoyle, J.C., Raistrick, H., Scadding, J.G., Tyler, W.H., Wilson, G.S. and D'Arcy, P., "Streptomycin treatment of pulmonary tuberculosis." *Brit Med J*, 1948. **2**: 769-782.

43.   Marks, H.M., *The Progress of Experiment: Science and Therapeutic Reform in the United States, 1900-1990.* Cambridge: Cambridge University Press, 1997, 122.

44.   Long, E.R. and Ferebee, S., "Controlled Investigation of Streptomycin Treatment in Pulmonary Tuberculosis." *Pub Health Reports*, 1950. **65**: 1421-1451.

45.   Ferebee, S.H. "Report on the USPHS Streptomycin Study Program." *Fifth Streptomycin Conference.* April 15-18, 1948. Chicago, IL: Veterans Administration Branch Office, Chicago, IL, 1948, 49.

46.   Letter from J.B. Amberson to E.R. Long, cited in Reference 43, page 124,

47.   Rothman, K.J. and Michels, K.B., "The continuing unethical use of placebo controls." *New Eng J Med*, 1994. **331**: 394-398.

48.   "Minutes." *Second Streptomycin Conference.* January 23-24, 1947. Chicago, IL: VA Branch Office #7, Chicago, IL, 1947b, 88.

49.   Tucker, W.B., "The evolution of the cooperative studies on the chemotherapy of tuberculosis of the Veterans Administration and Armed Forces of the U.S.A." *Adv Tuberc Res*, 1960. **10**: 1-68.

Chapter 6. The Atomic Medicine Program and the Birth of Nuclear Medicine

George Lyon and the Atomic Medicine program

One VA research area that took off quickly after World War II was research in the use of radioisotopes. During the autumn of 1946, General Hawley, the Chief Medical Director, became deeply concerned about the problems that atomic energy might create for the VA because of the possibility of nuclear warfare. He held a conference in his office on August 7, 1947, attended by key VA and military health officials, including officers who had worked on the Manhattan Engineering Project.[1] Attendees, besides himself, included Lt. Gen. Leslie R. Groves, Commander, and Col. James Cooney, Chief Medical Officer of the Manhattan Engineering District, the organization that developed the atomic bomb. Also attending were Maj. Gen. Raymond Bliss, Surgeon General, U.S. Army; Rear Admiral W.L. Wilcutts, Deputy Surgeon General, U.S. Navy; Maj. Gen. Malcolm Grow, Air surgeon, U.S. Air Force; Leonard Scheele, M.D., Surgeon General, U.S. Public Health Service; and George Marshall Lyon, M.D., former medical officer, Bikini atomic tests.

Dr. Lyon (Figure 6.1), a pediatrician from West Virginia, had been assigned to the Manhattan Project as a naval officer and was the ranking medical officer at the Bikini tests in the Pacific. Soon after Bikini, Lyon became the VA's expert on atomic energy. When he left the Navy, he retained the records of the military personnel who had been exposed in the various atomic tests. These were stored in a locked file in his office; when he left Central Office in 1956, they went with him.[2]

Dr. Lyon was recruited in 1947 as "Special Assistant to the Chief Medical Director for Atomic Medicine." His charge was to prepare the VA to handle claims for injuries associated with the atomic-bomb tests. As it turned out, few if any such claims were received, but the Atomic Medicine unit kept up with the literature on radiation effects. Soon, under Lyon's leadership, the VA set up a Radioisotope Section of the Research and Education Service, with Lyon as its chief. Lyon characterized the existence of the "Atomic Medicine" program as a secret, with emphasis on radioisotope research applications in the VA serving to divert interest from the nuclear warfare theme.[3] The VA became the lead agency for civil preparedness against an atomic attack, and staff of the radioisotope units in the hospitals were responsible for civil preparedness at the local level.[4]

Dr. Lyon, who knew most of the key people who had been in the Manhattan Project and the Navy atomic warfare program, used his personal contacts extensively in establishing the new VA radioisotope program. He quickly proceeded to set up radioisotope departments in as many VA hospitals as possible. At each of them, there was a physician chief and a radiation safety officer, generally a physicist with training in nuclear physics. These VA radiation physicists held courses for their communities on atomic preparedness and taught local police and fire departments how to handle Geiger counters. In 1949, the Atomic Medicine program published a *Training Guide for a Course in Radiological Defense.* By the summer of 1950, most VA staff physicians, nurses and dentists, as well as some 400 others had received this training.[1]

The physicians and scientists in these new VA radioisotope departments began to explore the uses of radioisotopes for diagnosis and treatment. In 1947, the Chief Medical Director established a Central Advisory Committee on Radiobiology and Radioisotopes.

Members of this committee, (Appendix IId and Figure 6.1) who were leaders in the use of radioisotopes in medicine and medical research, advised on all use of radioisotopes by the agency. But the committee also assisted in establishing the medical research program in general. Three of its members, who were especially close to Dr. Lyon, worked at a practical level to help establish VA radioisotope laboratories in different geographic areas. This committee was active from 1947 to 1961. It was not until 1955 that a similar advisory committee was appointed with responsibility for other aspects of the VA medical research program.

Figure 6.1: Meeting of the Central Advisory Committee on Radioisotopes
Left to right: Hugh Morgan, Perrin H. Long, George M. Lyon, Admiral Joel Boone (CMD), H.L.Friedell, Shields Warren, A.G.Moseley, Jr. Missing: Stafford Warren

The Radioisotope Laboratories

By the end of 1946, sites for six radioisotope laboratories had been identified, primarily based on the presence of staff and consultants who had been involved in the Manhattan Project.[5] The first of these to conduct routine clinical work with radioisotopes (as distinct from research studies) opened at Van Nuys, CA, in February 1948 with Mortimer E. Morton, M.D., as chief.[1] Others followed rapidly. By 1949, 12 radioisotope laboratories were functioning; by 1951, there were 14, employing 98 persons; and by the end of 1953, there were 33, with 202 employees. By 1960, 60 such laboratories had been established. In 1965, 86 VA hospitals were licensed under the Atomic Energy Commission to use radioisotopes; of them, 55 maintained separate Radioisotope Services. In time, these numbers grew until every VA medical center with an acute-care responsibility provided nuclear medicine services.

Figures 6.2 – 6.4: Relaxing at the 1949 Radioisotope conference in Washington, D.C.

Figure 6.2 Hudack, Henry Lanz, Raymond Libby, Bernard Roswit, Benedict Cassen, W. Saunders, Herbert Allen, George Meneely

Figure 6.3: Raymond Libby, Benedict Cassen, Mortimer Morton, Wallace Armstrong, Hymer Friedell, George Meneely, George Lyon

Figure 6.4: Benedict Cassen, Raymond Libby, Joe Meyer

In 1948, Dr. Lyon convened the first meeting of his Chiefs of Radioisotopes in VA Central Office. These meetings continued twice a year, later annually, until in the late 1950s they were subsumed in larger general annual VA research meetings (Chapter 3).

**Figure 6.5: Harold Weiler, George Lyon and Graham Moseley
lead the 1950 Radioisotope Conference**

**Figure 6.6: Attendees, Fifth Semiannual VA Radioisotope Conference, VAH
Framingham, 1950**

**Back row, left to right: H Allen, Jr., Henry Lanz, R. Chodos, ?, ?, ?, ?.
Middle row: M.E.Morton, H.Weiler, F.Wasserman, W.Saunders, Geo. Leroy, Leslie
Zieve, Wm Reilly, Ray Libby, Reginald Shipley.
Front row: Belton Burrows, Geo Meneely, Alfred Lawton, Gasser (Manager), George
Lyon, Joseph Ross, A.G.Moseley, Jr., Ed Williams (USPHS)**

So eager was Dr. Lyon to set up new radioisotope laboratories that he actively sought out good people in a variety of fields to start them. As a pediatrician, he did not hesitate to recruit fellow pediatricians. The majority of the early VA Chiefs were specialists in Internal Medicine, however, and this relatively heavy balance of internists continued in VA Nuclear Medicine for many years. In the VA, the Radioisotope Service in the field hospitals was an independent unit; this encouraged variety and individualism in its chiefs.

In 1950, Joseph Ross, M.D., at the Framingham (MA) VA Hospital, together with Herbert Allen, M.D., from Houston (TX), Reginald A. Shipley, M.D., from Cleveland (OH) and Leslie Zieve, M.D., from Minneapolis (MN), formed a group to plan a Cooperative Study of Radioiodine Therapy of Hyperthyroidism. Dr. Ross chaired the group and reported its early work at a meeting of VA Chiefs of Radioisotopes held in Central Office in June 1951. A Case Study Protocol was developed for use by all participating Radioisotope laboratories. At the next meeting, in Los Angeles in January 1952, the protocol was agreed upon by the participants and the study was launched. Its goals were to determine the relation between dose (in microcuries per gram concentrated by the thyroid) and the outcome of treatment, and to search for characteristics that might predict a patient's response to treatment. The group also proposed to follow patients over the long term to identify any adverse effects of the treatment, especially the development of thyroid cancer.[6] This study, performed on a purely voluntary basis with little urging from Central Office, succeeded in collecting an early body of data, but it failed to reach a definitive conclusion. Some of the chiefs objected to the degree of standardization required. Even more importantly, Dr. Ross became the founding Associate Dean at the new UCLA School of Medicine in 1954, and after that he lacked time to pursue the study.[7] Nevertheless, this study led to research within the VA to improve the thyroid dose estimate for radioiodine.[8, 9] It also set the pace for an extensive, more definitive, study to address these questions funded by the NIH in the late 1950s.[10]

While the radioisotope laboratories increasingly concentrated on providing the latest in patient care, they remained at the forefront of nuclear medicine research. At the Wadsworth VA Hospital in Los Angeles in the late 1940s, Herbert Allen developed a method to map the radioactivity in the thyroid gland by using a directional probe at many points along a grid over the neck.[11]

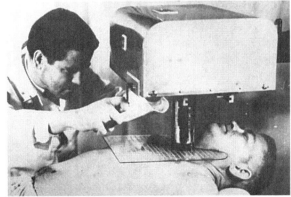

**Figure 6.7 Herbert Allen, M.D., manually scans
the radioactivity in a patient's thyroid gland**

This technique gave crude imaging information, but it took several hours to complete a study. Dr. Allen challenged Dr. Benedict Cassen, a physicist at UCLA, to develop an electrically driven scanner. The result was the first nuclear medicine scanner, developed in

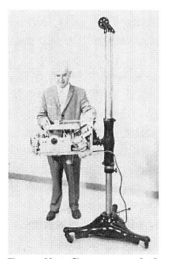

Figure 6.8: Benedict Cassen and the first radionuclide scanner

1950 by Drs. Cassen, Allen and Goodwin and used to study the thyroids of patients at Wadsworth.[12, 13] At the January 1952 meeting in Los Angeles, Drs. Franz Bauer, William E. Goodwin and Raymond L. Libby demonstrated this new device to "mechanically scan" radioiodine in the thyroid gland. This was the beginning of the imaging of radioisotope distribution in intact persons, a technique that has revolutionized the diagnostic and therapeutic approaches to many diseases of many organs and played a key role in improving patient care.

Later in the 1950s, Manuel Tubis, Ph.D., a radiochemist at Wadsworth, developed a variety of ^{131}I-labeled compounds, of which the most important was iodohippurate (hippuran), a compound that proved very useful in the study of kidney disorders.[14, 15]

Figure 6.9: Manual Tubis, Ph.D.

And in the late 1950s, Drs. Berson and Yalow of the Radioisotope Service at the Bronx VA Hospital announced their radioimmunoassay method (Chapter 11), a discovery that later won a Nobel Prize for Dr. Yalow. This technique has revolutionized the measurement of hormones, drugs and body chemicals in tiny samples of blood or tissue.

Local governance

A hospital Radioisotope Committee regulated the activities of the radioisotope laboratories at the local level. Research in these laboratories did not come under the control of the hospital Research and Education Committee until the separate Radioisotope Service in Central Office was dissolved in 1960, making the radioisotope research program a part of Research Service. After that, the hospital's Radioisotope Committee became a subcommittee of the Research and Education Committee, and approval of both of the local committees (Radioisotope and Research and Education) was needed before a research project involving radioisotopes could start. At first, the members of the Radioisotope Committee were exclusively non-VA consultants. Later, the committee also included VA staff experienced in radioisotope use.

By 1962, radioisotope use was widespread in the VA (Appendix Va), and patients could be examined through a wide variety of clinical radioisotope studies (Appendix Vb).

Graham Moseley

Shortly after he arrived in VA Central Office, Dr. Lyon recruited A. Graham Moseley to join him. Moseley had been on the chemistry faculty at Marshall University before World War II. During the war, he was in the Navy and was present with Lyon at the Bikini tests. At Bikini, he is reported to have detected high levels of ^{24}Na in a ship's onboard still used to prepare drinking water from sea water.

Figure 6.10: A. Graham Moseley

When Lyon became ACMD/R&E in 1952, he appointed Moseley to be Chief of the Radioisotope Program, which became a separate service when R&E became a recognized independent Office in 1953. Moseley continued to administer the program until he retired in 1967. He had an intimate knowledge of all of the radioisotope laboratories, and he used his considerable talents and knowledge of the "system" to expand the radioisotope program. He is remembered as "a delightful guy who ran the program and tried to give everyone what he needed to do a good job."[16]

When Ralph Casteel left Research and Education to become Special Assistant to the Chief Medical Director in 1956, Dr. Lyon assigned Moseley the additional duties of his "Special Assistant." Moseley continued as both Special Assistant to the ACMD/R&E and head of the Radioisotope Program until 1965, when Benjamin Wells, then the ACMD/R&E, arranged to have Moseley and the radioisotope program transferred out of the Research and Education Office and into the Professional Services Office.[18] Moseley's duties as Special Assistant to the ACMD/R&E were turned over to a new Deputy ACMD, James A. Halsted, M.D. This was the official beginning of the Nuclear Medicine Service in VACO as a clinical entity, with Moseley as its Director.

At that time, Moseley wrote to all of the Radioisotope Services asking for material to include in a brochure he intended to write about the radioisotope research program. The brochure itself seems to have disappeared, if it was ever completed, but many of the responses are still available. They paint a picture of a group of contented, productive, hospital-based clinicians and scientists, spending much of their effort on patient-oriented research but also conducting many types of bench research and establishing a rapidly increasing number of patient-care procedures. Their research contributed to many disciplinary areas that use the tracer principle.[19]

Richard Ogburn, Belton Burrows and Gerald Hine

When Graham Moseley retired in 1967, his position as Director of the Central Office Radioisotope Service was filled by Richard Ogburn, M.D., who had been Chief, Radioisotopes, at the Omaha VA Hospital and had set up the first hospital-based nuclear reactor, in addition to running an active clinical and research program. Sadly, Ogburn developed carcinoma of the pancreas and died shortly after he was appointed.

Figure 6.12: Richard Ogburn, M.D.

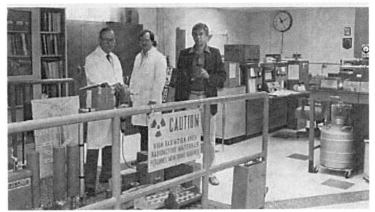

Figure 6.13: TRIGA reactor at the Omaha VAMC

After Ogburn's death, the Director position remained vacant. Concerned about this lack of leadership, four Nuclear Medicine Chiefs, William Blahd from Los Angeles, Irvin Kaplan from Hines (IL), Richard Peterson from Iowa City and Belton Burrows from Boston, formed a "search committee" and met with Lyndon Lee, the ACMD for Professional Services. They offered to take over the program on an interim basis in rotation. Burrows (Figure 6.6) received the first month's assignment. At the end of that month, the others persuaded him to continue. However, Burrows did not want to move to Washington or to give up his program in Boston. So, for the next five years, he commuted between Boston and Washington, managing the national clinical Nuclear Medicine program as well as the nuclear medicine programs at his hospital and at Boston University.[16, 20, 21] However, he was responsible only for the clinical Nuclear Medicine Service and not for leading research in the field, still the purview of Research Service. In 1969, Gerald Hine, Ph.D., a physicist who had worked with Burrows at Boston and then for the International Atomic Energy Commission, came to the Central Office Research Service as Program Chief for Radioisotope Research.[22]

Figure 6.14 Gerald Hine, Ph.D.

The place of nuclear medicine within the VA

Over the years, nuclear medicine in the VA has experienced a number of organizational changes. Although it started as a Section of the Atomic Medicine Division within Research and Education Service, it also originally enjoyed a direct line to the Chief Medical Director. In 1953, when Research and Education Service was elevated to a freestanding

Office, it contained three services, Atomic Medicine, Research and Education. In 1960, the Atomic Medicine Service (which was active only through its Radioisotope Section) was abolished, and the radioisotope research program was incorporated within Research Service.

Increasingly, with maturation of the field, more and more of the radioisotope work at the VA hospitals became established patient care procedures rather than pure research. Some clinical funding of the hospital-based program began in 1955. In 1965, as mentioned above, a clinical Nuclear Medicine Service was officially founded within Professional Services in VACO, though the hospital Radioisotope Services were still considered to be primarily research. Finally, in about 1971, when Mark J. Musser, M.D., was Chief Medical Director, Nuclear Medicine became a clinical service at the VA hospitals, with support of patient-care activities coming from clinical funds rather than research funds. By 1972, when James J. Smith, M.D., became Director of Nuclear Medicine in Central Office, the clinical Nuclear Medicine Service had become entirely independent of the Research Service.

Basic scientists in the Radioisotope Services

The physicists and other basic scientists recruited into the early radioisotope program served as a nucleus for later development of a corps of basic scientists for the VA research program as a whole. Stemming from their importance to the "atomic medicine" program, the nuclear medicine scientists commanded high salary grades, and this soon led to upgrading of all basic scientist positions in VA research.[4] Among the nonclinician scientists who started their VA work in the radioisotope program of the 1940s, 1950s and 1960s were Rosalyn Yalow at the Bronx, who won the Nobel Prize; Joe Meyer, later VACO Program Chief in Basic Sciences; David Cohn, later ACOS for Research and Development at Kansas City; Gerald Hine at Boston; Joseph Rabinowitz at Philadelphia; Helmut Gutman at Minneapolis; Charles C. Irving at Memphis; Raymond Lindsay at Birmingham; and Manuel Tubis, Nome Baker and Michael Shatz at Wadsworth.

Figure 6.15: Rex Huff, M.D.

Nuclear Medicine as a physician specialty

In 1955, the Society of Nuclear Medicine was founded by a small group of physicians and scientists, including Rex Huff, Chief of Radioisotopes at the Seattle VA Hospital. Huff

176

gave the first paper in the scientific session of the Society's first meeting, "Estimates of Cardiac Output by In Vivo Counting of I^{131} Labeled HSA." VA nuclear medicine physicians and scientists have been prominent in the Society of Nuclear Medicine ever since.

In 1969, nuclear medicine was one of the subject areas in which the VA's new Research and Education Training Program (Chapter 14) was established, with a distinguished selection committee.[22] Six of these formal training programs were in place in 1970, and their numbers grew over the next two years. These programs, funded by research money but administered by the Education Service, were designed to train physician trainees with at least two years of prior residency training in a related field in both the patient care and the research aspects of nuclear medicine. The intent was to provide an entry opportunity for physicians who wanted to enter academic nuclear medicine. This program arrived at an opportune moment for the field of nuclear medicine, which at that time had no specialty board and no formal residency programs. In the Nuclear Medicine Training Programs, young physicians learned both clinical and research skills. Many remained in the VA, enriching the program's research and clinical components. In 1972, this program was folded into the VA's regular residency program, and residency slots were added to hospitals' allocations to replace the lost trainee slots. In this way, the VA developed nuclear medicine residency programs well before most other institutions supported them.

The physicians who entered the early VA radioisotope program have been among the pioneers in the emerging specialty of nuclear medicine. Among the many physicians who contributed to the program in the 1950s and early 1960s and emerged as leaders in nuclear medicine practice and research were Solomon Berson, William Blahd, James Pittman, Leslie Zieve, Ervin Kaplan, Marcus Rothchild, Belton Burrows, Ralph Cavalieri, Robert Donati, Clayton Rich, Lindy Kumagai, Richard Spencer, Ralph Gorton, Gerald Denardo, David Baylink, Walter Whitcomb, Robert Meade, Francis Zacharewich, Leo Oliner and Robert Chodos. All of these physicians have made important contributions to medicine and medical science.

In 1972, the American Board of Nuclear Medicine gave its first certifying examination for physician specialists. At about the same time, access to nuclear medicine services became a requirement for hospital certification. The specialty of Nuclear Medicine had matured. It was now in the mainstream of American medicine. Within the VA, Nuclear Medicine services took their place next to the other clinical services.

Today, the primary job of a VA nuclear medicine physician is patient care. Many continue to be active in research, but their research is now under the same umbrella as that of other VA research investigators. Those who recall the early days take pride in the VA as the birthplace of their specialty.

References

1.   Lyon, G.W. "VA radioisotope program: Historical." *25th meeting of the Committee on Veterans Medical Problems.* Washington, DC: National Academy of Sciences, 1952, 553-554.

2.   Interview with Clo Gooding, May 2, 1988 at VA Central Office, Washington, DC.

3.   Lyon, G.W. "VA radioisotope program: General statement of objectives and principles." *25th meeting of the Committee on Veterans Medical Problems.* Washington, DC: National Academy of Sciences, 1952, 554-556.

4.   Interview with Joe Meyer, Ph.D., May 4, 1992 at Dr. Meyer's home in suburban Maryland.

5.   Interview with Herbert Allen, M.D., January 28, 1994 at Dr. Allen's office in Houston, TX.

6.   Ross, J. "Cooperative study of radioiodine therapy for hyperthyroidism." *25th meeting of the Committee on Veterans Medical Problems.* December 5, 1952. Washington, DC: National Academy of Sciences, 1952, 576-578.

7.   Telephone interview with Joseph Ross, M.D., February 1, 1990.

8.   Goodwin, W.E., Cassen, B. and Bauer, F.K., "Thyroid gland weight determination from thyroid scintigrams with postmortem verification." *Radiology,* 1953. **61**: 88-92.

9.   Bauer, F.K. and Blahd, W.H., "Treatment of hyperthyroidism with individually calculated doses of 131I." *Arch Intern Med,* 1957. **99**: 194-201.

10.   Dobyns, B.M., Sheline, G.E., Workman, J.B., Tompkins, E.A., McConahey, W.M. and Becker, D.V., "Malignant and benign neoplasms of the thyroid in patients treated for hyperthyroidism: A report of the cooperative thyrotoxicosis therapy follow-up study." *J Clin Endocrinol Metab,* 1974. **38**: 976-998.

11.   Allen, H.C., Libby, R. and Cassen, B., "The scintillation counter in clinical studies of human thyroid physiology using I131." *J Clin Endocrinol Metab,* 1951. **11**: 492-511.

12.   Cassen, B., Curtis, L., Reed, C. and Libby, R., "Instrumentation for I131 use in medical studies." *Nucleonics,* 1951. **9**: 46-50.

13.   Bauer, F.K., Goodwin, W.E., Libby, R. and Cassen, B., "Visual delineation of thyroid glands in vivo." *J Lab Clin Med,* 1952. **39**: 153-158.

14.   Tubis, M., Posnick, E. and Nordyke, R.A., "Preparation and use of I131 labeled sodium iodohippurate in kidney function tests." *Proc Soc Exp Biol Med,* 1960. **103**: 497-498.

15.   Nordyke, R.A., Tubis, M. and Blahd, W.H., "Use of radioiodinated hippuran for individual kidney function tests." *J Lab Clin Med,* 1960. **56**: 438-445.

16.   Interview with William Blahd, M.D., November 8, 1991 at Dr. Blahd's office in the VA Medical Center, Los Angeles, CA.

17.   Telephone interview with James Pittman, M.D., March 13, 1988.

18.   Interview with Ralph Casteel, May 3, 1988 at a restaurant in Bethesda, MD.

19.   Letters from Radioisotope Service Chiefs, collected by Clo Gooding., written in 1965 to A. Graham Moseley, Jr.

20. Interview with Ervin Kaplan, M.D., May 1, 1994 at Dr. Kaplan's home in Wilmette, IL.

21. Interview with Belton Burrows, M.D., October 27, 1992 at Dr. Burrows's home in Brookline, MA.

22. *Medical Research in the Veterans Administration, FY 1969*. Washington, DC: Government Printing Office, 1969, ix.

Part III. The VA research program takes off, 1954 - 1959

Chapter 7. The Intramural Research Program, 1954-1959

Research becomes a Service

In 1953, the Research and Education Service in the young VA Department of Medicine and Surgery (DM&S) was upgraded in status, becoming the new Research and Education Office with three Services: Research, Education and Atomic Medicine. George M. Lyon, M.D., the ACMD/R&E succeeding Dr. Cushing, headed the new Office[1] but did not give up his title of Director, Atomic Medicine Service. Although Graham Moseley actually ran the radioisotope program, Dr. Lyon continued his intense interest and, some felt, favored it.[2] John C. Nunemaker, M.D., was a very active Director of the Education Service after serving as acting Chief, Research Section, during 1952[3] when Alfred Lawton left.

Figure 7.1 John Nunemaker, M.D.

Figure 7.2 Martin Cummings, M.D.

Martin M. Cummings, M.D., becomes Director, Research Service

Shortly after the new Research Service was created, Martin M. Cummings, M.D., became its Director. Cummings had worked at the Tuberculosis Evaluation Center in Atlanta (part of the USPHS's Centers for Disease Control) from 1947 to 1950. Drs. Magnuson and Barnwell, after visiting Dr. Cummings in his laboratories, persuaded him to move to the Atlanta VA Hospital in 1950 to start a tuberculosis research laboratory and take over care of tuberculosis patients. In 1954, they recruited him to VACO.[4]

Research Service, 1954

When Cummings arrived in Central Office, his professional staff consisted of only three individuals. Harold Weiler (figure 6.11), a former high school science teacher, was "Chief, Research Laboratories," and worked on plans for building and equipping general medical research laboratories. Dr. Marjorie Wilson, "Chief of Contracts Research" left soon after Cummings's arrival and was succeeded by Dr. T. S. Moise. Cummings recalled that a large fraction of the contract budget went for prosthetics research. The third staff member, Graham Moseley, worked closely with Cummings even though he was not officially in the Research Service.

Research space remained a big issue. There was little point in increasing the budget unless intramural physicians and scientists had space to do their work. By this time, some research space was included in plans for new hospitals, and a great deal of effort went into preparing these plans. Cummings remembered this as a difficult but rewarding process, in which his initial plans usually ended up being significantly reduced by VA's own construction design section, as well as by review staff at the Bureau of the Budget. In some instances, he recalled, space for research was provided through a patchwork approach:

> "I remember the VA Hospital in Durham because the faculty at Duke was real gung-ho. They wanted to do a lot of work in the VA. After our construction plans had been trimmed way back, they put up a Quonset hut adjoining the VA and made that a research facility. A lot of the medical schools contributed a lot of space as well. I don't claim to have had any intimate influence on a design but I always fought for a strategic location and I fought for an adequate square footage."[4]

As a result of the efforts of Weiler and Nunemaker (while Nunemaker was responsible for Research)[5], Research Service could soon offer generic plans for laboratory renovation and lists of equipment for setting up new laboratories. To save money and paper work, Central Office bought some frequently-needed equipment in volume for distribution to laboratories. Cummings, Weiler, and Moseley worked together to design both medical research and radioisotope laboratories.[4]

The Research program reaches out

Cummings worked hard to improve VA affiliations with medical schools. For example, he rapidly opened negotiations with the new UCLA medical school, which lacked research laboratories for arriving faculty. Renovations at Wadsworth VA Hospital provided laboratories for these faculty members. Admiral Boone, the CMD, and Stafford Warren, the UCLA dean, reached an informal agreement which Cummings carried out.[4] The VA paid for setting up the laboratories but thereafter made very little financial contribution to the UCLA faculty programs using the labs. However, the presence of faculty members, working side by side with VA investigators, enriched Wadsworth's research program. Even after the UCLA Medical Center, which included faculty laboratories, opened in 1955, several full-time UCLA faculty members remained at Wadsworth. Meanwhile, as the intramural program at Wadsworth grew, it took over space developed for UCLA. A highly productive medical research program followed.

NIH grants become available to VA investigators

During a visit to Los Angeles to help implement the UCLA affiliation, Cummings talked with Samuel Bassett, M.D., a VA physician and investigator also on the UCLA faculty. Bassett complained that VA investigators were not allowed to compete for NIH funds.

Shortly after that visit, Cummings talked with Ernest Allen, the Associate Director of the Division of Research Grants at NIH. Allen told him that NIH had been receiving applications from VA investigators but had turned them all down administratively, owing to a lack of a funding precedent. After Cummings raised the issue, Allen looked into the policy history and checked the legal language. He found nothing in the law to forbid NIH from funding principal investigators from the VA. Shortly thereafter, Cummings and Allen went together to Philadelphia for an NIH site visit. They discussed the matter further and on the return trip drafted an agreement to allow VA people to compete for NIH funds through their affiliated universities.[4] Allen proceeded to make the change in policy at NIH. The new availability of research funding, which Cummings later described as a major incentive for recruitment and retention of VA physicians and scientists, was announced within VA in January 1954.[7]

Promoting VA Research

When John Barnwell became ACMD in 1956, he conceptually broadened the scope of the research program. It was natural that the tuberculosis studies grew more closely identified with Research Service during his period of R&E leadership. He encouraged interaction between his staff and other research leaders in VACO.

Barnwell was a good critical observer of research, even though he himself was not very active in research except for his interest in the tuberculosis cooperative studies. Barnwell was a humanist and philosopher. He remained current in his field and was also personally generous.[4]

Barnwell's predecessor, Dr. Lyon, had taken a rather conservative approach toward seeking support for VA research outside the agency. In contrast, Barnwell encouraged Cummings to "do anything honorable to improve the budget." Barnwell, as well as Dr. Middleton, who became Chief Medical Director in 1955, worked with Members of Congress and professional organizations toward this goal. Cummings and Barnwell made contact with Mary Lasker and Florence Mahoney. These influential research advocates arranged for meetings with Senator Lister Hill, Chairman of the Appropriations Committee, and other Congressmen who became interested in the VA research program.

Another strong supporter of VA research who was particularly influential with the Congress was prominent Houston surgeon Michael DeBakey, who had been active on the Committee for Veterans Medical Problems since its inception. De Bakey recalled that "in those early days, I was there every year testifying both in the House and the Senate for their appropriations for research and emphasizing ... this was the way to advance the quality of care in the VA—by putting in research and having these committee affiliations with medical schools an integral part of that activity."[8]

William Middleton, M.D.

William S. Middleton, M.D., the Chief Medical Director from 1955 to 1963, was a strong advocate for the VA research program. Dr. Middleton had been Dean of the University of

Wisconsin School of Medicine since 1935. He had pushed the concept of VA-medical school affiliation since the beginning of DM&S, and affiliations flourished during his term as Chief Medical Director. He viewed his role as physician leader. Each week while he was in Central Office, Middleton made clinical rounds at the Washington (DC) VA Hospital. He was a hard taskmaster, respected by all, loved by many and feared by some. He furthered the research program in any way he could, and his support was critical to the program's growth spurt during his years as Chief Medical Director.

Cummings called Middleton "the most extraordinary administrator that I ever met in the VA. If you were ever invited to travel with him and go to the field, he would do his duty and perform the necessary business with the hospital director and all of the staff, but you'd never get out of a VA hospital without making rounds with him and seeing patients. And he taught me a lot of medicine while we were both in an administrative job."[4]

Figure 7.3 William S. Middleton, M.D.

While he was in Central Office, Cummings ran a personal research laboratory and saw patients at Mt. Alto (Washington, DC) VA Hospital. He was also on the faculty of George Washington University Medical School and lectured there. But he spent more time at his Mt. Alto laboratory, where he was assisted by two technicians and a postdoctoral fellow in a study of sarcoidosis. Both Barnwell and Middleton encouraged these academic activities.

VA medical research becomes law

In 1955, Congress appropriated an explicit VA research budget for the first time. But, in dealings with Congress, Cummings discovered that a lack of legal authorization for research within the VA was a major impediment to improving the research budget. Middleton agreed to Cummings's efforts seeking legal authorization. The political dealings were successful. In September 1958, with passage of Title 38, USC, section 4101, the words "including medical research" were added to the legal definition of the mission of the DM&S.[9] This helped to justify increasing funding for VA medical research.

As a part of their efforts to educate Congress, Drs. Barnwell, Cummings and Nunemaker, with encouragement from Dr. Middleton, prepared *Medical Research in the Veterans Administration*, the first annual report to the Congress on the VA's research program. This first report, presenting material from Fiscal Year 1956, was published on March 5, 1957.[10] In his transmittal letter Dr. Middleton said, "The compelling force to accelerate medical research within the Veterans' Administration has been tempered only by difficulties in engaging qualified medical staff and in achieving the necessary expansion of laboratory space and related physical facilities." *Medical Research in the Veterans Administration* continued through 1975 as an annual report, describing all aspects of the VA medical research program, including research supported by patient care services and the Follow-up Agency. An annual "supplement" detailed individual research projects.

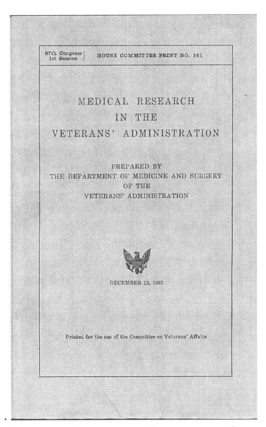

Figure 7.4 The VA's annual report to Congress on its research program

This report had evolved from a simple catalog inventory of research projects. When Middleton took Cummings on visits to hospitals, he would complain, "We don't have anything like the NIH Inventory of Research Projects." Cummings set out to create such an inventory. Marjorie Wilson, who returned to Central Office in 1956 as Assistant Director, Education Service, under John Nunemaker worked with Cummings on this effort. They received important help from Marguerite Duran of Medical Records, who indexed and classified the research projects. In 1956, this catalog contained over 3,600 projects and had increased to 5,000 by the time Cummings left Central Office in 1959. Cummings took this catalog with him whenever he went to Capitol Hill and used it as ammunition to show Members of Congress that the VA was conducting excellent research work.[4]

Beginnings of the Career Development Program

The VA Research Career Development Program, which received high acclaim through the years as a source of physician leadership in the VA and academia, began in 1956 with the Clinical Investigator Program. Drs. Cummings and Nunemaker, encouraged by Dr. Middleton, initiated the concept of providing young physicians with VA appointments to concentrate on research.[4]

When Marjorie Wilson returned to VA Central Office, her major task was to organize the Clinical Investigator program. In preparation, she reviewed programs of the NIH, the American Heart Association and other organizations and established a formal system of applications and an evaluation committee. The "Selection Committee for Clinical Investigators," forerunner of the long-standing Research Career Development Committee, was established in November 1956. Its founding members were J. Burns Amberson, M.D., from New York's Bellevue Hospital; Stanley E. Dorst, M.D., Dean, University of Cincinnati School of Medicine; Maxwell Finland, M.D., from Harvard Medical School; Carl A. Moyer, M.D., from Washington University, St. Louis and Harold G. Wolff, M.D., from Cornell. From its inception, this committee upheld high selection standards.[11] The selectees, from the very first group, made major contributions to academic medicine and the VA medical program.[12]

Dr. Wilson also started the Senior Medical Investigator program in 1959, modeled on programs for senior scientists such as the American Heart Association Established Investigator program. The Selection Committee for Clinical Investigators also reviewed the Senior Medical Investigators, but Central Office leadership played an active role in their selection. Drs. Auerbach, Gross and Freis,[13-15] among the earliest appointees, all recalled in interviews that they first heard of the program when they received calls, from Dr. Middleton or Dr. Cummings, inviting them to accept the appointment. Senior Medical Investigators could work independently on research of their choosing. They were permitted to accept teaching and patient care responsibilities, but their primary effort was on research. As with the Clinical Investigators, Senior Medical Investigators were supported directly from research funds.

New Central Office Research staff

Charles Chapple, M.D., came to the Central Office Research Service in 1956 as Chief of Clinical Studies (cooperative studies). Chapple, a pediatrician friend of Dr. Lyon, had previously been at Children's Hospital in Philadelphia and was Professor of Pediatrics at the University of Pennsylvania. He had been honored by election to the "Young Turks" and held several consultantships. In addition, Chapple was an accomplished amateur archeologist and botanist. While in the Navy in the Aleutians, he had discovered three new plant species, one named after him. He invented the Isolette infant incubator and a humidification device, which led to the Croupette.[4]

About 1958, Chapple took on special responsibility for furthering research in aging. An Advisory Committee on Problems of Aging was established in December 1955, with rotating membership of five leaders in the field. Abraham Dury, Ph.D., who served on this committee in the early 1960s, recalled that meetings dealt primarily with policy and strategic issues and did not review the science of ongoing projects.[16] This committee assisted Chapple in encouraging research relevant to aging, a problem of a special interest to Chief Medical Director Middleton.

W. Edward Chamberlain, M.D., came to VA Central Office in 1957 as "Special Assistant to the CMD for Atomic Medicine," apparently recruited by Dr. Lyon to be his successor.[17] A radiologist, Dr. Chamberlain had been Professor of Radiology at Temple University Medical School. He served on the Committee on Veterans Medical Problems from 1956 to 1958. From 1958 to 1960, Chamberlain's title was "Assistant Director (Plans), Research Service." In 1960, he received the Longstreth Medal from the Franklin Institute in Philadelphia for his earlier innovative contributions to radiology.[18]

The Research Advisory Committee

By the 1950s, the Committee on Veterans Medical Problems (Chapter 4) had become less active in advising the VA intramural research program. To fill this gap, in September 1955, six months after William S. Middleton became Chief Medical Director, the VA appointed its own Advisory Committee on Research. This committee (Appendix IIe) continued to be active until 1960, when it was reconstituted. It reviewed the research program and advised about new directions. Generally, a new program such as the Clinical Investigator program would be reviewed and approved by this committee before implementation. At times, especially in the early years, the committee met at individual hospitals to review the local research program. However, they did not review individual research projects.[2]

The annual Research Conference

The annual research conferences, started by Dr. Cushing at the Atlanta meeting in January 1952 (Chapter 3), continued to be well attended and popular. Invited were all ACOS/R&Es, Chiefs of the Radioisotope Services, Clinical Investigators and Senior Medical Investigators, as well as other VA research scientists whose papers were accepted for presentation.

The second annual research conference was held at the Houston VA Hospital and the next seven at the Memphis VA Hospital. By the December, 1959, tenth conference, the group was too large to meet in a VA facility and began meeting for the next eight years at the Netherlands Hilton Hotel in Cincinnati. By 1959, the Annual Research Conference required two concurrent sessions for presentation of 108 papers chosen from 288 submitted abstracts.[19]

At the 1959 conference, attendees established a Middleton Award for research accomplishment to recognize the importance of Dr. Middleton's support for the research program. "The managers of VA installations" were to nominate recipients, and a special committee with representatives from both the field and Central Office was to make the selection. The Middleton Award "is considered the highest honor that can be given by colleagues in recognition of outstanding quality in research."[20] Solomon A. Berson and Rosalyn S. Yalow, who later won the Nobel Prize, received the first Middleton award the following year at the annual research conference. The award is still given annually, and its recipients (Appendix I) reflect the spectrum of VA medical research.

Growth of the Cooperative Studies Program

More and more VA physicians began to recognize the potential of the VA as a site for cooperative clinical trials. By 1956, the studies on chemotherapy of tuberculosis (Chapter 5) had expanded to include studies of other pulmonary diseases and an intensive collaborative effort to develop and standardize pulmonary-function tests. These studies were extended to include coccidioidomycosis and histoplasmosis. Fifty-four VA and four military hospitals collaborated in these studies, and their reports were distributed to 35 foreign countries as well as throughout the United States. As a separate effort, eight VA hospitals collaborated in a study of possible effects of tranquilizing drugs on tuberculosis patients who were also psychotic.[21]

A study of the new antihypertensive drugs began in eight VA hospitals.[22] This study (Chapter 9), later brought the VA wide recognition and won Dr. Freis the Lasker Award and nomination for the Nobel Prize.

A new study of therapies for esophageal varices[23] compared medical methods to surgical procedures. This study group continued into the mid 1970s, comparing long-term results in patients who underwent portacaval shunts with a control group treated medically. The procedure was found to have no survival or life style benefit,[24] but study showed that portacaval shunt does decrease the hematological problems of hypersplenism.[25]

At the end of 1956, plans included cooperative studies on resistant staphylococcal infections, sarcoidosis and treatment of coronary artery disease.[26] Several cooperative studies on cancer chemotherapy were in progress.[27] The number of active studies grew rapidly; the FY 1960 annual report listed 34.[28]

By 1959, the VA cooperative studies on chemotherapy of psychiatric disorders (Chapter 8) were well under way. The independent cooperative study of patients diagnosed with psychosis and tuberculosis disbanded, reporting essentially negative findings: the combination of anti-tuberculosis drugs and various tranquilizers was not harmful and isoniazide, even in high doses, had no adverse effect on psychiatric status of patients in need of mental hospital care. Electric shock therapy combined with anti-tuberculosis drugs was found not to cause untoward complications, and management of these patients' disease on full activity without bed rest was effective. Therapeutic results for the patients' tuberculosis were very good, and the full activity program was believed valuable in management of the psychiatric condition. Annual chest x-rays for all patients in neuropsychiatric hospitals, with immediate isolation of actual or suspected tuberculosis cases, resulted in a marked decline in new cases. A randomized study of isoniazide administration to such patients was planned but not put into effect because of the small number of newly discovered cases.

Table 7.1. VA cooperative study groups active during the 1950s

Study	Years active
Chemotherapy of tuberculosis	1946-1974
Prefrontal lobotomy	1950-1956
Multiple sclerosis	1954-1963
Sarcoidosis	1954-1956
Pulmonary function testing	1954-1965
Antihypertensive drugs	1956-1975
VA cancer chemotherapy group	1956-1968
Western cancer chemotherapy group	1956-1964
Southwestern cancer chemotherapy group	1956-1964
Esophageal varices	1956-1975
Peptic ulcer surgery	1956-1972
Ruptured intervertebral disk	1956-1967
Surgery of Parkinsonism	1956-1968
Hospital infections	1956-1963
Coccidioidomycosis	1957-1961
Histoplasmosis	1957-1965
Blastomycosis	1957-1965
Tuberculosis in psychotic patients	1957-1959
Atherosclerosis	1957-1972
Lung cancer	1957-1975
Adjuvant Cancer Chemotherapy	1957-1975
Surgery of solitary pulmonary nodules	1957-1968
Lung cancer diagnosis	1957-1962
Surgery of coronary artery disease	1957-1975
Evaluation of analgesics	1957-1962
Chemotherapy in psychiatry	1957-1973
Psychology research	1957-1962
Diabetes mellitus	1958-1965
Endocrine disorders	1958-1966
University surgical adjuvant study	1958-1963
Early diagnosis of lung cancer – pilot	1958-1963
Outpatient psychiatry	1958-1964
Atrophic lateral sclerosis – assisting NINDB	1958-1961
Functional deafness	1958-1961
Gastroenterology (gastric ulcer)	1959 -1969
VA Prostate Cancer Chemotherapy Study Group	1959-1963
Midwestern cancer chemotherapy group	1959-1964

Each early cooperative clinical trial (Table 7.1) typically had a unique organizational structure. Involved would be one or more biostatisticians. Often they were based in Central Office, but university and other biostatisticians also participated. There was a board of consultants and a Central Office-based coordinator, most frequently a physician in one of the professional services. For example, Edward Dunner, M.D., who later joined Research Service but who was at that time a member of Tuberculosis Service, coordinated the studies on antihypertensive agents, diabetes mellitus and other endocrine diseases, and the pulmonary disease studies, outgrowths of tuberculosis trials. Lyndon E. Lee Jr., M.D., at that time a member of Surgery Service, coordinated all ten of the VA-funded cooperative surgery studies, as well as those funded by the National Cancer Institute. In 1956, VA hospitals participated in two regional cancer chemotherapy cooperative studies, involving eleven Eastern VA hospitals and five in the West. These NCI-funded studies involved both VA and university hospitals. In addition, several NCI-funded projects based entirely within the VA continued for many years. These included the VA study groups for cancer chemotherapy, lung cancer and surgical adjuvant cancer chemotherapy.

The endocrine disorders cooperative study did not produce the clinical answers desired but nevertheless made an important contribution. The original plan was to study adrenal insufficiency and other rare diseases, taking advantage of the huge VA-wide patient population for a more robust number set. To prepare for the clinical study, five steroid assay laboratories were established in medical centers. These laboratories developed standardized chemical procedures for assay of plasma 17-hydroxycorticosteriods and standardized the test for ACTH stimulation.[29] While the study never accrued enough patients to provide definitive results about Addison's disease, the reference laboratories' important work set standards for steroid hormone assays that were generally adopted.

Special Laboratories

In some cases, when a research project was judged to need centralized administration, it was formally established as a "Special Laboratory." The first of these, a laboratory at the Boston VA Hospital charged with the study of epilepsy, started in 1952; others followed quickly. These laboratories were specially funded from and reported directly to Central Office, in contrast with other research projects, that were controlled and funded through the hospital's Research and Education Committee. This seems to have been a transitional mechanism, brought into play when the concept of a hospital's intramural research program as a single "laboratory" became inappropriate. As hospital-based programs diversified and formal funding mechanisms were put in place, the Special Laboratories were no longer necessary. A number of the most productive leaders of the laboratories (Appendix VI) became Medical Investigators or Senior Medical Investigators (Chapter 14.) By 1970, almost all of the Special Laboratories had been closed or absorbed into other programs.

Examples of research by individual staff members at VA hospitals

By the close of the 1950s, the VA research program was still youthful, growing, and very much decentralized. Any VA staff member who wanted to conduct research generally could, though very likely on his or her own time. There was still room, in the VA and elsewhere, for a physician untrained in research to learn how to conduct research and to carry out the work. Some of this work proved to be important. The atmosphere encouraged innovation, but systems were not yet in place to discourage mediocrity. The result was a varied program that centered on clinical issues.

Many important VA research programs began during the 1950s: the development of radioimmunoassay by Berson, Yalow and their colleagues at the Bronx VA Hospital

(Chapter 11); the studies led by Edward Freis at the Washington VA Hospital that eventually proved the importance of pharmacotherapy of hypertension (Chapter 9); Oscar Auerbach's studies at the East Orange (NJ) VA Hospital proving that smoking causes lung cancer (Chapter 10); and the studies led from the Central Neuropsychiatric Research Laboratory at Perry Point (MD) VA Hospital that proved the efficacy of antipsychotic drugs (Chapter 8).

A brief sampling of a few other VA intramural research programs in progress during the 1950s includes:

Dallas – Diabetes research

When Roger Unger, M.D., arrived at the Dallas (TX) VA hospital in 1956, he found that Seymour Eisenberg, Leonard Madison and Willis Sensenbach were collaborating on studies of cerebral blood flow, using the Kety method in a variety of clinical conditions. Among other findings, they showed that cerebral blood flow in confused cardiac patients is markedly reduced.[30] Unger, who had been hired as a clinician, had little time for research, but Eisenberg gave him a corner of the laboratory for research.

Noting he had never had any specific training in doing research, Unger credited two technicians in the radioisotope laboratory, Mary McCall and Ann Eisentraut, with getting him started.

> "They were dying to do research, but they didn't know how to apply their skills. I had a lot of ideas but few skills. So we were able to work together. They were tremendously helpful."[31]

After a new Chief of Medicine freed some of Unger's time for research, he began his long and distinguished career as a diabetes researcher. He collaborated with Madison on a series of studies on the metabolic effects of insulin and of tolbutamide[32-37] and on a tolbutamide test for mild diabetes.[38, 39]

Figure 7.5 Roger Unger, M.D.

An important early contribution to diabetes research from Unger's group was developing a practical assay to measure glucagon. As he described this effort:

"I was interested in the pathophysiology of carbohydrate metabolism—diabetes. The big need in those days was to be able to measure peptide hormones in the plasma. . . .

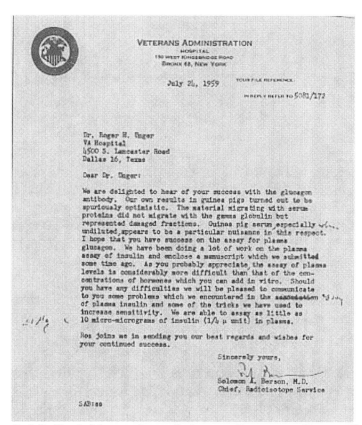

Figure 7.6 Collegial letter from Solomon Berson to Roger Unger

We tried to reproduce (a red cell) assay for insulin and glucagons. I had the idea that glucagon was a very important player in carbohydrate metabolism along with insulin, and we wanted an assay for both. We used this red cell immunoassay, and it was very, very insensitive. It only measured milliunits of insulin, so it was useless. But the idea of competitive inhibition using antibodies, I thought, was a good one. So in 1952 Berson published his first paper on detecting insulin antibodies in the plasma of insulin-dependent diabetics using labeled insulin, ^{131}I labeled insulin. So my idea was – well, instead of using red cells, why not use [131]I?"

Unger did not know Dr. Berson, but telephoned him anyway to discuss his idea. Unger related that he was invited to the Bronx VA Hospital, where Berson and Rosalyn Yalow were doing the research that would later lead to a Nobel Prize:

"I went up to the Bronx VA and . . . she (Dr. Yalow) came in with a pile of notebooks and she showed me the data. She had a beautiful curve for an insulin assay. They had already had this idea and finished it.

"So we published a paper in 1959,[40] which really, in terms of date, was the first RIA paper ever published. We knew that they (Berson and Yalow) were having publication problems with a prior article, so I wrote them to ask permission—could we go on ahead and publish this paper? There was no published record of their work that I could cite to give them the credit that they deserved. Their paper didn't come out until 1960. They did have a paragraph in *Advances in Nuclear Medicine* in 1958, I think, that I was able to cite to give them the proper credit, and they told me to go ahead. I offered to hold the paper back until after theirs was published, but they said 'No, go ahead.'"[31]

Oakland – Pathology

At the Oakland (CA) VA Hospital, set in an old hotel, Bruno Gerstl and his colleagues were systematically collecting increasingly sophisticated clinical data. Tuberculosis was still a clinical problem of great interest. Gerstl's group found that circulating antibodies of the common type were absent in pulmonary tuberculosis,[41] but that antibodies were detectable by a new method.[42] They studied the electrophoretic patterns of the lipoproteins in spinal fluid and the effects of diet on the pattern of unsaturated fats.[43, 44] They correlated x-ray findings with pathology, especially in pulmonary diseases.[45-47]

Los Angeles – Gastroenterology

At the Wadsworth VA Hospital in Los Angeles, James Halsted, Chief of Gastroenterology, was collaborating on studies of the effects of stress on the upper gastrointestinal tract.[48, 49] His most important contributions during this period were on the absorption of vitamin B_{12} and its relation to megaloblastic anemia, especially in diseases of the upper gastrointestinal tract.[50-58] In 1955, Halsted moved to the Syracuse VA Hospital as Director, Professional Services (later called the Chief of Staff), and Morton Grossman came to Wadsworth to head gastroenterology. Grossman was already beginning his work on gastrointestinal hormones,[59, 60] but his work during the 1950s reflected broad interests. He studied gastro-esophageal reflux,[61] experimental pancreatitis,[62] Laennec's cirrhosis[63, 64] and a new nuclear medicine test for intestinal absorption.[65] By the end of this period, he was working on his first dog model for experimental studies of gastric secretion for which he became famous.[66]

Boston – Nephrology

Among the enthusiastic staff Maurice Strauss recruited to the Boston VA Hospital was Solomon Papper, M.D. With his colleagues, Papper studied renal excretion of water and solutes in human subjects, as influenced by various conditions. They reported on sodium excretion in Addison's disease[67] and after sodium administration,[68] on ethanol effect on water diuresis,[69] and on the influence of Laennec's cirrhosis,[70-72] acute hepatitis[73] and myxedema[74] on kidney function.

Chicago Research Hospital – Physiology

In 1953, Francis Haddy joined the brand-new Chicago Research VA Hospital, where, together with Richard Ebert, Craig Borden, Ben Heller and John A.D. Cooper, Chief of Nuclear Medicine (Chapter 6), he set up the clinical and research facilities. He returned to the Research Hospital in 1957 as one of the early Clinical Investigators. Morris Lipton was then the ADPSR, a position he held until 1957, when Haddy assumed it until leaving in 1959.[75] Haddy and Lipton collaborated on studies of serotonin and its interaction with the catecholamines.[76, 77] Haddy expanded the work he had done in the Army[78] on factors influencing blood flow to a series of animal studies on regulation of blood flow.[79-85]

Thomas Starzl was at the Research Hospital at that time and was already transplanting livers in dogs, though as yet without success.[86] Starzl later achieved the first successful human liver transplant while at the Denver (CO) VA Hospital.

Des Moines – Surgery

At Des Moines, L.T. Palumbo, M.D., Chief of Surgery, published extensive follow-up evaluations of large series of patients treated by established and innovative surgical procedures: on the physiological changes caused by vagotomy, with or without gastrectomy,[87-89] and on results of various types of hernia repair (1650 cases).[90, 91] He worked extensively on methods to avoid Horner's syndrome when doing upper sympathectomy,[92-94] and studied the physiology of the sympathetic pathways to the eye.[95, 96]

Birmingham – Cardiology

At the Birmingham (AL) VA Hospital, E.E. Eddleman was studying, in humans and dogs, the motions made by the heart as measured externally by kinetocardiography or ballistocardiography.[97-104]

San Fernando – Mycology

At the San Fernando (CA) VA Hospital, a tuberculosis hospital later destroyed in an earthquake, Milton Huppert was beginning his research in mycology. Huppert later became known as an authority on coccidioidomycosis. From 1955 through 1959, he published on candida albicans infections,[105, 106] atypical mycobacteria[107, 108] and fungal infections of the skin,[109, 110] as well as on coccidioidomycosis.[111]

Chicago Westside – Hematology

Paul Heller, M.D., later acclaimed for his clinical and basic research on the hemoglobinopathies and made a Senior Medical Investigator in 1969, met Hyman Zimmerman when both were in Washington, D.C. Zimmerman (Chapter 3) recruited Heller to the Omaha (NE) VA Hospital in 1951 and then to the Chicago (IL) Westside VA Hospital at the beginning of 1954. After joining the VA, Heller collaborated with Zimmerman in an eclectic research program: clinical studies of hepatic dysfunction,[112-116] studies of nucleophagocytosis,[117, 118] serum enzyme patterns in disease[119-121] and Vitamin B12 distribution in the rat.[122] Encouraged by Zimmerman, Heller began to study and publish on the hemoglobins.[123-126] Heller's later work on abnormal hemoglobin diseases, especially sickle cell anemia and sickle cell trait, won him the Middleton Award.

Buffalo – The cardiac pacemaker

When Andrew Gage, fresh out of his residency, started work as a surgeon at the Buffalo VA Hospital about 1953, William Chardack was Assistant Chief of Surgery. Gage and Chardack organized a one-room animal research facility in an old laundry area. In that room, they housed dogs, kept apparatus, and set up the animal studies operating room. After about a year, they added another room and were able to house the dogs separately. One research employee took care of the animals, assisted at surgery and did every thing else.

About 1954, Gage and Chardack began to work on coronary revascularization and blood flow. They studied mortality in dogs after coronary ligation. Gage worked out a system of putting thrombogenic wires into coronary arteries.[127] After the dogs developed ischemia, they were used to study the Beck and Vineberg operations, early procedures directed to coronary artery stenosis.[128]

In 1958, Chardack and Gage started the work that led to developing an artificial pacemaker. In their coronary studies, they assembled a lot of physiology apparatus and were having problems with it. They hired Wilson Greatbatch, an electrical engineer, who was then a private consultant, to assist them. He asked them if there might be some use for a device to stimulate the heart. They said that they would be interested in seeing such a device. Greatbatch built one and brought it back. They attached it to a dog's heart, and it worked for twenty seconds before it failed. This was the beginning of the work that led to the clinically applicable pacemaker. The concept of pacing the heart had been tried in

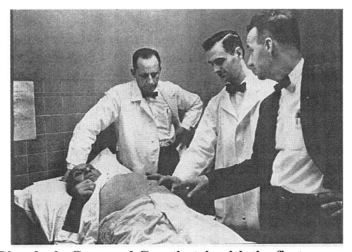

Figure 7.7 Chardack, Gage and Greatbatch with the first pacemaker patient

England and reported not to be feasible, but Gage and Chardack had not seen the paper.[129] During the following year, they studied many dogs with increasing success[130] in their tiny laboratory supported by VA general medical research funds. In 1959, they had a visit from John Kennedy, the Director of Surgery and Lyndon Lee, the Chief of Surgery Research, in

Central Office. They were able to show the visitors a dog with complete heart block that was kept alive with the pacemaker. Very impressed, Kennedy and Lee arranged for additional funds to enlarge the facility.

This successful implantable pacemaker[131] was first described at the December 1959 VA annual research meeting held in Cincinnati.[129]

The first NAS-NRC survey of VA research

In the late 1950's, at the request of the VA Administrator, the National Academy of Sciences-National Research Council (NRC) began the first of its three surveys of the VA's research program. Why the VA requested these surveys is uncertain, but it seems likely that its leaders wanted to be reassured of the value of the program and also to acquire an objective source to quote in support of the program.

While the NRC report was not published until June 1960, the actual review occurred in 1958 and 1959. In the process, hospitals were visited, deans and research investigators interviewed, and many documents reviewed. The report concluded that "There is no question but what the Veterans Administration has good reason to be proud of the quality of its research now."[132]

This report recommended that Central Office Research Service central coordination and decentralized administration be continued for the VA's medical research program. "It has proved both effective and efficient to give autonomy in the use of research funds and responsibility for the quality and pertinency of research to the local Veterans Administration stations."[133] This report also encouraged expansion of the Research Service staff in Central Office by the "addition of three or four persons who are highly skilled in research methods and research administration."[134]

The NRC report addressed other late 1950s problems in addition to the very small Central Office research staff: travel restrictions that hampered VA investigators and restrictions on the funding of publications and the purchase and distribution of reprints. During the 1960s, VA leadership cited report recommendations to correct these problems and to increase the research budget.

The NRC report compared the 1958 VA research publications in more prestigious journals with those from the NIH's intramural program. In general, more NIH publications appeared in basic journals such as *American Journal of Physiology* and *Journal of Biological Chemistry*, while more VA publications appeared in clinically oriented journals such as *Annals of Internal Medicine*, *JAMA*, *New England Journal of Medicine* and the AMA Archives series. Publication in the *Journal of Clinical Investigation* was similar for the two groups: the JCI published 23 NIH papers and 27 VA papers that year.[135]

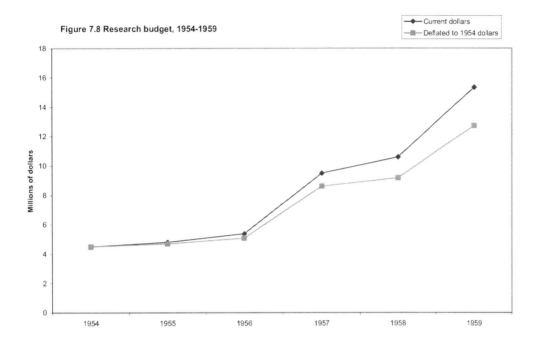

Figure 7.8 Research budget, 1954-1959

Current dollars
Deflated to 1954 dollars

VA research at the end of the 1950s

The NAS-NRC report provided an encapsulated description of the VA medical research program in 1959. There were 6,371 approved projects, with 1,780 described as general medical research, 1,761 as studies in aging, 1,711 as investigations of mental and nervous diseases, 642 as radioisotope research, 381 as tuberculosis studies and 96 as dental research. Nine special dental research laboratories and 12 other special laboratories reported directly to Central Office. In addition, 17 tuberculosis laboratories and 34 neuropsychiatric laboratories had special relations with their counterparts in Central Office. In all, 128 VA stations operated research programs. There were 28 ongoing cooperative studies, including the study of the chemotherapy of tuberculosis, which involved 58 hospitals.

Recalling the 1950s, Andrew Gage described the enthusiasm of VA researchers:

> "Research was motivated by academic drive and intellectual curiosity. It was easier in those days, because there was so much to be done and little to impede a motivated researcher. Devices needed to be built and physiologic studies done. One could have an idea and carry it out, and six months later a paper might be generated."[129]

In trying to pin a specific label on this era, one is tempted to refer to it as a "golden age" in the evolution of VA research. At the very least, it can be said that the VA research done in the 1950s certainly stands as the solid foundation upon which future progress was built.

References

1. Telephone Directory, Veterans Administration Central Office. 1954.

2. Interview with Martin Cummings, M.D., April 7, 1988 at Dr. Cumming's office in Washington, DC.

3. Lyon, G.M. "Medical research programs of the Veterans Administration." *25th meeting of the Committee on Veterans Medical Problems*. December 8, 1952. Washington, DC: National Academy of Science-National Research Council, Appendix II.

4. Interview with Martin Cummings, M.D., February 7, 1994 at Dr. Cummings' home in Florida.

5. Telephone interview with John C. Nunemaker, M.D., January 14, 1992.

6. Telephone interview with Ernest Allen, Ph.D., April 11, 1988.

7. Acting Chief Medical Director. "Appendix IV." *29th meeting of the Committee on Veterans Medical Problems*. December 8, 1952. Washington, DC: National Academy of Science-National Research Council, 633.

8. Interview with Michael DeBakey, M.D., January 28,1994 at Dr. DeBakey's office at Baylor Medical Center, Houston, TX.

9. *Medical Research in the Veterans' Administration. For the Year Beginning July 1, 1962 and Ending June 39, 1963 (Fiscal Year 1963)*. Washington, DC: U.S. Government Printing Office, 1963, 1.

10. *Medical Research in the Veterans' Administration. For the Year Beginning July 1, 1955 and Ending June 39, 1956 (Fiscal Year 1956)*. Washington, DC: U.S. Government Printing Office, 1957.

11. Interview with Stewart G. Wolf, M.D., 10/30/92 at Dr. Wolf's office in Tott's Gap, PA.

12. Interview with Marjorie T. Wilson, M.D., 4/29/88 at Dr. Wilson's office in Washington, DC.

13. Interview with Oscar Auerbach, M.D., October 30, 1992 at Dr. Auerbach's office at the East Orange, NJ VAMC.

14. Interview with Ludwig Gross, M.D., October 28, 1992 at Dr. Gross's office at the Bronx VAMC.

15. Interview with Edward Freis, M.D., April 8, 1993 at Dr. Freis's office at the Washington, DC VAMC.

16. Interview with Abraham Dury, P.D., February 8, 1994 at Dr. Dury's home in Florida.

17. Chamberlain, W.E., "Radiological health." *Newsletter: Research and Education in Medicine*, May, 1960. 17.

18. "Personals." *Newsletter: Research and Education in Medicine*, September, 1960. 28.

19. *Medical Research in the Veterans' Administration. For the Year Beginning July 1, 1959 and Ending June 30, 1960 (Fiscal Year 1960)*. Washington, DC: Government Printing Office, 1960, 37-81.

20. *Medical Research in the Veterans' Administration, FY 1960.* 1960, 11.

21. *Medical Research in the Veterans' Administration, FY 1956.* 1957, 8-9.

22. *Medical Research in the Veterans' Administration, FY 1956.* 1957, 10.

23. *Medical Research in the Veterans' Administration, FY 1956.* 1957, 12.

24. *Medical Research in the Veterans' Administration. For the Year Beginning July 1, 1973 and Ending June 30, 1974 (Fiscal Year 1974).* Washington, DC: U.S. Government Printing Office, 1975, 99.

25. Felix, W.R., Myerson, R.M., Sigel, B., Perrin, E.B. and Jackson, F.C., "The effect of portacaval shunt on hypersplenism." *Surg Gynecol Obstet,* 1974. **139**: 899-904.

26. *Medical Research in the Veterans' Administration, FY 1956.* 1957, 11-12.

27. *Medical Research in the Veterans' Administration, FY 1956.* 1957, 12-13.

28. *Medical Research in the Veterans' Administration, FY 1960).* 1960, 37-82.

29. *Medical Research in the Veterans' Administration, FY 1960.* 1960, 42.

30. Eisenberg, S., Madison, L.L. and Sensenbach, W., "Cerebral hemodynamic and metabolic studies in patients with congestive heart failure. II. Observations in confused subjects." *Circulation,* 1960. **21**: 704-709.

31. Interview with Roger H. Unger, M.D., January 27, 1994 at Dr. Unger's office at the Dallas VAMC.

32. Madison, L.L. and Unger, R.H., "Comparison of the effects of insulin and Orinase (tolbutamide) on peripheral glucose utilization in the dog." *Metabolism,* 1958. **7**: 227-239.

33. Madison, L.L. and Unger, R.H., "The physiological significance of the secretion of endogenous insulin into the portal circulation. I. Comparison of the effects of glucagon-free insulin administered via the portal vein and via a peripheral vein on the magnitude of hypoglycemia and peripheral glucose utilization." *J Clin Invest,* 1958. **37**: 631-639.

34. Unger, R.H. and Madison, L.L., "Comparison of response to intravenously administered tolbutamide in mild diabetic and non-diabetic subjects." *J Clin Invest,* 1958. **37**: 627-630.

35. Madison, L.L., Combes, B., Strickland, W., Unger, R.H. and Adams, R., "Evidence for a direct effect of insulin on hepatic glucose output." *Metabolism,* 1959. **8**: 469-471.

36. Madison, L.L., Combes, B., Unger, R.H. and Kaplan, N., "The relationship between the mechanism of action of the sulfonylureas and the secretion of insulin into the portal circulation." *Ann NY Acad Sci,* 1959. **74**: 548-556.

37. Unger, R.H., Madison, L.L. and Carter, N.W., "Relative effectiveness of newer oral agents in the regulation of diabetic patients imperfectly controlled by tolbutamide studied within the framework of a tentative subclassification of the disease." *Ann NY Acad Sci,* 1959. **82**: 570-584.

38. Unger, R.H. and Madison, L.L., "A new diagnostic procedure for mild diabetes mellitus; Evaluation of an intravenous tolbutamide response test." *Diabetes,* 1958. **7**: 455-461.

39. Unger, R.H. and Madison, L.L., "The intravenous tolbutamide response test in diagnosis of mild diabetes." *Ann NY Acad Sci,* 1959. **74**: 667-671.

40. Unger, R.H., Eisentraut, A.M., McCall, M.S., Keller, S., Lanz, H.C. and Madison, L.L., "Glucagon antibodies and their use for immunoassay for glucagon." *Proc Soc Exp Biol Med,* 1959. **102**: 621-623.

41.   Gerstl, B., Kirsh, D., Davis, W., Jr. and Barbieri, M., "Absence of circulating antibodies in patients with pulmonary tuberculosis." *Science*, 1954. **120**: 853-854.

42.   Gerstl, B. and others, "Detection of apparently absent circulating antibodies in tuberculous sera." *Am Rev Tuberc*, 1955. **72**: 345-355.

43.   Gerstl, B., Davis, W., Jr, Smith, J., Athineos, E. and Herold, G., "Effects of dietary fat upon polyunsaturated fatty acids in patients with multiple sclerosis." *Proc Soc Exp Biol Med*, 1959. **100**: 534-538.

44.   Smith, J., Gerstl, B., Davis, W., Jr. and Orth, D., "Lipoprotein patterns of spinal fluid obtained by electrophoresis." *Arch Neurol Psychiat*, 1956. **76**: 608-613.

45.   Epstein, E., Gerstl, B., Bark, M. and Belber, J., "Silica pregranuloma." *Arch Dermat*, 1955. **71**: 645-647.

46.   Jacobs, L. and Gerstl, B., "Effect of pulmonary tuberculosis on Roentgen shadow of heart." *Rock Mountain MJ*, 1956. **53**: 363-370.

47.   Jacobs, L., Gerstl, B., Hollander, A. and Berk, M., "Intra-abdominal egg-shell calcifications due to silicosis." *Radiology*, 1956. **67**.

48.   Halsted, J., "Emotional component in gastrointestinal disorders." *California Med*, 1954. **80**: 449-454.

49.   Bachrach, W., Smith, J. and Halsted, J., "Spasm of the choledochal sphincter accompanying sudden stress." *Gastroenterol*, 1952. **22**: 604-606.

50.   Halsted, J., Gasster, M. and Drenick, E., "Absorption of radioactive vitamin B12 after total gastrectomy; Relation to microcytic anemia and to site of origin of Castle's intrinsic factor." *N Eng J Med*, 1954. **251**: 161-168.

51.   Swendseid, M., Halsted, J. and Libby, R., "Excretion of cobalt 60-labeled vitamin B12 after total gastrectomy." *Proc Soc Exper Biol and Med*, 1953. **83**: 226-228.

52.   Swendseid, M., Gasster, M. and Halsted, J., "Limits of absorption of orally administered vitamin B12: Effect of intrinsic factor sources." *Proc Soc Exper Biol and Med*, 1954. **86**: 834-836.

53.   Halsted, J., "Megaloblastic anemia associated with surgically produced gastrointestinal abnormalities." *California Med*, 1955. **83**: 212-217.

54.   Halsted, J., Swenseid, M., Gasster, M. and Lewis, P., "Absorption of radioactive vitamin B12 in patients with disease of small intestine: Relation to macrocytic anemia." *Trans Amer Clin Climat Assn*, 1955. **66**: 18-36.

55.   Halsted, J., Swenseid, M., Lewis, P. and Gasster, M., "Mechanisms involved in development of vitamin B12 deficiency." *Gastroenterology*, 1956. **30**: 21-36.

56.   Halsted, J. and others, "Evaluation of fecal recovery method for determining intestinal absorption of vitamin B12." *J Lab Clin Med*, 1956. **48**: 92-101.

57.   Citrin, Y., DeRosa, C. and Halsted, J., "Sites of absorption of vitamin B12." *J Lab Clin Med*, 1957. **50**: 667-672.

58.   Halsted, J., Carroll, J. and Rubert, S., "Serum and tissue concentration of vitamin B12 in certain pathologic states." *N Eng J Med*, 1959. **260**: 575-580.

59.   Grossman, M., "The physiology of secretin." *Vitamins and Hormones, NY*, 1958. **16**: 179-203.

60.   Grossman, M., "Some properties of trypsin inhibitor of pancreatic juice." *Proc Soc Exp Biol Med*, 1958. **99**: 304-306.

61.   Tuttle, S. and Grossman, M., "Detection of gastro-esophageal reflux by simultaneous measurement of intraluminal pressure and pH." *Proc Soc Exp Biol Med*, 1958. **98**: 225-227.

62.   Grossman, M., "Experimental pancreatitis: Recent contributions." *JAMA*, 1959. **169**: 1567-1570.

63.   Grossman, M., "Hepatic coma." *Gastroenterology*, 1958. **34**: 667-674.

64.   Tuttle, S., Figueroa, W. and Grossman, M., "Development of hemochromotosis in a patient with Laennec's cirrhosis." *Am J Med*, 1959. **26**: 655-658.

65.   Grossman, M. and Jordan, P., Jr, "The radio-iodinated triolein test for steatorrhea." *Gastroenterology*, 1958. **34**: 892-900.

66.   Grossman, M., "Stimulation of secretion of acid by distention of denervated fundic pouches in dogs." *Gastroenterology*, 1961. **41**: 385-390.

67.   Rosenbaum, J., Papper, S. and Ashley, M., "Variations in renal excretion of sodium independent of change in adrenocortical hormone dosage in patients with Addison's disease." *J Clin Endocr*, 1955. **15**: 1459-1474.

68.   Papper, S., Saxon, L., Rosenbaum, J. and Cohen, H., "Effects of isotonic and hypotonic salt solutions on renal excretion of sodium." *J Lab Clin Med*, 1956. **47**: 776-782.

69.   Rosenbaum, J., Papper, S., Cohen, H. and McLean, R., "The influence of ethanol upon maintained water diuresis in man." *J Clin Invest*, 1957. **36**: 1202-1207.

70.   Papper, S., "The role of the kidney in Laennec's cirrhosis of the liver." *Medicine, Balt*, 1958. **37**: 299-316.

71.   Papper, S. and Saxon, L., "The diuretic response to administered water in patients with liver disease. II. Laennec's cirrhosis of the liver." *Arch Int Med*, 1959. **103**: 750-757.

72.   Papper, S., Belsky, J. and Bleifer, K., "Renal failure in Laennec's cirrhosis of the liver. I. Description of clinical and laboratory features." *Ann Intern Med*, 1959. **51**: 759-773.

73.   Papper, S., Seifer, H. and Saxon, L., "The diuretic response to administered water in patients with liver disease. I. Acute infectious hepatitis." *Arch Int Med*, 1959. **103**: 746-749.

74.   Bleifer, K., Belsky, J., Saxon, L. and Papper, S., "The diuretic response to administered water in patients with primary myxedema." *J Clin Endocr*, 1960. **20**.

75.   Telephone interview with Francis Haddy, M.D., Ph.D., April 6, 1988.

76.   Gordon, P., Haddy, F. and Lipton, M., "Serotonin antagonism of noradrenalin in vivo." *Science*, 1958. **128**: 531-532.

77.   Haddy, F., "Serotonin and the vascular system." *Angiology*, 1960. **11**: 21-24.

78.   Emanuel, D., Scott, J. and Haddy, F., "Effect of potassium on small and large blood vessels of the dog forelimb." *Amer J Physiol*, 1959. **197**: 637-642.

79.   Haddy, F., "Vasomotion in large and small blood vessels." *Illinois Med J*, 1958. **114**: 107-111.

80.   Haddy, F., "Effect of histamine on small and large vessel pressures in the dog foreleg." *Amer J Physiol*, 1960. **198**: 161-168.

81.   Haddy, F., "Local effects of sodium, calcium and magnesium upon small and large blood vessels of the dog forelimb." *Circ Res*, 1960. **8**: 57-70.

82.   Haddy, F., "Peripheral vascular resistance." *Amer Heart J*, 1960. **60**: 1-5.

83.   Haddy, F., "Effect of levarterenol upon venous pressure in the rabbit ear." *Angiology*, 1961. **12**: 486-490.

84.   Haddy, F., "Autoregulation of blood flow." *Amer Heart J*, 1961. **62**: 565-566.

85.   Haddy, F., Molnar, J. and Campbell, R., "Effects of denervation and vasoactive agents on vascular pressures and weight of dog forelimb." *Amer J Physiol*, 1961. **201**: 631-638.

86.   Starzl, T.E., *The Puzzle People: Memoirs of a Transplant Surgeon.* Pittsburgh and London: University of Pittsburgh Press, 1992, 62.

87.   Palumbo, L., "Physiological changes of upper gastrointestinal tract following combined partial gastrectomy and vagus resection." *Mississippi Valley Med J*, 1954. **76**: 56-60.

88.   Palumbo, L., Mazur, T. and Doyle, B., "Combined vagus resection and partial gastrectomy for duodenal and marginal ulcer." *Arch Surg*, 1954. **69**: 762-768.

89.   Palumbo, L., Mazur, T. and Doyle, B., "Partial gastectomy with or without vagus resection for duodenal or marginal ulcer." *Surgery*, 1954. **36**: 1043-1050.

90.   Palumbo, L. and Mighell, S., "Primary indirect inguinal hernioplasty." *Am J Surg*, 1954. **88**: 293-297.

91.   Palumbo, L. and Mighell, S., "Primary direct inguinal hernioplasty; Study of 275 Cases." *Surgery*, 1954. **36**: 278-282.

92.   Palumbo, L., "Upper dorsal sypmpathectomy without Horner's syndrome." *Arch Surg*, 1955. **71**: 743-751.

93.   Palumbo, L., "Anterior transthoracic approach for upper thoracic sympathectomy." *Arch Surg*, 1956. **72**.

94.   Palumbo, L., "New surgical approach for upper thoracic sympathectomy; a method to avoid Horner's syndrome." *Arch Surg*, 1958. **76**: 807-810.

95.   Palumbo, L., "A new concept of the sympathetic pathways to the eye; a new technique to avoid a Horner's syndrome." *Surgery*, 1957. **42**: 740-748.

96.   Palumbo, L. and Shapiro, S., "Physiological studies before and after upper dorsal sympathectomy." *Ann Surg*, 1958. **147**: 261-263.

97.   Eddleman, E.E., Jr. and Reeves, T.J., "Kinetocardiography." *Meth Med Res*, 1958. **7**: 107-118.

98.   Eddleman, E.E., Jr., "Kinetocardiographic changes as the result of mitral commissurotomy." *Am J Med*, 1958. **25**: 733-743.

99. Frederick, W.H. and Eddleman, E.E., Jr., "Genesis of the force ballistocardiogram of the dog." *J Appl Physiol*, 1958. **13**: 109-117.

100. Frederick, W.H. and Eddleman, E.E., Jr., "A simple bed suspension for ultra-low frequency ballistocardiography on dogs." *J Appl Physiol*, 1958. **12**: 347-348.

101. Suh, S.K., Cooper, W.H., Frederick, W.H. and Eddleman, E.E., Jr., "Force, work, and power ballistocardiography." *Am J Card*, 1958. **1**: 726-735.

102. Eddleman, E.E., Jr. and Thomas, H.D., "The recognition and differentiation of right ventricular pressure and flow loads." *Amer J Cardiol*, 1959. **4**: 652-661.

103. Eddleman, E.E., Jr., Hughes, M.L. and Thomas, H.D., "Estimation of pulmonary artery pressure and pulmonary vascular resistance from ultra low frequency precordial movements (kinetocardiograms)." *Amer J Cardiol*, 1959. **4**: 662-668.

104. Suh, S.K. and Eddleman, E.E., Jr., "Kinetocardiographic findings in myocardial infarction." *Circulation*, 1959. **19**: 531-542.

105. Huppert, M. and Cazin, J., Jr., "Pathogenesis of candida albicans infection following antibiotic therapy; Further studies of effect of antibiotics on in vitro growth of candida albicans." *J Bact*, 1955. **70**: 435-439.

106. Huppert, M., Cazin, J., Jr. and Smithe, H., Jr., "Pathogenesis of candida albicans infection following antibiotic therapy; Effect of antibiotics on incidence of candida albicans in intestinal tract of mice." *J Bact*, 1955. **70**: 440-447.

107. Huppert, M., Wayne, L. and Juarez, W., "Characterization of atypical mycobacteria and of nocardia species isolated from clinical specimens. II. Procedure for differentiating between acid-fast microorganisms." *Am Rev Tuberc*, 1957. **76**: 468-479.

108. Wayne, L., Krasnow, I. and Huppert, M., "Characterization of atypical mycobacteria and of nocardia species isolated from clinical specimens. I. Characterization of atypical mycobacteria by means of the microcolonial test." *Am Rev Tuberc*, 1957. **76**: 451-467.

109. Huppert, M. and Keeney, E., "Immunization against superficial fungous infection. II. Studies on human volunteer subjects." *J Invest Derm*, 1959. **32**: 15-19.

110. Keeney, E. and Huppert, M., "Immunization against superficial fungous infection. I. Studies on experimental animals." *J Invest Derm*, 1959. **32**: 7-13.

111. Huppert, M. and Walker, L., "The selective and differential effects of cyclohexamide on many strains of coccidioides immetis." *Am J Clin Path*, 1958. **29**: 291-295.

112. Heller, P., Korn, R. and Zimmerman, H., "Amebic hepatitis presenting as fever of unknown origin." *N Eng J Med*, 1953. **249**: 596-600.

113. Loomis, G., Heller, P., Hall, W. and Zimmerman, H., "Pattern of hepatic dysfunction in malaria." *Am J Med Sci*, 1954. **227**: 408-416.

114. Heller, P., Zimmerman, H., Rozengvaig, S. and Singer, K., "L.E. - cell phenomenon in chronic hepatic disease." *N Eng J Med*, 1956. **254**: 1160-1165.

115. Krasnow, S., Walsh, J., Zimmerman, H. and Heller, P., "Megaloblastic anemia in alcoholic cirrhosis." *Arch Int Med*, 1957. **100**: 870-880.

116.	Korn, R., Kellow, W., Heller, P., Chomet, B. and Zimmerman, H., "Hepatic involvement in extrapulmonary tuberculosis: Histological and functional characteristics." *Am J Med*, 1959. **27**: 60-71.

117.	Zimmerman, H.J., Walsh, J. and Heller, P., "Production of nucleophagocytosis by rabbit antileukocytic serum." *Blood*, 1953. **8**: 651-654.

118.	Heller, P. and Zimmerman, H., "Nucleophagocytosis; Studies of 336 patients." *Arch Int Med*, 1956. **97**: 208-224.

119.	West, M., Heller, P. and Zimmerman, H., "Serum enzymes in disease. III. Lactic dehydrogenase and glutamic oxalacetic transaminase in patients with leukemia and lymphoma." *Am J Med Sci*, 1958. **235**: 689-701.

120.	Zimmerman, H., West, M. and Heller, P., "Serum enzymes in disease. II. Lactic dehydrogenase and glutamic oxalacetic transaminase in anemia." *Arch Int Med*, 1958. **102**: 115-123.

121.	Heller, P., Weinstein, H., West, M. and Zimmerman, H., "Enzymes in anemia: A study of abnormalities of several enzymes of carbohydrate metabolism in the plasma and erythrocytes in patients with anemia, with preliminary observations of bone marrow enzymes." *Ann Int Med*, 1960. **53**: 898-913.

122.	Heller, P., Henderson, W., Bowser, E., JM, L. and Zimmerman, H., "The distribution of Co58-labeled vitamin B12 in the rat with fatty metamorphosis and cirrhosis of the liver." *J Lab Clin Med*, 1960. **55**: 29-37.

123.	Josephson, A.M., Singer, K., Singer, L., Heller, P. and Zimmerman, H., "Hemoglobin S-thalassemia and Hemoglobin C-thalassemia in siblings." *Blood*, 1957. **12**: 593-602.

124.	Oliner, H. and Heller, P., "Megaloblastic erythropoiesis and acquired hemolysis in sickle-cell anemia." *N Eng J Med*, 1959. **261**: 19-22.

125.	Heller, P., Weinstein, H., West, M. and Zimmerman, H., "Glycolytic, citric acid cycle, and hexosemonophosphate shunt enzymes of plasma and erythrocytes in megaloblastic anemia." *J Lab Clin Med*, 1960. **55**: 425-434.

126.	Yakulis, V., Heller, P., Josephson, A. and Singer, L., "Rapid demonstration of A2 Hemoglobin by means of agar gel electrophoresis." *Am J Clin Path*, 1960. **34**.

127.	Gage, A., Olsen, K. and Chardack, W., "Experimental coronary thrombosis in dog; Description of method." *Ann Surg*, 1956. **143**: 289-294.

128.	Gage, A., Olsen, K. and Chardack, W., "Cardiopericardiopexy: An experimental evaluation." *Ann Surg*, 1958. **147**: 289-294.

129.	Telephone interview with Andrew Gage, M.D., May 21, 1992.

130.	Chardack, W.M., "Recollections - 1958-1961." *PACE*, 1981. **4**: 592-596.

131.	Chardack, W., Gage, A. and Greatbatch, W., "A transistorized, self-contained, implantable pacemaker for the long-term correction of complete heart block." *Surgery*, 1960. **48**: 643-654.

132.	Committee on the Survey of Medical Research in the Veterans Administration *Medical Research in the Veterans Administration: Final Report.* National Academy of Science - National Research Council, 1960. 45.

133.   NAS Committee on VA Research *Final Report.* 1960. 2.

134.   NAS Committee on VA Research *Final Report.* 1960. 3.

135.   NAS Committee on VA Research *Final Report.* 1960. 102-103.

Chapter 8. The VA Psychopharmacology Trials Lead a Revolution in Psychiatric Practice

Postwar VA Central Office direction of psychiatric research

New enthusiasm for research in mental health emerged after World War II, with the establishment of the Department of Medicine and Surgery and the affiliations with medical schools that began in 1946 (Chapter 3). Even as hospitals retooled to care for increasing numbers of patients with psychiatric disorders (Figure 8.1), the Central Office leadership recognized a need to create research programs focused on mental health. Research Chiefs for both psychiatry and psychology were recruited. While they increasingly interacted with leaders of the fledgling Research Service, these chiefs were quite independent of Research Service and reported to their superiors in Neuropsychiatry Service (Chapter 3). The chiefs were charged with designing and supervising research of importance to the VA's neuropsychiatric patients.

Figure 8.1 Neuropsychiatric patients in VA hospitals

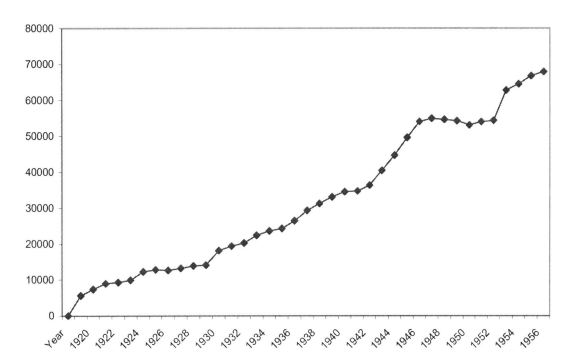

Background - the psychoactive drugs

Since the 1950s, the explosive growth of effective psychopharmacological agents has revolutionized care of the seriously mentally ill. Prior to 1950, no genuinely effective psychoactive drugs were available to psychiatrists. There were sedatives and hypnotics, such as barbiturates, hyoscine, and chloral hydrate for insomniac, violent, anxious, or agitated patients. However, few physicians seriously believed that these drug interventions actually treated psychiatric illness. At best, the medications relieved symptoms; at worst, they restrained patients chemically rather than physically and sometimes proved to be harmful.[1]

In 1950, this situation began to change when the French pharmaceutical firm Rhône-Poulenc synthesized chlorpromazine (Thorazine). Though originally synthesized for its antihistaminic properties, a number of physicians noticed its ability to create a "euphoric quietude" without undue sedation. Beginning in 1952, an increasing number of publications extolled chlorpromazine's virtue for treating psychiatric patients and, by the mid- to late 1950s, it had become one of the most successful pharmaceutical agents synthesized.[2] Almost simultaneously, Western physicians "discovered" derivatives of the alkaloid *Rauwolfia serpentina*, which had been used for centuries in India. Its Western use as an anti-hypertensive agent as well as a psychotropic agent briefly rivaled the perceived tranquilizing ability of chlorpromazine.[3] Also serendipitously, physicians in the early 1950s found that monoamine oxidase inhibitors could relieve depression and, in the mid to late 1950s, that depressed patients responded favorably to the tricyclic, imipramine. Thus, by the end of the 1950s, pharmaceutical companies had synthesized all major classes of what became a contemporary psychopharmacopoeia—including minor tranquilizers, such as the benzodiazepines.[4]

New psychopharmacologic agents intensified psychiatrists' growing recognition that they needed better methods for evaluating therapeutic interventions. In the 1930s, a surge of "revolutionary" therapies promised highly optimistic rates of cure, according to the best contemporary scientific evidence. For example, physicians of the 1930s and 1940s saw prefrontal lobotomy as the most scientifically validated therapy in their armamentarium, a belief reinforced when its inventor won the Nobel Prize in 1947.[5] Lobotomy's luster soon faded with the introduction of chlorpromazine and the realization that lobotomy may not have been as effective as originally believed.[6-8] Insulin shock therapy, too, faced a similar fate as investigators increasingly questioned its efficacy (Chapter 2). In short, psychiatrists, like their counterparts in general medicine, became aware of the pitfalls of simple clinical, albeit "expert," observation in deciding whether an intervention worked or not. Bias, the lack of valid comparison groups, and difficulties in objectively measuring outcomes made 1950s researchers increasingly wary of 1930s and 1940s studies of treatment outcome.[9]

With growing disillusionment about older remedies and the proliferation of new psychotropic drugs, psychiatric researchers began employing methods we now commonly associate with randomized controlled clinical trials. However, clinical trials posed particularly thorny problems because psychiatric disorders proved difficult to define clearly and outcomes were often vague and difficult to quantify. Further, many psychiatrists believed in the unique nature of the doctor-patient relationship that clinical trials appeared to efface.[10] However, VA investigators led the way in surmounting these difficulties, developing methodologies and carefully nurturing relevant studies. By the mid-1970s, large, multi-center clinical trials had become generally accepted as the unquestionable means for establishing preferred treatment of mental illness. VA researchers played a critical role in this process.

Early VA research in psychiatry
Before World War II, psychiatry research in the VA, as elsewhere, was limited in scope, despite the large and growing number of patients hospitalized for neuropsychiatric

illnesses. A centrally funded laboratory at the Northport (NY) VA Hospital carried out work on shock therapies as well as more basic studies (Chapter 2). In the1920s and early 1930s, articles in the V.A. *Medical Bulletin* reflected a thoughtful approach to psychiatric problems in some neuropsychiatric hospitals. But by the late 1930s and early 1940s there is little evidence of searches for better treatments. During World War II, a time when psychiatry generally received increasing recognition, VA psychiatry suffered from a severe shortage of psychiatrists. Many psychiatrists and other doctors joined the military services. VA research in general, and psychiatric research in particular, seems virtually to have ceased.

The lobotomy study

In this setting, in 1949, Richard L. Jenkins, M.D., Chief, Research in Psychiatry, and J. Quinter Holsopple, Ph.D., Chief, Research in Psychology, reviewed the records of some 1,500 VA patients who had received lobotomy operations. They concluded that, while there was "clear consensus that benefits did accrue to operated patients," "such benefits were not reflected with equal clarity in discharge rates or in social and economic independence."[11] Evaluation of lobotomized patients as seen in the literature still heavily depended on case reports and small, uncontrolled series. Jenkins and Holsopple sought a more objective evaluation and designed a study of the effects of prefrontal lobotomy. They recruited Maurice Lorr, Ph.D., VA Chief of Research in Outpatient Psychiatry, to design objective psychological scales to evaluate clinical status of study patients before surgery and at intervals after the operation.

Figure 8.2 Maurice Lorr, Ph.D.

In setting up this study and later in starting the psychopharmacology studies, they drew heavily on the experience of leaders of the early VA tuberculosis studies (Chapter 5). The research problems were similar: Most of the people carrying out the day-to-day aspects of the studies at the hospitals had little or no prior research experience. Psychiatric hospitals, like tuberculosis hospitals, tended to be isolated and generally were not affiliated with medical schools. The study outcome measures depended heavily on clinical observations; it was difficult to make them objective. And it was also difficult to conceal from evaluators which treatment a patient had received.

Despite these obstacles, Jenkins, Holsopple and Lorr designed a study that, in the context of its time and subject, has been described as "model science."[12] Six VA hospitals participated and, between 1950 and 1953, 373 patients were studied: 188 who received lobotomies and 185 controls. All patients were reviewed and judged appropriate for lobotomy before they were assigned to the group having the operation or the control group that did not undergo lobotomy. However, modern randomization methods were not followed strictly: many controls were those whose families refused the operation. "Controls were matched as closely as possible with the patients selected for lobotomy."[13] The operating surgeon decided on the type of surgery, so that the data analysis included four different types of operations, though 140 of the 188 operated patients received the "standard" lobotomy procedure.

Patients were studied prior to the operation, with the controls studied shortly after randomization, and at three months and one, two, three, four and five years after surgery or entry into the study. The key evaluation instrument, the Multidimensional Scale for Rating Psychiatric Patients (MSRPP), was developed for the study by Lorr and his colleagues. Other clinical and psychometric observations were also recorded.

During the study follow-up, chlorpromazine and other effective drugs came into increasing use in the treatment of schizophrenia. As time went on, more patients in the study were treated with these agents. At the time of the three-year follow up, one-fifth of the patients evaluated were on the drugs; by five years, two-thirds. Drug treatment made interpretation of lobotomy effects difficult.

On average, the lobotomy study showed some improvement in lobotomized patients compared to controls, as reflected in significantly higher discharge rates at three and four years. By five years, however, drug therapy had diluted the picture and the differences between the groups had diminished.

More important than its unimpressive conclusions, this study provided a template for the psychopharmacology studies that followed. It provided tools to evaluate results of psychiatric treatment. As Jenkins told the Committee on Veterans Medical Problems in December 1952, before the neuroleptic drugs were in widespread use:

"The VA lobotomy research project, under Dr. Holsopple and myself of Central Office, is being carried on in VA hospitals at Roanoke, Bedford, Northampton, Fort Custer, North Little Rock and American Lake, with very little special assistance. We regard it as significant, not only because it is yielding fairly clean-cut results upon the effects of lobotomy, but even more because we believe we have devised methods for determining and recording the effects of a treatment measure upon psychiatric patients more satisfactorily than it has been done before. These methods we believe to have an importance, which extends far beyond lobotomy. Central among them is the Multidimensional Patient Rating Scale, devised by Dr. Maurice Lorr of the Psychology Section, Central Office, which we believe to be a much more reliable, comprehensive and useful device for recording comparable data about different patients, and about the same patient at different times, than any other with which we are acquainted."[11]

The Central Neuropsychiatric Research Laboratory

In 1955, Holsopple and the lobotomy study staff moved from Central Office to the VA hospital at Perry Point on Chesapeake Bay in northern Maryland. The hospital's administration turned over a building for research purposes, and the Central Neuropsychiatric Research Laboratory (CNPRL) was started there, with Holsopple serving as its first chief. This move was a turning point in the VA's clinical psychiatric research program. The laboratory, though supported by Central Office, now became a distinct entity. It had more space than before and the staff now had access to patients and collaborations with physicians and psychologists at the hospital. Perry Point at that time was a neuropsychiatric hospital with a moderately active research program. Twenty-eight research studies involving 48 investigators were ongoing there at the time of the VA's first report to Congress for FY 1956.

The CNPRL was the focus for VA cooperative studies in psychiatry over the next two decades. Its staff, with their advisors, chose and designed studies, developed methodologies, and coordinated data collection and analysis. Together with Central Office colleagues, CNPRL managed the annual VA research conferences on chemotherapy in psychiatry. They came to know the clinicians at the participating hospitals and worked closely with them. The annual conferences and other contacts were important to morale and to assuring that these difficult studies were successful.

The first VA trial of chemotherapy in psychotic disease

Even before completion of the lobotomy study, Holsopple and Jenkins began to plan a similar study of the new psychotropic drugs appearing on the scene. During the 1950s, the use of drugs in major psychiatric illness increased rapidly. Like lobotomy, these new interventions achieved widespread use: a survey in January 1957 showed that 50% of the 57,000 patients with psychiatric diseases hospitalized in VA hospitals were receiving tranquilizing drugs. Of those on tranquillizers, 61% received chlorpromazine and 21% reserpine or other Rauwolfia extracts.[14]

On the other hand, in the early 1950s there was no clear evidence for the efficacy of these drugs. Dosage and administration schedules were empirical. It wasn't known for sure if they did more than simply sedate patients. One of the early studies of these drugs, rare in that it was a randomized blinded study, was conducted by an internist who later played an important role in the VA psychopharmacology cooperative studies. In 1953, Leo Hollister, M.D., Chief of Medicine at the Palo Alto VA Hospital, then a psychiatric facility, noted that when he gave reserpine to treat hypertension in patients who were also schizophrenic, the patients' schizophrenic symptoms seemed to improve. He learned that others were using reserpine to treat psychotic symptoms, and he decided to confirm his impressions with a double-blind study. He persuaded some of his psychiatrist colleagues to refer acutely ill schizophrenic patients to him. They were treated with reserpine or placebo, following a random assignment design blinded to the patient and the referring physician, and sent back to the referring psychiatrist for evaluation after three weeks of treatment on Hollister's ward. The reserpine-treated patients had improved dramatically. [15,16] When

Jenkins and Holsopple assembled a group to plan the new cooperative studies, Hollister was invited to participate.

Figure 8.3 Leo Hollister, M.D.

The group convened by Jenkins and Holsopple reflected a variety of interests and areas of expertise in behavioral science research. In addition to Hollister, Jenkins, Holsopple and Lorr, the original group included Gilbert Beebe (statistician) and Jonathan Cole (psychiatrist) from the National Academy of Sciences, Charles Chapple (internist) from Central Office Research Service, S.T. Ginsberg and Clyde Lindley from Central Office Psychiatry Service, Harry Goldsmith from the Baltimore Regional Office and Ivan F. Bennett, Eugene Caffey, Ian Funk, and Amedeo Marrazzi, psychiatrists from the VA hospitals at Coatesville (PA), Perry Point, Albany (NY) and Pittsburgh (PA). Their first task was to help design a study aimed at determining the efficacy of the new drugs. Biostatistician Gilbert Beebe of the Follow-up Agency (Chapter 4) advised them about study design.

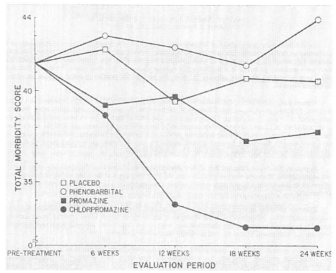

Figure 8.4 Results of the first study of the efficacy of the phenothiazide drugs in schizophrenia

A meeting of prospective participants was held at Downey (IL) VA Hospital in April 1956, and the first study, involving 37 hospitals, was launched. This study (Figure 8.4) compared chlorpromazine, promazine, phenobarbital and placebo. It clearly showed that chlorpromazine, and less so promazine, led to improvement. Phenobarbital was no better than placebo. This study proved that the antipsychotic effects of chlorpromazine were not solely the result of sedation.[17]

Such studies were difficult to perform. Sometimes patients who had been on drugs relapsed during the "washout" period before starting on study medication. Some patients refused their pills. Even though the drugs looked alike, ward staff often guessed what drug a patient was receiving, making it difficult to maintain the "blind" criterion for these studies. The planning group and CNPRL staff frankly discussed these problems and tried to find ways around them.[18]

Further role of the CNPRL

This first chemotherapy trial, which in turn built on experience from the lobotomy study, created the template for future VA cooperative trials in psychiatry. It also institutionalized the CNPRL as the central organizing agency in future trials. Underscoring its role as a central organizing agency for cooperative trials, the CNPRL remained directly funded by the VA Central Office Neuropsychiatry Service. In 1962, Edward Dunner, M.D., then Director, Research Service, attended the annual conference and enticed the group to join Research Service. After that, CNPRL was funded by Research Service as a Special Laboratory (Chapter 7) but retained close ties with Neuropsychiatry Service and its successors. The program remained much the same.

Holsopple, the founding chief, died in 1957, not long after launch of the chlorpromazine study and before completion of the prefrontal lobotomy study. N. Norton (Ned) Springer, Ph.D., followed him as Chief for a year, and then Julian J. Lasky, Ph.D. was Chief until he joined the Peace Corps in 1962.

Figure 8.5 James Klett, Ph.D.

At that point, C. James Klett, Ph.D., assumed leadership of CNPRL. Klett continued as Chief for the balance of its existence as the CNPRL and thereafter as a Cooperative Studies Program Coordinating Center. Klett had been recruited to CNPRL shortly after Holsopple's unexpected death. He was a young research and clinical psychologist from

Northampton (MA) VA Hospital, who had interviewed patients for the lobotomy study during his internship at the American Lake (WA) VA Hospital

Organization of the studies and of the CNPRL

The CNPRL quickly developed an organizational structure to design and implement cooperative trials. Early on, it acquired its own statistical staff, who often worked in collaboration with university consultants. The group of VA consultants who conceived the first study remained as an advisory committee, at first informal and later as a formal Executive Committee. Eugene Caffey, Jr., M.D., then a Staff Psychiatrist at Perry Point hospital, served on this committee from the beginning and remained on it after he moved to Central Office as Deputy ACMD for Professional Services. He and Hollister both served

Figure 8.6 The Executive Committee in 1966

through the Executive Committee's entire 20-year history. The current Director of Neuropsychiatry Service in Central Office, or its successor Services, was always on the Executive Committee and was deeply involved in the planning and execution of studies, even after the CNPRL and its studies officially joined Research Service in 1962. Most other Executive Committee members served for shorter terms. They represented many interests and disciplines and made important contributions to the success of the program.

How a study was created

Generally, the Executive Committee originated and approved the concept of a study in collaboration with the CNPRL staff. After concept approval, staff developed the complete protocol, which the Executive Committee would review. Once approved, the new study with its protocol would be announced in a letter sent to all VA psychiatric hospitals and others with large psychiatric patient populations. Participants were chosen from hospitals that expressed an interest in the study. The test drugs or placebos were furnished to the participants, but the only other tangible reward for study cooperation was attendance at the annual conference.

Starting with the second annual meeting, pharmaceutical firm representatives were invited to the annual meetings. The drug companies provided study drugs and matching placebos without cost, and sometimes they helped with packaging. Otherwise, they did not fund the CNPRL-sponsored studies, nor did they dictate or approve the study design.

CNPRL staff designed protocols, recruited participating hospitals, received data, analyzed results, planned the annual meetings of participants and generally nourished the program. As new methodologies were needed, they saw to it that they were developed. When it was time to publish results, they often wrote the papers. This was a different process from the simultaneous VA cooperative studies in medicine and surgery, which usually were initiated and designed by the field investigators who carried them out, assisted by biostatisticians from Central Office. It also differed from the present-day Cooperative Studies Program (Chapter 18), in which planning originates with staff members in the medical centers but is completed collaboratively together with one of the CSP Coordinating Centers.

There was active collaboration between the CNPRL and Dr. Lorr's laboratory in developing psychiatric rating scales and in research directed towards defining psychiatric syndromes by factor analysis and clustering techniques. In addition, psychologists in the CNPRL worked on evaluation scales. John Overall, Ph.D., was a member of the CNPRL staff from 1959 to 1961, having joined after a postdoctoral fellowship on psychometrics. When he arrived, data from the third cooperative study, a comparison of six phenothiazine derivatives, was just coming in. He and Donald Gorham, an older psychologist with a wealth of clinical experience, worked to simplify the Lorr MSRPP, using factor analysis of the MSRPP data from the third study. This involved laborious computer work, entering all of the data onto punched cards and waiting three months while a commercial computer firm programmed a matrix analysis, since the VA had no computers available for research at that time.[19] Eventually, combining Overall's knowledge of factor analysis and Gorham's clinical understanding, they produced the Brief Psychiatric Rating Scale (BPRS),[20] which is still in widespread use in psychiatric research.

Later studies sponsored by the CNPRL

The landmark chlorpromazine study was followed by a sequence of studies evaluating all the important antipsychotic drugs available at that time.[17, 21, 22] The cooperative group studied effects of different dosage schedules and "drug holidays" or even complete discontinuation of treatment.[23] They studied psychotherapy as an adjunct to or substitute for neuroleptic medication[24] and evaluated the long-term need for anti-Parkinson drugs by chronic patients.[25]

For a number of years, Dr. Lorr and the Outpatient group simultaneously studied the use of minor tranquilizers and psychotherapy in treatment of neurotic patients. These studies[26] shared the Executive Committee with the CNPRL.

The CNPRL also undertook some of the earliest investigations of antidepressant drugs. In 1954, Geigy Pharmaceuticals synthesized the first effective tricyclic antidepressant, imipramine. But not until the late 1950s did its antidepressant effects become recognized. VA researchers and clinicians saw the need to evaluate this class of drugs as well as the phenothiazines. A study comparing imipramine with isocarboxazid, amobarbital-dextroamphetamine and placebo showed the efficacy of imipramine but was confounded by the high rate of spontaneous improvement in all groups.[27]

In the late 1960s and 1970s, the CNPRL began branching out beyond its earlier focus on phenothiazines and antidepressant medications. About 1961, Samuel C. Kaim, M.D., came to Central Office Research Service as Program Chief in Psychiatry. He was especially interested in addictive disorders and sparked studies on alcoholism and drug abuse. Noteworthy was a double-blind study of 537 patients undergoing alcohol withdrawal that compared chlordiazepoxide, chlorpromazine, hydroxyzine, thiamine and a placebo, given for a 10-day detoxification period. As to general symptomatic improvement, no significant differences were found among treatments, but chlordiazepoxide (Librium) was clearly the most effective of the drugs studied for prevention of delirium tremens and convulsions.[28] In the late 1960s and early 1970s, the VA collaborated with SAODAP (the Special Action Office for Drug Abuse Prevention), an interagency group under the White House, in a study comparing a long-acting methadone analog, L-alpha-acetyl methadol, with two dosage levels of methadone in the treatment of heroin addicts. The new drug, administered three times a week, was as safe as daily methadone and compared favorably with high-dose methadone in efficacy.[29] The superiority of high-dose methadone over low doses in this study contributed to the ongoing controversy about appropriate maintenance dose. Several subsequent studies showed additional evidence of safety and efficacy of L-alpha-acetyl-methadol as well as guidance for induction and crossover schedules.

In the late 1960s, Jonathan Cole, who by then was head of the Psychopharmacology Center at the National Institute of Mental Health (NIMH), invited CNPRL to submit a grant application on the role of lithium in the treatment of manic depressive disorders and schizophrenia in 12 VA hospitals and 6 public hospitals. Dr. Caffey was designated as principal investigator. This jointly funded VA-NIMH study was reviewed by both agencies, coordinated by CNPRL and overseen by a joint Executive Committee chaired by Dr. Caffey. At the suggestion of the NIMH review committee, additional funds were provided to support a new position for an assistant at the CNPRL. Robert F. Prien, Ph.D., was recruited to the CNPRL and assumed essentially all responsibility for the study in both VA and non-VA hospitals. The study evaluated lithium compared with other active therapies in the affective disorders,[30] as prophylaxis against recurrence,[31] and for treatment of patients with schizoaffective disorder in the excited state.[32] Unlike other studies coordinated by the CNPRL, hospitals that collaborated in the lithium studies were funded. NIMH paid for the extra staffing and other expenses required by the study.[33]

The annual Research Conference on Chemotherapy in Psychiatry

These studies were enhanced by annual conferences that had an important effect on the spirit of the participants. In April 1956, the Central Office Psychiatry and Neurology

Service sponsored the first such conference at the Downey (IL) VA Hospital. Some 75 persons, including representatives from VA neuropsychiatric hospitals and other VA hospitals with large psychiatric sections, attended. CPNRL staff and key people from Central Office were also present.[34] This meeting became an annual event for 20 years. At the second meeting, 17 representatives of 10 pharmaceutical firms were among the more than 100 attendees.[35]

The Neuropsychiatry Service coordinated the annual meetings. They fostered cooperation between the hospitals and participating disciplines and catalyzed friendships among people from various hospitals and with Central Office and CNPRL staff. The social aspects were also important. Psychiatrists, psychologists, nurses, social workers and statisticians attended and participated. Clyde Lindley, the administrative officer for Neuropsychiatry Service, encouraged the studies and secured funding for the conference each year. He and others maintained a high standard for the scientific presentations that soon became the dominating feature of the conference.[36]

The flavor of these meetings is reflected in a description in the May 1961 *Research and Education Newsletter*:

> "About 250 scientists attended the Sixth Annual Conference of the VA Chemotherapy Studies in Psychiatry and Broad Research Approaches to Mental Illness, held at the Netherlands Hilton Hotel, Cincinnati, Ohio, March 27-29, 1961 . .
>
> "The Chief Medical Director, Dr. William S. Middleton, opened the conference with a brief address. Invited addresses were delivered by Dr. Carrol Keonig, VAH Chicago (Res), Illinois, Dr. R.G. Kuhlen, Syracuse University and Dr. J. T. Shurley, VAH, Oklahoma City, Oklahoma.
>
> "There were preliminary reports on the VA's Cooperative Study No. 5, Chemotherapy of Depression, and Study No. 6, an evaluation of several drugs in treating newly admitted schizophrenic patients. The NIMH made a preliminary report on a 9-hospital collaborative study evaluating drugs in treating acute schizophrenic patients. An initial report was made on the VA Cooperative Study with Psychiatry Outpatients, evaluating the effectiveness of early treatment with a tranquilizer. Thirty research papers were presented which covered a wide range of topics in the field of mental illness, from the neurophysiological to the effect of milieu therapy. Four symposia were presented to highlight significant research approaches to the field of mental illness."

In addition to VA attendees, representatives were present from the American Psychiatric Association, the Mental Health Institute at the University of Michigan, the New York Department of Mental Health and NIMH.[37]

These annual conferences, with name changes to reflect their increasingly broader scope, continued through the 20th annual conference in April, 1975, held shortly before Clyde Lindley retired from the VA[38] and when the CNPRL was transferring its operations to the

Cooperative Studies Program. That meeting had nearly 600 participants, offered CME credit, and covered such diverse topics as biofeedback, family therapy, suicide prevention and drug abuse, as well as the cooperative studies program.[39]

Impact of the CNPRL studies

In addition to proving the efficacy of drug treatment of psychiatric disorders, these studies had broad impact. The centrally directed program brought many physicians and psychiatrists into research. The studies' tests and scales became widely used in the VA and elsewhere. For example, the NIMH adopted the BPRS as part of the standard assessment battery in its Early Clinical Drug Evaluation Unit. Spin-off research projects were begun

Figure 8.7 Published Proceedings of the annual conferences

in hospitals where staff previously had little motivation or opportunity to carry out research. John Barnwell, who started the tuberculosis trials, said when he addressed the members of the first conference of this cooperative group in 1956:

> "When you bring together a considerable number of doctors into a cooperative study, you obviously gather a group of individuals of varying experiences and capacities. As with many graduates of medicine, some have never before participated in any investigation. Some have never distinguished between observed fact and the professor's opinion. A well-conducted cooperative study forces all to attempt to make this distinction and it helps us all to clarify and identify our problems. It may

make investigators out of some who never realized that the body of medical knowledge was a growing, living thing with its own diseases and relapses."[40]

CNPRL-coordinated studies involved many VA staff who otherwise would not have participated in research. Some who entered research through this program were later successful in their own research programs. Especially in the early days, the major motivation for hospital psychiatrists to take part in these trials was altruistic. They received little or no reward for participation. Some were invited to the annual study meetings, but few became authors of the resulting scientific papers. Their main reward was sharing the excitement of being part of an important venture to help patients. This opportunity was particularly important to those working in isolated, unaffiliated hospitals.

In 1972, when Cooperative Studies Program Coordinating Centers (CSPCCs) were set up to manage the administrative and statistical aspects of the cooperative studies (Chapter 18), a new CSPCC was established at Perry Point with Dr. Klett as its Chief. The CNPRL continued as a separate entity, Klett remaining its chief, until 1975. During this time, Dr. Prien completed the lithium studies and prepared several review papers. One important product is a 1975 monograph, an annotated program bibliography of publications from the two decades of the CNPRL existence.[26] Thereafter, new cooperative studies were handled by the Perry Point CSPCC. At first, this new CSPCC concentrated on neuropsychiatric protocols, but gradually it took on studies in other subject areas and soon entered the mainstream of the Cooperative Studies Program.

Impact of the VA psychopharmacology studies on psychiatry

Psychiatric science and practice have undergone enormous change since the 1950s. One of the most significant developments in psychiatry was the creation of VA multi-center cooperative studies for evaluation of psychiatric interventions described in this chapter. The basis of psychiatric clinical practice has moved from relying mostly on individual, expert judgment to learning from rigorous outcome studies. The VA has continued to sponsor Cooperative Studies directed to improving the treatment of its patients with serious mental illnesses. In recent years, VA psychopharmacology cooperative studies have included the recent generations of new antipsychotic drugs.

A major outcome of the VA studies, and of similar studies by others, was a massive exodus of psychiatric patients from state and federal institutions, the most dramatic change in American psychiatry over the last half of the twentieth century. From the mid-nineteenth century until the 1950s, the number of patients in psychiatric hospitals continually rose. At the 1955 peak, 559,000 individuals resided in state hospitals. VA institutions experienced similarly high growth in numbers of residential psychiatric patients (Figure 8.1). In the 1950s, psychiatric patients constituted nearly sixty percent of the VA patient population. Some forty years later, by 1997, the number of patients in state hospitals plummeted to 62,722, although the U.S. population had nearly doubled since the mid 1950s.[41] The VA's inpatient psychiatric population has declined in parallel.

The savings in cost and suffering made possible by the proper use of psychoactive drugs is immeasurable. The studies described in this chapter expedited and legitimized their use.

Acknowledgement

Joel Braslow, M.D., Ph.D., made important contributions to this chapter.

References

1. Braslow, J., *Mental Ills and Bodily Cures: Psychiatric Treatment in the First Half of the Twentieth Century.* Berkeley: University of California Press, 1997.

2. Swazey, J.P., *Chlorpromazine in Psychiatry: A Study of Therapeutic Innovation.* Cambridge, MA: MIT Press, 1974.

3. Ayd, F.J., "The Early History of Modern Psychophysiology. 29th (1990) Annual Meeting of the American College of Neuropsychopharmacology, San Juan, PR." *Neuropsychopharmacology*, 1991. **5**: 71-84.

4. Healy, D., *The Antidepressant Era.* Cambridge, MA: Harvard University Press, 1997.

5. Valenstein, E.S., *Great and Desperate Cures: The Rise and Decline of Psychosurgery and Other Radical Treatments for Mental Illness.* New York: Basic Books, 1986.

6. Appel, K., Myers, J.M. and Scheflen, A.E., "Prognosis in Psychiatry: Results of Psychiatric Treatment." *Arch Neur Psychiatry*, 1953. **70**: 459-468.

7. Barahal, H.S., "1000 Prefrontal Lobotomies - a Five-to-10-Year Follow-up Study." *Psychiat Quarterly*, 1958. **32**: 653-678.

8. Robin, A.A., "A Controlled Study of the Effects of Leucotomy." *J Neurol, Neurosurg and Psychiatry*, 1958. **21**: 262-269.

9. *Psychopharmacology: Problems in Evaluation.* Cole, J.O. and Gerard, R.W., eds.; Washington, DC: National Academy of Sciences, 1959.

10. Barsa, J.A., "The Fallacy of the 'Double Blind'." *Am J Psychiatry*, 1963. **119**: 1174-1175.

11. Jenkins, R.L. "Intra-VA Research in Neurology and Psychiatry." *25th meeting of the Committee on Veterans Medical Problems.* December 5, 1952. Washington, DC: National Academy of Sciences-National Research Council, Appendix IV.

12. Pressman, J.D., *Last Resort: Psychosurgery and the Limits of Medicine.* Cambridge, New York, Melbourne: Cambridge University Press, 1998, 394-397.

13. Ball, J., Klett, C.J. and Gresock, C.J., "The Veterans Administration Study of Prefrontal Lobotomy." *J Clin Exptl Psychopathology and Quarterly Rev Psychiatr Neurol*, 1959. **20**: 205-217.

14. Lindley, C.J. "VA Hospital Survey of Tranquilizing Drugs." *Second Research Conference on Chemotherapy in Psychiatry.* Downey, IL: Office of the Chief Medical Director, Veterans Administration, Washington, DC, 29-30.

15. Interview with Leo E. Hollister, M.D., January 29, 1994 at his residence in Houston, TX.

16. Hollister, L.E., Krieger, G.E., Kringel, A. and Roberts, R.H., "Treatment of Chronic Schizophrenic Reactions with Reserpine." *Ann NY Acad Sci*, 1955. **61**: 92-100.

17. Casey, J.F., Bennett, I.F., Lindley, C.J., Hollister, L.E., Gordon, M.E. and Springer, N.N., "Drug Therapy in Schizophrenia: A Controlled Study of the Relative Effectiveness of Chlorpromazine, Promazine, Phenobarbital, and Placebo." *Arch Gen Psychiat*, 1960. **2**: 210-220.

18. Hollister, L.E. "Discussion, First Plenary Session." *Second Research Conference on Chemotherapy in Psychiatry*. May 9-10, 1957. Downey, IL: Office of the Chief Medical Director, Veterans Administration, Washington, DC, 25-26.

19. Interview with John Overall, Ph.D., January 28, 1994 at Dr. Overall's office in Houston, TX.

20. Overall, J.E. and Gorham, D.R., "The Brief Psychiatric Rating Scale." *Psychol Rpts*, 1962. **10**: 799-812.

21. Casey, J.F., Hollister, L.E., Klett, C.J., Lasky, J.J. and Caffey, E.M., Jr., "Combined Drug Therapy of Chronic Schizophrenics: A Controlled Evaluation of Placebo, Dextroamphetamine, Imipramine, Isocarboxazid, and Trifluoperazine added to Maintenance Doses of Chlorpromazine." *Amer J Psychiat*, 1961. **117**: 997-1003.

22. Lasky, J.J., Klett, C.J., Caffey, E.M., Jr., Bennett, J.L., Rosenblum, M.P. and Hollister, L.E., "Drug Therapy of Chronic Schizophrenics: A Comparative Evaluation of Chlorpromazine, Chlorprothixene, Fluphenazine, Reserpine, Thioridazine, and Triflupromazine." *Dis Nerv Syst*, 1962. **23**: 698-706.

23. Caffey, E.M., Jr., Diamond, L.S., Frank, T.V., Grasberger, J.C., Herman, L., Klett, C.J. and Rothstein, C., "Discontinuation or Reduction of Chemotherapy in Chronic Schizophrenics." *J Chron Dis*, 1964. **17**: 347-358.

24. Gorham, D.R., Pokorney, A.D. and Moseley, E.C., "Effects of Phenothiazine and/or Group Psychotherapy with Schizophrenics." *Dis Nerv Syst*, 1964. **25**: 77-86.

25. Klett, C.J. and Caffey, E.M., Jr., "Evaluating the Long-Term Need for Antiparkinson Drugs for Chronic Schizophrenics." *Arch Gen Psychiat*, 1972. **26**: 374-376.

26. Abrams, S. and Ciufo, S., *Cooperative Studies in Mental Health and Behavioral Sciences*. Washington, DC: Department of Medicine and Surgery, Veterans Administration, 1975, ii.

27. Overall, J.E., Hollister, L.E., Pokorney, A.D., Casey, J.F. and Katz, G., "Drug Therapy in Depressions: Controlled Evaluations of Imipramine, Isocarboxazid, Dextroamphetamine-Amobarbital, and Placebo." *Clin Pharmacol Therapeut*, 1962. **3**: 16-22.

28. Klett, C.J., Hollister, L.E., Caffey, E.M., Jr. and Kaim, S.C., "Evaluating Changes in Symptoms During Acute Alcohol Withdrawal." *Arch Gen Psychiat*, 1971. **24**: 174-178.

29. Ling, W., Charavastra, C., Kaim, S.C. and Klett, C.J., "Methadyl Acetate and Methadone as Maintenance Treatments for Heroin Addicts." *Arch Gen Psychiat*, 1976. **33**: 709-720.

30. Prien, R.F., Caffey, E.M., Jr. and Klett, C., J, "Comparison of Lithium Carbonate and Chlorpromazine in the Treatment of Mania." *Arch Gen Psychiat*, 1972. **26**: 146-153.

31. Prien, R.F., Caffey, E.M., Jr. and Klett, C., J, "Factors Associated with Treatment Success in Lithium Carbonate Prophylaxis." *Arch Gen Psychiat*, 1974. **31**: 189-192.

32. Prien, R.F., Caffey, E.M., Jr. and Klett, C., J, "A Comparison of Lithium Carbonate and Chlorpromazine in the Treatment of Excited Schizo-Affectives." *Arch Gen Psychiat*, 1972. **27**: 182-189.

33. Interview with C. James Klett, Ph.D., January 11,1990 at a hotel lobby in Washington, D.C.

34. *First Research Conference on Chemotherapy in Psychiatry*. Downey, IL: Office of the Chief Medical Director, Veterans Administration, Washington, DC, 1956.

35. *Second Research Conference on Chemotherapy in Psychiatry*. Downey, IL: Office of the Chief Medical Director, Veterans Administration, Washington, DC, 1957.

36. Telephone interview with C. James Klett, Ph.D., March 12, 2001.

37. Kaim, S. and Lindley, C., *R&E Newsletter*, May, 1961, 14-15.

38. Klett, C.J. "Preface." *Highlights of the 20th Annual Conference, Veterans Administration Studies in Mental Health and Behavioral Sciences*, i.

39. *Highlights of the 20th Annual Conference, Veterans Administration Studies in Mental Health and Behavioral Sciences*. Klett, C.J., ed. Perry Point, MD: Veterans Administration, 1975,

40. Barnwell, J.B. "The Value of Cooperative Research." *First Research Conference on Chemotherapy in Psychiatry*. Downey, IL: Office of the Chief Medical Director, Veterans Administration, Washington, DC, 3-5.

41. Lamb, H.R., "Deinstitutionalization and Public Policy", in *American Psychiatry after World War II (1944-1994)*, Menninger, R.W. and Nemiah, J.C., Editors. 2000, American Psychiatric Press: Washington, DC 259.

Chapter 9. The Hypertension Studies

The relationship between hypertension, commonly referred to as high blood pressure, and adverse health effects has long been recognized. People with hypertension are more likely than others to have cardiovascular disease, heart attacks, stroke and heart failure. VA medical research over more than 60 years has significantly contributed to the improved treatment of hypertension.

In their 1948 review of young service men who had heart attacks during World War II, Yater and his colleagues at the Washington (DC) VA Hospital showed that enlistment blood pressures in men who had coronary attacks were higher compared with those of men who were later treated in the VA for amputations.[1] These authors reviewed earlier publications that also showed this effect. While the relationship between hypertension and vascular disease was already well established, it was by no means accepted that one led to the other. Many authorities thought that hypertension and vascular disease were simply different expressions of a common problem. Unless hypertension was causing obvious problems, such as the convulsions of eclampsia in pregnancy or the headaches and papilledema of malignant hypertension, hypertension was not widely believed to require treatment.

Early treatment of hypertension

Before effective drugs became available to lower blood pressure, other approaches were recommended in standard medical textbooks. In the 1925 tenth edition of Osler's *Principles and Practice of Medicine*, McCrae states that one should look for a correctable cause for hypertension. If no cause was found:

> "Any focus of infection should be removed --. Mental rest and quiet, so far as can be secured, are important. Long hours of physical rest are useful. Exercise, short of fatigue, is helpful, best in the form of walking, golf, etc. A good vacation, often one spent at one of the springs, is an advantage. One day a week in bed on a low diet is useful in more advanced cases.

> ". . . Bathing in tepid or warm water usually is best. The bowels should be kept well open, for which a saline before breakfast is often useful. A weekly dose of blue mass or mercury and chalk powder at bedtime for two successive nights is often beneficial. Some patients do well with irrigations of the colon once or twice a week in addition."[2]

This advice had not changed much by the 1947 sixteenth edition of the same text, now written by Christian. He advised, however, that: "The bowels should be kept normal; the oft advised free catharsis seems to the present author inadvisable." He went on to state that "A sedative, such as phenobarbital, generally is helpful."[3]

Edward Freis, M.D., of the Washington VA Hospital, whose later work was prominent in solving the hypertension problem, described the situation in 1951. He advised treating only patients with such severe hypertension that they were "almost certain to develop fatal complications within a few years". These were:

"1. Patients with hemorrhages, exudates and/or papilledema in the optic fundi.

2. Patients with diastolic blood pressures persistently above 120 mm. Hg. even after forty-eight hours of bed rest in the hospital.

3. Patients with repeated attacks of acute hypertensive encephalopathy associated with extreme elevations of blood pressure."[4]

The reason for this conservatism was that while the available effective treatments—surgical sympathectomy, Kaempner's "200 mg sodium diet" and toxic drugs—could be life-saving, were very hard on the patient. Freis and others searched for effective, less toxic drugs to lower blood pressure and within the next few years the search began to produce results.

Should hypertension be treated?

By the 1950s and 1960s, effective drugs for reducing blood pressure were becoming available. Mortality in patients with malignant hypertension who were treated with the new drugs was shown to be markedly reduced when compared to historical controls.[5] Increasing numbers of cardiologists favored drug treatment for severe or malignant hypertension.[6] But even that opinion was not universal, and there was no agreement about the best way to handle less severe cases, patients with diastolic blood pressures under 120 mm Hg.

Even though cardiology texts started advising drug therapy for severe hypertension, standard medical textbooks generally hesitated to advise drug therapy. A 1966 British textbook of medicine states:

"In the present status of therapy there is no justification in attempting to lower the blood pressure by drugs or operation in the absence of symptoms. An exception might be made in young subjects, especially men, with a high fixed level of blood pressure (e.g. diastolic exceeding 120 mm.). In such cases it may be felt that complications are likely to occur sooner rather than later and for this reason some reduction of the pressure with hypotensive drugs is justifiable. The level may be regarded as fixed when residual hypertension persists after 7 days' complete rest in bed with adequate sedation."[7]

The 1967 edition of the *Cecil and Loeb Textbook of Medicine*, by Beeson and McDermott, contained the following "philosophy of treatment":

"Be sure that the patient really needs treatment. Those over 70 years rarely do, whatever the level of pressure, and certainly should not be treated unless a definite indication such as pulmonary edema, angina pectoris, severe headache or marked shortness of breath on effort is present. It is sad to see a well preserved patient of 70 years with an arterial pressure of 190 systolic, 90 diastolic in mm. of mercury due to the presence of a rigid aorta receiving treatment for a headache or other symptoms that are manifestations of anxiety or depression. Age needs no additional therapeutic hazards."[8]

A 1966 book, *Controversy in Internal Medicine*, edited by Ingelfinger, Relman and Finland, included a strongly stated criticism by Goldring and Chasis of those who treated even severe hypertension. They stated, "We believe that we are now in an era of empiric treatment of hypertension, in which a huge uncontrolled clinical-pharmacological experiment may be masquerading as a clinically acceptable therapy." They commented:

"The effect of artificially lowered blood pressure on the occurrence of cerebral vascular accidents and myocardial infarction or failure has been reported, but only as a statistical relationship between these complications and the level of blood pressure. . . . Furthermore, there are sufficient reports in the literature indicating that coronary disease may progress in spite of artificially lowered blood pressure."

They even questioned the value of lowering blood pressure in "accelerated hypertension" or "malignant hypertension", with this conclusion:

"After about 15 years of data collecting, we believe that the alleged usefulness of antihypertensive drugs rests on conclusions drawn from notoriously uncertain statistical compilations compounded by equally uncertain estimates of morbidity and mortality in the natural history of a disease of highly unpredictable course."[9]

Two other papers in the same book[10, 11] placed more value on use of antihypertensive drugs. In his summarizing "Comments", Arnold Relman asks: "It is not difficult in most cases to lower blood pressure with various types of drugs, but does this prolong life or prevent serious cardiovascular complications?" His perspective was that:

"We need more controlled prospective studies. I suspect, however, that few will be forthcoming, so that the practicing physician is faced with a familiar dilemma." Relman concluded: "If he is prudent, I believe he will reserve drug therapy—for only those patients with moderate or severe hypertension whose blood pressures cannot be improved by simpler measures. While using drugs, the physician must be aware of the possible dangers of long-range toxic effects and of all the uncertainties implicit in the uncontrolled experiment he is conducting."[12]

To find answers to the questions and address skepticism about hypertension treatment, in 1956 Dr. Edward Freis, Chief of Medical Service at the Washington VA Hospital, assembled a group of colleagues from other VA facilities to start a cooperative study on antihypertensive drugs.

Edward D. Freis, M.D.

Freis, interested in research since childhood, published several clinical papers during his early medical training. While in an Air Force pathology laboratory in Lincoln, NE during World War II, he worked with I. Arthur Mirsky, M.D., who was already famous for his diabetes research. Mirsky shared a tremendous enthusiasm for research and taught Freis a lot about how to carry out medical investigation.[13] Together, they published a paper on shock induced by trypsin.[14]

Figure 9.1 Edward Freis, M.D.

After the war, Freis returned to Boston University to complete his residency under Chester Keefer. Keefer introduced him to James Shannon, of later importance to the NIH, who was then head of the Squibb Institute for Medical Research. Shannon wanted to study the chemotherapy of hypertension. His previous search for antihypertensives, which had not been successful, included work on the red pigment in lobster shells, since the Russians had reported that ground-up lobster shells reduced blood pressure.

Now, Shannon wanted to test pentaquine, an antimalarial drug used during World War II, which caused hypotension when given in large doses. Freis agreed to do the clinical trials. The hospital assigned a wing of a ward for a clinical trial of pentaquine in hypertensive patients. The drug produced severe side effects, but it did lower blood pressure and help some patients with the most severe hypertension.[15]

After that, Freis and his fellow resident Joseph Stanton learned about veratrum viride from a review paper by Otto Krayer of Harvard.[16] Veratrum viride had been used by American Indians in their initiation rites to cause vomiting and collapse as well as by nineteenth century physicians in Appalachia to treat eclampsia. Freis and Stanton studied it in their hypertensive patients. They found the therapeutic window was very narrow: the dose that lowered the blood pressure often caused bradycardia, sweating and projectile vomiting. They found the drug's effectiveness improved by combining it with a low-sodium diet. They followed up with a series of other studies of drugs having some benefit to patients with severe hypertension.

In 1949, Freis was recruited to Washington, DC, to be Assistant Chief of the Medical Service at the Washington VA Hospital and a faculty member at Georgetown University. At first his laboratory was primarily at Georgetown, but he gradually moved his base of operations to the VA. He found that VA patients were more cooperative in his clinical research than Georgetown clinic patients. Also, the VA had a good laboratory, partly in the same facility as the old Cardiovascular Research Laboratory that closed in 1949 (Chapter 2). There, Freis conducted hemodynamic studies, primarily on cardiac patients.

An important product of this period of research was the demonstration that cardiac output and stroke volume decreased in proportion to the severity of myocardial infarction. He worked with engineers from the National Bureau of Standards to develop the first monitoring equipment and other special equipment for cardiac patients.

All along, Freis continued his clinical research on drugs to counteract hypertension. The most important breakthrough, in 1957, was chlorothiazide, a new diuretic drug that quickly supplanted injection of mercurial diuretics in edematous patients. Freis had tried mercurials in severe hypertension and saw the potential of chlorothiazide therapy for hypertension. He quickly treated a series of hypertensive patients with this new drug and presented his results at the next meeting of the American Heart Association.

Beginnings of the VA cooperative studies on hypertension

Freis learned about the cooperative study approach to clinical research in the early 1950s. During a meeting of cardiologists in Europe, Freis joined a VA colleague, Hubert Pipberger, in a visit to Dr. Martini, a well-known medical statistician in Cologne, Germany. Together, they discussed Pipberger's interest in cooperative studies in vectorcardiography. Returning to the conference, Freis defended his use of drug treatment for hypertension and encountered opposition to his position. He concluded that his only alternative was to use multi-clinic trials in the fashion he and Pipberger had discussed with Martini.

At a VA Chiefs of Medicine meeting, Freis gained the interest of about 15 people in mapping out a plan to conduct such a study. His original thought was for a "very simple design—placebo versus treatment—the best treatment you had available at the time—and follow up for complications." But, everyone wanted to add to it. Freis described what he encountered:

> "The plan was made out by the doctors. There was no help yet at that stage from any statisticians, and it was a lousy plan. . . . Pretty soon it was loaded. . . . We were comparing different drugs at the same time we were studying effectiveness and mortality. Well, we learned after that that you can't have two main objectives in the same study."

Freis took the group's plan to VA Central Office. In a November 26, 1956, press release, the goal of the study was described as "determining how well newer drugs control high blood pressure and whether they can prevent hardening of the arteries, heart attacks, strokes and other complications of the disease."[17] The leaders in the cooperating VA hospitals, in addition to Freis, were Mark Armstrong and Walter Kirkendall of Iowa City, John Bakke and Harold Dodge of Seattle, Massimo Calebresi of West Haven (CT), Loyal Conrad of Oklahoma City, E.E. Edelman of Birmingham (AL), Rudolph Fremont of Brooklyn, David Littman of West Roxbury (MA), Clifford Pilz of Chicago West Side, Eli Ramirez of San Juan (PR), and David Richardson of Richmond (VA).

Results of the first series of studies by this group of investigators were reported in a series of papers in the *Annals of Internal Medicine* between 1960 and 1962.[18-20] These studies helped to establish the most effective ways to control hypertension using then-available agents, but they did not answer the central question of whether this led to prevention of the disease's complications.

Resolving hypertension's core question

In 1963, Freis and a group of investigators from earlier studies planned a study specifically designed to resolve the essential mystery surrounding hypertension treatment. This time, they planned closely with Lawrence Shaw,[21] the new head of research biostatistics at the VA Central Office, to keep the study design simple. From their work on available drugs, they chose what they considered to be the best regimen, a combination of hydrochlorothiazide, reserpine and hydralazine. They persuaded the drugs' pharmaceutical companies to provide placebo tablets. Additional special tablets, each with its own placebo, were available when doses of one or another drug needed to be adjusted because of side effects.

Patients were very carefully selected for this study. Veterans with hypertension were hospitalized for an initial workup before enrollment. Those whose diastolic blood pressures averaged between 90 and 129 mm Hg during days 4 through 6 of a hospital stay were considered for the study. They selected only patients who appeared motivated and had no existing severe hypertensive sequelae. As Freis recalled, although there was no formal consent process; the patient's preference to return to his usual practitioner was a formal basis for exclusion.

The investigators rigorously checked a patient's reliability before accepting him into the study. After hospital discharge and before randomization, patients received two placebo tablets, one of them containing riboflavin. During two subsequent clinic visits, pill counts were done and urine was checked by fluorescence for riboflavin content. Excluded from the study were patients who failed to keep both appointments and bring their pills, had incorrect pill counts, or had no riboflavin in their urine. With these precautions, noncompliance, probably the most important cause of treatment failure in ordinary practice, could be minimized.

This study began in April 1964 and only the statistical staff were aware of the results until they were "unblinded" in 1969. However, in early 1967, Shaw told Freis of his early analysis of results from patients with severe hypertension, defined as diastolic pressures 115 through 129. By this time, 143 patients with severe hypertension were enrolled in the study, 70 of them on placebo medication. Fifty-five patients with severe hypertension, 23 on placebo, had been followed more than two years. Analyzing this group of patients, Shaw found that the number of serious cardiovascular events was much greater in the placebo group, showing a convincing degree of statistical significance. Serious cardiovascular "events" had occurred in 27 of the placebo-treated severely hypertensive patients but in only two of those receiving active antihypertensive treatment. There was no question that reducing a markedly elevated diastolic blood pressure helped to protect the patient. Patients in this "severe hypertension" group were immediately dropped from the study, and those who had been on placebo received active treatment to reduce their blood pressures.

JAMA published the results in December 1967.[22] As Freis recalled, this paper on treatment of severe hypertension didn't cause much discussion. But he also recalls deciding against having a press release. Just as there were those who still needed to be convinced that treatment of hypertension is efficacious, there were others, convinced that lowering blood pressure protected patients, who criticized the group for doing a placebo-controlled study. And the more difficult question—whether treatment of mild and moderate hypertension is efficacious—still needed to be answered.

So the group continued to enroll patients with diastolic pressures up to 114 for another two years, until September 1968. The "blind" for these patients continued until after the last observations had been completed in October 1969. Three hundred eighty patients had been observed for one to five years, on average for more than three years.

As before, throughout the course of the study, the statistical group continued to monitor the "unblinded" data. They shared the results with Central Office officials. One Saturday in October 1969, Thomas Chalmers, M.D., ACMD for Research and Education and himself an authority on controlled clinical trials, was working at his desk in Central Office. He looked at the latest – significant – statistical analysis of results from the hypertension study. It was clear that reducing blood pressure prevented stroke and congestive heart failure. Immediately, Chalmers sent out instructions to the study clinics to put all patients on active treatment and to break the blind. Later, the group found that the significance of their findings was primarily due to the patients with moderate hypertension, diastolic pressures 105-114. It would take a later, much larger, study to prove the protective effect of treating even mild hypertension.

This VA report, by virtue of its randomized, double-blind, placebo-controlled design, presented the first definitive and convincing proof that treating moderate hypertension was beneficial in preventing or delaying many of its catastrophic health complications.

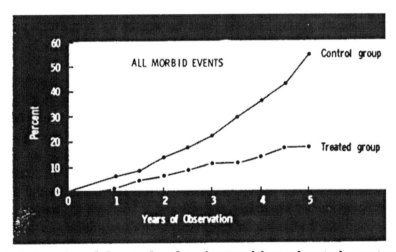

Figure 9.2 Results of the study of patients with moderate hypertension

<u>Response to the study</u>

The report of the study showing the efficacy of treatment of moderate hypertension appeared in *JAMA* in August 1970.[23] It provoked little immediate reaction. The Associated Press circulated the news, but not much was published in the general press. As Freis recalled, there was little immediate interest among physicians. However, the results were recognized in the 1971 edition of the Cecil-Loeb textbook: "Now that controlled trials of treatment in less severe grades of hypertension have been carried out, it is clear that improvement in outlook is conferred by successful treatment." Nevertheless, the textbook continued to advise against treating the elderly.[24]

In May 1971, Freis spoke at a special seminar on clinical trials held by the "Young Turks" (the American Society for Clinical Investigation) at its Atlantic City meeting. Mary Lasker heard about the study. Freis recalled that Lasker approached Secretary of Health, Education and Welfare Elliot Richardson with reprints of Freis's papers and publications. Richardson's father, a physician, had had hypertension and died of a stroke. He ordered the creation of a nationwide effort to publicize hypertension that became known as the National High Blood Pressure Education Program.

In November 1972, Freis received the Lasker Award for his contributions to clinical medicine.

The 1974 edition of *Controversies in Clinical Medicine* included a follow-up to the 1966 disagreement on the treatment of hypertension:

> "There has (in the first edition) been a difference of opinion in regard to the treatment of benign hypertension, but both Hollander and Relman stated the need for a carefully controlled prospective study. Such a study has now been done.

> "The results of a clinical trial conducted in the Veterans Administration and led by Freis conclusively demonstrated the value of treating patients with benign hypertension of a moderate or severe grade."[25]

Nevertheless, skepticism about benefit from treatment of hypertension waned slowly. Even in 1997, Moser wrote:[26]

> "Even as results of therapy in the 1950s and the early 1960s improved, progress was still held back by prevailing attitudes of therapeutic nihilism, popularized and given respectability by several leading medical authorities. It is hard to believe, but some experts still believed that arterial disease was the cause of the hypertension rather than the result. These opinions scoffed at the use of drug as treatment of the manometer or the 'numbers' rather than the patient. There was disbelief that benefit could be achieved by just paying attention to the numbers. In the mid 1950s at the New York Academy of Medicine, we presented 10 cases of malignant hypertension, who had experienced clearing of fundoscopic abnormalities and heart failure and as a result of blood pressure lowering. Two eminent authorities pronounced that this

probably represented the 'natural history' of some patients. When reversal of LVH was demonstrated on EKG, a well-known New York City electrocardiographer sent us a note, 'Ain't nature grand.' - he expressed disbelief that cardiac hypertrophy could be reversed by just lowering the blood pressure (paying attention to the manometer). In view of more recent data, this attitude seems strange indeed.

"But some hypertension experts in the 1990's still belittle the benefits of 'just lowering the blood pressure.' It may be true that modifying other risk factors in addition to lowering blood pressure will result in a greater reduction in morbidity and mortality than has been noted thus far in the clinical trials and clinical experience."

Later studies by the VA Cooperative Study Group on Antihypertensive Agents

More questions still needed answering. The VA group had proven that drug treatment helped the patients they studied who had moderate to severe hypertension. These patients were relatively young, averaging about 50 years of age. How about the elderly? How about patients with mild hypertension—should they also be treated? What is the significance of systolic hypertension when the diastolic pressure is normal? How do other drugs compare with the fixed combination used in the morbidity study? Can the drugs be stopped after the blood pressure is controlled? The group of research clinicians remained together as the "Veterans Administration Cooperative Study Group on Antihypertensive Agents" and carried out a series of studies, some of them supported by the NIH and pharmaceutical companies as well as by the VA.

Among their first efforts was a more detailed analysis of the data from the morbidity study on patients with mild to moderate hypertension. They found that the older the patient and the more cardiovascular or renal abnormalities present at entry, the greater the benefit from treatment. While the entry diastolic blood pressure had little effect on adverse outcomes in the treated group, treatment had a greater effect on the level of blood pressure in those with the greater entry blood pressures.[27]

In later studies, the group compared new drugs with established antihypertensive drugs in a series of carefully controlled studies.[28-35] They also studied the effectiveness of drug combinations when single drugs were not effective in sufficiently lowering blood pressure and found that combinations, especially those containing diuretics, are often effective when the same drugs given singly are not.[36] This finding has led to the recommendation that drug combinations be used routinely.[37]

A 1975 paper reporting an attempt to wean patients from antihypertensive drugs showed that only 15 percent of patients with drug-controlled hypertension remained normotensive when a placebo was substituted. However, a later study showed that dosage could frequently be reduced safely but not discontinued entirely.[38]

Following the VA group's original finding that treatment of the elderly reduced adverse events, a finding reinforced by other groups,[39-42] an NHLBI-funded study with VA participation showed that lowering systolic blood pressure below 160 mmHg in elderly persons with isolated systolic hypertension lowered the stroke rate by one-third.[40]

Implications of the hypertension studies

Proof that treatment of hypertension prevents its complications has led to widespread efforts to detect and control the condition. In 1972, anticipating that a large number of untreated hypertensive veterans would need treatment to prevent complications, the VA started the Hypertension Screening and Treatment Program (HSTP), which included 32 treatment clinics to detect and treat hypertension in veterans. H. Mitchell Perry, M.D., of the St. Louis VA Medical Center was chairman of the program. A law change in late 1973 permitted outpatient treatment of hypertension. Treatment visits to the HSTP clinics began in January 1974 and some of these clinics continue active to the present time. A 20-year review in 1998 showed that lowering blood pressure had been effective in 85 percent of patients and that early treatment had decreased incidence of end-stage renal disease by half.[43]

The VA cooperative studies on hypertension have led to a revolution in the care of those with this condition. Countless people have been spared the ravages of stroke and other consequences of uncontrolled hypertension.

References

1.   Yater, W.M., Traum, A.H., Brown, W.G., Fitzgerald, R.P., Geisler, M.A. and Wilcox, B.B., "Coronary artery disease in men eighteen to thirty-nine years of age." *Am Heart J*, 1948. **36**: 334-372.

2.   McCrae, T., *The Principles and Practice of Medicine. Originally Written by William Osler. Tenth Edition.* New York and London: D. Appleton and Company, 1925, 864.

3.   Christian, H.A., *The Principles and Practice of Medicine. Originally Written by William Osler. Sixteenth Edition.* New York and London: D. Appleton-Century Company, Incorporated, 1947, 1130.

4.   Freis, E.D., "An approach to the treatment of severe essential hypertension." *Medicine Illustrated*, 1951. **5**: 53-58.

5.   Perry, H.M. and Schroeder, H.A., "The effect of treatment on mortality rates in severe hypertension." *Arch Int Med*, 1958. **102**: 418-425.

6.   Leishman, A.W.D., "Merits of reducing high blood-pressure." *Lancet*, 1963. **1**: 1284-1288.

7.   Scott, R.B., *Price's Textbook of the Practice of Medicine.* London: Oxford University Press, 1966, 735.

8.   Beeson, P.B. and McDermott, W., *Cecil-Loeb Textbook of Medicine, Twelfth Edition.* Philadelphia, London, Toronto: W.B. Saunders Company, 1967, 665-666.

9.   Goldring, W. and Chasis, H., "Antihypertensive drug therapy: An appraisal", in *Controversy in Internal Medicine*, Ingelfinger, F., Relman, A., and Finland, M., Editors. 1966, W.B. Saunders Company: Philadelphia and London 83-91.

10.   Page, I.H. and Dustan, H.P., "The usefulness of drugs in the treatment of hypertension", in *Controversy in Internal Medicine.* 1966 92-95.

11.   Hollander, W., "The evaluation of antihypertensive therapy of essential hypertension", in *Controversy in Internal Medicine.* 1966 96-100.

12.   Relman, A.S., "Comment", in *Controversy in Internal Medicine.* 1966 101-102.

13.   Interview with Edward Freis, M.D., May 27, 1997 at Dr. Freis's office at the Washington, DC VAMC.

14.   Mirsky, I.A. and Fries, E.D., "Renal and hepatic injury in trypsin "shock"." *Proc Soc Exp Biol Med*, 1944. **57**: 278.

15.   Freis, E.D. and Wilkins, R.W., "The effects of pentaquine in patients with hypertension,." *Proc Soc Exp Biol Med*, 1947. **64**: 455-458.

16.   Krayer, O. and Acheson, G.H., "The pharmacology of the veratrum alkaloids." *Physiol Rev*, 1946. **26**: 282-446.

17.   Veterans Administration Central Office, *Future release.* 1956, Veterans Administration: Washington, DC.

18.   Veterans Administration Cooperative Study on Antihypertensive Agents, "A double blind control study of antihypertensive agents." *Arch Int Med*, 1960. **106**: 133-148.

19.   Veterans Administration Cooperative Study on Antihypertensive Agents, "A double blind control study of antihypertensive agents II." *Arch Int Med*, 1962. **110**: 222-229.

20.   Veterans Administration Cooperative Study on Antihypertensive Agents, "A double blind control study of antihypertensive agents III. Chlorothiazide alone and in combination with other agents; Preliminary results." *Arch Int Med*, 1962. **110**: 230-236.

21.   Interview with Lawrence Shaw, February 3, 1994 at Mr. Shaw's home.

22.   Veterans Administration Cooperative Study on Antihypertensive Agents, "Effects of treatment on morbidity in hypertension. Results in patients with diastolic blood pressures averaging 115 through 129 mm Hg." *JAMA*, 1967. **202**: 116-122.

23.   Veterans Administration Cooperative Study on Antihypertensive Agents, "Effects of treatment on morbidity in hypertension. Results in patients with diastolic blood pressures averaging 90 through 114 mm Hg." *JAMA*, 1970. **213**: 1143-1152.

24.   Beeson, P.B. and McDermott, W., *Cecil-Loeb Textbook of Medicine.* Philadelphia, London, Toronto: W.B. Saunders Company, 1971, 1058-1059.

25.   Ingelfinger, F.J., Ebert, R.V., Finland, M. and Relman, A.S., *Controversy in Internal Medicine II.* Philadelphia and London: W.B. Saunders Company, 1974

26.   Moser, M., *Myths, misconception, and heroics; The story of the treatment of hypertension from the 1930s.* Le Jacq Communications, Inc., 1997

27.   Veterans Administration Cooperative Study Group on Antihypertensive Agents, "Effects of treatment on morbidity in hypertension III. Influence of age, diastolic pressure, and prior cardiovascular disease; further analysis of side effects." *Circulation*, 1972. **45**: 991-1004.

28.   Veterans Administration Cooperative Study Group on Antihypertensive Agents, "Multiclinic controlled trial of bethanidine and guanethidine in severe hypertension." *Circulation*, 1977. **55**: 519-524.

29.   Veterans Administration Cooperative Study Group on Antihypertensive Agents, "Propranolol in mild HBP." *JAMA*, 1977. **237**: 2307-2310.

30.   Veterans Administration Cooperative Study Group on Antihypertensive Agents, "Comparative effects of ticrynafen and hydrochlorothiazide in the treatment of hypertension." *New Eng J Med*, 1979. **301**: 293-297.

31.   Veterans Administration Cooperative Study Group on Antihypertensive Agents, "Comparison of prazosin with hydralazine in patients receiving hydrochlorothiazide." *Circulation*, 1981. **64**: 772-779.

32.   Veterans Administration Cooperative Study Group on Antihypertensive Agents, "Comparison of propranolol and hydrochlorothiazide for the initial treatment of hypertension. I. Results of short-term titration with emphasis on racial differences in response." *JAMA*, 1982. **248**: 1996-2003.

33.   Veterans Administration Cooperative Study Group on Antihypertensive Agents, "Comparison of propranolol and hydrochlorothiazide for the initial treatment of hypertension. II. Results of long-term therapy." *JAMA*, 1982. **248**: 2004-2011.

34.   Veterans Administration Cooperative Study Group on Antihypertensive Agents, "Low-dose captopril for the treatment of mild to moderate hypertension. I. Results of a 14-week trial." *Arch Int Med*, 1984. **144**: 1947-1953.

35.   Materson, B.J., Reda, D.J., Cushman, W.C., Massie, B.M., Freis, E.D., Kochar, M.S., Hamburger, R.J., Fye, C., Lakshman, R., Gottdiener, J., Ramirez, E.A. and Henderson, W.G., "Single-drug therapy for hypertension in men. A comparison of six antihypertensive agents with placebo." *New Eng J Med*, 1993. **328**: 914-921.

36.   Materson, B.J., Reda, D.J., Cushman, W.C. and Henderson, W.G., "Results of combination anti-hypertensive therapy after failure of each of the components." *J Hum Hypertension*, 1995. **9**: 791-796.

37.   Freis, E.D., "Improving treatment effectiveness in hypertension." *Arch Int Med*, 1999. **159**: 2517-2521.

38.   Freis, E.D., Thomas, J.R., Fisher, S.G., Hamburger, R.J., Borreson, R.E., Mezey, K.C., Mukherji, B., Neal, W.W., Perry, H.M. and Taguchi, J.T., "Effects of reduction in drugs or dosage after long-term control of systemic hypertension." *Am J Card*, 1989. **63**: 702-708.

39.   Amery, A., Birkenhager, W., Brixko, P., Bulpitt, C., Clement, D., Deruyttere, M., De Schaipdryver, A., Dollery, C., Fagard, R., Forette, F., Forte, J., Hamdy, R., Henry, J.F., Joossens, J.V., Leonetti, G., Lund-Johansen, P., O'Malley, K., Petrie, J., Strasser, T., Tuomilehto, J. and Williams, B., "Mortality and morbidity results from the European Working Party on High Blood Pressure in the Elderly Trial." *Lancet*, 1985. **1**: 1349-1354.

40.   S.H.E.P. Cooperative Research Group, "Prevention of stroke by antihypertensive drug treatment in older persons with isolated systolic hypertension." *JAMA*, 1991. **265**: 3255-3264.

41.   The Management Committee, A.N.B.P.S., "Treatment of mild hypertension in the elderly." *Med J Aust*, 1981. **2**: 398-402.

42.   Coope, J. and Warrender, J.S., "Randomized trial of treatment of hypertension in elderly patients in primary care." *Br Med J*, 1986. **293**: 1145-1151.

43.   Perry, M., "Hypertension research in the VA." *unpublished*, 1998.

240

Chapter 10. Smoking and Lung Cancer

Arguably, the American public takes for granted the health warnings that are imprinted on the packages of tobacco products and appear in their advertising. Smokers and non-smokers alike readily accept the notion that the inhaling of burning tobacco fumes is not good for you. The issue was not always as settled as it appears today. Scientific and legal battles about tobacco dot the landscape of both medicine and commerce over the past 50 years. The public's and corporate acceptance of what many now consider to be a common-sense notion is a far cry from the days when smoking was considered a benign habit.

A vivid picture of just how far this subject has evolved requires no more than a glimpse of life among the troops of World War II. Smoking was so widespread in the military that small packages of cigarettes were routinely included in field rations. War-zone photos of soldiers at rest often caught men taking smoking breaks; the Bill Maudlin cartoon characters portraying typical GIs Willie and Joe frequently uttered their war-time wisdom past lips from which dangled a cigarette. Cigarette manufacturers routinely sponsored radio broadcasts; one that aimed its entertainment specifically to the Armed Forces announced prizes for military units in the form of hundreds of cartons of cigarettes. The phrase "smoke if you got 'em" remains well-known to most veterans. That the study of a connection between smoking and health first emerged from the then-obscure interests of a VA scientist seems more than just a coincidence.

Oscar Auerbach, M.D., was named one of the VA's first Senior Medical Investigators in 1959. A staff pathologist at the Halloran VA hospital on Staten Island (NY) from 1947 until 1952, when he moved to the new East Orange (NJ) VA Hospital, he remained on the staff at East Orange until 1980, keeping an office there until his death in 1997 at the age of 92.

Figure 10.1 Oscar Auerbach, M.D.

Auerbach was a central player in the VA tuberculosis trials (Chapter 5) and had been a pathologist at the Seaview tuberculosis hospital on Staten Island before joining the VA. He published landmark reports on the pathology of unusual types of tuberculosis based on his Seaview experience, tuberculous empyema,[1] tracheobronchial tuberculosis,[2] tuberculosis of the pleura, peritoneum and pericardium[3] and tuberculous meningitis.[4] After he joined the VA, he studied the effects of the new antituberculosis drugs on the pathology of the disease.[5-9]

Auerbach became a central figure in American medicine for his studies of the relationship between smoking and lung cancer, demonstrated by his use of "smoking dogs." He was a participant in the first Surgeon General's report on the effects of smoking and was written up in *Life Magazine*.[10]

The following are excerpts from the author's interview with Dr. Auerbach in his office at the East Orange VA Medical Center, on October 30, 1992.[11]

"When I was at Seaview, I published on tuberculosis. When I first went into the Veterans Administration, I published on the effects of antibiotic therapy (on tuberculosis). And one day, right here, I gave a CPC on an individual who had died of lung cancer. As a TB pathologist, used to taking many sections of the tracheobronchial tree, I saw in the many sections all of the preliminary stages of the lung cancer, including carcinoma in situ and early invasion. This individual was exposed to chromate, so I thought it was all due to chromate.

"I mused to the conference after my presentation that it would be interesting to see if we would find those same changes in the tracheobronchial tree that we saw here following smoking. So Charles Pfizer, for whom I had been a consultant, gave me money to pay four technicians overtime to work on that at night.

"When I was through with the preliminary report, somehow or other Ed Murrow got wind of it and sent his man up and asked me if I would go on his program, *See It Now*. I felt it was too preliminary and wouldn't do it. So I presented the preliminary changes at the American College of Chest Physicians in Atlantic City somewhere around 1952 or 1953. The Cancer Society became interested in our studies, and we had a press conference, and that was the beginning of the explosion as far as I'm concerned. It was really quite something.

"Everybody was interested. The American Cancer Society called a press conference, and asked me if I would appear at what was the then the Pennsylvania Hotel in New York. Around that table were all of the big reporters. They all were around the table and quizzed me. I never knew the power of the press until the next week. One of the people at the press conference was a column writer for the *New York Times*. There was a whole story on me on the op-ed page of the *New York Times*. It appeared in papers throughout the country.

"I presented my material to the American Cancer Society, and from then on all our studies were done with an epidemiologist at the American Cancer Society, Cuyler Hammond.

"The original results which I showed were the presence of these precancers. I drew no

242

conclusions. These were published in (the journal) *Cancer.*[12]

"As I said, we drew no conclusions. But there were sufficient changes in the tracheobronchial tree to warrant our going on with the study. I saw that we needed more material. That was a preliminary study with no conclusions drawn.

"I had been in the Navy with Charles Cameron, who was the Medical Director of the Cancer Society. Dr. Perdy Stout, who was my consultant at that time, and I went to see him. They brought in Dr. Hammond and Dr. Weaver, who was then the Research Director. And Dr. Hammond really began a dance all over the place. He said, 'What your slides are showing is what we have been saying epidemiologically, but they wouldn't listen to us.' And see, this was the proof. So he became very excited. And he said, would you let me work with you? I said that I would let him work with me on one condition, that he become a co-author. He said, 'That's very generous. You know, I've been asked by the Cancer Society to help you.' We made quite a team. So you notice that his name is on all the papers.

"The Cancer Society people were very excited. They said that they would support us. And for all the years after that, we were supported by the American Cancer Society.

"It was very, very, very interesting. I would go into the American Cancer Society, and I would sit down with Cuyler Hammond and with Lawrence Garfinkel, who took his place. E. Cuyler Hammond was the world's best and best-known epidemiologist in the field of smoking. No question about it. This all happened in the early 50s.

(Meanwhile, what were you doing at the VA?)

"I was a routine pathologist, carrying on with all my work. I did the research at home at night and on weekends. For years I did that. . . . It was all day Sunday. And I'd start about four in the morning and work until about six thirty. I would go home after work and sometimes work until ten o'clock at night. And all day Saturday, all day Sunday. It was something I loved. I enjoyed doing it. . . .

"Well, here's what would happen. I would go and see Cuyler Hammond at the American Cancer Society and we sat and we talked. And he said, 'Oscar, what are you trying to do?' I said, 'Simple. I am trying to see, in individuals who die of lung cancer, whether they show all the changes preliminary to the development of invasive carcinoma?[13] If I prove that, am I also able to see those same changes in individuals who die of causes other than lung cancer? And are they proportional to the amount of cigarettes they smoke?'[14]

"And those were the two studies all the way through, except one, which came later: What happens when individuals give up the smoking habit? That became the article that was published in the *New England Journal of Medicine*[15, 16] on former cigarette smokers."

"The first, 1964, Surgeon General's report on *Smoking and Health* includes a section on these anatomical studies.[17] That report reviewed the results of attempts up to that time to induce lung cancer in experimental animals from smoking. They concluded that all studies up to that time were inconclusive.[18]

(When did you decide to set up your experimental dog model?)

"I'll tell you what happened. There was an advertisement by one of the tobacco companies. A big full-page ad, which said that it is interesting that no animal model was used. That inspired me. And so I did one (preliminary) study on animals. They were all thoroughbred beagles. I did it with Cuyler. Ten smoking dogs versus ten non-smoking dogs.

(How did you get the dogs to smoke?)

"Tracheostomy. That study set the pace. It was at that time that we saw that we could produce the same changes in the tracheobronchial tree as we saw in human beings right up to invasion. And that was published.[19] Then we were beset by the tobacco industry. But that never bothered me and the tobacco industry never bothered me.

(What did they do?)

"Oh, the tobacco industry would always write articles. When I went to have articles published in the *Archives of Environmental Health*, they threatened the editor. They also went to the AMA and tried to have my article withdrawn.

(What kind of pressure could they use?)

"Oh, they would take their advertisements out of the papers. I had a story in *Life Magazine*. A very pretty young woman was doing the story for them. And the tobacco industry threatened *Life Magazine*, that if they wrote that story, they were going to withdraw their ads. She told me that the editorial board, all the editorial board, had a meeting and stated that they were completely behind the story that she wrote. And the article was published. . . .

"When we were studying the smoking dogs, they got the antivivisectionists after us.

(How did you decide to use dogs first of all?)

"I sat down with Cuyler Hammond and Arthur Purdy Stout. I said that, if we were going to do an animal model, the tracheobronchial tree must be large enough so that we could examine it. It must be one in which we could see the same changes as in the human being if they really occur. Dr. Hammond said that we want no variables. He insisted upon one breed and one sex, males.

"We found that using a tracheostomy was the best way to teach the dogs how to inhale. We later found out that they inhale by themselves after a while. But with the tracheostomy, we had complete control of how much smoke would go in . . . What happened (in the preliminary study) was that one died after 29 days. Another dog died after 200 some-odd days, another after 410 days, another after 415, and another after 420. We found that they were developing pulmonary infarcts. I called Cuyler Hammond, and said we'd better end this trial now while we still have good tracheobronchial trees to examine. So five dogs were sacrificed from 420 to 423 days. And we found that they developed pulmonary embolisms from thrombi that would develop in the right atrial appendage. The control dogs didn't have any changes.[19]

"We did the larynx. We did the esophagus. We did the lung parenchyma. Our studies on emphysema were equally as important as our studies on the tracheobronchial tree. All related to the smoking effects. Every study in the dog paralleled that of the human being.

"And always, I want you to know, we were pursued by the tobacco industry, but that was nothing. That didn't bother me. Never. They got hold of the Congressmen and Senators..... They wrote to Dr. Middleton and Dr. Middleton called me and said, 'Oscar, I want you to know they asked why the Veterans Administration was supporting a doctor who was killing an important industry in the southern states?' And his answer was, 'I never interfere in the scientific pursuits of the people who are under me.' I received the same support from Ben Wells, Jim Musser and Hal Engle. Bill Middleton knew everything I was doing. So did Jim Musser and Ben Wells."

Auerbach's definitive study of smoking dogs involved a total of 97 male beagles, eight nonsmoking controls with tracheostomies in place and the rest smoking various numbers of cigarettes, both filter-tipped and unfiltered. After almost three years, all the nonsmoking dogs had normal lungs. Histopathological changes had occurred in the lungs of all the smoking dogs, with the greatest changes in the lungs of dogs smoking unfiltered cigarettes most heavily.[20] Ten of the 24 dogs in the latter group developed invasive bronchiolo-alveolar tumors.[21] They also showed pulmonary fibrosis with emphysema.[22, 23] In another study, Auerbach demonstrated thickening of the arteriolar walls in the myocardia of smoking dogs and humans.[24]

Auerbach later studied other environmental effects on lung cancer. He collaborated with Geno Saccomanno, M.D., Ph.D., of the Grand Junction (CO) VA Hospital, who studied the factors leading to lung pathology among the uranium miners of the Colorado plateau.[25-32] He collaborated on studies of arsenic[33] and asbestos[34, 35] exposure and of inhalants[36] to lung cancer.

Auerbach's landmark contributions were the result of intense and laborious observation. His laboratory was lined floor to ceiling with slides. A typical study involved 208 serial section slides on each of 117 cases, each containing more than 24,000 slides and each studied, in most cases, by Auerbach himself. He also had expert statistical collaboration from his first studies on the lung cancer problem, and randomization and "blinding" were the rule. Auerbach's work has made a lasting impact on the health of millions.

References

1. Auerbach, O., "Empyema as a complication of chronic pulmonary tuberculosis." *Am Rev Tuberc*, 1949. **59**: 601-618.

2. Auerbach, O., "Tuberculosis of the trachea and major bronchi." *Am Rev Tuberc*, 1949. **60**: 604-620.

3. Auerbach, O., "Pleural, peritoneal and pericardial tuberculosis - a review of 209 cases uncomplicated by treatment or secondary infection." *Am Rev Tuberc*, 1950. **61**: 845-861.

4. Auerbach, O., "Tuberculous meningitis: Correlation of therapeutic results with the pathogenesis and pathologic changes." *Am Rev Tuberc*, 1951. **64**: 408-429.

5. Auerbach, O., Weiss, L. and Stemmerman, G., "Pathology of tuberculosis treated with streptomycin: A review of 34 cases." *Dis Chest*, 1951. **19**: 145-157.

6. Auerbach, O., Katz, H.I. and Small, M., "The effect of streptomycin therapy on the bronchocavitary junction and its relation to cavity healing." *Am Rev Tuberc*, 1953. **67**: 173-200.

7. Auerbach, O., Hobby, G., Small, M., Lenert, T. and Vaughn, L., "Effect of degree of healing upon persistence of tubercle bacilli within pulmonary lesions." *Am Rev Tuberc*, 1955. **72**: 386-389.

8. Auerbach, O., "Pulmonary tuberculosis after the prolonged use of chemotherapy." *Am Rev Tuberc*, 1955. **71**: 165-185.

9. Auerbach, O., Hobby, G., Small, M., Lenert, T. and Comer, J., "The clinicopathologic significance of the demonstration of viable tubercle bacilli in resected lesions." *J Thorac Surg*, 1955. **29**: 109-132.

10. "New cigarette-cancer link." *Life Magazine*, June 11, 1956, Cover and pp 129-130.

11. Interview with Oscar Auerbach, M.D., October 30, 1992 at Dr. Auerbach's office at the East Orange, NJ, VA Medical Center.

12. Auerbach, O., Petrick, T.G., Stout, A.P., Statsinger, A.L., Muehsam, G.E., Forman, J.B. and Gere, J.B., "The anatomical approach to the study of smoking and bronchogenic carcinoma." *Cancer*, 1956. **9**: 76-83.

13. Auerbach, O. and Stout, A.P., "Histopathological aspects of occult cancer of the lung." *Ann N Y Acad Sci*, 1964. **114**: 803-810.

14. Auerbach, O., Stout, A.P., Hammond, E.C. and Garfinkel, L., "Changes in bronchial epithelium in relation to cigarette smoking and in relation to lung cancer." *N Engl J Med*, 1961. **265**: 253-267.

15. Auerbach, O., Stout, A.P., Hammond, E.C. and Garfinkel, L., "Bronchial epithelium in former smokers." *N Engl J Med*, 1962. **267**: 119-125.

16. Auerbach, O., Stout, A.P., Hammond, E.C. and Garfinkel, L., "Smoking habits and age in relation to pulmonary changes: Rupture of alveolar septums, fibrosis and thickening of walls of small arteries and arterioles." *N Engl J Med*, 1963. **269**: 1045-1054.

17. Surgeon General of the United States *Smoking and Health: Report of the Advisory Committee to the Surgeon General of the Public Health Service.* U.S. Department of Health, Education and Welfare; Public Health Service, 1964. 167-173.

18. Surgeon General *Smoking and Health*. 1964. 165.

19. Auerbach, O., Hammond, E.C., Kirman, D., Garfinkel, L. and Stout, A.P., "Histologic changes in bronchial tubes of cigarette-smoking dogs." *Cancer*, 1967. **20**: 2055-2066.

20. Hammond, E.C., Auerbach, O., Kirman, D. and Garfinkel, L., "Effects of cigarette smoking on dogs: 1. Design of experiment, mortality, and findings in lung parenchyma." *Arch Environ Health*, 1970. **21**: 740-753.

21. Auerbach, O., Hammond, E.C., Kirman, D. and Garfinkel, L., "Effects of cigarette smoking on dogs. II. Pulmonary neoplasms." *Arch Environ Health*, 1970. **21**: 754-768.

22. Frasca, J.M., Auerbach, O., Parks, V.R. and Jamieson, J.D., "Electron microscopic observations on pulmonary fibrosis and emphysema in smoking dogs." *Exp Mol Pathol*, 1971. **15**: 108-125.

23. Frasca, J.M., Auerbach, O., Parks, V.R. and Jamieson, J.D., "Alveolar cell hyperplasia in the lungs of smoking dogs." *Exp Mol Pathol*, 1974. **21**: 300-312.

24. Auerbach, O., Hammond, E.C., Garfinkel, L. and Kirman, D., "Thickness of walls of myocardial arterioles in relation to smoking and age. Findings in men and dogs." *Arch Environ Health*, 1971. **22**: 20-27.

25. Saccomanno, G., Archer, V.E., Saunders, R.P., James, L. and Beckler, P.A., "Lung cancer of uranium workers on the Colorado Plateau." *Health Physics*, 1964. **10**: 1195-1201.

26. Saccomanno, G., Archer, V.E., Auerbach, O., Kuschner, M., Saunders, R.P. and Klein, M.G., "Histologic types of lung cancer among uranium miners." *Cancer*, 1971. **27**: 515-523.

27. Saccomanno, G., Archer, V.E., Auerbach, O. and Saunders, R.P., "Susceptibility and resistance to environmental carcinogens in the development of carcinoma of the lung." *Hum Pathol*, 1973. **4**: 487-495.

28. Saccomanno, G., Archer, V.E., Saunders, R.P., Auerbach, O. and Klein, M.G., "Early indices of cancer risk among uranium miners with reference to modifying factors." *Ann N Y Acad Sci*, 1976. **271**: 377-383.

29. Auerbach, O., Saccomanno, G., Kuschner, M., Brown, R.D. and Garfinkel, L., "Histologic findings in the tracheobronchial tree of uranium miners and non-miners with lung cancer." *Cancer*, 1978. **42**: 483-489.

30. Saccomanno, G., Yale, C., Dixon, W., Auerbach, O. and Huth, G.C., "An epidemiological analysis of the relationship between exposure to RN progeny, smoking and bronchogenic carcinoma in the U-mining population of the Colorado Plateau--1960-1980." *Health Phys*, 1986. **50**: 605-618.

31. Saccomanno, G., Huth, G.C., Auerbach, O. and Kuschner, M., "Relationship of radioactive radon daughters and cigarette smoking in the genesis of lung cancer in uranium miners." *Cancer*, 1988. **62**: 1402-1408.

32. Saccomanno, G., Auerbach, O., Kuschner, M., Harley, N.H., Michels, R.Y., Anderson, M.W. and Bechtel, J.J., "A comparison between the localization of lung tumors in uranium miners and in nonminers from 1947 to 1991." *Cancer*, 1996. **77**: 1278-1283.

33. Wicks, M.J., Archer, V.E., Auerbach, O. and Kuschner, M., "Arsenic exposure in a copper smelter as related to histological type of lung cancer." *Am J Ind Med*, 1981. **2**: 25-31.

34.   Auerbach, O., Hammond, E.C., Selikoff, I.J., Parks, V.R., Kaslow, H.D. and Garfinkel, L., "Asbestos bodies in lung parenchyma in relation to ingestion and inhalation of mineral fibers." *Environ Res*, 1977. **14**: 286-304.

35.   Auerbach, O., Garfinkel, L., Parks, V.R., Conston, A.S., Galdi, V.A. and Joubert, L., "Histologic type of lung cancer and asbestos exposure." *Cancer*, 1984. **54**: 3017-3021.

36.   Weiss, W., Moser, R.L. and Auerbach, O., "Lung cancer in chloromethyl ether workers." *Am Rev Respir Dis*, 1979. **120**: 1031-1037.

Chapter 11: Radioimmunoassay—A Revolutionary Advance in Medicine

If there has ever been any question or skepticism about the quality of medical research being done within the VA health-care system, such doubts were forever dispelled with a signal event in 1977. A dedicated and relentless physicist and a VA scientist studying hormones gained world attention with the winning of two Nobel Prizes. Rosalyn Yalow, Ph.D., of the Bronx VA Medical Center captured science's crown jewel for her groundbreaking work in the field of radioimmunoassay (RIA), a process by which substances in the blood can be measured with exquisite accuracy. Andrew F. Schally, Ph.D., earned the recognition for his research at the New Orleans VA Medical Center on hormone activity in the hypothalamus gland.

The breakthrough work by Yalow and her colleague Solomon Berson, M.D., was supported from its inception by the Radioisotope Service at the Bronx VA Hospital. The RIA achievement is a testimony to the skill of Drs. Yalow and Berson and to the value of the VA's policy of providing sustained support to talented and productive medical researchers.

RIA works by combining an unknown amount of the substance to be measured with an antibody that will bind to it in a reversible way, so that after a time the bound and unbound amounts of the substance will reach equilibrium. It is also mixed with a radioactive version of the material to be measured. Since the binding of the radioactive form competes with the stable form for binding on the antibody, the known radioactive form can be used as a "tracer" for the behavior of the unknown amount of the stable form and will achieve the same bound-to-unbound equilibrium as does the substance to be measured. When the amount of antibody present is enough to bind only part of the material to be measured, it will also bind only that same fraction of the radioactive tracer. The more substance to be measured, the more will be left after saturating the antibody binding. Since this is equally true for the tracer, one can measure the percent of bound tracer and thus accurately measure the unknown. The Nobel Prize announcement provided this example:

> "The percentage binding of labeled insulin to the antibodies is a function of the total insulin concentration in the solution...RIA is so sensitive that it allowed determination of insulin in amounts as small as 10-20 pg and ACTH in an amount less that 1 pg (or one thousand-billionth g) per ml."[1]

The discovery of RIA reaches back some 30 years before it culminated with the Nobel award. In late 1947, Bernard Roswit, M.D., set up a Radioisotope Unit at the Bronx VA Hospital, one of the original seven units started by Herbert Allen[2] (Chapter 6). Roswit's first hire, in December 1947, was the young physicist Rosalyn Yalow[3] who wanted to work with radioisotopes. Yalow's training was in nuclear physics, with a Ph.D. degree earned in 1945 at the University of Illinois. Her first job was working as an electrical engineer for International Telephone and Telegraph, a leading worldwide telecommunications company. Yalow next moved to teaching, joining the physics faculty at Hunter College in the Bronx.

Yalow very much wanted to pursue her interest in research even though Hunter possessed no such facilities. Her training in nuclear physics had fostered an interest in radioisotopes and a curiosity that was stimulated by her husband's use of radioiodine in the treatment of patients with thyroid disease. She visited Dr. Edith Quimby at Montefiore Hospital in New York, who agreed to teach her about radioisotopes and introduced her to Dr. G. Fialla. In addition to their research activities at Montefiore, Quimby and Fialla were radiology consultants at the Bronx VA Hospital. Through them, Yalow met Bernard Roswit, M.D., chief of Radiation Therapy at the VA.

At first, Yalow performed her VA work while "moonlighting" from her teaching job, but in 1949 she opened her own VA-based laboratory. Early papers were eclectic and reflected the interests of her clinician colleagues. With Roswit, she studied radioactive phosphorus (^{32}P) in diagnosis of testicular cancer[4] and radioactive iodine (^{131}I) in treatment of metastatic thyroid cancer.[5] With others, she studied dosimetry in diagnostic radiology,[6] variability of bone marrow biopsies,[7] and the clearance of radiosodium from skin and muscle.[8-11]

Figure 11.1 Rosalyn Yalow in her laboratory

In 1950, an opportunity arose to recruit a physician colleague for the Radioisotope Unit. Yalow recalled:

"It seemed to me. . . that the future of radioisotopes in medicine was not in radiotherapy, in spite of the 'atomic cocktail'. . . but that the way to go would be physiology—that we needed somebody trained in internal medicine. So I went to the Head of Medicine at the hospital here, Dr. Bernard Straus, and said, 'We'll take anybody you recommend.'

"And he said, 'I have a brilliant resident. He's already accepted the position at another VA Hospital but I'll send him down to you.' And so Sol came down, and we interacted very well, and he gave up the other job."

Solomon Berson, M.D., was just finishing his internal medicine residency in the Mt. Sinai—

Bronx VA affiliated program. He had already shown a talent for clinical research and was an author on papers about Hodgkin's Disease[12, 13] and rheumatoid arthritis.[14] For the first year or so after he joined the VA, he worked there only part time and also carried on a private practice. Soon, he gave up his practice and worked full time at the VA, because he found the work so exciting. In 1954, when the radioisotope unit was separated from Radiotherapy and became a separate Radioisotope Service at the hospital, Berson became its Chief.

Figure 11.2 Solomon Berson, M.D.

The first collaborative work by Berson and Yalow were studies of ^{32}P and ^{42}K labeled red blood cells for studies of blood volume and red-cell disorders.[15-17]

Soon they began to study the thyroid. Yalow developed an improved Geiger counter for detection of the ^{131}I gamma ray. They worked out a method for measuring iodine clearance by the thyroid gland and applied it to a variety of clinical conditions. In 1954, they published what was probably the first comprehensive model of thyroid iodine metabolism.[18-20]

Next their attention was directed to ^{131}I labeled human serum albumin, and they began studying albumin metabolism and blood volume in humans, both well and ill.[21-26] Two early research fellows in the lab, Marcus Rothschild, M.D., and Arthur Baumann, M.D.,[27] worked on the albumin studies, which Rothschild later extended to important work on albumin production by the liver.

Rothschild and Baumann also collaborated on the laboratory's first studies of metabolism of insulin, which Yalow labeled with ^{131}I. These studies were stimulated by Arthur Mirsky's theory that adult-onset (Type 2) diabetes was caused by an excessive rate of metabolism of insulin, since it was known that the pancreas of these patients contained insulin. Mirsky's theory would predict that insulin would disappear faster from the blood of diabetic patients than from the blood of normal subjects. Instead, the opposite occurred.

Yalow described how the process worked:

"We labeled the insulin with (radio)iodine, gave it intravenously, and noted that there was a slower disappearance in the adult diabetics, rather than faster, which the theory had predicted. Although there was an occasional patient who was a 'rapid disappearer' when his diabetes was first discovered, he then converted to a 'slow disappearer' after 3 months of insulin therapy. And then we had schizophrenic patients who had had insulin shock therapy who were also 'slow disappearers'. So we thought this was due to the development of antibody."

But the notion of an antibody to insulin was too iconoclastic for the medical establishment, and this led to difficulty in publication[28] of this pivotal discovery, the basis for the concept of radioimmunoassay:

"We were able to demonstrate that, yes, in the plasma of insulin-treated patients, the labeled insulin was bound to something that had the characteristics of a gamma globulin. We submitted the paper to *Science*; they rejected it. We submitted the paper to the *Journal of Clinical Investigation*; they rejected it . . . We reached a compromise with the (JCI) editor. Instead of calling it an antibody we called it a binding globulin, because they agreed that we had demonstrated it had the characteristics of a gamma globulin. But in those days *everybody* knew peptides smaller than 10,000 were not antigenic. Therefore, insulin could not be antigenic. Therefore we couldn't call it an antibody."

So the key publication reporting the binding of insulin to an antibody[28] used the term "binding globulin," but, within a year or so, the presence of insulin antibodies was well accepted.

Over the next 3 years, Berson and Yalow published elegant characterizations of these antibodies.[29-35] As they assayed the antibodies using various amounts of insulin, they realized that they could turn the process around. A fixed amount of antibody would bind a certain amount of insulin. If the balance between antibody and insulin were optimal, the fraction of the insulin (or radioactive insulin) that bound to the antibody would relate to the total amount of insulin present.

While this concept is as simple as it is elegant, carrying it forward to a usable assay required intense work and thought. The antibody had to be just right. The balance in the assay had to be correct. At first, they succeeded in measuring insulin added to human blood, but the assay was not sensitive enough to measure the insulin in normal serum. They were very careful, checking and crosschecking. Eventually, they were confident that they could measure insulin in normal human serum. A preliminary report showing insulin response to glucose in two human subjects appeared in *Nature* in 1959.[36] The definitive report presenting the radioimmunoassay of human insulin, including glucose response studies in 96 patients, appeared in the *Journal of Clinical Investigation* in 1960.[37]

Successful radioimmunoassay of insulin led to an explosion of assays. As Berson and Yalow continued refining their method, others were trying to apply the same concept to other hormones. The Radioisotope Service at the Bronx VA Hospital played an active role. Even before the 1960 paper was published, Berson and Yalow helped Roger Unger, who used the same concept to measure circulating glucagon in human subjects, to get started

(Chapter 7). Now many others sought their instruction. Yalow saw the two journal articles as the sparks that ignited more widespread interest in the field. She noted that:

" . . . over the next 4 or 5 years we gave four training programs in which, at no charge, we invited endocrinologists—anybody who wanted to come. And I think we trained 140 people. And . . . those people started to produce an awful lot of papers, and that's how immunoassay took off."[3]

In 1963, Seymour Glick and Jesse Roth, both fellows in the Berson-Yalow laboratory, together with Yalow and Berson, published a successful method to assay human growth hormone in normal human plasma.[38] In 1963, Berson and Yalow, together with Gerald Aurbach and John Potts of the NIH, published a report on radioimmunoassay of parathyroid hormone,[39] though this assay still required a lot of work before it could be used routinely.

The following year, with Glick and Roth, they published a preliminary report on the assay of ACTH extracted from plasma.[40] This was followed by years of painstaking development to increase the sensitivity of the assay, necessary since ACTH is present in very small concentrations in normal human plasma. Eventually, in 1968, they published a method for radioimmunoassay of ACTH in unextracted plasma, together with its application in a variety of physiological and clinical states.[41]

**Figure 11.3 Yalow and one of the guinea pigs
whose antibodies made radioimmunoassay possible**

Paralleling the development of assays and improvements in techniques, there was constant study of patients and physiological processes. As Yalow said, "We never developed assays to develop assays. We developed assays to deal with physiologic problems."[3] The insulin assay led to studies of insulin metabolism in normal people and diabetic patients.[42-45] Development of the human growth hormone assay was followed by studies of the physiology of growth hormone, made possible by this new tool. Most important was their demonstration that hypoglycemia caused a marked rise in growth hormone levels.[46, 47] In 1969 the group showed that different types of stress had different effects on ACTH and growth hormone response.[48]

In 1968, Solomon Berson left the VA to become the founding Chair of the Department of Medicine at the new Mount Sinai School of Medicine. However, he did not move his research to Mount Sinai, and Yalow remained at the Bronx VA Hospital, now as Chief, Radioisotope Service. From that time until his sudden death in 1972, Berson continued to work at the VA laboratory when he could, generally late at night, but Yalow managed the day-to-day operation of the research.

The laboratory entered a new field, the study of the gastrointestinal hormones, which Yalow and her colleagues studied over several years. The first was gastrin. At the same time, they produced an assay for the Australia antigen, the virus that causes hepatitis B. This assay made it possible for blood banks everywhere to detect the hepatitis B-causing virus in blood donations, to prevent the transmission of this virulent disease.

**Figure 11.4 Rosalyn Yalow, Roger Unger, Solomon Berson and Erik Jorpes at
the Nobel Conference on Gastrointestinal Hormones in 1970**

Yalow described how hepatitis B assay came about:

"When we described the gastrin assay, Mort Grossman was expecting John Walsh, who had been at the NIH, to come to him in the Career Development Program. And so he felt it would be a good idea if John Walsh came here to learn the gastrin assay before he went out to Mort Grossman. And I was in Washington, so I thought I ought to take John out to lunch and, you know, get to know him a bit."

Walsh expressed an interest in the Australia antigen's potential for an assay study of the hepatitis-causing virus. This led to a joint project:

> "We used ourselves and our technicians as our controls," she said. "And so I labeled the Australia antigen, and purified it on the G200 column, and then we added it to control plasma, and its behavior in my plasma was different from its behavior in the plasma of two of the technicians here. And it turned out that those two technicians had been sent to the South Pacific, during the War. They had the yellow fever vaccine which was contaminated with the virus. They had antibody. So we had an assay going, immediately. We didn't have to immunize a guinea pig."[3]

After Berson's death in 1972, Yalow continued to extend the radioimmunoassay to new uses. The laboratory was named the "Solomon A. Berson Research Laboratory," and a fellowship in Berson's name was established to support young researchers in the laboratory.

Yalow and Berson had been nominated for the Nobel Prize while Berson was still alive. Now that he was dead and so not eligible for the Prize, her work alone would have to earn the recognition. Over the next years, she and her young colleagues developed a major body of work on hormones and prohormones,[49-59] on the many locations of hormones previously associated with a single site,[60-62] and on hormones in malignancies.[63, 64] She and Ludwig Gross developed a radioimmunoassay for the mouse leukemia virus that Gross had discovered.[65] Yalow continued to make contributions, all from a modest laboratory in which she herself could vouch for every finding.

Throughout Yalow's research career, the VA consistently supported her research. She asserted that she had never applied for a grant from the NIH or other agencies. She in turn was most loyal to the institution that had nourished her career. In all her contacts, she proudly acknowledged the VA as her home base and the source of support for her research.

Figure 11.5 Rosalyn Yalow receiving the Nobel Prize

Finally, in 1977, Rosalyn Yalow received the Nobel Prize for the development of radioimmunoassays of peptide hormones. She was the second woman to win the award in "Physiology or Medicine."

The magnitude of her work was captured in the formal Nobel announcement:

> "RIA brought about a revolution in biological and medical research. We have today at our disposal a large number of RIA-like procedures, so-called ligand methods, for determination of almost anything we wish to measure: peptide hormones, hormones that are not peptides, peptides that are not hormones, enzymes, viruses, antibodies, drugs of the most different kinds, etc. This has brought about an enormous development in hitherto closed areas of research.

> " - - - Yalow's contributions were not limited to presenting us with RIA. In a series of classical articles she and her coworkers, with the aid of RIA, were able to elucidate the physiology of the peptide hormones insulin, ACTH, growth hormone, and also to throw light upon the pathogenesis of diseases caused by abnormal secretion of these hormones. Thus, they directed diabetes research into new tracks and gave it a new dimension. This was pioneering work at the highest level. It had an enormous impact. We were witnessing the birth of a new era in endocrinology, one that started with Yalow."[1]

The young physicist from a modest family, who, as a student had been urged to use stenography as a back door into science, had found in the VA her opportunity to thrive. and to make an important contribution.[66]

References

1. Karolinska Institutet, *The 1977 Nobel Prize in Physiology or Medicine*. 1977: Stockholm, Sweden.

2. Lyon, G., *Summary of Radioisotope Labs (Handwritten Notes)*. 1957.

3. Interview with Rosalyn Yalow, Ph.D., October 28, 1992 at her office at the Bronx VA Medical Center.

4. Roswit, B., Sorrentino, J. and Yalow, R., "Use of radioactive phosphorus (P32) in diagnosis of testicular tumors; Preliminary report." *J Urol*, 1950. **63**: 724-728.

5. Sorrentino, J., Roswit, B. and Yalow, R., "Thyroid carcinoma with multiple metastases and pathologic fracture, successfully treated with radioiodine; Report of a case." *Radiology*, 1951. **57**: 729-737.

6. Sorrentino, J. and Yalow, R., "Nomogram for dose determinations in diagnostic radiology." *Radiology*, 1950. **55**: 748-753.

7. Fadem, R.S. and Yalow, R., "Uniformity of cell counts in smears of bone marrow particles." *Am J Clin Path*, 1951. **21**: 541-545.

8. Conway, H., Roswit, B., Stark, R.B. and Yalow, R., "Radioactive sodium clearance as test of circulatory efficiency of tubed pedicles and flaps." *Proc Soc Exp Biol Med*, 1951. **77**: 348-351.

9. Wisham, L.H., Yalow, R. and Freund, A.J., "Consistency of clearance of radioactive sodium from human muscle." *Am Heart J*, 1951. **41**: 810-818.

10. Wisham, L.H. and Yalow, R., "Some factors affecting clearance of Na24 from human muscle." *Am Heart J*, 1952. **43**: 67-76.

11. Freund, J., Wisham, L.H. and Yalow, R.S., "Effect of priscoline on clearance of radiosodium from muscle and skin of man in normal and diseased limbs." *Circulation*, 1953. **8**: 89-97.

12. Straus, B., Berson, S.A., Bernstein, T.C. and Jacobson, A.S., "Guanazolo in therapy of Hodgkin's disease." *Blood*, 1950. **5**: 1059-1061.

13. Fadem, R.S., Berson, S.A., Jacobson, A.S. and Straus, B., "Effects of cortisone on bone marrow in Hodgkin's disease." *Am J Clin Path*, 1951. **21**: 799-813.

14. Guest, C.M., Kammerer, W.H., Cecil, R.L. and Berson, S.A., "Epinephrine, pregnenolone and testosterone in treatment of rheumatoid arthritis." *JAMA*, 1950. **143**: 338-344.

15. Yalow, R. and Berson, S.A., "Use of K42 tagged erythrocytes in blood volume determinations." *Science*, 1951. **114**: 14-15.

16. Berson, S.A. and Yalow, R., "Use of K42 or P32 labelled erythrocytes and I131 tagged human serum albumin in simultaneous blood volume determinations." *J Clin Invest*, 1952. **31**: 572-580.

17. Berson, S.A., Yalow, R.S., Azulay, A., Schreiber, S.S. and Roswit, B., "The biologic decay curve of P32 tagged erythrocytes. Application to study of acute changes in blood volume." *J Clin Invest*, 1952. **31**: 581-591.

18. Berson, S.A. and Yalow, R.S., "The effect of cortisone on the iodine accumulating function of the thyroid gland in euthyroid subjects." *J Clin Endocrinol Metab*, 1952. **12**: 407-422.

19.   Berson, S.A., Yalow, R.S., Sorrentino, J. and Roswit, B., "The determination of thyroidal and renal plasma I131 clearance rates as a routine diagnostic test of thyroid dysfunction." *J Clin Invest*, 1952. **31**: 141-158.

20.   Berson, S.A. and Yalow, R.S., "Quantitative aspects of iodine metabolism. Exchangeable organic iodine pool, and rates of thyroidal secretion, peripheral degradation and fecal excretion of endogonously synthesized organically bound iodine." *J Clin Invest*, 1954. **33**: 1533-1552.

21.   Berson, S.A. and Yalow, R.S., "Distribution of I131 labelled human serum albumin introduced into ascitic fluid: Analysis of kinetics of 3 compartment catenary transfer system in man and speculations on possible sites of degradation." *J Clin Invest*, 1954. **33**: 377-387.

22.   Rothschild, M.A., Bauman, A., Yalow, R.S. and Berson, S.A., "Effect of splenomegaly on blood volume." *J Appl Physiol*, 1954. **6**: 701-706.

23.   Schreiber, S.S., Bauman, A., Yalow, R. and Berson, S.A., "Blood volume alterations in congestive heart failure." *J Clin Invest*, 1954. **33**: 578-586.

24.   Vazquez, O.N., Newerly, K., Yalow, R. and Berson, S.A., "Estimation of trapped plasma with I131 albumin; Critique of methods." *J Appl Physiol*, 1954. **6**: 437-440.

25.   Bauman, A., Rothschild, M.A., Yalow, R. and Berson, S.A., "Distribution and metabolism of I131 labeled human serum albumin in congestive heart failure with and without proteinurea." *J Clin Invest*, 1955. **34**: 1359-1368.

26.   Rothschild, M.A., Bauman, A., Yalow, R. and Berson, S.A., "Tissue distribution of I131 labelled human serum albumin following intravenous administration." *J Clin Invest*, 1955. **34**: 1354-1358.

27.   Interview with Marcus A. Rothschild, M.D., February 8, 1994 at Dr. Rothschild's home in Florida.

28.   Berson, S.A., Yalow, R., Bauman, A., Rothschild, M.A. and Newerly, K., "Insulin-I131 metabolism in human subjects: Demonstration of insulin binding globulin in the circulation of insulin-treated subjects." *J Clin Invest*, 1956. **35**: 170-190.

29.   Berson, S.A. and Yalow, R.S., "Ethanol fractionation of plasma and electrophoretic identification of insulin-binding antibody." *J Clin Invest*, 1957. **36**: 642-647.

30.   Berson, S.A. and Yalow, R.S., "Studies with insulin-binding antibody." *Diabetes*, 1957. **6**: 402-405.

31.   Berson, S.A. and Yalow, R.S., "Insulin antagonists, insulin antibodies and insulin resistance." *Am J Med*, 1958. **25**: 13S-18S.

32.   Berson, S.A. and Yalow, R.S., "Species-specificity of human antibeef, pork insulin serum." *J Clin Invest*, 1959. **38**: 2017-2025.

33.   Berson, S.A. and Yalow, R.S., "Recent studies on insulin-binding antibodies." *Ann NY Acad Sci*, 1959. **82**: 338-344.

34.   Berson, S.A. and Yalow, R.S., "Quantitative aspects of the reaction between insulin and insulin-binding antibody." *J Clin Invest*, 1959. **38**: 1996-2016.

35.   Berson, S.A. and Yalow, R.S., "Cross reactions of human anti-beef, pork insulin with beef, pork, sheep, horse and human Insulins." *Fed Proc*, 1959. **18**: 11.

36. Yalow, R.S. and Berson, S.A., "Assay of plasma insulin in human subjects by immunological methods." *Nature*, 1959. **184 (Suppl 21)**: 1648-1649.

37. Yalow, R.S. and Berson, S.A., "Immunoassay of endogenous plasma insulin in man." *J Clin Invest*, 1960. **39**: 1157-1175.

38. Glick, S.M., Roth, J., Yalow, R.S. and Berson, S.A., "Immunoassay of human growth hormone in plasma." *Nature*, 1963. **199**: 784-787.

39. Berson, S.A., Yalow, R.S., Aurbach, G.D. and Potts, J.T., "Immunoassay of bovine and human parathyroid hormone." *Proc Natl Acad Sci USA*, 1963. **49**: 613-617.

40. Yalow, R.S., Glick, S.M., Roth, J. and Berson, S.A., "Radioimmunoassay of human plasma ACTH." *J Clin Endocrinol Metab*, 1964. **24**: 1219-1225.

41. Berson, S.A. and Yalow, R.S., "Radioimmunoassay of ACTH in plasma." *J Clin Invest*, 1968. **47**: 2725-2751.

42. Yalow, R.S. and Berson, S.A., "Plasma insulin concentrations in nondiabetic and early diabetic subjects. Determinations by a new sensitive immuno-assay technic." *Diabetes*, 1960. **9**: 254-260.

43. Yalow, R.S. and Berson, S.A., "Comparison of plasma insulin levels following administration of tolbutamide and glucose." *Diabetes*, 1960. **9**: 356-362.

44. Berson, S.A. and Yalow, R.S., "Plasma insulin in health and disease." *Amer J Med*, 1961. **31**: 874-881.

45. Berson, S.A. and Yalow, R.S., "Insulin antibodies and insulin resistance." *Diabetes Dig*, 1962. **1**: 4.

46. Roth, J., Glick, S.M., Yalow, R.S. and Berson, S.A., "Secretion of human growth hormone: Physiologic and experimental modification." *Metabolism*, 1963. **12**: 577-579.

47. Roth, J., Glick, S.M., Yalow, R.S. and Berson, S.A., "Hypoglycemia: A potent stimulus to secretion of growth hormone." *Science*, 1963. **140**: 987-988.

48. Yalow, R.S., Varsano-Aharon, N., Echemendia, E. and Berson, S.A., "HGH and ACTH secretory responses to stress." *Horm Metab Res*, 1969. **1**: 3-8.

49. Silverman, R. and Yalow, R.S., "Heterogeneity of parathyroid hormone. Clinical and physiologic implications." *J Clin Invest*, 1973. **52**: 1958-1971.

50. Yalow, R.S. and Wu, N., "Additional studies on the nature of big big gastrin." *Gastroenterology*, 1973. **65**: 19-27.

51. Yalow, R.S., "Radioimmunoassay methodology: Application to problems of heterogeneity of peptide hormones." *Pharmacol Rev*, 1973. **25**: 161-178.

52. Coslovsky, R. and Yalow, R.S., "Influence of the hormonal forms of ACTH on the pattern of corticosteroid secretion." *Biochem Biophys Res Commun*, 1974. **60**: 1351-1356.

53. Gewirtz, G., Schneider, B., Krieger, D.T. and Yalow, R.S., "Big ACTH: Conversion to biologically active ACTH by trypsin." *J Clin Endocrinol Metab*, 1974. **38**: 227-230.

54. Straus, E. and Yalow, R.S., "Studies on the distribution and degradation of heptadecapeptide, big, and big big gastrin." *Gastroenterology*, 1974. **66**: 936-943.

55. Straus, E., Greenstein, A.J. and Yalow, R.S., "Effect of secretin on release of heterogeneous forms of gastrin." *Gut*, 1975. **16**: 999-1005.

56. Straus, E., Urbach, H.J. and Yalow, R.S., "Comparative reactivities of 125I-secretin and 125I-minus 6-tyrosyl secretin with guinea pig and rabbit anti-secretin sera." *Biochem Biophys Res Commun*, 1975. **64**: 1036-1040.

57. Yalow, R.S., Hall, K. and Luft, R., "Immunoreactive somatomedin B in urine." *J Clin Endocrinol Metab*, 1975. **41**: 638-639.

58. Yalow, R.S., Hall, K. and Luft, R., "Radioimmunoassay of somatomedin B." *Adv Metab Disord*, 1975. **8**: 73-83.

59. Yalow, R.S., Hall, K. and Luft, R., "Radioimmunoassay of somatomedin B. Application to clinical and physiologic studies." *J Clin Invest*, 1975. **55**: 127-137.

60. Straus, E. and Yalow, R.S., "Studies on the distribution and degradation of heptadecapeptide, big, and big big gastrin." *Gastroenterology*, 1974a. **66**: 936-943.

61. Straus, E., Yalow, R.S. and Gainer, H., "Molluscan gastrin: Concentration and molecular forms." *Science*, 1975. **190**: 687-689.

62. Straus, E., Muller, J.E., Choi, H.S., Paronetto, F. and Yalow, R.S., "Immunohistochemical localization in rabbit brain of a peptide resembling the COOH-terminal octapeptide of cholecystokinin." *Proc Natl Acad Sci U S A*, 1977. **74**: 3033-3034.

63. Gewirtz, G. and Yalow, R.S., "Ectopic ACTH production in carcinoma of the lung." *J Clin Invest*, 1974. **53**: 1022-1032.

64. Ayvazian, L.F., Schneider, B., Gewirtz, G. and Yalow, R.S., "Ectopic production of big ACTH in carcinoma of the lung. Its clinical usefulness as a biologic marker." *Am Rev Respir Dis*, 1975. **111**: 279-287.

65. Yalow, R.S. and Gross, L., "Radioimmunoassay for intact Gross mouse leukemia virus." *Proc Natl Acad Sci U S A*, 1976. **73**: 2847-2851.

66. Yalow, R.S. "Nobel Autobiography." *Nobel Prize Awards, 1977*. Stockholm, Sweden.

Part IV. The roaring sixties

Chapter 12. The Intramural Research Program 1960-1967

Most of the decade of the 1960s was characterized by the rapid growth of medical research within the VA, and institutional recognition that it had both earned and deserved solid support by the agency. Congress had ratified the movement with budget allocations, dedicated space was being built or otherwise provided, and basic science was gaining a foothold. The agency's ties to academic institutions were gaining strength as well. VA's reputation for engaging in productive clinical studies was attracting ties for collaborative research even as less formalized joint efforts continued with renewed vigor. The era also brought about recognition for achievement, and the annual research conference continued to be an important medium for the presentation of scholarly and clinical information.

Growth of the VA research program

At the decade's beginning, the VA Medical Research program was experiencing a growth spurt. A $17 million budget supported over 6,000 projects, most of them in clinical research: 1,400 were related to neuropsychiatric disorders, 300 to tuberculosis, and the rest included almost every field of medical research.[1]

The 1960 annual report to Congress provided this definition of the agency's medical research program:

"For the purposes of the mission of the Research Service of the Department of Medicine and Surgery of the Veterans' Administration, medical research is defined as any study undertaken to test a hypothesis related to the etiology, pathogenesis, natural history, prevention, amelioration, or cure of human disease or deformity."[2]

The report laid out the basis upon which a VA with a strong research program was able to achieve and maintain a higher standard of medical care:

1. Attraction of top caliber staff
2. Improved clinical interest of nonresearch staff
3. Newer and better care for patients
4. Availability of expert consultation
5. Increase in prestige[3]

"Research in the VA system is considered a privilege," the report noted. "Any member of a VA hospital professional staff who is eager to do research presents his project as a proposal in competition for funds and space with other staff members. Because VA physicians participate in research only as it relates to their patient care responsibilities, it is evident that their research originates in the clinical problems which confront them at the bedside. Probably there can be no better direction of medical research than this."[4]

By this time, there was a growing body of basic research, only indirectly influenced by patient-care needs, in the VA research program. Nevertheless, the needs of the veteran patient continued to be a major motivation for VA researchers. For example, the development of the technique of radioimmunoassay, described in the previous chapter, required elegant, complex understanding and methodologies of basic science, but the impact on patient care proved to be enormous.

Need for laboratory construction

The 1960 annual Congressional report also made a strong case for providing adequately equipped laboratories to support research programs, pointing out that, in a recent year, 80 medical schools provided over $40 million for development of basic research laboratories, which allowed faculty members to obtain an additional $65 million in Federal grants. The physical plant was still the most pressing problem facing the VA research program.[5]

New Central Office leadership

The expanding budget started during Martin Cummings's time as Director, and the resulting opportunity for innovation attracted well-qualified leaders to Central Office Research Service.

Figure 12.1 Mark J. Musser, M.D.

Mark J. ("Jim") Musser, M.D.

In 1959, Dr. Musser replaced Dr. Cummings as Director, Research Service. Musser had previously been Professor of Medicine at the University of Wisconsin, where he knew Dean Middleton well. Later, Musser had been Chairman of the Department of Medicine at Baylor University in Houston. He brought to Research Service a rich network of friends in academic medicine and considerable political acumen and administrative talent. In 1962, he became ACMD/R&E, but left Central Office in 1965 to direct a Regional Medical Program in North Carolina. He returned to Central Office as Chief Medical Director at the end of 1969 and continued to champion the research program while leading the DM&S.

Benjamin B. Wells, M.D.

Dr. Wells was appointed to the post of ACMD/R&E in the spring of 1960. He had joined the VA in 1957 at the Hines (IL) VA Hospital and was Chief of Staff at the New Orleans VA Hospital before coming to Central Office in July 1958 as Director of the Education Service. He held an M.D. from Baylor University and a Ph.D. in biochemistry and physiology from the University of Minnesota and was a diplomate of both the American Board of Pathology and the American Board of Internal Medicine. As a graduate student, he had done important research on the adrenal cortical hormones, work that was extensively cited by Kendall in his *Cortisone*.[6] Before joining the VA, Wells was Chairman of Medicine at the University of Arkansas and at Creighton University and Dean of the School of Medicine at the University of Arkansas. He had also served as a journal editor and practiced medicine with an unaffiliated group. In addition to these accomplishments, he was reported to be an expert pianist.

Figure 12.2 Benjamin B. Wells, M.D.
Courtesy Archives, UC Irvine

Dr. Wells was described by those who knew him as small in stature and huge in intellect. A witty person, he got along well with people and was a skillful politician who spearheaded the VA's success in improving the research budget through the 1960s.

His sense of humor pervaded even official documents. The following passage in the fiscal year 1961 annual report to Congress was probably his:

> "The last annual report differed from most of the earlier numbers by the omission of the abstracts written by each investigator describing his research. These abstracts added little light and much bulk, so were abandoned."[7]

In the *Research and Education Newsletter*, he states:

> "The NEWSLETTER is not "staffed out." For those who may be new in the business, this is the process of intellectual emasculation in which a document is passed through

several hands and several echelons until it emerges in depersonalized and inanimate form, its wordage increased but its stimulating force reduced to an amplitude of zero."[8]

On another occasion he wrote:

"Perhaps it is all wrong, but society is not willing to give money for unidentified or undisclosed ventures. The fact that scientists find research an entertaining and gratifying way of life has little persuasive value."[9]

In 1962, Dr. Wells left Central Office to become the founding Dean of the California College of Medicine at Los Angeles (now the School of Medicine at the University of California, Irvine). In a parting tribute, Dr. Musser wrote:

"Certainly, in his quiet and gentle, yet refreshingly positive, way, Ben Wells had become one of the most respected and effective executives in the Department of Medicine and Surgery."

Wells returned to Central Office again as ACMD/R&E in 1965 when Musser went to North Carolina. A year later, Wells left once more to direct the Regional Medical Program in Alabama and then returned in 1969 as Deputy CMD under Musser.

James A. Halsted, M.D.

Dr. Halsted came to VACO in 1964 as Deputy ACMD/R&E. A graduate of Harvard Medical School, he had been in private practice before World War II. During the war, he served in North Africa and Italy. He began his VA career at the Wadsworth (Los Angeles) VA Hospital, where he was Chief of Gastroenterology from 1950 to 1955.

Figure 12.3 James A. Halsted, M.D.

While there, he married Anna Roosevelt, daughter of President Franklin and Eleanor Roosevelt.[10,11]

Later he moved to the Syracuse VA Hospital, was a Fulbright scholar for two years in Iran and then Director of Postgraduate Education of the University of Kentucky Medical

School. At the time of his recruitment to VACO, he was ACOS/R&E at the Dearborn (MI) VA Hospital and professor at Wayne State University.

Dr. Halsted had become interested in medical research during World War II while stationed in North Africa. He and his colleagues studied soldiers who developed peptic ulcers under the stress of battle. They demonstrated that these were exacerbations of preexisting ulcers and that new ulcers seldom resulted from battle stress.[12] While at Wadsworth, he and his colleagues studied the absorption of Vitamin B12, demonstrating its complete absence after total gastrectomy.[13, 14] He also showed that antibiotic treatment in "blind loop syndrome" reversed the malabsorption of Vitamin B12 seen in this condition.[15, 16] While at the Syracuse VA Hospital, he, together with Kenneth Sterling, demonstrated protein loss from the stomach in Menetriere's disease.[17] While in Iran, he and Ananda Prasad, later ACOS/R&D at the Allen Park (MI)VA Hospital, became interested in a group of dwarfs who had anemia and no sexual development. Eventually, they established zinc deficiency as the cause of this syndrome.[18]

In March 1966 after 2 years in Central Office, Dr. Halsted moved to the Washington (DC) VA Hospital, where he was ACOS/R&E and VA-wide coordinator for research in nutrition.[19]

Figure 12.4 Edward Dunner, M.D., center, with Ludwig Gross, M.D. of the Bronx VA Hospital, and Lucien Guze, M.D., COS/R&E at the Los Angeles Wadsworth VA Hospital, at the 1965 Annual Research Conference

Edward Dunner, M.D.

Dr. Dunner (Figure 12.4) had been in the VA since 1941 as a staff physician at the Palo Alto, San Fernando and Livermore hospitals in California. While at Livermore, he participated in the original tuberculosis trials under John Barnwell (Chapter 5). From 1950 to 1954, he was Area Chief for Tuberculosis in St. Louis. He came to Central Office Tuberculosis Service in 1954 and served as Chief of Tuberculosis Research and Executive

Secretary of the VA-Armed Forces Chemotherapy of Tuberculosis Cooperative Study from 1956 to 1958, at a time when more than 60 units participated in this study. In 1958, he joined the Central Office Research Service as Associate Director and Chief of the Clinical Studies Division. He was Director, Research Service, from 1962 to 1966, when he became Special Assistant to Dr. Wells, the ACMD/R&E.[20]

Local research management

By 1960, governance of the research program had stabilized. Each VA hospital with a research program had a Research and Education (R&E) Committee responsible for evaluating and approving staff research proposals and distributing the support money allocated by Central Office. Each hospital received a basic institutional research allocation to provide "equipment, supplies, technical support, and other facilities necessary for the proper pursuit" of research activities. When a research project was completed, R&E Committee approval was needed before results could be published. The Committee comprehensively reviewed the station's research program annually for quality and productivity and reported findings to Central Office. The position of "Assistant Director of Professional Services for Research (ADPSR)," renamed the "Associate Chief of Staff for Research and Education (ACOS/R&E)" in 1961, was established as Secretary to the R&E Committee and as full-time coordinator of the research program.[4]

Professional papers had required Central Office approval before submission for publication until 1957, when the review and approval responsibility moved to the R&E Committees. Two copies of the published papers were sent to Central Office, a practice that continued into the 1970s.[21]

Special Laboratories

In 1960, while the majority of the research carried out in VA laboratories was controlled by the R&E Committee, there continued to be Special Research Laboratories (Appendix VI), some of them new, others continuing since the 1950s. These laboratories were still controlled directly by Central Office Research Service with budgets earmarked and activities supervised by Central Office staff. By 1963, 22 laboratories were directly supervised by Central Office staff and carried out special projects in response to Central Office direction. However, in most cases, these were investigator-directed laboratories that functioned very much like program project grants, with a central theme but a number of projects initiated by the laboratory staff.

The radioisotope program

By 1960, radioisotope research at the local level had been completely integrated into the overall research program, and the hospital Radioisotope Committee was now a subcommittee of the R&E Committee. The Central Office now considered most research projects in the Radioisotope Services in relation to disease state or research problem, rather than the use of radioisotopes. Only 185 of the 6,569 research projects listed in the 1960 annual research report were classified as "radioisotope, not elsewhere classified."[22]

Extra-VA research funding

VA investigators successfully used the privilege achieved in 1954 to apply for non-VA monies through affiliated medical schools. Research grant support in 1960 was listed as $4.5 million in 717 projects.[23] The VA was responsible for approximately one-third of the National Cancer Institute's nationally integrated cancer chemotherapy research program.[24]

Epidemiology and biostatistics

A new division of Central Office Research Service, the Geographic Epidemiology Division, was activated in July 1959. Dr. E. Donald Acheson, who later held a high position in the British National Health Service, was its first Chief. After he left the VA in January 1960, Clifford A. Bachrach, M.D., was appointed to succeed him. This division was charged with using VA materials and resources to study geographic distribution of diseases. Early efforts focused on multiple sclerosis, regional ileitis, ulcerative colitis, and nonspecific lung diseases.[25] By the mid-1970s, it had become the only branch of the Central Office actually carrying out research.

In addition, a Central Office Research Statistics Division was established in 1959, apparently by transferring staff from the VA Controller's Office. Dr. Bachrach was also chief of this division, which included four other statisticians.[26] Many but not all of the cooperative studies received statistical support and coordination from this division. In 1962, Dr. Bachrach volunteered for service in Israel, and Donald V. Brown, Ph.D., of the Systems Development Corporation was recruited to head this Statistical Division with special responsibility for the new Research Support Centers.

The Cooperative Studies Program

In 1960, the tuberculosis and psychopharmacology studies (Chapters 4 and 8) were very active. A Tuberculosis Cooperative Study Laboratory in Atlanta was now operating as a central laboratory serving several new tuberculosis cooperative studies. This laboratory distributed standardized testing materials to all tuberculosis cooperative study units to improve comparability of test results. In addition, cooperative studies were started to study a variety of other medical problems. The hypertension study group (Chapter 9) published its first major report in 1960.

During the early 1960s, individual program chiefs directed Cooperative Studies. However, Lawrence W. Shaw, who came to VA Central Office in 1963 as a senior statistician, gradually worked into overall leadership of Cooperative Studies. [27,28] In 1966, the first meeting was held of the Cooperative Studies Evaluation Committee (CSEC), a general advisory committee for all Cooperative Studies. This Committee continues active to the present (Appendix VII). The first CSEC chairman was William Tucker, M.D., Director of Medical Service in VA Central Office. During the 1960s, CSEC reviewed most of the VA Cooperative Studies except the psychiatry studies coordinated by the CNPRL (Chapter 8) or those that were collaborative with the National Cancer Institute, reviewed by committees of the National Academy of Sciences (Chapter 4).

Publications

In 1960, a *Research and Education (R&E) Newsletter* debuted and continued to be published two to six times a year through 1968. The *Newsletter* and annual reports to Congress required a more formal publications process. Thus, in 1960 the position of Publications Editor was established, first in Research Service and later moved to the ACMD/R&E office. The initial Publications Editor was Mrs. L. Tracy Fetta, who had prepared a prospectus on Research in Aging. She prepared the 1959 and 1960 annual reports to Congress and the *R&E Newsletter*. However, Dr. Chapple (Chapter 7) played an active role in establishing the *Newsletter* and served as its editor.[29] He was officially designated Chief of Research Publications from 1962-1964. In addition to the annual report to Congress entitled *Medical Research in the Veterans Administration*, Research Service published occasional manuals and monographs (Appendix VII).

Budgetary management

Budgetary decision-making was generally straightforward. The Director, Research Service, had the authority to distribute research funds, and his decisions were honored. There was no advisory committee structure influencing individual decisions and there existed few bureaucratic "hoops" to master. The Director was responsible for the results of those decisions, good or bad.

Robert Efron, M.D., described his own experience with the accommodating way things sometimes worked, from the occasion when Marc J. Musser, M.D., recruited him to work for the VA:

> Efron had been working in his basement laboratory at the Medical Research Council (MRC) in London when Musser (then Director of the VA Research Service) was visiting the facility. His British hosts asked Musser if he would like to meet their young American scientist.
>
> After hearing about Efron's research, Musser asked him whether, when he came back to the U.S., he would like to work for the VA. He said to contact him when the time came. Not long afterward, Efron was recruited by Boston University Medical School to do patient care and research located in the Boston VA Hospital.
>
> Efron's lab equipment at MRC was specialized to his work, and it was decided that he could take it with him to the U.S. The delicate equipment required a huge, room-sized crate and very careful handling. Efron contacted Musser, and inquired whether the VA might be able to pay for the crating and moving cost.
>
> The VA research chief simply said it would be done. With no further action on the Efron's part, no supply forms, no applications, no paper work at all . . . the crating and shipping were accomplished. When the equipment was set up in his new VA lab, not

a single item had been damaged.[30]

Introduction of Program Chiefs

The 1960 National Academy of Sciences report on the VA Research program (Chapter 7) advised expansion of the Central Office professional staff. This advice, together with Dr. Middleton's support for the research program and Drs. Musser's and Wells's energetic leadership, led to a marked expansion of the Central Office Research Staff during the 1960s.

The concept of the Program Chief (Table 12.1) was introduced in this staffing expansion. Dr. Chapple, already responsible for the Research in Aging Division, became Chief of Research in Aging; and Lyndon Lee,M.D., already administering the surgical cooperative studies (Chapter 13), became Chief of Research in Surgery. Graham Moseley's position was redesignated as Chief of Research in Radioisotopes, and Joe Meyer, Ph.D., became Chief of the Research Laboratories Division, and later (in 1962) Chief of Research in the Basic Sciences. The first recruits specifically to positions of Program Chief were Samuel C. Kaim, M.D., who arrived in 1960 as Chief of Research in Psychiatry and Neurology, and Harold W. Schnaper, M.D. and H. Elston Hooper, Ph.D., who in 1961 became Chiefs of Research, respectively, in Internal Medicine and Psychology. Later in the 1960s, recruitment continued of subject matter specialists to administer their particular areas of research, with 19 new recruits between 1963 and 1971.

Program Chiefs were responsible for encouraging and coordinating research in their specific program areas. Each was allotted a portion of the total research budget, over which he or she had almost complete discretion. Typically, they traveled extensively, visiting laboratories and reviewing research in their program areas. They formed Research Program Committees to assist them in directing their efforts, and they also coordinated special Study Groups. They served as coordinators of the Clinical Investigator Program within their special areas and later of the Research Associate, Medical Investigator and Research and Education Trainee programs. In their fields, they served as Executive Secretaries of the Coordinating Committees for Cooperative Studies and later as Executive Secretaries of the Program Evaluation Committees.

Table 12.1. Program Chiefs

Lee, Lyndon E., Jr., M.D., Coordinator, Research in Surgery, 1957-1964
Chapple, Charles C., M.D., Chief, Research-in-Aging Division, 1958-1962
Moseley, A. Graham, Chief, Radioisotope Division, Research Service, 1958-1967
Kaim, Samuel C., M.D., Chief, Research in Psychiatry and Neurology, 1960-1970
Hooper, H. Elston, Ph.D., Chief, Research in Psychology, 1961-1965
Schnaper, Harold W., M.D., Chief, Research in Internal Medicine, 1961-1967
Meyer, Joe, Ph.D., Chief, Research in Basic Sciences, 1962-1968
Cass, Jules S, D.V.M., Chief, Research in Laboratory Animal Research and Care, 1963-198?
Feldman, W.H., D.V.M., Chief, Laboratory Research in Pulmonary Diseases, 1963-1967
Matthews, James H., M.D., Chief, Clinical Research in Pulmonary Diseases, 1963-1968
Filer, Richard N., Ph.D., Chief, Research in Psychology, 1965-1970
Rosenberg, Charles A., M.D., Chief, Research in Endocrinology and Metabolism, 1965-1968
Wolcott, Mark W., M.D., Chief, Research in Surgery, 1965-1970

Chauncey, Howard W., D.M.D., Chief, Research in Oral Diseases, 1966-1971
Nadel, Eli M., M.D., Chief, Research in Pathology and Laboratory Medicine, 1966-1968
Simons, David G., M.D., Chief, Research in Physical Medicine and Rehab., 1967-1971
Dury, Abraham, Ph.D., Chief, Research in Basic Sciences, 1968-1972
Cady, Allen B., M.D., Chief, Research in Gastroenterology, 1969-1971
Christianson, Lawrence G., M.D., Chief, Research in Neurology, 1969-1970
Hine, Gerald G., Ph.D., Chief, Research in Nuclear Medicine, 1969-1973
Loudon, Robert G., M.B., Ch.B., Chief, Research in Pulmonary&Infectious Dis., 1969-1970
Meyer, Leo M., M.D., Chief, Research in Hematology, 1969-1970
Oliner, Leo, M.D., Chief, Research in Endocrinology and Metabolism, 1969-1971
Adler, Terrine K., M.D., Chief, Research in Pharmacology, 1970-1972
O'Reilly, Sean, M.D., Chief, Research in Neurology, 1971-1972
Sisk, Charles W., M.D., Chief, Research in Arthritis and Rheumatism, 1971-1972

Research Program Chiefs (1960-1968)

Lyndon E. Lee, Jr., M.D.

Dr. Lee came to Central Office in 1957 as Coordinator for Surgical Research within Surgery Service. He graduated from Duke University School of Medicine in 1938 and completed postdoctoral training in surgery. Before coming to Central Office, he had wide experience in surgery, both clinical practice and research. In 1958, when Mr. Moise left the post of Chief of Extra VA Research, Lee transferred to Research Service. He and Dr. Barnwell negotiated with the Director of the National Cancer Institute (NCI) to initiate a joint program of research on cancer therapy. Lee became responsible for coordinating this joint VA-NCI research. He also continued to coordinate research in surgery and in 1963 became Program Chief in Research in Surgery. In 1964, he left Research Service to become Director, Surgery Service, but returned as Acting ACMD/R&E in 1970. In 1971, he became ACMD for Professional Services. Until he left Central Office in the late 1970s, he coordinated the joint VA-NCI research program, taking it with him as he went from post to post.[31]

Figure 12.5 Lyndon Lee, M.D.

Figure 12.6 Samuel Kaim, M.D., right, with Edward Dunner, M.D.

274

Samuel C. Kaim, M.D.

Dr. Kaim came to Central Office Research Service in 1960 as Program Chief in Psychiatry and Neurology. A New Yorker, he had done his undergraduate work at Western Reserve and studied medicine in Zurich. He had been in the private practice of psychiatry until 1950, when he joined the staff of the VA hospital at Coral Gables (FL), where he became Chief, Psychiatry and Neurology Service in 1958.[32]

H. Elston Hooper, Ph.D.

Dr. Hooper (Figure 16.2) was appointed Chief, Psychology Research, in 1961. After obtaining his bachelor's degree at UCLA in 1942, he served over 3 years in the Air Force as a research psychologist in the Air Crew Selection Program. He then entered the VA Clinical Psychology Program and received his Ph.D. from USC in 1950. He was staff psychologist at the Long Beach (CA) VA Hospital from 1950 to 1960. He then went to the Augusta (GA) VA Hospital to serve as Chief of the Central Research Laboratory for the Psychological Research Program for a year before going to VACO.[33] Except for a brief period in the mid-1960s as Chief of the Western Research Support Center at the Sepulveda (CA) VA Hospital, Dr. Hooper remained in Central Office Research Service until his retirement in 1978.

Harold W. Schnaper, M.D.

Dr. Schnaper was recruited to Central Office as Program Chief, Research in Internal Medicine, in 1961. Previously, he worked with Edward Freis, M.D., at the Washington, D.C. VA Hospital, serving as his Assistant Chief and an active partner in the early hypertension studies (Chapter 9). In 1965, he became Assistant Director of Research Service but also continued to coordinate research in internal medicine until he left Central Office to become a professor at the University of Alabama in 1966. He was Acting Director, Research Service after Dr. Dunner transferred to the ACMD office and before Lionel Bernstein arrived.[34]

Figure 12.7 James Matthews, M.D.

James H. Matthews, M.D.

Dr. Matthews came to the Central Office in 1961 as Secretary to the Committee on the Chemotherapy of Tuberculosis, then still a part of Professional Services. He had been a pulmonary specialist at the Oteen (Asheville, NC) VA Hospital and had participated in the tuberculosis cooperative studies. From his arrival in Central Office, he coordinated his activities closely with Research Service and by 1963 had transferred to Research Service as Program Chief for Clinical Research in Pulmonary Diseases. He gradually took on other responsibilities as well, becoming Chief of Research Communications in the ACMD office in 1965 and Assistant Director, Research Service, in 1968. In 1972, he left the VA to head the tuberculosis control program for the State of Virginia.[35, 36]

Lewis W. Carr, D.S.W.

Dr. Carr became Program Chief, Social Work Research, in 1963. His responsibilities were to "develop, promote and administer the social work research program," in response to a recommendation by an Ad Hoc VA Social Work Research Committee. Dr. Carr, a Doctor of Social Work from Washington University, was Clinical Social Worker in the Mental Hygiene Clinic at VA Regional Office, St. Louis, from 1957 to 1959 and Research Social Worker at the Houston VA Hospital and Assistant Professor of Social Work in the Department of Psychiatry, Baylor University, from 1961 to 1963. At the time of his appointment, he was a member of the National Association of Social Workers, The Academy of Certified Social Workers, The Council on Social Work Education, and The National Conference on Social Welfare.[37]

Figure 12.8 Charles Rosenberg, M.D.

Charles A. Rosenberg, M.D.

Dr. Rosenberg came to Central Office as Chief of Research in Metabolism and Endocrinology in 1964 from the Batavia (NY) VA Hospital, where he had been Chief of

Medicine and had established a Radioisotope Unit. Previously he was at the Nashville VA Hospital as Assistant Chief of Medicine and Chief of the Radioisotope Unit. In addition to endocrinology, Dr. Rosenberg took on responsibility for coordinating research in gastroenterology and hematology, taking some of the load from Harold Schnaper.[38] Dr. Rosenberg later became Director of Medical Service in Central Office and then Chief of Staff at the Miami VA Medical Center.

Mark W. Walcott, M.D.

Dr. Walcott, who had been Chief of Surgery at the Coral Gables (FL) VA Hospital, was Program Chief of Research in Surgery from 1964 to 1970. He took over this assignment when Lyndon Lee became Director of Surgery Service in Central Office. Lee, however, continued to be Chief of Extra-VA Research, a position in which he coordinated the NCI-funded VA Surgical Adjuvant studies and cancer research ward at the Washington, D.C. VA Hospital.

**Figure 12.9 Mark Walcott, M.D., center, with Joe Meyer, Ph.D.,
and Lyndon Lee, M.D. at the 1965 Research Conference**

Walcott was an active researcher and while in Central Office set up a hyperbaric oxygen chamber for mice at the Washington VA Hospital, where he carried out research on gas gangrene. He also practiced surgery at the hospital once a week. Such activities were encouraged. Hal Engle, the CMD during Walcott's later years in Research Service and a strong supporter of the VA research program, envisioned the possibility of academic affiliations for the Central Office DM&S, with close ties to the Washington VA Hospital.

Wolcott was later Chief of Staff at the Salt Lake City VA Hospital and set up the Regional Medical Education Center there. He served as ACMD for Professional Services during the 1980s.[39]

David G. Simons, M.D.

Dr. Simons became Program Chief of Research in Physical Medicine and Rehabilitation in 1965. He was a 20-year veteran of the Air Force, and Director of the Physiometrics Research Laboratory at the Houston VA Hospital. In 1962, he received the Aerospace

Medicine Honor citation from the American Medical Association. He continued to be based in Houston but frequently traveled to Washington.[40]

Margaret McCrindle Plymore, Ph.D.

Dr. Plymore became Chief, Research in Clinical Nursing, in 1965. Her office was located in the Boston VA Hospital, rather than Central Office. A sociologist by training, she had been on the faculties of Yale and Emory Universities before joining the Boston VA Hospital as its Chief Research Clinical Nurse.[40]

Howard W. Chauncey, Ph.D., D.M.D.

Dr. Chauncey became Program Chief of Research in Oral Diseases on October 1, 1965. His Ph.D. degree was in biochemistry from Boston University and his dental degree from Tufts. He had been active in dental research at Tufts, where he was Professor of Oral Pathology. Dr. Chauncey remained in Central Office until 1971, when he became ACOS/R&E at the Boston VA Outpatient Clinic.[41]

Eli M. Nadel, M.D.

Dr. Nadel joined Research Service in 1965 as Program Chief, Research in Pathology. Before coming to Central Office, he had been a career physician at NIH, most recently as Chief, Diagnostic Research Branch at the NCI.[41] He left the VA in 1970.

Figure 12.10 Abraham Dury, Ph.D.

Abraham Dury, Ph.D.

Dr. Dury had worked on the endocrinology of aging at the Pittsburgh VA Hospital and had chaired the VA's advisory committee on research in aging. He then moved to NIH into the new Institute for General Medical Sciences. When Joe Meyer decided to return to the laboratory in 1968, he persuaded Dury to move to the VA to replace him as Program Chief,

Basic Sciences. Dury stayed in VA Central Office as an important member of Research Service during the changes of the following years, until he retired in 1976.

Lawrence G. Christianson, M.D.

Dr. Christianson was Director of the Automatic Data Processing Staff when he was recruited to be Chief of Research in Neurology in 1969. He had been at the VA Hospital in Fort Meade, SD, before coming to VACO in February 1961 as Assistant Director, Medical Services. He spent only seven months in Research Service before returning to Medical Service.[42]

The Enhanced Career Development Program

In June 1961, the Clinical Investigator program, which until then had been coordinated by Research Service's sister service, Education Service, was officially transferred to Research Service. Dr. Schnaper coordinated awards in internal medicine and Dr. Lee in surgery. As new Program Chiefs arrived, they assumed coordination in their areas.

The Clinical Investigator program continued to be very active during the 1960s. As of February 1962, 47 awardees had completed their appointment. Forty of them remained in academic medicine, 15 in medical schools and 25 within the VA.

Shortly after they arrived, Drs. Kaim and Hooper established entry-level Research Associate programs in psychiatry and psychology to alleviate the shortage of psychiatrists and psychologists adequately trained in research. The training was 1 year for psychiatrists and 2 years for psychologists. The first Research Associates, three in psychiatry and four in psychology, entered their training in 1962.

The Research Associate in Psychology program continued as a 2-year program through the 1960s. The 1-year Research Associate program was later extended to include oral diseases, podiatry, and pathology, areas perceived to have major shortages of qualified research personnel. In these 4 programs, 13 Research Associates completed training during fiscal year 1965. In many cases, the 1-year appointments were extended a second year and the Research Associate appointment soon became established as a 2-year appointment. By 1967, 38 appointees participated in the physician Research Associate Program and applicants from all specialties were considered.

The early 1960s marked expansion of the Senior Medical Investigator (SMI) program. The VA research program had now matured to the point where many distinguished research physicians provided leadership. Appointment as an SMI conferred high honor on selected distinguished investigators in the VA hospital system. They worked independently on research of their own choosing. While they were permitted teaching and patient-care responsibilities, the major focus was to be on research activities, and they were supported directly from research funds. Their 4-year appointments were usually renewed after review, so this program conferred an unusual amount of continuity for the recipient.

Dr. Musser, as Director, Research Service, actively expanded the SMI program. Drs. Samuel Bassett (Chapter 3) and Edward Freis (Chapter 9) were appointed in 1959; Drs. Oscar Auerbach (Chapter 10) and Ludwig Gross (Chapter 3) in 1960; Dr. Jay Shurley in 1961; Dr. Morton Grossman (Chapter 7) in 1962; and Dr. Solomon Berson (Chapter 11) in 1963. Dr. Bassett died in 1962, leaving six active SMIs.

Jay Shurley, M.D., the only psychiatrist to hold an SMI appointment, had an eclectic research program. He had authored a 1948 VA Medical Bulletin on insulin shock therapy[43] and was engaged in research on sensory deprivation at the time he received the SMI appointment.

Figure 12.11: Jay Shurley, M.D.

Dr. Shurley's primary research interest involved the physiological, psychological, and behavioral effects of unusual environments. He did extensive studies of the effects of sensory isolation through water immersion and other controlled environments.[44, 45] He found that patients with insomnia were helped by use of an air-fluidized bed originally developed for burn victims.[46] In the late 1960's and 1970's Dr. Shurley studied the effects of the extreme environment at the Navy's South Pole Station.[47, 48] Much of this work focused on changes in sleep patterns.[49-51]

External advisors to VA research

The Committee on Veterans Medical Problems from the National Academy of Sciences (Appendix IIc) continued into the 1960s, but its advice was limited to negotiations with other agencies, industries and universities. At the beginning of 1960, four VA advisory committees advised the Research Service: the Advisory Committee on Research, begun in 1955 (Appendix IIe); the Advisory Committee on Radiobiology and Radioisotopes, begun in 1947 (Appendix IId); the Advisory Committee on Problems in Aging, begun in 1955; and the committee reviewing applicants for Clinical Investigator appointments, first called the Committee on Clinical Investigations and later the Research Career Development Committee (Appendix IIj). In 1960, the first three of these committees were abolished, and a new Advisory Committee on Research was established with membership from the three committees and other experts from outside the VA to advise on all aspects of the research program. This Advisory Committee on Research (Appendix IIf) remained active until 1968.

Internal advisors: the Research Program Committees

In November 1960, Research Service began to establish Research Program Committees, whose members were available to advise the Director, Research Service, and Program Chiefs on the status of the field and assist in broad planning and further development of the research program in their specialty. These Committees consisted primarily of VA field researchers with some outside consultants. Each committee had an Executive Secretary from Central Office, who was the Program Chief or a subject matter expert from another Central Office Service.[52]

In fiscal year 1964, Research Program Committees were in place for Basic Science, Cancer, Cardiovascular Disease, Infectious Disease, Oral Diseases, Psychiatry, Neurology and Psychology, and Pulmonary Disease (Appendix IIg).

The Program Evaluation Committees

In 1964, several chairmen of the Research Program Committees were asked to develop a mechanism for review of individual investigators' research programs. As a result of their recommendations, Research Evaluation Committees were established. Each principal investigator who was identified with a VA medical research laboratory or program was asked to document the scope, purpose, progress, and achievements of his or her research, to enable a critical scientific evaluation by panels of experts composed of VA and non-VA members. This program was announced in a Chief Medical Director's letter dated January 8, 1965, entitled "Evaluation of Medical Research Program". These committees reviewed brief proposals; their decisions were based on the productivity of the research or the apparent promise of the investigator. By 1968, Program Evaluation Committees in had been established in 12 subject areas (Appendix IIh.).

Study groups

In 1961, the VA established "Study Groups," small groups of VA investigators who met about twice a year to discuss individual research and exchange ideas and plans for new or extended Cooperative Studies.[53] In 1962, these groups were active in research on epilepsies, arthritis and rheumatic diseases, coccidioidomycosis, emphysema, oral diseases, physical medicine and rehabilitation, sarcoidosis, and social work.[54] By 1964 the Study Groups on epilepsies and sarcoidosis had disbanded; new groups studied chronic bronchitis, multiple sclerosis, psychological aspects of aging and nursing.[55] By fiscal year 1967, nine study groups were active. The emphysema and chronic bronchitis groups had disbanded. There were now groups studying endocrinology and "Restoration Centers, Intermediate Care Wards, Nursing Care Home Unit and Domiciliaries."[56] Subsequently, interest in these study groups waned. The annual reports of 1968 and 1969 listed only four groups. By FY 1973, only the group studying coccidioidomycosis remained active.[57] It continues to meet annually, though no longer primarily a VA group.

Research Support Centers

In 1962, Research Support Centers were established at the Hines (IL), Washington (DC) and Sepulveda (CA) VA Hospitals, known respectively as the Midwestern, Eastern and Western Research Support Centers. Their charge was to provide multidisciplinary consultation and assistance in:
        a. Research design, mathematical and statistical formulation
        b. Data acquisition, processing and analysis
        c. Storage, retrieval and transmission of scientific information
        d. Education and training

As originally envisioned, the center at Hines would primarily provide statistical and computational services and the one in Washington would emphasize medical instrumentation and automatic data processing.[58]

In January 1963, the Hines center presented the first of a series of courses for research investigators, covering problems in experimental design and applied statistical methods.[59]

In March 1964, a fourth center, the Southern Research Support Center, opened at the Little Rock (AR) VA Hospital. While this center had a broad mission— "biochemistry, physical chemistry, biophysics, statistics and data processing, research design, psychology, bioengineering and instrumentation," its 20 staff members, including 7 Ph.D. scientists, had particular expertise in instrumentation and design and construction of specialized research instruments. This center offered courses in biomedical instrumentation and atomic medicine.[60] During FY 1966, it developed procedures for a central research instrument program and became the site for the Central Research Instrumentation Pool (CRIP).[61]

In July 1965, a new Eastern Research Support Center opened at the West Haven VA Hospital.[62] The center at the Washington, D.C. VA Hospital became AHIS, dedicated to developing hospital information systems (Chapter 19).

In time, each support center developed special interests, while still trying to serve all of the regional needs of its researchers. By 1969, the Western Center had acquired expertise in information systems and became the site of data processing for the new Medical Research Information System. The Eastern and Midwestern centers became leaders in biostatistics, while the Southern center expanded its expertise in instrumentation.[63]

Outreach to other Federal agencies

During the 1950s and 1960s, the VA actively worked with other agencies. The medical research program was and remains represented on the Councils of the National Institutes of Health. Many NIH Study Sections include VA representatives. As of 1964, the VA also was represented on the President's Committee on Aging and the Committee on Scientific and Technical Information of the President's Federal Council for Science and Technology.[64]

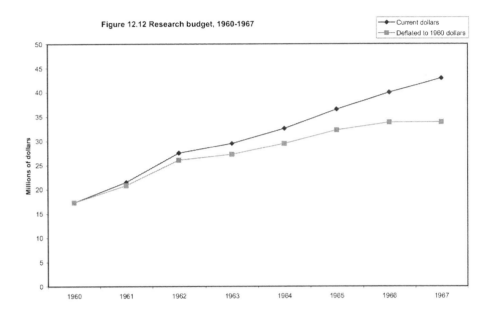

Figure 12.12 Research budget, 1960-1967

The Program expands and the budget soars

During the early 1960s, the VA research budget constantly expanded (Figure 12.12), helped by its good press and the favorable report from the National Academy of Sciences. Musser and Wells, strongly backed by Dr. Middleton, were politically very active.

The budgetary process then, as now, began with presentation and reviews of a budget through the VA hierarchy to the Bureau of the Budget, now called the Office of Management and Budget (OMB), before arriving at the Presidential budget. Within the VA, the budget was reviewed by the Chief Medical Director and then the Administrator's staff. The Bureau of the Budget auditors then completed a thorough review with an eye to saving money. Dr. Middleton as Chief Medical Director encouraged and vigorously defended growth of the research budget.[65] While his successor, Dr. McNinch, was less enthusiastic, Dr. H. Martin "Hal" Engle, the Chief Medical Director who followed McNinch, was also a strong advocate of research. William J. Driver, VA Administrator from 1965 to 1969, actively pushed the VA research program, using his direct contact at the White House when necessary.[66] Driver and Drs. Engle and Wells attended a meeting with President Lyndon Johnson to discuss federal funding of medical research (Figure 12.13).

Figure 12.13 White House meeting about Federal funding of medical research

With this degree of encouragement, the research budget was consistently favorable at the VA's submission stage but usually cut back by the Bureau of the Budget staff. Work at the congressional level was then necessary to restore the cuts. Here, Drs. Wells and Musser were the key players. Wells, especially, was described in interviews as a "consummate politician."

With increased resources, it was possible to expand the program as recommended by the NAS report. Efforts to build and improve the research physical plant and equipment at VA hospitals continued. During the early 1960s, the VA requested, and Congress appropriated, extra money for construction of badly needed VA research laboratories. Twice, the congressional appropriation had a special item for research laboratory construction. In 1961, the Research Service employed a full-time architect.[67]

Figure 12.14 Jules S. Cass, D.V.M.

VA pioneers better standards for veterinary care of research animals

Along with expanded basic science and more sophisticated clinical research programs, animal research facilities had been developed in most VA hospitals research programs. At that time, standards for the care and use of research animals were primarily subjective. In 1962, the VA appointed its first Chief of Research in Laboratory Animal Medicine and Care, Jules S. Cass, D.V.M. His charge was to develop a training program for animal care and to improve the quality of research with laboratory animals.

Since 1951 Dr. Cass had been at the University of Cincinnati as Assistant Professor of Industrial Health. He received his veterinary training and M.S. degree from Ohio State University and served a fellowship in medical entomology at the College of Veterinary Medicine of the University of Minnesota, where he remained as instructor. He also spent 2 years in the Communicable Diseases Center in Savannah, GA, where he was responsible for the health of the laboratory-animal colony.[68]

Under Dr. Cass's leadership, the VA developed training programs for animal technologists and pioneered in setting standards for veterinary care within animal research facilities. As accreditation standards developed in the general research community, the VA established a policy that all animal facilities must be accredited. Dr. Cass worked very closely with animal activists, particularly groups campaigning for humane care of laboratory animals.

The VA developed a reputation as a pace-setter in improving standards. Construction of animal facilities became an important part of the VA research construction program, a policy that continues to the present day.[69]

Medical research in the basic sciences

Until about 1960, most of the medical research in the VA was carried out by clinicians and was clinical in nature. As medical science progressed, however, the scientific base for medical research became increasingly important. Collaboration and interaction with full-time, specifically trained basic scientists became very desirable.

Up to this point, most of the independent basic scientists in the VA had entered through the Radioisotope Service. Since basic scientists were needed to handle the radiation safety program, from the beginning the Radioisotope Service had conferred high status on Ph.D. scientists and given them high grades in the Civil Service. However, elsewhere in medical research during the early days, the few Ph.D. scientists who entered the VA program were regarded and graded as "super technicians."[70] Largely as a result of Joe Meyer's efforts, this situation changed in the 1960s.

Joe Meyer, Ph.D.

Dr. Meyer (Figure 12.9) came to VA Central Office in 1960 as Chief of the Research Laboratory Division, succeeding Harold F. Weiler. Meyer, an organic chemist by training, served as a research chemist in Chicago before World War II. During the war, he worked on programs sponsored by the Office of Scientific Research and Development and later the

Manhattan Project. After the war, he worked as a chemist in the pharmaceutical industry but then went to Western Reserve in 1946 as a graduate student and Instructor in the new Biochemistry Department. He received his Ph.D. from Western Reserve in 1949 and then joined the VA as Assistant Director and Principle Scientist of the Radioisotope Unit at the Denver (CO) VA Hospital, with a faculty appointment in the Department of Biophysics at the University of Colorado Medical School. While at Denver, he was in charge of the program to train public employees, such as police and fire fighters, in radiation protection. In 1953, he moved to the New Orleans VA Hospital, where he installed the Radioisotope Unit and then served as its Associate Director, with an Associate Professor of Biochemistry appointment at the LSU Medical School. In 1959, he went to Houston as Chief of Medical Research Laboratories and Associate Professor of Biochemistry at Baylor University.[71]

After a short time as Chief of the Research Laboratories Division, Meyer perceived greater opportunities. The need to encourage development of basic science in the research program was recognized, and he had the background to do this. He suggested to Dr. Musser that he be made Program Chief for Basic Science, and this soon became his major responsibility. Drs. Middleton, Musser, and Wells all wanted a strong basic science component in the VA and gave Meyer the autonomy he needed to achieve this goal.[70]

One of the initiatives Meyer directed was Research in Aging. He apparently inherited this initiative from Dr. Chapple and relied on the Advisory Committee to help him identify areas of interest. To further this work, Meyer was urged to contact the renowned scientist Linus Pauling. Meyer visited Pauling, who agreed to collaborate with a VA scientist. They recruited Arthur Chernoff, Ph.D., who had an interest in aging. Pauling was about to announce his macromolecular theory at the Sepulveda (CA) VA Hospital, but the arrangement collapsed under political pressure stemming from Pauling's reputation of being a pacifist.[70]

Meyer, who had known Dr. Andrew Schally at Baylor University, worked with the New Orleans Hospital to recruit Schally into VA research. Meyer described his efforts to help:

> "One of the things I did was very useful to Andy. He needed all these hypothalami to work with, so Jim Musser said, 'Why don't you go up to Madison (WI) to the Oscar Meyer plant there and talk with them? Maybe they'll make pig hypothalami available to Andy.' So, I went up and talked with them and, sure enough, they made arrangements so we could put a technician up there. I am told . . . that they ended up with almost a million hypothalami, which is what made it possible for Schally to do his work."

Schally credited Meyer for making possible his Nobel Prize-winning work on the hypothalamic hormones. One of the first things he did after he won the Nobel Prize was to call Joe Meyer.

Meyer traveled extensively, pushing the importance of basic science as integral to the VA Medical Research program. He actively sought out distinguished and promising scientists, such as Paul Srere, who went to the Dallas VA Hospital and Claude Baxter, who went to

Sepulveda. Most of these new recruits were active academicians with appointments in affiliated universities. In addition, he encouraged promising young Ph.D.s already in the system to remain.[70]

Figure 12.15 Schally receiving the Nobel Prize

The VA annual medical research conference

During the early 1960s, the VA's popular annual research conference expanded. It was now held at the Netherlands-Hilton Hotel in Cincinnati. Concurrent sections for the scientific presentations became the norm.

The Agenda Committee was bombarded with abstracts for the program. All Clinical Investigators and Senior Medical Investigators were invited and held their own special subsection meetings. The Radioisotope Chiefs continued to attend and have their own special meetings, as did the Associate Chiefs of Staff for R&E. A description of the 1963 conference, from the January 1964 Research and Education Newsletter, follows:

"The 14th V.A.A.M.R.C. was as successful a conference as has been held by the VA in a perceptibly long while. For the last several years, the format of these conferences has been experimental but now it seems to have settled into a proper mold. The meeting was divided, like last year's, into separate quarter-day sessions but, unlike last year's, usually it was only the format which remained constant during each of these periods. The subjects were treated with a certain continuity, although this may not have been conspicuous in any but the plenary sessions.

"Tuesday evening, Clinical Investigators presented papers and Senior Medical Investigators led the discussions. Most Conferees, however, were not present but, instead, were sitting in administrative session, listening to matters discussed which touched on the specific and personal if it could be said that there was anything else at all during that evening meeting.

"The first session, the official opening of the general scientific meeting, on Wednesday before the entire body, was of good omen. Its welcomes were gracious, its introductions remarkably informative of the speakers' philosophies and remarkable backgrounds and the addresses themselves extraordinarily good and well received. These last were by the William S. Middleton award winner, Stanley Ulick, M.D. of the V. A. H. Bronx and by the Chief Medical Director, Joseph H. McNinch, M.D., who was appearing before the Conference for the first time. The welcomes were by L. H. Gunter, the VA Hospital Director of the long-time host-city whose team does most of the work of the Conference, and from Dr. Jackson Freidlander, the Area Medical Director. The introductions were by the Assistant Chief Medical Director for R&E in Medicine, Dr. M.J. Musser and by one of the co-winners of last year's W. S. Middleton award, Dr. Leslie Zieve, Associate Chief of Staff, Chief of the Radioisotope Service and Chief, Special Laboratory for Cancer Research of the V.A.H. Minneapolis, Minn. (This latter is reproduced here, in toto, by popular demand.)

"The second was a specialties-session during which four separate programs were conducted simultaneously in separate parlors. The largest of these was a combined medical-surgical series. The others were in psychology, pulmonary disease and the basic sciences.

"After lunch while research support (statistical and biological) was being described, about 20 large circular discs were brought into the theater-sized hall where they were set on legs, and chairs were placed around them. When this process was completed a sign, designating the topic to be discussed around it was placed on each and the round-table discussions were on their way. At one, the subject was so popular that it became clear at once that no peace or audibility would be possible around that table, so the members were led off by their leader to a parlor. At the rest of the round-tables the numbers were not so great, although still allowing little elbow-room but the enthusiasm and intensity around them had nothing to do with number and the discussions were unabated until closing time.

"Before dinner on Wednesday there was a cooperative reception. In this kind, as in the studies of the same name, the investigator can become involved to whatever degree he chooses. Nothing else was on the prescribed agenda for the evening.

"Thursday morning until the coffee break, the conferees again gathered and heard discourses as an assemblage. These were piloted by the only speaker from beyond the VA confines, Dr. Ewald Busse, Professor of Psychiatry, Medical School, Duke University, who spoke on Research in Aging and they were followed by the final period which was a second Specialties Session. This resembled the first one in all respects except that, where psychology had the front on Tuesday, psychiatry led the parlor on Wednesday. By 1:30 p.m. the 14th Veterans Administration Annual Medical Research Conference had joined the previous 13 in the cemetery for deceased Conferences and the 15th was being conceived."[72]

The Middleton Award (Chapter 7) was presented at each annual conference by the previous year's winner, and the awardee addressed the conference. After the 1960 award to Berson and Yalow, in 1961, Hubert Pipberger at the Washington (DC) VA Hospital received it for his work on computerization of the electrocardiogram (Chapter 13). In 1962, it went to collaborators Leslie Zieve and William Vogel at Minneapolis for their studies of phospholipids and phospholipases. In 1963, Stanley Ulick from the Bronx received the award for his work in the chemistry and metabolism of mineralocorticoid hormones. In 1964, Ulick presented it to Robert Becker for his identification of electrical control systems in living organisms, including man.

**Figure 12.16. Drs. Becker, Musser, Ulick and Wells at the time
Dr. Becker received the Middleton Award**

In 1965, Lucien Guze and George Kalmanson (Figure 12.17) from the Los Angeles VA Hospital received the Middleton Award for discerning the host-parasite relationship in chronic infectious kidney disease.

**Figure 12.17 Lucien Guze, M.D., and George Kalmanson, M.D.,
at the 1965 Middleton Award ceremony**

In 1966, Guze presented the Award to Leo Hollister of Palo Alto (Chapter 8) for his numerous significant contributions in the field of therapeutic drugs for mental illness (Figure 21.3).

The 1967 Middleton Award went to Leonard Skeggs, Ph.D., of the Cleveland VA Hospital for developing automated laboratory test devices and for his studies of the biochemistry of hypertension. The automated devices developed by Skeggs have revolutionized laboratory medicine.

Figure 12.18 Leonard Skeggs, Ph.D.
1967 Middleton Award winner

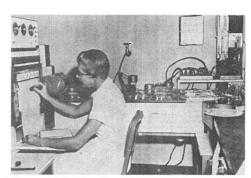

Figure 12.19 The Autoanalyzer
developed by Skeggs

The Central Research Instrumentation Pool

In the early 1960s, the *Research and Education Newsletter* listed equipment that users no longer needed. Persons who wanted the equipment contacted the Research Facilities office in Central Office Research Service for equipment transfer. The success of this popular program overloaded Central Office staff. The program was transferred to Supply Service, but that did not meet the need. In 1966, the VA piloted a regional exchange program under the direction of the Southern Research Support Center at Little Rock. In 1968, this expanded to the Central Research Instrument Pool, dubbed "CRIP," a nationwide instrument exchange program, that continued to be administered from the Little Rock VA hospital. Nationwide listings of available equipment were distributed regularly, and investigators needing the equipment applied for it through their hospitals. In cases of multiple requests for an item, CRIP made a decision based on justified need.[73] Generally, preference was given to appointees in the Career Development Program. The CRIP staff also brought disabled equipment to Little Rock for repair and distribution. This equipment pool later became a resource for training biomedical engineers.

Changes in Central Office leadership

After Edward Dunner left the directorship of Research Service in 1966, Harold Schnaper, M.D., who had been his deputy, served as Acting Director for several months, until Lionel Bernstein from the Chicago West Side VA Hospital came into the position (Chapter 15). Shortly after Bernstein's arrival, Dr. Wells resigned as ACMD/R&E to head a Regional Medical Program centered in Birmingham, AL. Bernstein became Acting ACMD/R&E and held that position until Thomas Chalmers, M.D., was appointed ACMD/R&E in 1968.

During this period, Bernstein encouraged the Research Evaluation Committees to work toward refining the quality of VA Research programs. However, it was not until after Chalmers's arrival in 1968 that, relieved of his double duty as both ACMD/R&E and

Director, Research Service, he moved to implement the major changes in the program attributed to him.

The Second National Academy of Sciences Study

During 1966 and 1967, the National Research Council of the National Academy of Sciences again reviewed the VA research program, this time reviewing the education program as well.

Their report, published in 1968, detailed the remarkable growth of the research program, both in terms of VA and non-VA monies. The number of publications from the VA research program had more than doubled between 1958 and 1966. As of FY 1966, 27 hospitals, all affiliated with medical schools, each were receiving $500,000 or more of VA Medical Research funds; 49 hospitals, 39 of them affiliated, were receiving between $100,000 and $500,000; and 84 hospitals, of which only 22 were affiliated, received less than $100,000. This report noted that the non-affiliated hospitals were at a disadvantage due to their remoteness from academic medical centers, but urged them to continue their roles in cooperative and collaborative studies. With that observation also came the recommendation that any new VA hospitals be built in close proximity to medical schools.[74]

In its review of research management, the report describes the decentralized program. During the 1961-1966 period, institutional allocations to VA hospitals averaged 83% of the funds requested, suggesting that activity had been "more limited by existing investigative competence and facilities than by lack of funds."[74] The report lauds the activities of the Program Evaluation Committees that since 1965 had been reviewing individual research programs. It states: "In due course, it may be expected that all programs supported by Veterans' Administration funds will be subject to review by an evaluating committee."[74]

The 1968 NAS report reviewed the activities of the four active Research Support Centers. Some review committee members doubted that "modestly staffed and equipped centers" such as these could "deliver the wide range of services stated in their mission." In the course of site visits, the committee members received mixed reviews from research investigators about the type of help they were receiving from the centers. It seemed that research personnel at a hospital close to a center sought assistance more frequently than those in more remote institutions. The committee recommended,

> "That the Veterans' Administration review the programs and accomplishments of its four Research Support Centers to determine whether they are accomplishing the purposes for which they were established and how their assistance to individual investigators can be enhanced."[75]

This report endorsed the Annual Research Conference, as well as the Study Groups, as excellent devices for fostering the intellectual satisfaction and research interest in the staff. The report was very favorable toward the Research Career Development Program and formally recommended program continuation.

In review of the quality of the research program, the committee once more concluded that,

> "The research program compares favorably with other broad national programs of biomedical research. It shares with them a significant quota of uninspired investigations but, on the whole, the Veterans Administration is to be commended on maintaining relatively high standards of quality of relating its program to its primary mission during a period of rapid growth."[76]

This second 1968 NAS report, with its recommendations, was both stimulus and justification for many of the changes begun in 1968.

References

1. *Medical Research in the Veterans Administration, FY 1960.* Washington, DC: Government Printing Office, 1960, 3-4.

2. *Medical Research in the Veterans Administration, FY 1960.* 1.

3. *Medical Research in the Veterans Administration, FY 1960.* 1-2.

4. *Medical Research in the Veterans Administration, FY 1960.* 5.

5. *Medical Research in the Veterans Administration, FY 1960.* 5-6.

6. Kendall, E.C., *Cortisone.* New York: Charles Scribner's Sons, 1971, 83-93.

7. *Medical Research in the Veterans Administration, FY 1961.* Washington, DC: Government Printing Office, 1961, xi.

8. *Research and Education Newsletter, July, 1960.* Washington, DC: Research and Education Office, VACO, 1.

9. *Research and Education Newsletter, July, 1965, Vol 6, 4.*

10. Telephone interview with Charles H. Halsted, M.D., son of James Halsted, M.D., March 12, 1992.

11. Telephone interview with John T. Farrar, M.D., March 26, 2001.

12. *The Harvard Medical Unit.* Finland, M. and Castle, W.B., eds.; Boston, MA: for the Countway Library, Harvard Medical School, 1983, 307-308.

13. Halsted, J., Gasster, M. and Drenick, E., "Absorption of radioactive vitamin B12 after total gastrectomy; relation to microcytic anemia and to site of origin of Castle's intrinsic factor." *N Eng J Med*, 1954. **251**: 161-168.

14. Swendseid, M., Halsted, J. and Libby, R., "Excretion of cobalt 60-labeled vitamin B12 after total gastrectomy." *Proc Soc Exper Biol and Med*, 1953. **83**: 226-228.

15. Halsted, J., "Megaloblastic anemia associated with surgically produced gastrointestinal abnormalities." *California Med*, 1955. **83**: 212-217.

16. Halsted, J., Lewis, P. and Gasster, M., "Absorption of radioactive vitamin B12 in syndrome of megaloblastic anemia associated with intestinal stricture of anastamosis." *Am J Med*, 1956. **20**: 42-52.

17. Citrin, Y., Sterling, K. and Halsted, J., "The mechanism of hypoproteinemia associated with giant hypertrophy of the gastric mucosa." *N Eng J Med*, 1957. **257**: 906-912.

18. Halsted, J.A., Ronaghy, H.A., Abadi, P., Haghshenass, M., Amirhakemi, G.H., Barakat, R.M. and Reinhold, J.G., "Zinc deficiency in man. The Shiraz experiment." *Am J Med*, 1972. **53**: 277-284.

19. *Research and Education Newsletter, March-April, 1966.* 18-19.

20. *Research and Education Newsletter, September, 1962.* 4.

21. *Research and Education Newsletter, May, 1962.* 3.

22.   *Medical Research in the Veterans Administration, FY 1960.* 643-659.

23.   *Medical Research in the Veterans Administration, FY 1960.* 6.

24.   *Medical Research in the Veterans Administration, FY 1960.* 11.

25.   *Medical Research in the Veterans Administration, FY 1960, 28.* 28.

26.   *Research and Education Newsletter, May, 1960.* 16.

27.   *Research and Education Newsletter, November, 1962.* 7-9.

28.   Interview with Mr. Lawrence Shaw, February 3, 1994 at Mr. Shaw's home, Gainesville, FL.

29.   *Research and Education Newsletter, May, 1960.* 2.

30.   Telephone interview with Robert Efron, M.D., 1988.

31.   Interview with Lyndon Lee, M.D., April 7, 1988 at a restaurant in Bethesda, MD.

32.   *Research and Education Newsletter, September, 1960.* Washington, DC: Research and Education Office, VACO, 28.

33.   *Research and Education Newsletter, May, 1961.* 24.

34.   Telephone interview with Harold W. Schnaper, M.D., January 26, 1992.

35.   Telephone interview with James H. Matthews, M.D., May 25,1988.

36.   Letter from James H. Matthews, M.D. to author, written at Richmond, VA, April 14, 1988.

37.   *Research and Education Newsletter, November, 1963.* Washington, DC: Research and Education Office, VACO, 15.

38.   *Research and Education Newsletter, February, 1965.* Vol. 6. Washington, DC: Research and Education Office, VACO, 1965, 4.

39.   Interview with Mark Walcott, M.D., April 5, 1988 at VACO.

40.   *Research and Education Newsletter, November, 1965.* Vol. 6. 1965, 4.

41.   *Research and Education Newsletter, November, 1965.* 5.

42.   Interview with Lawrence G. Christianson, M.D., May 4, 1992 at Dr. Christianson's home in suburban Maryland.

43.   Shurley, J.T. and Bond, E., "Insulin shock therapy in schizophrenia." *Medical Bulletin,* 1948.

44.   Serafetinides, E.A., Shurley, J.T., Brooks, R. and Gideon, W.P., "Electrophysiological changes in humans during perceptual isolation." *Aerosp Med,* 1972. **43**: 432-434.

45.   Serafetinides, E.A., Shurley, J.T., Brooks, R. and Gideon, W.P., "Sensory versus perceptual isolation: a comparison of their electrophysiological effects." *Aerosp Med,* 1973. **44**: 539-541.

46.   Miller, W.C., Jr. and Shurley, J.T., "Treatment of insomniac patients with the air-fluidized bed." *Am J Psychiatry,* 1972. **128**: 1147-1149.

47.   Popkin, M.K., Stillner, V., Osborn, L.W., Pierce, C.M. and Shurley, J.T., "Novel behaviors in an extreme environment." *Am J Psychiatry*, 1974. **131**: 651-654.

48.   Serafetinides, E.A., Shurley, J.T. and Brooks, R.E., "EEG and the effects of photic stimulation at the South Pole." *Aerosp Med*, 1971. **42**: 52-53.

49.   Natani, K., Shurley, J.T., Pierce, C.M. and Brooks, R.E., "Long-term changes in sleep patterns in men on the South Polar Plateau." *Arch Intern Med*, 1970. **125**: 655-659.

50.   Joern, A.T., Shurley, J.T., Brooks, R.E., Guenter, C.A. and Pierce, C.M., "Short-term changes in sleep patterns on arrival at the South Polar Plateau." *Arch Intern Med*, 1970. **125**: 649-654.

51.   Natani, K. and Shurley, J.T. "Disturbed sleep and effect in an extreme environment. In: Sleep Physiology, Biochemistry, Psychology, Pharmacology, Clinical Implications." *First European Congress on Sleep Research.* Apr. Basel, Switzerland: S. Karger, Basel, 1972, 426-430.

52.   *Medical Research in the Veterans Administration, FY 1961.* 12-14.

53.   *Medical Research in the Veterans Administration, FY 1961.* 68-70.

54.   *Medical Research in the Veterans Administration, FY 1962.* Washington, DC: Government Printing Office, 1962, 78-84.

55.   *Medical Research in the Veterans Administration, FY 1964.* Washington, DC: Government Printing Office, 1964, 82-86.

56.   *Medical Research in the Veterans Administration, FY 1967.* Washington, DC: Government Printing Office, 1967, 99-103.

57.   *Medical Research in the Veterans Administration, FY 1973.* Washington, DC: Government Printing Office, 1974, 94-95.

58.   *Research and Education Newsletter, May, 1962.* 7-8.

59.   *Research and Education Newsletter, March, 1963.* Vol. 4. 13.

60.   *Research and Education Newsletter, April, 1965.* 8-9.

61.   *Medical Research in the Veterans Administration, FY 1966.* Washington, DC: Government Printing Office, 1966, 87.

62.   *Research and Education Newsletter, April, 1965.* 9-10.

63.   *Medical Research in the Veterans Administration, FY 1969.* Washington, DC: Government Printing Office, 1969, 72-78.

64.   *Medical Research in the Veterans Administration, FY 1964.* 4.

65.   Interview with Martin Cummings, M.D., April 7, 1988 at Dr. Cummings' office in Washington, DC.

66.   Interview with Thomas Chalmers, M.D., July 29,1992 at a hotel lobby in Boston, MA.

67.   *VA Telephone Directory.* Washington, DC: 1962

68. *Research and Education Newsletter, September, 1962.* Washington, DC: Research and Education Office, VACO, 7-8.

69. Interview with Jules Cass, D.V.M., May 8, 1992 at the Cosmos Club in Washington, DC.

70. Interview with Joe Meyer, Ph.D., May 4, 1992 at Dr. Meyer's home in suburban Maryland.

71. *Research and Education Newsletter, September, 1960.* 28-29.

72. *Research and Education Newsletter, January, 1964.* 1.

73. *Medical Research in the Veterans Administration, FY 1969.* 78.

74. NAS-NRC, *Evaluation of Biomedical Research and Education in the Veterans' Administration.* Washington, DC: National Academy of Sciences, 1968, 28.

75. NRC, *Evaluation of Biomedical Research and Education in the VA.* 1968, 30.

76. NRC, *Evaluation of Biomedical Research and Education in the VA.* 1968, 34.

Chapter 13. The VA Cooperative Studies Program of the 1960s

The veterans' health care system is such an excellent venue for cooperative clinical trials that it is understandable that VA is often—if erroneously—credited with being the birthplace of this form of clinical research. In fact, a few cooperative studies had been performed by others even before the landmark VA tuberculosis trials (Chapter 5), and the British Medical Research Council ran tuberculosis trials at about the same time as the VA trials. It is certainly accurate to say that VA clinicians were among the first to understand the power of this important tool for evaluating and improving patient treatment, and VA clinicians have applied its methodology to many clinical problems.

In a cooperative study, investigators at different hospitals analyze a clinical problem by following exactly the same protocol and controlling as many factors as possible. Since there are inevitable differences between hospitals, even those within the VA system, the unique aspect stemming from one local environment becomes less important than it would be in a study conducted in a single hospital. Also, by working together, investigators can study many more patients affected by the condition under scrutiny in a shorter time than would be possible in a study limited to the patient population of a single hospital. Moreover, economies of scale make it practical to include professional coordination and statistical support.

The earliest VA Cooperative Studies include the tuberculosis trials (Chapter 5), the psychopharmacology studies and the predecessor study of prefrontal lobotomy (Chapter 8), the hypertension studies (Chapter 9), and the earliest of the truly randomized VA studies, evaluation of the effect of isoniazide on multiple sclerosis conducted jointly with the Follow-up Agency (Chapter 4). VA groups outside of Research Service spearheaded these early studies, but Research Service soon became involved, providing in differing degrees monetary, administrative or statistical support. By the early 1960s, the Research Service had assumed general responsibility for cooperative studies. Edward Dunner, M.D., who became Chief of the Clinical Studies Division of Research Service in 1958 (Chapter 12), brought the tuberculosis studies with him, formalizing a collaboration that had increased since the beginning of that research.

Statistical support for VA Cooperative Studies

The VA Central Office statisticians who supported the early tuberculosis and hypertension trials worked for the agency's Controller's Office. In 1957, a Research Statistics Division consisting of five statisticians and headed by Clifford Bachrach, M.D., was established in that Office.

Bachrach had graduated from medical school in 1941 and served as an Army doctor during World War II. After the war, he had earned an M.P.H. degree from Johns Hopkins University, taking "all the statistics courses they offered." Subsequently, he was a Hopkins faculty member for 10 years, teaching statistics and epidemiology before joining the VA. He organized a dedicated staff to begin collecting and sorting data and contributing their analyses of the clinical implications. In a 1992 interview, Bachrach described the character of working with research statistics in those early days:

> "I had a shop with about ten or a dozen people. . . four of them were college graduates with some degree of training in statistics . . . (and there were) about seven or eight clerical people and a secretary.

> "The state of the art was 80-column punch (IBM) cards. . . . You had to write up your specifications (for a computer run) and you were behind the administrative parts of the VA in priority . . . a difficult way to work."

In view of the administrative barriers to using the fledgling data processing equipment, Bachrach expressed a continuing affinity for the simple 3 by 5 card.

> "I still think it (the 3 by 5 card) is a wonderful device, for a number of reasons. I have always been strong on having people rub their noses in the data. I don't like this business of putting it all into the machine and putting in a program that does an analysis of variance and getting out some things at the end, without looking at the distributions, looking at the peculiarities of the data that you see when you look at them one by one."[1]

In 1962, Dr. Bachrach left the VA to accept a U.S. Public Health Service assignment in Israel. At about that time, the research statistics unit was moved to Research Service and became part of the Clinical Studies unit under Edward Dunner. Lawrence W. Shaw was recruited to the position of head statistician.

Shaw had previously been Chief of the Records and Statistics Unit in the tuberculosis program of the U.S. Public Health Service, studying the epidemiology of BCG vaccination. His initial appointment in the VA was to the Research Statistics Division in Research Service, and he was to be responsible for the statistical aspects of the cooperative studies that had formerly been under Dr. Bachrach. Shaw had graduated from Ohio Wesleyan University, earned an M.S. from the University of Pennsylvania and had pursued other graduate studies at Ohio State and Columbia Universities. Prior to joining the Public Health Service in 1945, he had been a statistician with the War Department.

In the early 1960s, the source of statistical support for the Cooperative Studies program varied markedly, depending on the type of study and the preferences of the investigators. Statisticians in Central Office supported the medical studies. The ongoing surgical and cancer studies used contract statisticians, based at a university or employed by the Follow-up Agency. The psychiatric studies received their planning, administrative and statistical support from the Central Neuropsychiatric Research Laboratory (CNPRL) at the Perry Point (MD) VA Hospital.[2]

When the Research Support Centers (Chapter 12) were established, they were intended to support only individual research. However, they became sites of statistical expertise, and as time went on, the Eastern Research Support Center assumed statistical support for some of the Cooperative Studies. At the same time, the statisticians in Central Office who left were not replaced. By the end of the 1960s, the only statistician left was Shaw. His role became primarily one of coordinating studies rather than that of hands-on statistician. However, the hybrid system, with many of the cooperative studies receiving statistical support from contractors overseen by Central Office coordinators, was well-established, and it continued into the 1970s.

Governance of a Cooperative Study in the early 1960s

Each cooperative study consisted of a Chairman who was a VA clinician from one of the participating hospitals, a principal investigator at each hospital, a Coordinator from VA Central Office, generally from Research Service, and a statistician. In most studies, consultants from outside the VA also met with the group. Usually, an executive committee of the key people in the study (the chairman, the VACO coordinator, the statistician and selected participants) met frequently to review results and plan future strategy. In some studies, the chairman and coordinator served this function without a committee. All participants met once or twice yearly. Decisions were made by consensus. Generally, the participants themselves made the key decisions about the direction of their study, and overall guidelines were flexible. Before 1966, no centralized or other systematic external review process existed for cooperative studies.

Funding for cooperative studies competed directly with individual research projects in a disciplinary area. The Program Chief for that area was responsible for distributing the funds within that area, using his best judgment as to whether a cooperative study or an individual investigator's project should receive higher priority.[3]

The Cooperative Studies Evaluation Committee (CSEC)

In 1966, CSEC (Appendix IIi) was formed. Shaw and others felt a need for guidance for the Cooperative Studies Program. As Shaw described it:

> "My opinion was that the evaluation of quality research in the VA had proceeded along lines where there were field committees established to advise the VA on the quality of each and every research field (the Research Evaluation Committees) . . . I thought that trend was very good, and it moved progressively through all domains of VA research enterprises. There was no similar thing for cooperative studies. Cooperative studies were largely influenced by the VA coordinator, . . . but (we proposed) to set up an evaluation committee that would work with all proposed new cooperative studies and comment on the wisdom of (the plan)."

William Tucker, M.D., Director of Medical Service and a long-time participant in the tuberculosis trials, chaired the first meeting of CSEC on March 11, 1966. At this meeting, the group reviewed the current structure of Research Service and where the Cooperative Studies Program fit into the Service. They accepted as their charge to "consider current cooperative studies and new proposals for cooperative studies in all fields of medical research and related specialties." The Director of the Research Service would decide which studies were to be evaluated.

Table 13.1 VA Cooperative Studies listed in annual reports, 1960-1970

Name of Cooperative Study	Years listed
Antihypertensive agents (Chapter 9)	1956–1975
Atherosclerosis	
Cardiology section	
Anticoagulant	1957–1971
Drug cholesterol lowering	1961–1962
Drug lipid	1962–1971
Neurology section	
Anticoagulant	1957–1962
Drug cholesterol lowering	1961–1962
Drug lipid	1962–1971
Estrogen	1963–1970
Diet section	
Low fat and unsaturated fatty acids	1957–1961
Automatic cardiovascular data processing	1960–1974
Diabetes mellitus	1958–1965
Endocrine disorders	1958–1966
Functional (nonorganic) deafness	1961
Gastroenterology (gastric ulcer)	1959–1969
Hepatitis	1967–1975
Osteoporosis	1967–1969
Arthritis – ankylosing spondylitis	1968–1970
Nephrosis	1966
Aging in men	1963–1964
Endocrine morphology in aging	1965–1967
Chemotherapy in psychiatry	1957–1973
Outpatient psychiatry	1958–1964
Multiple sclerosis	1957–1963
Microbiology in multiple sclerosis: pilot study	1960–1962
Amyotrophic lateral sclerosis	1958–1961
Psychological research	1957–1962
Chemotherapy of tuberculosis	1946–1974
Chemoprophylaxis of tuberculosis	1963–1974
Pulmonary function testing	1956–1965
Coccidioidomycosis	1957–1961
Fungus diseases (blasto-, histo-& cryptococcosis)	1957–1972
Oral exfoliative cytology	1961–1963
Hospital infections study	1956–1963
Coronary artery disease surgery	1957–1975
Parkinson's syndrome surgery	1956–1968
Esophageal varices	1956–1975
Solitary pulmonary nodules	1957–1968
Ruptured intervertebral disk	1956–1967
Techniques for early diagnosis of lung cancer	1957–1962
Peptic ulcer surgery	1956–1972
Evaluation of analgesics	1964–1975
Peripheral vascular disease	1963–1968
Esophageal cancer	1963–1972
VA cancer chemotherapy study group	1956–1968
Lung cancer chemotherapy study group	1957–1975

VA cooperative urological group	1959–1975
VA surgical adjuvant cancer chemotherapy study	1957–1975
Infusion substudy	1963–1967
University surgical adjuvant study	1958–1963
Western cooperative cancer chemotherapy group	1961–1963
Pacific VA Cancer chemotherapy group	1961–1971
Southwest cancer chemotherapy group	1956–1964
Midwest cooperative chemotherapy group	1959–1964

At its first meeting, CSEC reviewed a proposal for a new cooperative study on osteoporosis. It did not approve the proposal as written but made extensive suggestions for improvement and recommended going ahead with a proposed pilot study. In this case, the pilot study did not lead to a complete study.[3] After that, CSEC met three times a year for some time and then settled into semiannual meetings. In VA today, this committee continues to be active under a different name, and its recommendations are routinely accepted as guidelines for funding new and continuing cooperative studies.

Between 1960 and 1970, a total of 54 VA Cooperative Studies were listed in the annual reports to Congress (Table 13.1). In 1960, 34 were in progress; in 1970, 21, with 12 studies in progress continuously throughout this period. These studies covered a wide range of disciplines.

A number of cooperative studies grew out of the tuberculosis trials (Chapter 5) and the annual conference they stimulated. These studies became independent of the tuberculosis trials themselves, though often the same investigators were involved. They included studies of the solitary pulmonary nodule, pulmonary function testing and fungal diseases of the lungs.

The solitary pulmonary nodule

As a part of the transition of the VA-Armed Forces studies from studies specifically of tuberculosis to studies of pulmonary disease in general, the surgeons in the group became interested in solitary pulmonary nodules that were discovered on routine chest x-rays. In 1957, a study of patients with such nodules began under the leadership of John Steele, M.D., of the San Fernando (CA) VA Hospital.

Dr. Steele died before the final 10-year follow-up period was completed, and George Higgins, M.D., and statisticians from the group at the Follow-up Agency completed the final analysis. Patients included in the study were male patients with *asymptomatic*, previously undiagnosed solitary pulmonary nodules less than 6 cm in diameter. All underwent surgery. In this group, 370 of the lesions proved to be malignancies that could be removed. These patients were then followed for 10 years after surgery. The 5-year survival was 38.5 percent; that at 10 years, 20.1 percent. Survival was longer in younger patients and patients with smaller nodules. Comparing this series with a different series of VA patients who had resectable but *symptomatic* lung cancer, who had a 26.3 percent 5-year survival, indicated the advantage of removing the cancer before it became symptomatic.[4]

Chemoprophylaxis of tuberculosis 1963–1974

Another study spun off from the tuberculosis trials was a trial of isoniazid in the prevention of recurrence of tuberculosis in patients with tuberculosis in remission. This trial, based on a study that showed a significant rate of reactivation of tuberculosis in VA patients with inactive disease, was a randomized double-blind study with three regimens, two with isoniazid and one with placebo only. A total of 7,036 patients with inactive disease, including some who had received prior chemotherapy, were treated for 2 years and then observed for 5 more years. In previously untreated patients, isoniazid led to fewer reactivations than experienced by patients receiving placebo, but previously treated patients, who had a very low rate of reactivation, showed no difference.[5]

Fungal diseases

Groups from VA and Armed Services hospitals in areas endemic for systemic fungal diseases started cooperative studies of coccidioidomycosis, histoplasmosis and blastomycosis in the late 1950s. In their severe forms, these diseases, while rare, pose serious management problems. The cooperative approach was the only feasible way to conduct studies with the potential to yield definitive answers about the best treatment.

Coccidioidomycosis (1957–1961, then a study group)

An example of the easy transition during the 1960s between a cooperative study and a loose coalition of persons interested in a problem involved the disease coccidioidomycosis. Especially in the Southwest and the deserts and valleys of California, where it is endemic, this disease was important in the differential diagnosis of tuberculosis and was treated by the same pulmonary specialists who treated tuberculosis. In 1957, a group interested in this disease met at the annual tuberculosis meetings and formed a cooperative study group. As a first step, they created a registry of patients with systemic coccidioidomycosis and began meeting annually to discuss this disease. By the early 1960s, it had become apparent that the only effective treatment, amphotericin B, was very toxic and that a randomized trial was not feasible at that time. Instead, the group became a VA Study Group and continued their annual meetings to share clinical experiences and the results of basic research.

At the fourteenth meeting of this group, in 1970, attendees included representatives from the VA Hospitals at Fresno, Long Beach, Los Angeles, San Fernando, San Diego, Oakland, and Sepulveda, CA, from Tuscon and Phoenix, AZ and from the Western Research Support Center and VACO. Two Army hospitals, two Air Force hospitals, the Centers for Disease Contro at Atlanta, the NIH, UC Davis, USC, San Diego State University and Kern County, California General Hospital were also represented. By this time, the group had won the sponsorship of local pulmonary professional groups to add to VA's primary support.[6] This group has continued, no longer sponsored by the VA but with VA members. John N. Galgiani, M.D., of the Tucson VA Medical Center was its secretary from 1986 to 1997.[7]

Histoplasmosis (1957-1972)

In this study, 85 patients with chronic pulmonary histoplasmosis were treated with amphotericin B, but the dose was randomized. Endpoints were the elimination of histoplasma from the sputum and the occurrence of amphotericin B toxicity. Both were related to dosage and duration of therapy. The relatively small dose of amphotericin B, 0.5g given over the course of 3.5 weeks, controlled the infection in only two-thirds of the patients. Even at this low dose, 80 percent had toxic reactions, but these did not require interrupting the treatment, and re-treatment of patients who failed to respond was uniformly successful. On the other hand, a dose of 2.5 g given over the course of 17 weeks controlled the infection in all patients, but toxicity was reported in 86 percent of the patients, and in 29 percent toxicity was so severe that therapy was discontinued. Participants in the study concluded that the best approach to using this drug was to employ a dose intermediate between the two that they had tested or to use a small dose followed by re-treatment when necessary.[8]

Blastomycosis (1957–1972)

This group carried out a randomized trial comparing two potential treatments for this rather rare systemic fungal disease. Of 84 patients with North American blastomycosis entered into the study, 41 were treated with amphotericin B and 43 received 2-hydroxystilbamidine. The results showed that pulmonary blastomycosis of a noncavitary nature, which was not extensive in its degree of involvement and was either not disseminated to other organs or disseminated only to the skin, responded well to either drug. When pulmonary involvement was extensive or associated with cavities, amphotericin B was the more effective agent. Involvement of any organ other than the lung or skin was best treated with amphotericin B.[9]

Cooperative groups developing diagnostic methods

Several groups of hospitals were involved in collaborative efforts to improve diagnostic methods. Prominent among them were the Pulmonary Function Study, the study of Endocrine Disorders and the Automatic Cardiovascular Data Processing group.

Pulmonary function testing (1956–1965)

A cooperative study was developed to standardize techniques and establish normal values for the multiple tests that were in use to evaluate pulmonary function. The group critically evaluated tests for measuring ventilation, lung volumes and alveolar capillary diffusion and then applied them to diagnostic and prognostic studies of patients with emphysema and those undergoing thoracic surgery.

Endocrine disorders (1958–1966)

This group at ten VA hospitals started with the intention of using the randomized clinical trial method to study rare endocrine diseases such as Addison's disease. However, they agreed that standardization of diagnostic methods was needed first. They developed the ACTH stimulation test for diagnosis of adrenal hypofunction or hyperfunction. Based on data from over 6,000 such tests, they set the "gold standard" for these diagnoses.

By the mid-1960s, the group developed a cluster of four subcommittees that contributed technical leadership in specific areas for development of cooperative study protocols. Pilot studies evaluated the effects of human growth hormone in renal failure, obesity and osteoporosis. They developed immunoassays for insulin, growth hormone, parathormone, TSH and ACTH, with help from their consultants, Drs. Berson, Yalow, and Unger.[10]

In 1966, this group was redesignated a "Study Group" and charged with identifying possible future cooperative studies. While such studies were never accomplished, the contributions of this group to endocrinology were profound. The standardized ACTH test was widely used for diagnosis of adrenal disease until radioimmunoassay of the adrenal compounds became reliable. And the improved availability of radioimmunoassay of the hormones benefited millions of patients.

Automatic cardiovascular data processing (1960–1974)

Computerization of the electrocardiogram (EKG or ECG) is now an accepted technology, assisting in the routine diagnosis of heart disease. One of the pioneers in this field was Hubert Pipberger, M.D., at the Washington (DC) VA Hospital. By the late 1960s, Dr. Pipberger had assembled a group of collaborators from eight VA hospitals to collect patient EKG data using his program for automatic analysis and to advise him on improvements in the program. The following excerpts from the annual *Medical Research in the Veterans Administration* give the flavor of this work:

1969: "Electrocardiograms of a series of 405 patients with pulmonary emphysema of moderate or severe degree were studied. Using a variety of statistical techniques, optimal ECG measurements were determined for the differentiation of pulmonary emphysema ECG'S from normal.

"They were divided into those which can be conveniently obtained through visual record analysis and those of a more complex nature obtained by digital computation. Using 14 ECG measurements with a multivariate statistical technique, more than 80 percent of the emphysema cases could be classified correctly with a false positive rate of only 5 percent. Thus, the electrocardiogram could be improved substantially as a diagnostic tool for the recognition of pulmonary emphysema which represents an increasing health hazard.

"A similar study was performed on 452 ECG records from patients with ventricular conduction defects. They were divided into those with and without a history of myocardial infarction. Recognition of infarcts in the presence of ventricular conduction defects has always been a most difficult problem in electrocardiography. Using multivariate statistics more than 50 percent of the infarcts could be classified correctly. The results were confirmed in 89 autopsy cases.[11]

1974: "In long-distance telephone transmissions of electrocardiograms, excessive noise interference is frequently encountered. When records were transmitted from the VA Hospital West Roxbury, Mass. to the VA Hospital, Washington, D.C., over a three-year period, data could not be successfully processed by computer because of high noise levels in approximately 8 percent of the cases. A digital filter was designed and tested, therefore, which led to elimination of most of the interference without substantial distortions of the EGG data proper. No more records were lost after application of the filter.

"Electrocardiograms from 191 patients with mitral stenosis were studied and compared with 510 records from normal subjects. Using a computer program based on multivariate analysis, it was possible to diagnose correctly 74 percent of the cases, which compared very favorably with the 44 percent recognized by conventional hand measurements.

"A new computer program was developed for the diagnosis of myocardial infarcts in the presence of ventricular conduction defects. When tested on 847 patients, it was possible to identify records from patients with infarcts correctly in 61 percent of the cases."[12]

During the 1970s, Pipberger and his colleagues compared in patients with clear diagnoses independent of the EKG the accuracy of the computerized analysis with that of nine experienced electrocardiographers. The human interpreters had an accuracy of 54 percent, which improved to 62 percent when they were shown the results of the automated interpretation. The computer analysis was 76 percent accurate in the same cases. The superiority of computer analysis was attributed to the use of a Bayesian classification method and multivariate analysis by the computer.[13]

Analgesia and anesthesia (1963–1975)

This study involved a group of VA hospitals standardizing the effects of both new and established drugs for the relief of pain. It was led by William Forrest, M.D., an anesthesiologist at the Palo Alto (CA) VA Hospital, and involved the cooperation of five VA hospitals. Byron Brown, Ph.D., at Stanford University, was the consulting statistician. The group developed practical questionnaires to assess pain and collaborated with trained nurse observers. In general, morphine was used as the comparison standard for parenteral agents; codeine for oral agents. This group collaborated with the National Academy of Sciences' National Research Council, Committee on Drug Addiction and Narcotics, which selected the important drugs to test, as well as with pharmaceutical companies that supplied the blinded agents. Many agents were evaluated during the course of this study. A subcommittee on animal anesthesia compiled a manual of anesthetic techniques for commonly used laboratory animals.

This group pioneered in the computer analysis of the complex data generated from this type of study. In 1964, they reported:

"Statistical methods of handling the data from the participating hospitals have been refined such that rapid computer analysis is now possible. Statistical tests have been applied to the computer method and the data has been examined by several methods with consistent results showing little variability."

These methods were later used in other cooperative studies, the transition expedited by Kenneth James, Ph.D., a statistician for the analgesia studies, who later joined the Hines CSP Coordinating Center and then was founding Chief of the Coordinating Center at Palo Alto.

Diabetes (1958–1965)

The new oral drugs to control diabetes in patients with non-insulin-dependent diabetes mellitus were the subject of this study. Eleven VA hospitals cooperated in a randomized, double-blind study comparing chlorpropamide, tolbutamide and placebo. The patients were highly selected, with only 121 chosen out of the 3,493 screened. Chlorpropamide controlled the diabetes in more patients than did tolbutamide (83 percent vs 60 percent), but both drugs were more effective than placebo (26 percent). This study, together with similar studies by others, helped establish these drugs in the care of diabetes.[14]

Atherosclerosis

Included in this study group were investigators especially interested in heart disease or neurovascular disease. The cardiology group focused on dietary control, and their efforts were soon concentrated on a diet study in the domiciliary at the Los Angeles VA Hospital under the leadership of Seymour Dayton, M.D.

The neurology group carried out a series of studies aimed at lowering the risk of stroke in patients with cerebral atherosclerosis. Their first effort, completed in 1960, was a study of anticoagulants. Investigators in 9 VA hospitals studied 155 patients with documented cerebrovascular disease, either cerebral ischemia or cerebral infarction. They were divided equally on a random basis between treatment and control groups and observed for an average period of about 9 and 12 months, respectively, after entering the study. Although anticoagulation appeared to decrease the number of attacks of cerebral ischemia, there was no reduction in the incidence of new or recurrent strokes. A higher mortality rate was found in the treated patients, due in part to hemorrhagic complications. The study concluded that long-term anticoagulation is neither a practical nor effective method of treatment for the majority of patients with cerebrovascular disease caused by atherosclerosis.[15] An independent study, supported by the NIH, reported similar findings at the same time.

Next, the group studied the effect of estrogens in preventing repeat stroke. Fifteen VA hospitals studied 572 men who had suffered cerebral infarctions, assigning them randomly by a double-blind protocol to placebo, to 1.25 mg Premarin daily or to 5 mg Premarin daily. They found that estrogen administration did not reduce the incidence of cerebral infarction, transient cerebral ischemia or death due to vascular disease. In fact, the use of hormones was associated with an overall higher death rate. This was due to cancer and vascular disorders, such as pulmonary embolism, mesenteric thrombosis and heart failure and various other diseases. On the other hand, incidence and death from myocardial infarction was decreased in treated patients compared with control patients. The investigators concluded that men with cerebral infarction received no benefit from estrogens given in moderate amounts for as long as 5 years.[16]

Another group of 20 VA hospitals studied the effect of clofibrate, a lipid-lowering drug, in 532 patients who had suffered cerebral infarction or transient cerebrovascular ischemic attacks (TIA). Patients were assigned to clofibrate 2 gm daily or to a placebo following a randomized double-blind design and followed for up to 4½ years. Contrary to expectations, recurrence of cerebral infarction actually increased in patients receiving clofibrate as compared to controls. The incidence of new myocardial infarction and new TIA was similar in both groups. Despite the more frequent strokes in treated patients, they had a decrease in mortality, partially explained by a lower death rate from these recurrences. There was no correlation between pretreatment lipid (cholesterol and triglyceride) values and the result of therapy. Use of clofibrate, however, was associated with a slight reduction of cholesterol and a sustained fall in triglyceride. The investigators concluded that this was not an effective way to prevent repeat vascular insults in stroke patients.[17]

Gastric ulcer

Gastroenterologists in 16 VA hospitals studied 638 patients with gastric ulcers that were not considered to be malignant on x-ray. Patients were hospitalized and treated with antacids and diet, the standard treatment for peptic ulcer at that time. The 111 patients whose ulcers did not heal sufficiently within 12 weeks of treatment were randomized either to immediate surgery or another 12 weeks of medical treatment.

This interesting study was published as a special supplement to the journal *Gastroenterology.*[18] Morton Grossman summarized the complex and inconclusive results. Of those patients with unhealed ulcers randomized to further medical treatment, 42 percent healed completely in the second 12 weeks of therapy. However, there was a high rate of recurrence of the ulcers in the medically treated patients during the 2-year observation period. Cancer was found in 3.9 percent (25) of the 638 patients, but the indicators for cancer were not clear-cut. Grossman concluded that, despite the tremendous effort and careful design of the study, its fundamental question, whether medical or surgical treatment is better for gastric ulcers that don't heal promptly, remained unanswered.[19]

Surgery for duodenal ulcer (1956–1972)

A cooperative group of VA surgeons started tracking the results of different types of surgery for duodenal ulcer in 1956. They published their retrospective analysis as a monograph in 1963.[20] After reviewing their findings, they concluded that a prospective randomized study was needed to establish the best type of surgical operation for this disease.

For the prospective study, patients were selected who needed surgery for their ulcers. They were not randomized until, during surgery, the surgeon had made sure that any of the four operations under study could be performed safely. At that point, a sealed envelope was opened in the operating room to identify the operation for the particular patient. In 17 VA Hospitals, 1,358 patients with duodenal ulcer requiring operation were randomly assigned to vagotomy and drainage, vagotomy and distal antrectomy, vagotomy and hemigastrectomy, or gastric resection alone.

The post-operative mortality and morbidity rates were least with vagotomy and drainage, but the incidence rate of recurrent ulcers during the 2 years after operation was highest with this procedure. The late sequelae tended to be more frequent and severe in relation to the amount of stomach removed. No statistically significant differences in the frequency of good and excellent results, as estimated by the surgeon, the patient, or an independent physician, were found among the four surgical procedures.[21]

Esophageal varices (1956–1975)

This very difficult clinical problem was studied by a group of surgeons who attempted a randomized study comparing portacaval shunt surgery with medical treatment. They studied patients who had known varices that had not yet bled and also patients who had already bled from their varices. They found that half of the medically treated patients would die from bleeding either from the varices or from other sources during the 3½-year follow-up period. While the operative mortality (13.5 percent) was not itself a primary factor in survival after a prophylactic shunt, there were serious complications. Liver failure and ulcer disease were the most serious threats to the shunted patient if he survived 1 year after surgery. An operation in the setting of established liver disease was still incompatible with a lengthened survival. They concluded that the portacaval shunt was not recommended in the nonbleeding, established cirrhotic patient with recent ascites, jaundice or encephalopathy.[22]

In the even more dismal context of the patient who has already had bleeding from his esophageal varices, 155 patients were randomized, 78 to medical treatment and 77 to shunt surgery. They were followed for an average of 5½ years. Of the medically treated patients, 37 percent survived the observation period, as did 55 percent of the shunted patients. The group concluded that "irrespective of the frequency or degree of previous or recent hemorrhage from varices, and previous or recent hepatic failure, the stabilized cirrhotic patient has a more favorable opportunity for a prolonged survival if he receives a portacaval shunt. Age, varying values of standard liver function tests, histological changes in the liver, the threat of peptic ulcer, the ravages of hepatic failure and post-shunt encephalopathy affect but do not appear to significantly alter this outcome, especially when the alternative is a conservative approach to a threat of lethal rehemorrhage."[23]

In the discussion after this study was presented, Ronald A. Malt, M.D., of Boston, commented, "The enormous amount of data in the complete manuscript, and the objectivity with which Dr. Jackson and his colleagues have analyzed it, sets a new standard in this area. And I am afraid that the rest of us who are interested in portal hypertension are going to have to work a lot harder just to try to keep up with it."

Coronary artery surgery studies

Angina pectoris and myocardial infarction, caused by obstruction of the coronary arteries, become increasingly important as the patient ages. Attempts to improve coronary circulation surgically came into common use in the 1960s, but no objective studies had been done to prove whether the techniques in use helped the patient.

In 1960, a group of VA surgeons designed a cooperative study to evaluate the Beck procedure, in which powder was introduced into the pericardial sac to cause adhesions between the pericardium and the heart. About 150 patients were randomized either to surgery or to medical treatment. After following for them for 4 years, the group concluded that the outcome of surgery was no better than that of medical treatment.[24]

Next, the group studied the Vineberg operation, at that time the most widely used operation for coronary artery disease. In this procedure, the internal mammary artery was implanted into the ischemic myocardium. A pilot study of the Vineberg procedure began in 1966 and was expanded to a full study in 1968. In all, 146 patients were enrolled. The long-term results showed no significant effect on survival after an average follow-up of 9.3 years.[25]

By 1970, coronary artery bypass surgery had come into frequent use, and the group began a pilot study of that procedure (Chapter 18).

Studies supported by the National Cancer Institute (NCI)

Another important group of studies involved collaboration with the NCI. These included the Surgical Adjuvant studies, the studies on medical treatment of inoperable lung cancer and the studies on treatment of prostate cancer.

The VA-NCI Surgical Adjuvant Studies

Shortly after Lyndon Lee, M.D. (Figure 12.5), arrived in VA Central Office in 1957 as Research Coordinator in Surgery Service, John Barnwell introduced him to Rodney Heller, Director of the National Cancer Institute. Heller placed Lee on one of his Advisory Groups, and together they negotiated a collaborative program[26] to study the effects of adjuvant (supplementary) treatments given patients at the time of surgery for primary cancers. A group of interested VA surgeons were assembled and the Follow-up Agency agreed to provide statistical support.

Over the next 25 years, this group studied almost 12,000 patients undergoing primary surgery for cancers of the lung, pancreas, esophagus, stomach, colon and rectum.[28-27] As promising new treatments were identified, the group would decide whether to start a new protocol to test them. The statisticians from the Follow-up Agency would design the protocols for the trial, always with strict randomization: new treatment plus surgery compared with surgery alone. Possible dangers of the treatments were tracked carefully, and a protocol was discontinued if patients on the adjuvant treatment did not respond as well as the control group.

Some of the most important findings of this group turned out to be those with negative results. Adjuvant chemotherapy did not improve the outcome of surgery for cancers of the stomach, pancreas, esophagus or lung, findings that since have been repeatedly confirmed. Similarly, despite its popularity at the time, preoperative radiation did not improve the outcome of surgery for lung cancer. These negative findings spared patients the dangers, discomfort and cost of futile efforts to improve their chances of cure.

On the other hand, this group showed that preoperative radiation did improve the chance of cure in rectal cancer and that 5-fluorouracil adjuvant chemotherapy increased the numbers of disease-free patients as well as the overall survival of patients with colon cancer.[27]

Treatment of inoperable lung cancer

This cooperative study group, also supported by the NCI, systematically evaluated the effect of therapies on patients with inoperable pulmonary carcinoma. This series of carefully controlled clinical trials involving over 9,000 patients began in February 1958 and continued until 1975.

At first, the group used an inert compound as a control against the agent to be tested because no valid evidence was available that any form of therapy prolonged the survival of patients with inoperable lung cancer. After cyclophosphamide was found to have a slight effect in prolonging survival in patients with extensive disease, cyclophosphamide became the standard against which other therapeutic modalities were compared. The group's first protocol showed that cortisone had a deleterious effect. In patients with disease limited to the thorax, they found that radiotherapy prolongs survival slightly. Cyclophosphamide and BCNU had similar effects, a statistically significant but slight improvement in prognosis.

Taking into account histologic type, they found that nitrogen mustard has its greatest effect on patients with highly and moderately differentiated squamous cell types, while cyclophosphamide was more effective in patients with undifferentiated small cell type of lung cancer. This differential effect of alkylating agents had been suspected before but had rarely been demonstrated with solid tumors such as bronchogenic carcinoma.

In addition to its careful use of randomized treatment comparisons, this group kept meticulous clinical records and performed intensive histologic analysis of the tumors. Their work improved the understanding of lung cancer pathology and identified patient characteristics that influence survival and response to treatment.[12]

Prostate cancer (1959–1975)

This NCI-supported VA cooperative study group studied some 5,000 patients with prostate cancer. Their early results conclusively showed that, while administration of stilbestrol in daily doses of 1.0 to 5.0 mg has a therapeutic effect on metastatic prostatic cancer, it causes cardiovascular complications. While these complications are dose-related, they disappear only when ineffective doses of stilbestrol are given. They also found bilateral orchiectomy to be of questionable value in any stage of prostatic carcinoma.

They concluded that, owing to the cardiovascular complications, treatment with estrogens should be withheld in prostatic carcinoma with regional spread until the development of symptoms severe enough to warrant the risk of cardiovascular complications. They also concluded that, in early focal prostatic cancer of elderly men, no treatment should be given, since these tumors are very slow-growing and the complications associated with surgical or hormonal treatment outweigh any possible benefit of treatment.

While more recent advances have furthered the treatment of prostate cancer since these studies were completed, the finding of the cardiovascular adverse effect of high-dose stilbestrol had a profound effect on practice in the 1970s.

Outpatient psychiatry

Associated with the psychopharmacology group (Chapter 8) but separate from them were a cooperative group who worked in the outpatient clinics in the VA's freestanding Regional Offices, coordinated by Maurice Lorr of VA Central Office. This group conducted single-protocol studies intended to improve the treatment of psychiatric outpatients. Their studies took advantage of the rating scales that Dr. Lorr was developing and led to development of other rating scales.

In a 1960 study by this group, 23 VA mental hygiene clinics collaborated in a 12-week, double-blind study of meprobamate and chlorpromazine to learn whether individual psychotherapy with a tranquilizer added would be more effective in reducing anxiety and hostility than psychotherapy alone or psychotherapy with either of 2 control substances. Accepted for the study were 180 patients who were randomly assigned to 5 treatment groups. Comparative analysis after 8 weeks of treatment revealed that neither chlorpromazine nor meprobamate used adjunctively had an advantage over psychotherapy alone, or over psychotherapy with either of two control substances in reducing anxiety and hostility. Both patients and therapists agreed with this finding.

A 1962 study evaluated the short-term effects of a new tranquilizer, chlordiazepoxide, on the anxiety and tension of newly accepted patients. The 4-week project was conducted double-blind in 23 VA mental hygiene clinics on 150 male patients referred for psychiatric care. Each patient was randomly assigned to one of six treatment groups. The effects of treatment were evaluated by means of 10 initial and terminal tests and on the basis of weekly self-reports on an adjective rating scale. In addition, patients assigned to psychotherapy were evaluated before and after treatment by their therapists. Patients on the drug reported significant reduction in anxiety and increased vigor during the first week, but these effects disappeared by the close of the study. However, psychotherapists reported that patients receiving the drug were significantly less severely ill and that their rapport with others was increased. The prescribing physician also judged patients receiving the drug to be improved. On the other hand, all patients receiving a capsule, whether a placebo or an active drug, reported greater reduction in anxiety and depression and greater overall improvement than those not receiving a capsule.[28]

Comments on the cooperative studies of the 1960s

Most of the studies described here show features characteristic of VA cooperative studies of the 1960s, characteristics that decreased or disappeared in later years. In general, such studies were products of an ongoing coalition of investigators focused on a general clinical problem. When one study was completed, the group, which by that time had formulated new questions, often moved on to another related study. This blurred the boundaries between studies, in contrast to the crisply defined studies begun in the 1970s and later.

Many of these studies were coordinated and analyzed by contract statisticians, rather than by the VA's. In some, protocol changes occurred by consensus rather than by decision of a formal review group. A large number of protocols were carried out, with continuity being provided by the group of physicians performing the studies rather than in the protocols themselves. A remarkable feature was the loyalty of the groups to their goals. Even the experience of one disappointment after another (as for the lung cancer treatment group) failed to discourage them from seeking reliable ways to improve the outlook for their patients.

Obsolescence of a drug or procedure is a problem that remains important in deciding which of these very ambitious and expensive studies to undertake. If something better comes along, the study is no longer relevant. But if something better doesn't appear, learning whether the intervention will benefit the patient is an obvious step forward. Some cooperative studies begun in the 1960s were abandoned after a short period, either by the investigators themselves or by CSEC, when it appeared that further benefit from continuing the study would not be worth the cost.

References

1.   Interview with Clifford Bachrach, M.D., May 7, 1992 at Dr. Bachrach's home in Gaithersburg, MD.

2.   Interview with Lawrence W. Shaw, M.S., February 3, 1994 at Mr. Shaw's home in Florida.

3.   Mimeographed document provided by Mr. Lawrence Shaw. "Highlights of the First Meeting of the Cooperative Studies Evaluation Committee." 1966

4.   Higgins, G., Shields, T. and Keehn, R., "The solitary pulmonary nodule: Ten-year follow-up of Veterans Administration-Armed Forces Cooperative Study." *Arch Surg*, 1975. **110**: 570-575.

5.   Falk A and Fuchs, G.F., "Prophylaxis with isoniazid in inactive tuberculosis. A Veterans Administration Cooperative Study XII." *Chest*, 1978. **73**: 44-48.

6.   Salkin, D. and Huppert, M. "Progress report of the Veterans Administration - Armed Forces Coccidioidomycosis Study Group, 1970." *Veterans Administration - Armed Forces Coccidioidomycosis Study Group*. San Francisco, CA: VA Hospital, San Fernando, 1970,

7.   Telephone interview with John N. Galgiani, M.D., September 27, 2002.

8.   Sutliff, W.D., "Histoplasmosis Cooperative Study V. Amphotericin B dosage for chronic pulmonary histoplasmosis." *Am Rev Resp Dis*, 1972. **105**: 60-67.

9.   Busey, J.F., " Blastomycosis III. A comparative study of 2-hydrostilbamidine and amphotericin B therapy." *Am Rev Resp Dis*, 1972. **105**: 812-818.

10.   *Medical Research in the Veterans Administration, FY 1966*. Washington, DC: Government Printing Office, 1966, 73-74.

11.   *Medical Research in the Veterans Administration, FY 1969*. Washington, DC: Government Printing Office, 1969, 81.

12.   *Medical Research in the Veterans Administration, FY 1974*. Washington, DC: Government Printing Office, 1974, 92-93.

13.   Milliken, J.A., Pipberger, H., Pipberger, H.V., Araoye, M.A., Ari, R., Burggraf, G.W., Fletcher, R.D., Katz, R.J., Lopez, J., E.A., McCans, J.L. and Silver, A.M., "The impact of an ECG computer analysis program on the cardiologist's interpretation. A cooperative study." *J Electrocardiology*, 1983. **16**: 141-150.

14.   Katz, H.M. and Bissel, G., "Blood sugar lowering effects of chlorpropamide and tolbutamide. A double blind cooperative study." *Diabetes*, 1965. **14**: 650-657.

15.   Veterans Administration Cooperative study of Atherosclerosis Neurology Section, "An evaluation of anticoagulant therapy in the treatment of cerebrovascular disease." *Neurology*, 1961. **11**: 132-138.

16.   Veterans Administration Cooperative study of Atherosclerosis Neurology Section, "Estrogenic therapy in men with ischemic cerebrovascular disease: effect on recurrent cerebral infarction and survival." *Stroke*, 1972. **3**: 427-433.

17.   Veterans Administration Cooperative Study of Atherosclerosis Neurology Section, "The treatment of cerebrovascular disease with clofibrate." *Stroke*, 1973. **4**: 684-693.

18.   Littman, A., "The Veterans Administration cooperative study on gastric ulcer." *Gastroenterology*, 1971. **61**: 567-640.

19.   Grossman, M.J., "Resume and comment in The Veterans Administration cooperative study on gastric ulcer." *Gastroenterology*, 1971. **61**: 635-640.

20.   Postlethwait, R.W., *Results of surgery for peptic ulcer; a cooperative study by twelve Veterans Administration hospitals.* Philadephia: W.B. Saunders Company, 1963

21.   Price, W.E., Grizzle, J.E., Postlethwait, R.W., Johnson, W.D. and Grabicki, P., "Results of operation for duodenal ulcer." *Surg Gynec Obstet*, 1970. **131**: 233-244.

22.   Jackson, F.C., Perrin, E.B., Smith, A.G., Dagradi, A.E. and Nadal, H.M., "A clinical investigation of the portacaval shunt: II. Survival analysis of the prophylactic operation." *Am J Surg*, 1968. **113**: 22-42.

23.   Jackson, F.C., Perrin, E.B., Felix, W.R. and Smith, A.G., "A clinical investigation of the portacaval shunt: V. Survival analysis of the therapeutic operation." *Ann Surg*, 1971. **174**: 672-701.

24.   *Medical Research in the Veterans Administration, FY 1968.* Washington, DC: Government Printing Office, 1968, 85.

25.   Bhayana, J., Gage, A.A. and Takaro, T., "Long-term results of internal mammary implantation for coronary artery disease. A controlled trial by the participants of the Veterans Administration Coronary Bypass Surgery Cooperative Study Group." *Ann Thorac Surg*, 1980. **29**: 234-242.

26.   Interview with Lyndon Lee, M.D., April 7, 1988 at a restaurant in Bethesda, MD.

27.   Hrushesky, W.J.M., "The Department of Veterans Affairs' unique clinical cancer research effort." *Cancer*, 1994. **74**: 2701-2709.

28.   *Medical Research in the Veterans Administration, FY 1962.* Washington, DC: Government Printing Office, 1962, 66.

Chapter 14. The Research Career Development Program

One of the major obstacles the VA medical research program confronted in its early days after World War II was the shortage of clinicians with advanced training in research. Funds were available to support meritorious research, and by the mid-1950s the problems of inadequate space had begun to be addressed. Some of the very successful clinician investigators who started their research in the 1950s–Roger Unger and Solomon Berson, for example–had no research training before they joined the VA. But many of them were outstanding individuals with energy, stamina, and intelligence, and the humility to learn from their colleagues and technicians and to persist beyond early mistakes. Many others who tried to enter research without the needed preparation soon became discouraged. Somehow, the VA itself would have to find a way to attract and keep promising candidates if the research program was to grow and flourish.

The Clinical Investigator program

In 1956, Martin Cummings, M.D., Director of the Research Service, together with John Nunemaker, M.D., Director of the Education Service, supported by the new ACMD for Research and Education, John Barnwell, M.D., and the new Chief Medical Director, William Middleton, M.D., started a program to address the shortage of clinical researchers. Thus began what was to become the Research Career Development Program, which aimed to create an elite leadership corps of clinician researchers within the VA. They persuaded Marjorie Wilson, M.D., who had left Central Office in 1953 to complete her clinical training, to return to the VA and start this program.[1]   She reviewed similar programs then in existence and tried to incorporate their best features.   The result was the Clinical Investigator program.

The VA FY 1957 annual report to the Congress *Medical Research in the Veterans Administration* describes this new program:

> "Because of a national shortage of scientific manpower, the Veterans Administration undertook a program to train specially qualified and interested physicians in research methodology.   Known as VA Clinical Investigators, 23 young physicians were selected for special training in disciplines of medical research with special reference to basic studies in problems of aging.   These young scientists are nominated by the medical school Deans' Committees after a local competition.   The nominees are screened in national competition by a central selection committee.   Those who are accepted will receive up to 3 years' training in research under the guidance of a senior preceptor while at the same time sharing clinical work as a member of the staff of a VA hospital.   A modest amount of money is provided for supplies, equipment, and technical assistance to their work.   This new program has been favorably commented upon by leaders of academic medicine."[2]

Clinical Investigators were treated as an elite corps.   Dr. Wilson serving as their advisor, would visit them in their labs and help them when they had administrative problems.

All Clinical Investigators were invited to attend the annual VA research meetings, while other investigators had to compete for places on the program. In conjunction with these meetings, they held special meetings of their own. At first, these were informal; the Clinical Investigators would get together to discuss mutual concerns.[1] Later, these meetings became scientific sessions of increasing formality.

The Clinical Investigator program developed into a huge success. Academic medical centers competed for its graduates for their faculties. Nevertheless, many Clinical Investigators elected to remain in the VA. The FY 1960 annual report to the Congress about the VA research program notes that "The original purpose of the program was realized in the assignment of 16 previous Clinical Investigators to regular full-time staff positions by July 1 of this year."[3]

During its formative period, the Clinical Investigator program, though funded from the Research budget, was administered by Education Service and perceived primarily as a training program. It soon became apparent that the awardees were already serious researchers, and in June 1961 the *Research and Education Newsletter* announced that, "The latest in a series of changes places the responsibility for the Clinical Investigator Program in Research Service instead of the Education Service."[4] Although the awardees were not the beginners originally envisioned when the program was started, the Clinical Investigator appointment was key to their entering independent research careers, and most of them did so.

The Senior Medical Investigator program

In 1959, the Senior Medical Investigator program was begun to provide a small nucleus of well-established, highly successful clinician scientists to serve as role models for younger research physicians. Dr. Wilson also initiated this program, modeling it on similar programs run by NIH and private foundations.[1] The first two Senior Medical Investigators, Drs. Samuel Bassett and Edward Freis, were appointed in 1959. Senior Medical Investigators were expected to spend the majority of their time on research, while maintaining a clinical presence in the host hospital. They attended the annual research meetings with the Clinical Investigators and served as a critical audience for their research papers.

The accomplishments of individual Senior Medical Investigators (Table 14.1) made important contributions to medical science and most continued in the VA for the remainder of their careers. Five of them (Freis, Gross, Yalow, Schally, and Oldendorf) won Lasker Awards and Yalow and Schally each won a Nobel Prize.

In the early days of this program, appointing Senior Medical Investigators was a very personal affair. Sometimes, the candidate did not even know that he had been nominated until he was informed of the selection.[5, 6] Notification was by a personal phone call from Dr. Middleton or another high official in Central Office. Each Senior Medical Investigator reported directly to the Central Office and received the highest possible personnel classification in the system. Central Office negotiated directly about individual needs, including funds that would be directly earmarked for each program.

Table 14.1. Senior Medical Investigators

	Year appointed	Specialty
Edward Freis, M.D.	1959	Cardiology (Chapter 9)
Samuel Bassett, M.D.	1959	Nephrology
Ludwig Gross, M.D.	1960	Hematology — oncology
Oscar Auerbach, M.D.	1960	Pathology — pulmonary (Chapter 10)
Morton Grossman, M.D.	1962	Gastroenterology
Solomon Berson, M.D.	1963	Nuclear med — endocrinology (Chapter 11)
Jay Shurley, M.D.	1967	Psychiatry
Paul Heller, M.D.	1969	Hematology
Rosalyn Yalow, Ph.D.	1972	Nuclear medicine (Chapter 11)
Sidney Ingbar, M.D.	1973	Endocrinology
Andrew Schally, Ph.D.	1973	Endocrinology
William Oldendorf, M.D.	1978	Neurology
Roger Unger, M.D.	1979	Endocrinology
Leo Hollister, M.D.	1982	Psychopharmacology (Chapter 8)
George Sachs, M.D.	1984	Gastroenterology
Jeremiah Silbert, M.D.	1990	Endocrinology – aging

The Research Associate program

Even though the Clinical Investigator appointment had been intended as an entry position, the successful applicants for it generally had already achieved some research experience. In some subject areas it was especially difficult to gain enough experience to compete for these awards. A bridge was needed between the clinical training period and the Clinical Investigator appointment, an opportunity to gain enough research experience to demonstrate that a candidate was likely to become a successful researcher. The advocates for certain research areas were successful in establishing programs to meet the clinician researcher shortages in their own areas. The first of these were in psychiatry and psychology.

In 1961, the VA announced a new program planned to alleviate the shortage of psychiatrists adequately trained for research. Directed by Samuel Kaim, M.D., the Research Associate in Psychiatry program involved a 1-year period of training for psychiatrists in the techniques of laboratory and clinical experimentation under the overall guidance of a preceptor. The first two Research Associates in Psychiatry were appointed in March 1962, and a third began his work in June 1962.[7]

At about the same time, a similar program of Psychology Research Associates was begun with four appointments under the direction of H. Elston Hooper, Ph.D.[8] This program of 2-year appointments for psychologists wishing to become research psychologists was announced late in 1961. During its time as a separate program, 87 psychologists benefited from this training, described as "one of the most desirable postdoctoral experiences in the Nation."[9]

Shortly afterwards, Research Associate openings were announced in other physician specialties in which a shortage of research talent was identified: pathology, physical medicine and rehabilitation, orthopedics, oral diseases, and gastroenterology.[10] Advocates of additional specialty areas made cases for establishing the Research Associate in their specialties, and by 1968, it had become a 2-year program available to all physician specialties. By the early 1970s, the Psychology Research Associate program had merged with the physician Research Associate program, which was now open to all VA doctoral-level clinicians.

The Medical Investigator program

By 1968, many distinguished physician-scientists in the VA were considered to be too experienced for the Clinical Investigator appointment but not yet at the level of seniority of the Senior Medical Investigator. At that time, a new position was introduced in the Research Career Development Program, the Medical Investigator, an appointment intermediate between Clinical Investigator and Senior Medical Investigator. The first five appointments were made the following year. This position was described as one that "provides established, successful investigators an opportunity to pursue research activities for a major portion of their time (at the discretion of the investigator) with the remaining (time) spent in teaching and patient care. Candidates selected will be those for whom the VA can anticipate continued productivity."[11] This new position was well-received, and 5, 7 and 13 appointments were made in 1969, 1970, and 1971, respectively.

With the Medical Investigator position in place, a "research career ladder" was now available to the career clinical scientist, though to move from one rung of the ladder to the next required approval of the review committee, and such approval was usually difficult to achieve.

In 1972, budgetary problems prompted a rethinking about the expensive Medical Investigator program. A senior-level salary plus substantial research support ($40,000 per year) went with the appointment. James Pittman, M.D., the ACMD/R&E at that time (Chapter 15), decided to place a moratorium on the program.[12] From 1973 through 1976, only eight appointments, including three reappointments, were made.

In 1975, Thomas Newcomb, M.D., ACMD/R&D (Chapter 15) and Marguerite T. Hays, M.D., Director, Medical Research Service (Chapter 16), decided to revive the Medical Investigator program under new guidelines, discarding the "ladder" concept. The new Medical Investigator position was a 6-year appointment that was not immediately renewable. An awardee could apply for renewal only after serving a year as staff clinician at his/her medical center. In 1977 and 1978, five new appointments under the new guidelines were made annually. Appointment as Medical Investigator continued to be a rare honor throughout the existence of the program.

Research and Education Trainee program (1968-1972)

Even with the Research Associate program, there was still no "fellowship" level in the research career ladder envisioned by Bernstein and Schoolman. To remedy this lack, they established a fellowship program for young clinicians in 1968. Called Research and Education Trainees, these were physicians who had completed an internship and at least 2 years of an approved residency. The traineeship allowed them to receive specialty training, including research experience. The research experience of these trainees was the responsibility of a "chief trainer" at the hospital, who selected the trainees and monitored their training experience. This program was funded by Research Service but administered by Education Service. A separate selection committee for each of 14 specialty areas reviewed applications from hospitals wanting to establish Traineeship programs. This program grew over several years, and by the end of FY 1971, 67 Traineeship programs had been established in 35 VA hospitals. These traineeships were abruptly discontinued during FY 1972, reportedly due to a decision by the Office of Management and Budget to terminate such programs, including those at the NIH as well as the VA. Fortunately, the VA residency program was large enough to absorb the trainees into specialty residencies, and incumbent trainees were able to complete their programs.

The Associate Investigator program

By the middle of the 1970s, competition for Research Associate positions had grown so keen that the qualifications of successful candidates were at an extremely high level. Persons with substantial bibliographies and established success in research began to edge out those wishing to enter a research career but who had not yet had the opportunity to do so. At the same time, the VA research traineeship program, intended to meet this need, had been disbanded. To provide an entry level in the Research Career Development Program, a new position, the Associate Investigator, was established in 1976. To assure that this position remained targeted to entry-level applicants, it came with certain restrictions. Awardees received a lower salary than they would have received as staff physicians, and they were not eligible for a bonus being paid to VA physicians. There was a limit on the amount of research training and experience that a candidate could have had before applying. Despite these restrictions, large numbers of excellent candidates continued to apply for the few positions available.

The review process for Research Career Development Program applicants

At the time that the Clinical Investigator program was initiated in 1956, the VA appointed a distinguished committee of outside academicians to review applications for appointment and recommend program policy (Appendix IIj). At first, this committee was called the Selection Committee for Clinical Investigators. In 1964, presumably because they also reviewed nominations for Senior Medical Investigator positions, the committee became the Selection Committee for Clinical and Senior Investigators. In 1971, in recognition of the increased complexity of the program it reviewed, it became the Research Career Development Committee. In the late 1970s, a few VA scientists were added to the committee to present the intramural viewpoint, but the committee continued to be largely an outside group.

From the beginning, this committee concerned itself primarily with assuring that awardees' research experience was the best possible, both for the awardee and the VA.

Compensation of Research Career Development awardees

Initially, Clinical Investigators and Research Associates received lower salaries than they would have earned as full-time staff clinicians. In 1961, the Clinical Investigator earned $9,000 per year.[5] The July-August, 1966 *Newsletter* contains the information that Research Associates were ordinarily staffed at Full Grade, Step 1, though in some cases they were given Intermediate Grade. Clinical Investigators entered at Intermediate Grade, Step 3, if board eligible, or Step 6 if board certified.[15] At the same time, clinicians were being recruited one or two grades higher. This discrepancy in salary was apparently causing enough concern that it remained under review with consideration being given to making appointments at a grade level that would equal those of staff physicians. Within the next several years, this transition was made, and subsequently these appointees received the same VA base salary as did their full-time clinician counterparts.

However, in 1975, when VA physicians began to receive a salary bonus, Career Development awardees (except Senior Medical Investigators) were denied the bonus, as there was no demonstrable shortage of candidates for the appointments. This led to turmoil in the program, with some appointees moving into patient-care positions, others accepting the lower salary, and others receiving salary compensation from their affiliated universities to make up the difference. Despite this problem, the program continued to be vigorous. The number of highly motivated, well-qualified candidates always exceeded the number of vacancies to be filled. During the 1980s, the administration of the physician's bonus was liberalized to permit some bonus salary for Research Associates and Clinical Investigators and the full bonus for Medical Investigators, as well as for Senior Medical Investigators.

Administration of the Career Development Program

After initiating the Clinical Investigator Program, Dr. Marjorie Wilson administered it from her position in Education Service until she left Central Office in 1960. The first Senior Medical Investigators were appointed during her tenure, and she set up the review committee and established guidelines. After she left, the program administration shifted to Research Service. Dr. Harold Schnaper became coordinator for Internal Medicine awardees, and Dr. Lyndon E. Lee, Jr., for Surgery awardees. Later in the 1960s, as Program Chiefs were recruited to Central Office in the various clinical and research specialties (Chapter 12), the Program Chiefs became the primary Central Office contacts for the Career Development appointees in their particular fields. In 1965, Dr. Eli Nadel assumed responsibility for overall coordination of the program.

In 1968, the Directors of Research and Education Services, Drs. Lionel Bernstein and Harold Schoolman, formalized their concept of a research career ladder for clinicians, starting with the Traineeship and culminating in the Senior Medical Investigator appointments. In recognition of the importance of this program, a formal Career Development Section was established within Research Service but with responsibility for the Traineeship program of Education Service. Dr. Chester de Long was its Chief. In 1971, this Section became a part of a new Career Development and Program Review Division in Research Service under Dr. de Long.

Figure 14.1 Chester DeLong, Ph.D.

In 1972, Ms. Darlene Whorley became Chief of the Career Development Section within that Division, and in 1973 Career Development again became a separate division in the new Medical Research Service, with Ms. Whorley continuing as its Chief.

Figure 14.2 Darlene Whorley

Figure 14.3 David Thomas

In 1978, when Ms. Whorley left Central Office for the San Diego VA Medical Center, Mr. David Thomas became Chief, Career Development Section, a position he held until 1990.

Follow-up of Research Career Development Appointees

From the beginning of the Research Career Development Program, the VA was concerned with determining whether the initial goal of enhancing the VA's cadre of expert clinician researchers had been met. The agency wanted to know if it was contributing its share to the nation's medical research manpower. To answer these questions on a continuing basis, careful records were kept of all appointees to the program, with a systematic follow-up every few years. Retention in the VA or in a university position was considered a measure of success. From the beginning, retention was very good. As time went on, attrition occurred, but many of the graduates spent their entire career in the VA.

In 1968, the current status of the 187 persons who had completed the Clinical Investigator program was listed in the VA's Annual Report to the Congress. Of the 182 former Clinical Investigators still alive and located, 68 were currently in the VA and 5 were in other Federal institutions (40 percent in Federal employment). Sixty-six (36 percent) were in universities or private research institutes. Eight (4 percent) were receiving further training and 35 (19 percent) were employed in primarily non-research situations. [16] Compared with the outcome of similar programs to provide research experience for junior clinician-researchers, this was considered to be an excellent result.

The most recent systematic follow-up of Career Development Program awardees was carried out in 1990. At that time, 1,781 of the 1,858 persons who were or had been in the program were located. Many of them had been appointed at more than one appointment level. They included 16 present or former Senior Medical Investigators, 70 Medical Investigators, 548 Clinical Investigators, 1,016 Research Associates and 428 Associate Investigators. Of the 1,742 living, non-retired appointees located, 834 remained in the VA, yielding an overall retention of 48 percent. Another 369 (21 percent) were in universities. Seventeen (1 percent) were in governmental positions other than VA, including the NIH. Sixteen (1 percent) were in industry and 506 (29 percent) were in private practice. Altogether, of those still active professionally, 70 percent held government or academic positions.

Looking more closely at the 1,212 former Career Development appointees who had been in the program prior to 1981, 1,143 were located. Thirteen were retired and 24 had died. Of the remaining 1106, 401 (36 percent) were still in the VA and 14 (1 percent) were in other government service. Two hundred seventy six (25 percent) were at universities, 13 (1 percent) were in industry and 402 (36 percent) were in private practice. [17]

Hence, 10 to 34 years after they began their assignments in the Career Development Program, 62 percent of Career Development Program awardees still active professionally were in government or academic positions. The program had not only achieved its original goals, it had done so to a remarkable degree. Of those who remained in the VA, many had become leaders, holding such titles as ACOS/Research (19), VA Service Chief (45), Chief of Staff (6), and many clinical section chiefs.

References

1. Interview with Marjorie Wilson, M.D., April 29, 1988 at Dr. Wilson's office in Washington, DC.

2. *Medical Research in the Veterans Administration, FY 1957.* Washington, DC: Government Printing Office, 4.

3. *Medical Research in the Veterans Administration, FY 1960.* Washington, DC: Government Printing Office, 25.

4. *R&E Newsletter*, June 1961. 15.

5. Interview with Paul Heller, M.D., March 3, 1993 at Dr. Heller's office at the Chicago Westside VA Medical Center.

6. Interview with Oscar Auerbach, M.D., October 30, 1992 at Dr. Auerbach's office at the East Orange, NJ VAMC.

7. *R&E Newsletter*, May, 1962. 19.

8. *R&E Newsletter*, November, 1962. 14.

9. *Medical Research in the Veterans Administration FY 1968.* Washington, DC: Government Printing Office, 16-17.

10. *Medical Research in the Veterans Administration FY 1967.* Washington, DC: Government Printing Office, 53.

11. *Medical Research in the Veterans Administration FY 1969.* Washington, DC: Government Printing Office, 14.

12. Interview with James Pittman, M.D., February 27, 1992 at Dr. Pittman's office at the University of Alabama.

13. *R&E Newsletter*, July 1962. 8-9.

14. *R&E Newsletter*, January 1966. 2-3.

15. *R&E Newsletter*, July-August 1966. 4.

16. *Medical Research in the Veterans Administration, FY 1968.* Washington, DC: Government Printing Office, 15.

17. Thomas, D. *Review of Career Development Graduates.* Medical Research Service, 1990.

Part V. Maturation, 1968-1980

Chapter 15. Transition years, 1968 – 1973

The late 1960s and 1970s saw the maturation of the VA Medical Research Service and the beginnings of today's Health Services Research and Development Service and the Rehabilitations Research and Development Service.

Medical Research experienced a rocky and controversial transition, from a program personally governed by managers with close familiarity with the investigators and their projects, to one based on peer review and objective criteria. Until about 1968, funding of projects in the VA was based on results of previous work. Budget was not a serious problem; money was available for programs that the experts in Central Office considered worth supporting. Even correcting for inflation, the budget was increasing enough to accommodate new programs without jeopardizing existing ones. There was encouragement to continue productive programs.

In 1968, new leaders committed to excellence in science introduced a program of peer review modeled after that of the NIH. Individual research programs received grant-type reviews. This system, imposed on an intramural program that had been relatively stable, led to turmoil and dramatic policy reversals. Over the next decade, the VA Medical Research program gradually transformed itself into the peer-review-driven program that exists today.

New leadership in the Research and Education Office

In 1966, Lionel Bernstein, M.D., a gastroenterologist who had been ACOS/R&E at the Hines VA Hospital in Chicago and then Chief of Medicine at the Chicago West Side VA, joined Central Office as Director, Research Service. At about the same time, Harold (Hack) Schoolman, M.D., who had been Chief of the VA Midwest Research Support Center at Hines, became Director, Education Service.

Figure 15.1 Lionel Bernstein, M.D., Ph.D. Figure 15.2 Harold Schoolman, M.D

Bernstein and Schoolman were good friends and considered themselves a team. For a time, each served as the other's deputy. They were well acquainted with Lucien Guze, the influential Chief of Staff for Research and Education at the Wadsworth VA Hospital in Los Angeles. Bernstein and Schoolman were hired into their VACO positions by Ben Wells, but both believed Guze played a key role in recruitment.[1, 2]

In late 1968, Thomas Chalmers, M.D., came to Central Office as ACMD/R&E. Bernstein and Schoolman had actively recruited Chalmers and enlisted Chief Medical Director H. Martin Engle to help bring him to their team. Chalmers had been serving on the Cooperative Studies Evaluation Committee.[3] Together with Bernstein and Schoolman, he was dedicated to assuring high quality in the research program.

Figure 15.3 Thomas Chalmers, M.D.

End of the Annual Research Conferences

The VA's annual research conferences were becoming very large and costly in both money and effort. Bernstein and Schoolman believed that the investigators would be better served by using the money to send them to meetings in their own specialties. After 1967, Research Service (later Medical Research Service) held only conferences for research administrators and advisors. Discontinuing the annual meetings meant that another setting was needed for presenting the agency's Middleton Award. A suitable event in the recipient's hometown was selected for the 1968, 1969 and 1970 awards. Dr. Middleton himself presented the 1971 and 1972 awards, at an Atlantic City, NJ, meeting of VA research administrators[4] and at the American Federation for Clinical Research; and for the 1973 award a ceremony was held in VA Central Office, where the Administrator and Chief Medical Director did the honors.

The Middleton Awardees, 1968-1973

The 1968 Award went to Thomas Starzl, M.D., of the Denver VA Hospital for his pioneering surgical transplantation of kidneys and other human organs, including the development of anti-lymphocyte serum and globulin to suppress the rejection of transplanted organs. He later accomplished the world's first successful liver transplant.

Figure 15.4 Thomas Starzl, M.D., Ph.D.

Roger Unger, M.D., (Chapter 7) received the 1969 award "for his conception of the physiology of metabolism of fats and carbohydrates, to better therapy for diabetes patients."

Andrew V. Schally, Ph.D., who later received the Lasker Award and Nobel Prize for the isolation and synthesis of hypothalamic hormones, won the 1970 award "for his investigations of the physiology and biochemistry of hypothalamic neurohormones."

Figure 15.5 Andrew S. Schally, Ph.D. receiving the Middleton Award from Emmanuel Bresler, M.D., ACOS/R&E, New Orleans VAMC

In, 1971, Marcus Rothschild, M.D., was honored "for basic and clinical research on the pathological biochemistry of the liver in alcoholism and other types of liver disease."

**Figure 15.6 Marcus Rothschild, M.D. receiving the Middleton Award
from Dr. Middleton**

The 1972 Middleton Award went to Kenneth Sterling, M.D., for his important work with radioactive tracers. He was cited for developing the ^{51}Cr labeling of erythrocytes for *in vivo* study as a clinical tool, using labeled human serum albumin to determine albumin turnover rate and for his use of radioactive thyroid hormones to study the disposal and turnover of thyroxine and triiodothyronone in humans.

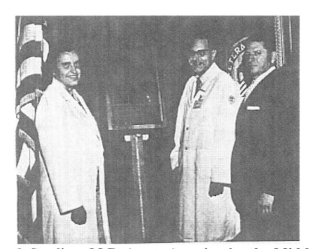

**Figure 15.7 Kenneth Sterling, M.D. (center) posing by the Middleton Award with
Rosalyn Yalow, Ph.D. (Chapter 11) and Harold Jaffrey, the Bronx VAMC Director.**

Ludwig Gross, M.D. (Chapter 3) received the 1973 Award "for demonstrating viral etiology of leukemia in mammals."

Figure 15.8 Ludwig Gross and Thomas Newcomb by the Middleton Plaque

A new approach to allocating research funds

Before the late 1960s, Central Office officials ran the research program in a very personal way, making most of the decisions about how much research money each hospital would receive.

In the earliest days of the post-World War II VA research program, the Committee on Veterans' Medical Programs (CVMP) (Chapter 4) had reviewed requests for individual VA research projects along with requests for research contracts from medical schools. These projects received peer review by the advisory committees of the National Research Council. At the same time (Chapter 3), "research laboratories" were being established at VA hospitals, each with a chief, equipment, laboratory space and employees. From the late 1940s on, these "laboratories" were under the jurisdiction of a hospital Research and Education (R&E) committee. As these laboratories recruited capable researchers, they grew and expanded into hospital-based intramural research programs, still under the jurisdiction of a local R&E Committee. The laboratory chief, first called the Assistant Director of Professional Services for Research (ADPSR) and later the Associate Chief of Staff for Research and Education (ACOS/R&E), was the secretary of the R&E Committee. In the late 1940s and early 1950s, the funding for a hospital's research "laboratory" was in a stable, annualized budget. When new money was needed, the investigator submitted a request to Central Office through the R&E Committee and hospital management. The request was generally reviewed by the CVMP. If the CVMP recommended funding, Central Office would send the additional money to the hospital.

This mechanism, considered to be unduly complicated, was discontinued in late 1952.[5] After that, the R&E Committee at a VA hospital approved and recommended to Central Office, through the hospital manager, that additional research funds be made available to the hospital in a specified amount—for a specified purpose. Nevertheless, an attempt was made to provide each VA hospital engaging in research a definite annual research budget that it could count on.

By April 1954, the CVMP recognized that the VA had changed its research focus from extramural to intramural. Contractual research was being phased down. The Committee questioned the value of the NRC concerning itself with the VA intramural program, although there was a feeling that governmental funded research should have a disinterested civilian group checking work quality and direction. At the time, Dr. George Marshall Lyon, the VA ACMD/R&E, explained that money was allotted to intramural programs according to such factors as:

1. Institution size or site
2. Quality of proposed work
3. Available patients
4. Degree of emphasis on particular fields
5. Local capabilities

Dr. Lyon felt that help was needed at the policy level, but he did not invite review of individual research projects.[6]

The first NRC survey of the VA medical research program (Chapter 7), in 1960, describes it as highly decentralized, with four expert committees to advise the Chief Medical Director on national-level Medical Research policy and programming. The NRC recommended that "the staff of the Research Service in the Veterans Administration's Central Office should be strengthened by the addition of three or four persons who are highly skilled in research methods and research administration."

At the local level, scientific review by the Research and Education Committee and/or the Deans Committee was a local option. Records from the 1950s at one hospital, Palo Alto (CA), document R&E Committee review of investigators' written and oral presentations in defense of requests for support. But the review process was variable and undoubtedly was less complete at some hospitals. The hospital's annual requests to Central Office were generally based on historic funding plus additions for proposed recruitments. Since the overall research budget was increasing during those years, money was available to support most worthwhile recruitments, and there was no compelling impetus to phase out less-productive programs.

During the 1960s, VACO Research Service responded to the NAS recommendations and other pressures by boosting the scientific expertise in VA Central Office. Program Chiefs in various disciplines were appointed (Chapter 12). At the beginning of each fiscal year, the Director, Research Service, would allocate money to each of the Program Chiefs. They could use this money to recruit new investigators in their field and supplement the budgets of promising projects. Typically, the Program Chiefs traveled extensively, visiting individual investigators and potential recruits at the hospitals. When they were convinced that a new program was meritorious, they would provide funding for it, which would later be annualized into the hospital's research budget. The Program Chiefs participated actively in annual meetings, both for VA-wide research and in their particular disciplines. In some cases, they arranged meetings of VA investigators at national specialty research meetings to discuss mutual concerns, especially policy matters.

Some Program Chiefs established expert advisory committees in their disciplines to give general advice about research administration and some scientific review (Appendix IIg). This concept was focused and strengthened in 1965 when Drs. Musser and Dunner established 10 Research Evaluation Committees, each under the leadership of a Program Chief from Central Office. These Committees (Appendix IIh) generally reviewed investigators' progress reports, as well as brief protocols for future research. Their advice helped the Program Chiefs to allocate funds and the hospital R&E Committee to distribute the research money received at the hospital.

A second NRC report, released in 1968, noted that: "The Central Office has appointed in the last two years a number of evaluation committees that, in the near future, will examine all research supported by the Central Office." It was recommended that the VA enhance the role of its Research Evaluation Committees and, as appropriate, seek the advice of other outstanding peer-review groups to assure itself that its individual research projects were worthy of support.[7]

Funding considerations in 1967

By 1967, many knowledgeable observers felt that a change was needed. At the NIH and elsewhere, a system of peer-review-based project funding was well established, and many felt that the VA should undertake a similar type of program.

This opinion was by no means universal. VA research was intramural, carried out by VA staff in VA hospitals. In this sense, it was similar to the NIH intramural program: At NIH, considerable scientific review existed within and across institutes, but NIH intramural research was not subject to a grant-type review. Some excellent work was being done in the VA under the existing system. VA researchers flourished in an environment where they could count on consistent support for their research, even when they ventured into new, perhaps risky, areas or followed up on ideas not hammered out in the peer review system.

The hospital-based research programs often were still conceptualized as large "laboratories," each with the ACOS/R&E serving as its chief. Some ACOSs had built up huge and flourishing research programs at their hospitals. These were flourishing under what was, usually, a benign dictatorship. New and continuing support of an investigator's projects was the prerogative of the R&E Committee, whose Secretary was the ACOS. In most cases, a simple memo or brief protocol was all that was required to justify funding a project. Newly hired staff members who entered the VA research program found it easy to get started. When new money was needed to set them up, a simple request to the Program Chief or Director of Research in Central Office usually sufficed.

On the other hand, it was difficult to control the way research money was spent. While some exchange with clinical services – clinical use of research facilities or research use of clinical facilities – was to be expected, some research projects seemed to have stopped advancing knowledge. The rapid growth of the research budget during the late 1950s and early 1960s showed signs of stabilizing, while the roster of qualified and motivated investigators grew. Money needed to be redistributed from unproductive programs to more promising ones. These concerns led to establishment of a revolutionary concept, the "Part 1 – Part 2" system.

The Part 1 - Part 2 System

In 1967, Lionel Bernstein introduced a new approach to VA research budgetary administration that became known as the "Part 1 – Part 2" plan.

Under this plan, Central Office "Part 1" funds were awarded to a hospital specifically for a VA investigator's project. The amount of support was based on the advice of one of the Research Evaluation Committees. With a 20 percent allowance for local adjustments, these funds were earmarked for the specific research project. The plan was eventually to dispense about half of VA Research funds in this manner.[2]

"Part 2" funds, on the other hand, were to be distributed as institutional allocations, partially following the historical model in place prior to that time. These funds continued to be dispensed locally on the advice of the local hospital R&E Committee. However, redistribution of Part 2 funds between VA hospitals was to be based on an institutional site visit. This review would determine how well Part 2 funds were used for recruiting new personnel, starting research programs and establishing common facilities, and how well it all combined to help the patient care program.

Figure 15.9 Leon Bernstein, M.B, Ch.B.

To implement this Part 1-Part 2 concept, Lionel Bernstein established a Program Evaluation Section within Research Service and in late 1967 recruited Leon Bernstein (no relation) from the Program Projects Grant Division of the National Heart Institute to be its Chief. Leon Bernstein, who had been a professor of physiology at the University College Hospital in London, had come to the Baltimore (MD) VA Hospital, where he was Acting ACOS/R&E, "acting" because he was not yet a U.S. citizen. He then moved to San Francisco, where he ran a laboratory at the VA hospital there and was briefly ACOS/R&E.

From San Francisco, he moved to NIH but left there only a year later when Lionel Bernstein recruited him.[8]

The Part 2 program

With a system for evaluation of individual projects by the Research Evaluation Committees already in place, Leon Bernstein's first effort was to establish a system to review institution-wide programs of individual VA hospitals, those to be funded by Part 2 money. Two large central committees (Appendix IIk) were established to oversee the Part 2 program reviews. Members of these committees served on audit teams that were to visit each hospital. In composing the team for a given hospital, the Central Office staff tried to assure that it included representatives of all major areas of research at that hospital. The plan was that these committees would visit hospitals on a 3-year rotation basis, interviewing each hospital's Research and Education Committee and all of its funded investigators. After this visit, the committee would recommend an amount for the Part 2 funding for that hospital for the next 3 years. This review was directed entirely at how well the hospitals were spending their "Part 2" monies, the undesignated general support research money they were receiving. Emphasis was placed on both the quality of research supported and the role of research in improving patient care. Projects that had passed "Part 1" review were exempted from Part 2 review.

Plans and implementation did not always match. For example, in advance of the Part 2 group's visit to Buffalo in 1970, the ACOS/R&E received a long, complex form to be completed. He instructed the research investigators to write brief project summaries, about one page per project. The investigators did not understand that this site visit was going to determine their future —they had become accustomed to the system of Central Office Program Chiefs' visits, which generally resulted in more funds for a specific program and did not threaten other parts of the program.

The site visitors, led by Leon Bernstein himself, spent two days at Buffalo, interviewed all the investigators and met with the R&E Committee and top hospital administration. They toured the research space and asked penetrating questions. When the site visit report ultimately arrived at Buffalo, it analyzed all elements of the program with specific funding recommendations for each project, the total amounting to Buffalo's entire Part 2 budget for the next 3 years. The casually assembled one-page summaries, together with a short interview between the investigator and the visitors, resulted in specific funding decisions.

As the first round of Part 2 reviews progressed, a number of hospitals that had managed to build up large programs during the past 10 years were visited. In several, the emphasis on building up common resources had led to large amounts of money being placed under the control of the ACOS/R&E. As one ACOS/R&E expressed it, the site visitors "admired my extensive common resources very much, and then cut the budget."[9] A number of very vocal ACOS/R&Es complained vigorously about the Part 2 program. Lionel Bernstein, the Director, supported Leon Bernstein and refused to make any alterations in the committees' decisions. Failing to find a sympathetic ear in the Research Office, the complainers went to higher officials in Central Office. Soon, Central Office was full of polarized opinions for and against the Part 2 program.

Part 1 reviews

Once Part 2 program visits were well underway, Leon Bernstein turned his attention to reviewing individual research projects. The old Program Evaluation Committees were disbanded. One round of reviews was skipped to allow a "settling down."[8] Then a new group of Research Evaluation Committees (Appendix IIh) began to review projects.[10, 11] Applicants received elaborate, complex instructions with which to present their projects. When instructions were not properly carried out, the proposals were returned to the investigator without review. At the same time, these new committees received clear mission instructions to be much less permissive than the old Program Evaluation Committees. For the first time, major emphasis was on the prospective research plan as well as evaluation of the investigator's research accomplishments. Scientists who had been accustomed to a cursory review of their research plan, resulting in continuation and expansion of their funding, suddenly found their projects being disapproved. Again, protests arose from the field. But leadership in Research Service stood firmly behind its new peer review system, followed by people complaining elsewhere in Central Office. The division of opinions within Central Office became even more pronounced. Officials responsible for patient-care services worried that these changes in research policy were hurting important clinicians at the hospitals.

Downfall of the Part 1 – Part 2 program

Bernstein, Schoolman and Chalmers had sought to use a much scaled-down version of the NIH national grants peer-review methodology within the context of a nation-wide intramural system of 170 VA hospitals. Their aim was both to support high-quality research and to enhance the effect of research on VA patient care and on medical schools affiliated with the VA hospitals. Many observers applauded their goals. But by late 1969 and early 1970, the Part 1-Part 2 system was generating protests. Many considered the review process too rigid. Some of the most powerful ACOS/R&Es found their power bases eroding and objected strenuously.[12,13] The resulting controversy in Central Office eventually led to abrupt policy and leadership changes in the Research and Education Office and in Research Service.

Leadership changes

In January 1970, Mark (Jim) Musser, M.D., who had previously been Director, Research Service, and ACMD/R&E, became VA's Chief Medical Director (CMD). He recruited Benjamin Wells, M.D., also a former ACMD/R&E, to return to Central Office as his Deputy. Musser and Wells had been keeping in touch with Research Service while they were at the Regional Medical Programs. They were concerned about the dissatisfaction in the field stirred up by the new Part 1-Part 2 program. They did not object to the peer review principle; indeed, the Program Evaluation Committees had started during their research leaderships. However, they were troubled by the rigidity of the present program and the abruptness of changes it imposed on the field.[14]

On his first day as CMD, Musser met with Thomas Chalmers (the ACMD/R&E) and told him that there were to be major changes in running the research program. Chalmers contacted NIH the same day, and accepted an appointment they had offered him earlier.[3] A short time later, Lionel Bernstein and Harold Schoolman received memos to the effect that they were to be reassigned from their present positions. During the next month or so, Lionel Bernstein reviewed VA needs in Health Services Research and Development and wrote a prospectus for this program (Chapter 17). He then moved to the Department of Health, Education and Welfare. A few months later, Leon Bernstein was reassigned from his position as Chief, Program Evaluation Section, to head up a Health Services Research and Development program.[15]

Musser appointed Lyndon Lee, M.D., his old deputy from Research Service, to be the new ACMD/R&E. Lee held that position for about a year, until he became ACMD for Professional Services in February 1971. Lee was as unhappy as Musser about the way Part 1 - Part 2 program was being administered. Lee appointed as his deputy Laurence Foye, M.D., who had been Director of Education Service, and Foye then served as Acting ACMD/R&E during the 1971 interim between Lee and his successor, James Pittman, M.D. During the interim until John Bailer, M.D., was recruited as Director, Research Service, at the end of 1970, James Matthews, M.D. and Abraham Dury, Ph.D. "held the Research Program together."[13] Basic institutional research support of the medical centers was held more or less constant, with adjustments upward after successful Part 1 reviews, but no response to unsuccessful reviews. After Leon Bernstein left Research Service, Chester de Long, Ph.D., assumed responsibility for Program Review while continuing to run the Career Development program. He recruited Gerald Libman to be responsible for Program Review and Darlene Whorley for Career Development.

Under de Long, the same basic system of Part 1 review was continued. The major difference was in its implementation. Minor irregularities in the applications were permitted, and deadlines were stretched in hardship cases. Also, an adverse Part 1 review did not result in a decrease in a hospital's research budget. Only a recommendation for start-up of a new Part 1 program or an increased support of an ongoing one affected the hospital's budget.[16]

"Total Institutional Review"

Lyndon Lee recruited John Bailar, M.D., from the National Cancer Institute to be Director of Research Service. Bailar had worked with the VA on the NCI-funded VA urology cooperative studies, including the important study of use of stilbestrol in prostate cancer which showed a 5mg/day dose to cause cardiovascular morbidity.[17, 18] Lee hoped that Bailar, who had a strong background in epidemiology, would lead the VA into becoming a giant in that area.[15]

Working together with de Long, Bailar started a program of "Total Institutional Review." Under this program, the entire hospital research budget would be determined by a site visit made to the hospital every 3 years. In their budgetary recommendations, site visitors were to take into account currently approved Part 1 programs, existing common resources left from the Part 2 program, and a projection of the hospital's needs over the next three years as determined at the site visit and in consultation with representatives from the affiliated medical school. The Part 1 funds were merged into this total hospital research budget, and new funding was not to be expected until the next site visit. The Regional Coordinators organized and staffed these site visits. The visiting teams were made up of VA investigators and ACOS/R&Es, as well as deans and other leaders from affiliated medical schools. These were full-dress affairs, not much different from the old Part 2 visits, except that the visitors now took into account the hospital's Part 1 experience. In addition, they attempted to sort through the optimistic input from the hospitals and medical schools to arrive at a realistic projection of expected growth over the ensuing 3 years.

At the initiation of this institutional review program, the Part 1-Part 2 system, that had been "on hold," was terminated. Hospital budgets were frozen at the level where they stood and remained essentially stable until the institutional site visit under the new system. Centralized Part 1 review was discontinued and the hospital Research and Education Committees were expected to undertake peer review of their own research applications.[19]

At the time this new program began and the totally decentralized budgets had been allocated, there was inadequate funding to include all of the new Part 1 programs recently approved. These were funded at only 30 percent of approved levels, causing considerable hardship for "growing" programs. These programs had recently succeeded in recruiting "stars," new investigators whose programs were reviewed at that time. As a result, during the next several years of total decentralization, growing programs found it hard to make ends meet.

The institutional site visits continued with few problems until the visit to one of the largest research programs in the country. On that particular site visit, after a key visitor had to drop out at the last minute, enough controversy about the process arose that Dr. Musser decided to place a moratorium on that program as well.[20-22]

With review of institutional and individual projects on hold, the responsibility of the ACOS/R&E and the R&E Committee at the hospital was now more clearly defined than before. The R&E Committees were expected to undertake their own peer review of programs and be accountable for the quality of research. Various systems were worked out, generally involving ad hoc reviews. Some groups of hospitals collaborated to review each other's projects or set up regional peer review. No one, however, was pleased with the situation.[23]

James A. Pittman, M.D., and Thomas F. Newcomb, M.D.

Dr. Pittman came to Washington from Birmingham, Alabama to become ACMD/R&E in mid-1971 and remained until 1973, when he returned to Birmingham as Dean of the University of Alabama Medical School. An endocrinologist and nuclear medicine physician, since 1956 he had been Chief of Nuclear Medicine at the Birmingham VA Hospital, as well as at the University of Alabama at Birmingham. He was also a highly respected investigator in endocrinology. He recruited Lawrence Hobson, M.D., Ph.D., an expert in clinical pharmacology, to be his Deputy.

Figure 15.10 James Pittman, M.D.   Figure 15.11 Lawrence Hobson, M.D., Ph.D.

A few months after Bailar returned to the National Cancer Institute, Pittman persuaded Thomas F. Newcomb, M.D., a hematologist and ACOS/R&E at the Gainesville, Florida VA Hospital, to come to Washington as Director, Research Service.[21]

Figure 15.12 Thomas Newcomb, M.D.

Newcomb and Pittman Reestablish Peer Review

Newcomb had been concerned about the problems he was encountering as ACOS/R&E at Gainesville stemming from the total decentralization of research funding. The R&E Committee was expected to use peer review in allocating their funds but was provided no guidance or help from Central Office in doing so. Newcomb had been trying to form a consortium of east coast VA hospitals that would work together to substitute their own peer-review system for the absent Central Office peer-review mechanism. One of Newcomb's first acts after arriving in Washington was to re-establish peer-review committees, now known as Merit Review Boards, to evaluate individual programs.

Decisions of these committees were advisory to the hospital R&E Committees and at first did not directly affect funding.

Re-establishing these review committees was made more difficult by a new law requiring that all Federal committees be chartered by the Office of Management and Budget (OMB). Newcomb worked with the OMB to charter a new group of Merit Review Boards, but he also went ahead and set up individual peer review, even without a charter. For the first year or so, these Boards functioned ad hoc, without a charter. For one round of review, travel monies of the board members were denied. Deliberation was by conference call. However, in the beginning, he continued the system of decentralized total hospital funding with some adjustments in response to new Merit Reviews. It was not until 1974 that the new Merit Review Boards were actually chartered (Appendix II l).[23]

The RRAG's and the RAC

Newcomb was bombarded with visitors who wanted him to help solve new problems at the hospitals, especially ones centered on meeting the needs of their new recruits. Other visitors described problems unanticipated by the institutional review group when their 3-year budget was established. Other hospitals had not been visited before the moratorium and were still functioning with the same budgets they had in 1969. To address these diverse situations, Newcomb created a new advisory mechanism, the Regional Research Advisory Committees, the RRAG's, later called the RAG's.[23] As initially conceived, the RRAG's were four committees, one from each of the four geographic research regions, each charged with reviewing proposals from another region. At first, the RRAG's met simultaneously every 2 months in Central Office. Each RRAG was set up as a three-person committee, with 3-year rotations, chaired by the member in his or her final year of RRAG service.

The first assignment to the RRAG's was to review a backlog of administrative requests that Newcomb had been deliberating. These were generally sketchily documented, and the RRAG groups often found it difficult to decide whether a proposal had scientific merit. A major concern was whether the requested funding would be beneficial for the hospital's patient-care program. After a few meetings, the basic RRAG guideline was established that a proposal submitted for approval needed to meet a baseline of scientific merit as determined by an ad hoc review. If the proposal met this criterion, then the RRAG's decision would be based on the expected impact of the requested funding on the hospital.

Newcomb also formed an in-house Research Advisory Committee (RAC), which initially consisted of the four RRAG chairpersons, the chair of the Cooperative Studies Evaluation Committee and representatives from Professional Services, Health Services Research and Rehabilitation Research. This committee met immediately after the RRAG meetings, reviewed the RRAG findings, and made recommendations about them. It also discussed research policy and the needs of the research program.

Regional Coordinators

Even during the1960s, there were always vacancies in the roster of Program Chiefs; programs in those subject areas did not have a direct advocate in Central Office. As budgetary authority moved away from the Program Chiefs, most of them left Central Office. Also, there was a need for an entity in Research Service to relate to the ACOS/R&E and through the ACOS to the hospital's research program as a whole. To meet this need, in 1969 Lionel Bernstein appointed five of the program chiefs to double duty as "Regional (Research) Coordinators." Later, the five regions were reduced to four, and, with attrition, the number of Regional Coordinators shrank. By 1974, two remained. Just as the Program Chiefs had been perceived by the field to have the real power during the early 1960s, the Regional Coordinators were now so perceived. The ACOS/R&E at a hospital worked mostly with the Regional Coordinator and his assistant. They advised new ACOS/R&Es on how to learn their jobs and which hospitals would be good programs to visit to see how a research program should be administered. They listened sympathetically to pleas and helped when they could.

Figure 15.13 Four of the five Regional Coordinators in 1968: Richard Filer, Ph.D., Elston Hooper, Ph.D., James Matthews, M.D. and Mark Walcott, M.D. (Howard Chauncey not shown)

Program Specialists

By the time Newcomb came to Central Office, all of the Program Chiefs had departed. Drs. Dury, Hine, Matthews, and Hooper, who had been Program Chiefs, now had other responsibilities. Matthews was Newcomb's Deputy, and when Matthews left, Dury became the Deputy Director, Research Service. Hooper and Hine continued as Regional Coordinators but were now expected to cover the whole country. Research investigators in the field complained that they no longer had someone in Central Office who was both interested in and knowledgeable about their particular fields of scientific interest. Also, Central Office needed specialists in various research areas to carry on some of the former Program Chiefs' functions. To meet these needs, Newcomb established the position of Program Specialist.

Program Specialists were chosen from successful VA research investigators in the subject area fields. They were based at their field hospitals and spent only a minority of their time as Program Specialist. Their function was to serve as liaison between individual investigators and VA Central Office. Initially, their major activities were as ombudsmen, tasked with helping research investigators with problems. They also surveyed the VA research in their fields and provided input for the annual report. Later, the Program Specialists were also asked to perform ad hoc scientific reviews of RRAG requests and suggest ad hoc scientific reviewers for Merit Reviews and Career Development applications.

The amount of work asked of the Program Specialists varied considerably from field to field. As partial compensation for this extra, unpaid work, the busier Program Specialists were given funds to hire a secretary to help them. In time, new Program Specialists were nominated from the field on 3-year rotations.

Basic scientists

Early in Newcomb's tenure as Director, Research Service, he faced turmoil among the basic scientists at several hospitals. Under the totally decentralized budgeting process, the R&E Committee had full responsibility for distribution of all institutional research funds and space. A few clinical leaders who didn't accept the value of basic scientists to the hospital attempted to displace these scientists from their jobs and laboratories by pressuring the R&E Committees to remove them. Many of these displaced scientists were distinguished, academically acclaimed researchers and, not surprisingly, they objected loudly and strongly. Newcomb sent Abraham Dury, previously the Program Chief for Basic Sciences, on site visits to meet with the scientists to try to resolve these problems. The R&E Committees' decisions were overruled, and the scientists were protected. As a result of these problems, Dury established an informal advisory group, including representatives from these and other medical centers, to present the viewpoint of the Ph.D. scientists.

Another outcome was the establishment of budgetary cost center 104. During the 1960s, the Program Chiefs had protected the basic scientists. But with total decentralization, they needed other salary protection. Cost center 104 was formed separately in the hospital research budget to pay the salaries of non-clinician principal investigators. Cost Center 104 funds could not be used for other purposes. Dury later received the VA's highest honor, the Exceptional Service Award, partly in recognition of his work in stabilizing the role of the basic scientist within the research program.

The Research Career Development Program (Chapter 14)

In 1969, Chester de Long, Ph.D., was recruited from NIH to be Chief of the newly expanded Research Career Development program. His appointment was in Research Service, but he also reported to the Director of Education Service, as his responsibilities included the Research and Education Trainee program. De Long worked with the Career

Development Committee to define the various "rungs" of the research career "ladder."

In early 1973, the OMB made the decision that research training programs were not in the best interests of the government. Along with NIH training grants, the VA research and education trainee program was discontinued. In addition, Pittman and his staff looked at the cost of the Medical Investigator Program and decided that it was too expensive. They placed a moratorium on appointment of new Medical Investigators.

Phase-out of the Regional Research Support Centers

By the time Pittman became ACMD/R&E, the four Research Support Centers had been operating for 7 to 9 years. Different Centers had developed specific specialties, but all had responsibility for supporting research in all of the hospitals in their section of the country. Unfortunately, the effectiveness of this support appeared to be in inverse proportion to the distance of the Center from the hospitals served and it became increasingly apparent that much of the function of the Support Center was local rather than general. Also, scientists in the Support Centers wanted to *do* research, not just support it. Moreover, these centers constituted a rather large and conspicuous budget item. The 1968 NAS-NRC review of VA research had recommended "That the Veterans Administration review the programs and accomplishments of its four Research Support Centers to determine whether they are accomplishing the purposes for which they were established and how their assistance to individual investigators can be enhanced."[7]

At the same time, it had become apparent that statistical support beyond what was provided by Central Office was needed for the Cooperative Studies program. Up to this point, studies had been receiving statistical support from many sources: statisticians from Central Office, the Follow-up Agency, universities and special VA laboratories. To standardize the statistical support of the Cooperative Studies, the West Haven (CT) and Hines (IL) Research Support Centers were transformed into Cooperative Studies Program Coordinating Centers (CSPCCs). This transformation was gradual. At first, they continued to do what they had been doing before, but increasingly more of their efforts were directed to Cooperative Studies.

The Western Research Support Center, which had emphasized bioengineering and computing, became the site of the Medical Research Information System (MRIS).[4] For a time, it continued to offer courses in bioengineering and computing, but these tapered off with increasing demands of the information system. The Southern Research Support Center at Little Rock was disbanded, but some of its staff continued to run the Central Research Instrumentation Pool (CRIP).[24]

In summary, the 1968-1973 period featured strong Central Office attempts to find a research administration design that incorporated peer review and streamlined and rationalized oversight. The goal was to achieve predictably high-quality research while protecting necessary basic research, clinical applications, and promising avenues of research. This time of rapid administrative change, much of it controversial, set the stage for the stabilization that followed. At the same time, the research carried out in VA hospitals continued to prosper in the face of the new initiatives. High-quality staff had been hired through the Career Development Program, along with other scientists and clinicians. These factors led to the continuing development of laboratories and research programs in fields important to the care of the veteran patient.

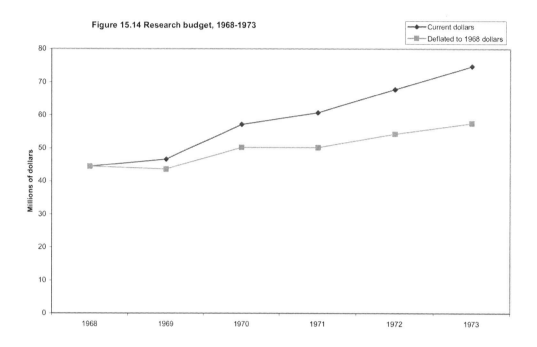

Figure 15.14 Research budget, 1968-1973

References

1. Telephone interview with Harold Schoolman, M.D., March 1, 1988 and April 26, 1988.

2. Interview with Lionel Bernstein, M.D., Ph.D., November 1, 1988 at Dr. Bernstein's office in Chicago, IL.

3. Interview with Thomas Chalmers, M.D., July 29,1992 at a hotel lobby in Boston, MA.

4. Benjamin B. Wells, M.D., "Circular 10-71-264. VA Medical Research and Education Conference, RCS 15-32-S." 12/9/71.

5. National Academy of Sciences - National Research Council. "Minutes, 25th Meeting of the CVMP." December 5, 1952. Washington, DC: National Research Council, 1952, 522.

6. National Academy of Sciences - National Research Council. "Minutes, 29th Meeting of the CVMP." April 20, 1954. Washington, DC: National Research Council, 1954, 536.

7. National Academy of Sciences - National Research Council "Evaluation of Biomedical Research and Education in the Veterans Administration." National Research Council, 1968. 29.

8. Interview with Leon Bernstein, P.D., April 29, 1988 at Dr. Bernstein's home in Alexandria, VA.

9. Interview with Leslie Zieve, M.D., September 21, 1992 at Dr. Zieve's home near Minneapolis, MN.

10. Thomas C. Chalmers, M.D., "R&E Letter 69-5. Institution of new procedures for requesting designated support for individual (research) programs, as Part I of the institutional (research) allocation." 4/15/69.

11. Thomas C. Chalmers, M.D., "R&E Letter 69-9. VA categorical research evaluation committees - Structure, functions and roster of members." 9/11/69.

12. Interview with Gerald Libman, May 5, 1992 at Mr. Libman's home in suburban Maryland.

13. Interview with Abraham Dury, P.D., February 8, 1994 at Dr. Dury's home in Florida.

14. Interview with Ralph Casteel, May 3, 1988 at a restaurant in Bethesda, MD.

15. Interview with Lyndon Lee, M.D., April 7, 1988 at a restaurant in Bethesda, MD.

16. Interview with Chester DeLong, P.D., May 7, 1992 at Dr. DeLong's Office in VACO.

17. Bailar, J.C., 3rd, "Estrogen therapy for prostatic cancer." *Prog Clin Cancer*, 1970. **4**: 387-392.

18. Interview with John Bailar, M.D., April 29, 1988 at Dr. Bailar's office in Washington, DC.

19. Telephone interview with Thomas Newcomb, M.D., March 15, 1988 and May 28, 1988.

20. M.J. Musser, M.D., "Chief Medical Director's Letter IL 10-71-17. Revision of VA Research Program." 3/9/71.

21. Interview with James Pittman, M.D., February 27, 1992 at Dr. Pittman's office in the Dean's Office at the University of Alabama School of Medicine.

22. Lyndon E. Lee, M.D., "R&E Letter. Phase out of disapproved Part I research programs." 7/10/70.

23.   Interview with Thomas Newcomb, M.D., March 29, 1992 at a hotel lobby in Washington, DC.

24.   Benjamin B. Wells, M.D., "R&E Letter 66-3. Central Research Instrument Pool." 6/21/66.

Chapter 16. Medical Research in the VA Comes of Age, 1974–1980

On the heels of increasingly complex organizational demands, a time had come for a genuine maturation of research as an institutional entity within the VA. Although new opportunities to acquire personnel and funding had been widely welcomed, they had been accompanied by inevitable growing pains. A crucial era had arrived. VA's leaders would be tested to effectively shape the research program into stability that would not only encourage its participants, but would foster recognition and support for the future.

During this time, a subtle but significant change was made in the nomenclature of facilities within the VA health-care system. The long-standing term "hospital" was abandoned in favor of "medical center," seen as more representative of the range of activities, including research, that was present at most VA locations.

Reorganization of Research and Development

As the activities of the Research Service, and simultaneously the Education Service, expanded and became more diverse, demands on the ACMD for Research and Education increased. There was a feeling, especially among the Education Service staff, that the needs of Research Service received preference in the R&E Office. Laurence Foye, M.D., Director of Education Service, campaigned to establish a separate Office of Academic Affairs.[1] He was successful when the Department of Medicine and Surgery was reorganized during the Nixon Administration. This reorganization coincided with James Pittman's departure in mid-1973 to become Dean of the Medical School at the University of Alabama. After the reorganization, the Offices of Academic Affairs and Research and Development were separate, with Foye and Thomas Newcomb as their respective ACMDs. The new office of Research and Development now comprised two Services and maintained a "staff office", soon to become a third Service The Medical Research Service, the former Research Service, searched for a new Director to replace Newcomb. Carleton Evans, M.D., directed a revitalized Health Services Research and Development Service (Chapter 19), an outgrowth from the old administrative research and hospital computer programs. The Prosthetics Research Program, the staff office, soon became a separate Service (Chapter 20).

Organization of Medical Research Service in 1974

In April 1974, the author joined VA Central Office as Director, Medical Research Service. Her former position—ACOS/R&D at the Buffalo VA Hospital—had provided experience for working within the VA research milieu, and appointment to several advisory groups and site visit teams, including chairing one of the original RRAG groups, added specific familiarity with the Central Office Research staff.

In 1974, the Medical Research Service staff was much slimmer than the Research Service of the 1960s. Program Chiefs no longer provided a strong professional presence, and their support staffs had been reassigned. In fact, the new Medical Research Service had only two physicians, a veterinarian and three Ph.D. scientists. Abraham Dury, Ph.D., who had previously been Program Chief for Basic Sciences (Chapter 12), was the Deputy Director and had been effectively running the Service, since the new ACMD/R&D, Dr. Thomas Newcomb, was focused on building new programs. Four staff assistants, one for each geographic region, handled day-to-day funding decisions, after consulting with Dury. Darlene Whorley was quietly and effectively running the Career Development Program, and Gerald Libman, assisted by two other executive secretaries and a small support staff, had stabilized the Merit Review program.

Figure 16.1 Marguerite Hays, M.D.

James Hagans, M.D., Ph.D., was heading the Cooperative Studies program from his Miami office, assisted by Marian Brault in Washington. He worked vigorously to mold this program, which changed in many ways during the 1970s (Chapter 18).

Figure 16.2 H. Elston Hooper, Ph.D.

The Field Operations section administered the undesignated research funds sent to the hospitals, which made up most of the budget. A hospital's research budget was still largely based upon precedent, derived from the previous year's budget, with adjustments that took into account new RRAG and Merit Review approvals. Even though many new funding decisions could now rely on RRAG recommendations, requests for new funding abounded. During the first few months after the author arrived, numerous visits were made by special pleaders; it was essential to stabilize the funding mechanism. The author appointed Elston Hooper, Ph.D., who had long experience and a deep understanding of the research program, to be Chief, Field Operations. In this new position, Hooper assumed the role that in the 1960s was that of the four Regional Coordinators and more recently of Dr. Dury himself. Hooper served as a buffer between the author and the "special pleaders."

The Central Office staff members were bombarded by requests for expensive new and replacement equipment, finding them difficult to evaluate. Another early decision was to appoint Gerald Hine, Ph.D., an instrumentation expert in his discipline of nuclear medicine, to review and administer research instrumentation.

Figure 16.3 Gerald Hine, Ph.D

Based on her experience as ACOS/R&D at Buffalo, the author was primarily concerned about two problems with the administration of the Medical Research Service. The first was its relative lack of flexibility: a hospital's research budget tended to remain stable even though its programs varied. This made it difficult for a growing program to emerge successfully. On the other hand, the status quo was a highly satisfactory situation for a well-established research program and, especially, for one with declining activity. A budgeting scheme was needed that was "transparent"—one based on discernable factors, reflecting a hospital's current research activities.

Another concern was the general confusion in the field resulting from the many recent major policy changes. Most of the ACOSs were themselves unclear about current research policy and that uncertainty was amplified in the minds of the investigators they were supposed to be guiding. The program needed consistent policies, acceptable to all interested parties in Central Office, acceptable in the field, and understood by all. It was vital that those most affected by policy change—hospital researchers—have a clear understanding of the policies that would govern them.

The Central Office Medical Research staff devoted considerable effort to describing policies explicitly and distributing the information to the field in clearly stated circulars and letters. Research was still officially functioning under a 1962 procedural manual so outdated that no one ever referred to it. It took the coordinated efforts of many within Central Office to completely review and process needed changes culminating in the issuance of a new manual in the early 1980s.

Establishing a management information system as the basis for the research budget

To make hospital research budgets more responsive to current activity, the author, Dury and Hooper worked with the staff of the Sepulveda (CA) Bioengineering and Computer Center (BECC) to expand and upgrade the Medical Research Information System, MRIS, (soon expanded to include all of R&D and renamed the Research and Development Information System, RDIS.)[2]

Figure 16.4 Frederick Weibell, Ph.D. Chief of the BECC

At that time, except for the AHIS system at the Washington, D.C. VA Hospital (Chapter 19), no management information system existed in the VA medical program, and a Congressional restriction forbade the purchase of new computers. Fortunately, Research already owned a computer at the BECC. Although antiquated—it used punched cards and was programmed in Fortran[2]—it was available. So this was the machine drafted to support the original RDIS.

In the new information system, each project was simultaneously reported to RDIS and the Smithsonian Science Information Exchange (SSIE). SSIE coded the projects and sent project summaries and their codes to the BECC. Each project was then cross-tabulated in budgetary reports to a specific part of the medical center's research budget. Other parts of the new system provided information about the numbers of principal investigators, the numbers of users engaged in animal studies, and the numbers of users of common resources at each hospital. Over several years, the system was revised until it was possible to combine this information with the results of Merit Review, RRAG review, the salaries of basic research scientists, Career Development Awards, Cooperative Studies activities and special laboratories, to establish a total hospital research budget.

Common resources

The major "soft" area in this budgetary scheme, and the most controversial, was the amount of core support or "common resources" to be allocated to each medical center's research budget. These "common resources" were the residual from the old "Part 2" funds and sometimes they constituted the majority of a hospital's research budget. Working with advisors, the Medical Research Service established formulas for the appropriate funding for each common resource, based upon such factors as the number of investigators using that particular resource, and the size of the total program. Using this analysis, the BECC calculated the projected funding for common resources for the various medical centers and then compared the result with a particular hospital's existing funding level. In some cases, the discrepancies were great. It was decided to make gradual adjustments toward achieving equity, aiming for full implementation of the formula within 5 years.

The more alert ACOSs quickly caught on to this new system. New common resources began to appear in their annual reports. When these were the same as in most other hospitals, they were simply added into the formula. However, unique common resources also appeared, and it was difficult to decide whether they were appropriate. The RRAG groups tried to advise about them, but they found doing so difficult without on site investigation. Later, site visits by the Research Advisory Committee helped influence these decisions.

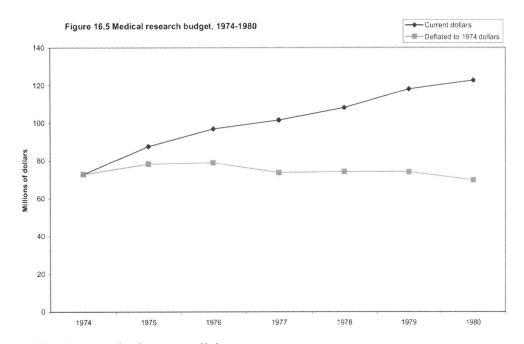

Figure 16.5 Medical research budget, 1974-1980

Establishing new budgetary policies

In the late 1970s, one budget crisis occurred after another. At the same time that inflation-corrected dollars were shrinking (Figure 16.5), the number of qualified researchers seeking support was increasing. For several years, these budgetary strictures were met primarily by cutting back on non-Merit Reviewed programs. Under the decentralized program of the early 1970s, Merit Review success had been rewarded with increased funding, yet lack of success had not resulted in decreases. A number of investigators continued to be supported from the "basic institutional support" at the medical centers, without applying to the Merit Review program, a carryover from "Part 2" funds. Many of these persons had never applied for Merit Review approval of their research.

The author worked with Dr. Newcomb to communicate with others in Central Office about the problems and how they were addressing them. Policy changes were openly debated within Research and Development. At that time, John Chase, M.D., the CMD, held daily staff meetings, which were attended by all the ACMDs as well as other key officials. These meetings provided an opportunity to discuss significant new events and possible policy changes. Newcomb received early feedback from those who were unhappy with proposed changes, allowing room to negotiate. They also talked to many ACOSs, in visits in both directions, phone calls, and formal meetings. The ACOSs' annual meetings included extensive open discussion of policy issues.

A system gradually evolved in which most of a hospital's research funding was based upon Merit Review. The first step in this process was simply to inform the hospitals how their budgets had been calculated. The BECC group performed these calculations, using the RDIS budget report, which showed the calculations, including details about common resources. Funding for investigators appeared in various columns: "RAG," "Merit Review approved," "Merit Review disapproved," and "not reviewed." Some ACOS's strongly protested identifying their budgets in this degree of detail, preferring the previous vagueness, which allowed more room for manipulation. But most seemed to prefer a transparent budgeting system.

Once the basis of the budget was explicit, budget policy shifted. Except for very small programs, continuing programs were required to undergo Merit Review. Once this requirement had been widely announced and had survived intense debate, programs that had not yet been submitted for review were not funded. This caused turmoil among those who believed they could rely on political considerations to retain their funding. While the author and Dr. Dury tried to be as flexible and empathetic as possible in enforcing these new policies, they did indeed enforce them. Unlike the situation faced by the research leaders of the late 1960s, whose policies were reversed by their organizational superiors, Newcomb and CMD Chase were consistently supportive and never reversed decisions made in Medical Research Service, despite political pressure to do so.

Once the principle of peer review for all individual programs was firmly in place, programs that failed peer review had to be dealt with. This was even more traumatic for participants than the actual review. Support of disapproved programs was tapered off gradually, to give investigators another chance to apply without closing down the project. The goal was to maintain the continuity important to an intramural program.

In 1974, when this change in funding policy began, the National Academy of Sciences (NAS) was just beginning its third review of the VA Research program. Their review was eventually published in 1977, which, in retrospect, was an unfortunate time for a review since funding policies were in flux. Some of the policies the committee criticized had already changed by the time of their final report. The NAS group was particularly concerned that disapproved programs were being supported at the local level.

As funding grew tighter, money was insufficient to fund even approved programs fully. Agencies funding extramural programs deal with this problem by funding only programs receiving the best evaluations from their reviewers. However, the author and Dury believed, as had Lionel Bernstein and Leon Bernstein, that an intramural program should fund all of its peer-review-approved projects. If a program was not good enough to fund, the Merit Review Board should disapprove it. But when there is not enough money to fund all meritorious programs fully, the only alternatives are to exclude some of them or to reduce the amount of money awarded to each, the choice made by Medical Research Service. To do this, a sliding scale reflecting the priorities assigned by the Merit Review Boards was built into the computer program used in calculating the budget

After 1975, the budget was a constant problem. The VA was working hard to upgrade its patient-care program, and attention was directed to medical care rather than to the research program. Some years, the research budget seemed a "sacrificial lamb" to achieve badly needed increases in the patient-care budget. This budgetary squeeze finally led, in 1978, to a proposal that the VA cut off funding to many hospitals with small research programs (Chapter 17).

The OMB study of VA peer review

A problem arose in gaining OMB charters for the Merit Review Boards. OMB staff began to feel that the VA, through its Merit Review Boards, was mimicking the NIH and its grants program. Newcomb's response was that the VA merit review system was simply the application of quality control in an intramural system, which was very different from NIH's extramural grants program.

During the negotiation with OMB that eventually led to chartering the Merit Review Boards in 1972, the OMB staff required that the VA and NIH conduct a joint "experiment" on peer review. This study, conducted in 1974 and 1975, compared the work of the VA Merit Review Boards with that of NIH Study Sections. Gerald Libman and his VA Program Review staff worked with the Executive Secretaries at the NIH to perform a blinded double review of VA projects. Applications to the NIH by VA staff were duplicated and sent to the VA, with VA cover sheets. Comparable VA Merit Review applications were sent to the NIH, with NIH cover sheets, to enter into the NIH review process.[3] Eventually, the NIH abandoned the study; many NIH staff were involved, often each with only one study project to handle, and they found the experiment to be too time-consuming and confusing for them. Anecdotally, in reviewing the results of the aborted study, the VA was reassured about the quality of its Merit Review Boards. In most cases, the two agencies' reviews were similar. When they differed, discrepancies tended to balance out, with some VA projects receiving better VA reviews and others better NIH reviews.[4] Though funding of VA applications was based only on the VA results, some investigators felt that they were placed under double jeopardy. By the time the experiment was abandoned, the staff at the OMB had changed; the new staff did not pursue the study and allowed continuation of the Merit Review Boards.[5]

Changes in the Merit Review system

Secondary review

As the results of Merit Review grew increasingly important to VA's medical centers, a great deal of interest naturally centered on them. In the early days, considerable pressure was applied to use the Director's executive authority to reverse disapproval decisions. In the mid-1970s, Medical Research Service established a second level of review, the "Medical Research Council," consisting of Medical Research Service senior staff and others in Central Office interested in research. The Council members reviewed all Merit Reviews, scrutinizing Merit Review Board recommendations one by one. When reviewers felt that the Board's recommendation might have gone astray, they would recommend that the proposal be returned for additional review, perhaps by a different Board. The final decision was left to the Director, and on rare occasions the author reversed a disapproval decision.

Investigators in medical disciplines that lacked a Merit Review Board specifically in their subject areas frequently complained that they felt they were not receiving a fair review, even though staff always sought expert reviewers. This problem plagues all peer-review systems, even at NIH. For the VA, it was more severe because fewer Boards existed, so that each Board was expected to cover a broad subject area. Since most nuclear medicine proposals were cross-disciplinary, they were generally reviewed by whatever specialty board seemed best suited to review them. After one round of Merit Review in which the performance of nuclear medicine proposals had been dismal, a special advisory group of nuclear medicine specialists re-reviewed the proposals. These reviewers were informed of the actions of the primary boards and were asked to look for possible areas of unfairness. In virtually every case, however, they endorsed the Boards' original decision. There is no way to know what their decisions would have been had they served as the primary review group.

Appeals

With so much now depending on Merit Review Board decisions, an investigator needed to be able to appeal a Board decision. But since unjustified appeals could swamp the system, only limited types of appeal were allowed.[6] An in-house committee reviewed appeals with advice from the Program Specialists. But this mechanism did not work very well, and with staff members not enthusiastic about appeals very few appeals were upheld.

Types 2, 3 and 4 Merit Review proposals

Another innovation that was not very successful was the introduction of three new types of Merit Review proposal. In addition to the standard ("Type 1") proposal, which includes a full description of proposed research, the new Type 2 and Type 3 proposals were to be reviewed retrospectively. Type 2 proposals were for small projects funded at less than $25,000 yearly, in which the request was simply for continued funding at the existing level. Any ongoing program under $25,000 was eligible for Type 2 review. To be eligible for Type 3 review, the retrospective review of larger programs, the Principal Investigator needed to have been funded in the VA's research program at least 10 years. Type 4 proposals were for pilot projects costing less than $25,000.

The retrospective review of Type 3 programs fit the concept that a senior investigator who is consistently productive should be supported based on track record without the need to present a complex prospective research program. Some of the leading ACOSs favored this approach, and Rosalyn Yalow was a strong advocate. There was enthusiasm in the field, and Central Office received many Type 3 proposals. However, the Merit Review Boards turned them down frequently, owing to the absence of a prospective proposal. Even though Board members had been instructed about the criteria for Type 3 proposals and understood that they were supposed to be reviewing them retrospectively, they were uncomfortable not to have a complete prospective proposal to review. Other mechanisms for reviewing these proposals were considered, such as a bibliographic analysis. For one round, the RAG groups, rather than the Merit Review Boards, reviewed them. The RAG groups, however, were also uncomfortable with this new assignment. Eventually, early in the 1980s, the retrospective review alternatives were abandoned. As with the appeals mechanism, Type 2, 3 and 4 reviews failed primarily because they were not well accepted by those whose job it was to implement them.

The Research Career Scientist program

After a few years of the new budget policies, a number of independent Ph.D. scientists whose salaries had been built into their hospitals' budgets lost their research funding. This presented the anomaly of a person being paid to conduct research who had no support for his research program. As most of these researchers had been hired into government career appointments, it was not possible simply to terminate their appointments. Yet one could not justify continuing to pay their salaries. In 1977, Medical Research Service notified the medical centers where these unfunded scientists were located that unless they had achieved peer reviewed research funding (VA or non-VA) by the beginning of the following fiscal year, the hospitals would receive no money for their salaries. Approximately 25 individuals were affected, and this decision generated great concern. However, the medical centers handled this crisis very well. Some of the scientists who were eligible to retire did so. Others stepped into other jobs at the hospital. A number of them said later that they were happier in their new positions.

Clearly, it was desirable to avoid a recurrence of this situation. A new policy stated that, in the future, new non-clinician scientists could be hired into a career appointment only if they qualified for a new category entitled Research Career Scientist.[7, 8] A Research Career Scientist appointment honored the most successful non-clinician scientists already within the VA and provided a means of recruiting new "superstars." A new committee reviewed applications, using criteria similar to those used by universities evaluating candidates for tenure. This committee set such high standards VA hospitals soon boasted an elite corps of research "stars" (Appendix VIII).

The Research Career Development Program

In 1975, the VA physician's salary bonus was introduced. Previously, VA physicians' salaries had been fixed at the same level as other employees in the equivalent Civil Service grade. As a consequence, their salaries lagged so far behind those of physicians at other institutions that it was becoming very difficult to hire first-rate physicians into the VA. The research program at that time was essential for recruiting and retaining physicians, and withholding research funds from an important clinician was controversial. The introduction of a bonus, however, made physicians' salaries competitive with academic salaries, at least for a time. As a result, outstanding physician-scientists flocked into the VA, and Medical Research Service had many new applications from talented investigators. This influx of talent occurred at the same time that the budget's spending power began to decline.

One problem imposed by the physician's bonus affected the Research Career Development Program. Since the bonus was specifically directed to correct recruitment problems and vigorous competition existed for Career Development positions, there was no problem in recruiting persons into that program. For this reason, CMD Chase made an agreement with OMB staff that, if they would approve the physician's bonus, he was willing to exclude from that bonus certain categories of physicians.[9] These categories included the Career Development physicians. Suddenly, Research Associates, Clinical Investigators and Medical Investigators, who had been paid the same as their peers in the clinical services at their hospitals, were being paid considerably less. The consequence was a significant exodus from the program, particularly among the more senior persons, who took high-level positions at their medical centers, positions eligible for the bonus. Some hospitals that had been active in nominating persons into the Career Development Program dropped out. Others, particularly when an affiliated medical school was willing to help make up the salary difference, continued to present outstanding candidates for Career Development positions. It turned out that many highly qualified young physicians were sufficiently interested in a research career that they were willing to accept smaller salaries in exchange for having extra time for research. The program continued to flourish.

The Research Career Development program had become so popular that the qualifications of successful candidates continued to escalate. When the Clinical Investigator program had been introduced in the late 1950s, it was considered to be an entry-level program (Chapter 7). But as Clinical Investigator positions became increasingly competitive, and applicants' qualifications grew increasingly impressive, a gap was left at the entry level. In the 1960s (Chapter 12), this gap was filled by applicants for the Research Associate position. By the mid-1970s, qualification for the Research Associate position had escalated to the point that it was no longer accessible to truly entry-level persons. In fact, the rather modest research support that came with the appointment was only a fraction of the total support of some successful candidates. Most of them also applied for Merit Review and many for other sources of funding. In some instances, Clinical Investigators were running huge laboratories with a large number of staff, quite inappropriate for a person still in a developmental career phase. In hopes of discouraging fully independent investigators from pushing the "developing" investigators out of the Research Associate and Clinical Investigator slots, limits were placed on their funding. While this discouraged some over-qualified individuals, these positions continued to be very popular among well-qualified researchers.[10]

Once again there was a need for entry-level positions in the Research Career Development Program. In setting up the new appointment level, constraints were placed to prevent its also escalating and becoming filled with over-qualified incumbents. Only clinicians without research training except that incidental to their residencies were eligible. This new position was a 2-year appointment, with 1-year appointments available to those who had completed one-year research fellowships. Those with both the M.D. and the Ph.D.degrees were not eligible, as they had already benefited from research training. To further emphasize this as a junior position, successful candidates were salaried lower than the usual staff-physician levels and were ineligible for the physician's bonus.[11]

Despite these constraints, good candidates soon applied for appointment to this new position of Associate Investigator. A major problem in their review was the nature of the research protocol itself. It was understood that these inexperienced candidates needed some help in writing their proposals. It became obvious that in some cases the preceptor had actually written the proposal; in others, the candidates themselves wrote it. Given this disparity, it was sometimes hard for the Career Development Committee to assess candidates. Increasingly, they emphasized their preference for a *good* (but not necessarily polished) proposal with evidence that the candidate had written it.

The Career Development program was always considered important, and it received preferential funding. Until the mid-1970s, all approved applications were funded. However, with the budget squeeze of the 1970s, it became necessary to use priority cutoffs that became progressively restrictive. By the time the Associate Investigator position was introduced, even it required a priority cutoff, though it was more lenient than for the more senior positions. So it was introduced in a modest way, and funding of Associate Investigator positions was always very competitive.

Newcomb and the author decided to reintroduce the Medical Investigator position, which had been under a moratorium for new appointments, by accepting limited numbers of applications, starting in 1975. One problem had been that these expensive positions tended to be grouped in a few successful hospitals. This did not seem equitable, particularly since these mature and successful clinician scientists could be important influences in hospitals with small research programs. In reintroducing the Medical Investigator position, they changed its character in a number of ways: (1) Only clinicians already on the VA staff could apply. (2) Each hospital had a limit of two Medical Investigators at any one time. (3) The appointment was for six years and could not be renewed unless the investigator had spent at least 1 year on the clinical staff at the completion of the earlier appointment. (4) In nominating a Medical Investigator, the hospital management had to promise to rehire that person on the clinical staff at the end of the appointment. In addition, at that time Medical Investigators were ineligible for the physician's bonus. Nevertheless, once the position was reopened, applications flooded in. Generally, not more than one or two of these expensive appointments were made at each semiannual round of Career Development reviews.

Changes were also made in the Senior Medical Investigator program. Ludwig Gross and Oscar Auerbach both reached their 70th birthdays in 1975 and faced the then-mandatory retirement from the VA. They could no longer be Senior Medical Investigators, but the VA honored them as Senior Medical Investigator Emeriti and as Distinguished Physicians, an appointment available to retirees. Both continued to conduct research at their hospitals. These two vacancies made it possible to think about appointing new Senior Medical Investigators. William Oldendorf at Brentwood (CA) was made Senior Medical Investigator in 1978, and Roger Unger, from Dallas (TX), previously ACOS for Research, received the appointment in 1979.[12]

<u>Middleton Awardees</u>

The 1974 and 1975 Middleton Awards were presented in VA Central Office with key officials present.

The 1974 awardee was Paul Srere, Ph.D., from the Dallas VA Hospital, for his biochemical accomplishments on key cellular metabolic pathways regulating lipid and carbohydrate synthesis and storage. Dr. Srere was in one of the first group of Research Career Scientists to be appointed and was an active and valued advisor of the research program.

In 1975, Paul Heller, M.D., of the Chicago West Side VA Hospital was honored with the Award. Heller was a Czech who, after 6 years in Nazi concentration camps, had been able to come to the United States to finish his training and had then made a career in the VA. He led the VA's important cooperative study on the sickle-cell trait. The Middleton Award honored him for his research in hematology, immunology, enzymology and metabolism, including findings on the mechanism of immunologic deficiency in multiple myeloma.

Figure 16.6 Chief Medical Director Chase, Middleton Awardee Paul Srere and Administrator Richard Roudebush

For the next 3 years, the award was presented at a celebration held in conjunction with a meeting of research administrators and advisors. In 1976, it went to William Oldendorf, M.D., from the Brentwood VA Hospital in Los Angeles for his development of nuclear techniques in clinical neurology. These included the first description of computerized tomography, the development of techniques of cerebral blood flow measurement, elaboration of cerebrospinal fluid functions and characterization of blood brain barrier permeability. The first of these was the basis of his 1975 Lasker Award and his later nomination for the Nobel Prize.

Figure 16.7. William Oldendorf accepting the Middleton Award as Administrator Max Cleland smiles

Oldendorf's introduction to VA research while he was Chief of Neurology at the Los Angeles VA Hospital clearly reflected the less structured, more personal approach to funding sometimes seen in earlier years. In a 1991 interview, he described being approached by Morton Grossman, the hospital's acting research chief, who asked, "Bill, you're interested in Research aren't you?" Oldendorf recalled what happened when he confirmed he was interested in doing research, with the simple answer, "yeah".

"He (Grossman) said, 'Have you got any funding?' and I said, 'No.' Then he asked, 'Could you use 3,000 dollars?'

"Could I! And so I had an account of 3,000 bucks set up. With that, I got a double sodium iodine head detector made up. And I did all that old work with the boluses measuring blood flow going through the head. And I used the same funds to build the first CT scanner. . . .Did everything myself."[13]

Figure 16.8 The prototype for the CT scanner

Figure 16.9 Oldendorf in his den in 1961 with the prototype

Oldendorf conceived the idea for the CT scanner as a way to avoid the pain and complications suffered by patients who had to be studied by pneumoencephalography to detect brain lesions. He set up the prototype scanner in the den at his home, using, among other things, an old model railroad train track.

In 1977, Charles Lieber of the Bronx VA Medical Center received the Middleton Award for his studies of the toxicity of alcohol, including elucidation of its interaction with drug, lipid and uric-acid metabolism, and the pathogenesis of fatty liver and cirrhosis in man and nonhuman primates.

Figure 16.10. Charles Lieber, M.D.

The 1978 award went to Victor Herbert, M.D., also of the Bronx, for "developing scientific tools to diagnose nutrient deficiencies, measure nutrient binding proteins, demonstrate selective deficiency of nutrients in one cell line but not another, and applying the scientific criteria of safety and efficacy to nutrition folklore."

In 1979, Edward Freis, M.D. (Chapter 9) received the Award for his "studies of hypertension that proved the efficacy and life saving qualities of medical treatment."

Norman Talal, M.D., a Medical Investigator at the San Francisco VA Medical Center, received the 1980 award in a VACO ceremony from Acting Administrator Rufus Wilson. He was cited "for the development of immunological concepts derived from the study of patients and animal models for autoimmune and endocrine systems which has led to new theoretical and therapeutic considerations for human diseases."

New honors for VA researchers

In addition to the VA's own Middleton Award, in the 1970s VA researchers were honored by many prestigious awards, including five Lasker Awards and two Nobel Prizes.

The Lasker Awards

After the Nobel Prize, the Lasker Award is arguably the top honor for an American medical researcher. Edward Fries, M.D., received the award in 1972 for "his demonstration of the life-saving effectiveness of drugs in the treatment of moderate hypertension" (Chapter 9). Ludwig Gross, M.D., of the Bronx, won it in 1974 for "his original discovery of leukemia- and cancer-inducing viruses in mammals, and the elucidation of their biology and epidemiology" (Chapter 3). And recognizing his original concept of the principles demonstrating the feasibility of computerized tomographic scanning, William Oldendorf, M.D., won it in 1975 for "discoveries which have envisaged a revolution in radiology".

According to the Lasker Foundation, more than half of those honored with the Lasker Award for Basic Medical Research since 1962 later received the Nobel Prize. This was true of the VA's Nobel Prize laureates, Rosalyn Yalow and Andrew Schally, both also honored with Lasker Awards. Schally won the Lasker Award in 1975, cited as one "whose research has expanded our knowledge of the interplay between the hypothalamus and the endocrine system." Yalow's 1976 Lasker Award was "for the discovery and development of the technique of radioimmunoassay" (Chapter 11).

Figure 16.11. Celebration at the Bronx VA Medical Center the day Rosalyn Yalow heard she had won the Nobel Prize: l-r: Ludwig Gross, Bernard Roswit, Rosalyn Yalow, Thomas Chalmers (dean Mt. Sinai School of Medicine), Julius Wolf (chief of staff), Bernard Straus (former Chief of Medicine who had helped Yalow recruit Berson), Marguerite Hays and Herbert Rose (ACOS/R&D).

The Nobel Prize winners

In 1977, Rosalyn Yalow from the Bronx and Andrew Schally from New Orleans were awarded the Nobel Prize. This was a time of great excitement in VA's Research and Development office. On the day the prizes were announced, the author went to the Bronx for a celebration in the afternoon and both she and Newcomb attended an evening celebration in New Orleans. Later, the VA held a reception at the Capitol in honor of its Nobel laureates. Schally was received by the King of Spain shortly after the Prize ceremony. Both later received many honorary degrees.

**Figure 16.12. Andrew Schally (second from left) next to
King Juan Carlos I of Spain**

The two winners had rather different reactions to the honor. Schally quickly dug back into his laboratory, determined, as he put it, to win a second Nobel Prize. Yalow, on the other hand, took her prize as an opportunity to support the VA research program that had supported her. She declared widely that she had never applied for NIH funding but had depended entirely on the VA for support of her laboratory. Yalow campaigned at the level of Administrator in the VA, and also with Congress. To the Central Office Research staff, her efforts were a mixed blessing. Certainly, the VA research effort needed the publicity and the exposure she provided. On the other hand, she was strongly opposed to the use of peer review for evaluation of research and expressed her opinion freely and in high places.

After discussions with Yalow about research administration, VA Administrator Max Cleland appointed a special research advisory committee, which Yalow chaired. The committee included Edward Rall, head of the intramural program at NIH, Julius Axelrod, Nobel Prize winner from NIH, Morton Grossman, VA Senior Medical Investigator, and a few others of similar distinction. The committee reviewed the medical research program, its current status and the way it was administered. They learned about the Career Development Program, Cooperative Studies, and the new high-priority programs, but their primary interest was the Merit Review system. The committee reviewed it in considerable detail, paying particular attention to the way the results were used. In the end, the committee not only rejected the idea of abolishing the Merit Review program, but some of the visitors favored abruptly discontinuing disapproved programs.

Personnel changes

Abraham Dury retired in 1976 and, after a nationwide search for a new Deputy Director of Medical Research Service, Elston Hooper assumed the position. In 1978, Betty Uzman, M.D., who was then the ACOS/R&D at Shreveport offered to come to Central Office if she were needed. For a person of her talents, there certainly was a need, though there was no appropriate staff opening at the time. She joined Central Office as "Assistant Chief of Field Operations." Soon, the incumbent Chief transferred to a different job and Uzman became Chief. Under her guidance, the Field Operations program became systematic and responsive to the field. She saw to it that policies were clear and decisions as fair as possible. Uzman was a strong advocate of peer review and opposed any administrative adjustment to Merit Review recommendations.

Figure 16.13. Betty Uzman, M.D.

Figure 16.13. Earl Freed, Ph.D.

When Elston Hooper retired in late 1978, Earl Freed, Ph.D., became the new Deputy Director of Medical Research Service. In his previous position of research coordinator in the Mental Health and Behavioral Sciences Service in Central Office, Freed had achieved good relations with Medical Research Service. He had been a successful research investigator for many years at the Lyons (NJ) VA Hospital and consequently understood the needs of psychology research and the research needs of the unaffiliated hospitals.

Figure 16.14. Dennis Roth and Wayne Tippets

Wayne Tippets, Administrative Officer for Medical Research Service from 1974 to 1978, entered the program to become a Medical Center Director, and Dennis Roth became Administrative Officer. Roth later became Administrative Officer for the ACMD/R&D and remained in that taxing position into the 1990s.

Figure 16.15. Jane Schultz, Ph.D.

Figure 16.16. Howard Berman

When Gerald Libman moved in 1977 from his position as Chief of the Program Review Division, the unit that administered the Merit Review program, Jane Schultz, Ph.D., a scientist from the Ann Arbor (MI) VA Medical Center, became Chief. When she returned to her laboratory in 1979, Howard Berman assumed the leadership of that complex operation.

In the summer of 1978, Newcomb left Central Office for San Antonio (TX) to be Chief of Staff at the VA Medical Center there and Associate Dean of the medical school. At about the same time, Dr. Chase completed his 4-year term as CMD and left Central Office. After a search that lasted several months, Administrator Cleland named James C. Crutcher, M.D., from the Atlanta VA Medical Center, as CMD. Crutcher was an unexpected choice, as he had no Central Office experience. He had been Chief of Medicine for many years at Atlanta and more recently had been ACOS for Education. He was also a Brigadier General in the Army Reserve. Laurence Foye had left shortly before Chase, so the Deputy CMD position was also vacant. Crutcher asked Donald Custis, M.D., a retired Navy vice admiral, at that time Deputy ACMD for Academic Affairs, to serve as Deputy CMD. After he had been in Washington for several months, Crutcher appointed the author to the ACMD/R&D position. Betty Uzman then became Director, Medical Research Service.

The Innovative Research Program

In the course of her appointment to the ACMD/R&D position, the author, together with Crutcher and Cleland, met with Senator Alan Cranston. Cranston, chairman of the Senate Veterans Affairs Committee, was a very powerful figure in veterans' politics. Rosalyn Yalow had many conversations with him about her ideas on research. Cranston's keen interest in the VA research program was apparent, as he inquired about research philosophy and, in particular, about attitudes toward peer review. He asked how the research leaders were making allowances for innovative programs that might not be recognized by the peer-review groups. Later, Cleland learned that the Senator was willing to agree to the author's appointment on the condition that two percent of the VA research budget be set aside for "innovative programs."

Uzman and the author worked together to establish an "Innovative Research" program within the constraints of the research budget and the peer-review system. Much of this requirement could be met within the current Merit Review system by identifying particularly innovative programs with the help of the Merit Review Boards; these innovative programs would then be funded preferentially. A separate category in the RDIS budgeting system was established to accommodate this preferential funding.

The Research Program Specialists sorted through the current projects in their areas searching for innovative programs. The Merit Review Boards identified projects they considered particularly innovative. A letter to the field announced this new "innovative research" program and invited persons who felt their research to be particularly innovative to write. An "Innovative Alcoholism" initiative was started. While these projects never quite added up to the Senator Cranston's two percent requirement, making inquiries from his staff a bit awkward, a sincere attempt was made to meet it without violating the principle of peer review.

Special Emphasis Areas

An effort had always been made to direct VA research money to solving the health problems of most importance to veterans. The centrally directed research programs of the 1920s and 1930s narrowly focused on such problems. During the post-World War II period, with university affiliations, this effort was less direct. Pragmatically, if a VA doctor could justify a research project on scientific grounds, the VA supported it. In most cases, these projects were relevant to the veteran, because veterans were the patients of these doctors. In addition, special efforts were made in some key areas, including those of the Advisory Committee on Aging Research and the centralized programs on prosthetics, tuberculosis and psychiatric disease.

Nevertheless, by the mid-1970s, with implementation of peer review and depletion of Central Office professional research staff, little effective effort was being devoted to boosting VA-supported research in the areas of particular importance to the veteran patient. It became difficult to respond constructively to the ever-present pressures from Congress and influential groups to divert research funds into their areas of particular interest. It seemed wise to define some explicit research priorities oriented to the special needs of the VA patient.[14] The first approach to this task was to identify the VA's most prevalent patient-care problems. These were categorized as "Special Emphasis Areas," which were announced in a 1977 Research and Development Letter to the field[15] specifically inviting cooperative studies in these Special Emphasis Areas.

High Priority Research Programs

In addition to encouraging research in these Special Emphasis Areas, a few High Priority areas were selected for preferential funding. These High Priority Areas were intentionally narrow and never consumed a large part of the budget, to avoid depleting the general funds supporting the Merit Review program. During the late 1970s, High Priority programs were begun in aging, the biology of alcoholism, the biology of schizophrenia and tissue regeneration.

In defining its original High Priority areas, the VA deliberately stayed away from areas heavily emphasized by other agencies. Even though the VA had large numbers of patients with cancer and heart disease, these areas of research were being well funded by the NIH, so that a small, directed initiative by the VA did not seem appropriate.

Aging

The High Priority Area in aging was already in place, as research in the Geriatric Research Education and Clinical Centers (GRECCs) was receiving preferential funding. The original GRECC program, spearheaded by Paul Haber, M.D., while he was ACMD for Extended Care, had been passed into law and funded, together with money to support research staff within the GRECCs. But the research staff needed support to carry out their research. The original GRECC units were "tooling up" when the author arrived in VA Central Office in 1974, and Haber lobbied hard to have her provide earmarked research support. The Medical Research leadership, however, insisted that these new programs be peer reviewed. A compromise was reached: GRECC research projects were required to undergo Merit Review, but, if approved, they would be fully funded even if other research budgets were being cut. This arrangement lasted into the 1980s, when budget constraints made its continuance impractical. By that time, research in the GRECCs had been well established.

The GRECCs, in their educational effort, sponsored Geriatric Fellowships for clinicians wanting to specialize in geriatrics. In 1980, as a part of the Aging High Priority program, Medical Research Service offered a 1-year research extension of these fellowships, handled within the Associate Investigator program.[16]

Aging research outside of the GRECCs, quantitatively much greater than that within the GRECCs, was considered to be in a Special Emphasis Area but received no budgetary preference.

New High Priority Areas: Alcoholism, Schizophrenia and Tissue Regeneration

VA patient demographics guided the choice of the next two High Priority areas. Alcoholism and its related diseases caused the most VA hospital admissions. Schizophrenia was clearly responsible for the largest number of patients occupying beds in the VA medical system at any given time. To leverage the existing strengths of VA research without duplicating research being done elsewhere, the biology of these conditions was selected for focused VA programs.

Figure 16.17. Matthew Kinnard, Ph.D., Chief, Field Operations and Robert Allen, Ph.D., Coordinator for High Priority Areas

To coordinate the High Priority programs from the Central Office, Robert Allen, Ph.D., was recruited from the NIH. He organized conferences and meetings, took charge of tracking all the defined High Priority areas to assure their protected budget lines, and interacted with the individuals in the programs. Allen became the glue holding these programs together and kept them pointed toward their goals.

Alcoholism

David Rutstein, M.D., at that time a VA Distinguished Physician in Boston, visited Newcomb in 1977 and urged that the VA follow up on recent interesting studies on the familial incidence of alcoholism. Stimulated by Rutstein's enthusiasm, CMD Chase held a meeting at which Sir Hans Krebs (who was interested in the biology of alcohol and friend of Paul Srere, Ph.D., from Dallas), Rutstein, Srere and a number of other VA scientists were present, along with a sprinkling of Central Office staff. One outcome of this meeting was a conference on the biology of alcoholism held in Florida in January 1978. The consensus was that the greatest need was to recruit competent scientists from other areas into the area of alcoholism.

Marcus Rothschild, Chief of Nuclear Medicine at the Manhattan (NY) VA, and a Middleton Award winner for his research on the liver, was interested in this problem. He agreed to spend 3 months in Central Office where he started a program of "Alcoholism Scholars". Scientists, those with M.D. or Ph.D. degrees, who were not currently working for the VA, were invited to present applications for 3-year fellowships to work in a VA laboratory on the biology of alcoholism. This program received 85 applicants in its first review cycle. Rothschild formed a special committee to review the applications, and 13 Alcoholism Scholars were chosen. The following year, VA scientists as well as non-VA scientists were permitted to apply, and 6 more Alcoholism Scholars were selected from 60 applicants.

These Alcoholism Scholars (Appendix IX), most quite young, were treated as an elite corps. They received their appointment certificates in ceremonies attended by the VA Administrator and Chief Medical Director. They were brought together to share their research experiences. Of the 13 Scholars in the first round, all recruited from outside the VA for this program, 9 continued with VA careers after their appointments expired.

A third round in this program, the Innovative Alcoholism program, was directed to innovative proposals from VA laboratories. Announcement of this program aroused much interest from VA researchers who were not primarily in the field of alcoholism research and generated 97 letters of intent, followed by 63 full proposals. After review by special committees in June 1981, 11 projects were selected as both innovative and highly meritorious scientifically. Owing to a budget shortfall, their funding was postponed until October 1982.

A task group reviewed the program in early 1982 and recommended that the VA alcohol research program be expanded to include clinical research that would combine the basic work under way with studies incorporating the VA's large patient-care effort in this area. In response, the Medical Research Service announced a competition for Clinical Research Centers in Alcoholism. After extensive review, the first such center was awarded to San Diego VA Medical Center, with Mark Schukit, M.D., one of the original Alcoholism

Scholars, as its Chief.

Schizophrenia

Claude Baxter, Ph.D., from the Sepulveda (CA) VA Medical Center, spent 6 months in Central Office to launch the High Priority research program in schizophrenia. Baxter, a neurochemist well known for his work with GABA in the brain, reviewed the literature on the biology of schizophrenia, which he found to be large and complex. He then identified the experts in the field, both within the VA and from universities in the United States and abroad.

**Figure 16.18. Attendees at the Harper's Ferry meeting
on schizophrenia research, 1979**

First row: C.E. Beck, E.D. Bird, Hiatt, Betty Uzman, Robert Allen, Janowski, A.L. Goldstein, Joseph Zubin. Second row: Phillip May, J.E. Kleinman, Sheri Buchsbaum, Monte Buchsbaum. Third row: Earl Freed, W.T. Carpenter, Jr., Savage, Zahn, Jack Ewalt, J.R. Perez-Polo, D.R. Weinberger, F.A. Henn, Arthur Yuweiler, T. Melnechuk, Philip Berger, Collins, Brown, N.R. Schoolar, Nazrallah, J.O. Cole, Gfeller, D.H. Ingvar, T.M. Itil, J.W. Mason, Claude Baxter, Loren Mosher, Marguerite Hays, J.M. Davis, Canoso, Singh.

Many of these scholars were invited to a conference held at Harper's Ferry, WV in April 1979, where they presented formal papers, subsequently edited in a *Proceedings* volume.[17] This meeting reviewed the state of the art in research on the biology of schizophrenia. The participants also considered how the VA could best launch a focused attack on the problem. The conference consensus was that the VA should establish centers of excellence in the biology of schizophrenia initially directed toward the classification of the various types of schizophrenia, since a meaningful biologic approach to the disease was possible only if classification were improved.

Proposals for Schizophrenia Biologic Research Centers (SBRCs) were formally solicited in September 1979.[18] Nineteen medical centers sent letters of interest, seven were invited to submit full applications, and six did so. The Bronx VA Medical Center was chosen for funding of an SBRC, with Kenneth L. Davis, M.D., as its Chief. Funding actually began in

January 1981. During 1981, after another competition, a second SBRC was selected at the Palo Alto VA Medical Center. Staff in both of these SBRCs published widely on schizophrenia and other mental illnesses, but the original goal of biologically based classification proved elusive.

Regeneration

VA Administrator Max Cleland, a Vietnam veteran who had lost both legs and one arm in a grenade explosion, was interested in the prospects of limb regeneration. The VA defined "tissue regeneration" as a High Priority research area. Vernon Nickel, Director of the Rehabilitation Engineering Research and Development Service (Chapter 20), together with Robert O. Becker, M.D., Middleton Award-winning orthopedic surgeon at the Syracuse (NY) VA Medical Center, organized a conference on "The Mechanisms of Growth Control." Becker was a pioneer in this area, having studied the effects of electrical stimulation on bone growth and repair. The conference, held September 26–28, 1979, was widely attended by scientists and others interested in tissue regeneration from all over the United States, and from Russia, Japan and Canada.

The Paralyzed Veterans of America service organization was strongly supportive of research in the area of spinal-cord regeneration. At the same time, basic neurobiology studies, many being carried out within the VA research program, suggested that such regeneration might no longer be in the realm of science fiction. Betty Uzman, whose scientific specialty was neurobiology and who knew most of the principal players in the area of nerve regeneration, assumed responsibility for the regeneration High Priority area.[19]

The formal VA regeneration program began taking form in 1980, when Dr. Uzman chaired a planning committee that met in Palo Alto, CA, and recommended that the VA establish an Office of Regeneration Research. A competition ensued for this office, which was established at the Portland (OR) VA Medical Center in early 1981, with Frederick Seil, M.D., a neurologist with an active research program in nerve regeneration, as its Chief.[20] During the 1980's and 1990's, this Office coordinated regeneration research in the VA, defined which VA research projects fit into the High Priority concept for preferential funding, published a newsletter and later established a training program in regeneration research. Through Dr. Seil and his office, the VA held biennial conferences on regeneration research that were well attended and encouraged collaborations in the field. Most of the effort was in the area of neural regeneration, work supported in collaboration with the Paralyzed Veterans of America and the VA Rehabilitation Research Service as well as Medical Research Service.

How useful was the concept of High Priority programs?

Even though the amount of extra money earmarked for these high-priority programs was relatively small, the programs proved productive. In addition to their scientific contributions, they helped to satisfy some of the special interest groups that wanted to divert VA resources to areas of their particular concern, since the VA areas of special emphasis were chosen as those most unique to the VA's patient-care needs.

Tissue regeneration

The conferences, newsletter and personal encouragement from the Office of Regeneration Research supported expansion of VA research in this field and led to some early successes in regeneration in the central nervous system.

One of the leaders in this field is Stephen Waxman, M.D., Ph.D., who was a part of the original planning group for this initiative. Dr. Waxman was Chief of Neurology at the Palo Alto VA Medical Center until 1985, when he became Chair of Neurology at Yale. The Eastern Paralyzed Veterans of America donated a Neuroscience Research Center on the West Haven VA campus to house the joint VA-Yale program of regeneration research under Dr. Waxman's leadership. Beginning while he was in Palo Alto, Waxman's laboratory studied the South American knife fish, *Sternarchus*, which has the ability to regenerate the spinal cord in its tail when the tail is bitten off by a predator. This process was studied in the laboratory in normal and tail-amputated *Sternarchus*, including anatomic, electron microscopic and cell culture studies. The source of the regeneration was identified as the ependymal cells of the center of the spinal cord. This seminal work has been expanded in other laboratories to produce some nerve regeneration in some mammals. While still a long leap to regeneration of cells in a severed spinal cord in the human, the outlook is considered no longer hopeless.[21, 22]

Schizophrenia

The Bronx Schizophrenia Biologic Research Center remained active long after Dr. Davis became Chairman of Psychiatry at the Mt. Sinai School of Medicine. The VA program became fully integrated with that of the medical school and the site of a large group of researchers in biologic psychiatry. One of its most important findings has been the correlation of homovanillic acid with schizophrenic symptoms. The group studied the genetics of schizophrenia and, through a gene bank, established pedigrees of schizophrenic families. A bank of brains donated by deceased schizophrenic patients led to the finding that schizophrenic brains are depleted of dopamine. The group also studied Alzheimer's disease, devised scales for its assessment, and developed tacrine, its first approved effective treatment.[23]

Biology of alcoholism

The 19 Alcoholism Scholars appointed in 1979 and 1980 (Appendix IX) were still publishing scholarly papers when contacted more than 20 years later (2002), and 15 were conducting research on the biology of alcoholism.

Marc Schukit, M.D., of the original group of Scholars, had won many awards for his genetic studies of alcoholism. His laboratory was now working to identify the specific genes involved. He described the significance of his most important findings as a key to formulating a theory that the genetic causes would be heterogeneous, selecting a particular marker of risk, showing that the marker, a low level of response to alcohol, related to a family history of alcoholism and predicted alcoholism 15 years later. His group had studied a group of 453 subjects and was now studying their 444 offspring. "I also hope that some of my work in comorbid psychiatric disorders in the context of alcohol and drug dependence has been useful to the field."[24]

Boris Tabakoff, Ph.D., who spent 1984-1990 in high positions at NIAAA, was now chair of the Department of Pharmacology at the University of Colorado where he was studying the cellular effects of alcohol. Tabakoff said:

"I believe that we were the first to link brain vasopressin and vasopressin-like peptides to the development of tolerance to alcohol. We described different forms of alcohol tolerance (those that involved learning and conditioning and those that did not involve components of learning). We demonstrated that one could, with manipulation of brain vasopressin peptides and modulation of brain noradrenergic systems, control the learned forms of tolerance, while leaving the other components of tolerance intact."

Tabakoff also demonstrated the involvement of the NMDA (N-methyl-D-aspartate) glutamatergic systems in the acute and chronic effects of ethanol with initial results that showed that ethanol was significantly and potently inhibiting NMDA receptor function. He noted that:

"My ideas were then extended to encompass the chronic effects of ethanol. These results substantiated that the NMDA receptor system responds (adapts) to ethanol administration by an upregulation of receptor number and receptor function."

Tabakoff extensively studied the effects of ethanol on the dopamine receptor-stimulated adenyl cyclase activity.

"The work continued with demonstrations of the chronic effects of ethanol, and the adenylyl cyclase systems and the observation that human alcoholic subjects had lower platelet adenylyl cyclase activity compared to controls. This clinical study was done while I was at the Westside VA in Chicago.

"More currently, in the adenylyl cyclase area, we have created transgenic animals and null mutant mice, as well as utilizing selective breeding techniques and QTL analysis which all point to the role that adenylyl cyclase plays in the etiology of alcohol tolerance and dependence."[25]

Carrie Randall, Ph.D., who was recruited into the Alcoholism Scholars program at the Charleston (SC) VAMC, received the Distinguished Alcohol Research Award from the Research Society on Alcoholism in 1998 and the Keller Award from NIAAA in 2000. She stated that the VA Alcoholism Scholar award allowed her to "build an independent research program from the ground up." She remained in the VA for 14 years, until she was recruited to the State University of South Carolina. Randall studied the role of prostaglandins in the etiology of Fetal Alcohol Syndrome and was now studying the relationship between social anxiety and the use/misuse of alcohol.[26]

Adron Harris, Ph.D.'s work focused on the study of drug addiction with emphasis on alcoholism. He clarified several molecular targets of alcohol action in the brain and studied actions of ethanol on GABA receptors.[27]

Raj Laksman, Ph.D. at the Washington (DC) VA Medical Center made significant contributions in the field of alcoholic hyperlipidemia. He found that the condition is partly due to the formation of abnormal triglyceride-rich remnant particles that are defectively cleared by the liver.[28]

Anna Taylor, Ph.D., of the Brentwood (CA) VA Medical Center and UCLA, focused her research on the neurobiology of alcoholism. She was among the first to demonstrate that prenatal exposure to ethanol produces a consistent pattern of enhanced neuroendocrine and behavioral responses to stress and psychoactive drugs, including ethanol, in adult fetal alcohol-exposed offspring. Recognizing that alcohol affects neural and endocrine systems that are intimately involved in immunological responses, her team of investigators demonstrated adverse effects of alcohol on immune competence following prenatal as well as adult exposure.[29]

Ladislav Volicer, M.D., Ph.D., was one of the Alcohol Scholars who later moved into a different field, but one also of great importance to the VA. He continued his basic neuropharmacological research and also initiated some clinical studies looking at factors influencing genetic predisposition to alcoholism. Volicer became the medical director of a Dementia Special Care Unit at the GRECC in Bedford, MA, and developed a palliative care program for patients with advanced dementia. This program was among the first to consider advanced dementia a terminal disease; its description was published in *JAMA*.[30]

John Crabbe, Ph.D., of the Portland (OR) VA Medical Center was an early proponent of genetic animal models and provided insight about the relationships among the different behavioral components of the overall alcoholic syndrome. For example, we now know that alcohol consumption and severity of alcohol withdrawal are negatively genetically coupled in rodents.[31]

Comment on the High Priority programs

One of the advantages of a relatively small, in-house research program like the VA Medical Research program was found in its administrative flexibility. All that was necessary to start these programs was an initial decision to proceed, recruitment of the staff and expertise needed and setting aside the money. Later, when it seemed to those in charge that these programs no longer were necessary, they could be abandoned in favor of other new initiatives. These small High Priority programs that were started in the late 1970s have well served the VA and its patients.

References

1. Telephone interview with Laurence Foye, M.D., March 12, 1988.

2. Foye, L.V., Jr., M.D., "10-77-219 Circular. FY 1977 VA R&D Information Systems (RDIS)." September 23, 1977.

3. Newcomb, T.F., M.D., "IL 15-74-12 R&D Letter. V.A.-NIH Review Feasibility Study." June 4, 1974.

4. Interview with Howard Berman, May 1, 1992 at Mr. Berman's office in the Westbard Building of NIH.

5. Interview with Thomas Newcomb, M.D., March 29, 1992 at a hotel lobby in Washington, DC.

6. Jacoby, W.J., Jr., M.D., "10-80-34 Circular. Merit Review Appeal Process." February 19, 1980.

7. Foye, L.V., Jr., M.D., "10-77-61 Circular. PhD Scientist Appointments in Medical Research (Program 821)." March 15, 1977.

8. Foye, L.V., Jr., M.D., "10-77-60 Circular. Research Career Scientist." March 14, 1977.

9. Foye, L.V., Jr., M.D., "10-75-277 DM&S Circular. Special pay for physicians and dentists." November 12, 1975.

10. Newcomb, T.F., M.D., "IL 15-75-5 R&D Letter. Medical Research Service Career Development Program." July 30, 1975.

11. Newcomb, T.F., M.D., "IL 15-77-16 R&D Letter. R&D Career Development Program." November 18, 1977.

12. Thomas, D. "Data base of information about Career Development appointees." 1989.

13. Interview with William H. Oldendorf, M.D., November 5, 1991 at Dr. Oldendorf's office at Brentwood VA Medical Center.

14. Newcomb, T.F., M.D., "10-76-177 Circular. R&D Priority Assessment." August 17, 1976.

15. Newcomb, T.F., M.D., "IL 15-77-8 R&D Letter. Planning and Development of Cooperative Studies in Special Emphasis Areas." June 24, 1977.

16. Jacoby, W.J., Jr., M.D., "10-80-186 Circular. Opportunity of research training for geriatric fellows." August 29, 1980.

17. *Perspectives in Schizophrenia Research*. Baxter, C.F. and Melnechuk, T., eds.; New York, NY: Raven Press, 1980.

18. Hays, M.T., M.D., "IL 15-79-11 R&D Letter. Solicitation of Letters of Intent for Schizophrenia Biologic Research Centers." September 5, 1979.

19. Uzman, B.G., M.D., "A report on progress in research High Priority Areas." *Newsletter: Research and Development in Health Care*, Washington, DC, December, 1979. 7.

20. Hays, M.T., M.D., "IL 15-80-4 R&D Letter. VA Regeneration Research." May 21, 1980.

21. Anderson, M.J. and Waxman, S.G., "Neurogenesis in adult vertebrate spinal cord in situ and in vitro: a new model system." *Ann NY Acad Sci*, 1985: 213-233.

22. *Form and Function of the Brain and Spinal Cord.* Waxman, S.G., ed. Cambridge, MA: MIT Press, 2001, 231-233.

23. Interview with Kenneth Davis, M.D., November 9, 1993 at Washington, DC hotel lobby.

24. Letter from Marc Schuckit, M.D. to author, written at San Diego, CA, March 18, 2002.

25. Letter from Boris Tabakoff, Ph.D. to author, written at Denver, CO, April 1, 2002.

26. Letter from Carrie Randall, Ph.D. to author, written at Charleston, SC, May 10, 2002.

27. Letter from Adron Harris, Ph.D. to author, written at Austin, TX, April 28, 2002 (Email).

28. Letter from Raj Lakshman, Ph.D. to author, written at Washington, DC, April 19, 2002.

29. Letter from Anna Taylor, Ph.D. to author, written at Los Angeles, CA, July 9, 2002.

30. Letter from Vladislav Volicer, M.D., Ph.D. to author, written at Bedford, MA, May 10, 2002.

31. Letter from John Crabbe, Ph.D. to author, written at Portland, OR, March 14, 2002.

Chapter 17. Meeting funding challenges: "Project Scissors"

In November of 1977, VA's medical research program encountered a crisis, as pressures to restrict Federal budgets and growing demand for research funding collided in a way that sent shock waves through the community of investigators, VA research managers, hospital administrators and medical school affiliates.

The immediate, precipitating factor was arrival at the VA of the President's budget for fiscal year 1979, which proposed a cut in the Medical Research budget to well below current (FY 78) operating dollars. The Research Service believed that most of the "fat" already had been cut out of the program and that it would be impossible to operate under the proposed budget with a "business as usual" approach. Something more drastic would be necessary; aggressive reductions would have to be made, in an effort that would become informally known as "Project Scissors".

Although the President's budget does not represent final funding decisions (the actual budget is ultimately determined by Congressional appropriation, a lengthy process worked out over several months), VA was obliged to prepare to operate at the proposed, lower level. Before the actual budget figure for the next fiscal year would be known, several developments would take place:

- The program's national leaders thoroughly explored cost-cutting options, and formulated a new policy that would eliminate or curtail research funding at many VA hospitals that appeared unproductive;
- Criteria were established to weigh relative productivity of research, such as instances of findings being published;
- An unprecedented series of nearly three-score site visits by small teams of researchers and administrators were made to evaluate ongoing projects;
- An ad hoc national "caucus" took place, at which investigators and administrators from throughout the system expressed concerns, debated solutions, and, ultimately, reached a level of consensus on the logic and fairness of the evolving funding process; and
- A new method of supporting research at smaller facilities was established, in the form of two regional research and development offices.

The problem had been brewing for some time, as a cost-conscious period in Federal budgeting had led to 3 years of relatively "straight line" funding for VA's medical research program. At the same time, the VA was recruiting many excellent physician scientists, willing and able to do needed research. To deal with these pressures, they had already increased peer review and, on advice of the Merit Review Boards, gradually phased out programs. This was a painful process, as VA research is an intramural program and the people losing funding were the VA's own employees. The cuts had clearly triggered reassignments, resignations, and retirements.

The Medical Research Service was supporting research programs in 123 VA medical centers with a total annual budget of $123 million. Ninety percent of the support was concentrated in 56 medical centers with large research enterprises. The other medical centers conducting research fell into several categories. In some cases, research support had started at modest levels when the medical center participated in a Cooperative Study or was given another special assignment. When that purpose was fulfilled, some of the "core" support remained and often paid for the salaries of one or two employees. In other cases, especially those distant from a medical school, one or two individuals consistently carried out high-quality research; they continued productive and received Merit Review Board approval despite their isolation. The monies sent to those distant medical centers supported the productive investigators and included additional "core support" for local research administration. There also were situations where a highly affiliated hospital, with academically qualified physicians, was small enough that the justifiable number of research physicians was small. And then there were situations of an emerging program on its way up or a declining program on its way down.

Despite changes over the preceding decade, administration of research money remained highly decentralized. The medical center's Research and Development Committee had much of the responsibility for deciding how best to use the money sent. As for review from Central Office, larger projects underwent individual Merit Review and the research of newly recruited investigators was reviewed by the Research Advisory Groups (RAG). Site-visit teams had been reviewing the overall research programs at medical centers with medium- and large-sized research budgets. Except for occasional Central Office staff member administrative site visits, medical centers with total budgets below $550,000 per year had not ordinarily been visited. Central Office staff often were not familiar with how these smaller research programs were using their money.

Medical Research Service staff wanted to protect the two most highly regarded programs, the Research Career Development and Cooperative Studies Programs. Both had been maintained at constant budgets during the recent budget squeeze.

The VA's medical research budget had grown steadily during the 1950s and 1960s but had leveled off after fiscal year 1975. At the same time, the program, which received Congressional attention in earlier days, was now relatively "invisible." While the Department of Medicine and Surgery and the Administrator's Office spoke of the importance of the program, they did not seek increased budgets. Research received relatively little attention in the VA's congressional hearings. Despite all the publicity and recognition on Capitol Hill that had been generated, even the 1977 Nobel prizes won by VA scientists Rosalyn Yalow and Andrew Schally, the picture had not changed.

Settling on a plan

After they learned of the proposed FY 1979 budget cut, the Medical Research Service staff evaluated three potential response options:
   1. A year of "no new initiatives." With this plan, they would make no new starts in high priority programs, not start research where it didn't already exist (including in newly constructed hospitals), nor support new affiliations or newly recruited staff.
   2. Redirect funds by a variety of budgetary manipulations, including restricting dollar

support for any individual investigator or any medical center. Some advisors felt they should cut off funds of part-time VA staff. Others recommended a retroactive application of a merit review "pay line." All these options involved reneging on a commitment made after peer review approval of the research's scientific merit. All but the last, they believed, would undercut the research of some of the VA's best investigators.

3. The third approach, that which earned the sobriquet "Project Scissors," was to entirely cut off funding from medical centers with marginal programs. The rationale was that a research program needs a "critical mass" of scientists in order to maintain quality. The National Research Council of the National Academy of Sciences in its 1976 report, *Biomedical Research in the Veterans Administration*, had recommended withdrawing research support from hospitals not affiliated with medical schools. Other advisors agreed with that approach. Review of funding patterns showed that, with few exceptions, hospitals with small research programs put proportionally more support into common resources and into projects that had been approved only locally, with less support provided for Merit Review-approved research.

Of the three options considered, cutting off smaller programs involved the fewest Merit Review-approved programs and was the approach chosen. Many medical centers would be affected. Depending on which were finally identified, approximately 55 with the smallest research budgets would need to be cut to save the necessary monies. In response to advice from the Research Advisory Committee, Medical Research Service also decided to place a $100,000 limit on the VA support of any investigator's program.

The author was prominently involved in these deliberations and actions, having been Director of VA Medical Research for more than three years. Thomas Newcomb, M.D., the ACMD/R&D, worked closely with the author in evaluating options and agreed on this approach. It next needed to be discussed with those higher in the VA administration. Newcomb asked Hays to present the plan to Dr. Chase, the Chief Medical Director and Dr. Thomas Fitzgerald, the deputy in charge of medical center operations. The three discussed the adverse effects expected from each cost-cutting measure. Chase asked the author for her recommendation. She proposed cutting the small programs and offered to exercise care. She also recommended placing a $100,000 limit on the large individual programs, reasoning that these programs could remain viable and probably find other support. Chase agreed and said he would bring the matter to Administrator Cleland's attention, cautioning that they could not talk publicly about the budget until after the President's budget message of January 23, 1978.

Choosing the "Scissors" medical centers

To identify which medical centers' research programs to cut, the Medical Research Service staff decided that except for a few places with so little research support that they could persuade their management to accept an administrative decision, they would first visit the targeted sites.

The 75 medical centers with the least research funding were the likely candidates. The BECC staff at the Sepulveda (CA) VAMC, who handled the R&D Information System, coded and retrieved information about the abstracts, papers and books published by research investigators at these 75 medical centers. For balance, information was gathered about the 3 centers with the most research money. They decided to site visit all but one of the medical centers on the list that received total funds of less than $300,000. The exception, a medical center with only $150,000, had produced so many publications in prestigious journals that they eliminated it from the "at risk" list. In the group with funding between $300,000 and $550,000, the decision to visit was made primarily on the basis of an index of medical journal publications used to score work being done at each location. After an analysis of the index, 11 medical centers, 10 of them with research funding over $300,000 per year, escaped further review.

Eight medical centers with research funding under $12,000 per year were "zeroed out" after the author called the Medical Center Director to discuss the situation. The Director of a ninth medical center that had received only $936 that year persuaded the author to make a site visit because of their pending medical school affiliation.

The 58 medical centers to be site visited included all the others with research funding below $150,000, 16 of the 17 with funding between $150,000 and $300,000 and 7 of 17 with research funding between $300,000 and $550,000.

The site visit teams

Twelve teams of site visitors were selected. Each team consisted of two members, an Associate Chief of Staff for Research and Development (ACOS/R&D) from a VA medical center and a VA clinician scientist. All of the site visitors had Merit Review funding of their own research. Generally, one team member was from a medical center with a large research program and one from a modest program. Each site visitor made three to five visits, some with one partner and others with another partner.

Site visitors were recruited by telephone. They were asked to commit time during late January and early February and also to attend a meeting in Central Office February 22 and 23, 1978. Despite the amount of time requested, the embargo on budget information prevented any of them from knowing the purpose of their visits.

By Christmas, all site visitors had received information about their partners and which hospitals they would visit. Medical Research Service had formally requested permission for their participation from their medical center directors and had also notified those programs that would be site visited, telling them when the visit would be and who would be visiting. They could not, of course, be told *why* they were being visited. During January, materials for site visitors were compiled. The BECC group at Sepulveda assembled packets showing each hospital's funding pattern for the past four years and listing all investigators with their funding histories, roles in the medical center, salary source, publication histories and the amount of time they reported spending on research. These information packets were sent to the medical centers for verification and updating. The updated information was ready for the site visitors when they arrived. A site visitors' questionnaire was developed to help them make succinct evaluations.

Announcing "Project Scissors"

In early January, other persons in Central Office were notified about these plans, including the list of the medical centers to be site visited between January 23 and February 20. Representatives of the other major offices in the Department of Medicine and Surgery were invited to the February 22-23 meeting.

On January 23,1978, President Carter announced his budget plan to Congress. That morning, the author read this message on a conference call to all the research programs:

"As you may know, today is the day that President Carter announces his Fiscal Year 1979 budgetary recommendations to the Congress. This budget has been prepared by the Office of Management and Budget after considering the needs of all parts of the executive branch of the government. The President's budget request for Fiscal Year 1979 will impose a severe constraint on the medical research budget. This means that drastic action has become necessary. A number of options are possible, and they have been discussed, not only within R&D but with the Chief Medical Director and the Administrator.

"Two decisions have been made. The first is that, with but a few exceptions in high priority research areas, we will place a $100,000 ceiling on the funding of programs of individual investigators. The second, more far-reaching decision is to terminate medical research funding in many health-care facilities. In a few cases, I have already talked to the Directors of the facilities and informed them that no FY 1979 funds will be sent. The other facilities are still in process of being identified.

"Site visits to selected hospitals will occur during the next month. The visitors are being asked to assemble as strong a case as they can for maintaining medical research funding at the hospitals they visit. I'm sure that those of you who are being visited will help them to do this. On February 22 and 23, there will be a meeting here in Washington at which the site visitors will present their findings. As a result of this meeting, we will assemble a listing of the facilities, ranking them according to our best assessment of the relative importance of maintaining the medical research program.

"As things look now, basic institutional medical research funding will have to be terminated in the majority of the facilities being site visited. This is a process that will be very painful. We would like to assist investigators at the facilities where funding is to be discontinued who have high priority merit review approvals, and who wish to do so, to transfer to facilities with continuing programs. If those of you who are not being site visited during the next month, and hence who are not in jeopardy of losing your medical research programs, will inform us of your staffing needs, we may be able to help you locate some fine investigators.

"In addition to this stricture on our operating budget, the current FY 1979 construction budget contains no major or minor research construction.

"There is still hope, of course, that the final budget allocation from the Congress will make this entire effort needless. I sincerely hope that, in the end, it turns out to have been a waste of time and effort. But we have no real reason to believe that this hope has any basis. We have, therefore, no choice but to proceed on the assumption that the current budget is to be the final budget."

The announcement left people stunned. While many site visitors had suspected something like this was in the wind, others were shocked to be involved in such an unpleasant process. People at the affected medical centers were understandably upset.

Medical Research Service prepared a letter to site visitors, for distribution coinciding with the President's budget announcement, explaining what was going on and containing a suggested agenda. If the program was affiliated, they were asked to visit the medical school or to talk to its representatives. They were expected to meet with the Research and Development Committee to review their procedures and attitudes and to try to interview all of the research investigators. Site visitors were asked to orient their visits to the positive. They were to serve, in the late February meeting, as advocates for medical centers they had visited. Obviously, salient negative aspects should be included. However, their primary role was to present reasons the program *should* be continued, rather than the opposite.

The next month was one of frantic activity. A number of site visitors became so upset by the turmoil their visits caused at medical centers that they protested.

The caucus

By the February 22-23 meeting, emotions among site visitors had reached a high pitch. One ACOS/R&D devised a plan by which site visitors would agree to vote unanimously a top score to all programs reviewed. This would, in effect, eliminate the possibility of using site visit results. He decided to drop this approach when another ACOS organized a February 21 caucus of site visitors to consider a joint stand. He proposed that the caucus consider stating that:

"1. The site visitors are unwilling and unable to advise Research Service in Central Office about which individual hospitals should have their research programs completely eliminated.
2. The administrative officers in Central Office Research Service who have decided on this policy should implement it themselves without help.
3. They should evaluate the adverse effects of this implementation.
4. The caucus members understand that other alternative policies might well result in significant restrictions of funds to their own institutions."

This caucus met as planned and later asked the author to join the meeting for her response to the sentiments expressed by the group. She explained that all were hoping that none of the process would prove necessary, as work was being done on a number of fronts to try to influence Congress to increase the budget. However, it was necessary to prepare for the possibility of no increase. She explained that their descriptive input was critical to the meeting, but that their votes, while helpful, were not essential. She again asked them to present all of the arguments they could muster in favor of retaining research at each of the medical centers they represented.

The group agreed jointly to vote a simple yes-no question. For each medical center, each attendee would vote that the program be retained or discontinued. If all site visitors wanted to vote for continuing all programs, their input would nevertheless be useful to other attendees in making decisions. The author pointed out that, in their presentations, the comment that "I would gladly give up money from my own program to retain this program" would indeed be a strong argument. After considerable discussion, this approach was accepted. The author agreed to put the caucus resolutions on the agenda first thing in the morning.

The Meeting

The next days' meetings were attended by 95 persons, site visitors, representatives from other parts of Central Office and most VA Medical Research field advisors. Each was given information about the medical centers to be reviewed and asked to vote either to retain or discontinue each program. The medical centers were reviewed in groups relatively comparable to each other, eight or nine in a group. For each medical center, the site visit team leader and his partner described their visit. At the end of each group of presentations, the assemblage reviewed the medical centers in the group and made an effort to rate them against each other. Attendees rated the medical centers as they heard about them, and also reviewed their ratings at the end of the second afternoon in light of what they had heard about the entire group. The site visitors were true to their task of presenting the positive side, but, in some cases, it became apparent that some research money was indeed being wasted. As time went on, site visitors and other attendees began to work from the same viewpoint.

By the end of the second day, a consensus had emerged about a number of issues:

- Even at medical centers with the smallest programs and a fair degree of mediocrity, there were occasional bright lights. Individual scientists managed to carry out excellent research despite lack of a supportive environment. There was general consensus that these persons should be allowed to continue.
- Frequently, money allocated outside of peer review, for administrative support and small projects, was not being used well.
- Smaller research programs would benefit from outside support of the type provided by the university in closely affiliated medical centers. The group considered pairing smaller centers with stronger ones.

Also by the end of the second day, a proposal emerged that the VA set up Regional Offices to administer smaller research programs. These offices would take over administrative chores now being done at each medical center. Administrative monetary support would be given to the Regional Offices to support the assigned research programs, rather than directly to the medical centers. The Regional Offices would also provide scientific support and "know-how" for their research programs.

Waiting

Over the next few months, the threatened program cutoffs received considerable attention. The impact was brought up in congressional hearings, stimulating specific research program hearings by the Senate Veterans Affairs Committee. Medical Research Service was invited to defend its position in meetings with a number of Members of Congress. Contacts with Senators and Representatives were coming from many of the affected medical centers and Cleland was being pressured to have the White House reconsider VA's research budget.

The next months were anxious times for the medical centers at risk as they waited for final resolution of the budget in Congress. It was not until almost the beginning of the next fiscal year that the final budget was signed containing a $10 million increase for Medical Research. As a result, it was possible to continue medical research funding at all of the medical centers that had been visited.

One year later

Toward the end of fiscal year 1979, the author wrote to the visited medical centers, requesting feedback about the effects of the review process. Research at 49 of the site-visited medical centers had now come under the jurisdiction of the two new Regional Offices; as a result they had little or no local discretionary research monies. On the other hand, the Chiefs of the Regional Research and Development Offices had, by this time, visited them all. Responses about the Regional Offices ranged from "it is another level of bureaucracy" and "the loss of our autonomy is bad" to "it is our only source of hope," and "it was the major positive effect of the process."

One of the medical centers, which subsequently showed an increase in both funding and activity, complained of the enormous amount of time required for preparation for the site visit. But the outcome was generally positive, as the research program had received significant support from top hospital management, substantive support from its affiliated university, input from the veterans' organizations, and strong support from their Members of Congress. The director of one hospital with a small research program, that had decided to close out research entirely, said the site visit had helped set their priorities when they realized they were not an appropriate site for a research program.

Another medical center, which reported decreases in funding and activity since the site visit, said that their program was in serious difficulty now and had lost five people. They said that the top hospital administration had assumed that their program would be discontinued and the affiliation was in jeopardy. On the other hand, a comparable hospital in the same funding range reported increased activity. Their medical school and community support had increased, and they had made the decision to push their affiliation. Another medical center that had increased its research activity since the visit described the severe negative effect on local morale, despite having received a great deal of support from medical center management, the school, the community, and Members of Congress.

With regard to the site visit process itself, a number of hospital officials wrote that it had been instructive and helpful and had improved communications with Central Office.

Many, however, complained of the long period of uncertainty, and pointed out that a written game plan would have been helpful. They described the drain on the time of the ACOS's seeking personnel replacements. "We cannot over-emphasize the negative effect resulting from ambiguous communications from Central Office. Obviously the whole system would work better if Central Office provided continuous encouragement rather than continued threat of withdrawal of financial support." And "The period of time between notification of the site visit and receipt of fiscal year 1979 budget information was fraught with uncertainty, dampening of research activities and resigning of research staff."

The individual impact on members of the research program included personal stress and discouragement. Some continued to feel pessimistic despite the restoration of their funds. There was resentment about the threat that small programs were to be cannibalized by the large, well-organized, well-staffed and well-funded research centers. Some responders said that it was now hard to interest physicians in research and that the enthusiasm among clinicians to engage in relatively minor direct-care-related projects had been dampened. "There's a feeling among the clinical staff . . . that VACO is unsympathetic to their commitment to the VA and the contributions they have made to this hospital." On the other hand, another hospital reported that the process had increased the support for research by the patient-care elements. They have "closed the ranks between various professions and focused attention on the need for research." Another said, "Many individuals involved in patient care, but only peripherally concerned with research, expressed great dismay about possible loss of the research program and felt they could not remain affiliated with a VA Medical Center where research was not done."

Other hospitals reported that "to the extent that the department chairmen, dean, and faculty of the school were unified in their support of the research program, the site visit was beneficial in making school officials recognize the critical need for research support for full-time academic faculty recruited to the VA."

With regard to the lessons learned, respondents discussed reassessment of their priorities and recognition of the need to improve their procedures and accountability. They had also learned from site visitors about the importance of RAG and Merit Review and exploration for extra-VA funds. A number also mentioned an increased awareness of the value of maintaining good communications with veterans groups and Congressional representatives. As one respondent said, "Now that the eyes of many are on us, if we do not deliver, with some haste, a high level of productivity, then time may not grant us a second respite."

Ten years later

In the aftermath of "Project Scissors," 49 research programs were assigned for their administrative support to the Eastern Research and Development Office at Perry Point (MD) with William Pare, Ph.D. as Chief, or to the Western Research and Development Office at Livermore (CA) with Werner Schlapfer, Ph.D., Chief. Of the 49 medical centers whose research was originally assigned to the regional offices, 23 had no Merit Review or RAG programs in 1978 and so were funded only through the Regional Research and Development Offices. The other 26 programs had one or more approved RAG or Merit Review programs and continued to receive funds. But the regionalized medical centers received no other direct funding. Instead, they were dependent for their support from the Regional Offices.

By 1988, 15 of the site-visited medical centers originally "zeroed out" had abandoned research. On the other hand, 13 medical centers that had received no research funds at all in fiscal year 1978 (and had not been reviewed in Project Scissors) were now receiving research funds. In most cases, the Regional Offices had played a major role in helping those "new" medical centers to establish research programs.

Three programs originally not regionalized became so weak that they were subsequently added to the Regional Offices' responsibility. One of them, after working closely with the Regional Office for 4 years, revived and regained independence in 1986. Another program that was originally regionalized was made independent in 1982, and a third was expected to become independent late in 1988. There were a few rather spectacular successes. One program that had no research at all in 1978 had three funded Merit Reviews, two RAG's, and one Clinical Investigator in 1988. Another had four Merit Review approved investigators in 1988, and a third had three. Another hospital, just beginning its affiliation in 1978 and with only one investigator, now had eight funded investigators receiving more than $400,000 in annual support.

Fifteen medical centers site-visited during Project Scissors were not assigned to regional offices. Their research programs seemed to be large enough to constitute a "critical mass" and to be well administered locally. Comparing the relative funding positions 5 and 10 years later for these 15 medical centers with those of 11 medical centers in approximately the same funding range that were not site visited, there was surprisingly little difference between the two groups of medical centers. If we assume that publication productivity is a reasonable predictor, we would have expected the medical centers that were site visited to do considerably less well than those that were spared. It is possible that the experience of being site visited under threatening circumstances stimulated the success of some of their research programs.

Total number of funded medical centers

Perhaps the most unexpected outcome of Project Scissors was stabilization of the total number of medical centers receiving research funds. This number had been declining year by year just before 1978. In fiscal year 1978, 127 medical centers received Medical Research money; in 1988, there were 125. This stabilization most likely can be credited to the Regional Office Chiefs, who actively encouraged and helped investigators from small research programs who wished to compete in research to do so.

Policy impact of Project Scissors

The general principles suggested by the Project Scissors site visitors, and later endorsed by other advisors, remained in place 10 years later and continued in subsequent years. A qualified and motivated person at any VA medical center, with local approval, may compete for research funds through the peer review processes. While the medical centers that have done well usually continue to be those with strong medical school affiliations, no restriction exists on opportunities for investigators from the other medical centers.

Chapter 18. The Cooperative Studies Program of the 1970s

As the 1960s progressed, Lawrence Shaw increased his role as Chief of the Cooperative Studies program. He brought together the program, establishing both a strong Cooperative Studies Evaluation Committee (CSEC) and Cooperative Studies Program Coordinating Centers (CSPCCs). By the end of his tenure in 1972, while he had not yet brought psychiatry studies under the centralized program, the program had become fairly well unified. Shaw had come up through the ranks in Central Office. His manner was rather low-key; the success of his leadership depended on eliciting cooperation from those willing to cooperate.[1]

After Shaw retired in the spring of 1972, a search committee sought a new chief. Meantime, William Best, M.D., from Hines (IL), acted as chief. He commuted back and forth to Washington, trying to hold the Cooperative Studies program together. Best was on the search committee and contacted James Hagans, M.D., Ph.D., to see if he would be interested in taking the job.[2] Hagans had personal reasons to stay in Miami, and turned down the job. However, because the Chief of the Cooperative Studies program spends considerable time away from his office, it was finally decided that the office need not be based in Washington as long as the Chief made frequent trips to Central Office. So, Hagans was approached again, this time with the prospect of establishing an office in Miami from which to administer the Cooperative Studies Program. Dr. Thomas Newcomb, who had recently accepted the position of Director, Research Service, and had not yet come to Washington, was attending a meeting in Hollywood, FL. He arranged to meet Hagans, who presented him with an overall plan for how he would run the Cooperative Studies program. The two reviewed it carefully, and Newcomb agreed that it seemed viable. Hagans accepted the position and immediately began to exert strong leadership in guiding the program in the direction he considered best.[3]

Figure 18.1 James Hagans, M.D., Ph.D.

Organizational changes

Hagan's first effort was to strengthen support of Cooperative Studies by the CSPCCs. In addition to the CSPCCs that had evolved from the old Regional Research Support Centers at Hines and West Haven, CT (Chapter 15), he started a CSPCC at Perry Point (MD). From the beginning, CNPRL, the Central Neuropsychiatric Research Laboratory, (Chapter 8) at Perry Point had handled statistical and planning support for cooperative studies in psychiatry. The Perry Point CSPCC evolved from that part of CNPRL's activities. Initially, it concentrated on psychiatric cooperative studies, but, as time went on, the responsibilities of the various CSPCCs became evenly distributed.

The CSPCCs at Hines and West Haven, reflecting their experience as Regional Research Support Centers, were still supporting local and regional research in addition to the Cooperative Studies. At first, Hagans forbade this. The incumbent chiefs of the centers were reluctant to change from their old missions, and there were gradual changes in leadership. Later, once the centers were functioning effectively in support of the nationwide Cooperative Studies, Hagans relaxed this rule to permit some support of the local research program in exchange for hosting the centers.

By 1978, the three CSPCCs were working at capacity, and Hagans decided that a new CSPCC was needed on the west coast. After a competition among medical centers wanting to host such a center, Palo Alto (CA) was chosen as the site for the fourth CSPCC. By 1980, all four CSPCCs were receiving new studies in rotation covering all types of disciplines. The four chiefs and their administrators met regularly. Guidelines were established and accepted by all. Administration of the studies was predictable and carefully supervised.

A central pharmacy was established in 1972 at the Washington (DC) VA Medical Center. This pharmacy now coordinated all studies using drugs or experimental devices, instead of the ad hoc systems of the past. By the late 1970s, the central pharmacy had outgrown its space at the Washington hospital and was moved to the Albuquerque (NM) VA Medical Center. This Cooperative Studies Program Clinical Research Pharmacy Coordinating Center (CSPCRPCC) has grown to become an important player in the program, participating in study design, manufacturing study drugs, keeping close track of study drugs and devices and reviewing the protection of human subjects at the various study sites.[3]

Under Hagans, the Cooperative Studies Program evolved from the rather relaxed program of past times, largely decentralized and encouraging individual initiative, to a much more centralized program with strict attention to statistics and experimental design. Some study groups with a longstanding record of one study after another became less active. As funding became increasingly limited, Hagans worked to find other sources of funds, especially from the NIH. He accepted some funds from private firms, but with very careful controls to prevent conflicts of interest.

Dr. Hagans introduced a structured system in which an investigator with an idea for a cooperative study first submitted a "précis," a brief description of the proposed study. A triage group reviewed it; many proposed studies were rejected at this stage. If approved by triage, the proposal was assigned to one of the CSPCCs and a formal planning process began. A committee, including the investigator and other subject-area experts as well as statisticians from the CSPCC, met several times to complete a plan. The polished proposal eventually went before the Cooperative Studies Evaluation Committee (CSEC) for review. If approved by CSEC (Appendix IIi), it joined a queue for funding.

Hagans insisted that, in the Cooperative Studies Program, separate groups perform the research, direct the project, and evaluate it. Hence, he arranged meetings of the groups of investigators from the cooperating hospitals, the people actually carrying out the research. In addition, an "Operations Committee" reviewed data at regular intervals and directed the project. Of the participants in a Cooperative Study, only the chairman also served on this committee, which made such critical decisions as when a participating hospital was not performing adequately and should be dropped, when an arm of the study should be changed or dropped owing to interim statistical results and when the study had achieved its goal. Evaluation was by CSEC, which reviewed proposed projects and also ongoing projects to determine if, after 3 years, they warranted continuation.

In addition, each CSPCC maintained a Human Rights Committee to review each project annually for the protection of subjects. This committee served as an additional protection, adding a second human rights review to that performed by the Institutional Review Board at each participating medical center.

The studies

The cooperative studies begun in the 1970s (Table 18.1) differed from earlier studies. Each now had a crisply defined goal and clear endpoint. Though some pilot studies were completed, they were limited in scope and limited to defining the feasibility of a specific study. Whereas earlier study groups set their own goals and sometimes freely departed from their primary studies, now an outside group carefully monitored each variation in study design. Some of the longstanding study groups adapted to this new system; others closed.

The group of hypertension researchers (Chapter 9) continued to conduct new studies under the new system, as did the group of cardiologists and surgeons studying the impact of coronary artery surgery on patients with coronary artery disease. On the other hand, the pulmonary study group that had started with the 1946 tuberculosis trials (Chapter 5) held its last published meeting in 1972 and completed its last report in 1974. The studies of analgesics (Chapter 13) and of psychopharmaceuticals (Chapter 8), that had performed one study after another without CSEC review, closed during the mid-1970s, in part because their leaders found it more difficult to work within the new system.

Table 18.1. Cooperative studies started during the 1970s

Medical
Antihypertensive drugs

Propranolol	1972–1975
Bethedine vs guanethedine in severe hypertension	1972-1975
Efficacy of treatment of mild hypertension (pilot)	1974–1977
Prazosin vs hydralazine	1976–1977
Oxyprenolol vs propranolol	1976–1977

Ticrynafen vs hydrochlorothiazide	1977–1978
Propranolol vs hydrochlorothiazide as first hyptertension rx	1978–1980
Low dose reserpine with chlorthalidone	1978–1980
Captopril	1980–1982
Nadolol	1980–1981
Hepatitis	
Immune vs hyperimmune globulin in needlestick	1972–1976
Immune vs hyperimmune serum globulin in post-transfusion	1973–1976
Hepatitis and drug abuse (observational)	1973–1976
Hepatitis and dentistry	1979–1981
Alcoholic hepatitis	1978–1983
Sickle cell trait	1972–1976
Crohn's Disease	
Prednisone, sulfasalazine, azathioprine, placebo	1972–1977
Sulfasalazine plus prednisone vs prednisone	1976–1977
Medical treatment of heart disease	
Aspirin therapy in unstable angina	1974–1982
Vasodilator therapy of myocardial infarction	1974–1981
Vasodilators in chronic heart failure	1980–1985
Renal failure self-care dialysis	1975–1981
Platelet aggregation in diabetes (aspirin and persantine)	1977–1983
Anticoagulants in the treatment of cancer	1977–1981
Urinary tract infections	1976–1978
Nafcillin therapy in staphylococcal bacteremia	1979–1981
Antiepileptic drugs	1978–1984

Surgical

Surgery of coronary artery disease	
Stable angina (vein bypass)	1970–1974+20yr FU
Unstable angina (vein bypass)	1976–1982+10yr FU
Radiotherapy vs surgery vs delayed hormonal rx in prostate ca	1974–1981
Bowel preparation for colon operations	
Placebo vs active therapy	1975–1976
Oral vs oral plus iv	1976–1982
Heart valve replacement	1977–1995
Surgical shunt vs medical treatment in alcoholic cirrhosis ascites	1979–1984

Neuropsychiatric

Drugs and sleep	1975–1977
Treatment of psychotic patients	
Hospital vs community foster care	1970–1974
Day treatment in aftercare	1973–1977
Characteristics of effective ward milieu	1975–1978
Community vs VA nursing home vs hospital	1978–1982
Aphasia	
Individual vs group therapy	1973–1977
Hospital vs home treatment	1979–1983
Alcohol and drug dependence	
LAAM-methadone	1973–1975
Antabuse in rx of alcoholics on methadone maintenance	1977–1980
Antabuse in the treatment of alcoholism	1979–1983
Lithium in alcoholics (pilot)	1979

Dental

Plaque control	1978–1982
Dental implants	1978–1990
Alloys for dental restorations	1980–1990

Sickle cell trait

An important study begun in 1972 determined the clinical importance of sickle cell trait (Hb AS) and glucose-6-phosphate dehydrogenase deficiency (G-6-PD). The chair was Paul Heller, M.D., of the Chicago West Side VA Medical Center. While the homozygous abnormality (Hb SS), known as sickle-cell anemia, causes a well-known illness, it was not known whether the heterozygous Hb AS caused any problems. G-6-PD also is fairly common in African Americans, and its impact was also unknown. Anecdotal reports had suggested that sickle-cell trait would cause an increase in pulmonary infarctions, vascular complications of diabetes, deaths from myocardial infarction and prolonged hospitalization after surgery. G-6-PD was thought to be associated with increased infections, especially pneumonia. Patients with both abnormalities were expected to have longer hospital stays and increased mortality.

This prevalence study screened 65,154 African-American patients at 15 VA medical centers for these two abnormalities. Sickle cell trait was present in 7.8 percent, G-6-DP in 11.2 percent and both abnormalities in 0.9%. Clinical data were retrieved from the VA centralized Patient Treatment File on 4,900 patients with sickle cell trait, 1,422 with hemoglobin C trait, 6,741 with G-6-PD and 18,294 with normal hemoglobin. Contrary to expectations, the only significant effects of sickle cell trait were found to be essential hematuria and a small increase in the incidence of pulmonary infarction. G-6-DP and hemoglobin C trait had no adverse effect at all.

This study made possible the reassurance of the many patients found to have sickle-cell trait among those screened for sickle-cell disease and the alleviation of anxiety of patients with hemoglobin C and G-6-DP. It also provided important information about the frequency of hemoglobin abnormalities, including some of the rarer types. One previously undescribed abnormal hemoglobin (Hemoglobin Arlington Park) was identified among the 65,154 patients screened.[4]

Hepatitis

A series of studies of transfusion-related hepatitis also had an important impact. A study begun in 1969 compared the effectiveness of a preparation of immune serum globulin (ISG) in preventing transfusion-related hepatitis. Incidence of hepatitis was significantly reduced with ISG. Of especial importance was the finding that only a quarter of the cases of hepatitis were due to the hepatitis B virus. The others were caused by a previously unrecognized virus, originally called nonA-nonB hepatitis, now known as hepatitis C. When investigators traced the origins of the transfused blood, they found that the nonA-nonB virus was associated with commercially available blood but not with donated blood. This important finding, confirmed in later studies, led to the effort to fill needs for blood from healthy volunteer donors rather than from paid donors who were more likely to carry the nonA-nonB virus.[5]

These findings were confirmed in studies comparing ISG with a serum globulin hyperimmune to hepatitis B (HBIG) in preventing post-transfusion hepatitis B and also needlestick hepatitis.[6] HBIG was more effective than ISG in preventing hepatitis B but not in preventing nonA-nonB hepatitis.

These investigators also searched for evidence of liver disease in asymptomatic parenteral narcotic drug abusers. They found that the majority had laboratory evidence of liver disease and determined that repeated liver biopsies would be needed to screen adequately for liver disease in these patients.[7]

Another group studied the efficacy of 30 days of treatment with either a glucocorticosteroid (prednisolone) or an anabolic steroid (oxandrolone) in moderate or severe alcoholic hepatitis. Of the patient population studied, 132 with moderate disease and 131 with severe disease were randomly assigned to one of three treatments: prednisolone, oxandrolone, or placebo. In the 30-day period, mortality did not differ significantly in the groups receiving steroid therapy from mortality in the placebo group: 13 percent of moderately ill patients and 29 percent of severely ill patients died. But although neither steroid improved short-term survival, oxandrolone therapy was associated with improved long-term survival, especially in patients with moderate disease. Among those who survived for 1 or 2 months after the start of treatment the 6-month death rate was 3.5 percent after oxandrolone and 19–20 percent after placebo (P = 0.02). No consistent long-term effect was associated with prednisolone therapy.[8]

A study of hepatitis and dentistry conducted at 126 VA dental clinics between 1979 and 1981 enrolled 963 dental personnel. At that time, universal precautions (gloves and mask) were not yet widespread in dentistry, and exposure to hepatitis-infected blood and saliva from patients was likely. The study showed that serological evidence of hepatitis B infection increased with the number of years working in the dental environment, from 7.4 percent for those working 5 or fewer years to 17.8 percent for those working more than 30 years. As a result of this study, immunization to hepatitis B was strongly recommended for dental workers.[9]

Cardiology studies

Surgery of coronary artery disease

Although the group that had been evaluating surgical operations for coronary artery disease (Chapter 13) began to include patients undergoing coronary artery bypass surgery (CABG) in 1970, they began their definitive study of this procedure in 1972. Between 1972 and 1974, 686 patients were enrolled by 13 VA hospitals.

The criteria for enrolling a patient in this protocol were carefully defined, and only eligible patients were invited to participate. Randomization to medical or surgical treatment was done centrally by the West Haven (CT) CSPCC.

Soon after intake into the study was completed in December, 1974, preliminary statistical analysis showed that the 91 patients who had obstruction of the left main coronary artery had a better survival rate if they received surgery than if they were maintained on medical treatment. This result was published and well received.[10]

However, the results of studying the remaining 595 patients, followed on an average of 36 months, showed no significant difference between the surgically and medically treated groups.[11] This report stimulated a vigorous response from advocates of the procedure, and considerable controversy.[12]

However, the VA supported its cooperative study group, who continued their studies to further refine the circumstances that warranted surgery in this condition. After longer follow-up and further study, they defined other "high risk" conditions, in addition to left main coronary artery obstruction, that favored surgery. The results of these studies, and of subsequent work by others, led to guidelines for the selection of patients who would benefit from CABG.[13]

Aspirin in unstable angina

Twelve VA medical centers participated in a double-blind, placebo-controlled randomized trial of aspirin treatment (324 mg in buffered solution daily) taken for 12 weeks by 1,266 men with unstable angina (625 taking aspirin and 641 placebo). The incidence of death or acute myocardial infarction was 51 percent lower in the aspirin group than in the placebo group, with no difference in gastrointestinal symptoms or evidence of blood loss between the two groups.

This study showed that aspirin has a protective effect against acute myocardial infarction in men with unstable angina.[14] This was among the first of over 100 studies of the effect of antiplatelet therapy in preventing myocardial infarction and death in patients with unstable angina. It has been cited countless times in support of using aspirin in these patients, a therapy that has become standard in medical practice.

Acute myocardial infarction with left ventricular failure

Between 1975 and 1981, 11 VA medical centers cooperated in a study of whether the vasodilator nitroprusside would improve the outcome in patients with acute myocardial infarctions complicated by increased left ventricular filling pressure. While nitroprusside was already in widespread use in this situation, it carried the risk of decreased coronary blood flow. An objective study of its risks and benefits was needed. The randomized double-blind, placebo-controlled trial assessed the efficacy of a 48-hour infusion of sodium nitroprusside in 812 men with presumed acute myocardial infarction and left ventricular filling pressure of at least 12 mm Hg who volunteered for the study. The results were complex. Overall mortality rates at 21 days (10.4 percent in the placebo group and 11.5 percent in the nitroprusside group) and at 13 weeks (19.0 percent and 17.0 percent, respectively) were not significantly affected by treatment. However, timing was critical: The drug had a deleterious effect in patients whose infusions were started within 9 hours of the onset of pain (mortality at 13 weeks, 24.2 percent vs. 12.7 percent; $P = 0.025$), but it had a beneficial effect in those whose infusions were begun later (mortality at 13 weeks, 14.4 percent vs. 22.3 percent; $P = 0.04$). The investigators concluded that nitroprusside should probably not be used routinely in patients with high left ventricular filling pressures after acute myocardial infarction, but that patients with persistent pump failure might receive sustained benefit from short-term nitroprusside therapy.[15]

Chronic congestive heart failure

Congestive heart failure continues to be a major cause of death among veterans as well as in the general population. In 1980, 11 VA medical centers undertook a study to see whether treatment with vasodilators would improve the life span of patients with this disorder. They randomly assigned 642 consenting men with impaired cardiac function and reduced exercise tolerance who were already taking digoxin and a diuretic for their heart failure to receive additional double-blind treatment. This involved placebo, prazosin (20 mg per day) or the vasodilating combination of hydralazine (300 mg per day) and isosorbide dinitrate (160 mg per day). Follow-up averaged 2.3 years (range, 6 months to 5.7 years). At 2 years, mortality was reduced by 34 percent among patients treated with hydralazine and isosorbide dinitrate ($P<0.028$), 25.6 percent in the hydralazine-isosorbide dinitrate group versus 34.3 percent in the placebo group; at 3 years, mortality was reduced 36 percent (36.2 percent versus 46.9 percent). Mortality in the prazosin group was similar to that in the placebo group. Left ventricular ejection fraction, a measure of left ventricular function, rose significantly at 8 weeks and at one year in the group treated with hydralazine and isosorbide dinitrate but not in the placebo or prazosin groups.

This study showed that the addition of hydralazine and isosorbide dinitrate to the therapeutic regimen of digoxin and diuretics in patients with chronic congestive heart failure can have a favorable effect on left ventricular function and mortality.[16]

Valvular heart disease

Improvements in cardiac surgery have allowed patients with damaged heart valves to receive valve replacements that correct their disorder. Both mechanical valves and animal (porcine) valves have been used, and both have their advantages and disadvantages. Mechanical heart valves are durable but are thrombogenic (tend to cause clotting), requiring that patients take anticoagulants. In contrast, bioprosthetic valves are less thrombogenic but are of limited durability owing to tissue deterioration. To compare the advantages and disadvantages of these two approaches, between 1977 and 1982 13 participating VA medical centers randomized 575 patients who needed replacement of their mitral or aortic heart valve to receive either a mechanical or porcine valve.

During an average follow-up of 11 years, no difference was found between the two groups in the probability of death from any cause or of any valve-related complication. A much higher rate of structural valve failure was experienced by patients who received bioprosthetic valves (11-year probability, 0.15 for aortic valves and 0.36 for mitral valves) than was experienced by those who received mechanical valves (no valve failures; $P<0.001$). However, this difference was offset by a higher rate of bleeding complications in patients with mechanical valves than in those with bioprosthetic valves (11-year probability, 0.42 and 0.26, respectively; $P<0.001$) and by a greater frequency of periprosthetic valvular regurgitation in patients with mechanical mitral valves than in those with mitral bioprostheses (11-year probability, 0.17 and 0.09, respectively; P = 0.05).

From the results of this study and the review of similar studies by others, the authors were able to provide guidance about which type of valve is better for a particular patient.[17]

Antibiotic prophylaxis in colon surgery

During the 1970s, some surgeons were using oral antibiotics to supplement mechanical bowel cleansing in preparing patients for surgery of the colon and rectum. This use, however, was controversial. In general, using antibiotics to prevent infection rather than treat it was considered unwise: bacterial flora were likely to become resistant to the antibiotics used, promoting the spread of resistant organisms in the individual patient and in the environment. On the other hand, small studies of the use of prophylactic oral antibiotics suggested that these fears were unfounded and that many infections could be avoided by prophylactic use of antibiotics.

To gain a better understanding of the potential value of antibiotic prophylaxis, a cooperative study was designed in which oral antibiotics (neomycin and erythromycin) or placebo were given the day before surgery in addition to vigorous mechanical cleansing of the bowel. The original plan had been to study 287 patients, the number projected for a clear-cut answer if infection rates were 20 percent without oral antibiotics and 10 percent with them. The difference revealed by the study was even more dramatic. Forty-three percent of patients in the placebo group developed infections, while only 9 percent of those receiving antibiotics the day before surgery did so.

This study reflected the wisdom of the system Hagans had established. Only the monitoring committee, the Operations Committee, saw the data and its statistical analysis on a periodic basis. The members of the Operations Committee did not actually enroll or follow the patients in the study, so there was no way that their knowledge of the preliminary results could affect the objectivity of the study. When the Operations Committee reviewed the data from the first 116 patients, the answer to the study question was clear: antibiotic treatment conferred a benefit. At that point, the Operations Committee announced the results and stopped the study. Henceforth, patients were no longer jeopardized by receiving the less favorable treatment.[18] All would receive the benefit of prophylactic antibiotics to reduce the likelihood of infection.

On the other hand, a later study, which examined the benefit of adding intravenous antibiotics to the established preparatory regimen of mechanical bowel cleaning together with oral antibiotics, failed to show a significant advantage. In order to establish this negative finding, it was necessary to study 1,128 patients over a 5-year period. Even then, the results with added IV antibiotic were somewhat better, though not significantly so. A doubt remained that an even larger study might uncover a small preference for adding the IV antibiotic. Unlike the first study, which changed the practice of surgeons both in the VA and elsewhere, despite the tremendous effort it involved, this later study had much less impact.[19]

Recurrent urinary infections in men

The natural history and treatment of recurrent urinary infections in women had been well studied by the 1970s, but appropriate treatment in men was still not established. Studies in women had shown that antibiotic treatment of bladder infections was effective after only 10 days of treatment, while infections of the upper urinary tract required prolonged therapy. At 3 VA medical centers, 38 male patients with recurrent urinary infections, most with prostatic infection, were treated in a double blind study with either 10 days or 12 weeks of antibiotic therapy. The cure rate was better with 12 weeks, but the difference failed to reach significance (p=.06). Most patients given only 10 days treatment had recurrences with the same organism within 4 weeks.[20]

Anticoagulants in the treatment of cancer

By the end of the 1970s, considerable evidence had accumulated implicating blood coagulation reactions in the growth and spread of malignancy. It was found that platelets may accumulate on embolic tumor cells and facilitate their adhesion to the endothelium at distant sites, perhaps by enhancing blood coagulation reactions. Another possibility was that platelets may promote tumor cell proliferation by contributing a growth-promoting factor or through interactions mediated by prostaglandins. Inhibition of tumor growth and spread by platelet-inhibitory drugs had been demonstrated in several experimental tumor systems, and preliminary data suggested that similar effects were seen in human malignancy.[21]

To evaluate the importance of this evidence that spread of malignancy is associated with blood clotting mechanisms, between 1976 and 1981 thirteen VA medical centers studied the effect of warfarin anticoagulation on outcome in patients with cancer of the lung, colon and rectum, prostate, and head and neck. The most dramatic finding was that warfarin doubled the survival time of patients with small-cell carcinoma of the lung. Median survival for 25 control patients was 24 weeks; for 25 warfarin-treated patients, it was 50 weeks. This difference could not be accounted for by differences between groups in performance status, extent of disease, age, or sex. The survival advantage associated with warfarin administration was observed both for patients with extensive disease and for those who failed to achieve complete or partial remission. The warfarin-treated group also demonstrated a significantly increased time to first evidence of disease progression. These results suggested that warfarin was useful in the treatment of small-cell carcinoma of the lung and also supported the hypothesis that the blood coagulation mechanism is involved in the growth and spread of cancer in man. This result was so definitive that the Operations Committee decided to stop adding patients in the arm of the study involving small-cell lung cancer.[22]

On the other hand, no differences in survival were observed between warfarin-treated and control groups for the other cancers studied.[23]

Care of schizophrenic patients

Psychotropic drugs (Chapter 8) revolutionized the care of schizophrenic patients, but they did not cure them. A series of cooperative studies carried out in the 1970s, led by Margaret Linn, Ph.D., a social worker at the Miami VA Medical Center, studied the post-hospital treatment of these patients. One of the most important of these studies compared the effect of differing characteristics of day treatment programs. In this study, conducted in ten VA Day Treatment Centers between 1973 and 1977, schizophrenic patients who were eligible for day treatment at the time of hospital discharge were randomly assigned to receive day treatment plus drugs or drugs alone. They were tested before assignment and at 6, 12, 18, and 24 months on social functioning, symptoms, and attitudes. Community tenure and costs were also measured. The Day Treatment centers were described on process variables every 6 months for the 4 years of the study.

Some centers were found to be more effective than drugs alone in treating chronic schizophrenic patients, and others were not, although all of the Day Treatment centers improved the patients' social functioning. Six of the centers were found to significantly delay relapse, reduce symptoms, and change some attitudes. Costs for patients in the successful centers were not significantly different from costs for the group receiving only drugs. The centers with the most successful outcomes offered more occupational therapy and a sustained reassuring environment. Centers with a treatment philosophy encouraging high patient turnover had poorer results. Surprisingly, poorer results were also associated with centers that had more professional staff hours and group therapy.[24]

References

1. Interview with Lawrence W. Shaw, M.S., February 3, 1994 at Mr. Shaw's home in Gainesville, Florida.

2. Interview with William Best, M.D., April 26, 1994 at a hotel lobby in Washington, DC.

3. Telephone interview with James Hagans, M.D., Ph.D., April 24, 1988.

4. Heller, P., Best, W.R., Nelson, R.B. and Becktel, J., "Clinical implications of sickle-cell trait and glucose-6-phosphate dehydrogenase deficiency in hospitalized black male patients." *N Eng J Med*, 1979. **300**: 1001-1005.

5. Seeff, L.B., Wright, E.C., Zimmerman, H.J. and McCollum, R.W., "VA cooperative study of post-transfusion hepatitis, 1969-1974: incidence and characteristics of hepatitis and responsible risk factors." *Am J Med Sci*, 1975. **270**: 355-362.

6. Seeff, L.B., Wright, E.C., Finkelstein, J.D., Greenlee, H.B., Hamilton, J., Leevy, C.M., Tamburro, C.H., Vlahcevic, Z., Zimmon, D.S., Zimmerman, H.J., Felsher, B.F., Garcia-Pont, P., Dietz, A.A., Koff, R.S., Kiernan, T., Schiff, E.R., Zemel, R. and Nath, N., "Efficacy of hepatitis B immune serum globulin after accidental exposure." *Lancet*, 1975: 939-941.

7. Seeff, L.B., Zimmerman, H.J., Wright, E.C., Schiff, E.R., Kiernan, T., Leevy, C.M., Tamburro, C.H. and Ishak, K.G., "Hepatic disease in asymptomatic parenteral narcotic drug abusers: a Veterans Administration collaborative study." *Am J Med Sci*, 1975. **270**: 41-47.

8. Mendenhall, C.L., Anderson, S., Garcia-Pont, P., Goldberg, S., Kiernan, T., Seeff, L.B., Sorrell, M., Tamburro, C.H., Weesner, R., Zetterman, R., Chedid, A., Chen, T., Rabin, L. and Veterans Administration Cooperative Study on Alcoholic Hepatitis, "Short-term and long-term survival in patients with alcoholic hepatitis treated with oxandrolone and prednisolone." *N Engl J Med*, 1984. **311**: 1464-1470.

9. Schiff, E.R., de Medina, M.D., Kline, S.N., Johnson, G.R., Chan, Y.-K., Shorey, J., Calhoun, N. and Irish, E.F., "Veterans Administration cooperative study on hepatitis and dentistry." *JADA*, 1986. **113**: 390-396.

10. Takaro, T., Hultgren, H.N., Lipton, M.J., Detre, K.M. and participants in the study group, "The VA Cooperative Randomized Study of Surgery for Coronary Arterial Occlusive Disease II: Subgroup with significant left main lesions." *Circ*, 1976. **54**: III-107-117.

11. Murphy, M.L., Hultgren, H.N., Detre, K.M., Thomsen, J., Takaro, T. and Participants, "Treatment of chronic stable angina: A preliminary report of survival data of the randomized VA cooperative study." *New Engl J Med*, 1977. **297**: 621-627.

12. Jones, D.S., "Visions of a cure; visualizations, clinical trials and controversies in cardiac therapeutics, 1968-1998." *Isis*, 2000. **91**: 504-541.

13. Kirklin, J.W., Akins, C.W. and Blackstone, E.H., "ACC/AHA guidelines and indications for coronary artery bypass surgery. A report of the American College of Cardiology/American Heart Association Task Force on Assessment of Diagnostic and Therapeutic Cardiovascular Procedures (Subcommittee on Coronary Artery Bypass Surgery)." *Circ*, 1991. **83**: 1125-1173.

14. Lewis, H.D., Davis, J.W., Archibald, D.G., Steinke, W.E., Smitherman, T.C., Doherty, J.E., Schnaper, H.W., LeWinter, M.M., Linares, E., Pouget, J.M., Sabarwal, S.C., Chesler, E. and DeMots, H., "Protective effects of aspirin against acute myocardial infarction and death in men with unstable angina." *N Engl J Med*, 1983. **309**: 396-403.

15. Cohn, J.N., Franciosa, J.A., Francis, G.S., Archibald, D.G., Tristani, F., Fletcher, R., Montero, A., Cintron, G., Clarke, J., Hager, D., Saunders, R., Cobb, F., Smith, R., Loeb, H. and Settle, H., "Effect of short-term infusion of sodium nitroprusside on mortality rate in acute myocardial infarction complicated by left ventricular failure. Results of a Veterans Administration Cooperative Study." *N Engl J Med*, 1982. **306**: 1129-1135.

16. Cohn, J.N., Archibald, D.G., Ziesche, S., Franciosa, J.A., Harston, W.E., Tristani, F., Dunkman, W.B., Jacobs, W., Francis, G.S., Flohr, K.H., Goldman, S., Cobb, F.R., Shah, P.M., Saunders, R., Fletcher, R., Loeb, H., Hughes, V.C. and Baker, B., "Effect of vasodilator therapy on mortality in chronic congestive heart failure." *N Engl J Med*, 1986. **314**: 1547-1552.

17. Hammermeister, K.E., Sethi, G.K., Henderson, W.G., Oprian, C., Kim, T., Rahimtoola, S. and Veterans Administration Cooperative Study on Valvular Heart Disease, "A comparison of outcomes in men 11 years after heart-valve replacement with a mechanical valve or bioprosthesis." *N Engl J Med*, 1993. **328**: 1289-1296.

18. Clarke, J.S., Condon, R.E., Bartlett, J.G., Sherwood, L., Gorbach, L., Nichols, R.L. and Ochi, S., "Preoperative oral antibiotics reduce septic complications of colon operations." *Ann Surg*, 1977. **186**: 251-259.

19. Condon, R.E., Bartlett, J.G., Greenlee, H.B., Schulte, W.J., Ochi, S., Abbe, R., Caruana, J.A., Gordon, E., Horsley, S., Irvin, G., Johnson, W., Jordan, P., Keltzer, W.F., Lempke, R., Read, R.C., Schumer, W., Schwartz, M., Storm, R.K. and Vetto, R.M., "Efficacy of oral and systemic antibiotic prophylaxis in colorectal operations." *Ann Surg*, 1983. **118**: 496-502.

20. Smith, J.W., Jones, S.R., Reed, W.P., Tice, A.D., Deupree, R.H. and Kaijser, B., "Recurrent urinary tract infections in men. Characteristics and response to therapy." *Ann Int Med*, 1979. **91**: 544-548.

21. Zacharski, L.R., Henderson, W.G., Rickles, F.R., Forman, W.B., Cornell, C.J., Jr., Forcier, R.J., Harrower, H.W. and Johnson, R.O., "Rationale and experimental design for the VA Cooperative Study of Anticoagulation (Warfarin) in the Treatment of Cancer." *Cancer*, 1979. **44**: 732-741.

22. Zacharski, L.R., Henderson, W.G., Rickles, F.R., Forman, W.B., Cornell, C.J., Jr., Forcier, R.J., Edwards, R., Headley, E., Kim, S.H., O'Donnell, J.R., O'Dell, R., Tornyos, K. and Kwaan, H.C., "Effect of warfarin on survival in small cell carcinoma of the lung. Veterans Administration Study No. 75." *Jama*, 1981. **245**: 831-835.

23. Zacharski, L.R., Henderson, W.G., Rickles, F.R., Forman, W.B., Cornell, C.J., Forcier, J., Edwards, R.L., Headley, E., Kim, S.-H., O'Donnell, J.F., O'Dell, R., Tornyos, K. and Kwaan, H.C., "Effect of warfarin anticoagulation on survival in carcinoma of the lung, colon, head and neck, and prostate." *Cancer*, 1984. **53**: 2046-2052.

24. Linn, M.W., Caffey, E.M., Klett, C.J., Hogarty, G.E. and Lamb, H.R., "Day treatment and psychotropic drugs in the aftercare of schizophrenic patients." *Arch Gen Psychiatry*, 1979. **36**: 1055-1066.

Chapter 19. Beginnings of Health Services Research and Development in the VA

Today's VA Health Services R&D Service is a major player in the overall research effort in the VA and a leader in its field. It took shape in its present form during the 1970s, and its major growth occurred after 1990. However, the recent program has its roots in multiple earlier efforts.

Maximizing both the quality and cost effectiveness of medical care has always been a central concern for the VA. As early as 1929, the Veterans' Bureau's Medical Council (Chapter 1) asked the Bureau's Research Section to compare the standards of medical care in Bureau hospitals with civilian hospitals. After reviewing the data presented to them by the Research Section, the Council concluded: "There exist at present no satisfactory standards according to which treatment can be appraised. Neither civilian nor bureau institutions rate treatment according to the same, let alone uniform, standards."[1]

Today, the Bureau's descendant, the Department of Veterans Affairs, maintains a vigorous and well-coordinated program of Health Services Research and Development (HSR&D). It employs an interdisciplinary approach that draws upon all relevant scientific methodologies and applies the scientific method to evidence-based management to assure that health care decisions will be based on fact. Improving the practice of medicine within the context of reality is its central goal.

This approach is the result of the combination and evolution of many methodologies. These include the operations research methods developed during World War II, psychometrics (the mathematical, especially statistical, design of psychological tests and measures), economics, decision analysis and management theory as well as aspects of computer science and other disciplines. This chapter traces some of these methodologies and their early intertwining into the emerging HSR&D program of the 1970s.

The Fort Howard Program and the Management Systems and Standards Service

Signs of the VA's first formal effort to conduct research in how to improve health services appear in 1958, when a research program was launched by Dr. Linus Zink, head of the administrative section in the Central Office Department of Medicine and Surgery. To organize and direct this program, he recruited John Willoughby, then Assistant Manager at the Ann Arbor (MI) VA Hospital. The charge of this new Management Systems and Standards Service was to conduct research in how to develop efficient hospital systems, an effort fully backed by the Director of Professional Services at that time, Dr. Irving Cohen.

Willoughby directed the new Service from the Washington office, where Peter Korstad performed generalized hospital studies. For more innovative studies, Willoughby set up a unit at the Fort Howard (MD) VA Hospital. This unit's original responsibility was to work with hospital staff to minimize waste. Although there were concerns among the local staff that the findings could lead to layoffs, Cohen made it clear that the Fort Howard group's mission was not to achieve local savings, but to develop data that might be used in developing national priorities. Initially, the Fort Howard group did not address professional areas such as physician staffing, even though Cohen expressed the intention of extending the studies in that direction.[2]

Leon Gintzig, who held a Ph.D. in Hospital Administration, started and led the Fort Howard operation. About February 1960, John Peters was assigned to Fort Howard as associate director of what was now called the Health Services R&D (HSR&D) Service. The plan was to locate HSR&D on a research floor at the new Washington, D.C., VA hospital, which was under construction. Until it was completed, the group worked at Fort Howard.

At the Fort Howard Hospital, the HSR&D unit established the VA's first intensive-care unit to test the value of individual monitoring. They also tested a concept for reorganizing smaller hospitals by centralizing the administrative management into a single service. This was tried out at a half dozen test facilities.

Aware of the need to have medical information stored in a manner enabling easy extraction and analysis of data, they also tried to get a medical information system keyed into a computer but lacked the requisite technical competence to do this effectively. After the program was later moved to the new Washington, DC VA Hospital, this effort evolved into the Automated Hospital Information System (AHIS).[3]

The Central Office Administrative Research Program

In 1963, a Committee on Administrative and Developmental Research was formally announced to the field, with Peter Korstad as Chairman and seven other members including Charles Chapple of Research Service; Clyde Lindley, from the psychopharmacology studies; and Daniel Rosen, the highly respected head of the statistics program. The committee was charged to "review projects submitted for administrative and developmental research to recommend priorities for their initiation throughout the VA system." This included plans for the administrative and developmental research laboratory at the VA Hospital in Washington, DC.[4] Three years later, in 1966, this committee was replaced by an Administrative Research Committee charged with general advice and proposal review[5] and whose members were mostly ACMDs. At that time, Korstad was made an alternate to the chairman, and R.E. Smith, of the Administrative Research Staff, became Executive Secretary.

By 1966, the Administrative Research Program had been placed within the Systems and Standards Service with Dr. John M. Buchanan as Director and Dr. William H. Kirby as Deputy Director.[6] Its mission included conducting formal studies to test hypotheses related to the administrative aspects of a health services operation. The program also was expected to conduct basic research, defined as "investigative activity directed toward an increase in knowledge (in fields relevant to VA's goals) rather than a practical application thereof". In addition, the Administrative Research Program's mission included involvement in developmental research in the form of "investigative activity in which the systematic use of knowledge is directed toward the production of more useful services, devices, systems and methods."[7]

During the following year, the Administrative Research Program solicited cooperation in a survey of job attitudes being undertaken by a group of Ph.D. scientists at the VA Hospital in Downey, IL. A project reviewing utilization and efficacy of Incentive Therapy programs was announced in 1965.[8]

In 1968, the Administrative Research Committee was abolished, with the explanation that: "With the reorientation of the Administrative Research program to emphasize central planning and direction, the Committee is no longer essential."[9] The next year, a circular soliciting suggestions for Health Services Research and Development projects was distributed to field hospitals.[10]

The Automated Hospital Information System (AHIS)

Meanwhile, the efforts at computerization begun at Fort Howard were expanding at the new Washington (DC) VA Hospital, which boasted a new computer system far more powerful than the one the Fort Howard unit had tried to use. The envisioned goal was to find a means to contend with a major problem: "the reams of paperwork connected with providing medical care and treatment for veterans (that) have always been the bane of doctors, nurses and other professionals in the Veterans Administration."[11]

During the 1957-1961 period under VA Administrator Sumner Whittier, a major effort was made to automate the paperwork activities of the VA's Insurance and Veterans Benefits departments.[11] The staggering load of paperwork in the patient care program was a compelling reason to try to extend this technology to the VA hospital system. In 1961, Chief Medical Director Middleton set in motion projects to use computer technology to increase efficiency and quality in VA hospitals, with the goal of total automation of the hospitals' information systems. Among its many positive effects would be that all necessary information concerning a patient - admission to discharge - would be recorded electronically. Armed with this information, the admitting physician would then give the veteran an examination to determine the needs for hospitalization. If the examination confirmed the need, the system would automatically check availability of a suitable bed, and indicate the location (ward, building, etc.) of that bed to the admitting physician. Other relevant services within the hospital would simultaneously be notified about support services that were needed. Subsequently, instructions concerning patient needs (prescriptions to the pharmacy, dietetic needs, etc.) would continue to flow through the system.

Regional data processing centers were planned to assemble all this information and service the information needs of designated VA medical installations within specific geographical areas.[11]

Work toward this utopian goal began in 1961, when, under a VA contract, the Systems Development Corporation in Los Angeles (SDC) began work on computerizing clinical care. It analyzed data from the Los Angeles VA Hospital and set up simulations of ward activities, bed control, laboratories and other hospital functions.

That same year, work toward this automation goal also began in VA Central Office. Lawrence Christianson, M.D., who had been Chief of Medicine and Chief of Staff at the Fort Meade (SD) VA Hospital, came to Central Office in early 1961 as Assistant Director of Medical Service. Later that year, he was put in charge of the 50-member data processing staff that was charged with developing automated systems for payroll, personnel, management control, clinical applications and research.

By 1965, the two projects were combined to form the Automated Hospital Information System (AHIS), now using an up-to-date computer facility located at the new Washington VA Hospital.

Working closely with nurses and doctors at the hospital in designing, developing, and programming simulations of all hospital activities, their goal was to create a prototype for a nationwide management information system.

The first AHIS applications, for admissions and discharges, presented little difficulty. But the study of pharmacy operations required complex interaction with the medical staff, nurses, pharmacists and the administrative staff working in the pharmacy. While the hospital was enthusiastic about this effort, Central Office officials were nervous about it, so programmers' efforts were redirected to automating radiology. In retrospect, this system, requiring expensive mainframe hardware, was ahead of its time. According to Dr. Christianson, "Someone did a cost-benefit analysis of this system about 1969 and found that the whole system might save 2 FTEE (employees)."[12]

During his period as ACMD/R&E (1968-1969), Thomas Chalmers, M.D., had some acquaintance with AHIS during the day he spent each week at the Washington hospital. At that time, Chalmers championed the effort to computerize all patient information, but in retrospect he felt that the initiative was premature since the available hardware and software weren't up to the job.[13]

In 1969, Christianson moved to Research Service as Program Chief in Neurology and Regional Coordinator for the Northeast Region. Orin Skouge, who had left his position as Deputy Chief Medical Director after a change in administrative leadership, spent most of 1970 at the Washington hospital working on AHIS. By this time, the administrative records had been automated and the AHIS staff were working on automating the professional records. Skouge also expressed the opinion that the technology for this task simply hadn't been there. Another problem was that doctors refused to use a keyboard to enter patient information. To make matters worse, maintaining the large IBM computer consumed several hundred thousand dollars annually.[14]

By 1972, when Al Gavazzi became Director of the Washington, D.C. VA Hospital, the Administrative Research Program there had been split into three groups. The first group was working on the automation of direct patient-care problems, led by Hubert Pipberger, M.D., who had begun computerizing EKGs while the hospital was still located in the Mt. Alto section of Washington. Other hospital clinicians also saw computers as the answer to patient-care problems and were trying to perfect various types of patient-care systems.

The second group, the AHIS central group, included people with administrative interests who were trying to place medical administration and medical records on the computer and make the computerized system clinically useful.

The third group, the former Health Systems Research unit that had moved from Ft. Howard to Washington when the new hospital opened, now comprised a staff of seven people headed by Leon Gintzig. They were addressing practical problems of hospital layout.

Wendell Musser, M.D., who became ACMD for Planning and Evaluation in 1970, was responsible for Central Office coordination of AHIS as well as for other aspects of Health Services R&D. In his opinion, AHIS was "a huge bottomless pit." By 1970, it had already cost $2.4 million, with little to show in the way of visible product or value added to administrative efficiency or care. A formal review of AHIS brought unfavorable results, and in 1972 the decision was made to reduce support for further AHIS development.

After that, there was little widespread support for AHIS, and funding became difficult. The core of its funding came from the Department of Data Management in Central Office and the Washington hospital's medical staff, who had remained enthusiastic about the project.

The first effort under Gavazzi involved placing computers in nursing stations to allow for computerizing orders to pharmacy, lab and then radiology. They also tried to centralize the patient record. Staff physicians, especially Paul Schaeffer, M.D., a neurosurgeon, devoted considerable time to this effort.

Central Office officials who felt that the AHIS project was ill-advised called this system of local support the "Underground Railway." But according to Gavazzi, this Central Office opposition was not universal. Key officials such as Pittman and Chase, and later Custis and Jacoby, were supportive.[15]

Walter Whitcomb, M.D., recalled that when he arrived in VACO in 1979 to head the medical computer program, his whole team spent some time at the Washington VA Medical Center learning about AHIS. Terminals were in use on all the clinical units. By this time, the ICU had been automated. Whitcomb recalled that two or three MUMPS programmers at the medical center were working on AHIS. It was a very expensive program, and as computer technology advanced, it was increasingly viewed as archaic.[16]

Nevertheless, AHIS continued to function at Washington VA Hospital through the 1970s and into the early 1980s, and the staff at the facility supported it. According to Jack Divers, who joined the AHIS team in 1975 as a programmer in IBM assembly language, the program ran on an IBM 360-40 mainframe computer with all code in IBM assembly language. Well before Divers's arrival, the program had been completed and was then in its maintenance phase. The 52 terminals scattered throughout the hospital handled a variety of tasks, including administrative matters (patient admissions, discharges and transfers);

clinical laboratory tests, which could be ordered on the computer from the wards and results sent to the ward computer terminals; and radiology scheduling.

No health-care provider was specifically assigned to AHIS, so each clinical service designated its own coordinator and the AHIS staff would meet with doctors to talk about their needs. Many physicians recognized the potential of the AHIS for improving health care in myriad ways; the Chief of Radiology would meet with technicians to discuss improvements that could be made to the radiology subsystem, and other groups of subject-matter specialists would also get together to discuss their needs.

The computer system proved to be very cumbersome. Six times a day, it was necessary to close it down for ten minutes, in order to back it up onto tape. And it was very demanding: a staff of 20 were on hand simply to maintain the program. The development phase had ended, but at its peak at least 50 people worked on the system. Still, in Divers's opinion, the actual design of the system was very good.

An audit staff of VA people not associated with AHIS reviewed all proposed changes to the system. If a hospital service requested a change, an auditor reviewed it and then passed it on to a programmer. The resulting change was again reviewed by the auditor, who then might give permission to implement it on the system. Testing any part of the system, however, was very expensive. No duplicate system existed, so all changes had to be implemented onto a test set of disks. At 2 a.m., the system was shut down until 5 a.m., to allow time to install the test system.

In 1975, the AHIS staff started a long-term plan to replace the hardware, which was by then grievously outdated. Procurement problems, however, prevented their getting new equipment and the AHIS systems was forced to continue to run on the old equipment.

The system-wide computerized hospital information system eventually developed by the VA differs from AHIS, but much of the basic design for data flow used in AHIS remains embedded in the current system.[17]

Health Services Research and Development Service in VA Central Office

Despite these efforts, the Central Office leadership identified a need for more progress in the study of health-care delivery. In 1971, Dr. Lionel Bernstein, former Director, Research Service, was given a special assignment to review hospital operations. His review resulted in a paper that identified the need for a more active program in Health Services Research. Leon Bernstein, Ph.D., who also had just left Research Service, was assigned to be Director of a newly constituted Health Services Research and Development (HSR&D) Service that incorporated the Administrative Research Service as well as other functions.[18]

In October 1972, Carleton Evans, M.D., succeeded Leon Bernstein as Director of the HSR&D Service, which continued to be located in the Office of Planning and Evaluation, under Wendell Musser, M.D. Evans had been at the San Francisco VA Hospital, where he had built up an outpatient department. While there, a medical school classmate, Dr. Gerald

Charles, returned from the military as a resident. Charles and Evans collaborated on a Health Services Research and Development study of physician extenders. They trained ghetto youths to perform triage using protocols and to function as physician's assistants. Charles had learned about this approach in the Army, where trained corpsmen successfully performed triage. The study was funded by the Federal Model Cities Program. When Wendell Musser heard about this activity, he visited San Francisco and recruited Evans. At that time, recalled Evans, HSR&D Service focused primarily on "industrial engineering." Without any money of its own, when the Service wanted to do something beyond the routine, it was forced to seek CMD approval. Consequently, very little research was going on and, in his opinion, the studies being done when he arrived in Central Office were mundane.

Figure 19.1 Carleton Evans, M.D.

In 1973, the new Office of Research and Development (Chapter 16) was established, and a newly conceptualized Health Services Research and Development (HSR&D) Service moved into it with Evans as Director. Thomas Newcomb, M.D., who had been Director, Research Service and was now ACMD/R&D, was Evans's new boss. At first, the HSR&D Service, which had a staff of some 125 people, was given responsibility for the VA's computer design and installation throughout the agency in addition to establishing health services research as a vigorous activity. Most of its computer staff, however, lacked the requisite training and appropriate experience for the task, and it seemed unlikely that they were up to the job. By 1976, the computer responsibility had moved to a separate office, making it possible to concentrate on starting a true research program of Health Services Research.

Until then, HSR&D lacked its own budget, and, except for a handful supported from Medical Research funds, projects were supported by the patient care budget. Newcomb and Evans worked strenuously to achieve a line item in the Congressional budget to support HSR&D. In 1976, some funds were found to support new programs, and in October 1976 (for the fiscal year 1977 budget), HSR&D was written into the VA's legislation with the addition of the words "including... health services research." The 1977 HSR&D budget was $3.6 million, and it remained at about $3 million until its gradual rise began in 1983.

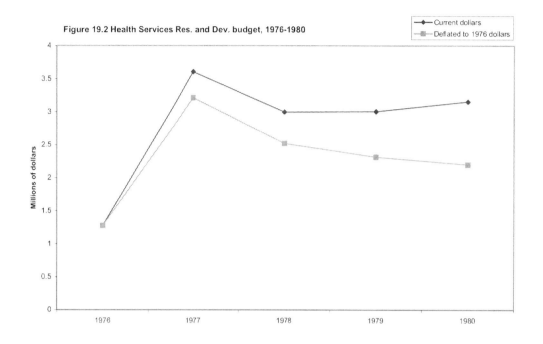

Figure 19.2 Health Services Res. and Dev. budget, 1976-1980

Current dollars
Deflated to 1976 dollars

Millions of dollars

The HSR&D Service continued to respond to short-term needs of the medical department with "management-type" studies conducted by Central Office staff or by contractors, until a field-based research program was introduced in the mid-1970s. In 1975, VA hospitals were invited to apply for support of projects ("investigator-initiated research.") A committee of experts assembled to provide peer review, and the first review meeting was held in June 1975. The results were disappointing: The proposed investigators were inexperienced in health-services research and lacked guidance on how to prepare a health-services research protocol. The committee provided extensive advice to the authors of those proposals that seemed to have potential merit. Some of these were rewritten and resubmitted for the next meeting of the committee, which continued to hold semiannual review meetings. By October 1976, when funds to support projects were in hand, 7 projects of the 55 that were reviewed were ready to be funded. Over the next 4 years, submission rates remained modest, and funding was similarly selective (Table 19.1). The review board held to a high standard; any project that was funded had met that standard.

Table 19.1. Beginnings of Investigator-Initiated Health Services Research and Development

	Fiscal Year				
	1976	1977	1978	1979	1980
Investigator-initiated projects*					
Number reviewed	55	64	74	60	44
Number funded	7	9	15	14	8
Percent funded	13	14	20	23	18

*Information provided by Carol Girard of the Management Decision and Research Center, VA Boston Healthcare System, October 11, 2001.

In addition to this nascent intramural program, the young Health Services Research program supplemented its intramural efforts with contracts, just as the early medical research program had depended heavily on contracts to investigators outside of the VA. Contracts were negotiated when there were "emergent high-priority research needs."[19]

The main challenge of health-services research in the 1970s was to build capacity, the same challenge that had faced the medical research program in the 1940s and 1950s. Without increased capacity, expansion of intramural research was impossible. Evans tried several approaches to meet this challenge. In the Investigator-Initiated Research program, the early review committee provided instruction as well as evaluation for aspiring researchers. In addition, a program of university affiliations was established, with an associated training program.

Table 19.2. Affiliations of VA hospitals with University Centers for Health Services Research*
            1975-1981

University	Affiliated VA Hospital
University of California at Los Angeles	Brentwood
	Wadsworth
University of Washington	Seattle
University of Michigan	Ann Arbor**
University of Missouri	Columbia, MO**
Johns Hopkins University	Perry Point
University of North Carolina	Fayetteville
	Durham
University of Pennsylvania	Philadelphia
Yale University	West Haven**
Massachusetts Institute of Technology	Boston
University of Florida	Gainesville**

*The university centers were funded by the National Center for Health Services Research of the Department of Health, Education and Welfare.[19]

**These centers had Health Services Research Training Programs, funded by Education Service.

In 1975, the National Center for Health Services Research of the Department of Health, Education and Welfare issued a grant solicitation for health-services research centers to "conduct health services research, provide educational opportunities, develop research agendas responsive to regional and local needs, and render technical assistance." [19] VA hospitals were invited to work with their medical school affiliates in preparing these applications. When the university affiliate's center was funded, the VA received enough support for a small unit (Table 19.2).

The staff of these units, assisted by their university affiliate, were then expected to apply for more research support from the VA and other funding agencies. Four of these VA hospitals also received positions for trainees. While the program of the National Center for Health Services Research terminated after its initial 5-year funding period, some of the VA-university partnerships established in these centers served as the basis for the VA Centers of Excellence in Health Services Research started in the 1980s.

Figure 19.3 Richard Greene, M.D., Ph.D.

In 1978, Evans recruited Richard Greene, M.D., Ph.D., to be a staff physician in HSR&D Service. Greene had been working with a group consulting in health-services research and had most impressive credentials. Previously, he had been a Ph.D. molecular biologist in the NIH intramural program. In addition to his medical and scientific education, he held an MPH from Johns Hopkins University. Not long after Greene arrived in 1979, Evans left for an intergovernmental detail to the National Academy of Sciences, and Greene became Director of Health Services R&D Service. A few months later, Vernon Nickel, the founding Director of Rehabilitative Engineering Research and Development Service, left to become a professor in San Diego; Greene also served as Acting Director of that Service while a search was on for a replacement. Next, Betty Uzman left to go to the Memphis VA Hospital, and Greene became Acting Director of Medical Research as well, later becoming permanent Director of Medical Research Service.   Later in the 1980s, Greene became ACMD/R&D.

References

1.   "Report of group in research in conjunction with committee on treatment and cure of veterans." *US Veterans' Bureau Medical Bulletin*, 1929. **5**: 230.

2.   Interview with Mr. John Willoughby, May 4, 1992 at Mr. Willoughby's home.

3.   Interview with Mr. John Peters, February 27, 1992 at Mr. Peters's office at the University of Alabama at Birmingham.

4.   H. Martin Engle, M.D., "Memorandum No. 10-63-25.   Committee on Administrative and Developmental Research." 8/14/63.

5.   H. Martin Engle, M.D., "Memorandum No. 10-666-3.   Administrative Research Committee." 2/25/66.

6.   *VA Central Office Telephone Directory*. Washington, DC: 1967, 32.

7.   Orin T. Skouge, M.D., "Circular 10-66-279. The Administrative Research Program." 12/22/66.

8.   Benjamin B. Wells, M.D., "R&E Letter 65-2. Request for cooperation in research project." 2/26/65.

9.   H. Martin Engle, M.D., "Memorandum No. 10-68-7.   Abolishment of Administrative Research Committee." 4/4/68.

10. Orin T. Skouge, M.D., "RCS 13-109-5.   Survey of Suggested Health Services Research and Development Projects." 7/8/69.

11. Adkins, R.E., "The Automated Hospital Information System", in *Medical Care of Veterans*. 1967, U.S. Government Printing Office: Washington, DC 390-391.

12. Interview with Lawrence Christianson, M.D., May 4, 1992 at Dr. Christianson's home in suburban Maryland.

13. Interview with Thomas Chalmers, M.D., July 29, 1992 at a hotel lobby in Boston, MA.

14. Telephone interview with Orin Skouge, M.D., August 3, 1992.

15. Interview with Mr. Al Gavazzi, May 6, 1992 at Mr. Gavazzi's home in suburban Virginia.

16. Telephone interview with Walter Whitcomb, M.D., August 11, 1992.

17. Telephone interview with Mr. Harold (Jack) Divers, January 14, 1994.

18. Interview with Leon Bernstein, M.D., April 29, 1988 at Dr. Bernstein's home in suburban Virginia.

19. Kruegel, D. and Evans, C., "The organization of health services research in the Veterans Administration." *J Med Systems*, 1981. **5**: 157-162.

Chapter 20. VA Research in Rehabilitation

Before October 1, 1973, when the Research and Development Office, including Prosthetics Research, was established, VA research in prosthetics and sensory aids was the responsibility of the clinical service that served veterans who needed these devices. Only in 1976 did research in rehabilitation become a Service in its own right.

Postwar research guided by NRC committees

In the first 31 years after World War II, from 1945 to 1976, the National Research Council (NRC) of the National Academy of Sciences played an active role in encouraging and supporting research in prosthetics and sensory aids, both in the VA and elsewhere. NRC committees reviewed proposals for contracts in support of prosthetics research, held meetings to review state-of-the-art prosthetics and advise on new directions and interacted directly with contractors. Funds supporting contracts came from the Office of Scientific Research (OSRD) and the War Department from 1945 to 1947; after that, the VA provided the funding. Public Law 729, 80th Congress, June 19, 1948, formally authorized VA research in the fields of prosthetics and sensory devices and provided a budget of $1 million per year. The law required the VA to "make available the results of such research so as to benefit all disabled people." The budget remained flat until 1962, when the $1 million funding ceiling was lifted by Public Law 87-572, which authorized "such funds as were necessary" for the program.[1]

Before the mid-1970s, the VA research program in prosthetics and sensory aids consisted primarily of contracts funded by the VA, supervised by VA staff and reviewed by NRC committees.[2]

The NRC committee structure in support of this program changed from time to time (Appendix IIm), with shifts in the perception of needs and changes in the agencies (including the VA) supporting research in prosthetics and sensory aids. NRC involvement began with a meeting held January 30–February 1, 1945 at Northwestern University to review the needs of amputees, sponsored by the Army at the request of the NRC. The 1945 meeting has been described as the beginning of modern research in prosthetics.[3] It was held just after the annual meeting of the American Academy of Orthopedic Surgeons in Chicago and orthopedic surgeons were well represented, including Henry Kessler and Paul Magnuson. The attendee representing the OSRD was Paul Klopstag, a physicist at Northwestern University and Director of Research at Northwestern's Technological Institute.

An outcome of this meeting was a Committee on Prosthetic Devices formed by the NRC in April of that year. In October, the wartime OSRD transferred its Committee on Sensory Devices to the NRC. From then until 1975, the NRC continued to play a key role in guiding research in prosthetics and sensory devices, a large fraction of it supported by the VA.

Through subsequent reorganizations, these committees were guided in the early days by the Executive Director, Brig. Gen. F.S. Strong, Jr. An early assistant to General Strong was Eugene Murphy, who played a key role in the VA program.[4]

Eugene Murphy, Ph.D.

Murphy, himself paraplegic as a result of childhood poliomyelitis,[5] was a mechanical engineer. He spent World War II on leave from his graduate studies at the Illinois Institute of Technology teaching mechanical engineering students at the University of California in Berkeley and conducting research, supported by OSRD, on the stability of bonded wire in strain gages. These gages were used to measure the stretching of reinforcing bars in steel structures such as bridges and large ships.

Figure 20.1 Eugene Murphy, Ph.D.

Murphy was a friend of Howard D. Eberhart, professor of civil engineering at Berkeley, who lost a leg in a wartime research accident in 1944. Ironically, Eberhart had gained an interest in prosthetics research and knew the men he would come to work with in this field, before the accident made him a user—as well as developer—of the technology. Already acquainted with Murphy through professional engineering interests, he had been consulted by Dr. Verne Inman, an orthopedic surgeon at UC Medical School in San Francisco, concerning the biomechanics of the shoulder joint. After Eberhart's injury, Dr. Inman became Eberhart's surgeon.

The accident that caused the loss of Eberhart's leg occurred while he was studying the stress on concrete from landing aircraft. While trying to develop more efficient reinforcing patterns for the concrete, to facilitate building longer runways for bombers with less material, he was run over by a trailer weighted to represent the landing gear of a B-29.

At the Mare Island Naval Hospital, under the guidance of Navy physician Henry Kessler— a leading expert in prosthetics—Eberhart was fitted with a conventional wooden foot and mechanical ankle joint prosthesis. In visits from Murphy, the two became interested in measuring the stresses involved in using this particular type of artificial leg. Back at the

416

civil engineering laboratory in Berkeley, they rigged up various rudimentary measuring devices as Eberhart walked about as a test subject. Their research indicated strains on the prosthetic limb were far greater than initially supposed, and the two engineers realized that more sophisticated techniques were needed to measure the complexities involved in the dynamic motion of simple walking.

Murphy described their experience to key people at the NRC, pointing out that little was really known about the mechanics of walking—knowledge critical to developing prosthetic lower limbs. The NRC officials were sufficiently impressed that Murphy became an assistant to Gen. Strong, helping to launch the NRC's initial effort in prosthetics research. Eberhart and Inman were given a contract for a formal research project, which endured for the next 35 years, leading to significant progress and understanding in the field of prosthetics.[4]

Prosthetics and Sensory Aids Service in the VA

In 1948, after Public Law 729 from the 80th Congress provided funding to the VA in support of prosthetics research, Murphy moved from his staff job with the NRC to the VA. Research in prosthetics and sensory aids in the VA was administered by the new Prosthetics and Sensory Aids Service in VA Central Office. Its first Director was Augustus Thorndike, M.D., a prominent orthopedic surgeon at Harvard, who never moved to Washington. Dr. Thorndyke was well connected in the medical community, and he used his contacts in the American Medical Association, the American College of Surgeons, and other professional organizations to help raise the profile of VA's work in prosthetics and sensory aids. The Assistant Director for Operations, Robert E. Stewart, D.D.S., was based in the Central Office in Washington, DC. After Thorndike retired in 1955, Dr. Stewart became Director, a position he held until he retired in 1973.

Figure 20.2 Augustus Thorndike, M.D.   Figure 20.3 Robert E. Stewart, D.D.S.

Murphy, as Assistant Director for Research, was based in New York City at the VA Regional Office. A "Prosthetics Testing and Development Laboratory" had been established in New York in 1945 by Walter Bura, who was in charge of the VA's clinical prosthetics program from 1945 to 1948. This unit was independent of the NRC effort.

The VA Prosthetics Center in New York

In 1955, Dr. Stewart, by then Director of the Prosthetics and Sensory Aids Service, visited the Sunnybrook Hospital in Toronto, where he learned about its prosthetics center that served eighteen centers throughout Canada and also engaged in research. He felt that a similar center would benefit the VA. In 1956, he established the VA Prosthetics Center (VAPC) in New York. This Center combined a clinical operation with the research and evaluation effort already ongoing under Dr. Murphy. Later, it established satellite stations at several VA hospitals.[6]

The research carried out at the VAPC constituted most of the VA's intramural research in Prosthetics and Sensory Aids before the 1973 reorganization that brought Prosthetics Research into the Office of Research and Development. While the VAPC carried out a variety of practical projects, primarily to improve upper and lower limb prostheses, it became increasingly involved in the evaluation of devices developed by others. It established a network of VA Prosthetics Service units at VA hospitals willing and able to evaluate new devices. In some cases, when the new device was clearly of benefit, it would be adopted in the VA for general clinical use. The VAPC also played an active role in prosthetics education. Its activities were extensively discussed in the review of the prosthetics and sensory aids program by Stewart and Bernstock published in 1973[7] and were regularly reviewed in the *Bulletin of Prosthetic Research*.

Dr. Murphy's role

While he supervised the intramural research at the VAPC, Eugene Murphy's most important role was to coordinate the contracts program. Frank Coombs, who joined the program in the 1970s, described Murphy as a superb expeditor, the "bee in the flower garden, cross-pollinating things," who exchanged and furthered ideas. When he learned what one person was doing, he was quick to think of who that person ought to talk to and would get them together, and then he would follow up on it. [4,8]

The *Bulletin of Prosthetics Research*

A key contribution led by Murphy was starting and continuing publications to share information among the prosthetics and sensory aids community. From 1954 to 1972, with VA support, the NRC published a journal called *Artificial Limbs*. To cover the broader field of research included in its Prosthetics and Sensory Aids research program, the VA started its own *Bulletin of Prosthetics Research* in 1964. Murphy continued as its editor until he retired in 1983.

The *Bulletin of Prosthetics Research* presented VA-sponsored research, both as progress reports and original articles. It also presented other research in the field. Recognized as a primary source of state-of-the–art information about research in prosthetics and sensory aids, by 1983 the *Bulletin* had expanded to include all areas of rehabilitation and changed its title to reflect its broader scope. Today known as the *Journal of Rehabilitation Research and Development*, this journal continues to expand and contribute to its field.

Early prosthetics research supported by the VA

University of California at Berkeley (UC Berkeley)

Work under the contract with UC Berkeley under Inman and Eberhart was begun even before the VA took over funding of contracts in 1947. They conducted classic fundamental studies on human locomotion, or gait analysis. Their early studies included limb and pelvis motion during locomotion and patterns of muscle activities in the lower limbs and trunk. To investigate these phenomena, they developed glass walkways and force plates. They used three-dimensional cinematography along with the force plates to greatly expand knowledge of human walking. This work had national and international impact on the field of motion analysis. The team also performed materials testing and made studies of structural design which led to improvements in artificial-limb alignment and suction-socket design that reduced pain in amputee fittings. Later products completed under this long-lasting contract were the development of casting techniques and plastic laminates for sockets, improvement in the suction socket, a casting technique for total contact sockets for above-knee amputees, a patellar-tendon-bearing socket for below-knee amputees, a safety-lock knee and a pneumatic swing-control knee. Inman and Eberhart's work also resulted in the prosthetic foot that became the standard for its time, the Solid-Ankle Cushion-Heel (SACH) foot.[9]

Mauch laboratories

Another long-time contractor was Hans Mauch, who developed hydraulic swing-control knees and ankles and who also worked on reading machines. Mauch had played a major role in developing Germany's V1 missile, and came to the U.S. with Werner von Braun.

Frank Coombs described Mauch as a "hydraulics wizard". He applied his expertise to the process of biomechanically replicating the motion of the human knee and ankle. The knee is far more sophisticated than a simple hinge; mechanically recreating its motion requires a variable center of rotation. Mauch's hydraulic configuration allowed the leg to swing forward normally during walking; then it would dampen its stopping point and suppress any backward motion. Mauch applied the same technology to the ankle joint by constructing a variable mechanical replica that adjusted to variations in up and down angles.[8]

University of California at Los Angeles (UCLA)

Another early contract that continued for many years was with UCLA. In the early years, the UCLA investigators collaborated with Northrup Aircraft, in Hawthorne, CA. The UCLA-Northrup group did classic studies of upper-extremity motion comparable to those of the lower limb done at UC Berkeley. They identified the basic requirements for upper-extremity prostheses and developed improved models.

Table 20.1. Comparison of rehabilitation research projects funded in 1973 with those funded in 1980 [10, 11]
      (1973 funding included where known [12])

Intramural projects active in 1973, terminated by 1980

Orthopedics and prosthetics

Moore et al	VAMC, San Francisco	Immediate postoperative prostheses	
McDowell	VAMC, Richmond	Immediate postoperative arm orthoses	

Spinal cord injury

Davis	VAMC, Miami	Paralysis, spasticity and pain	

Extramural projects active in 1973, terminated by 1980

Oversight

McLaurin	Nat'l Academy of Sciences	Advisory committee	$167,000

Sensory aids

Causey et al	University of Maryland	Hearing aid research	55,000
Carhart, Olsen	Northwestern University	Test proced, binaural hearing aids	
Benham et al	Bionic Instruments, Inc.	Laser cane for blind	35,000
Cooper et al	Haskins Laboratory, Inc.	Speech output- reading machine	134,400
Mauch, Smith	Mauch Laboratories	Reading machines	145,600
Weisgerber	Am. Inst. Res., Palo Alto	Training - Mauch Stereotoner	
Hathaway, Butow	Hadley School for Blind	Reading machine training	20,000

Orthopedics and prosthetics

Mauch	Mauch Laboratories	Hydraulic limbs	110,000
Bennett	New York University	Evaluation of prostheses	20,930
Lyman et al	University of California, LA	Externally powered arm	49,800
Sarmiento et al	University of Miami	Improved fitting procedure-leg	59,000
Graupe	Colorado State University	EMG-act contr for art upper arm	15,600
Perry	Rancho Los Amigos	Clinical gait analyzer	

Spinal cord injury

Newell, Leavitt	Texas A&M Engineering	Automotive adaptive equip	
Scott	Mobility Engineering	Passenger safety, vehicle for handicap	
Perry, Allen	Rancho Los Amigos	Bed-chair	

Other

Cochran	St. Lukes Hosp, NYC	Electrical stimulation of bone healing	
Chase, Babb	Univ Calif, LA	Lit search on electrode implantation	

Intramural projects active both in 1973 and 1980

Orthopedics and prosthetics

Burgess, Lippert	Seattle VAMC	Improved amputation and prostheses

  (Contract to University of Washington in 1973, Seattle VAMC in 1980)

Sensory Aids

Acton, De L'Aune	West Haven VAMC	Reading and mobility aids
Malmazian, Farmer	Hines VAMC	Reading and mobility aids
Hennessey et al	Palo Alto VAMC	Reading and mobility aids

Other
Schweiger, Lontz   Wilmington VAMC   Maxillofacial materials
  (Contract to Temple University in 1973, Wilmington VAMC in 1980)
Lee et al   Castle Point VAMC   Hemodynamic evaluation in amputees
Hoaglund et al   San Francisco VA   Lower limb prostheses, locomotion
  (Contract to UC Berkeley in 1973, San Francisco VAMC in 1980)

Extramural projects active both in 1973 and 1980

Orthopedics and prosthetics
Thompson, Childress   Northwestern Univ.   Powered prostheses
Seamone, Schmeisser   Johns Hopkins   Ext powered arms, robots, wheel chair
  Hall, Rostoker   Southwest Res Inst   Permanent artificial limbs

Intramural projects active in 1980, started after 1973

Rehabilitation Research and Development Centers
??   Hines VAMC   Multidisciplinary program
Leifer   Palo Alto VAMC   Multidisciplinary program

Sensory Aids
Kelly   Atlanta VAMC   Wheelchairs, reading and mobility
Linvill et al   Palo Alto VAMC   Communication system for the blind

Orthopedics and prosthetics
Cochran et al   Castle Point VAMC   Electrical stimulation of bone transplants
Mears   Pittsburgh VAMC   Joint wear particles
Murray   Wood VAMC   Normal and abnormal motion
Marsolais   Cleveland VAMC   Engineering – Orthotics and prosthetics
Fortune, Leonard   Wash, DC VAMC   Grouting materials
Spadaro   Syracuse VAMC   Electrical stimulation of hard tissue
Cooper   Iowa City VAMC   Foot biomechanics
Lippert, Burgess   Seattle VAMC   Below-knee physiological suspension
Weinstein   New Orleans VAMC   Orthopedic implant retrieval
Golbranson   San Diego VAMC   Gait analysis
Malone et al   Tuscon VAMC   Postoperative prosthesis, arm and leg

Spinal cord injury
Perkash, Motloch   Palo Alto VAMC   Seating systems
Vistnes   Palo Alto VAMC   Pressure sores
Rossier   West Roxbury VA   Wheelchair – Myoelectric control
Weibell et al   Sepulveda VAMC   Wheelchair power steering
Bohlman et al   Cleveland VAMC   Spinal cord monitoring
Sypert, Munson   Gainesville VAMC   Spinal cord regeneration
Peckham   Cleveland VAMC   FES – upper extremity
Hussey, Rosen   West Roxbury VA   Muscle control by electrical stimulation

Other
Goldstein et al   Gainesville VAMC   Artificial larynx
Hood, Schoen   Gainesville VAMC   Lung reaction to biomaterials
Griffin, Schiavi   Nashville VAMC   Neuromuscular deficit techniques

Sensory Aids
Clark, Savoie	Telesensory Systems	Speech output for reading aid

Orthopedics and prosthetics
Swanson	Blodgett Med Ctr	Grommet bone liner
Banks	NASA Lewis Res	Finger joint grommets
Matsen	Univ. Washington	Neuromuscular structure viability

Spinal cord injury
Roemer et al	UC Santa Barbara	Bladder volume determination

But probably the UCLA group's most important contribution, which began in 1953 with VA prosthetics research funding, was starting a university-level prosthetics education course. This was soon followed by similar courses at New York University and Northwestern University. They taught up-to-date methods and worked to make prosthetics a profession. These programs, while not strictly centered on research, provided formal accreditation for prosthetists, a qualification that soon was required by the VA.[13]

Northwestern University and the Rehabilitation Institute of Chicago

Northwestern University had been the cradle for modern prosthetics research, hosting the seminal 1945 meeting and providing the original NRC committee staff. In those early days, Northwestern had a contract for reviewing the literature and patents related to artificial limbs that led to a lengthy report on the state of the art. The University's researchers also worked on methods for testing artificial legs.

In 1954, largely as a result of the personal efforts of the VA's Dr. Paul Magnuson, the Northwestern-affiliated Rehabilitation Institute of Chicago (RIC) was founded in downtown Chicago. In 1958, a VA-sponsored Prosthetics Research Center was set up within the RIC. Its chief was an orthopedic surgeon, Dr. Clinton Compere, one of the key professionals sustaining the new RIC. Dr. Compere, a combat surgeon in the South Pacific, had been chief of an Army amputee unit following WWII and knew Dr. Magnuson. The new program was charged with evaluating special amputation situations to facilitate the development and fit of appropriate devices. From its inception, the Prosthetics Research Program worked with the nearby Chicago Research VA Hospital, later called the Chicago Lakeside VA Medical Center, drawing clinical collaboration from the VA hospital as well as from its host, the RIC.

A wide variety of prosthetic devices were developed at the Northwestern unit. Early on, its engineers became interested in use of external power in prosthetics. In 1966, Dr. Dudley Childress, an electrical engineer, joined the staff. In 1968, he and his associates fitted the first self-contained and self-suspended trans-radial myoelectric prosthesis. It was also the first such system designed in the United States. With this system, which later became commercially available, the amputee activates the same muscles that had controlled the original arm. Electrodes on the skin then pick up the muscle activation signal which is electronically amplified to control small motors in the artificial arm. The first person ever fitted with such a device later became a successful New York banker who continued to use later generations of the myoelectric hand. A large cadre of individuals were fitted in this way in Chicago, and they provided design feedback to Childress and his team.

Figure 20.4 Dudley Childress, Ph.D.

The Prosthetics Research Laboratory, attached to VA Lakeside Hospital, became known world wide for practical and elegant myoelectric systems. The VA held a national educational course at Northwestern University's prosthetics school in the early 1970s, enrolling approximately 50 students, where VA clinicians learned how to fit the new prostheses. This event launched myoelectric prosthetics for American veterans. Subsequently, Childress designed a new prehension mechanism that used two motors acting in synergy. Thirty years later, the principle was still employed in three commercially available prosthetic systems. The Myo-Pulse modulation scheme that Childress created for the myoelectric signal processor was revolutionary because of its high performance and simplicity of design. The modulation principle, which essentially eliminates delays in the electronics, enables a prosthesis to respond instantly to its wearer's wishes.

Childress and John Billock had good success using the Northwestern socket that Billock designed for persons with trans-radial amputations. They also had success with transhumeral amputations by using a body-powered elbow and myoelectric hand controlled with a myoelectric signal from the biceps and triceps brachii. This fitting method is standard today in VA and civilian prosthetics facilities. They also developed a multi-state myoelectric arm that allowed the biceps and triceps to control four degrees of freedom of the arm.

Childress and his team at the RIC Prosthetics Research Center were also leaders during the 1970s and 1980s in the development of many rehabilitation-engineering systems for people with spinal cord injuries. They were the first to design and commercially introduce the "sip and puff" wheelchair controller for persons with high-level quadriplegia. Margaret Pfrommer, who had significant quadriplegia, had a 25-year tenure in their laboratory as a laboratory assistant. The group developed a wide range of assistive equipment for persons with similar significant disabilities. Such equipment is now common and much advanced, but during the 1970s and early 1980s very few devices of this kind were available. Ms. Pfrommer used the "sip and puff" wheelchair, and the Childress team designed many devices around this control concept. Items developed and marketed through a national company included the first solid-state environmental control system for office and/or home and the first (1973) dedicated computer that allowed a person to serve as a receptionist and office assistant. Pfrommer demonstrated the effectiveness of this equipment in her home as well as in the laboratory. Her home was adapted so that she could live alone, with caregivers needed only in the morning and evening. Childress integrated her rocking bed with a positive pressure ventilator. She became a strong advocate for technology in rehabilitation and was a compelling spokesperson and example for what persons with disability could do if given the proper tools.[14, 15]

University of Washington: The Prosthetics Research Study, Seattle

In 1964, Ernest Burgess, M.D., an orthopedic surgeon in Seattle and chief of the amputee clinic at the Seattle VA Hospital, organized a VA-sponsored study of the theoretical and practical aspects of Immediate Postsurgical Prosthetic Fitting (IPPF). This technique had recently been described by a Polish surgeon, Professor M. Weiss. On hearing about Weiss's work, Burgess organized a national workshop of VA clinic team directors and other leaders in the prosthetic and amputee rehabilitation field to review this new technique. After this workshop, the VA funded Burgess and his coworkers to undertake a clinical investigation. A laboratory was established at the Pacific Northwest Research Center, and the clinical base for the program was centered on the Seattle VA Hospital campus but involved all of the hospitals affiliated with the University of Washington.

The first cases of IPPF, patients cared for by a team with Dr. Burgess as the surgeon, were successful. Within a few months, it had become apparent that patients had less postoperative pain and their rehabilitation was faster than in the past. However, it also became clear that many areas called for further research. In subsequent years, this group studied surgical and casting techniques, materials, wound healing, measurement of tissue circulation, selection of amputation site and many related issues. It redefined the surgical procedure of amputation as a part of the rehabilitation procedure and introduced a new family of surgical techniques directed toward surgical reconstruction and a series of new prosthetic devices.[16]

During the 1980s, collaborating with engineers at Boeing Aerospace, this laboratory developed the Seattle Foot system, incorporating light-weight, responsive materials that capture an amputee's natural movement. Dr. Burgess is personally credited with having strongly advocated one particularly distinctive attribute of the system: an energy saving and return feature. As the wearer brings the foot down, the structure absorbs and briefly stores excess energy from the downward momentum; as the wearer begins lifting the foot for the next step, the stored energy is released to spring the foot up, giving the wearer a positive sense of "pushing off".[17]

Combining this system with computer-aided design and manufacture, the Seattle group developed a method for producing better-fitting prostheses more quickly and inexpensively than was possible before. This system, the CAD-CAM system, is now being used widely in the VA and elsewhere. It is being used successfully to provide inexpensive and comfortable limbs for amputees in Vietnam and other countries that have been ravaged by land mines from recent wars.[18]

Sensory-Aids research

The need for improved care of those who became blind or deaf as a result of their military service concerned the wartime Committee on Medical Research of the OSRD. In January 1944, the OSRD formed a Committee on Sensory Devices. This committee was transferred to the NRC in October 1945, when the OSRD closed down its operations. In 1950 it sponsored a book titled *Blindness: Modern Approach to the Unseen Environment* that reviewed the state-of-the-art with respect to assistive technology for limited vision. In a 1954 NRC reorganization, this committee was dissolved and its activities ceased. The NRC did not review or support sensory-aids research for the next 10 years. In 1964, at the request of the VA, the NRC established a new Subcommittee on Sensory Aids under its Committee on Prosthetics Research and Development.[19] Administration of sensory aids research in the VA was a part of the prosthetics research program, led by Eugene Murphy in the New York office during the entire period up to and for several years after the 1973 reorganization of the VA. While some contracts related to hearing aids were consistently in the portfolio, the major effort was aimed towards blindness.

The VA's specialized care of the blinded veteran began with the establishment of the first center for rehabilitation of the blind at the Hines VA Hospital in Chicago. In this program, selected blind veterans were trained in a variety of skills.[20] This center, and the Blind Centers later established at other VA Hospitals, provided the VA with a focus and willing participants in efforts to improve life for veterans and others with severe visual impairment.

Mobility aids for the blind

Development of an effective obstacle detector to help blind persons navigate has long been a challenge. The VA began supporting research directed to this problem in the 1940s.

In 1948, the VA bought 25 "Signal Corps Devices," single-channel obstacle detectors built by RCA. The VA contracted for their evaluation with Thomas A. Benham, a blind faculty member at Haverford College. Professor Benham reported on his results and suggested improvements in a 1952 report. In 1953, the VA contracted with Haverford to allow Benham to oversee development of an improved device. Haverford subcontracted work to a commercial firm, Bionic Instruments. Over the next 16 years, under VA contract, 10 devices were developed, ultimately including practical laser canes for the blind. The 1975 product, the C-5 Laser Cane, emitted three pulses of infrared light, directed up, down and straight ahead. The light is reflected from an object in front of it and detected by a photodiode placed behind a receiving lens. The angle made by the reflected ray passing through the lens indicates the distance of the object detected. The cane makes a sound when the downward beam detects a drop-off or the upward beam detects an overhead barrier. Sounds of different frequencies indicate the barriers ahead, in front of and above the user. The VA developed the training programs necessary for proper use of this device. It proved to be appropriate only in certain circumstances, for highly motivated users and for training of the newly blind, who later were able to maneuver without it. The cost and skills required were substantial, but they were less than those needed for use of a guide dog.[21]

Reading machines

The early contracts from the NRC supporting research on reading machines for blind veterans involved attempts to translate printed material to sound. This work ended in 1954 when the Committee on Sensory Devices was dissolved.[22] Between 1954 and 1958, the VA and the NRC sponsored a series of five conferences bringing together people interested in further development of reading machines, but there was essentially no governmental support of research to advance the field during that period. These conferences attracted wide attention: from 11 attendees at the first conference in 1954 to 68 at the fifth in 1958. The conferences stimulated new ideas, even though funding had lapsed in 1954.[23]

In 1957, the VA started a funded program to develop reading machines for persons with severe visual impairment. The earliest product of this new program was the improved Optophone, developed at Battelle Memorial Institute by upgrading and transistorizing a device that had been developed by RCA during the 1940s. This device translated the printed word into a series of nine tones representing portions of the letters in each word. Five prototypes were produced and a group of blind students and adults learned to use it. Several blind VA employees became experts in its use, but reading was very slow. The Battelle device was never widely distributed, but it led to other devices that were more widely accepted.[24]

In the Mauch Laboratories, in addition to the prosthetics development described earlier, Hans Mauch started a reading-machine project in 1957 that lasted 20 years. His first contract from the VA was to contribute to the Batelle Optophone. His first assignment was to develop an improved tracking device, which he called the Colineator. Soon, he and his colleagues were working on a machine that produced speech-like sounds in response to letter shapes. When this did not prove practical, he moved to the use of recorded phonemes based on letter shapes, using the "spelled speech" system being developed under VA contract by Professor Milton Metfessel of the University of Southern California. This "Cognodictor" went through a number of modifications leading to a field prototype that was delivered in 1969 and to further improvements up to 1976.

Meanwhile, Mauch was also developing a hand-held probe that gave tactile responses to letters, a device called the Visotactor. It was like a miniature version of the Optophone, except that its output was tactile rather than auditory. Mauch then changed the output to a system of sounds instead of the tactile output, producing the Visotoner. The Visotactor, Visotoner and the Optophone were all practical for reading when used by well-motivated, thoroughly trained and intelligent blind users. At best, however, reading was slow. Mauch continued improving these small, relatively inexpensive, "direct translation" devices and in 1972 produced the Stereotoner, which took advantage of a double array of detectors to speed the letter recognition process by producing its tones binaurally. The Visotactor, Visotoner and Stereotactor were originally intended to be useful components in the development of the Cognodictor. In fact, in the hands of trained users, they were more practical when used directly, and they continued to be used by a few blind readers, while the Cognodictor never entered the practical-use phase of development.[25, 26]

Franklin Cooper of the Haskins Laboratory in New York (later in New Haven, CT) and his colleagues had worked on the reading machine concept in the 1940s under the Committee on Sensory Devices. They had developed a device that produced a tone pattern in response to the shapes of letters. However, Cooper's interest had turned more and more to the problem of production of standard English and the laboratory conducted fundamental linguistic research toward that end. When the VA started funding its reading machine program in 1957, Haskins received a contract to produce "audible outputs of reading machines for the blind." For a shorter-range product, they had a second contract, for an interim device—a reading machine that could recognize a vocabulary of up to 7,200 words. Since optical character recognition was not yet developed, for input they used a punched-tape system from the printing industry. Ability to read these tapes would, in principle, make a wide variety of printed material accessible to blind persons. The short-range project never reached the clinical testing phase, but the long-range project, production of synthetic speech from the written word, led to important theoretical advances.

Mauch's group developed a system of linguistic rules to synthesize speech, leading to their primary product, Speech Synthesis by Rule. Eventually, in 1973, they produced a prototype reading machine that provided a version of synthetic speech. It depended on a commercially available optical character reader and on four Haskins developments: a text-to-phoneme dictionary look-up, stress and intonement assignment, Speech Synthesis by Rule, and a parallel resonance synthesizer. Editorial corrections were needed at several points in the process. While a usable reading machine did not result from the many years of research that the Haskins Laboratory carried out with VA funding, the basic knowledge gained was important to the ultimate development of a practical reading machine in the mid-1970s.[27, 28]

The VA was active in reading-machine development until 1978, but none of the devices developed under VA contract was ultimately successful in the market. The first commercially successful devices were the Optacon, a tactile Braille-like instrument using air jets, developed by James Bliss and John Linvill at Stanford Research Institute and Stanford University, and Raymond Kurzweil's Reading Machine, which produced electronic speech in response to text. The Optacon was a direct competitor for the Stereotoner, and comparative testing showed both to be useful. However, the Optacon was marketed, and the Stereotoner never reached the open market, even though it was less expensive.[29]

Even though they themselves were not initially funded by the VA, the successful developers of reading machines benefited from the work that had been done under VA contract. The Kurzweil machine took advantage of the linguistic knowledge gained in the basic research done by the Haskins group. Both the Optacon and the Kurzweil Reading Machine were evaluated in the VA's Blind Centers. Linvill, in fact, was a coinvestigator of a VA intramural project at the Palo Alto VA Medical Center's Blind Rehabilitation Center during the late 1970s,[30] and Bliss and Linvill's company, Telesensory Systems, Inc., had a VA contract in 1980 to develop a speech output for the Optacon.[31] All of the important devices designed to assist blind persons in reading have been tested and compared in the VA centers.[32]

Emergence of a new Rehabilitation Engineering R&D Service, 1973–1980

When the VA reorganized its research and education program in 1973, setting up a new office, the Office of Research and Development, with Thomas Newcomb, M.D., as the first ACMD/R&D, the old Prosthetics and Sensory Aids Service was divided. Its clinical responsibility remained in the Professional Services, its training activities became a part of the Academic Affairs program and its research and development became a Prosthetics Research Program in the new Office of Research and Development. At that time, Dr. Stewart, who, as Director of the Prosthetics and Sensory Aids Service had taken an active interest in the research program, retired. Dr. Murphy and the VA Prosthetics Center remained in New York, but the center of research administration for the program moved to Washington. Thomas Radley, M.D., Assistant Director of Surgery Service in Central Office, became the Acting Director of the new Prosthetics Research Program under Dr. Newcomb.[33]

Newcomb believed that VA research in rehabilitation needed increased status and support and that these could be gained if the program were administered by a separate Service in the R&D Office. He gained the support of the veterans' service organizations that were especially interested in people with disabilities and of others in the VA Central Office.[34] His effort was rewarded when, in 1976, the Prosthetics Research Program was given Service status and renamed the Rehabilitation Engineering Research and Development Service.[35] This new designation reflected the understanding that research needs in rehabilitation transcended the scope of prosthetics and sensory aids alone.

The budget increases

The new Service, set up with Congressional approval and with a new mission, was rewarded with more money to spend. The veterans' service organizations were enthusiastic about the new direction, and the national climate favored improving the lot of people with disabilities.

The 1947 congressional appropriation of $1 million for the VA Prosthetics Research program had not been increased at all by 1976, after inflation was taken into account. Now the VA requested and received new money to support this new effort. Between 1976 and 1980, the Rehabilitation Engineering R&D Service's congressional appropriation had more than doubled. Even taking into account the high rate of inflation in those years, this 4-year increase was substantial (Figure 20.5) and made it possible to move in new directions.

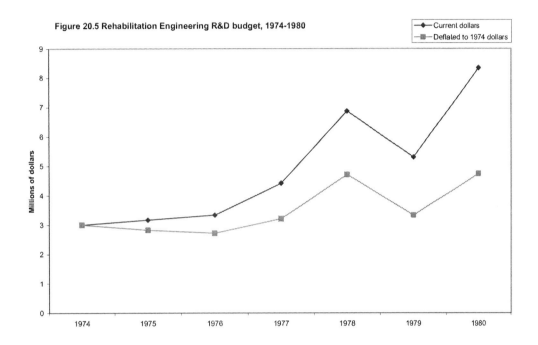

Figure 20.5 Rehabilitation Engineering R&D budget, 1974-1980

The program moves from contracts to intramural research

By the late 1970's, things were very different in the VA than they had been when the contractual prosthetics research program began in 1947. Medical Research had become a vigorous intramural program, recognized widely as beneficial to the VA's veteran patients. Newcomb and his colleagues were convinced that the VA would benefit more from an intramural program of rehabilitation research than from a purely contractual program. It was also felt that VA patients would be more likely to receive direct benefits if the research were done in VA hospitals. A major policy change was agreed upon: In the future, where possible, VA research funds for rehabilitation research would be allocated to VA investigators.[34] When feasible, the contracts that remained would be supervised by a VA investigator and assigned to a VA medical center.[8]

By 1980, the majority of the research supported by the VA Rehabilitation Engineering R&D budget either was being carried out either in VA hospitals or involved VA staff (Table 20.1).

The VA forms its own peer-review system for research in rehabilitation

From its inception, peer review for the VA rehabilitation research program was by the NRC's Committee on Prosthetics Research and Development (CPRD). By the mid-1970s, change was felt to be desirable.[8] Although the membership of the committee rotated regularly, it became difficult to find qualified members with no conflicts of interest, and reappointments were frequent. In 1975, Newcomb offered a contract to NAS to review the activities of its CPRD. The Academy declined the contract, and the following year, by mutual agreement, the CPRD disbanded.[34]

This left the VA with a need for a peer-review mechanism for its rehabilitation research program. At first, Dr. Murphy supervised the review process from his New York base, primarily using ad hoc written reviews. But by this time, both Medical Research Service and Health Services R&D Service had systems of Merit Review Boards meeting regularly to review proposals. In 1976, the new Rehabilitation Engineering R&D Service held its first Merit Review Board meeting.[8]

The first two Rehabilitation Engineering R&D Centers begin

To create an academic base to boost VA rehabilitation research, Newcomb and his advisors decided to set up centers of excellence in rehabilitation research at VA hospitals that had close affiliations with schools of engineering. In 1976, Dr. Chase, the CMD, signed a Request for Proposals sent to all VA hospitals, describing the criteria envisioned for such centers:

> "a. Close proximity to and preferably location on premises of a VA health care facility with substantial clinical programs in important areas of rehabilitation, e.g., spinal cord injury, blind rehabilitation, amputee clinic, geriatric medicine, maxillo-facial restoration, prosthetics and orthotics clinics, etc.
> b. Ready access to engineering expertise preferably from a major academic institution.
> c. Close proximity to a medical school.
> d. Association with allied health schools such as physical and occupational therapy with expertise in electromyography, biomechanics, kinesiology, etc."[36]

A committee of experts reviewed the applications and site visited the leading candidates. The application from the Hines (IL) VA Medical Center, in affiliation with the Illinois Institute of Technology, received the committee's highest recommendation. In second place was the application from the Palo Alto (CA) VA Medical Center and the Stanford School of Engineering. Since only one Center could be approved, in 1977 Hines was awarded the first Center, together with support for renovation of space and funds to hire a cadre of investigators and support staff. Soon, however, Palo Alto also got a Rehabilitation Engineering R&D Center.[34]

Rehabilitation Engineering R&D Service recruits its first Director

Shortly after Rehabilitation Engineering R&D became a Service, the search for a Director began. Vernon Nickel, M.D., from Ranch Los Amigos Hospital in Downey, CA, near Los Angeles, became intrigued with the potential of the new Service and eventually agreed to accept the Directorship in late 1977. He saw the appointment as an opportunity to "build something new," and he approached it with great enthusiasm.[17]

Frank Coombs, an engineer who had joined the Service a few months before Nickel arrived, served as Nickel's assistant. Coombs was an organized person capable of making changes smoothly. He and Nickel had complementary talents that made for an effective start of the new organization.

Figure 20.6 Vernon Nickel, M.D.

Nickel traveled extensively, meeting with VA investigators and with others interested in the program. He took seriously the responsibility to expand the program beyond the limits of prosthetics and sensory aids. Under his leadership, the program grew and became more and more intramural, and it also began to encompass extensive work in the rehabilitation of spinal cord injury, including development of robotic "servants" for the severely paralyzed, improved wheelchairs, electrical stimulation of paralyzed muscles and prevention of pressure sores. New programs began in restorations for persons with mutilating facial deformities and for those with loss of the larynx. Also started were a number of more basic research programs related to rehabilitation (Table 20.1).

In 1979, the Rehabilitation R&D Service joined with Medical Research Service in identifying tissue regeneration as a high priority research area. Basic research in regeneration was encouraged, as well as more attempts to apply current science to achieving regeneration, especially of nerves and the spinal cord. The first of a series of conferences, organized by Medical Investigator Robert Becker, an orthopedic surgeon who used electrical stimulation to enhance bone healing, was held in Syracuse NY in 1979. The attendees reviewed the state-of-the-art and recommended that the VA undertake an organized effort in this area. Tissue regeneration has since been a long-term VA research priority, still supported by the two Services.

During 1980, Dr. Nickel left Central Office to return to the west coast. The new Service was beginning to grow and flourish. In 1983, its name was simplified, and it is now the Rehabilitation R&D Service. Later Directors have encouraged the growth that began in the 1970s and have continued to guard the quality of the rehabilitation research supported by the VA.

References

1.   Stewart, R. and Bernstock, W., *Veterans Administration prosthetic and sensory aids program since World War II.* Washington, DC: U.S. Government Printing Office, 1977, 66.

2.   Stewart and Bernstock, *VA prosthetic and sensory aids program.* 1977, 31-109.

3.   Interview with Dudley Childress, Ph.D., April 8, 2001 at Dr. Childress's home in Wilmette, IL.

4.   Interview with Eugene F. Murphy, Ph.D., October 29, 1992 at Dr.Murphy's home in New York, NY.

5.   Childress, D., Ph.D., "Eugene F. Murphy (1913-2000): Polymath of prosthetics." *Capabilities*, 2001. **10**: 1-2.

6.   Stewart and Bernstock, *VA prosthetic and sensory aids program.* 1977, 125.

7.   Stewart and Bernstock, *VA prosthetic and sensory aids program.* 1977

8.   Interview with Frank Coombs, May 4, 1992 at Techworld RRD Office in Washington, DC.

9.   Stewart and Bernstock, *VA prosthetic and sensory aids program.* 1977, 34-41, 70-74.

10.   Nickel, V.L., "Veterans Administration rehabilitative engineering research and development programs." *Bulletin of Prosthetics Research*, 1980. **17**: 65-143.

11.   Murphy, E.F., "Highlights of other VA research programs." *Bulletin of Prosthetics Research*, 1974. **11**: 109-173.

12.   Letter from Director, Prosthetic and Sensory Aids Service to Director, Supply Service, 1/30/73.

13.   Stewart and Bernstock, *VA prosthetic and sensory aids program.* 1977, 51-52, 91.

14.   Stewart and Bernstock, *VA prosthetic and sensory aids program.* 1977, 86-87.

15.   Childress, D., Ph.D., personal communication with author, February 6, 2002.

16.   Stewart and Bernstock, *VA prosthetic and sensory aids program.* 1977, 93-96.

17.   Interview with Vernon L. Nickel, M.D., January 15, 1992 at a restaurant in San Diego, CA.

18.   Interview with Ernest Burgess, M.D., November 4, 1992 at Dr. Burgess's office in Seattle, WA.

19.   Stewart and Bernstock, *VA prosthetic and sensory aids program.* 1977, 30-31.

20.   Haugen, J.S., *Reading Machines for the Blind: A study of Federally supported technology development and innovation, 1943-1980.* Blacksburg, VA: Virginia Polytechnic Institute and State University, 1995, 47.

21.   Stewart and Bernstock, *VA prosthetic and sensory aids program.* 1977, 102-104.

22.   Haugen, *Reading Machines for the Blind.* 1995, 13-20.

23.   Haugen, *Reading Machines for the Blind.* 1995, 50-54.

24.   Haugen, *Reading Machines for the Blind.* 1995, 62-68.

25.   Stewart and Bernstock, *VA prosthetic and sensory aids program*. 1977, 98-100, 105-109.

26.   Haugen, *Reading Machines for the Blind*. 1995, 69-97.

27.   Stewart and Bernstock, *VA prosthetic and sensory aids program*. 1977, 104-105.

28.   Haugen, *Reading Machines for the Blind*. 1995, 98-118.

29.   Haugen, *Reading Machines for the Blind:*. 1995, 8.

30.   Nickel, V.L., "Veterans Administration rehabilitative engineering research and development programs." *Bulletin of Prosthetics Research*, 1980. **17**: 113-115.

31.   Nickel, V.L., "Veterans Administration rehabilitative engineering research and development programs." *Bulletin of Prosthetics Research*, 1980. **17**: 111-112.

32.   Telephone interview with Gregory Goodrich, Ph.D., January 29, 2002.

33.   Stewart and Bernstock, *VA prosthetic and sensory aids program*. 1977, 3-4.

34.   Interview with Thomas Newcomb, M.D., March 29, 1992 at a hotel lobby in Washington, DC.

35.   Chase, J.D., M.D., "IL 10-76-2 Chief Medical Director's Letter. Rehabilitation Engineering R&D Service." January 20, 1976.

36.   Chase, J.D., M.D., "IL 10-76-40 Chief Medical Director's Letter. Rehabilitative engineering research and development center." August 5, 1976.

<u>Examples</u>

<u>Part VI Research in individual VA medical centers</u>

Chapter 21. Research at the Palo Alto VA Medical Center

The present Palo Alto VA Medical Center (now called the VA Palo Alto Health Care System) has three campuses and a number of clinics. The Livermore Division, located in Livermore, CA in the hills east of the San Francisco Bay, was a separate hospital until a recent merger. Its research activity has always been modest, though it housed the Western R&D Office (Chapter 17) until that office was closed in 2001, and it was one of the sites of the early tuberculosis treatment studies (Chapter 5).

The Menlo Park Division is the original Palo Alto VA Hospital. The area where it is located, while now a part of the City of Menlo Park and in a different county from the City of Palo Alto, was called North Palo Alto in 1917, when the original hospital was built. The current Palo Alto Division, which is indeed located in Palo Alto, opened in 1960.

This chapter discusses the research carried out at the Palo Alto VAMC through 1980. Coverage of the huge research enterprise that developed after 1980 must be left to another effort.

The Palo Alto VA Hospital before World War II

The campus of the original Palo Alto VA Hospital, now called the Menlo Park Division, was on grounds of a World War I Army hospital, the Camp Fremont base hospital. It was expanded by purchase of land with money raised by the Palo Alto Chamber of Commerce (Chapter 1). At first it was a Public Health Service hospital and was transferred to the Veterans Bureau in 1922. Originally the hospital primarily treated tuberculosis, but it had several wards for general medicine and surgery, and was a referral center for patients with medical and surgical problems. In 1924, a new unit of nine modern hospital buildings designed for care of neuropsychiatric patients opened. Patients "were sent in by train loads and in a short time the new wards were full."[1] While primarily a psychiatric hospital after 1924, the Palo Alto Veterans' Hospital had a full range of services until the San Francisco VA Hospital opened in 1934.

In 1928 the Palo Alto Veterans' Hospital was designated a Diagnostic Center, largely due to the efforts of Ray Lyman Wilbur, M.D., President of Stanford University and chairman of the Veterans' Bureau Medical Council. By 1929, a Postgraduate School for specialized training of Bureau physicians was functioning at Palo Alto.

The hospital is described in an "Annual Report" published (using a donated press, the work done by patients) in 1924.[2] The new psychiatric wards had recently been completed and housed 1296 patients. Half (648) of the psychiatric patients were diagnosed with "dementia praecox" (schizophrenia). Sixty-five had syphilitic disease of the nervous system. Only three diagnoses of "drug addiction" were reported. The report states that:

"The treatment given is along modern lines and consists of hydrotherapy and electrotherapy, calisthenics, occupational therapy and habit training, the purpose of all these being to keep the patient physically fit and to re-educate him to more normal ways of living. Contrary to the popular concept of mental diseases so far as prognosis is concerned a considerable percentage of the cases admitted to this service are enabled, after a period of treatment, to make a satisfactory adjustment and are discharged to their homes as improved. In a smaller percentage of these cases actual recovery takes place."[3]

The tuberculosis service was located in eight of the wards of the old Camp Fremont Base Hospital until it was moved to the new Livermore hospital in 1925. There were 180-190 tuberculosis patients, most of them on bed rest, the sickest even being fed by nurses. When allowed up, patients rested on porches in reclining chairs donated to the hospital.[4]

Figure 21.1 The building for tuberculosis patients.

The hospital had a farm, used primarily for training of patients, but the food raised fed the sickest patients. There were 5000 laying hens, fifty brood sows and 200 breeding ducks, as well as extensive gardens.[5]

The Clinical Laboratory was under the direction of Dr. T.H.T. Wight, whom Ray Lyman Wilbur described in 1924 as having "an instinct for research" (Chapter 1). The laboratory force included Dr. Wight, one "laboratorian" and two "boys", one of whom "is on his way to becoming a fair technician." "Both boys excel in catching and bleeding our sheep for Wasserman day." In addition to some 25,000 clinical tests annually, the laboratory "continually" tested the hospital's milk, water and food supplies. There was an animal house, with two sheep, 50 rabbits, 100 guinea pigs and numerous white rats and mice, all used for clinical tests.[6]

The earliest publications from the hospital were by Dr. Wight. He became interested in an organism called "Councilmania lafleuri" that had been reported in 1921 as a new intestinal parasite. After extensive examination of hundreds of stools from patients "from all over the world," Wight concluded that this organism was simply a variant of E. Coli.[7] In the same journal issue, he published a method for producing "rainbow medium", for studying

438

chemical reactions in bacterial flora of the gastro-intestinal tract.[8] The Councilmania controversy was further detailed, with extensive photomicrographs, in a joint paper with L.H. Prince, M.D., of the Veterans' Bureau Pathological Unit at the Army Medical Museum, confirming Wight's earlier thesis.[9]

In a 1926 report on 1341 stool examinations, Wight found Endamoeba histolytica in 92 patients, only 31 of whom were symptomatic. He urged treatment of carriers, to prevent further spread of this organism.[10] Also in 1926, collaborating with Prince, Wight published a report and discussion of a case of renal cell carcinoma.[11] In 1929, he published about the "Gregerson test" for detection of occult blood in the stool,[12] and in 1930 about the importance of iron in the medium for culturing typhoid organisms.[13]

Staff of the early Palo Alto Veterans' Hospital published clinical papers on ophthalmic signs observed in neuropsychiatric diseases,[14] on "inadequate behavior,"[15] "toxic psychosis,"[16] hysteria,[17] early symptoms of brain tumor,[18] amnesia,[19] "paraphrenia,"[20] schizoid mechanisms[21] and on improved dental techniques.[22]

On March 17, 1928, the hospital's new Diagnostic Center, the third in the Veterans' Bureau, was dedicated. General Hines, the Administrator, attended and inspected the facilities. The Medical Director of the Veterans' Bureau, Dr. B.W. Black, spoke, describing the Diagnostic Center as the "Supreme Court" on medical matters for veterans in the West. Ray Lyman Wilbur spoke for the Medical Council.[23] Dr. Wilbur was credited with "valuable assistance in its establishment."[24]

Figure 21.2. The Diagnostic Center

The Diagnostic Center (Figure 21.2) occupied 50 beds in a building that also housed the hospital's surgery, eye, otolaryngology, dental, radiology and laboratory facilities and the pharmacy. There were also 100 beds in this building for "general medical and surgery" patients, who were under treatment after discharge from the Diagnostic Center. Professional staff of the Diagnostic Center included 14 full time physicians, most of them specialists, as well as 26 part time and consulting specialists drawn from the medical school faculties of the University of California and Stanford University. Patients admitted to the Diagnostic Center received a large battery of examinations by the full time staff and many radiological and laboratory studies. The ward surgeons observed them frequently. As soon as results of the various tests and examinations were available, a patient's case would be reviewed at a daily case conference, where there was open discussion to reach a consensus about the diagnosis. After this "staff diagnosis" had been established, the case was assigned to a consultant. The consultant's report was then reviewed at another staff conference, comparing his opinion with that of the staff. Typically, this process could be completed within 30 days![25]

Publications from the Diagnostic Center emphasized clinical observations: multiple sclerosis,[26] narcolepsy,[27] etiology of epilepsy,[28] tetany from overbreathing,[29] conversion hysteria,[30] gall bladder disease,[31] panniculitis,[32] suppurative phlebitis,[33] coarctation of the aorta,[34] cardiac response to vagal stimulation,[35] splenic abscess,[36] meningitis,[37] epidemic encephalitis,[38, 39] esophageal stricture,[40] gastrointestinal lesions in psychoneurosis, bronchial spirochetosis,[41] elliptical erythrocytes,[42] myeloid leukemia,[43] meningo-encephalitis,[44] diencephalic lesions[45] and transverse myelitis.[46] The laboratory reported on methods for blood typing and on a new method to prepare gold solution for colloidal gold tests of spinal fluid.[47, 48] The surgeon discussed a new approach to thyroidectomy.[49]

Meanwhile the physicians in the neuropsychiatric section of the hospital were exploring new treatments for their patients. Carbon dioxide inhalation appeared to help some catatonic patients,[50] as did a carefully supervised regimented routine.[51] Sodium amytal was found to help calm acutely agitated patients.[52] A case demonstrating the difficulty in diagnosing tertiary syphilis in the presence of schizophrenia was reported,[53] as was a case of psychosis associated with alcoholic pellagra.[54] The legal aspects of psychiatry were discussed.[55]

Treatment of neurosyphilis (paresis) with malaria in addition to antisyphilitic drugs began in 1926; in 1931 the first 42 patients were reviewed. Nine of these patients had been discharged and were reported to be adjusting well.[56] The following year, six paretic patients with marked agitation were reported much improved by malaria treatment.[57] For patients unresponsive to antisyphilitic treatment and malaria, ultraviolet light exposure followed by injections of autogenous blood appeared to help.[58] A comprehensive review in 1934 of 304 paretic patients treated intensively with antisyphilitic drugs and malaria, reported that 16 had been discharged from the hospital and 85% of the others were considered improved.[59, 60]

More theoretical reports included a discussion of the role of affect in psychotic behavior[61] and the significance of schizoid mechanisms in the manic-depressive syndrome.[62]

In the early 1930s, the hospital established a Medical Society that held monthly meetings. The 37th such meeting was held on April 19, 1934. Dinner was served in the nurses' dining hall at 6:30, followed by the scientific program in the personnel dining hall. Approximately 75 physicians attended, including members of the San Mateo County Medical Society.[63] The papers at these meetings were usually given by one or two faculty members from the medical schools at the University of California or Stanford University, followed by discussion. The Society also met with the Santa Clara County Medical Society. Physicians from nearby, including the Livermore VA Hospital, generally attended.

In the Postgraduate School, visiting physicians spent four months in special training. Five physicians were assigned to the session that began in October 1932.[64]

In 1934, the Diagnostic Center moved from Palo Alto to the new VA hospital in San Francisco. This arrangement was much more convenient for the consultants from the medical schools, both of which were in San Francisco, 40 miles from Palo Alto. All of the medical and surgical patients as well as 10 doctors and 11 nurses were transferred to San Francisco, leaving only the neuropsychiatric units at Palo Alto. The Diagnostic Center building was refurbished to accommodate some of the many psychiatric patients on the waiting list for admission.

From then through World War II, the character of the hospital seems to have changed. Staff authored only a total of 16 publications of any type during the 1936-1945 period. The aftermath of the Great Depression hit hospital funding; many staff entered the military at the beginning of the war. By 1946, the Palo Alto VA Hospital had slipped to the point that Paul Magnuson, then ACMD for Research and Education, wrote sadly of his visit there (Chapter 3).

The postwar Research Program before 1960

This dismal situation began to turn around when new educational and research programs started in 1946 under the new Department of Medicine and Surgery. An active psychiatry residency program began in 1946 at the Palo Alto VA Hospital, even though the affiliated medical schools were located in San Francisco. A large psychology internship program was in place by 1947.[65] It was associated with the Stanford University clinical psychology program, already located on Stanford's Palo Alto campus. The Palo Alto VA Hospital soon became the central site for VA psychology training programs for the west coast.[66] Psychology interns were encouraged to participate in research projects at the hospital. The hospital leaders tried to hire staff who could enhance these educational programs.[67] In December 1948, a Research Committee was established, with representatives from both Stanford University and the University of California.[68]

By 1950, the hospital had research programs in psychology, ethnology, biochemistry and pathology. The psychology research program grew in prominence during the 1950s. By 1960, the Menlo Park campus is said to have had one of the most eminent groups of academic psychologists in the country. They were housed in a Quonset hut during the early 1950s, and later in a remodeled dormitory building. When the Palo Alto Division opened in 1960, some of the most active psychology research laboratories moved to the new division.

Between 1949 and 1960, the research program grew steadily in personnel and funds, though the funding remained very modest. The number of professional staff members and trainees involved in research projects varied from 40 to 60 during the 1950s. Among them were 6 to 16 psychology trainees and 1 to 5 psychiatry residents. Funding decisions before 1956 were made by the Research Committee, which met in the Schoolhouse and deliberated such requests as $250 for a tachistoscope (1952) and a typewriter (1953). Even small supply items were preapproved by the Committee. In FY1953, the total Palo Alto VA research budget was $8,809, including $6,454 in salaries for two GS3 clerks. By FY 1959, there were 13.1 FTEE employees, with salary costs of $68,352 and a total VA research budget of $81,120. Non VA funding in FY1953 was $5,833. In FY1959, it was $46,770. (Records provided by Paul McReynolds, Ph.D.) The Research Committee had a broad representation, including administrative leaders and active researchers. It met once or twice a month. Investigators gave talks on their proposed research and received feedback from the committee members. They also presented completed projects. The meetings were open to all interested persons; sometimes there was a large attendance. In addition, at least for a time, there were bimonthly research seminars.

About 1956, in anticipation of Stanford's move of its medical school to Palo Alto, the VA dropped the hospital's academic affiliation with the University of California and strengthened its affiliation with Stanford University. As a part of its increased interest, the new Stanford Dean's Committee appointed a Research Subcommittee to overview the hospital's research program. This Subcommittee defined its role as: 1. To approve or disapprove research proposals forwarded by the hospital Research Committee and to assign funding priorities. 2. To provide advice of a consultative nature. The hospital Research Committee was "to stimulate the initiation of research projects by the personnel of the hospital and to help formulate these projects in the best possible way. These activities should be carried on without regard to the relationship of budgetary request to available funds, although specific budgetary items should be questioned if their relevancy to the scientific aspects of the project are not clear."[69] At the instigation of the Dean's Committee, the Research Committee was reconstituted to be smaller, consisting primarily of service chiefs.[70]

The Dean's Committee Research Subcommittee met once or twice a year, and reviewed any projects not already funded, requiring a formal written application. On at least one occasion, Dr. Raffel, the Subcommittee chair, visited VA Central Office on behalf of the research program.[71] He also persuaded the Acting Dean to write to Dr. Middleton on the Dean's Committee's behalf, urging an increase in the budget.[72]

In 1956, the Dean's Subcommittee denied a request from Gregory Bateson for additional funds for a project primarily funded by a grant, on grounds that the grant should support the whole effort. Bateson responded with a letter pointing out the importance of a policy

442

precedent that would discourage VA staff from applying for funds from other sources.[73] By a split vote, the Subcommittee reversed its position.[74]

Research investigators recruited to the Menlo Park Campus

Paul McReynolds, Ph.D.

Dr. McReynolds began working at the Palo Alto VA Hospital on a part time basis in 1947, while he was a graduate student in the Stanford clinical psychology program. When he finished his Ph.D. in 1949, he was hired as a full-time clinical psychologist, and soon became Chief of Psychology Research. He recalled that, when he was hired, he was the only psychologist doing research, but that Virginia Cull, a biochemist and chief of Laboratory Service, was doing research, as were others in pathology. He was appointed Executive Secretary of the Research Committee, and functioned as the administrative head of the research program. He set agendas for the Research Committee, kept its minutes, and handled research funds. He continued to carry out that responsibility until 1960 when, with the opening of the new Palo Alto Division, Leo Hollister was appointed full-time Associate Chief of Staff for Research and Education (ACOS/R&E).

McReynolds recruited Robert McFarland, Ph.D., as his assistant in about 1951. When McFarland left for the Chicago Research VA Hospital after a few years, Robert Weiss, Ph.D. replaced him. Weiss later went to the University of Oregon. McFarland and his colleagues studied the nature of schizophrenia. They developed psychological tests to evaluate schizophrenic patients. In collaboration with J. Ferguson, M.D., a psychiatrist, they published the Hospital Adjustment Scale. They worked on the Rorschach test, setting up norms for its use in psychotic patients. They developed the Rorschach Concept Evaluation Technique, and standardized it at Palo Alto during the early 1960s. McReynolds helped plan the early centralized cooperative studies that were coordinated by the Perry Point group (Chapter 8).

When the new Palo Alto Division opened in 1960, McReynolds, Weiss, and others in the Psychology Research group moved to Building 4 on the new campus. The group now included Al Helavy, Ph.D., a biochemist, and Hugh Conn, Ph.D., a psychologist who did EEG research. Each year, they had a research fellow who was funded by Central Office. There were a half dozen of these research assistants. This group remained active until McReynolds moved to the University of Nevada in 1969.[65]

Gregory Bateson

In 1949, John Prusmak, M.D., the Chief, Professional Services, of the Palo Alto VA Hospital, arranged to recruit Gregory Bateson, a famous British anthropologist, to join the hospital's staff with the title "Ethnologist". Bateson's assignment was to teach the psychology and psychiatry trainees about cross-cultural behavior and to carry out his own research on communication.[67] He was disheveled in appearance, looked "like an unmade bed." He was an excellent raconteur and described as "very nice." He "could make a long conversation out of a casual comment." As former residents described him to the author, he was brilliant and very interesting, but hard to follow, often trying to explain cybernetics to them.[75, 76] He had an informal weekly evening meeting at his home, largely attended by residents, in which the discussion was wide-ranging, from individual patient cases to major philosophic problems.

Bateson attempted therapy on a few VA patients, primarily in an attempt to understand them better. He became very much interested in schizophrenic communication[77] and developed a theory (the double bind theory) that schizophrenia stemmed from communication "traps", especially with the mother, in childhood. This theory led to experiments in treatment of family interactions and was the beginning of the current field of family therapy. Later, while still at Palo Alto, Bateson expanded his interests to animal behavior and worked with zoo animals. He even attempted to communicate with octopi, which he housed at the hospital and at his home. He would go to the ocean to get brine shrimp to feed the octopi.[78] The FY 1961 Annual Report of Research Activities lists a 300 square foot "octopus laboratory" among the hospital's assets.[79] After Bateson left Palo Alto in 1961 to study dolphin communications in Hawaii, the research team he had set up formed a privately funded institute in Palo Alto, where they developed the field of family therapy.[80]

Leo Hollister, M.D.

In 1952, Leo Hollister, M.D., an internist, was transferred to Menlo Park from the San Francisco VA Hospital, where he had been working as the personnel physician since leaving the military after service in the Korean War. Dr. Prusmak was sent to him for a physical examination as a part of his promotion to Manager of the Palo Alto hospital. In their conversation, Dr. Prusmak learned that Dr. Hollister lived in Palo Alto; there was an internist on the Palo Alto staff who lived in San Francisco. They arranged a trade.

Figure 21.3. Leo Hollister (second from left) at the time he received the Middleton Award. Also shown are (left to right) Chief Medical Director Engel, Hollister's parents and Lucien Guze.

444

Hollister found himself the Chief of the Medical Service in this psychiatric hospital, in charge of a large ward of psychiatrically ill patients who also had medical illnesses.

Many of his patients were hypertensive. He tried the new antihypertensive drug, reserpine, and noticed that his patients' psychotic signs seemed to improve. Hollister arranged with Dr. Prusmak to do a blinded trial of reserpine for schizophrenic patients. He asked interested psychiatrist colleagues to send him patients for treatment, and he gave the patients either reserpine or a placebo. Neither the patient nor the referring psychiatrist knew what the patient was receiving. The referring psychiatrist then decided whether the patient had improved. This study showed that reserpine caused dramatic improvement.[81]

Shortly afterwards, Hollister met Mark Altschule of Harvard, who was interested in schizophrenia and had used the new drug chlorpromazine. Hollister decided to test its effectiveness, using the same randomized approach as he had used with reserpine. By the end of 1954, the results were in. His presentation at a meeting of the AAAS was enthusiastically received.[82]

In 1955, Clyde Lindley of Central Office came to Palo Alto to meet with Hollister. Together, they designed a survey of VA hospitals to see what the experience had been with the new psychoactive drugs. They had a 100% response, confirming the dramatic improvement.

The Central Office leadership wanted to use a scientific approach to learning how best to use the new psychotherapeutic drugs. The early use of these drugs was empirical. Good studies were needed to establish their effectiveness, the relative potencies of different drugs, their risks and proper dosage regimens. Hollister was active in all of the activities of the early group that started the VA Cooperative Studies in Psychopharmacology (Chapter 8).

Hollister continued his interest in medical problems. He studied hyperlipidemia states[83-87] and, collaborating with pathologist Virginia Cull, he reported on chronic thrombosis of the pulmonary arteries.[88]

In 1960, when the new Palo Alto Division opened, Hollister moved there and became ACOS/R&E. He started a group of new studies together with a subgroup of the Cooperative Studies group, doing early evaluations of new psychoactive drugs, comparable to the present Phase 2 studies.

During the 1960s and early 1970s, Hollister and his collaborators became interested in the hallucinogenic drugs[89-99] and marijuana and its analogs, and studied them in normal subjects and psychiatric patients under an FDA license.[100-144] Author Ken Kesey, who was working as a ward aide on a psychiatric ward, volunteered for one of the LSD experiments. Hollister recalled that Kesey had a very rich fantasy response. As it turned out Kesey had received a placebo![77]

Jered Tinklenberg, M.D., who worked with Hollister in the 1970s and early 1980s, described him an excellent mentor, who would encourage the development of new hypotheses followed up by protocols. According to Tinklenberg, Hollister was absolutely honest, but also uncompromising. He did not recognize boundaries, and was willing to try anything. Hollister was a "bedside doc." He insisted on clinical observations and did not trust gadgets. He insisted that the researcher must be active and hands on. If one tried a drug on a subject one tried it first on oneself.[145]

Hollister received the VA's Middleton Award in 1966 "For numerous, significant contributions in the field of therapeutic drugs for mental illness." In 1970, he was honored with appointment as Medical Investigator and, in 1982, as Senior Medical Investigator. His work ranged from continued clinical studies to experimental use of new drugs in human and animal subjects, to studies of the cellular mechanisms of drug effects in mental illness. His laboratory graduated many leaders in academic psychiatry.

Leonard Krasner, Ph.D. and Leonard Ullman, Ph.D.

Dr. Krasner entered the VA as a psychologist in the Brooklyn VA Mental Health Clinic. He went to the Lexington, KY VA Hospital in 1951 as Assistant Chief of Psychology and in 1953 came to the Palo Alto VA Hospital as director of the VA Psychology Training Program. His responsibilities actually covered all of the VA-funded psychology training programs on the west coast. These trainees were involved with research. He brought in consultants from Stanford and U.C. Berkeley. Later, Krasner became Assistant Chief of Psychology.

Leonard Ullman, one of the early trainees, began research collaboratively with Krasner at Palo Alto even before receiving his Ph.D. degree. In 1956, after a year of postdoctoral fellowship, Ullman joined the Palo Alto staff as the local head of the Psychology Evaluation Project, a multihospital project funded by the VACO's Psychiatry Service, headed by Lee Gurel, Ph.D.[146]

Krasner and Ullman squeezed time from their regular duties and spent long hours on collaborative research. Their particular interests were nonverbal communications, verbal conditioning and behavior modification. They sought and received a Public Health Service grant through their Stanford courtesy appointments and hired Robert Weiss. Then Weiss assumed a VA appointment and was replaced on the grant by Paul Eckman. This group worked on verbal conditioning and found that they could very quickly bring out schizophrenic symptoms, which could then be dealt with by behavior modification. A book, *Case Studies in Behavior Modification*, by Ullman and Krasner (Holt, 1965), resulted from this work. They also worked on nonverbal communications and published their findings in another book, *Behavior Influence and Personality*.[66, 147]

George Fairweather, Ph.D.

Dr. Fairweather came to the Palo Alto VA Hospital in 1957. For two years previously, he had been at the Perry Point VA Hospital, where he worked on a project on the outcomes of treatment programs. He became interested in a group of psychiatric patients who adapted poorly, and he wanted to work with these people. Shortly after he arrived in Palo Alto, he met Robert S. Mowry, M.D., a psychiatrist, whom Fairweather described as "a renegade and a real hero." Mowry was excited about Fairweather's ideas on how to improve treatment of the chronic patients who did not adapt well. Together, Fairweather and Mowry worked to set up a research ward, with the support of Dr. Prusmak, who by then was the Hospital Director, and of the Research and Education Committee.

In this research, patients were asked to volunteer to be randomized either to the experimental community or to the usual ward milieu. Fifty percent of the patients in the group of chronically mentally ill maladapted patients volunteered. The volunteers were matched in pairs, one of each pair being placed in the usual ward situation and the other in the experimental community.

This program began in 1959 or 1960 and remained on the Menlo Park campus after the new Palo Alto Division opened. Initially the investigators studied shared management of the ward as the research intervention. The patients were evaluated with 120 measures for each patient. They found that the patients did very well in the hospital, but that once they were separated from the group they failed. This observation led to the decision to move the group into the community.

The first Lodge was established in 1961. Patients in the experimental ward were trained for one or two months in community life, and then were moved out from the hospital and into the community as a group. They set up a community living arrangement (a "Lodge"), from which they managed a business. This effort was supported by an NIMH grant. The business they set up was called the 49er Janitorial Service, and their living quarters were called the 49er's Lodge. At the end of four years, they had $400,000 in the bank and owned two businesses.

Melvin Lerner, a young social psychologist, worked with Fairweather. He had been in a postdoctoral position at Stanford and became interested in Fairweather's program. His special concerns were: How should the groups be composed? Should there be a professional included in the group? They compared groups that did and did not have professionals within them. They gave individual and group awards for certain accomplishments. They found that in general the all-patient group solved problems better than those that included a professional, but with a slower learning curve. When a professional was involved, the learning was rapid but never reached as high a level as when the group was entirely made up of patients. Also, the all-patient group developed cohesiveness, which was important to their well-being.

They found that for these groups to be successful they needed to have a distribution of leadership and social activity. It was also important that the verbal activity be distributed, with at least some patients being actively verbal, even if the verbal activity was speaking to hallucinations.

Figure 21.4. John Prusmak, M.D., Hospital Director who recruited Gregory Bateson, encouraged research and opened the new Palo Alto Division in 1960.

Dr. Prusmak, the Hospital Director (Figure 21.4), was very much interested in the Lodge. He would call every two to three months to see how things were going. Fairweather recalled that, after the Lodge was set up and funded by NIMH through Stanford, Stanford lawyers advised the residents about how to protect themselves. Among other things, they told them not to allow anyone whom they had not authorized to come into their house. Some time after that, Prusmak brought a visitor to show off the program. The residents didn't know him, and called the police. Prusmak was a very understanding person and did not hold it against the Lodge once he understood the situation.

While he was at Palo Alto, Fairweather, together with Tom Kennelley, the Chief of Psychology Service, studied the attitudes of the hospital toward this innovative program. They found that there was an increase in support as the research began to show results.

Fairweather has published two books based on this experience.[148, 149] Later, he was able to expand this study into a national program over a five year period. This later research was also directed toward methods to induce hospitals to change their programs. The Lodge concept has been widely adopted, though it has not been used much in the VA. The State of Texas alone has adopted 45 or 46 of the Lodge Societies.[150]

Irene and Fred Forrest

Fred Forrest, M.D. and Irene Forrest, Ph.D., a husband-wife team, became interested in the psychopharmacological agents even before Fred joined the VA at the Montrose, NY VA Hospital. Fred, a practicing psychiatrist, was a strong believer in the pharmacologic treatment of schizophrenia, stating that "the brain can get sick just like any other organ".

He felt a need for a practical test to establish whether patients were taking their medications. Irene, a chemist, took on the challenge of developing such a test. She traveled to the Woods Hole library, where she went through nineteenth century German reports on the chemistry of the phenothiazide compounds to gain the background necessary to develop a simple urine test for phenothiazide-containing drugs (most of the antipsychotic drugs in use at that time.) This was the beginning of a continuously
productive research program on the antipsychotic drugs that the Forrests soon moved to the new Brockton VA Hospital. In 1961, they transferred to the Menlo Park campus of the Palo Alto VA Hospital. Half of a Quonset hut was converted to laboratory space for

Figure 21.5. Irene Forrest, Ph.D., about 1979

Irene, the other half devoted to monkey research by sleep researcher William Dement (below). After Dement closed his VA laboratory, Irene Forrest's research filled the whole Quonset hut. There, she continued to expand knowledge about the pharmacology and chemistry of these compounds even after her retirement in 1978. In 1981, when it
was decided to demolish her Quonset hut, she and Fred built a room onto their home, where she continued her research well into her eighth decade.[151] Among her other honors was dedication of a book on the phenothiazines:

> "Although there is some controversy as to who is the father--or, to avoid charges of sexism, the parent--of <u>clinical</u> phenothiazine-ology, there is little question as to who is the parent of <u>laboratory</u> phenothiazine-ology: Irene S. Forrest. In hospitals and laboratories throughout the world, whenever there is a question of patient compliance with regard to ingestion of a phenothiazine, the almost universal procedure is to request a "Forrest's test" on the patient's urine. When there is a discussion of the number of metabolites of chlorpromazine, the standard reply is that Irene Forrest has indicated that there are 168 (even though this ignores the fact that Dr. Forrest has been demonstrating more and more chlorpromazine metabolites in recent years)."[152]

Figure 21.6. Forrest and Dement Quonset hut and research staff

The Palo Alto Division of the Palo Alto VA Hospital

In July 1960, the new division of the hospital opened in south Palo Alto. It was located on land owned by Stanford, but some 5 miles from the new Stanford University hospital and 9 miles from the old Menlo Park Division. This location was the result of a compromise. As Frederick Eldridge, M.D., who was on the Stanford faculty at the time, remembered it, when Stanford planned their move from San Francisco to Palo Alto, they realized they needed more clinical beds than their new hospital would provide. They went to the VA leadership, asking that they build a new hospital. The VA said that they did not need more medical and surgical beds, but they were planning a new psychiatric hospital. A compromise was reached in which there would be 250 medical-surgical beds in the new VA hospital.

The VA wanted to place this hospital next to the Medical School and the University Hospital. When word got to the Stanford faculty that there was going to be a psychiatric hospital next to their Medical School, they were alarmed, and blocked the plan. Finally, another compromise was reached: There was a "friendly condemnation suit" in which a piece of land near the edge of Stanford property, far distant from the Stanford Medical Center, was condemned and transferred to the Federal government for $525,193.[153, 154] This suit made it possible for Stanford to transfer the land to the Federal government. All this was necessary because the California State Constitution, thanks to the efforts of

450

Senator Leland Stanford at the founding of the University, forbade Stanford University from selling any of its property unless it had been condemned by a governmental institution.[155]

When it opened, the new hospital had, in addition to the 250 medical-surgical beds, 140 neurological beds, 200 geriatric beds and about 400 acute psychiatric beds. Chronic psychiatric patients and those who were undergoing rehabilitation in preparation for discharge were to be housed at the Menlo Park Division.[156]

On July 1, 1960, Dr. McReynolds, Dr. Ullman and their group moved to the new hospital. Dr. Hollister also moved, but not as Chief of Medicine. Instead, he took over McReynolds's research administration duties and became Assistant Director, Professional Services, Research and Education, the position that was renamed "Associate Chief of Staff" the following year. He received a courtesy appointment in Internal Medicine at Stanford, but his research became increasingly oriented toward psychopharmacology.

When Hollister became ACOS/R&E, Prusmak suggested that he approach Frank Hevern, retired Assistant Manager of the hospital, to be his Administrative Officer. Hollister hired him on his own research grant moneys. Hollister recalled that Hevern turned out to be extremely talented in developing a research program. The hospital had been built with little research space, and Hevern succeeded in uncovering all sorts of areas which could be converted into research laboratories. He persuaded the various administrative services to help him and used moneys from any available source to convert space to laboratories. Over the first 5 years of the 1960s, they created approximately 20,000 square feet of research space, 15,000 of it within the first year.[157] An area in Building 1, the medical-surgical building on the Palo Alto campus, that had been intended for a patient dining room under the original plan for a psychiatric hospital, was renovated into laboratories.[155] Space intended for staff quarters on the top floor were gradually converted for research.

Nevertheless, it was apparent that more wet laboratory space was needed. About 1964, plans began for a new research wing on Building 1. Visits from VA and Stanford staff to VACO resulted in visits to Palo Alto by VACO engineers and architects. To maximize space while staying within budget, the new wing, the E wing, was built without windows. It opened in 1970.

Resident physicians from Stanford rotated through the VA in medicine, surgery and neurology. The psychiatry residency, which had been based only at the VA, became a Stanford residency. However, there were problems. Frederick Eldridge, M.D, the first Chief of Medicine at the new division, recalled fighting to persuade the hospital to provide food for residents and students who were on call. Under the previous system, there was a single Officer of the Day who would be fed, but under the Stanford plan there were multiple residents and students on call. It seemed reasonable that they should all receive food, but it required a new type of administrative thinking. There was also a battle over space for the cardiac catheterization lab, even though money was available from Central Office. Stanford also was undergoing stressful changes and could not always help.[155]

Psychiatry and psychology continued to be the major areas of research in the 1960s, but research in other fields emerged during that decade as new, academically-oriented, staff arrived. By the end of the decade, there were active programs in psychiatry, psychology, pathology, neurology, internal medicine, anesthesiology and surgery. Young clinicians were recruited through the Career Development Program (Chapter 14). Between 1962 and 1969, 16 new appointments were made in that program, five of them in psychology, three in psychiatry, but also three in surgery, one in pathology and four in various fields of internal medicine.

<u>Psychiatry and psychology research begun at the Palo Alto Division in the 1960s</u>

In 1961, David Hamburg, M.D., became chairman of the Department of Psychiatry at Stanford. He wanted to develop the new psychiatric unit at the Palo Alto Division as an academic unit. He recruited George Solomon, M.D., whose interest was in psychoimmunology, to become chief of a "Stanford" service.[158] At the same time, Rudolf Moos, Ph.D., a psychologist who had been collaborating with Solomon on the psychosomatic aspects of cancer and rheumatoid arthritis, became a Stanford faculty member based at the VA. Also recruited in 1962 was psychiatrist David Daniels, M.D

Daniels was very much interested in the work being done by George Fairweather's group at the Menlo Park division on the "lodge" concept for rehabilitation of seriously ill psychiatric patients. After trying various systems on the ward under his charge, he assembled an interested group to try a new approach. They formed the DANN Corporation, which included an employment agency. They helped patients to find jobs in the community, and they also did some in-house manufacturing. The patients remained on the wards, but were gone during the day to their jobs. (Daniels remembered that the Dietetic Service began to balk at making so many box lunches.) The staff visited the patients on the job in order to make sure that they were doing well.

The corporation got contracts for various services, such as repairing credit card machines. One problem was that the staff didn't know how to run a business. Business people from the community consulted with them. Syntex gave them a seminar on business methods.

From 1966 to 1969 Daniels had a large NIMH grant, about $100,000 a year, to enhance this program and to evaluate it. For comparison, there was a control ward, under George Gulevich, with similar patients but with a "kinder, gentler" treatment. They found that, while the patients were more satisfied with the control ward, they did better on the experimental ward. They also found that the patients were actually healthier when they were in the hospital than after they were discharged. For that reason, Daniels also started a community housing project, and his staff continued to assist patients after they went into the housing project. They had alumni meetings of the patients and found that at 6 and 12 months' follow-up the improvement was sustained.[159]

Sleep research in psychiatry

In 1963, George Gulevich, M.D., a psychiatrist, joined the staff. In addition to running the comparison ward for Daniels's study, he opened the first clinical research sleep program. He collaborated with William C. Dement, M.D., Ph.D., who had come to Stanford in 1961, and whose research facility at Stanford consisted only of a small closet-sized room. Gulevich worked with Dement there, where they did REM deprivation studies on medical students. Gulevich set up a clinical sleep program on ward 4B2. He had an office and a two-bed patient room with a one-way mirror between. He studied schizophrenic patients during sleep with EEG monitoring. Typically, he would do his full ward duties by day, go home for dinner, and then come back to study a patient. This involved staying up all night, as he had no one to help him with these studies. At the end of the night, he would take the patient out to breakfast as a sort of thank you. During these studies, he did partial REM deprivations on schizophrenic patients, involving REM-depriving them for a couple of nights, and then studying the rebound. He showed that there is an abnormal rebound in schizophrenics.[160]

About 1965, Dement opened a basic science sleep lab in half of a Quonset hut at Menlo Park. Some of his studies required monkeys. One Saturday morning some of the monkeys escaped with electrodes in place. However, they were recovered.[161]

In 1966, Vincent Zarcone, M.D., still a resident, began to work with Gulevich. When Gulevich moved to Stanford in 1967, Zarcone took over the VA sleep program. Between 1967 and 1972 he continued the work on REM deprivation. He found that there was a failure of REM rebound in acute schizophrenia, whereas, when the patients were in remission, the REM rebound was exaggerated. He collaborated with Dement at his Menlo Park Quonset hut, studying an animal model for this phenomenon. These were cats that had been treated with a chemical to deplete serotonin; the animals appeared psychotic. They showed abnormal aggression and their REM sleep became very abnormal, with spikes at different stages of sleep and even when awake. Treatment with chlorpromazine reversed these changes. In these studies, they REM-deprived cats. The cat would be placed on a brick surrounded by water. The brick was small enough so that the cat could sit but not lie down. Each time it would fall asleep, it would get wet, and that would wake it up. Hence it was not necessary to intervene in order to REM-deprive the animals. Later, as mentioned above, Dement moved his basic studies to Stanford, and Irene Forrest, who had shared the Quonset hut, took over his space.

During the 1970s, Zarcone, with Kate Benson, Ph.D., who joined him in 1974, studied sleep in alcoholics. They showed that alcohol caused a decrease in 5-hydroxyindoleacetic acid, a serotonin precursor, in cerebrospinal fluid, indicating decreased serotonin metabolism. These subjects had prolonged REM sleep and abnormalities in slow wave sleep. Zarcone and Benson went on to do basic studies of sleep and its relationship to the cerebrospinal fluid chemistry. They found that there was a very strong correlation between 5-hydroxyindoleacetic acid levels in the cerebrospinal fluid and stage three and four sleep.[162]

New research laboratories for psychiatry

In addition to Dement's primates at Menlo Park, there was also a monkey colony at the Palo Alto Division, part of construction in Building 4 for psychiatric research. The monkey colony was said to be a part of a plan to attract Jane Goodall to the institution, a plan that fell through. There was also a primate research center under James Dewson studying sensory processing in monkeys. While a few such studies were done, eventually the monkeys were moved out and the space reassigned. The project of which it was a part, however, prepared over 3000 square feet of space, essentially the entire first floor of Building 4, for research. Hamburg is given credit for bringing about this major step, which prepared Psychiatry Service for later hosting an NIMH-funded Clinical Research Center and a VA-supported Schizophrenia Biologic Research Center. Hamburg had been at NIMH, and his intent was to build a well-run unit on the same plan as NIMH's intramural program.

The Evoked Potential Laboratory

Bert Kopell, M.D., was recruited by Hamburg in 1964. He had just finished his residency at the University of Colorado, and was interested in biologic psychiatry, a field not then in vogue. Hamburg used some of his own grant money to send Kopell to the Langley Porter Clinic in San Francisco to learn how to do evoked potentials. Kopell then set up an evoked potential laboratory in Building 4. At that time Kopell did all the research himself. All that he needed was the equipment and subjects. He gradually built up the laboratory until the Palo Alto VA had the best equipped evoked potential lab anywhere. It was completely computer controlled.[163]

This facility later attracted other young psychiatrists, who started out in the evoked potential laboratory and then went into other areas of biological psychiatry. Adolf Pfefferbaum came as an assistant professor in 1974.[164] In the late 1970s, stimulated by the VA's announcement of a competition for a schizophrenia biologic research center (Chapter 16), which included imaging, he began to do brain imaging. Steven Stahl, M.D., and Terry Jernigan, Ph.D., joined in this effort. They worked with the PET instrument at the Donner Laboratory in Berkeley, transporting acutely ill schizophrenics from Palo Alto to Berkeley for the studies. This work was an important factor leading to the hospital's acquiring its own PET camera in the early 1980s.

Walton T. (Tom) Roth was another young psychiatrist recruited to Kopell's evoked potential laboratory. While a fellow at St Elizabeth's Hospital, he studied evoked potentials, and demonstrated that the P300 was decreased in schizophrenic patients, and he continued this work after he came to Palo Alto in 1971. Studying cognitive evoked potentials, he showed changes in schizophrenics and on drugs, and that this technique clearly differentiates the apparent dementia of schizophrenia from senile dementia. Roth later focused his research on anxiety disorders and panic attacks.[165]

Another young psychiatrist recruited by Hamburg was Jered Tinklenberg, M.D. He met Hamburg while he was still a medical student in Iowa and visited Stanford in 1964, during his senior year. After a psychiatry residency at Stanford, he joined the VA. As a resident, he started working with Leo Hollister and Hollister's colleagues Hamp Gillespie and Saul Kanter, and helped to link the Kopell laboratory with Hollister's. He worked on the early studies of cannibis, done on volunteer subjects. Many of their first subjects were persons with professional contact with marijuana, such as judges and guidance counselors.

Tinklenberg began to develop an independent research program centered on drug effects on cognition. Initially, he studied drugs that reduced cognition, such as cannabis, alcohol, and the barbituates. Then he began studying drugs to improve memory, drugs with potential benefit in Alzheimer's disease. In recent years, he has concentrated on the problems of geropsychiatry.[145]

The Social Ecology Laboratory

Rudolph Moos, Ph.D., who became a part of the VA group in 1962 (though salaried by Stanford until 1974), came with the charge to develop a psychiatry research program. He served as a collaborator, advisor and expeditor for psychiatry research. He "ran a psychiatrist research training program". He tried to help the psychiatrists to get their own research programs going, and advised them in all aspects of research methodology.

Moos became interested in process and outcomes studies. One of the early studies was Daniels's therapeutic community, discussed above. There he became interested in the effects of ward milieu on therapy. This led him to study ward atmosphere. He developed two scales that have had a major impact, a scale of ward atmosphere and another on community-oriented programs' environment. His ward atmosphere scale was used in a VA Cooperative Study on ward milieu. The process of developing these scales was prolonged and complex. First, in the "anthropologic" phase, he studied a diverse group of wards to get information about the entire field to be covered by the scale. Then, a preliminary version was devised incorporating observations that might be items in the scale. Then a number of different versions were pretested. They would ask everyone on the ward the same question and then compare the answers. The major pretest scale for the ward atmosphere scale had 206 items in it. Finally, they would determine whether an item differentiated between wards and would study item distributions and intercorrelations.

In the mid 1970s, Moos prepared an evaluation scale for geriatric wards. Paul Haber, M.D., who started the Geriatric Research, Education and Clinical Centers in the VA, came to Palo Alto and asked him to undertake this project. It was one of the first field projects funded by Health Services Research and Development (HSR&D) Service. Much of what Moos had been doing fitted into what was now being defined as health services research, and by the 1980s this had become his major focus. He and Harold Sox, M.D., an internist who also was involved in health services research, applied for, and eventually received funding for, an HSR&D Field Program, which has become increasingly prominent at Palo Alto VAMC.[166]

Figure 21.7. The Social Ecology Laboratory staff in 1977

Research in pathology

Charles Conley, M.D., who had been at the Menlo Park hospital before 1960, moved to the new Palo Alto Division as Chief of Laboratory Service, but he left a year later and was replaced by Bruno Gerstl, M.D., who had been at the Oakland VA Hospital (Chapter 3). Jon Kosek, M.D., did his final year of pathology residency under Conley and stayed as a staff pathologist under Gerstl.[167] Gerstl recruited Lawrence Eng, Ph.D. as his chief chemist.

Lawrence Eng, Ph.D.

Dr. Eng was a Ph.D. student in biochemistry at Stanford in the late 1950's. In August 1961, at the time that Bruno Gerstl came to Palo Alto from the Oakland VA, Eng was hired to train residents in basic Clinical Chemistry, to supervise Dr. Gerstl's research program and to develop clinical chemistry tests.

As time went on, he also began to do animal experimentation, and, collaborating with Marion Smith, developed a method to separate proteins from myelin. About 1970 he acquired independent research funding and his own laboratory. In 1971, he and his coworkers isolated glial fibrillary acidic protein (GFAP) from the plaques of multiple sclerosis patients. They produced an antibody to GFAP that has been shared (without cost) with thousands of laboratories throughout the world.

In recent years, Eng has had great recognition. He received the Middleton Award in 1988. His award plaque cited him "For identification, characterization and immunocytochemical

456

studies of glial fibrillary acidic protein (GFAP), the intermediate filament protein of differentiated astrocytes. GFAP has become a prototype antigen in central nervous tissue identification and a standard marker for fundamental and applied neurobiology at an interdisciplinary level. Antibodies to GFAP are used routinely in medical centers throughout the world to assist in the diagnosis of brain tumors."

Eng served on an NIH study section for 6 years and did a term on the Neurobiology Merit Review Board which he completed in 1990. Later he served a term on the Council of the Neurologic Institute of NIH.[168] At the time of his retirement in 2004, an issue of *Neurochemical Research* was dedicated to him as a festschrift.

Luis Fajardo, M.D.

Dr. Fajardo joined the Palo Alto VAMC as a staff pathologist in 1966. When Dr. Gerstl retired in 1977, Fajardo became Chief of the Laboratory Service. He has collaborated widely in studies of radiation effects and of the pathology of parasitic diseases. He summarized his most important research contributions as:

"a. The characterization of heart injury produced by therapeutic radiation of adjacent thoracic tumors. We studied a large number of patients treated for lymphomas - mainly Hodgkin's disease - and coined the term Radiation Induced Heart Disease (RIHD), which is used today for a constellation of lesions including pericardial and myocardial fibrosis, and coronary artery disease. In addition we developed a model of RIHD in the New Zealand white rabbit (which develops pericardial and myocardial lesions identical to those of humans) and used it to determine the mechanisms of the myocardial fibrosis. These studies have resulted in modifications in the treatment of thoracic malignancies.[169, 170]
b. Study of radiation injury in multiple organs and in several mammalian species, resulting in many articles. These observations are compiled in two books.[171, 172]
c. Invention of a novel in-vivo system for the study and quantification of angiogenesis. The Disc Angiogenesis System (DAS), has been used in numerous experiments in mice to study the effects on angiogenesis of ionizing radiation and also the effects of hyperthermia, neoplasms and cytokines such as Tumor Necrosis Factor (TNF-alpha) and Transforming Growth Factor (TGF-beta-1)[173, 174]
d. Discovery that in mammals malaria parasites (plasmodia) not only invade red cells but also platelets.[175]
e. Demonstration, in a mouse model, that cerebral malaria (the most severe complication of malaria, often fatal) is mediated by the cytokine Tumor Necrosis Factor (TNF-alpha). Maneuvers to inhibit or block TNF are being tried.[176]
f. Discovery of a new form of parasitic infection: lethal invasive cestodiasis. Subsequent classification of these parasites by molecular techniques."[177, 178]

Neurology

William Hofmann, an assistant professor at Stanford, became Chief of the large Neurology Service in 1960, and he recruited Lysia Forno, M.D. as a neuropathologist. The following year, he recruited Ronald Angel, M.D., a clinical neurologist, and Marion Smith, Ph.D., who set up a basic neurochemistry laboratory.[179]   Dr. Forno became an authority on the neuropathology of Parkinson's Disease, and continued to do merit-review funded research well into her 80s.   Drs. Hofmann and Angel both published extensively in clinical neurology and also in human neurophysiology.

Figure 21.8. Marion Smith, Ph.D.

Dr. Smith collaborated widely and trained many successful neuroscientists. She received important recognitions, including dedication of an issue of *Neurochemical Research*.[161] During the late 1960s, she demonstrated that myelin, previously thought simply to provide structural support to neurons, has an active turnover. Her work on myelin metabolism and turnover led to improved understanding of the demyelinizing diseases such as multiple sclerosis. Her later work, some of it collaborative with Dr. Eng, included studies of astrocytic cytoskeletal proteins in demyelinating disease.

Internal medicine

Frederick Eldridge, M.D., who had been on the Stanford faculty in San Francisco, replaced Hollister as Chief of Medicine when the Palo Alto Division opened. At first, there was only one other staff physician in Medicine, Frederick Glazener, who continued to collaborate with Hollister. Eldridge, a specialist in pulmonary diseases and cardiology, soon set up a cardiac catheterization laboratory for both clinical and research use.[155]

In 1963, Thomas Merigan, M.D. came to Stanford and the Palo Alto VAMC from the NIH. He had been studying the role of proteins in genetic control. While at the VA, he studied human interferon and developed an assay for interferon.[180-185]   One practical outcome of his studies while at the VA was the demonstration that the interferon induced by measles vaccination inhibited the effectiveness of smallpox vaccination give shortly thereafter.[186, 187]   In 1966, he moved to Stanford to become Chief of Infectious Diseases.[188]

Peter Rowley, M.D., also arrived at the Palo Alto Division in 1963. His research interest was in hemoglobin synthesis as a model for the regulation of genetic control. Halsted Holman, M.D., Chairman of the Stanford Department of Medicine, recruited him, as well as Merigan, in a move to build up a genetics research program. Rowley had a lab in the space that had been renovated from staff quarters, where he carried out basic studies of protein synthesis in maturating erythrocytes that were published in important journals.[189,190]

Ed Hershgold, M.D., a hematologist, was at the Palo Alto VAMC in the late 1960s and early 1970s. His research interest during that period was hemophilia and Factor VIII.[191-196] and his work improved the treatment of patients with Factor VIII deficiency.

About 1968, the Dean at Stanford Medical School, Robert Glazer, M.D., became convinced that improved integration with the VA would benefit the medical school, and he persuaded Holman to move more vigorously in that direction. Since Dr. Eldridge planned a sabbatical leave and would step down as Chief of Medicine at that time, Holman started a search for a new Chief. The search committee included Keith Taylor, M.D., a gastroenterologist, Gerald Reaven, M.D., an endocrinologist, and Roy Maffly, M.D., a nephrologist. After a period of reviewing candidates, Glazer persuaded Taylor, Reaven and Maffly to move to the VA, with joint appointments at Stanford and with Taylor as the new Chief of Medical Service. At about the same time, Herbert Hultgren, M.D., who had been Chief of Cardiology at Stanford, moved to the VA as did Robert Swenson, M.D., a junior colleague of Maffly.

With this move from Stanford to the VA came new laboratory space from renovations that Taylor recalled were funded by VACO. For a time after this influx from Stanford, Grand Rounds alternated between Stanford and the VA and some of the Stanford division chiefs were based at the VA.

Taylor's research while at the VA was primarily devoted to studies of the metabolism and absorption of intrinsic factor and on immune factors in gastrointestinal disease.[197-213] He also tried to set up a clinical nutrition program, but did not feel that that was very successful.[214]

Roy Maffly had the laboratory that had previously been assigned to Merigan.[215] There, he studied ion transport by the toad bladder, a model for the renal tubule.[216-221] He studied the role of microtubules on the mechanism of action of the antidiuretic hormone, work done in collaboration with Eve Reaven, Ph.D. (see below.)[222-224]

Robert Swenson had just finished his fellowship with Maffly studying the toad bladder[216] when he moved to the VA in 1968. Then he turned his attention to glucose metabolism in uremia, work in which he collaborated with Gerald Reaven.[225-232] He received VA Research Associate and Clinical Investigator awards. At the end of these, he applied for and received a VA dialysis unit that supported him and two other physicians.[233] He set up the dialysis unit as a basis for research, recruiting research-oriented physicians. About 1980, Swenson moved to Stanford to head its dialysis unit. In the late 1980s, he served as

Chief of Staff of the Livermore VAMC, expediting its affiliation with Stanford prior to its merger with the Palo Alto VAMC.

Gerald Reaven, M.D., also joined the VA staff in 1968. He had been at Stanford since 1959 but attended in Medicine at the Palo Alto VA Hospital. He had been studying calcium metabolism at Stanford but turned to glucose metabolism (studies for which he became renowned) because the calcium machine broke and repairs were delayed. In 1971, Reaven was awarded a Medical Investigator appointment. In the mid 1970s, he helped to plan a proposed Geriatric Research, Education and Clinical Center (GRECC) and became its Chief about 1978. In 1987, he received the Middleton Award "For demonstration of the relationship between degree of hyperglycemia and insulin response to oral glucose, for the conceptual definition, subsequent quantification, and major development of the idea that insulin resistance is a major factor in the pathogenesis of NIDDM, for bringing understanding to the abnormal lipoprotein metabolism characteristic of diabetics, and for persistent leadership in the application of research knowledge to the treatment of diabetes."

Herbert Hultgren, M.D., had been at Stanford since 1949 and had been its Chief of Cardiology for ten years before moving to the VA Hospital in 1968. At the VA, he set up a separate Cardiology section and worked closely with the cardiac surgeons, in particular William Angell (see below). Hultgren became an early and active participant in the VA's Coronary Artery Surgery Cooperative Studies. He also had a long-term interest in the cardiovascular aspects of high altitude medicine and the metabolic aspects of space flight, areas in which he contributed throughout his long career.[234-244]

Cardiac surgery

Among the early laboratories built under the administration of Leo Hollister and Frank Hebern was an animal facility set up for surgical research. There, a group of surgeons worked on cardiac transplantation. Stanford pioneer surgeon Norman Shumway headed the group; its main VA participant was William Angell, M.D., who headed the VA thoracic surgery program after finishing a residency under Shumway in 1967. Angell continued to do research in cardiac surgery after leaving Palo Alto in the mid 1970s and was later affiliated with the Tampa VAMC. While at Palo Alto, he was a participant in the early Coronary Artery Surgery Cooperative Studies.

Neurosurgery

While young surgical subspecialists often spent only a few years at the VA before returning to full time positions at Stanford, Frances K. Conley, M.D., a distinguished neurosurgeon, spent her entire research career at the Palo Alto VAMC. During the late 1990s, she served as Chief of Staff at the medical center. Her research was aimed at conquering malignant brain tumors. As she described it:

"The underlying research goal of the laboratory was to develop an immunotherapy protocol that would stop the development and growth of the highly malignant brain tumor, the glioblastoma.

"Toxoplasma gondii (Toxo) is a parasitic organism that must invade a host cell in order to multiply, and infection with Toxo is known to stimulate the immune system. Infected animals have the ability to resist a lethal dose of other diverse infections as well as to retard growth of a variety of tumors in systemic locations. In 1977 we extended these observations to the brain. Toxo has a predilection for the brain, and, once there, is capable of inciting a cellular immune response that markedly inhibits the development and subsequent growth of implanted malignant brain tumors.[245]

"In order to overcome criticism that a model of implanted tumor necessitates initial violation of the brain, which, in itself, might permit entry of immune cells, we developed a reliable model of metastatic malignant brain tumor by injecting the left side of the heart with tumor cells. 30% of cardiac output goes to the brain, and lodges tumor cells into brain vasculature where they grow into tumor nodules. By selective in vivo/in vitro cloning we developed a "brain-homing" tumor line that produced multiple metastatic tumors in the brain and very few tumors elsewhere in the body.[246, 247] We next determined that chronic infection with Toxo virtually stopped all growth of metastatic tumors in the brain and elsewhere, while treatment with another potent immunomodulating agent, Corynebacterium parvum (Cp) had no effect on the growth of brain tumors, but did stop metastatic tumors in other parts of the body.[248, 249]

"Infection with Toxo is always accompanied by inflammatory (immune) cells and exists in two forms: the infective tachyzoite, and the chronic tissue cyst which forms late in the course of infection. The tachyzoite is extremely difficult to visualize using normal histological stains; tissue cysts are very prominent with the most basic of stains. Given our findings of such spectacular brain tumor inhibition, we needed to know the relationship of the infective tachyzoite to the influx of immune-function cells that are responsible for the tumor killing. We adapted the powerful peroxidase-anti-peroxidase staining technique (PAP) developed by Sternberger to demonstrate the tachyzoite (and cysts) and follow the course of Toxo infection in the brain. The tachyzoites break through tiny brain blood vessels and invade adjacent brain cells and start multiplying. A plethora of immune cells rapidly follows, determined to kill the foreign, dividing tachyzoites as well as any adjacent tumor cells. In turn, the Toxo organisms, in order to survive, force their host cell to become a thick-walled cyst impervious to the cellular onslaught. Thus, a symbiotic relationship develops between invader and host with the immune cells keeping watch over the cysts, ready to attack should the cyst rupture and release their infective tachyzoites.[250, 251]

"1981 was the start of the AIDS epidemic, and it rapidly became apparent that cerebral infection with Toxo, heretofore thought to be benign, was a deadly disease in AIDS patients. HIV infection destroys cellular immunity and without immune cell surveillance, pre-existing Toxo cysts in the brain rupture and release hordes of infective tachyzoites which rapidly spread through the brain and cause fatal infection. Because of our pioneer work with the PAP stain, our laboratory received slides from all over the world for staining and became a reference laboratory for the diagnosis of early Toxo infection.[249, 252-255]

"Returning to developing immunotherapy for brain tumors, we used a direct intralesional approach with two potent, but toxic, immunostimulating agents, CP and interleukin-2 (IL-2).[256] By adding a collagen carrier the two agents could be injected directly into the brain with minimal toxicity and high efficacy as the collagen permitted the agents to remain in the vicinity of the tumor for a prolonged period. In both mouse and rat models of highly malignant brain tumors, this combination resulted in cures[257] and lead to an FDA approved Phase 1 trial in humans with recurrent glioblastoma. The treated patients lived far longer than expected but all died of recurrent disease, not at the primary tumor site where tumor cells were not visualized, but at multiple foci elsewhere in the brain. Malignant glioblastoma cells travel throughout the brain, and can probably only be stopped with an agent(s) that can immunologically stimulate the entire brain (like infection with Toxo) but not cause disability or disease in and of itself."

Anesthesiology

John Welden Belleville, M.D., a Stanford clinical pharmacologist, started a program to study analgesic medications both in animals and in human subjects. William H. Forrest, M.D. worked with him while Forrest was a research fellow at Stanford in 1962-1963. They started multihospital studies of the analgesic and hypnotic drugs. Forrest was offered a faculty appointment at Stanford, but needed to pay his medical school debts, so he went into private practice in Sacramento for three years before returning to the Palo Alto VAMC as Chief, Anesthesiology. Even while he was in Sacramento, he continued to collaborate with Belleville.

Soon, Forrest was chairing a group of seven VA hospitals that tested a series of drugs, standardizing their effects against known agents. They developed techniques to quantify the subjective drug effects, using nurse observers and standardized scales. A national advisory committee provided oversight and new drugs were identified by a committee of the National Academy of Sciences (Chapter 13).

In 1969, Richard I. Mazze, M.D., joined Forrest on the clinical Anesthesiology Service. Mazze had been doing clinical research studies on the effect of anesthesia on the kidney while he was in the Army. He became interested in the effects of methoxyfluoride, which had been reported to be toxic to the kidney. His clinical studies confirmed this finding and demonstrated it to be associated with markedly increased levels of fluoride in patients receiving this anesthetic. Among the toxic effects was production of large numbers of oxylate crystals in the urine. The makers of methoxyfluoride, angry about these findings, reviewed Mazze's results. After they became convinced, they funded additional studies of smaller concentrations. These also showed the effects to persist. These studies led to methoxyfluoride fading from the market and many patients being spared its damage to their kidneys.

Mazze and his colleagues, especially Michael Cousins, M.D., then studied other fluorinated anesthetics, developing in vitro assays for them that helped to predict whether they would defluorinate. After the most likely agents were identified, they did animal studies to test further for toxicity.[258]

After Forrest stepped down, Mazze became Chief of Anesthesiology Service. In 1988, he moved to Stanford to be Associate Department Chair, responsible for building up the research program. He returned to the VA as Chief of Staff after Franklin Ebaugh's death in 1992.

Nuclear Medicine

Joseph Kriss, M.D., the prominent chief of the nuclear medicine program at Stanford recruited Gerald L. DeNardo, M.D., in 1965 to come to Palo Alto as a part of the Stanford program, to initiate a nuclear medicine service at the VA. The local hospital leadership had received funding from VACO for equipment, which was quite up-to-date, but construction was delayed. This was the time when control of Nuclear Medicine had shifted in VACO from Research to the Patient Care services (Chapter 6), and space criteria had not yet been established. While at the VA, DeNardo collaborated with Lawrence Crawley, Chief of Surgery, on liver blood flow in dogs,[259] and with William Hofmann in Neurology on the effects of digitalis on muscle cell flow of sodium and potassium.[260] In 1967, DeNardo moved to Stanford. Later he became the founding Chief of Nuclear Medicine at the new medical school at the University of California, Davis. David Goodwin, M.D. replaced him as Chief at the Palo Alto VAMC.[261]

Goodwin, a Canadian, had trained in Montreal and had then spent two years at Johns Hopkins. When he arrived at the Palo Alto Hospital, the nuclear medicine service was active clinically and had facilities for research. When the VA's Research Traineeship program began in the late 1960s, he successfully competed for one; after the traineeships were transferred to residencies, the VA nuclear medicine residency program became integral to that at Stanford.[262]

Goodwin remained at the Palo Alto VAMC through the balance of his career, collaborating widely in both clinical studies and research. In the mid1970s, he began to collaborate with Claude Meares, Ph.D., a chemist at UC, Davis, who was interested in chelates. Their joint work eventually led to methods for improved targeting of specific radioactive agents for imaging and treatment of various malignancies, work which continues to promise important improvements in the treatment of cancer with radioactive agents.[263-271]

Blind rehabilitation

The Western Blind Rehabilitation Center (WBRC) at the Palo Alto VAMC opened in 1967, as the second such center in the VA.[272] (The first opened at Hines in 1948.)

From its onset, the WBRC has provided a clinical research "laboratory" in which many prototype devices for improving the function of both blind and low vision veterans have been tested and refined. Among the earliest were closed circuit televisions,[273] electronic calculators designed to be used by the visually impaired,[274] electronic mobility devices which serve as obstacle detectors for blind travelers,[275, 276] night scopes to aid night blind travelers,[277] reading machines that convert print to tactile or sound patterns[278] sensed and interpreted by touch or sound and eventually machines which literally read print.[279] Staff of the WBRC, collaborating with Staff Ophthalmologist Michael Marmor, developed the Wide Angle Mobility light based upon the design of a scuba diving light. This light, which could be worn using a shoulder and belt strap, provided a low cost night travel aid that proved to be more effective than other current, more expensive, electronic night vision aids.[280]

In the early 1980s, as personal computer technology began to emerge, the WBRC undertook a series of studies to evaluate the potential role of speech and large print technology in vision rehabilitation services.[281, 282]

Most recently the WBRC has begun evaluating the use of bright, high-resolution displays for applications in low vision reading aids.[283] These displays, which project an image directly onto the retina, may allow individuals with severe low vision to visually read and perform other daily living tasks, tasks that were previously beyond their visual ability.

One of the areas in which the WBRC has played a cutting-edge role is in the development of assessment and training procedures to train patients with limited vision to optimize use of their residual vision.[284, 285]

The 1970s

In 1970, the new research wing discussed above (the E wing) opened in the medical-surgical hospital building, making room for recruitment of more research-oriented staff.

Leo Hollister received a Medical Investigator award that year and stepped down from the ACOS/R&E position. The new ACOS/R&D was James Elliot, M.D., a urologist with an interest in kidney stones. Elliot had been at the Oakland VA Hospital since 1960 and had moved to Martinez when the new VA Hospital there replaced the Oakland VA Hospital in 1963. He had been Acting Chief of Staff and later ACOS/R&D at Martinez,[286] and he volunteered to take on the duties of ACOS/R&D when he arrived at Palo Alto in 1970. He held that position for two years.

In 1972, Clayton Rich, M.D., Dean of the Stanford School of Medicine, helped to recruit Franklin Ebaugh, M.D. to the Palo Alto VA Medical Center, to be Chief of Staff for Research and Education. Ebaugh was a hematologist who had a distinguished record in academic medicine. He had been Dean of the Boston University School of Medicine, and was Dean of the medical school at the University of Utah at the time he was recruited to Palo Alto. In addition to his VA appointment, Ebaugh became Associate Dean for VA Affairs at Stanford. After the incumbent Chief of Staff for the Palo Alto Division, Franklin Johnson, M.D., retired, Ebaugh also took on responsibility for the Stanford-affiliated patient care services at the Palo Alto Division, in addition to research and education at both divisions. In the early 1980s, Associate Chiefs of Staff were recruited for Research and Education, but Ebaugh, as Chief of Staff, continued to play an active role until his death in 1992.

Under Ebaugh's vigorous leadership, the research program flourished. Recruitment of staff in the clinical services was closely coordinated with Stanford, and research credentials were an important element in recruitment decisions. About 1975, Palo Alto competed successfully for one of the original Geriatric Research, Education and Clinical Centers. In the late 1970s, Palo Alto became the site of the VA's second Rehabilitation Engineering R&D Center (Chapter 20). Research programs were in place in all of the clinical services and most of the subspecialties, and the researchers competed successfully in the peer review process. By 1980, Palo Alto had the largest VA R&D funding in the system.

During the 1970s, appointments to the Career Development Program continued, with a wider distribution than in the 1960s. Leo Hollister and Gerald Reaven became Medical Investigators. There were two psychiatrists and six other internists, as well a one surgeon and one psychologist, appointed to the Career Development Program during the 1970s.

Geropsychiatry

Jerrold Yesavage, while a medical student at Stanford, worked for Leo Hollister, assisting in his studies of marijuana effects. After a Stanford psychiatry residency, he took a geriatrics fellowship with Hollister and then joined the VA in 1978. He was in charge of ward 5C4, the "flight deck," with the most acutely psychotic patients. This was a biologically oriented unit, where he did pharmacokinetic studies and studied tardive dyskinesia. He found that neuroleptic drug metabolism slowed with age.

Yesavage, himself a pilot, became interested in flight simulation. He studied the effects of marijuana and, more recently, the effects of alcohol. He found that even small amounts of residual alcohol and other drugs affect a pilot's performance. Hormonal status has little effect.

In 1983, Yesavage and Tinklenberg, with Terrence Brink, developed the Geriatric Depression Scale, which has become a standard of practice and has been translated into many languages. It is on the Web and gets about 3000 "hits" per month.

Since 1985, Yesavage has been chief of a Geriatric Psychiatry Center, now funded by the National Institute on Aging. This Center follows a core of 400 patients with Alzheimer's Disease. They have been studying the deterioration in the sleep cycle that occurs in that condition. The patient becomes agitated at night – "sundowning" - as the disease progresses. Staff of the Center are currently studying the effects of bright light, and also of melatonin, on helping this syndrome.[287]

Smoking cessation

In 1978, Robert G. Hall, Ph.D., began studying and treating patients at the Palo Alto VAMC who want to stop smoking. In particular, he studied an aversive technique called rapid smoking. Under supervision, smokers were asked to smoke every 6 seconds until about to pass out or vomit. When the smokers could go no further they were told to stop. After a few moments of rest the procedure was resumed. The patient was sent home after the second trial and told not to smoke until they returned for the next visit the next day. Treatment was scheduled daily for three days, skipped a day, then was repeated on the fifth and the eighth day. By that time most smokers found they were able to abstain.

Critics charged this procedure was dangerous to patients with cardiac and pulmonary disease. Studies in normal persons and in patients with mild to moderate cardiac and pulmonary disease showed no increase in PVCs or CO-Hb between a normal smoking phase, inhaling every 60 seconds, and rapid smoking. Hall and his colleagues concluded this was a safe technique to use.[288-290] It was a remarkably effective intervention when tailored to each individual. Hall's sample of patients with mild to moderate cardiac disease had a 50% abstinence rate 5 years after treatment.

Psychotic patients are widely known for heavy smoking and resistance to quitting. Hall's group[291] interviewed 300 psychotic patients followed by the VA, who were living in Boarding Houses and Board and Care Homes. Forty-two (14%) had quit smoking on their own. Only one patient quit in a conventional stop smoking program. When they examined the difference between former smokers and persons who continued to smoke, they found the former smokers to be less psychiatrically impaired on several measures. They concluded that improvements in smoking cessation in this population would mirror improvements in treating psychosis.

Ophthalmology

Michael F. Marmor, M.D. was Chief of the Ophthalmology Section at the Palo Alto VAMC from 1974 until 1984 and studied retinal function and disease in his research laboratory. In 1984, he moved to Stanford as Chairman of the Department of Ophthalmology.

His research focused on a layer of cells called the retinal pigment epithelium (RPE) that lies directly beneath the retina. Although RPE cells have been known anatomically for centuries, their role in retinal function and disease had been obscure. Marmor and his associates looked particularly at the role of RPE in maintaining adhesion of the retina (to prevent detachment) and in controlling the environment of the retina. They were first to report the metabolic requirements for adhesion to be maintained,[292, 293] and to quantify the role of the RPE in maintaining a healthy fluid environment for the retinal photoreceptor cells.[294, 295] Other studies looked at experimental models of retinal disease to show implications of this knowledge for retinal aging and detachment.[296, 297] They explored electrical responses that can be used clinically to monitor the function of retina and RPE,[298, 299] and did collaborative studies with David Gaba, M.D. of the Anesthesia Service on oxygen requirements of the RPE.[300]

This work was seminal in raising ophthalmologic awareness of the role of the RPE in retinal health and disease, and was summarized in a book[301] that remained the major reference source on RPE for nearly two decades. The many applications to patient care mostly derive from enhanced awareness of the range of RPE functions that are critical to retinal health. RPE dysfunction is very much a part of the pathophysiology of age-related macular degeneration, macular dystrophies, retinitis pigmentosa, retinal detachment, and drug toxicity of the retina -- and new therapies are beginning to utilize this knowledge.

Nephrology

Michael Weiner, M.D., a nephrologist, joined the VA as a Research Associate in 1974. As Weiner wrote:

"I am about as much a product of the VA as anyone can be. As a med student at Upstate Medical Center, I did about half my medical rotations at the Syracuse VA. Subsequently I was a resident and a postdoc fellow at the West Haven VA. After postdocing at the Institute for Enzyme Research at U Wisc in Madison, I was offered my first job at the Madison VA. I applied for and was given a VA Research Associate at the ripe old age of 31 in 1971, and thus began my career as an Asst Prof. In 1974, I applied for and was awarded a VA Clinical Investigatorship. I was recruited to the Palo Alto VA where I worked for 6 years, writing papers on kidney biochemistry. [302] I won the Young Investigator Award of the American College of Cardiology for this work. - - -

"I had the idea to put a rat in a NMR machine in order to obtain 31P NMR spectra from the kidney using an implanted RF coil. This turned out to be one of the first whole animal NMR experiments. When I came to San Francisco, I continued NMR experiments at UCSF, and had the foresight to recognize the coming of MRI which really was the same thing as NMR."[303]

Weiner moved to the San Francisco VAMC in 1980, where he remains and has been deeply involved in imaging techniques. He now heads a group of some 65 scientists, studying neurodegenerative diseases.

Growth of the Palo Alto research program after 1980

By the early 1980s, the Palo Alto VA Medical Center was among the most diverse of those in VA medical centers and had the largest VA funding for its R&D program. Its new Rehabilitation R&D Center grew and became an important player in the community. In 1984, an HSR&D Center of Excellence was started, a center that has grown and flourished. The Cooperative Studies Program Coordinating Center, started in 1979 (Chapter 18), gradually expanded to play an important role both locally and nationally.

The medical research program continued to pride itself on its diversity. There was funded research in virtually every field of internal medicine and surgery, and also in radiology and nuclear medicine. Research thrived in the areas of rehabilitation and, increasingly, in health services research.

Many researchers who had started in the earlier, formative, years of the medical center continued their work and served as senior colleagues for younger staff recruited jointly with Stanford. Many received honors for the research they did at the Palo Alto VAMC.

A new building was constructed to house an updated, fully approved, animal research facility. After the buildings at the Palo Alto Division, where research space had been laboriously eked out, were damaged in the Loma Prieta earthquake of 1989, many laboratories moved to temporary space and later to the new hospital building that replaced Building 1 in 1998. The research facilities are now modern and well-equipped, an attraction to the next generation of medical researchers.

References

1.   Smith, F.C., "History of Hospital and Staff Organization", in *Annual Report 1924, U.S. Veterans Hospital No. 24, Palo Alto, California*, Leslie, F.E., Editor. 1924, U.S. Veterans Hospital no. 24, Palo Alto, California: Palo Alto, CA 1-3.

2.   Leslie, F.E., *Annual Report 1924, U.S. Veterans Hospital No. 24, Palo Alto, California*. Palo Alto, CA: U.S. Veterans Hospital no. 24, Palo Alto, California, 1924

3.   Melvin, G.M., "The Neuro-Psychiatric Service", in *Annual Report 1924, U.S. Veterans Hospital No. 24, Palo Alto, California*, Leslie, F.E., Editor. 1924, U.S. Veterans Hospital no. 24, Palo Alto, California: Palo Alto, CA 4-5.

4.   Purinton, C.O., "Tuberculosis Service", in *Annual Report 1924, U.S. Veterans Hospital No. 24, Palo Alto, California*, Leslie, F.E., Editor. 1924, U.S. Veterans Hospital no. 24, Palo Alto, California: Palo Alto, CA 6-9.

5.   Clark, E.B., "The Farm", in *Annual Report 1924, U.S. Veterans Hospital No. 24, Palo Alto, California*, Leslie, F.E., Editor. 1924, U.S. Veterans Hospital no. 24, Palo Alto, California: Palo Alto, CA.

6.   Wight, T.H.T., "Clinical Laboratory", in *Annual Report 1924, U.S. Veterans Hospital No. 24, Palo Alto, California*, Leslie, F.E., Editor. 1924, U.S. Veterans Hospital no. 24, Palo Alto, California: Palo Alto, CA 18-20.

7.   Wight, T.H.T., "Notes on Councilmania Lafleuri (Kofoid-Swezy 1921)." *Proc Soc Exp Biol Med*, 1925. **22**: 517-522.

8.   Wight, T.H.T., "Revised Formula for the Rainbow Medium." *Proc Soc Exp Biol Med*, 1925. **22**: 522-523.

9.   Wight, T.H.T. and Prince, L.H., "Artifacts in Endamoebae Which Have Led to the Naming of a New Genus and Species." *Am J Trop Med*, 1927. **5**: 287-309.

10.   Wight, T.H.T., "Routine Stool Examination for Protozoa at a United States Veterans' Hospital." *United States Veterans' Bureau Medical Bulletin*, 1926. **2**: 557-563.

11.   Wight, T.H.T. and Prince, L.H., "Adenocarcinoma - Primary in the Renal Tubules." *United States Veterans' Bureau Medical Bulletin*, 1926. **2**: 987-991, 1095-1098.

12.   Alvarez, R.S. and Wight, T.H.T., "The Gregerson Test." *United States Veterans' Bureau Medical Bulletin*, 1929. **5**: 888-890.

13.   Wight, T.H.T. and Meehan, W., "Value of Media Containing Certain Iron Compounds in Differentiating the Typhoid-Colon Group of Organisms." *United States Veterans' Bureau Medical Bulletin*, 1930. **6**: 493-495.

14.   de River, J.P., "Some Important Ophthalmic Signs in Diseases of the Nervous System." *United States Veterans' Bureau Medical Bulletin*, 1925. **1**: 26-31.

15.   Carlisle, C.L., "The Interpretation of Inadequate Behavior through Neuropsychiatric Symptoms." *United States Veterans' Bureau Medical Bulletin*, 1926. **2**: 230-248.

16.   Kellum, H.J., "The Infection, Exhaustion, and Toxic Psychosis." *United States Veterans' Bureau Medical Bulletin*, 1926. **2**: 369-372.

17. Stewart, N.E., "The History of Hysteria." *United States Veterans' Bureau Medical Bulletin*, 1926. **2**: 1151-1152.

18. Carlisle, C.L., "Early Symptoms of Brain Tumor." *United States Veterans' Bureau Medical Bulletin*, 1927. **3**: 321-328.

19. Covey, C.B., "Notes on Amnesia." *United States Veterans' Bureau Medical Bulletin*, 1927. **3**: 356-362.

20. Carlisle, C.L., "Paraphrenia, Its General Consideration in Relation to Schizophrenia." *United States Veterans' Bureau Medical Bulletin*, 1927. **3**: 676-686.

21. Carlisle, C.L., Heffner, W.J., Adams, F., Eltinge, R.L., Cullins, J.G. and Gates, G.R., "Schizoid Mechanisms with Manic-Like Symptoms." *United States Veterans' Bureau Medical Bulletin*, 1927. **3**: 1193-1208.

22. Canine, F.G., "A Technique for the Construction of a Cast Gold Crown." *United States Veterans' Bureau Medical Bulletin*, 1927. **3**: 147-148.

23. "The Third Diagnostic Center." *The Live Oak*, 1928. **6, no.6**: 1-2.

24. "Establishment of a New Diagnostic Center." *United States Veterans' Bureau Medical Bulletin*, 1928. **4**: 287.

25. Swackhamer, W.B., "Organization and Procedure in United States Veterans' Diagnostic Center." *United States Veterans' Bureau Medical Bulletin*, 1929. **5**: 947-950.

26. Crouch, E.L., "Multiple Sclerosis." *United States Veterans' Bureau Medical Bulletin*, 1928. **4**: 839-845.

27. Crouch, E.L., "Narcolepsy." *United States Veterans' Bureau Medical Bulletin*, 1930. **6**: 371-377.

28. Carlisle, C.L., "The Etiology of Idiopathic (Nonorganic) Epilepsy." *United States Veterans' Bureau Medical Bulletin*, 1929. **5**: 161-163.

29. Read, J.M., "Tetany from Overbreathing." *United States Veterans' Bureau Medical Bulletin*, 1929. **5**: 491-493.

30. Brann, H.W., "Conversion Hysteria." *United States Veterans' Bureau Medical Bulletin*, 1929. **5**: 798-800.

31. Johnson, P.E., "The Clinical Symptomatology of Diseases of the Gall Bladder and Biliary Ducts." *United States Veterans' Bureau Medical Bulletin*, 1930. **6**: 684-687.

32. Mella, H., "Panniculitis." *United States Veterans' Bureau Medical Bulletin*, 1930. **6**: 697-698.

33. Baker, R.E., "Suppurative Phlebitis of the Femoral Vein." *United States Veterans' Bureau Medical Bulletin*, 1930. **6**: 809-810.

34. Hein, G.E., "Aortic Stenosis." *United States Veterans' Bureau Medical Bulletin*, 1931. **7**: 209-211.

35. Sanders, A.O., "Observations of the Heart Action under Vagus Stimulation." *United States Veterans' Bureau Medical Bulletin*, 1931. **7**: 212-217.

36. Baker, R.E., "Abscess of the Spleen." *United States Veterans' Bureau Medical Bulletin*, 1931. **7**: 264-266.

37. Mella, H., "The Use of Subarachnoid Lavage and Ethylhydrocupreine in Meningitis." *United States Veterans' Bureau Medical Bulletin*, 1931. **7**: 77-78.

38. Fisher, S.G., "Epidemic Encephalitis." *United States Veterans' Bureau Medical Bulletin*, 1931. **7**: 379-382.

39. Fisher, S.G., "Stramonium in Encephalitis." *United States Veterans' Bureau Medical Bulletin*, 1931. **7**: 864-865.

40. Barnard, L.J., "Esophageal Stricture." *United States Veterans' Bureau Medical Bulletin*, 1931. **7**: 435-440.

41. Burkett, J.A., "Bronchial Spirochetosis, with Report of a Case." *United States Veterans' Bureau Medical Bulletin*, 1932. **8**: 26-37.

42. Terry, M.C., "Elliptical Human Erythrocytes: Report of Two Cases." *United States Veterans' Bureau Medical Bulletin*, 1932. **9**: 7-17.

43. Terry, M.C. and Sanders, A.O., "A Case of Myeloid Leukemia Treated with Luminal and Amidopyrine." *Proc Soc Exp Biol Med*, 1934. **31**: 1154-1156.

44. Schultz, E.W., Terry, M.C., Brice, A.T. and Gebhardt, L.P., "Bacteriological Observations on a Case of Meningo-Encephalitis." *Proc Soc Exp Biol Med*, 1934. **31**: 1021-1023.

45. Mella, H., "Loss of Associated Locomotor Movements in Diencephalic Lesions." *United States Veterans' Bureau Medical Bulletin*, 1931. **7**: 762-763.

46. Grady, G.W., "Transverse Myelitis." *United States Veterans' Bureau Medical Bulletin*, 1934. **10**: 246.

47. Terry, M.C., "Blood Grouping and the Selection of Donors for Transfusion." *United States Veterans' Bureau Medical Bulletin*, 1930. **6**: 930-938.

48. Hartinger, A.O., "Preparation of Gold Solution." *United States Veterans' Bureau Medical Bulletin*, 1934. **10**: 337-338.

49. Johnson, P.E., "Bilateral Blocking of the Cervical Plexus for Surgery of the Front of the Neck; Report of a Thyroidectomy by This Method." *United States Veterans' Bureau Medical Bulletin*, 1930. **6**: 968-970.

50. Lasche, P.G. and Rubin, H., "Carbon Dioxide-Oxygen Inhalation in Catatonic Dementia Praecox." *United States Veterans' Bureau Medical Bulletin*, 1930. **6**: 1037-1041.

51. Robinson, J.A., "Institutional Care in Catatonic Dementia Praecox." *United States Veterans' Bureau Medical Bulletin*, 1931. **7**: 152-153.

52. Mella, H. and O'Neil, R.T., "Intravenous Administration of Sodium Amytal in Acute Psychotic Episodes." *United States Veterans' Bureau Medical Bulletin*, 1933. **9**: 271-275.

53. Robinson, J.A., "Undiagnosed Syphilis in Psychotic Patients." *United States Veterans' Bureau Medical Bulletin*, 1931. **7**: 583-585.

54. Kennedy, J.A., "Psychosis with Alcoholic Pellagra." *United States Veterans' Bureau Medical Bulletin*, 1933. **10**: 155-158.

55. Pittock, H.J., "Legal Psychiatry." *United States Veterans' Bureau Medical Bulletin*, 1931. **7**: 1050-1052.

56. O'Neil, R.T., "Treatment and Course of Neurosyphilis; Case Reports." *United States Veterans' Bureau Medical Bulletin*, 1931. **7**: 1107-1120.

57. O'Neil, R.T., "Malaria Therapy in Agitated Cases of Paresis." *United States Veterans' Bureau Medical Bulletin*, 1932. **8**: 291-294.

58. Mella, H. and O'Neil, R.T., "Ultraviolet Irradiation in General Paresis." *United States Veterans' Bureau Medical Bulletin*, 1932. **9**: 29-32.

59. Carlisle, C.L. and O'Neil, R.T., "Results of Extra-Intensive Treatment of General Paresis of the Insane." *United States Veterans' Bureau Medical Bulletin*, 1934. **11**: 31-58.

60. Carlisle, C.L. and O'Neil, R.T., "Results of Extra-Intensive Treatment of General Paresis of the Insane." *United States Veterans' Bureau Medical Bulletin*, 1934. **10**: 309-336.

61. Carlisle, C.L., "The Role of Affect in Psychotic Behavior." *United States Veterans' Bureau Medical Bulletin*, 1931. **7**: 202-207.

62. Carlisle, C.L., "The Significance of Schizoid Mechanisms in the Manic-Depressive Syndrome." *United States Veterans' Bureau Medical Bulletin*, 1932. **8**: 93-98.

63. "Meeting of Medical Societies." *United States Veterans' Bureau Medical Bulletin*, 1934. **11**: 64-65.

64. "Postgraduate Schools." *United States Veterans' Bureau Medical Bulletin*, 1933. **9**: 323.

65. Telephone interview with Paul McReynolds, Ph.D., February 11, 1992.

66. Interview with Leonard Krasner, Ph.D., January 24, 1992 at Palo Alto VAMC.

67. Telephone interview with John Prusmak, M.D., February 19, 1992.

68. Waldron, A.W., Manager, VA Hospital, Palo Alto "Research Committee." 1949.

69. Raffel, S. "Subcommittee on Research of the Dean's Committee, Veterans Hospital." 1956.

70. Letter from Prusmack, J.J. to Chief Medical Director., written February 19, 1957.

71. Letter from Sydney Raffel, M.D. to Roy S. Hubbs, M.D., written March 2, 1958.

72. Letter from Robert Alway, M.D. to Dr. William S. Middleton, written April 2, 1958.

73. Letter from Gregory Bateson to Sidney Raffel, M.D., written November 15, 1956.

74. Letter form S. Raffel to John Prusmak, Director, written December 20, 1956.

75. Interview with Mildred Ashe, M.D., January 10, 2000 at Dr. Ashe's home in Palo Alto, CA.

76. Interview with Mark Graeber, M.D., September 4, 1991 at Dr. Graeber's Office at the Menlo Park Division of Palo Alto VAMC.

77. Interview with Leo Hollister, M.D., January 29,1994 at Dr. Hollister's home in Houston, TX.

78. Interview with Marion Barry, February 14, 1992 at the author's office.

79. "Veterans Administration Hospital Palo Alto, California Annual Report of VA Medical Research Activities for Fiscal Year 1961." July, 1961.

80. Interview with John Weakland, March 19, 1992 at Mr. Weakland's office in Palo Alto, CA.

81. Hollister, L.E., Krieger, G.E., Kringel, A. and Roberts, A.H., "Treatment of Chronic Schizophrenic Reactions with Reserpine." *Ann NY Acad Sci*, 1955. **61**: 92-100.

82. Hollister, L.E., Jones, K.P., Brownfield, B. and Johnson, F., "Chlorpromazine Alone and with Reserpine: Use in Treatment of Mental Diseases." *California Med*, 1955. **83**: 218-221.

83. Hollister, L.E. and Wright, A., "Diurnal Variation of Serum Lipids." *J Atheroscler Res*, 1965. **5**: 445-450.

84. Hollister, L.E., "The Effect of Adrenergic Blocking Agents (Including Chlorpromazine) on Serum Lipid Levels of Patients with Disorders of Fat Metabolism." *J Chronic Dis*, 1957. **6**: 234-243.

85. Hollister, L.E. and Glazener, F.S., "Serum Lipid Levels in Geriatric Patients Treated with a Dietary Supplement of Unsaturated Fatty Acids." *J Am Geriat Soc*, 1959. **7**: 327-334.

86. Hollister, L.E., "Reduced Serum Lipids after Liothyronine Administration Combined with Diet High in Unsaturated Fat." *Amer J Clin Nutr*, 1962. **10**: 114-118.

87. Hollister, L.E. and Kanter, S.L., "Essential Hyperlipemia Treated with Heparin and with Chlorpromazine." *Gastroenterology*, 1955. **29**: 1069-1076.

88. Hollister, L.E. and Cull, V.L., "Syndrome of Chronic Thrombosis of Major Pulmonary Arteries." *Am J Med*, 1956. **21**: 312-320.

89. Hollister, L.E., Prusmack, J.J., Paulsen, A. and Rosenquist, N., "Comparison of Three Psychotropic Drugs (Psilocybin, Jb-329, and It-290) in Volunteer Subjects." *J Nerv Ment Dis*, 1960. **131**: 428-434.

90. Hollister, L.E., "Clinical, Biochemical and Psychologic Effects of Psilocybin." *Arch int Pharmacodyn*, 1961. **130**: 42-52.

91. Hollister, L.E. and Hartman, A.M., "Mescaline, Lysergic Diethylamide and Psilocybin Comparison of Clinical Syndromes, Effects on Color Perception and Biochemical Measures." *Compr Psychiat*, 1962. **3**: 235-242.

92. Hollister, L.E., Degan, R.O. and Schultz, S.D., "An Experimental Approach to Facilitation of Psychotherapy by Psychotomimetic Drugs." *J Ment Sci*, 1962. **108**: 99-100.

93. Hartman, A.M. and Hollister, L.E., "Effect of Mescaline, Lysergic Diethylamide and Psilocybin on Color Perception." *Psychopharmacologia*, 1963. **65**: 441-451.

94. Hollister, L.E., "Clinical Syndrome from LSD-25 Compared with Epinephrine." *Dis Nerv Syst*, 1964. **25**: 427-429.

95. Hollister, L.E. and Sjoberg, B.M., "Clinical Syndromes and Biochemical Alterations Following Mescaline, Lysergic Acid Diethylamide, Psilocybin and a Combination of the Three Psychotomimetic Drugs." *Compr Psychiatry*, 1964. **20**: 170-178.

96. Hollister, L.E., "Chemical Psychoses." *Ann Rev Med*, 1964. **15**: 203-214.

97.   Hollister, L.E., Macnicol, M.F. and Gillespie, H.K., "An Hallucinogenic Amphetamine Analog (DOM) in Man." *Psychopharmacologia*, 1969. **14**: 62-73.

98.   Hollister, L.E., Shelton, J. and Krieger, G., "A Controlled Comparison of Lysergic Acid Diethylamide (Lsd) and Dextroamphetmine in Alcoholics." *Am J Psychiatry*, 1969. **125**: 1352-1357.

99.   Hollister, L.E., Kanter, S.L. and Dronkert, A., "Antidiuresis in Man Following Lysergic Acid Diethylamide and Mescaline." *Behav Neuropsychiatry*, 1970. **2**: 50-54.

100.   Hollister, L.E., Richards, R.K. and Gillespie, H.K., "Comparison of Tetrahydrocannabinol and Synhexyl in Man." *Clin Pharmacol Ther*, 1968. **9**: 783-791.

101.   Hollister, L.E. and Gillespie, H.K., "Marihuana, Ethanol, and Dextroamphetamine. Mood and Mental Function Alterations." *Arch Gen Psychiatry*, 1970. **23**: 199-203.

102.   Hollister, L.E., "Tetrahydrocannabinol Isomers and Homologues: Contrasted Effects of Smoking." *Nature*, 1970. **227**: 968-969.

103.   Hollister, L.E., Moore, F., Kanter, S. and Noble, E., "1 -Tetrahydrocannabinol, Synhexyl and Marijuana Extract Administered Orally in Man: Catecholamine Excretion, Plasma Cortisol Levels and Platelet Serotonin Content." *Psychopharmacologia*, 1970. **17**: 354-360.

104.   Melges, F.T., Tinklenberg, J.R., Hollister, L.E. and Gillespie, H.K., "Marihuana and Temporal Disintegration." *Science*, 1970. **168**: 1118-1120.

105.   Tinklenberg, J.R., Melges, F.T., Hollister, L.E. and Gillespie, H.K., "Marijuana and Immediate Memory." *Nature*, 1970. **226**: 1171-1172.

106.   Melges, F.T., Tinklenberg, J.R., Hollister, L.E. and Gillespie, H.K., "Temporal Disintegration and Depersonalization During Marihuana Intoxication." *Arch Gen Psychiatry*, 1970. **23**: 204-210.

107.   Hollister, L.E., "Actions of Various Marihuana Derivatives in Man." *Pharmacol Rev*, 1971. **23**: 349-357.

108.   Hollister, L.E., "Marihuana in Man: Three Years Later." *Science*, 1971. **172**: 21-29.

109.   Melges, F.T., Tinklenberg, J.R., Hollister, L.E. and Gillespie, H.K., "Marihuana and the Temporal Span of Awareness." *Arch Gen Psychiatry*, 1971. **24**: 564-567.

110.   Hollister, L.E., "Hunger and Appetite after Single Doses of Marihuana, Alcohol, and Dextroamphetamine." *Clin Pharmacol Ther*, 1971. **12**: 44-49.

111.   Pivik, R.T., Zarcone, V., Dement, W.C. and Hollister, L.E., "Delta-9-Tetrahydrocannabinol and Synhexl: Effects on Human Sleep Patterns." *Clin Pharmacol Ther*, 1972. **13**: 426-435.

112.   Hollister, L.E., Kanter, S.L., Moore, F. and Green, D.E., "Marihuana Metabolites in Urine of Man." *Clin Pharmacol Ther*, 1972. **13**: 849-855.

113.   Kanter, S.L., Hollister, L.E., Moore, F. and Green, D., "Cannabinoids in the Urine of Man after Single and Subchronic Oral Doses of Marihuana." *Int Pharmacopsychiatry*, 1972. **7**: 205-213.

114.   Tinklenberg, J.R., Kopell, B.S., Melges, F.T. and Hollister, L.E., "Marihuana and Alcohol, Time Production and Memory Functions." *Arch Gen Psychiatry*, 1972. **27**: 812-815.

115. Hollister, L.E. and Gillespie, H.K., "Delta-8- and Delta-9-Tetrahydrocannabinol Comparison in Man by Oral and Intravenous Administration." *Clin Pharmacol Ther*, 1973. **14**: 353-357.

116. Hollister, L.E., "Cannabidiol and Cannabinol in Man." *Experientia*, 1973. **29**: 825-826.

117. Hollister, L.E. and Tinklenberg, J.R., "Subchronic Oral Doses of Marihuana Extract." *Psychopharmacologia*, 1973. **29**: 247-252.

118. Roth, W.T., Tinklenberg, J.R., Whitaker, C.A., Darley, C.F., Kopell, B.S. and Hollister, L.E., "The Effect of Marihuana on Tracking Task Performance." *Psychopharmacologia*, 1973. **33**: 259-265.

119. Hollister, L.E., Kanter, S.L., Board, R.D. and Green, D.E., "Marihuana Metabolites in Urine of Man. III. Unchanged Delta-9- Tetrahydrocannabinol." *Res Commun Chem Pathol Pharmacol*, 1974. **8**: 579-584.

120. Kanter, S.L., Hollister, L.E., Moore, F. and Green, D.E., "Marihuana Metabolites in Urine of Man. IV. Extraction Procedures Using Diethyl Ether." *Res Commun Chem Pathol Pharmacol*, 1974. **9**: 205-213.

121. Kanter, S.L., Hollister, L.E., Moore, F. and Green, D.E., "Marihuana Metabolites in Urine of Man. II. Undescribed Metabolite Following Oral Ingestion of Delta-9-Tetrahydrocannabinol." *Res Commun Chem Pathol Pharmacol*, 1974. **7**: 79-84.

122. Hollister, L.E. and Reaven, G.M., "Delta-9-Tetrahydrocannabinol and Glucose Tolerance." *Clin Pharmacol Ther*, 1974. **16**: 297-302.

123. Hollister, L.E., "Structure-Activity Relationships in Man of Cannabis Constituents, and Homologs and Metabolites of Delta9-Tetrahydrocannabinol." *Pharmacology*, 1974. **11**: 3-11.

124. Hollister, L.E., Overall, J.E. and Gerber, M.L., "Marihuana and Setting." *Arch Gen Psychiatry*, 1975. **32**: 798-801.

125. Kanter, S.L., Hollister, L.E. and Moore, F., "Marihuana Metabolites in Urine of Man. V. Characterization and Separation of Polar Metabolites of Delta-9-Tetrahydrocannabinol." *Res Commun Chem Pathol Pharmacol*, 1975. **10**: 215-219.

126. Hollister, L.E. and Gillespie, H., "Interactions in Man of Delta-9-Tetrahydrocannabinol. II. Cannabinol and Cannabidiol." *Clin Pharmacol Ther*, 1975. **18**: 80-83.

127. Lombrozo, L., Kanter, S.L. and Hollister, L.E., "VI. Separation of Cannabinoids by Sequential Thin Layer Chromatography." *Res Commun Chem Pathol Pharmacol*, 1976. **15**: 697-703.

128. Kanter, S.L. and Hollister, L.E., "Marihuana Metabolites in Urine of Man. VII. Excretion Patterns of Acidic Metabolites Detected by Sequential Thin Layer Chromatography." *Res Commun Chem Pathol Pharmacol*, 1977. **17**: 421-431.

129. Kanter, S.L. and Hollister, L.E., "Marihuana Metabolites in Urine of Man. Ix. Identification of Delta9- Tetrahydrocannabinol-11-Oic Acid by Thin-Layer Chromatography." *J Chromatogr*, 1978. **151**: 225-227.

130. Kanter, S.L., Hollister, L.E. and Loeffler, K.O., "Marihuana Metabolites in the Urine of Man. Viii. Identification and Quantitation of Delta9-Tetrahydrocannabinol by Thin-Layer Chromatography and High-Pressure Liquid Chromatography." *J Chromatogr*, 1978. **150**: 233-237.

131. Kanter, S.L., Musumeci, M.R. and Hollister, L.E., "Quantitative Determination of Delta 9-Tetrahydrocannabinol and Delta 9- Tetrahydro-Cannabinolic Acid in Marihuana by High-Pressure Liquid Chromatography." *J Chromatogr*, 1979. **171**: 504-508.

132. Ohlsson, A., Lindgren, J.E., Wahlen, A., Agurell, S., Hollister, L.E. and Gillespie, H.K., "Plasma Delta-9 Tetrahydrocannabinol Concentrations and Clinical Effects after Oral and Intravenous Administration and Smoking." *Clin Pharmacol Ther*, 1980. **28**: 409-416.

133. Ohlsson, A., Lindgren, J.E., Wahlen, A., Agurell, S., Hollister, L.E. and Gillespie, H.K., "Plasma Levels of Delta 9-Tetrahydrocannabinol after Intravenous, Oral, and Smoke Administration." *NIDA Res Monogr*, 1981. **34**: 250-256.

134. Kanter, S.L., Hollister, L.E. and Zamora, J.U., "Marijuana Metabolites in Urine of Man. Xi. Detection of Unconjugated and Conjugated Delta 9-Tetrahydrocannabinol-11-Oic Acid by Thin-Layer Chromatography." *J Chromatogr*, 1982. **235**: 507-512.

135. Kanter, S.L., Hollister, L.E. and Musumeci, M., "Marijuana Metabolites in Urine of Man. X. Identification of Marijuana Use by Detection of Delta 9-Tetrahydrocannabinol-11-Oic Acid Using Thin- Layer Chromatography." *J Chromatogr*, 1982. **234**: 201-208.

136. Ohlsson, A., Lindgren, J.E., Wahlen, A., Agurell, S., Hollister, L.E. and Gillespie, H.K., "Single Dose Kinetics of Deuterium Labelled Delta 1-Tetrahydrocannabinol in Heavy and Light Cannabis Users." *Biomed Mass Spectrom*, 1982. **9**: 6-10.

137. Magliozzi, J.R., Kanter, S.L., Csernansky, J.G. and Hollister, L.E., "Detection of Marijuana Use in Psychiatric Patients by Determination of Urinary Delta-9-Tetrahydrocannabinol-11-Oic Acid." *J Nerv Ment Dis*, 1983. **171**: 246-249.

138. Reeve, V.C., Grant, J.D., Robertson, W., Gillespie, H.K. and Hollister, L.E., "Plasma Concentrations of Delta-9-Tetrahydrocannabinol and Impaired Motor Function." *Drug Alcohol Depend*, 1983. **11**: 167-175.

139. Zimmerman, E.G., Yeager, E.P., Soares, J.R., Hollister, L.E. and Reeve, V.C., "Measurement of Delta 9-Tetrahydrocannabinol (Thc) in Whole Blood Samples from Impaired Motorists." *J Forensic Sci*, 1983. **28**: 957-962.

140. Yesavage, J.A., Leirer, V.O., Denari, M. and Hollister, L.E., "Carry-over Effects of Marijuana Intoxication on Aircraft Pilot Performance: A Preliminary Report." *Am J Psychiatry*, 1985. **142**: 1325-1329.

141. Johansson, E., Ohlsson, A., Lindgren, J.E., Agurell, S., Gillespie, H. and Hollister, L.E., "Single-Dose Kinetics of Deuterium-Labelled Cannabinol in Man after Intravenous Administration and Smoking." *Biomed Environ Mass Spectrom*, 1987. **14**: 495-499.

142. Hollister, L.E., "Marijuana and Immunity." *J Psychoactive Drugs*, 1988. **20**: 3-8.

143. Hollister, L.E., "Cannabis--1988." *Acta Psychiatr Scand Suppl*, 1988. **345**: 108-118.

144. Johansson, E., Agurell, S., Hollister, L.E. and Halldin, M.M., "Prolonged Apparent Half-Life of Delta 1-Tetrahydrocannabinol in Plasma of Chronic Marijuana Users." *J Pharm Pharmacol*, 1988. **40**: 374-375.

145. Interview with Jared R.Tinklenberg, M.D., January 7, 1991 at Palo Alto VAMC.

146. Telephone interview with Lee Gurel, Ph.D., July 27, 1992.

476

147.   Telephone interview with Leonard Ullman, Ph.D., February 10, 1992.

148.   *Social Psychology in Treating Mental Illness*. Fairweather, G.W., ed. New York: John Wiley&Sons, Inc., 1964,

149.   Fairweather, G.W., Sanders, D.H., Maynard, H., Cressler, D.L. and Bleck, D.S., *Community Life for the Mentally Ill*. Chicago: Aldine Publishing Company, 1969

150.   Telephone interview with George Fairweather, P.D., January 24, 1992.

151.   Interview with Irene Forrest, Ph.D., January 10, 1992 at Dr. Forrest's home in Menlo Park, CA.

152.   *Phenothiazines and Structurally Related Drugs: Basic and Clinical Studies*. Usdin, E., Eckert, H. and Forrest, I.S., eds.; New York, Amsterdam, Oxford: Elsevier/North Holland, 1980.

153.   Letter from Herbert Brownell, A.G. to Honorable Harvey V. Higley, A., Veterans Administration, written at Washington, DC, April 17, 1956.

154.   *United States of America, Plaintiff, V. Certain Land Situated in the County of Santa Clara, State of California, the Board of Trustees of the Leland Stanford Junior University, a Body Having Corporate Powers, City and County of San Francisco, a Municipal Corporation, Count of Santa Clara, Et Al., and Unknown Owners, Defendants*. 1955, United States District Court in and for the northern district of California, southern division.

155.   Telephone interview with Frederick Eldridge, M.D., January 30, 1992.

156.   "Palo Alto Va Hospital Is Self-Contained Community." *Palo Alto Times*, Palo Alto, CA, May 12, 1960. 2.

157.   Interview with Leo E.Hollister, M.D., September 6, 1991 at Palo Alto VA Medical Center.

158.   Interview with George Freeman Solomon, M.D., November 7, 1991 at Sepulveda VA Medical Center, Dr. Solomon's office.

159.   Interview with David N. Daniels, M.D., January 8, 1992 at Dr. Daniels's office in Palo Alto, CA.

160.   Interview with George Gulevich, M.D., January 21, 1992 at Palo Alto VAMC.

161.   *Neurochemical Research*. Vol. 21. New York and London: Plenum Press, 1996, 393-535.

162.   Interview with Vincent P. Zarcone, M.D., February 10, 1992 at Palo Alto VAMC.

163.   Interview with Bert Kopell, M.D., December 10, 1991 at Palo Alto VAMC.

164.   Interview with Adolf Pfefferbaum, M.D., January 10, 1992 at Palo Alto VAMC.

165.   Interview with Walton Thomas Roth, M.D., August 1, 2002 at Dr. Roth's office at the Palo Alto VAMC.

166.   Interview with Rudolf Moos, P.D., September 24, 1991 at Palo Alto VAMC.

167.   Interview with Jon Kosek, M.D., September 17, 1991 at Palo Alto VAMC.

168.   Interview with Lawrence Eng, P.D., October 15,1991 at Palo Alto VAMC.

169. Fajardo, L.F. and Stewart, J.R., "Experimental Radiation-Induced Heart Disease. I. Light Microscopic Studies." *Am J Pathol*, 1970. **59**: 299-316.

170. Fajardo, L.F. and Stewart, J.R., "Pathogenesis of Radiation-Induced Myocardial Fibrosis." *Lab Invest*, 1973. **29**: 244-257.

171. Fajardo, L.F., *Pathology of Radiation Injury*. New York: Masson Publishing USA, Inc., 1982

172. Fajardo, L.F., Berthrong, M. and Anderson, R.E., *Radiation Pathology*. Vol. 187. Oxford University Press, 2001, 1962-1966.

173. Fajardo, L.F., Kowalski, J., Kwan, H.H., Prionas, S.D. and Allison, A.C., "The Disc Angiogenesis System." *Lab Invest*, 1988. **58**: 718-724.

174. Fajardo, L.F., Kwan, H.H., Kowalski, J., Prionas, S.D. and Allison, A.C., "Dual Role of Tumor Necrosis Factor-Alpha in Angiogenesis." *Am J Pathol*, 1992. **140**: 539-544.

175. Fajardo, L.F., "Letter: Malarial Parasites in Mammalian Platelets." *Nature*, 1973. **243**: 298-299.

176. Grau, G.E., Fajardo, L.F., Piguet, P.F., Allet, B., Lambert, P.H. and Vassalli, P., "Tumor Necrosis Factor (Cachectin) as an Essential Mediator in Murine Cerebral Malaria." *Science*, 1987. **237**: 1210-1212.

177. Santamaria-Fries, M., Fajardo, L.F., Sogin, M.L., Olson, P.D. and Relman, D.A., "Lethal Infection by a Previously Unrecognised Metazoan Parasite." *Lancet*, 1996. **347**: 1797-1801.

178. Olson, P.D., Yoder, K., Fajardo, L.F., Marty, A.M., van der Pas, S., Olivier, C. and Relman, D.A., "Lethal Invasive Cestodiasis in Immunosuppressed Patients." *J Infect Dis*, 2003. **187**: 1962-1966.

179. Interview with William Hofmann, M.D., September 5, 1991 at Palo Alto VAMC.

180. Merigan, T.C., "Purified Interferons: Physical Properties and Species Specificity." *Science*, 1964. **145**: 811-813.

181. Baron, S., Merigan, T.C. and McKerlie, M.L., "Effect of Crude and Purified Interferons on the Growth of Uninfected Cells in Culture." *Proc Soc Exp Biol Med*, 1966. **121**: 50-52.

182. Freshman, M.M., Merigan, T.C., Remington, J.S. and Brownlee, I.E., "In Vitro and in Vivo Antiviral Action of an Interferon-Like Substance Induced by Toxoplasma Gondii." *Proc Soc Exp Biol Med*, 1966. **123**: 862-866.

183. Joklik, W.K. and Merigan, T.C., "Concerning the Mechanism of Action of Interferon." *Proc Natl Acad Sci U S A*, 1966. **56**: 558-565.

184. Merigan, T.C., Gregory, D.F. and Petralli, J.K., "Physical Properties of Human Interferon Prepared in Vitro and in Vivo." *Virology*, 1966. **29**: 515-522.

185. Merigan, T.C., Jr., "Interferon's Promise in Clinical Medicine. Fact or Fancy?" *Am J Med*, 1967. **43**: 817-821.

186. Petralli, J.K., Merigan, T.C. and Wilbur, J.R., "Action of Endogenous Interferon against Vaccinia Infection in Children." *Lancet*, 1965. **40**: 401-405.

187. Petralli, J.K., Merigan, T.C. and Wilbur, J.R., "Circulating Interferon after Measles Vaccination." *N Engl J Med*, 1965. **273**: 198-201.

188. Interview with Thomas Merigan, M.D., December 17, 1991 at Dr. Merigan's office at Stanford Medical Center.

189. Rowley, P.T., "Protein Synthesis in Reticulocytes Maturing in Vivo." *Nature*, 1965. **208**: 244-246.

190. Rowley, P.T. and Morris, J.A., "Protein Synthesis in the Maturing Reticulocyte." *J Biol Chem*, 1967. **242**: 1533-1540.

191. Hershgold, E.J., Pool, J.G., Pappenhagen, A.R. and Nuenke, J.M., "A More Potent Human Antihemophilic Globulin Concentrate: Preparation and Clinical Trial." *Bibl Haematol*, 1965. **23**: 1214-1218.

192. Pool, J.G., Hershgold, E. and Pappenhagen, A., "Treatment of Hemophilia A." *Bibl Haematol*, 1965. **23**: 1315-1316.

193. Hershgold, E.J., Pool, J.G. and Pappenhagen, A.R., "The Potent Antihemophilic Globulin Concentrate Derived from a Cold Insoluble Fraction of Human Plasma: Characterization and Further Data on Preparation and Clinical Trial." *J Lab Clin Med*, 1966. **67**: 23-32.

194. Hershgold, E.J., Davison, A.M. and Janszen, M.E., "Human Factor VIII (Antihemophilic Factor): Activation and Inactivation by Phospholipases." *J Lab Clin Med*, 1971. **77**: 206-218.

195. Hershgold, E.J., Davison, A.M. and Janszen, M.E., "Isolation and Some Chemical Properties of Human Factor VIII (Antihemophilic Factor)." *J Lab Clin Med*, 1971. **77**: 185-205.

196. Stites, D.P., Hershgold, E.J., Perlman, J.D. and Fudenberg, H.H., "Factor 8 Detection by Hemagglutination Inhibition: Hemophilia a and Von Willebrand's Disease." *Science*, 1971. **171**: 196-197.

197. Baur, S., Fisher, J.M., Strickland, R.G. and Taylor, K.B., "Autoantibody-Containing Cells in the Gastric Mucosa in Pernicious Anaemia." *Lancet*, 1968. **2**: 887-894.

198. Ashworth, L.A., Strickland, R.G., Koo, N.C. and Taylor, K.B., "Effect of Ph on Intrinsic Factor and Nonintrinsic Factor Vitamin B12 Binding in Human Gastric Juice Neutralized in Vivo." *Gastroenterology*, 1969. **57**: 506-510.

199. Fisher, J.M. and Taylor, K.B., "The Intracellular Localization of Castle's Intrinsic Factor by an Immunofluorescent Technique Using Autoantibodies." *Immunology*, 1969. **16**: 779-784.

200. Hausamen, T.U., Halcrow, D.A. and Taylor, K.B., "Biological Effects of Gastrointestinal Antibodies. I. The Production of Antibodies to Components of Adult and Fetal Guinea Pig Gastric and Colonic Mucosa." *Gastroenterology*, 1969. **56**: 1053-1061.

201. Hausamen, T.U., Halcrow, D.A. and Taylor, K.B., "Biological Effects of Gastrointestinal Antibodies. 3. The Effects of Heterolous and Autoantibodies on Deoxyribonucleic Acid Synthesis in the Stomach and Colon of Guinea Pigs and Rabbits." *Gastroenterology*, 1969. **56**: 1071-1077.

202. Hausamen, T.U., Halcrow, D.A. and Taylor, K.B., "Biological Effects of Gastrointestinal Antibodies. Ii. Histological Changes in the Stomach Induced by Injection of Specific Heterologous Antibodies." *Gastroenterology*, 1969. **56**: 1062-1070.

203. Strickland, R.G., Ashworth, L.A., Koo, N.C. and Taylor, K.B., "Intrinsic Factor, Nonintrinsic Factor Vitamin B12 Binder, and Pepsinogen Secretion in Normal Subjects. Quantification Using Intragastric Neutralization and Inorganic Phosphate as a Marker." *Gastroenterology*, 1969. **57**: 511-517.

204.	Strickland, R.G., Baur, S., Ashworth, L.A. and Taylor, K.B., "Gastric Autoimmunity in Pernicious Anaemia." *Gut*, 1970. **11**: 980.

205.	Ashworth, L.A. and Taylor, K.B., "Rat Intrinsic Factor. Partial Purification and Characterization." *Biochim Biophys Acta*, 1971. **230**: 468-478.

206.	Fisher, J.M. and Taylor, K.B., "The Significance of Gastric Antibodies." *Br J Haematol*, 1971. **20**: 1-7.

207.	Rapp, W., Goldmann, K. and Taylor, K.B., "An Immunological and Chromatographic Comparison of Human Intrinsic Factor and the Acid-Stable Gastric Esterase Vi A." *Clin Exp Immunol*, 1971. **9**: 11-20.

208.	Strickland, R.G., Baur, S., Ashworth, L.A. and Taylor, K.B., "A Correlative Study of Immunological Phenomena in Pernicious Anaemia." *Clin Exp Immunol*, 1971. **8**: 25-36.

209.	Taylor, K.B., "Immunologic Disorders of the Gastrointestinal Tract." *Postgrad Med*, 1973. **54**: 117-123.

210.	Porteous, J.R., Fisher, J.M., Lewin, K.J. and Taylor, K.B., "Induction of Autoallergic Gastritis in Dogs." *J Pathol*, 1974. **112**: 139-146.

211.	Taylor, K.B., "Nutrition and Diseases of the Gastrointestinal Tract." *Prog Food Nutr Sci*, 1975. **1**: 225-243.

212.	Lewin, K.J., Dowling, F., Wright, J.P. and Taylor, K.B., "Gastric Morphology and Serum Gastrin Levels in Pernicious Anaemia." *Gut*, 1976. **17**: 551-560.

213.	Wright, J.P., Callender, S.T., Grumet, F.C., Payne, R.O. and Taylor, K.B., "Hla Antigens in Addisonian Pernicious Anaemia: Absence of a Hla and Disease Association." *Br J Haematol*, 1977. **36**: 15-21.

214.	Interview with Keith Taylor, M.D., January 8, 1992 at Dr. Taylor's home, Stanford, CA.

215.	Interview with Roy Maffley, M.D., January 9, 1992 at Office of Student Affairs, Stanford University School of Medicine.

216.	Swenson, R.S. and Maffly, R.H., "Effect of Sodium Transport and Vasopressin on the Respiratory Quotient of the Toad Bladder." *Nature*, 1968. **218**: 959-961.

217.	Mamelak, M., Weissbluth, M. and Maffly, R.H., "Effect of Chlorpromazine on Permeability of the Toad Bladder." *Biochem Pharmacol*, 1970. **19**: 2303-2315.

218.	Coplon, N.S. and Maffly, R.H., "The Effect of Ouabain on Sodium Transport and Metabolism of the Toad Bladder." *Biochim Biophys Acta*, 1972. **282**: 250-254.

219.	Taylor, A., Hess, J.J. and Maffly, R.H., "The Effects of Propionate on Sodium Transport by the Toad Bladder. Evidence for a Metabolic Mode of Action." *Biochim Biophys Acta*, 1973. **298**: 376-392.

220.	Taylor, A., Hess, J.J. and Maffly, R.H., "On the Effects of Tricarboxylic Acid Cycle Intermediates on Sodium Transport by the Toad Bladder." *J Membr Biol*, 1974. **15**: 319-329.

221.	Hess, J.J., Taylor, A. and Maffly, R.H., "On the Effects of Propionate and Other Short-Chain Fatty Acids on Sodium Transport by the Toad Bladder." *Biochim Biophys Acta*, 1975. **394**: 416-437.

222. Taylor, A., Maffly, R., Wilson, L. and Reaven, E., "Evidence for Involvement of Microtubules in the Action of Vasopressin." *Ann N Y Acad Sci*, 1975. **253**: 723-737.

223. Reaven, E., Maffly, R. and Taylor, A., "Evidence for Involvement of Microtubules in the Action of Vasopressin in Toad Urinary Bladder. III. Morphological Studies on the Content and Distribution of Microtubules in Bladder Epithelial Cells." *J Membr Biol*, 1978. **40**: 251-267.

224. Taylor, A., Mamelak, M., Golbetz, H. and Maffly, R., "Evidence for Involvement of Microtubules in the Action of Vasopressin in Toad Urinary Bladder. I. Functional Studies on the Effects of Antimitotic Agents on the Response to Vasopressin." *J Membr Biol*, 1978. **40**: 213-235.

225. Swenson, R.S., Silvers, A., Peterson, D.T., Kohatsu, S. and Reaven, G.M., "Effect of Nephrectomy and Acute Uremia on Plasma Insulin- 125 I Removal Rate." *J Lab Clin Med*, 1971. **77**: 829-837.

226. Weisinger, J., Swenson, R.S., Greene, W., Taylor, J.B. and Reaven, G.M., "Comparison of the Effects of Metabolic Acidosis and Acute Uremia on Carbohydrate Tolerance." *Diabetes*, 1972. **21**: 1109-1115.

227. Reaven, G.M., Lindley, T.S., Weisinger, J.R. and Swenson, R.S., "A Paradoxical Effect of Chlorpropamide on the Plasma Glucose and Immunoreactive Insulin Response to Intravenous Glucose in Normal Dogs." *Diabetes*, 1973. **22**: 367-371.

228. Swenson, R.S., Peterson, D.T., Eshleman, M. and Reaven, G.M., "Effect of Acute Uremia on Various Aspects of Carbohydrate Metabolism in Dogs." *Kidney Int*, 1973. **4**: 267-272.

229. Weisinger, J.R., Reaven, G.M., Coplon, N.S. and Swenson, R.S., "The Effect of Dialysis on True Plasma Glucose Tolerance in Uremia." *Trans Am Soc Artif Intern Organs*, 1973. **19**: 277-281.

230. Reaven, G.M., Weisinger, J.R. and Swenson, R.S., "Insulin and Glucose Metabolism in Renal Insufficiency." *Kidney Int Suppl*, 1974: 63-69.

231. Swenson, R.S., Weisinger, J. and Reaven, G.M., "Evidence That Hemodialysis Does Not Improve the Glucose Tolerance of Patients with Chronic Renal Failure." *Metabolism*, 1974. **23**: 929-936.

232. Reaven, G.M., Sageman, W.S. and Swenson, R.S., "Development of Insulin Resistance in Normal Dogs Following Alloxan-Induced Insulin Deficiency." *Diabetologia*, 1977. **13**: 459-462.

233. Interview with Robert Swenson, M.D., January 2, 1992 at Palo Alto VAMC.

234. Hultgren, H.N. and Grover, R.F., "Circulatory Adaptation to High Altitude." *Annu Rev Med*, 1968. **19**: 119-152.

235. Hultgren, H.N., "Letter: Furosemide for High Altitude Pulmonary Edema." *Jama*, 1975. **234**: 589-590.

236. Hultgren, H.N. and Marticorena, E.A., "High Altitude Pulmonary Edema. Epidemiologic Observations in Peru." *Chest*, 1978. **74**: 372-376.

237. Hultgren, H.N., "High-Altitude Edema." *Jama*, 1978. **239**: 2239.

238. Hultgren, H.N., "High Altitude Medical Problems." *West J Med*, 1979. **131**: 8-23.

239. Bock, J. and Hultgren, H.N., "Emergency Maneuver in High-Altitude Pulmonary Edema." *Jama*, 1986. **255**: 3245-3246.

240. Hultgren, H.N., "The Safety of Trekking at High Altitude after Coronary Bypass Surgery." *Jama*, 1988. **260**: 2218-2219.

241. Sutton, J.R., Reeves, J.T., Groves, B.M., Wagner, P.D., Alexander, J.K., Hultgren, H.N., Cymerman, A. and Houston, C.S., "Oxygen Transport and Cardiovascular Function at Extreme Altitude: Lessons from Operation Everest II." *Int J Sports Med*, 1992. **13 Suppl 1**: S13-18.

242. Hultgren, H.N., "High-Altitude Pulmonary Edema: Current Concepts." *Annu Rev Med*, 1996. **47**: 267-284.

243. Hultgren, H.N., Wilson, R. and Kosek, J.C., "Lung Pathology in High-Altitude Pulmonary Edema." *Wilderness Environ Med*, 1997. **8**: 218-220.

244. Hultgren, H.N., "High Altitude Pulmonary Edema: Hemodynamic Aspects." *Int J Sports Med*, 1997. **18**: 20-25.

245. Conley, F.K. and Remington, J.S., "Nonspecific Inhibition of Tumor Growth in the Central Nervous System: Observations of Intracerebral Ependymoblastoma in Mice with Chronic Toxoplasma Infection." *J Natl Cancer Inst*, 1977. **59**: 963-973.

246. Conley, F.K., "Development of a Metastatic Brain Tumor Model in Mice." *Cancer Res*, 1979. **39**: 1001-1007.

247. Conley, F.K., "Metastatic Brain Tumor Model in Mice That Mimics the Neoplastic Cascade in Humans." *Neurosurgery*, 1984. **14**: 187-192.

248. Conley, F.K., "Effect of Corynebacterium Parvum and Chronic Toxoplasma Infection on Metastatic Brain Tumors in Mice." *J Natl Cancer Inst*, 1979. **63**: 1237-1244.

249. Conley, F.K., "Effect of Immunomodulation on the Fate of Tumor Cells in the Central Nervous System and Systemic Organs of Mice. Distribution of [125I]5- Iodo-2'-Deoxyuridine-Labeled KHT Tumor Cells after Left Intracardial Injection." *J Natl Cancer Inst*, 1982. **69**: 465-473.

250. Conley, F.K. and Jenkins, K.A., "Immunohistological Study of the Anatomic Relationship of Toxoplasma Antigens to the Inflammatory Response in the Brains of Mice Chronically Infected with Toxoplasma Gondii." *Infect Immun*, 1981. **31**: 1184-1192.

251. Conley, F.K., Jenkins, K.A. and Remington, J.S., "Toxoplasma Gondii Infection of the Central Nervous System. Use of the Peroxidase-Antiperoxidase Method to Demonstrate Toxoplasma in Formalin Fixed, Paraffin Embedded Tissue Sections." *Hum Pathol*, 1981. **12**: 690-698.

252. Luft, B.J., Brooks, R.G., Conley, F.K., McCabe, R.E. and Remington, J.S., "Toxoplasmic Encephalitis in Patients with Acquired Immune Deficiency Syndrome." *Jama*, 1984. **252**: 913-917.

253. Moskowitz, L.B., Hensley, G.T., Chan, J.C., Gregorios, J. and Conley, F.K., "The Neuropathology of Acquired Immune Deficiency Syndrome." *Arch Pathol Lab Med*, 1984. **108**: 867-872.

254. Wanke, C., Tuazon, C.U., Kovacs, A., Dina, T., Davis, D.O., Barton, N., Katz, D., Lunde, M., Levy, C., Conley, F.K. and et al., "Toxoplasma Encephalitis in Patients with Acquired Immune Deficiency Syndrome: Diagnosis and Response to Therapy." *Am J Trop Med Hyg*, 1987. **36**: 509-516.

255. Israelski, D.M., Araujo, F.G., Conley, F.K., Suzuki, Y., Sharma, S. and Remington, J.S., "Treatment with Anti-L3t4 (CD4) Monoclonal Antibody Reduces the Inflammatory Response in Toxoplasmic Encephalitis." *J Immunol*, 1989. **142**: 954-958.

256. Kennedy, J.D. and Conley, F.K., "Effect of Intracerebrally Injected Corynebacterium Parvum on Implanted Brain Tumor in Mice." *J Neurooncol*, 1989. **7**: 89-101.

257. Conley, F.K., Adler, J.R., Jr., Duncan, J.A., Kennedy, J.D. and Sutton, R.C., "Intralesional Immunotherapy of Brain Tumors with Combined Corynebacterium Parvum and Recombinant Interleukin-2 in Mice." *J Natl Cancer Inst*, 1990. **82**: 1340-1344.

258. Interview with Richard I. Mazze, M.D., December 12, 1991 at Palo Alto VA Medical Center.

259. DeNardo, G.L., Crowley, L., Pardoe, R. and Weintraub, R., "Animal Studies with Se75 Selenomethionine." *J Nucl Med*, 1967. **8**: 350.

260. Hofmann, W.W. and DeNardo, G.L., "Sodium Flux in Myotonic Muscular Dystrophy." *Am J Physiol*, 1968. **214**: 330-336.

261. Telephone interview with Gerald L. DeNardo, M.D., October 28, 1991.

262. Interview with David Goodwin, M.D., at Palo Alto VAMC.

263. Goodwin, D.A., Mears, C.F., McTigue, M. and David, G.S., "Monoclonal Antibody Hapten Radiopharmaceutical Delivery." *Nucl Med Commun*, 1986. **7**: 569-580.

264. Goodwin, D.A., "Tumor Imaging with Indium-Labeled Biotin." *J Nucl Med*, 1991. **32**: 750-751.

265. Goodwin, D.A., Meares, C.F., McTigue, M., Chaovapong, W., Diamanti, C.I., Ransone, C.H. and McCall, M.J., "Pretargeted Immunoscintigraphy: Effect of Hapten Valency on Murine Tumor Uptake." *J Nucl Med*, 1992. **33**: 2006-2013.

266. Goodwin, D.A., Meares, C.F., Watanabe, N., McTigue, M., Chaovapong, W., Ransone, C.M., Renn, O., Greiner, D.P., Kukis, D.L. and Kronenberger, S.I., "Pharmacokinetics of Pretargeted Monoclonal Antibody 2d12.5 and 88y-Janus-2-(P-Nitrobenzyl)-1,4,7,10-Tetraazacyclododecanetetraacetic Acid (Dota) in Balb/C Mice with Khjj Mouse Adenocarcinoma: A Model for 90y Radioimmunotherapy." *Cancer Res*, 1994. **54**: 5937-5946.

267. Goodwin, D.A., Ransone, C.M., Diamanti, C.I. and McTigue, M., "Rapid Synthesis and Quality Control of 68Ga-Labeled Chelates for Clinical Use." *Nucl Med Biol*, 1994. **21**: 897-899.

268. Goodwin, D.A., "Tumor Pretargeting: Almost the Bottom Line." *J Nucl Med*, 1995. **36**: 876-879.

269. Goodwin, D.A., Meares, C.F. and Osen, M., "Biological Properties of Biotin-Chelate Conjugates for Pretargeted Diagnosis and Therapy with the Avidin/Biotin System." *J Nucl Med*, 1998. **39**: 1813-1818.

270. Goodwin, D.A. and Meares, C.F., "Pretargeted Peptide Imaging and Therapy." *Cancer Biother Radiopharm*, 1999. **14**: 145-152.

271. Watanabe, N., Yokoyama, K., Shuke, N., Kinuya, S., Aburano, T., Tonami, N., Seto, H. and Goodwin, D.A., "Experimental Investigation of I-123 Iodoamphetamine in the Detection of Lung Cancer." *Lung Cancer*, 1999. **25**: 1-6.

272. Apple, L.E. and Goodrich, G.L., *Flight to Freedom, 1967-1992: a History of the First 25 Years of the Western Blind Rehabilitation Center*. Washington, DC: Blinded American Veterans Foundation, 1992

273. Goodrich, G.L., Mehr, E.B. and Darling, N.C., "Experience with Closed-Circuit Television in the Blind Rehabilitation Program of the Veterans Administration." *Am J Optometry and Arch Am Acad Optometry*, 1980. **57**: 881-892.

274. Goodrich, G.L., Bennett, R.R. and Wiley, J.K., "Electronic Calculators for Visually Impaired Users: An Evaluation." *J Visual Impairment and Blindness*, 1977. **71**: 154-157.

275. Darling, N.C., Goodrich, G.L. and Wiley, J.K., "A Follow-up Study of Electronic Travel Aid Users." *Bull Prosthetic Res*, 1977. **10**: 82-91.

276. Morrissette, D.L., Goodrich, G.L. and Hennessey, J.J., "A Follow-up Study of the Mowat Sensor: Applications, Frequency of Use and Maintenance Reliability." *J Visual Impairment and Blindness*, 1981. **75**: 244-247.

277. Morrissette, D.L. and Goodrich, G.L., "The Night Vision Aid for Legally Blind People with Night Blindness: an Evaluation." *J Visual Impairment and Blindness*, 1983. **77**: 67-70.

278. Wiley, J.K. and others, "Clinical Application Study of Reading and Mobility Aids for the Blind." *Bull Prosthetic Res*, 1976. **BPR-10-26**: 272-273.

279. Goodrich, G.L. and others, "Partial Evaluation of the Kurzweil Reading Machine." *J Visual Impairment and Blindness*, 1979. **73**: 389-399.

280. Morrissette, D.L., Goodrich, G.L. and Marmor, M.F., "A Study of the Effectiveness of the Wide Angle Mobility Light." *J Visual Impairment and Blindness*, 1985. **79**: 109-111.

281. Goodrich, G.L., "Application of Microcomputers by Visually Impaired Persons." *J Visual Impairment and Blindness*, 1984. **78**: 408-414.

282. Goodrich, G.L., "Applying Video and Microcomputer Technology in a Low Vision Setting." *Ophthalmology Clin N America*, 1994. **7**: 177-185.

283. Goodrich, G.L. and others, "A Comparative Study of Reading Performance with a Head Mounted Laser Display and Conventional Low Vision Devices." *J Visual Impairment and Blindness*, in press, 2004.

284. Holcomb, J.G. and Goodrich, G.L., "Eccentric Viewing Training." *J Am Optimetric Assn*, 1976. **47**: 1438-1443.

285. Ludt, R. and Goodrich, G.L., "Change in Visual Perceptual Detection Distances for Low Vision Travelers as a Result of Dynamic Visual Assessment and Training." *J Visual Impairment and Blindness*, 2002. **96**: 7-21.

286. Interview with James Elliot, M.D., February 11, 1992 at Palo Alto VAMC.

287. Interview with Jerome Yesavage, M.D., August 1, 2002 at Dr. Yesavage's office at the Palo Alto VAMC.

288. Sachs, D.P., Hall, R.G. and Hall, S.M., "Effects of Rapid Smoking. Physiologic Evaluation of a Smoking-Cessation Therapy." *Ann Intern Med*, 1978. **88**: 639-641.

289. Sachs, D.P., Hall, R.G., Pechacek, T.F. and Fitzgerald, J., "Clarification of Risk-Benefit Issues in Rapid Smoking." *J Consult Clin Psychol*, 1979. **47**: 1053-1060.

290. Hall, R.G., Sachs, D.P., Hall, S.M. and Benowitz, N.L., "Two-Year Efficacy and Safety of Rapid Smoking Therapy in Patients with Cardiac and Pulmonary Disease." *J Consult Clin Psychol*, 1984. **52**: 574-581.

291. Hall, R.G., Duhamel, M., McClanahan, R., Miles, G., Nason, C., Rosen, S., Schiller, P., Tao-Yonenaga, L. and Hall, S.M., "Level of Functioning, Severity of Illness, and Smoking Status among Chronic Psychiatric Patients." *J Nerv Ment Dis*, 1995. **183**: 468-471.

292. Marmor, M.F., Abdul-Rahim, A.S. and Cohen, D.S., "The Effect of Metabolic Inhibitors on Retinal Adhesion and Subretinal Fluid Resorption." *Invest Ophthalmol Vis Sci*, 1980. **9**: 893-903.

293. Marmor, M.F. and Maack, T., "Local Environment Factors and Retinal Adhesion in the Rabbit." *Exp Eye Res*, 1982. **34**: 727-733.

294. Frambach, D.A. and Marmor, M.F., "The Rate and Route of Fluid Resorption from the Subretinal Space of the Rabbit." *Invest Ophthalmol Vis Sci*, 1982. **22**: 292-302.

295. Marmor, M.F., Negi, A. and Maurice, D.M., "Kinetics of Macromolecules Injected into the Subretinal Space." *Exp Eye Res*, 1985. **40**: 687-696.

296. Negi, A. and Marmor, M.F., "Experimental Serous Retinal Detachment and Focal Pigment Epithelial Damage." *Arch Ophthalmol*, 1984. **102**: 445-449.

297. Negi, A. and Marmor, M.F., "Helaing of Photocoagulation Lesions Affects the Rate of Subretinal Fluid Resorption." *Ophthalmol*, 1984. **91**: 1678-1683.

298. Lurie, M. and Marmor, M.F., "Analysis of the Response Properties and Light-Integrating Characteristics of the C-Wave in the Rabbit Eye." *Exp Eye Res*, 1980. **31**: 335-349.

299. Wu, L., Lurie, M. and Marmor, M.F., "Experimental Observations on the C-Wave of the Electroretinogram." *Chinese J Ophthalmol*, 1981. **17**: 193-196.

300. Marmor, M.F., Donovan, W.J. and Gaba, D.M., "Effects of Hypoxia and Hyperoxia on the Human Standing Potential." *Doc Ophthalmol*, 1985. **60**: 347-352.

301. Zinn, K. and Marmor, M.F., *The Retinal Pigment Epithelium*. Cambridge: Harvard University Press, 1979

302. Weiner, M.W., "Uncoupling Agents Distinguish between the Effects of Metabolic Inhibitors and Transport Inhibitors." *Science*, 1979. **204**: 187-188.

303. Weiner, M.W., Greene, K., Vreman, H., Wemmer, D., Jardesky, N.W. and Jardesky, O., "NMR Measurements of Metabolites in Organs of Live Animals Using Chronically Implanted Radiofrequency Coils." *IRCS Medical Science*, 1980. **8**: 671.

485

Chapter 22. Research at the Oteen/Asheville VA Medical Center
Timothy Takaro, M.D.

This hospital is unique in both its location and character, and the two are inextricably entwined. Following each of the two World Wars, a spurt of hospital-building activity commenced to house and treat the large numbers of returning veterans in need of medical care. The Oteen VA Hospital was the direct result of the construction, in 1918, on a large tract of land seven miles east of the city of Asheville, NC of U. S. Army Hospital No. 19 (O'Reilly General Hospital.)[1, 2] It was transferred to the US Public Health Service in 1920, when it began to house and treat veterans thought to have pulmonary tuberculosis, a major public health problem in those years. When bed rest and fresh air were about the only modalities available for treating this condition, Asheville had been a favored resort area in the Blue Ridge Mountains of western North Carolina for "taking the cure."

In 1922, the hospital became part of the newly-established Veterans Bureau, and in 1930, it was formally incorporated into the renamed Veterans Administration. In contrast to the facility's original cantonment-type housing ultimately reaching 3000 beds, between the two wars permanent structures were built with a bed capacity of between 850 and 1264. Twelve hospitals in the VA system were devoted to the management of patients with tuberculosis, with Oteen thought to be the largest.[3] Occasionally referred to locally as the Azalea Hospital—a railroad depot in the valley about a mile below the hospital was called Azalea — it later acquired the name of Oteen. The derivation of this name is obscure. Some have attributed it to a Cherokee Indian term variously taken to mean "chief aim" or "health and cheer," but the term does not appear as such in a Cherokee syllabary.[4]

Figure 22.1. The Moore General Army Hospital

After World War II, a second cantonment-type Army Hospital of 1,000 beds (Moore General Hospital) was constructed eight miles farther east, in Swannanoa. This facility was eventually turned over to the Oteen VA Hospital and operated in conjunction with it until 1960, when the Moore General hospital was closed. As tuberculosis was brought under control with the advent of effective pharmacologic agents (streptomycin and the subsequent train of chemotherapeutic drugs), a large new general hospital was constructed on ground adjacent to the permanent buildings of the older Oteen tuberculosis hospital. It opened in 1967. Many of the old buildings were sold to local governmental agencies and private developers. In 1975, the hospital's name was changed to the Asheville VA Hospital and soon after to the Asheville VAMC.

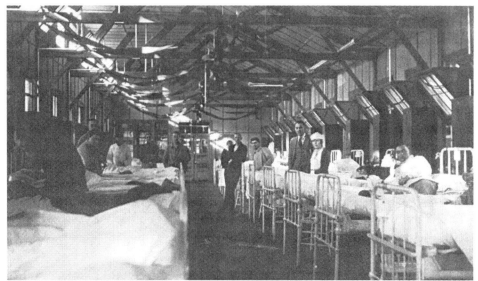
Figure 22.2. Open ward in the Army hospital

This account of the research activities at the Oteen/Asheville VAMC through 1980 is divided into decades and highlights the main foci of investigative interests during each period, briefly profiles major researchers and describes some of the research laboratories.

The Early Years (late 1940s and the decade of the 1950s)

From Oteen's beginnings, it was natural that the initial research interests of its physicians focused on the treatment of pulmonary tuberculosis. Thanks to its size, the Oteen VA Hospital was one of the major contributors to the seminal cooperative chemotherapy trials for tuberculosis treatment that began during this period and are reviewed in Chapter 5. The magnitude and intensity of tuberculosis activities at this site also explains the establishment of a surgical service devoted primarily to thoracic surgery. In 1946, a thoracic surgical residency training program was added. One of the earliest thoracic surgical residency programs in the country, it was unaffiliated with any medical school, making it the only free-standing such program within the VA system.

Medical research, which was mainly concerned with the chemotherapy of tuberculosis, was pursued primarily by two prominent pulmonologists, W. Spencer Schwartz M.D., and Ralph Moyer, M.D., and their colleagues. Separately and together, they published at least nine papers during this period and more in the 1960s, many presented at the VA/Armed Forces Conferences on the Chemotherapy of Tuberculosis.[5-9] For many years, the Oteen VA Hospital played a key role at these regularly recurring research conferences.

The first director of the Surgical Service, James D. Murphy, M.D., was a conscientious investigator from the beginning. Throughout this early period, he and his first resident (and later second-in-command) Harry E. Walkup, M.D., actively engaged in surgical research. In spite of marked differences in personality and temperament (Dr. Murphy quiet-spoken and reserved, Dr. Walkup ebullient and gregarious), these two physicians worked well together, helping train a cadre of several dozen residents, including the author of this chapter. They inculcated a spirit of inquiry, self-examination and candor in many of their trainees that became a lasting part of the institution. Together with their residents they published almost 50 papers on various aspects of the surgical management of pulmonary tuberculosis and its complications.[10-12]

Figure 22.3. W. Spencer Schwartz   **Figure 22.4. James D. Murphy**

A very early report on the rehabilitation of patients with tuberculosis was also published during this period by B. B. Bagby, M.D.[13]

With the gradual decline in the use of surgical treatment for tuberculosis, Oteen surgeons turned their attention increasingly to the newly emerging specialties of cardiac and vascular surgery. The first sustained "open heart" surgical program in Western North Carolina was begun at the very end of this decade by Stewart Scott, M.D. His initial success, an aortic valve replacement on August 4, 1959, was reported in a headlined article in the local newspaper that showed not only a photograph of the patient beside the massive apparatus that was the pump-oxygenator, but also reported the names of all 23 donors whose blood

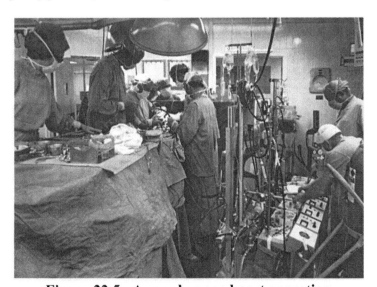

Figure 22.5. An early open heart operation

489

was used to prime the pump. The surgical team remained appropriately anonymous.[14] The next operation was also news. These efforts were aimed at recruiting blood donors for the large amounts of blood needed for each operation—40 years before the bloodless disposable plastic bags in use today as oxygenators became available.

Early Oteen investigators

Even before 1960, Oteen attracted a number of important researchers, many of whom played important roles through the years:

Julian Moore, M.D.

Dr. Moore was the first fully trained thoracic surgeon in Western North Carolina when he arrived in Asheville as a private practitioner in 1930. He received his surgical training at the University of Pennsylvania in Philadelphia and the University of Michigan at Ann Arbor, under the tutelage of John Alexander, one of the nation's pioneer thoracic surgeons. He served vital roles as surgical consultant at the VA Hospital by assisting Dr. Murphy in the more complicated surgical cases and in training surgical residents, including this writer. He authored or co-authored at least half a dozen papers with members of the VA Hospital staff on a variety of thoracic surgical subjects, many involving the treatment of tuberculosis.[15-19] In addition to his VA work, he was Director of Surgery at the North Carolina State-run Black Mountain Sanatorium, as well as being one of the busiest and most prominent surgeons in private practice in Asheville. Many of Asheville's leading surgeons apprenticed with him. He helped found the Buncombe County Medical Society Library. He died suddenly, in 1959, at the age of 63 of a massive pulmonary embolus after a long day of surgery; his body was found resting on his own examining table.

Ralph E. Moyer, M.D.

Dr. Moyer joined Oteen in 1940 as a staff physician and rose to become Chief of the Pulmonary Diseases Service. Trained at the University of Minnesota School of Medicine, he was one of the three important early investigators in the field of tuberculosis at Oteen, along with Drs. Murphy and Schwartz, and a major participant in the VA-Armed Forces chemotherapy trials for the treatment of this disease. He authored or co-authored some 30 papers on the subject,[5, 8, 9] but also studied the problems of pulmonary sarcoidosis, pneumoperitoneum and silicotuberculosis.[20, 21] He died in 1964.

James D. Murphy, M.D.

The founder of the surgical program at the Oteen VA Hospital, Dr. Murphy (Figure 22.4) came to Asheville from the VA Hospital in San Fernando, California, in 1943. He received his medical school training at the University of Washington and Northwestern University, interned at Cook County Hospital and completed residency training at the Passavant Memorial Hospital, both in Chicago. As Chief of the Surgical Service at Oteen, over the next 13 years, along with his assistant (and first resident) Harry E. Walkup, M.D., he developed a residency training program in thoracic surgery independent of any medical school affiliation. Several dozen surgeons trained in this unusual program. A founding member of the Board of Thoracic Surgery, Dr. Murphy later helped found and was the first president of the Southern Thoracic Surgical Association.[22]

His research interests were focused mainly on the surgery of pulmonary tuberculosis and its complications. The first research reports emanating from the Oteen VA Hospital were his.[23, 24] He studied every aspect of this subject, including even the conduct of anesthesia[25] and the design of an appropriate operating table,[26] authoring or co-authoring approximately 40 papers. For the next five and a half decades, his productive example set the pattern at this institution for an investigative style of surgical practice. Endlessly innovative in the surgical treatment of tuberculosis, he was also assiduous in tracking down causes of the complications of surgical therapy.[10-12] He also studied a wide variety of non-tuberculous conditions including mycotic infections of the lung,[18, 27] cystic disease of the lung,[28] lung abscess, and constrictive pericarditis.[16]

Dr. Murphy became the General Manager of the VA Hospital in Baltimore, Maryland, in 1956 (the title was later changed to Director) and returned to the Oteen VA hospital as Director in 1959. He died of hepatitis in 1964.

Harry E. Walkup, M.D.

Dr. Walkup was architect of the plan to transform the Oteen VA Hospital from a hospital devoted to the treatment of tuberculosis to a hospital with major emphasis on cardiovascular diseases. In 1946, when he came to Oteen from a residency in St. Joseph's Hospital in Baltimore, he became the first thoracic surgical resident in the only unaffiliated thoracic surgical training program in the eastern United States. After receiving additional training in general surgery at the University of Pennsylvania, he returned to Oteen in 1949 as Assistant Chief of the Surgical Service under Dr. Murphy. Following a brief trial in private practice with Dr. Julian Moore, he returned to the VA in 1951.

Dr. Walkup's research interests lay primarily in thoracic diseases, about which he authored or co-authored at least 10 published papers.[11, 12, 19, 29-32] He was appointed to the Executive Committee of the VA's Research Conferences in Pulmonary Diseases (Chapter 5).

Figure 22.6. Harry E. Walkup

491

Hoping to expand the residency training program to include cardiovascular surgery, Dr. Walkup recruited Oteen's first cardiac surgeons, Drs. Edward Munnell and Tom Crymes, who performed the earliest mitral and aortic valvular commissurotomies at this hospital. The initial attempts at open heart surgery were carried out by Dr. Crymes. Dr. Walkup's most successful recruit was Dr. Stewart M. Scott, who established the first permanent cardiac surgical program in Western North Carolina and one of the earliest in the entire Veterans Administration.

Dr. Walkup remained as Chief of the Surgical Service until 1961 when he left for the VA Central Office. Later, he became Director of Research for the American Thoracic Society, and, finally, served as Director of the Wilmington, Delaware VAMC, until his retirement.

Philip Morganstern, M.D.

Among the very earliest of clinical investigators at Oteen and one of the handful of physicians on the Medical Service active in research, Dr. Morgenstern was Chief of Medicine at Oteen's Swannanoa Division in 1948 and 1949. He trained at George Washington University School of Medicine in Washington, D.C., and Bellevue Hospital in New York City. Not surprisingly, his research interests at Oteen all related to pulmonary conditions.[33-36] He moved to the VA Hospital in Newington CT in 1953 to become Chief of Gastroenterology, and later Assistant Professor of Internal Medicine at the University of Connecticut Medical School.

John E. Rayl, M.D.

Dr. Rayl came to Oteen in 1949 from the Medical College of Virginia, for two years of training in thoracic surgery and a year on the surgical staff. After two more years of general surgical training at the VA hospital in Johnson City, TN, he returned as Section Chief of Thoracic Surgery in 1951 and remained at Oteen for the next eleven years. His chief research interests focused on thoracic surgery, including surgery for pulmonary tuberculosis,[19, 37] and on bronchoscopy and bronchography,[38] which led to his creating a series of scientific motion pictures and training films involving cinefluorography. He helped establish the distinction between cylindrical ("non-surgical") and saccular (or"surgical") bronchiectesis.[39] After leaving Oteen in 1962, he continued this work at the Lake City VA Hospital in Florida and the University of Florida in Gainesville. After he retired from the VA, he returned to Asheville, where he died in 2000.

W. Spencer Schwartz, M.D.

In 1949, Dr. Schwartz (Figure 22.3) joined Oteen, where for 22 years he served as Chief of Professional Services. (The title was later changed to Chief of Staff.) A graduate of the Ohio State Medical School, he then served on the staff of the Trudeau Sanatorium in Lake Saranac, NY. Along with Drs. Moyer and Murphy, he was among the earliest investigators of the treatment of pulmonary tuberculosis, and particularly in the search for more effective chemotherapeutic regimens for this disease. Author or co-author of some 40 papers and book chapters in this area,[5-9, 40-42] he also provided reviews for the *Journal of the American*

Medical Association on the management of tuberculosis and other common pulmonary diseases.[43, 44] He died unexpectedly in 1971.

Oscar Kanner, M.D.

Dr. Kanner was Chief of Laboratory Services at Oteen from 1950 to 1963. A native of Czechoslovakia, he received his medical education at the University of Vienna and the Pasteur Institute in Paris. Before coming to Oteen, he taught pathology at Loyola University. Possessed of an unusually analytic and questioning mind, he published over a dozen papers while at Oteen, on subjects ranging from the expected (those relating to pulmonary tuberculosis)[45] to the unexpected, (the rejection of observations;[46] contamination risk with screw-capped centrifuge tubes;[47] and the evaluation of diagnostic tests—the concept of inverse probability.)[48] His temperament was excitable, and the greater the intensity of his passion about a subject, the more pronounced became his distinctive Viennese accent, making memorable his clinico-pathologic conferences, which all surgical residents were required to attend. He died in 1965.

Robert. G. Fish, M.D.

Dr. Fish, one of the key players in Oteen's cardiovascular surgical program, was a graduate of the University of Michigan School of Medicine at Ann Arbor and completed his residency training at its University Hospital. He came to Oteen in 1952 and became Chief of Medicine the following year. Almost all of his investigational studies revolved around his strong interest in cardiology and in the surgical management of angina pectoris. He co-authored one of the earliest reports in the literature on the effects of internal mammary artery ligation for the treatment of angina.[49]

He also helped develop a number of diagnostic procedures for cardiac conditions.[50-52] His support in providing accurate diagnostic assistance and his physical presence in the operating room during the early phases of the cardiac surgical program were of vital importance in its establishment.

Figure 22.7. Robert G. Fish

493

Dr. Fish was a Principal Investigator in two VA Cooperative Studies of Surgery for Coronary Arterial Occlusive Disease (the Internal Mammary Artery Implant and the Coronary Artery Bypass Graft Studies). He authored or co-authored at least 16 papers, most on cardiac conditions[53-58] and remained Chief of the Medical Service for over 20 years (1953–1974). He then was appointed Chief of Staff and remained in that position until his retirement in 1983. He died in 1985.

Daniel E. Smith, M. D.

Dr. Smith came to the Oteen VA Hospital in 1955 for its thoracic surgical training program. He had taken general surgical training in residencies in Bryn Mawr, Pennsylvania, Parkland Hospital, Dallas, Texas and the VA Hospital in Johnson City, Tennessee. Upon completing his residency, he joined the staff at Oteen and within five years became Chief of the Surgical Service. His research interests included working with Dr. John Rayl in bronchography,[38] with Dr. James Matthews in fungal infections of the lungs,[59] with Dr. Kjell Christianson in canine lung transplantation and bronchogenic carcinoma[60, 61] and with a number of colleagues on the problems of bronchial stump healing after pneumonectomy.[62] He left Oteen to take up the position of Chief of Surgery at the VA Hospital in Albuquerque, New Mexico., and an appointment on the faculty at the University of New Mexico.

Stewart M. Scott, M.D.

Dr. Scott (Figure 22.8) established the first "open heart" surgical program in Western North Carolina at Oteen.

He came to Oteen as a resident in thoracic surgery from the Harrison Department of Surgical Research at the University of Pennsylvania. Clearly, an interest in investigation was a strong early influence in his career. After his residency, he took additional training in cardiac surgery for two years at the Allegheny General Hospital under Dr. George Magovern. Although a few attempts had been made to perform "open heart" surgery just before his return, Dr. Scott established Oteen's first sustained cardiac surgical program, which he headed for the next 35 years.

His research interests were broad and varied, reflecting the state of the art in the 1960s and 1970s, when many young thoracic surgeons began to perform cardiac surgery as well as vascular surgery. The evidence of these diverse interests is his many publications, approximately one-third on cardiac subjects,[54-58, 63-74] one third on vascular topics,[75-81] and one third on thoracic and miscellaneous surgical subjects.[82-86] Dr. Scott made lasting contributions in at least three areas: the design and function of cardiac prosthetic valves, pioneering valve replacement as definitive treatment for acute aortic insufficiency due to bacterial endocarditis, (a radical concept at that time;)[55] in co-chairing two VA Cooperative studies of Surgery for Obstructive Coronary Artery Disease; and in his investigations of the hemodynamics and ultrastructure of the endothelial lining of small-caliber vascular prosthetic grafts.[79]

Dr. Scott published more than a dozen studies investigating various aspects of cardiac valvular surgery, including the efficacy of the Magovern sutureless aortic valve, Starr-Edwards valves, the DeBakey Surgitool valve and others. The complications following valve replacement, including operative mishaps, valve durability, stent fracture, embolization of poppets and other valve parts were all investigated. Probably his greatest contribution to this center was establishing cardiac surgery on a firm footing.

Before his untimely death in 1996, Dr. Scott authored or co-authored over 100 papers, abstracts and book chapters in the broad areas of thoracic and cardiovascular surgery. He held the teaching appointment of Clinical Professor of Surgery at Duke University School of Medicine at the time of his death.

Timothy Takaro, M. D.

The author came to Oteen in 1951 from a Fellowship in general surgery at the Mayo Clinic. Following a two-year thoracic surgical residency at Oteen came a three-year stint in Western India as Director of Surgery at a tuberculosis sanatorium under the auspices of the Presbyterian Church. In 1957, he returned to Oteen as a staff surgeon, participating in the early stages of "open heart surgery," with many training sessions on the pump-oxygenator with his predecessor, Dr. Tom Crymes. He served as Dr. Scott's assistant in the first several years of the cardiac surgical program. He became Chief of the Surgical Service in 1962.

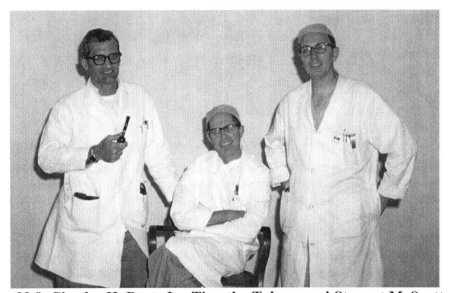

Figure 22.8. Charles H. Dart, Jr., Timothy Takaro and Stewart M. Scott, 1973

A three-month visit to Moscow in 1962 under the auspices of a US-USSR Scientific and Cultural Exchange Agreement allowed Dr. Takaro to pursue his research interests in mechanical suturing devices[87, 88] and to sort out the practical from the impractical.[89] His further studies back at Oteen led to the adoption of the lung stapling instrument as a useful adjunct in thoracic surgery.[62, 83, 90] A major research effort of the Surgical Service in which he participated was in the area of ischemic heart disease. These efforts culminated in the series of VA's important multicenter cooperative studies of surgery for coronary artery disease (Chapter 18) .

Supported by an NIH-sponsored travel grant to Nagoya, Japan in 1967, where ultra-fine focal spot Xray tubes made magnification angiography possible, he investigated the angiographic appearances of the small vessels of the heart,[91] lungs,[92] kidneys,[93] lymphatics[94] and extremities.[95] By the 1980s, the usefulness of this technology was supplanted by the development of computerized scanning and magnetic resonance imaging.

His basic investigations of the ultrastructure of the lungs in experimentally–induced emphysema [96] as well as clinical pulmonary emphysema led to the discovery of a number of features of canine and human lungs not previously described. He held the appointment of Clinical Professor of Surgery at Duke University School of Medicine at the time of his retirement in 1988. He served as Chief of Staff from 1983 to 1988.

John T. Joyner, III, M.D.

In 1958, Dr. Joyner came to the Oteen VA Hospital from a residency in Medicine at Emory University Hospital, having previously attended the Bowman Gray School of Medicine. He took special training in Nuclear Medicine at Oak Ridge, Tenn. and at the Mayo Foundation. He was named Chief of the Medical Service in 1974 and remained at the VA Hospital until his retirement in 1991.

His research interests paralleled those of his colleagues with whom he authored or co-authored half a dozen papers.[39, 53, 97]

The 1960s

The most active period in the history of research at Oteen probably occurred in this decade, which saw the publication of over 230 papers, abstracts and book chapters. This fine frenzy of activity was the outcome of the serendipitous confluence of a number of factors: the simultaneous presence of staff physicians and surgeons with a bent toward research, plus a cadre of talented residents; the overlapping areas of interest of several researchers, which stirred both competition and cooperation among them; generous funding for investigational studies and an institutional climate favorable to such activities. In addition to the various non-tuberculous conditions affecting the lungs and the esophagus, the principle areas of research interest were then in: cardiac diagnostic techniques;[50-52] angiography, especially coronary arteriography;[91, 98, 99] surgery for obstructive coronary artery disease;[53, 100, 101] cardiac valvular surgery;[54, 55] surgical treatment of peripheral vascular diseases;[75, 102] use of surgical stapling devices[62, 87, 88] and development of prosthetic vascular grafts.[103] Following in this hospital's tradition of cooperation with other VA and Armed Forces hospitals in the chemotherapy trials for pulmonary tuberculosis, it also seemed quite natural to pursue cooperative studies of randomized controlled trials in investigating the management of cardiac diseases, especially those involving the coronary arteries.

Figure 22.9. Surgical resident and physician staff about 1961. Front row, left to right: Thomas Crymes, Anthony Karich, John Rayl, Harry Walkup, Daniel Smith, Kjell Christianson, David Reiner. Back row: Wesley Morgan, Alan Grantham, William Sewell, Timothy Takaro, Stewart Scott, Ray Hunt.

The most prolific researcher during this period was the Clinical Investigator William H. Sewell, M.D. During his six-year tenure at this hospital, his work resulted in an astonishing 38 papers plus a book.[53, 99, 100, 104] His presence had a reciprocal effect: he applied for a Clinical Investigatorship at Oteen because of its existing interest in surgery for obstructive coronary artery disease, and his work provoked further strong stimulus among other investigators to explore the field even more vigorously. His certainty about his theories was challenged by the skepticism of his colleagues.

Figure 22.9. William H. Sewell

Charles H. Dart, Jr. (Figure 22.8) investigated internal mammary arteriography and studied internal mammary artery blood flow;[56, 57] and Drs. Joginder Bhayana and Gulshan Sethi reviewed the results of implant operations on two series of patients.[105, 106] Finally, the hospital's demonstrated interest in studying the surgical treatment of ischemic heart disease led to the series of multicenter trials of the variety of surgical approaches being proposed at

497

the time, including the Beck poudrage operation, the Vineberg/Sewell pedicle operation, and coronary bypass graft surgery.

The testing of various regimens for the treatment of tuberculosis continued to be of great interest to clinicians in the first half of this decade and resulted in the publication of 26 papers and abstracts. These studies helped to further refine the management of pulmonary tuberculosis.[40-43, 107] During this period, Seth Gilkerson, M.S., a microbiologist working in Dr. Oscar Kanner's Clinical Laboratory, developed an extremely useful technique for the rapid identification of tubercle bacilli in the sputum of patients by applying the fluorescent dye auramine to slides of specimens.[45] Interest in this methodology continues to this day.

Many patients initially thought to have pulmonary tuberculosis were found on further study to have one of a variety of fungal infections of the lungs. These patients were studied intensively when better diagnostic techniques and definitive new therapies emerged for coccidioidomycosis, histoplasmosis, North American blastomycosis, and sporotrichosis, spawning ten publications.[59, 82, 108-110]

From the very beginning, the problem of bronchial stump healing following pulmonary resections for tuberculosis was of significant interest and concern to Oteen surgeons. Bronchopleural fistulae, especially following pneumonectomy, were significant complications which could be accompanied by substantial mortality.[111, 112] During the 1960s, the problem was studied closely since, even after streptomycin became available to "cover" surgical resections, the problem persisted.

In the late 1950s, during a thaw in the Cold War with the USSR, American surgeons visiting Moscow were shown a variety of surgical stapling devices at the Scientific Institute for Surgical Apparatus and Instruments. One visitor, Ivan Brown, M.D., of Duke University's Department of Surgery, returned with a number of such instruments and loaned the Oteen VA hospital two of them for use in closure of the bronchial stump or the lung parenchyma. These were first tested in the Oteen laboratory on 40 dogs and subsequently used with good results in pulmonary resections in patients.[62] The author, another visitor to the USSR, further investigated the concept of using stapling devices in surgery,[89] and over the next several years, laboratory and clinical research in the uses of both blood vessel and bronchial staplers was fairly intense at Oteen. Although it was concluded that none of the devices for anastomosing blood vessels were of much clinical use, an exception was the lung-stapling device. In fact, an American surgical instrument company, the US Surgical Corporation, made the instruments much more practical, and their use in lung surgery in this country is now standard practice.[83] Some 13 papers were published on both vascular and bronchial staplers during this period.[62, 83, 87-90, 113]

With the establishment of the cardiac surgical program by Stewart Scott, M.D., experimental and clinical studies in this area were carried out by him and his colleagues that produced four papers during this period.[54, 55, 63, 64] Of especial interest were studies designed to shorten the duration of cardio-pulmonary bypass with use of the sutureless aortic valves, though these were subsequently displaced by more effective technology. Another advance was the recognition that early intervention and valve replacement in aortic insufficiency due to acute bacterial endocarditis was both effective and curative.[55] Members of the medical staff, in particular Robert G. Fish, M.D., Chief of Medicine, participated actively in these investigations.

Another bit of serendipity brought Edgar Hines, M.D., co-author of the classic textbook *Peripheral Vascular Diseases* from the Mayo Clinic to retirement in Asheville and a position as Consultant to the VA Medical Center.[114] Dr. Hines authored or co-authored half a dozen papers during his tenure at Oteen, including one on the use of angiographic magnification for digital arteriography.[95, 115, 116] Other members of the Medical Service were also responsible for investigations of various conditions: Irving Chofnas, M.D., on the non-surgical treatment of Pott's Disease and on the relation of the post-gastrectomy state to tuberculosis;[117, 118] and Ben Sandler, M.D., and his colleagues on pulmonary cavitation in polyarteritis.[119]

Clinical and laboratory studies in peripheral vascular diseases led to the publication of 15 reports. Several focused on the phenomenon of the "subclavian steal" syndrome, in which an atheromatous narrowing of the artery proximal to the origin of the vertebral artery can reverse cranial blood flow, potentially causing fainting and even stroke. Carl Williams, M.D., a surgical resident, showed that this condition could be corrected by endarterectomy and patch grafting.[76]

In thoracic surgery, Takeshi Okano, M.D., and Harry Walkup, M.D., examined problems with the management of tuberculous empyema.[120] The advanced cinefluorographic studies[39] of John Rayl, M.D., and his colleagues demonstrated the distinguishing features between so-called "surgical" and "medical" bronchiectasis. Kjell Christianson, M.D., a surgical resident, and Chief of Surgery Daniel E. Smith, M.D., reviewed the hospital's experience with bronchogenic carcinoma,[61] and also developed a technique for homologous lung transplantation in dogs before much was known about how to prevent organ rejection.[60]

Diseases of the esophagus received attention as well: Randall Bradham, M.D., another surgical resident, reported on neuromuscular disorders of the esophagus as well as on spontaneous perforation of the esophagus.[121] The author and his colleagues reviewed problems of the etiology and management of esophago-pleural fistulas.[122] Albert H Bridgman, M.D., and his colleagues explored the feasibility of cryosurgery for endobronchial lesions to palliate inoperable bronchogenic carcinoma.[123]

A prodigious effort involving hundreds of animals was made by Dr. Scott, his chief laboratory technician, Lee Gaddy, and others, to perfect the techniques of heart transplantation. Studies included methods of combating rejection,[85] with some animals surviving up to three or four months. The experiments were abandoned when this hospital was not designated as one of a handful of VA hospitals authorized to perform heart transplants in humans.

In 1967, Oteen's independent thoracic surgical residency training program began to be phased out when Dr. David C. Sabiston, Chairman of the Dept. of Surgery at Duke

University School of Medicine and a strong supporter of surgical research, sent a resident for the first time to this hospital. Dr. Newland Oldham initiated Oteen's affiliation with Duke, which, after a seven-year trial, was formalized in 1975 and continues, now including most of the other surgical subspecialties as well.[58]

Facilities improvements during the 1960s

Major improvements in research opportunities at this medical center during this decade included enhancement of the animal research facilities and establishment of modern electron microscopy facilities.

Animal Research Laboratories

Oteen had no facilities for animal research until a small laboratory specifically designated for this purpose was set up in an out-building in the 1950s to test the newly developed "heart-lung" machines on the canine model. This was necessary to ensure that extra-corporeal circulation for cardiac surgery would be safe for clinical use. In time, a more complete facility with room for several dozen animals, large and small, and a fairly well-equipped operating room using furnishings salvaged from the old Oteen tuberculosis hospital—operating room lights, cabinets, instruments—was established in the basement of a former nurses' home.

An enlarged laboratory, again in the basement of one of the nearby administrative buildings (Bldg 14), was constructed at the time the new Oteen VA Hospital was opened in 1967. In addition, space within the new hospital was allotted for a fully equipped animal operating room, a small post-operative recovery room, an X-Ray lab and facilities for chemistry and histology. This animal laboratory was fully accredited by AAALAC (the American Association for the Accreditation of Laboratory Animal Care.) Additional research space for a transmission electron microscope and, later, a scanning electron microscope was added to the lab in Bldg.14.

Figure 22.11. Open air exercise areas for dogs

The Electron Microscope Laboratory

The hospital's Laboratory Service acquired a transmission electron microscope in 1967, for both clinical and research use. Initially, the equipment was used to examine needle biopsies of the liver and kidneys for diagnostic purposes. Edith Hapke, M.D., a pulmonologist, was successfully recruited to Oteen in part by the opportunity it gave her to use the electron microscope as a research tool.[124] The laboratory was under the direction of Ms. Saundra Cordell Parra during most years of its operation. A working relationship developed between the chief technician of the Electron Microscope Laboratory, Sylvia Mast, and Dr. James Parker, the Director of Research of the Akzona Corporation in nearby Enka, North Carolina. This relationship resulted in the acquisition in 1977 of a scanning electron microscope donated by the Milliken Research Corporation of Spartanburg, South Carolina. Over the next two and a half decades, the Electron Microscope Laboratory was engaged primarily in clinical and laboratory investigations of the ultrastructure of human lungs as well as those of experimental animals in the study of clinical and experimental pulmonary emphysema. The second focus of attention was on the study of the endothelial lining of small-caliber vascular prostheses. Approximately a dozen reports of the results of this work were published after 1980.

New research investigators of the 1960s

Research investigators recruited to Oteen during the 1960s included:

William H. Sewell, Jr., M.D.

After completing his medical studies at Yale, Dr. Sewell joined the Oteen VA Hospital in 1960. Even as a medical student, he had distinguished himself by devising a pump to bypass the right side of the heart in the dog. This device was considered so innovative and ingenious—it was built from erector set parts for less than $25—that it eventually found a place in the Smithsonian Institution alongside the pump created by Lindbergh and Carrel.[125]

After time spent at the National Naval Medical Center in Bethesda, Maryland, and at Emory University in Atlanta, he was awarded a three-year Clinical Investigatorship by the Veterans Administration. After completing it, he joined the surgical staff for an additional two and a half years.

An unusually focused investigator, Dr. Sewell operated on more than 900 dogs during his research career. He was responsible for the early advantage enjoyed by this hospital's staff in mastering coronary cinearteriography ahead of many other centers. His focus on surgery for obstructive coronary artery disease further benefited the hospital by sparking the need to conduct randomized controlled trials of surgical procedures for this disease. In addition, a group of talented technicians whom he helped train in the animal laboratory and the radiology department were later able to assist in many other research endeavors at the medical center.

After having published 38 papers and a book on his work,[53, 91, 99, 100, 104] Dr. Sewell left Oteen in 1966 and joined the staff of the Guthrie Clinic in Sayre, Pennsylvania. He died in 1993.

Albert H. Bridgman, M.D.

Dr. Bridgeman came to Oteen as a resident in thoracic surgery in 1965, having attended LSU Medical School in New Orleans, interned at Touro Infirmary, and completed a residency at Charity Hospital, also in New Orleans. He had also wintered-over for one season in Antarctica as a Naval Medical Officer before coming to Oteen. In 1967, he left the VA Hospital to serve as a medical missionary in South Korea, returning to join the staff in 1971. His research interests were primarily in thoracic and peripheral vascular subjects. He published over a dozen papers during the subsequent two and a half decades, including studies in cryosurgery of the lung,[123] diagnostic procedures in thoracic surgery,[86] bronchoplastic procedures for benign and malignant tumors,[126] and carotid artery surgery.[127] At the time of his retirement from the VA in 1996, he held the teaching appointment of Clinical Professor of Surgery at Duke University School of Medicine.

Charles H. Dart, Jr., M.D.

Dr. Dart (Figure 22.8) came to the Oteen VA Hospital from the surgical program at Chapel Hill North Carolina in 1968. During the five years he spent at this center, he was a very industrious and productive investigator, publishing well over a dozen papers and abstracts on cardio-thoracic subjects. His most significant expertise lay in measuring blood flow in internal mammary artery implants and visualizing them by means of arteriography.[56, 57] By demonstrating unequivocally the lack of correlation between measured blood flow and arteriographic evidence of vascular connections between the internal mammary implant and the coronary circulation, he cast serious doubt on the efficacy of implants to increase circulation to the myocardium and lent significant impetus to the recognition of the need for a randomized controlled trial of this operation and, by extension, all surgical procedures purporting to improve survival in patients with coronary artery disease.

His other research interests included experimentally induced pulmonary hypertension in the rat; the relief of angina pectoris through carotid sinus nerve stimulation;[74] the use of bronchial staplers;[83] and more aggressive mediastinal exploration prior to thoracotomy for bronchogenic carcinoma.[86] He left Asheville in 1973 for private practice in Oxnard, California.

Stephen V. Kishev, M.D.

In 1964, Dr. Kishev came to the United States as a political refugee from Sofia, Bulgaria. He was educated in Vienna and taught in Tubingen, Prague and Sophia, where he was Chief of the Section on Urology at the Medical School for eleven years. He assumed the same title when he came to the Oteen VA Hospital in 1968. At Oteen, he helped train residents in urology from Duke University Medical Center and perfected several innovative surgical procedures involving urethroplasties as well as the repair of post-prostatectomy urinary incontinence. He published 20 papers on these and related subjects, using his own illustrations, and contributed a chapter on surgery for male urinary incontinence to the second edition of Glenn's *Urologic Surgery* (1975).[128-133] In 1977, he transferred to the VA Hospital in Salisbury, North Carolina, as head of the Section in Urology. At the time he left Asheville, he held the teaching appointment of Clinical Associate Professor at Duke University School of Medicine.

The 1970s

Oteen clinicians interested in clinical and basic research continued their vigorous efforts during this decade, the hospital's second most productive in terms of numbers of publications. These included 175 papers, abstracts and book chapters. The first results of the VA Cooperative Study of Surgery for Chronic Stable Angina began to be published during this period, and these reports, plus the subsequent controversy which they stirred up, accounted for over 50 publications authored or co-authored by Asheville VA Medical Center staff.

Of equal interest during this period was the search for the ideal prosthetic cardiac valve, which was conducted by Dr. Scott and his colleagues. At least four varieties were tested - the Magovern Sutureless Valve, the Starr Edwards and DeBakey Surgitool valves, and the Hancock Bioprosthesis.[65, 66] Unfortunately, significant complications of one type or another (silastic ball variance, strut fracture, cloth embolization) were recognized with most of them.[67-69] Other complications of valve surgery - acute pancreatitis, opportunistic endocarditis, coronary stenosis, and acquired left ventricular-right atrial fistula - were also reported.[70,71,133,134]

The publications resulting from these studies lent support to the idea of conducting a systematic clinical trial of cardiac valves. Accordingly, in 1977 a cooperative study was begun under the chairmanship of Drs. Gulshan Sethi (then still at the Asheville VA Medical Center) and Karl Hammermeister (at the VA Medical Center in Seattle WA) to compare long-term survival and valve-related complications of bioprosthetic and mechanical heart valves. The study included 575 men undergoing single aortic or mitral valve replacement at 13 VA Medical Centers randomly assigned to receive either a bioprosthetic or a mechanical valve.[135]

After 15 years of follow-up, a mechanical valve, despite its more frequent bleeding complications stemming from the need for long-term anticoagulant therapy, was found to produce a better survival rate in patients having undergone aortic valve replacement owing to a higher frequency of bioprosthetic valve failure. The finding applied only to patients younger than 65 years of age; for those 65 or older, there was no significant difference in valve failure rates between bioprosthetic and mechanical valves.[136]

Next most important, if judged by the numbers of published papers, were the 22 from the Urology Section of the Surgical Service. A number reported on studies of cryosurgery of the prostate gland, which had been undertaken earlier by James Dow, M.D.[137-139] Most were the work of Stephen Kishev, M.D., an original thinker and creator of innovative operative procedures for intractable urologic problems ranging from urethral strictures to incontinence.[128-133]

Several papers were published on projects involving the search for the ideal small-caliber arterial substitute, most of them by Dr. Scott. The clinical problem of femoro-popliteal obstructions had been described in an earlier report.[75] During the seventies, various graft materials were tested in animals and patients. These included collagen tubes of bovine origin[140] as well as pyrolytic carbon-coated grafts,[141] and, in later years, woven double velour and collagen-coated Dacron grafts. The hemodynamics, or flow properties, of grafts were investigated with computer models.[77, 78] Also in later years, basic investigations were conducted into the role of circulating cells involved in the healing of the flow surface of grafts. These, among the last of Dr. Scott's studies, which demonstrated that circulating stem cells were probably capable of differentiation into the endothelial monolayer, contributed significantly to our understanding of the way small caliber prosthetic grafts are incorporated into the body.[79]

An experimental study on the effects of intra-aortic balloon pumping on organ perfusion in cardiogenic shock, by Joginder N. Bhayana, M.D., and his colleagues was published late in the decade.[142] Papers were also published on miscellaneous subjects in cardiac, thoracic, and vascular surgery and on various other topics by the General and Orthopedic Surgical Sections,[143-148] the Medical Service and the Laboratory Service.[80,97,149,150]

Research investigators who joined the Asheville VAMC during the 1970s included:

Gulshan K. Sethi, M.D.

Dr. Sethi completed the thoracic surgical program at Latter Day Saints Hospital in Salt Lake City UT before joining the surgical staff of the Oteen VA Hospital in 1972. He remained at Oteen for the next 15 years. His research interests were wide-ranging, including thoracic,[151,152] vascular[81,153-160] and cardiac surgical subjects.[65,66,68-71,105,134] He participated in two VA Cooperative Studies of surgery for coronary artery disease and co-chaired another involving cardiac valvular surgery. He was co-chairman of still another VA Cooperative Study in Structures, Processes and Outcomes in Cardiac Surgery. He served as Associate Chief of Staff for Research from 1984 to 1987. While at Oteen, he was the author or co-author of 45 papers and abstracts and contributed several chapters to textbooks of surgery.[101,161] He was Clinical Professor of Surgery at Duke University School of Medicine.

Dr. Sethi left Asheville in 1987 for the Tucson VA Hospital and the University of Arizona Medical Center, where he became Professor of Surgery and continued a productive career in academic medicine.

Amir A. Neshat, M. D.

Dr. Neshat, a native of Iran who attended the Isfahan University Medical School and took his surgical training at Union Memorial Hospital in Baltimore and at the Memorial Hospital for Cancer in New York, arrived at the Oteen VA Hospital in 1973 as a staff surgeon. His principal research interests while here were in general surgery (particularly the surgical management of morbid obesity) and oncology. He was involved with a number of protocols involving ascites tumors in mice, metastatic liver cancer, and prostatic and lung cancers, authoring or co-authoring eight papers on these subjects.[143-146] He retired from the VA in 2000.

Figure 22.12. The modern Asheville VA Medical Center. A: The old tuberculosis hospital, a cluster of buildings constructed between 1924 and 1934. B: The General Hospital, opened in 1967. C: The Extended Care and Rehabilitation Facility, opened in 1996. D: The Ambulatory Care Addition, opened in 2002.

Summary and Conclusions

For the first 30 years of its existence, this hospital functioned in a caretaker role for its thousands of patients with pulmonary tuberculosis. However, soon after WWII when definitive medical treatment became available in conjunction with surgical management, both modalities were extensively studied by the staff. Multi-center cooperative trials of chemotherapy were undertaken, and during the subsequent two decades tuberculosis was virtually eradicated. Research interest then shifted to non-tuberculous chest diseases, to cardiovascular diseases, and to "open heart" surgery. Hospital staff members helped organize multi-center cooperative trials of surgery for coronary artery disease as well as cardiac valvular diseases. (In the 1990s, the multicenter cooperative studies technique was extended to a variety of other clinical conditions, and a research corporation was established to allow private pharmaceutical manufacturers to fund research studies on VA patients.)

For those privileged to have had a part in past programs, the duties and responsibilities of conducting medical research have been amply rewarded by the satisfaction of seeing some intractable problems yield to solutions and, to quote physicist Richard Feynman, "in the pleasure of finding things out."

References

1. Wagner, I.R., "Veterans Administration Facility, Oteen, N.C." *Dis Chest*, 1937. **3**: 20, 26.

2. "Application Form to US Dept. Of the Interior National Park Service's National Register of Historic Places Inventory - Nomination Form, Item No. 8."

3. "Oteen Hospital Is Largest Government Institution of Its Kind." *Asheville Citizen-Times*, Asheville, NC, Nov. 1, 1936.

4. Holmes, R.B. and Smith, B.S., *Beginning Cherokee*. Norman, Okla.: Univ. of Okla. Press, 1976

5. Schwartz, W.S. and Moyer, R.E., "Management of Massive Tuberculous Pneumonia." *Am Rev Tuberc*, 1951. **64**: 41-49.

6. Schwartz, W.S., "Recent Drug Therapy in Diseases of the Chest, Including Tuberculosis." *JAMA*, 1952. **148**: 600-602.

7. Schwartz, W.S., "Chemotherapy of Tuberculosis." *N Eng J Med*, 1953. **248**: 717-720.

8. Schwartz, W.S. and Moyer, R.E., "Chemotherapy Treatment of Pulmonary Tuberculosis with PZA Used Alone or in Combination with SM, PAS, or INH." *Am Rev Tuberc*, 1954. **70**: 413-422.

9. Schwartz, W.S. and Moyer, R.E., "Use of INH Alone in the Treatment of Pulmonary Tuberculosis." *Am Rev Tuberc*, 1954. **70**: 924-925.

10. Murphy, J.D., "Streptomycin in the Surgery of Pulmonary Tuberculosis." *Surg Gynec Obstet*, 1948. **87**: 546-548.

11. Murphy, J.D., Elrod, P.D., Walkup, H. and Koontz, E.R., "Surgical Treatment of Residual Cavities Following Thoracoplasty for Tuberculosis." *Dis Chest*, 1948. **14**: 694-706.

12. Walkup, H. and Murphy, J.D., "Extrapleural Pneumonolysis with Plombage Thoracoplasty." *Dis Chest*, 1949. **16**: 18-20.

13. Bagby, B.B., "Swannanoa Plan for Rehabilitation of Tuberculous Veterans." *Ann Phys Med*, 1950. **31**: 450-452.

14. "First WNC Open-Heart Surgery at Oteen Is Teamwork Miracle." *Asheville Citizen-Times*, Asheville, NC, August 30, 1959.

15. Moore, J.A. and Murphy, J.D., "Spontaneous Rupture of the Esophagus - One Case with Recovery." *J Thorac Surg*, 1948. **17**: 632-638.

16. Moore, J.A. and Murphy, J.D., "Constrictive Pericarditis with Tuberculous Intrapericardial Abscess Treated by Streptomycin; Case Report." *Ann Surg*, 1948. **127**: 685.

17. Moore, J.A., Murphy, J.D. and Elrod, P.D., "Use of Streptomycin in Pulmonary Resection." *S Clin North America*, 1948. **28**: 1543-1555.

18. Moore, J.A., Murphy, J.D. and Ward, E.E., Jr., "Lobectomy in Coccidioidomycosis. Report of Two Cases." *J Thorac Surg*, 1949. **18**: 484-492.

19. Moore, J.A., Walkup, H.E., Rayl, J.E. and Chapman, E.P., Jr., "End Results of Pulmonary Resection for Tuberculosis." *Ann Surg*, 1958. **147**: 659-667.

20.   Moyer, R.E. and Ackerman, A.J., "Sarcoidosis." *Am Rev Tuberc*, 1952. **61**: 299-322.

21.   Moyer, R.E., Sears, L.H. and Williams, M.H., "Pneumoperitoneum." *Am J Nursing*, 1953. **53**: 332-335.

22.   Seiler, H.H., "The Early Years of the Southern Thoracic Surgical Association." *Ann Thorac Surg*, 1972. **14**: 113-122.

23.   Murphy, J.D., "Thoracoplasty for Tuberculosis." *Med Bull VA*, 1944. **21**: 140-143.

24.   Murphy, J.D., "Thoracoscopy with Pneumonolysis." *Dis Chest*, 1947. **13**: 631-635.

25.   Murphy, J.D., "Ether Anesthesia in Pulmonary Tuberculosis." *Am Rev Tbc*, 1944. **49**: 251-254.

26.   Murphy, J.D. and Sword, B.C., "Adaptation of Albe-Comper Table to Improve Position for Thoracic Surgery." *Anesthesiol*, 1948. **9**: 58-61.

27.   Murphy, J.D. and Bornstein, S., "Mucormycosis of the Lung." *Ann Intern Med*, 1950. **33**: 442-453.

28.   Murphy, J.D. and Piver, J.D., "Cystic Disease of the Lung." *Dis Chest*, 1951. **19**: 454-472.

29.   Walkup, H. and Murphy, J.D., "A Modern Evaluation of Extrapleural Pneumonolysis in the Treatment of Tuberculosis with Special Reference to Methylmethacrylate "Plombage". Review of 26 Cases." *Dis Chest*, 1949. **16**: 456-472.

30.   Walkup, H.E. and Wolcott, M.W., "Surgical Treatment of Bullous Emphysema." *Dis Chest*, 1955. **28**: 638-650.

31.   Wolcott, M.W., Shaver, W.A., Walkup, H.E. and Peasley, E.D., "Mesotheliomas of the Pleura." *Dis Chest*, 1959. **36**: 119-126.

32.   Murphy, J.D., Walkup, H. and Cheek, J.M., "Evaluation of Streptomycin as Protective Agent against Spreads, Reactivations and Wound Infections Following Thoracoplasty for Pulmonary Tuberculosis." *Surg Clin N America*, 1948. **28**: 1555.

33.   Pine, I. and Morganstern, P., "Post-Thoracoplasty Pulmonary Hernia: Report of Four Cases." *Am Rev Tbc*, 1948. **57**: 511-518.

34.   Morganstern, P. and Dewing, S.B., "Insulin in the Treatment of Tuberculous Patients with Anorexia; a Modified Technique." *Am Rev Tbc*, 1949. **60**: 25-31.

35.   Morganstern, P. and Pine, I., "Pulmonary Cavities "Below the Diaphragm"; Phenomenon Sometimes Seen in Pneumoperitoneum Treatment of Pulmonary Tuberculosis." *Am J Roent*, 1948. **59**: 677-681.

36.   Study, R.S. and Morganstern, P., "Co-Existing Pulmonary Coccidiodomycosis and Tuberculosis." *New Eng J Med*, 1949. **238**: 837-.

37.   Rayl, J.E. and Murphy, J.D., "Large-Scale Jury Type of Review of Indications for Surgery in Pulmonary Tuberculosis." *Am Rev Tbc and Pulm Diseases*, 1956. **73**: 191-218.

38.   Rayl, J.E. and Smith, D.E., "Recent Advances in Bronchography." *Dis Chest*, 1958. **33**: 235-250.

39.   Rayl, J.E., Peasley, E.D. and Joyner, J.T., "Differential Diagnosis of Bronchiectasis and Bronchitis." *Dis Chest*, 1961. **39**: 591-600.

40. Schwartz, W.S., "VIII. Kanamycin in the Treatment of Pulmonary Tuberculosis, Including Studies of Drug Toxicity. (a Report of the Cooperative Study by Veterans Administration Hospitals)." *Am Rev Respir Dis*, 1960. **81**: 105-107.

41. Schwartz, W.S. and Moyer, R.E., "Streptomycin 0.5 Gm Daily with INH and Para-Aminosalicylic Acid Used as a Re-Treatment Regimen in Pulmonary Tuberculosis." *Am Rev Respir Dis*, 1960. **81**: 941-942.

42. Schwartz, W.S. and Moyer, R.E., "One-Half Gram of Streptomycin Daily with Isoniazid and PAS Used as a Re-Treatment Regimen in Pulmonary Tuberculosis." *Am Rev Respir Dis*, 1961. **83**: 268-271.

43. Schwartz, W.S., "Developments in Treatment of Tuberculosis and Other Pulmonary Diseases." *JAMA*, 1961. **178**: 43-50.

44. Schwartz, W.S., "Management of Common Pulmonary Diseases." *JAMA*, 1962. **181**: 134-141.

45. Gilkerson, S.W. and Kanner, O., "Improved Technique for the Detection of Acid-Fast Bacilli by Fluorescence." *J Bacteriology*, 1963. **86**: 890-891.

46. Kanner, O., "Rejection of Observations." *Am J Clin Pathol*, 1964. **41**: 626-627.

47. Kanner, O., "Contamination Risk with Screw-Capped Centrifuge Tubes." *Am Rev Respir Dis*, 1965. **91**: 439.

48. Kanner, O., "Evaluation of Diagnostic Tests - the Concept of Inverse Probability." *N Carolina Med J*, 1965. **26**: 321-328.

49. Fish, R.G., Crymes, T.P. and Lovell, M.G., "Internal-Mammary Artery Ligation in Angina Pectoris; Its Failure to Produce Relief." *N Eng J Med*, 1958. **259**: 418-420.

50. Crymes, T.P., Fish, R.G., Smith, D.E. and Takaro, T., "Complications of Transbronchial Left Atrial Puncture." *Am Heart J*, 1959. **58**: 46-52.

51. Fish, R.G., Takaro, T. and Crymes, T.P., "Left Atrial Pressure Pulses in the Presence of Myxoma." *Circulation*, 1959. **20**: 413-418.

52. Scott, S.M., Fish, R.G. and Takaro, T., "A Double-Needle Technic for Transbronchial Left Heart Catheterization." *Circulation*, 1960. **22**: 976-978.

53. Sewell, W.H., Sones, F.M., Jr., Fish, R.G., Joyner, J.T. and Effler, D.B., "The Pedicle Operation for Coronary Insufficiency: Technique and Preliminary Results." *J Thorac Cardiov Surg*, 1965. **49**: 317-329.

54. Scott, S.M., Fish, R.G., Takaro, T. and Sewell, W.H., "Aortic Valve Surgery Using the Magovern Prosthesis." *Ann Thorac Surg*, 1965. **92**: 463-465.

55. Scott, S.M., Fish, R.G. and Crutcher, J.C., "Early Surgical Intervention for Aortic Insufficiency Due to Bacterial Endocarditis." *Ann Thorac Surg*, 1967. **3**: 158-161.

56. Dart, C.H., Jr., Kato, Y., Scott, S.M., Fish, R.G., Nelson, W.M. and Takaro, T., "Internal Thoracic (Mammary) Arteriography. A Questionable Index of Myocardial Revascularization." *J Thorac Cardiovasc Surg*, 1970. **59**: 117-127.

57. Dart, C.H., Jr., Scott, S., Fish, R. and Takaro, T., "Direct Blood Flow Studies of Clinical Internal Thoracic (Mammary) Arterial Implants." *Circulation*, 1970. **41**: II 64-72.

509

58.   Oldham, H.N., Jr., Scott, S.M., Dart, C.H., Jr., Fish, R.G., Claxton, C.P., Dillon, M.L., Jr. and Sabiston, D.C., Jr., "Surgical Correction of Ventricular Septal Defect Following Acute Myocardial Infarction." *Ann Thorac Surg*, 1969. **7**: 193-201.

59.   Smith, D.E., "Amphotericin B." *Pediatric Clinics N America*, 1961. **8**: 1099-1103.

60.   Christiansen, K.H., Smith, D.E. and Pinch, L.W., "Homologous Transplantation of Canine Lungs." *Arch Surg*, 1963. **86**: 495-499.

61.   Christiansen, K.H. and Smith, D.E., "Bronchogenic Carcinoma: A Sixteen Year Study." *J Thorac Cardiovasc Surg*, 1962. **43**: 267-275.

62.   Smith, D.E., Karish, A.F., Chapman, J.P. and Takaro, T., "Healing of the Bronchial Stump after Pulmonary Resection." *J Thorac Cardiovasc Surg*, 1963. **46**: 548-556.

63.   Magovern, G.J., Kent, E.M., Cromie, H.W., Cushing, W.B. and Scott, S.M., "Sutureless Aortic and Mitral Prosthetic Valves." *J Thorac Cardiov Surg*, 1964. **48**: 346-361.

64.   Takaro, T. and Scott, S.M., "Aortic Valve Replacement Using a Stapling Device. An Experimental Study." *Angiology*, 1966. **17**: 726-731.

65.   Scott, S.M., Sethi, G.K., Flye, M.W. and Takaro, T., "The Sutureless Aortic Valve Prosthesis: Experience with and Technical Considerations for Replacement of the Early Model." *Ann Surg*, 1976. **184**: 174-178.

66.   Scott, S.M., Sethi, G.K., Bridgman, A.H. and Takaro, T., "Experience with the DeBakey-Surgitool Aortic Prosthetic Valve." *Ann Thorac Surg*, 1976. **21**: 483-486.

67.   Scott, S.M., "Editorial. The Durable Poppet." *Ann Thorac Surg*, 1970. **10**: 288.

68.   Scott, S.M., Sethi, G.K., Paulson, D.M. and Takaro, T., "Insidious Strut Fractures in a DeBakey-Surgitool Aortic Valve Prosthesis." *Ann Thorac Surg*, 1978. **25**: 382-384.

69.   Crawford, F.A., Sethi, G.K., Scott, S.M. and Takaro, T., "Systemic Emboli Due to Cloth Wear in a Starr-Edwards Model 2320 Aortic Prosthesis." *Ann Thorac Surg*, 1973. **16**: 614-619.

70.   Sethi, G.K., Scott, S.M. and Takaro, T., "Iatrogenic Coronary Artery Stenosis Following Aortic Valve Replacement." *J Thorac Cardiovasc Surg*, 1979. **77**: 760-767.

71.   Silverman, N.A., Sethi, G.K. and Scott, S.M., "Acquired Left Ventricular-Right Atrial Fistula Following Aortic Valve Replacement." *Ann Thorac Surg*, 1980. **30**: 482-486.

72.   Paulson, D.M., Scott, S.M. and Sethi, G.K., "Pulmonary Hemorrhage Associated with Balloon Flotation Catheters: Report of a Case and Review of the Literature." *J Thorac Cardiovasc Surg*, 1980. **80**: 453-458.

73.   Purut, C.M., Scott, S.M., Parham, J.V. and Smith, P.K., "Intraoperative Management of Severe Endobronchial Hemorrhage." *Ann Thorac Surg*, 1991. **51**: 304-306; discussion 306-307.

74.   Dart, C.H., Jr., Scott, S.M., Nelson, W.M., Fish, R.G. and Takaro, T., "Carotid Sinus Nerve Stimulation Treatment of Angina Refractory to Other Surgical Procedures." *Ann Thorac Surg*, 1971. **11**: 348-359.

75.   Scott, S.M., "Femoropopliteal Obstruction." *N Carolina Med J*, 1966. **27**: 326-330.

510

76. Williams, C.L., Scott, S.M. and Takaro, T., "Subclavian Steal." *Circulation*, 1963. **28**: 14-19.

77. Wilson, B.S. and Scott, S.M., "Hemodynamic Design Considerations for an Improved Artery Shunt Prosthesis." in *First Mid-Atlantic Conference on Bio-Fluid Mechanics*, Schneck, D.J., Editor. 1978, VPI Press: Blacksburg 93-98.

78. Scott, S.M. and Wilson, B.S., "The Mechanical Design of Vascular Prostheses." in *Hemodynamics of the Limbs. I.*, Puel, P., Boccalon, H., and Enjalbert, A., Editors: Toulouse, France 251-259.

79. Scott, S.M., Barth, M.G., Gaddy, L.R. and Ahl, E.T., Jr., "The Role of Circulating Cells in the Healing of Vascular Prostheses." *J Vasc Surg*, 1994. **19**: 585-593.

80. Gomez-Uria, A. and Pazianos, A.G., "Syndromes Resulting from Ectopic Hormone-Producing Tumors." *Med Clin North Am*, 1975. **59**: 431-440.

81. Sethi, G.K., Scott, S.M. and Takaro, T., "Effect of Intra-Arterial Infusion of PGE1 in Patients with Severe Ischemia of Lower Extremity." *J Cardiovasc Surg (Torino)*, 1980. **21**: 185-192.

82. Scott, S.M., Peasley, E.D. and Crymes, T.P., "Pulmonary Sporotrichosis. Report of Two Cases with Cavitation." *New Eng J Med*, 1961. **265**: 453-457.

83. Dart, C.H., Jr., Scott, S.M. and Takaro, T., "Six-Year Clinical Experience Using Automatic Stapling Devices for Lung Resections." *Ann Thorac Surg*, 1970. **9**: 535-550.

84. Bradham, R.R., Bridgman, A.H., Scott, S.M. and Betts, R.H., "Spontaneous Esophageal Perforation. Management of the "Intermediate" Phase." *Ann Thorac Surg*, 1967. **3**: 6-14.

85. Gilkerson, S.W., Scott, S.M. and Gaddy, L., "Titers of Antilymphocytic Sera Determined by Immunofluorescence." *Am J Clin Pathol*, 1970. **53**: 928-931.

86. Dart, C., Jr., McWilliams, H., Scott, S., Takaro, T. and Bridgman, A., "More Aggressive Mediastinal Exploration before Thoracotomy for Lung Carcinoma." *South Med J*, 1973. **66**: 359-361.

87. Takaro, T., "A Simple Stapling Device for the Anastomosis of Blood Vessels." *J Thorac Cardiov Surg*, 1960. **40**: 673-684.

88. Williams, C.L. and Takaro, T. "An Evaluation of the Russian Stapler in Small Artery Anastomosis and Grafts." *Thirteenth Annual VA Medical Research Conference*, 1962, 209.

89. Takaro, T., "Institute for Experimental Surgical Instruments in Moscow." *Science*, 1968. **142**: 195-199.

90. Betts, R.H. and Takaro, T., "Use of Lung Stapler in Pulmonary Resection." *Ann Thorac Surg*, 1965. **24**: 197-202.

91. Takaro, T., Scott, S.M. and Sewell, W.H., "Experimental Coronary Arteriography Using Roentgenographic Magnification." *Amer J Roentgen*, 1962. **87**: 258-264.

92. Takaro, T. and Scott, S.M., "Angiography of the Minute Vessels of the Lung." *Dis Chest*, 1964. **45**: 28-35.

93. Takaro, T., "Experimental Renal Angiography." *Surg, Gynec and Obstet*, 1965. **121**: 579-584.

94. Takaro, T. and Kivirand, A.I., "Experimental Renal Venography." *Surg Forum*, 1965. **16**: 342-344.

95. Takaro, T. and Hines, E.A., Jr., "Digital Arteriography in Occlusive Arterial Disease and Clubbing of the Fingers." *Circulation*, 1967. **35**: 682-689.

96. Takaro, T. and White, S.M., "Unilateral Severe Experimental Pulmonary Emphysema." *Am Rev Respir Dis*, 1973. **108**: 334-342.

97. Joyner, J.T., "Abnormal Liver Scan (Radiocolloid "Hot Spot") Associated with Superior Vena Caval Obstruction." *J Nucl Med*, 1972. **13**: 849-851.

98. Sewell, W.H., Takaro, T., Rayl, J.E. and Quinn, R.P., "A Technique Using Coronary Cinearteriography for Surgical and Physiologic Studies in Dogs." *Amer J Roentgen*, 1962. **88**: 49-56.

99. Sewell, W.H., "The Use of Cinearteriography for Estimation of the Relative Flow in the Anterior Descending Coronary Artery in Dogs after Experimental Surgical Constriction." *Am J Roent. Radium Therapy and Nucl Med*, 1963. **89**: 261-268.

100. Sewell, W.H., "Results of 122 Mammary Pedicle Implantations for Angina Pectoris." *Ann Thorac Surg*, 1966. **2**: 17-30.

101. Sethi, G.K., Scott, S.M. and Takaro, T., "Myocardial Revascularization by Internal Thoracic Arterial Implants: Late Follow-Up", in *Coronary Artery Medicine and Surgery: Concepts and Controversies*, Norman, J.C., Editor. 1975, Apple-Century-Crofts: New York.

102. Williams, C.L. and Takaro, T., "Subclavian Arterial Occlusion." *Ann Surg*, 1963. **157**: 48-55.

103. Daugherty, C.O., Clark, T. and Takaro, T., "Impregnation of Vascular Sutures and Grafts with Radioactive Phosphorus." *J Cardiovasc Surg (Torino)*, 1969. **10**: 282-286.

104. Sewell, W.H., *Surgery for Acquired Coronary Disease*. Springfield, IL: Charles C. Thomas, 1967

105. Sethi, G.K., Scott, S.M. and Takaro, T., "Myocardial Revascularization by Internal Thoracic Arterial Implants: Longterm Follow-Up." *Chest*, 1973. **64**: 235-240.

106. Bhayana, J.N., Gage, A.A., Takaro, T. and Participants of the VA Cooperative Study, "Long-Term Results of Internal Mammary Artery Implantation for Coronary Artery Disease: A Controlled Trial by the Participants of the Veterans Administration Coronary Bypass Surgery Cooperative Study Group." *Ann Thorac Surg*, 1980. **29**: 234-242.

107. Matthews, J.H., "Pyrazinamide and INH Used in the Treatment of Pulmonary Tuberculosis." *Am Rev Respir Dis*, 1960. **81**: 345-351.

108. Takaro, T., "Mycotic Infections of Interest to Thoracic Surgeons." *Ann Thorac Surg*, 1967. **3**: 71-93.

109. Matthews, J.H., "Histoplasmosis." *W Va Med J*, 1960. **36**: 157-162.

110. Walkup, H. "Treatment of North American Blastomycosis." *Transactions of 20th VA-Armed Forces Research Conference in Pulmonary Diseases*, 1961, 284-286.

111. Murphy, J.D., Becker, B.B. and Swindell, H.V., "Complications and Results in Treatment of Bronchopleural Fistula Following Resection for Tuberculosis." *J Thorac Surg*, 1952. **24**: 578-586.

112. Murphy, J.D. and Becker, B.B., "Intermediate Report of 102 Streptomycin Protected Pulmonary Resections." *Am Rev Tbc*, 1953. **67**: 22-28.

113. Takaro, T., "The American and the Russian Vascular Staplers; a Comparison." *Arch Surg*, 1964. **89**: 536-539.

114. Allen, E.V., Barker, N.W. and Hines, E.A., *Peripheral Vascular Diseases, Third Edition*. Philadelphia, Pa.: W.B. Saunders, 1962

115. Hines, E.A., Jr., "The Differential Diagnosis of Chronic Ulcer of the Leg." *Circulation*, 1963. **27**: 989-996.

116. Hines, E.A., Jr., "Hypotension", in *Cyclopedia of Medicine, Surgery, Specialties*. 1964, F.A. Davis Co.: Philadelphia, Pa. **4** 269-281.

117. Chofnas, I. and Love, R.W., Jr., "Postgastrectomy State and Tuberculosis." *Arch Surg*, 1966. **92**: 704-706.

118. Chofnas, I., Surrett, N.E. and Severn, H.D., "Pott's Disease Treated without Spinal Fusion." *Am Rev Respir Dis*, 1964. **90**: 888-898.

119. Sandler, B.P., Matthews, J.H. and Bornstein, S., "Pulmonary Cavitation Due to Polyarteritis." in *Rare Diseases in Internal Medicine*, Stern, N.S., Editor. 1966, Thomas: Springfield, Ill. 108-109. Report #219.

120. Okano, T. and Walkup, H., "Chronic Purulent Tuberculous Empyema and Pulmonary Tuberculosis Treated by Decortications and Resections." *J Thorac Cardiovasc Surg*, 1962. **43**: 752-761.

121. Bradham, R.R. and Sealy, W.C., "Collective Review: Neuromuscular Disorders of the Esophagus." *Ann Thorac Surg*, 1967. **3**: 460-483.

122. Takaro, T., Walkup, H.E. and Okano, T., "Esophagopleural Fistula as a Complication of Thoracic Surgery. A Collective Review." *J Thorac Cardiov Surg*, 1960. **40**: 179-193.

123. Bridgman, A.H., King, B.K., Dunn, R.C. and Takaro, T., "Experimental Freezing of Intrathoracic Organs." *Cryosurgery*, 1968. **1**: 193-196.

124. Scott, S.M. and Hapke, E.J. "Pulmonary Function and Ultrastructural Changes in the Ischemic Lung,." *Thirtieth VA-Armed Forces Pulmonary Diseases Research Conference*. Jan. 25-26, 1971. Cincinnati, Ohio, 1971,

125. Sewell, W.H. and Glenn, W.W.L., "Experimental Cardiac Surgery I. Observations on the Action of a Pump Designed to Shunt the Venous Blood Past the Right Heart Directly into the Pulmonary Artery." *Surgery*, 1950. **28**: 474-494.

126. Lowe, J.E., Bridgman, A.H. and Sabiston, D.C., Jr., "The Role of Bronchoplastic Procedures in the Surgical Management of Benign and Malignant Pulmonary Lesions." *J Thorac Cardiovasc Surg*, 1982. **83**: 227-234.

127. Schwartz, L.B., Bridgman, A.H., Kieffer, R.W., Wilcox, R.A., McCann, R.L., Tawil, M.P. and Scott, S.M., "Asymptomatic Carotid Artery Stenosis and Stroke in Patients Undergoing Cardiopulmonary Bypass." *J Vasc Surg*, 1995. **21**: 146-153.

128. Kishev, S.V., "A New 'Thumb' Urethroplasty." *J Urol*, 1971. **106**: 231-235.

129. Kishev, S.V., "New Elements in the Technique of Perineal Prostatectomy." *Der Urologe, Ausgabe A*, 1972. **11**: 130-134.

130. Kishev, S.V., "Surgical Repair of Stricture of the Membranous Urethra. I. Methods Applied through the Anterior Approach." *Urol Internat*, 1972. **27**: 1-11.

131. Kishev, S.V., "Surgical Repair of Stricture of the Membranous Urethra. II. Posterior Approach to the Membranous Urethra." *Urol Internat*, 1972. **27**: 12-23.

132. Kishev, S.V., "Transsacral Cystectomy." *J Urol*, 1973. **109**: 835-837.

133. Panebianco, A.C., Scott, S.M., Dart, C.H., Jr., Takaro, T. and Echegaray, H.M., "Acute Pancreatitis Following Extracorporeal Circulation." *Ann Thorac Surg*, 1970. **9**: 562-568.

134. Norenberg, R.G., Sethi, G.K., Scott, S.M. and Takaro, T., "Opportunistic Endocarditis Following Open-Heart Surgery." *Ann Thorac Surg*, 1975. **19**: 592-604.

135. Sethi, G.K., Miller, D.C., Souchek, J., Oprian, C., Henderson, W.G., Hassan, Z., Folland, E., Khuri, S., Scott, S.M., Burchfiel, C. and others, "Clinical, Hemodynamic, and Angiographic Predictors of Operative Mortality in Patients Undergoing Single Valve Replacement. Veterans Administration Cooperative Study on Valvular Heart Disease." *J Thorac Cardiovasc Surg*, 1987. **93**: 884-897.

136. Hammermeister, K., Sethi, G.K., Henderson, W.G., Grover, F.L., Oprian, C. and Rahimtoola, S.H., "Outcomes 15 Years after Valve Replacement with a Mechanical Versus a Bioprosthetic Valve: Final Report of the Veterans Affairs Randomized Trial." *J Am Coll Cardiol*, 2000. **36**: 1152-1158.

137. Dow, J.A., "Effects of Surgical Capsular Temperature on Cryosurgery of the Prostate." *J Urol*, 1968. **100**: 66-71.

138. Dow, J.A. and Waterhouse, K., "An Experimental Study in Lethal Freezing Temperatures of the Prostate Gland." *J Urol*, 1970. **103**: 454-457.

139. Dow, J.A. and Waterhouse, K., "Effects of Thermal Conductivity and Solute Concentration on Cryosurgery of the Prostate." *Int Surg*, 1970. **53**: 251-257.

140. Dillon, M.L., Scott, S.M., Vasquez, M.D., Postlethwait, R.W. and Dart, C.H., "Tissue Response to an Arterial Substitute of Bovine Origin." *Arch Surg*, 1972. **105**: 577-581.

141. Scott, S.M., Gaddy, L.R. and Parra, S., "Pyrolytic Carbon-Coated Vascular Prostheses." *J Surg Res*, 1980. **29**: 395-405.

142. Bhayana, J.N., Scott, S.M., Sethi, G.K. and Takaro, T., "Effects of Intraaortic Balloon Pumping on Organ Perfusion in Cardiogenic Shock." *J Surg Res*, 1979. **26**: 108-113.

143. Neshat, A., "Self-Induced Lipid Granuloma of the Rectum." *Dis Colon and Rectum*, 1974. **17**: 696-699.

144. Neshat, A.A. and Flye, M.W., "Early Formation of Gallstones Following Jejunoileal Bypass for Treatment of Morbid Obesity." *Am Surg*, 1975. **41**: 486-491.

145. Neshat, A.A., Price, H.P. and Parra, S., "Liver Failure and Death after Jejunoileal Shunt for Morbid Obesity." *Iranian J Surg*, 1978. **1**: 262-274.

146. Neshat, A.A. and Sethi, G.K., "Management of Postoperative Pharyngocutaneous Fistulae." *Iranian J Surg*, 1978. **1**: 81-89.

514

Examples

515

Chapter 23. VA Research in Gastroenterology
John Farrar, M.D.

The marvelously rapid transformation by 1952 of the pre-WWII VA health system from a few unaffiliated hospitals to many excellent affiliated Deans Committee hospitals is documented elsewhere. This chapter demonstrates how very important the VA research program was during the period between 1948 and 1980 to advances in gastroenterology, the study of the organs of digestion including the liver.

It is difficult to document the precise clinical and economic importance of specific basic and clinical research. We in the medical profession depend heavily on the fact of publication of new information in medical journals because publication in good journals virtually always depends on peer review, review of the article by other physicians or scientists to judge whether it is an important contribution to our knowledge. It is rare that there is a direct link between a single scientific advance and a new cure or a new treatment. When in this chapter there is such a link between the research done in the VA after World War II and the specific effects on patients, this will be mentioned.

Gastroenterology in the late 1940s and early 1950s

The largest and oldest organization of gastroenterologists in the United States is the American Gastroenterological Association (AGA). Founded in 1897; the AGA has always been devoted to the acquisition of new knowledge. Accordingly, a review of the attitudes of its leaders offers a useful way to assess the attitudes and aspirations of this sub-specialty of internal medicine. This chapter also describes important contributions of surgeons who have contributed to research on the alimentary tract and liver, many of whom were members of the AGA as well as of their own surgical societies.

An assessment of the state of gastroenterological knowledge in the 1940s reveals that the field was lagging behind cardiology, infectious diseases, nephrology and oncology. Gastroenterologists possessed few new techniques or treatments to cope with peptic ulcer, viral hepatitis, cirrhosis, pancreatitis or ulcerative colitis. This would soon change. In 1941, the American Board of Gastroenterology offered its first sub-specialty examination; in 1943, the AGA launched a new journal, *Gastroenterology*; and in 1945, the AGA appointed a national committee to study peptic ulcer.[1] Interest in gastroenterology training was growing, prompting calls for more research into both clinical and basic mechanisms of disease. As a result, in the early 1950s a General Medicine Study Section was formed at the National Institutes of Health which included Thomas Almy, Franz Ingelfinger, Joseph Kirsner, Julian Ruffin, Wade Volwiler and Stewart Wolf, all prominent gastroenterologists.[2] To many of these leaders, the VA research programs in digestive diseases owe their later vigor. As a measure of the readiness of the gastroenterological community for the flowering of the VA research program, Dwight Wilbur, M.D., AGA President in 1954–55, devoted his presidential address to an urgent plea for more research to be conducted in both clinical and basic gastroenterology.[3]

The stage was set for the post-WWII surge of interest in all medical training for physicians returning from battle; the trainers were ready, and the VA was tooling up with unprecedented construction of new facilities. The result of these efforts would be very important for the VA, for veterans and for the nation.

Earliest post-WWII VA researchers in gastroenterology

From 1946 to 1950, four medical scientists interested in digestive diseases joined the VA and helped to pave the way for others to soon follow. These researchers were: Thomas Warthin, M.D., Hyman Zimmerman, M.D., James Halsted, M.D., and Leslie Zieve, M.D.

Dr. Thomas Warthin was a medical statesman who made a substantial impact on medicine in Boston and its early acceptance of the post-war VA as a first-rate operation. After graduating from Harvard Medical School in 1934, he interned at the Harvard Service of Boston City Hospital with such great figures as George Minot, Soma Weiss, Chester Keefer and Henry Jackson, Jr. After fellowships at Yale and Johns Hopkins and a brief stint of private practice, in 1944 he joined the Army as a Flight Surgeon. On returning to civilian life in 1946, he headed a joint Harvard-Tufts medical service at the Boston Veterans Hospital.[4] Within a short time, he was named Chief of Medicine at the Harvard-affiliated West Roxbury VA Hospital, where he served until 1975.[5] Tom Warthin served on the American Board of Internal Medicine and had a major impact as an early gastroenterologist in the VA in Boston. The author's mentor from 1951 to 1955, Dr. Franz J. Ingelfinger, was an enthusiastic weekly gastroenterological consultant at the West Roxbury VA Hospital. Dr. Warthin's productivity was modest, but he published 18 papers in peer-reviewed journals including papers on amebic abscess of the liver,[6] management of upper gastrointestinal hemorrhage[7,8] and the treatment of idiopathic hemochromatosis.[9]

Hyman J. Zimmerman received his M.D. from Stanford University in 1942, and during World War II served as a physician in the Army. An important early figure in the post-war VA, from 1948 to 1978, Hy Zimmerman worked in Veterans Hospitals in the District of Columbia, Omaha, Chicago and Boston. Devoted to the acquisition of knowledge, he was a superb Chief of Medicine (Washington VA 1971-78) and helped advance the research careers of others. Between 1948 and 1951, Zimmerman published a number of papers including an early study of fatty liver and other histologic abnormalities in the liver of diabetics.[10, 11] While in Omaha, he continued to write papers on a subject to which he would make seminal contributions—liver enzymes and liver function tests in various diseases.[12-14] During his 30-year-career in the VA, Zimmerman published more than 100 scientific papers in peer-reviewed journals. His later years were replete with papers on the hepatotoxicity of various drugs and he was considered by many to be the reigning U.S. expert on hepatotoxicity. In discussions with his colleagues,[15] he frequently mentioned that he was "enormously proud of the VA" and that he viewed the VA system as a "marvelous phenomenon." He did his share to make his perception reality.

As noted earlier, Zimmerman was the Chief of Medicine at the VAMC in Washington. In that capacity, he facilitated the careers of three outstanding researchers, James Finkelstein, M.D., Jay Hoofnagle, M.D., and Leonard Seeff, M.B., Ch.B.

Finkelstein received his M,D. from Columbia College of Physicians and Surgeons in 1958 and after training with Dr. David Schacter moved to the NIH in 1963 to work with Doctors Leonard Laster and Harvey Mudd. Initially, their focus was homocystinuria but their research was expanded to demonstrate three pathways for homocysteine metabolism. Finkelstein soon moved to the Washington VA, where he was a VA Clinical Investigator (1965-68); Medical Investigator (1965-69); Chief of Gastroenterology (1970-7), ACOS/R&D (1975-1979) and, finally, for two decades Chief of Medicine (1979-99). This talented academician and investigator published more than 40 papers in peer-reviewed journals, many in prestigious basic science journals, between 1967 and 2001.[16-19] A marvelous example of the way the "clinic and the bench" should work together, in addition to continuing his NIH work on cystathionine synthase deficiency (homocystinuria) and cystathionase deficiency (cystathioninuria), he also participated in demonstrating defects in the following: methylenetetrahydrofolate reductase (homocystinuria), methionine adenosyltransferase (hypermethioninemia) and glycine methyltransferase (a variant of hypermethioninemia).[20, 21]

Dr. Jay Hoofnagle received his M.D. degree from Yale in 1971, trained for three years at the University of Virginia; and spent 1975-76 at the Bureau of Biologics in the NIH. In 1976, exemplifying how excellence attracts excellence in medicine, he joined Zimmerman, Finklestein and Leonard Seeff as a trainee/research fellow, at the VA Hospital in Washington.

Hoofnagle had already published extensively (33 papers) almost exclusively on hepatitis. While at the Washington VA, he published or co-authored nine papers; noteworthy was the first demonstration of transmission of non-A, non-B hepatitis from man to a chimpanzee;[22] demonstration of hepatitis after transfusion with blood containing antibody to hepatitis B core antigen;[23] and a paper on passive active immunity from hepatitis B immune globulin.[24] All of his studies were performed in collaboration with one of both of his colleagues, Doctors Seeff and Zimmerman. In 1978, Hoofnagle moved to the NIH as an investigator and leader and has continued to be extremely productive. He now serves as Director of the Digestive Diseases and Nutrition Section of the National Institute of Digestive Diseases and Kidney Diseases.

Dr. Leonard B. Seeff earned his M.B. and Ch.B. from the University of Witwatersrand in South Africa in 1961. After three years of internship and residency in South Africa, he completed another residency at Mt. Sinai Hospital in Chicago, after which in 1966 he joined the Washington VA Hospital. Thus began an outstanding career as a clinical investigator in liver disease, first collaborating with Zimmerman and then as one of the leaders in research on hepatitis, particularly hepatitis C. To review Leonard Seeff's many publications is to be struck by his ability to cooperate with and lead his colleagues. He was the lead author on a series of VA cooperative studies: one 1978 study demonstrated that Hepatitis B immune globulin (HBIG) was significantly better than immune serum globulin (ISG) in preventing hepatitis B after needle-stick exposure;[25] another cooperative study on 2204 patients proved that post-transfusion hepatitis can be most effectively reduced by eliminating commercial blood and screening volunteer donors.[26] Seeff was the lead author on one of the definitive articles confirming the importance of acetaminophen in causing hepatotoxicity in alcoholics.[27] This is clinically important because it has influenced clinicians worldwide to caution their patients not to take acetaminophen (Tylenol) when drinking alcohol.

As noted above, in 1978 Seeff and Hoofnagle worked with others to show transmission of non-A, non-B hepatitis from man to chimpanzee. After the nebulous agent was finally identified in 1989 as Hepatitis C, Seeff focused largely on the disease caused by this virus and became one of the world's experts.[28, 29] Seeff and his colleagues conceived one study that was especially fascinating. They got wind of the presence of frozen serum specimens at Warren Air Force Base in Wyoming that had been collected between 1948 and 1955 from healthy servicemen by Doctor Rammelkamp and colleagues in studies on group A streptococci. Seeff and his co-workers studied the serum of these 8568 recruits for hepatitis C and then did follow-ups on the clinical outcome. Patients who harbored the virus 45 years ago may have a lower incidence of chronic liver disease, hepatocellular carcinoma and death than is suggested by current studies.[30] In addition to the articles cited, Leonard Seeff published more than 90 other articles in peer-reviewed journals, offering a fine example of how an active, talented, yet very modest investigator can effectively pursue his own innovative ideas while cooperating with colleagues and leading others in additional research efforts.

The work of Leonard Seeff and others on hepatitis C has been very important because it has shown that this liver disease has a very wide distribution worldwide and is a common cause of chronic liver disease and cancer of the liver. Seeff's studies have helped to stimulate pharmaceutical companies to produce drugs to control or cure Hepatitis C.

In some ways, the experiences of Zimmerman, Finklestein and Seeff are unusual. In most other affiliated VA Hospitals (for example, Durham, Boston, Richmond), their affiliated medical schools have been actively helpful to investigators, providing salary supplements and other types of support. The Washington, D.C. VA Hospital-affiliated universities (Georgetown, George Washington and Howard), however, were neither noted for their research productivity nor for their support of the Washington VA and its research staff. Fortunately, the VA team proceeded splendidly virtually on its own.

The third of the early gastroenterological researchers to join the VA after World War II was Dr. James A. Halsted. He received his M.D. from Harvard in 1930. After a two-year internship at Massachusetts General Hospital (MGH), he had an assistant residency in Cleveland at the Lakeside Hospital of Case Western Reserve Medical School. After several years of private practice in Dedham, Massachusetts, Halsted became a member of the MGH Sixth General Army Hospital, serving in North Africa and Italy. During his wartime experience, he published ten papers, mostly on functional intestinal disorders. In 1950, Roger Egeberg, Chief of Medicine at Wadsworth Veterans Administrative Hospital in Los Angeles and a friend from Cleveland days, offered Halsted a position as Head of the Gastrointestinal Division at Wadsworth. During the five years Halsted held that position, he set up his own laboratory and studied ulcerative colitis.[31-33] He also developed a productive research relationship with Dr. Marion Swenseid to study vitamin B12 physiology and deficiency after gastrectomy and in other disorders.[34-38] The results of these investigations were important contributions to our knowledge at that time and early evidence of the felicitousness of the VA environment upon the research output of this unusually curious scientist.

In 1955, Halsted relocated to the Syracuse VA Hospital as Director of Professional Services, where he published five papers, including an early report on the mechanism of hypoproteinemia in gastric mucosal hypertrophy.[39] In 1958, he took a leave of absence to accept a two-year Fulbright professorship in Iran, where he initiated studies on zinc deficiency geophagia and dwarfism. Upon returning to the United States, he became Deputy Assistant Chief Medical Director for Research and Education in VACO from 1964 to 1966, and from 1966 to 1971 he was Associate Chief of Staff for Research and Education at the Washington VA Hospital. During these seven years in Washington, he continued to publish papers from the VA on nutrition and zinc deficiency.[40-43] During his illustrious career, he published 66 papers in peer-reviewed journals, the majority written during his 19 years with the VA. In addition, in 1968 he co-edited with Zimmerman a volume of the Medical Clinics of North America devoted to articles by gastroenterological investigators based at VA Hospitals.[44] Jim Halsted was an excellent physician, a very productive researcher and a "wonderful and very caring person"[45] whose frequent career moves call to mind those of the great Paracelsus. For the VA's support of Halsted, it was the recipient of his boundless energy, altruism and curiosity.

Leslie Zieve, the last of these early gastroenterological researchers who joined the VA just after World War II, received his M.D. from the University of Minnesota in 1942. After a stint in the Army, he was discharged in 1946 and served his residency at the Minneapolis VA Hospital under Richard Ebert. In 1950, he was made chief of the Radioisotope Service and subsequently Chief of Gastroenterology and then Associate Chief of Staff for Research and Education. Ebert's choice of Zieve for de facto director of Research was demonstrated to have been very wise, judging from Zieve's future contributions and those of his colleagues. One early fellow, Daniel Gregory, said: ". . . he (Zieve) energized the investigative environment, procured the resources, set the standards and monitored productivity. There seemed to be no limit to his energy, wisdom and ability to obtain or achieve that which he believed essential for a successful program."[46]

Zieve's own work was very impressive, numbering 150 papers in peer-reviewed journals published between 1950 and 1992. His principal achievements were many excellent studies on liver function tests,[47-51] several studies on residuals of hepatitis[52, 53] and studies on the biochemistry of hepatic encephalopathy.[54-57]

Zieve's influence on younger colleagues was also very important. On two occasions, he was an important factor in motivating a trainee to pursue a career in investigative gastroenterology either in the VA or elsewhere. One trainee, Paul Webster, had graduated from Bowman-Gray School of Medicine in 1956, trained at Boston City Hospital and the Army and then taken a residency at the University of Minnesota and the VA from 1960 to 1963. He published three papers with Zieve,[58-60] apparently just enough to whet Webster's appetite for discovery. (Webster's career will be discussed below, in connection with the

Durham VA Hospital.) A second individual inspired by Les Zieve was Daniel Gregory. After receiving his M.D. at the University of Virginia in 1962, he took an internship at the Medical College of Virginia and then three years of residency, mostly at the Minneapolis VA Hospital, followed by a Fellowship at the Veterans Hospital. Strongly influenced by the excellence of the Chair, Dr. Cecil Watson, and more directly by Zieve, while there, Gregory published eleven papers in very good journals.[61-63] (Gregory's career will be reviewed below during discussion of the Richmond VA Hospital and bile acid research.)

Leslie Zieve served on the Minneapolis VA staff from 1950 until his retirement in 1979. In addition to inspiring short-term fellows such as Webster and Gregory, he and the hospital attracted an extremely impressive and productive group of investigators, among them Doctors Jack Vennes, Stephen Silvis, William Duane, John Bond and Michael Levitt. All received their M.D. degrees from the University of Minnesota except for John Bond, whose was from the University of Pennsylvania where he transferred after two years at North Dakota University. All five trained at Minnesota and some had faculty time at the University before completing their careers at the VA Hospital.

Jack Vennes, who joined the VA in 1955, published until 2000; as did Stephen Silvis, who joined the VA staff in 1966. For years, these two physician-researchers constituted the forefront of clinical research in gastrointestinal endoscopy in the United States. Specifically, Vennes and Silvis were the leading early proponents in this country for endoscopic retrograde cholangiopanceatography (ERCP). In the early 1970s, the Japanese had reported on the use of ERCP. Leslie Zieve, recognizing the clinical importance of this procedure, sent Jack Vennes to Japan to learn all he could. Shortly thereafter, Vennes and Silvis were the first to publish on ERCP in this country.[64-67]

Stephen Silvis was a most productive clinical investigator, publishing 116 peer-reviewed articles during his VA career, of which 32 shared authorship with Jack Vennes. These include multicenter trials,[68, 69] many technical articles and a presidential address on "Research in gastrointestinal endoscopy."[70] Although Vennes and Silvis were highly respected clinical researchers, the most important quality of their program at the Minneapolis VA Medical Center was their willingness to teach. They welcomed people from throughout the United States to visit Minneapolis, cooperate on research and learn from them.

The other three members of this Minneapolis VA team joined full-time in the 1970s, William Duane in 1975, John Bond in 1976 and Michael Levitt in 1978. Levitt divided his time between the University Hospital and the VA from 1968 to 1978.

Duane compiled a great record at the Minneapolis VA. By 2001, he had published more than 75 papers, most of them in the leading peer-reviewed U.S. journals of "bench" research (e.g., *Journal of Clinical Investigation, Journal of Lipid Research, New England Journal of Medicine, Gastroenterology, Journal of Laboratory and Clinical Medicine, American Journal of Physiology, Hepatology*) and often with his colleagues (Levitt, Bond, Vennes and Silvis). Duane's principal interests have been bile acid metabolism[71-76] and biliary secretion.[77, 78]

John Bond also compiled an impressive record of research and publication that is more diverse and more clinical than Duane's. Between 1977 and 2001, Bond published more than 90 papers in excellent peer-reviewed journals, often with colleagues, i.e. on intestinal gases[79-81] with Mike Levitt and on the jaundiced patient with Vennes.[82] Bond has written scholarly and thoughtful articles on endoscopy,[83, 84] colonic polyps and carcinoma,[85-88] as well as on many other subjects that might be expected to win the attention of a curious, talented and energetic investigator in a nurturing research milieu.

Michael Levitt spent four years training with Franz Ingelfinger at Boston University before coming to Minneapolis. In 1978 when Leslie Zieve retired, he was named Associate Chief of Staff for Research and Development at the Minneapolis VA Medical Center. Levitt has performed a great service to this impressive unit both by his own contributions and by his leadership. Between 1978 and 2001, he published approximately 172 articles in peer-reviewed journals. He studied intestinal gas (methane and hydrogen) production,[89-91] and hyperamylasemia,[92-94] and he published a variety of excellent papers on ethanol absorption[95] and mechanics of intestinal absorption.[96] His success reflects not only his ability but also the high quality of the VA Medical Center, the University of Minnesota and his colleagues.

The second "wave" of gastroenterologic investigators (1953–1955).

Gastroenterologists joining the VA system in the 1953–55 period included Ben Eiseman in 1953 at the Denver VA Hospital; Angelo Dagradi and Stephen Stempien in 1954 at Long Beach VA; Malcolm Tyor at the Durham VA Hospital in 1955; Morton Grossman in 1955 at the Los Angeles VA Hospital; and Marcus Rothschild in 1954 at the New York VA Hospital.

Research in gastroenterology has always included those whose primary training was surgical. During the middle years of the last century, the President of the American Gastroenterological Association would occasionally be a surgeon. One of the early talented recruits to the VA was a surgeon, Ben Eiseman, who conducted very important research on the digestive system. Eiseman received his M.D. degree from Harvard in 1943; after three years in the Army, he trained at Barnes Hospital and Washington University in St. Louis with Dr. Evarts Graham from 1946 to 1952. In 1953, he joined the Denver VA Medical Center. After five years (1961–1966) at the University of Kentucky, in 1967 he returned to the Denver VA Medical Center where for 41 years he remained very productive, until 2002. During his publishing career, which extended to 2000, he published more than 300 scientific papers on many subjects. Those relating to the digestive system made major contributions to the understanding of hepatic coma,[97-101] hypothermia in peritonitis,[102-104] peptic ulcer,[105, 106] pancreatitis[107, 108] and extra-corporeal liver support for hepatic failure and transplantation.[109-113] In the opinion of one outstanding surgical colleague, "Ben Eiseman had a tremendous impact on gastroenterological research in the VA."[114]

Eiseman's admirer, Tom Starzl, is himself a very important person in the history of VA research. Starzl received his M.D. and Ph.D. from Northwestern University in 1952, his residency training at Johns Hopkins from 1952 to 1956 and then two years in Miami. In June 1958, Starzl moved to Northwestern for a fellowship in chest/cardiac surgery with Dr. F. John Lewis. Within his first few days in Chicago, Starzl began performing allograft transplantation in dogs at the Chicago VA Research Hospital. For a year, using only VA contingency funds and no permanent personnel, Starzl undertook at least one procedure a week in the surgical research laboratory. These experiments laid the foundation for the eventual clinical use of liver transplantation.[115, 116] In 1961, Starzl moved to Denver where he became Chief of Surgery at the VA Hospital and continued his pioneering research on liver transplantation. An early important paper from the VA revealed the potential of and problems associated with human transplantation.[117] Four of the six authors on this classical paper were full-time VA employees.

Key advances in liver transplantation made at the Denver VA included recognition of the importance of adrenocortical steroids,[118] the development of homograft tolerance,[119] preservation techniques for the storage of liver homografts,[120] and the use of cyclosporin A in transplantation.[121] The first successful human liver transplant was done there.[122] Even after Starzl moved to the University Hospital as chair of surgery in 1972, he retained his VA laboratory until 1980, when he moved to Pittsburgh. At the University of Pittsburgh, Starzl continued his transplant research both at the University and at the Pittsburgh VA Medical Center.[123] Between 1995 and 1998, Starzl was a VA Distinguished Physician, a fitting tribute to a remarkable man who has given much to many patients and colleagues.[124]

In the late 1940s, gastrointestinal endoscopy was attracting attention in this country, in large part owing to the invention in the 1920s by Rudolph Schindler, a German physician, of a semi-flexible gastroscope. The scope was produced in 1932 by George Wolf, a leading instrument maker in Berlin. An excellent account of this important development is given by Dr. William Haubrich.[125]

Dr. Walter Lincoln Palmer arranged in 1934 for Schindler to be a Visiting Professor at the University of Chicago where Schindler continued his teaching and developed U.S.-made endoscopes. In 1943, Schindler moved to Los Angeles, where he taught at the College of Medical Evangelists (now Loma Linda University) and was a consultant at the Long Beach VA Hospital. It was probably Schindler's influence plus the presence of two VA physicians, Drs. Stempien and Dagradi, that made the VA the principal site of intensive endoscopic clinical studies in the United States.

Dr. Stephen Stempien received his M.D. at Case Western Reserve University in 1937. After an internship in Cleveland, he had residencies at Willard Parker in New York City and two years of medicine at the Boston City Hospital. His first documented VA publication, in 1948 from the Van Nuys, California VA Hospital, addressed gastroscopy under pentothal-curare anesthesia.[126] Stempien continued to publish significant clinical papers in peer-reviewed journals, from Van Nuys and from the new Long Beach VA Hospital. In 1952, he was joined by Dr. Angelo E. Dagradi. The two physicians were a dynamic team. Dagradi had received his M.D. from Long Island University in 1940 and completed his internship and residency in pathology at the Long Island College Hospital and his internal medicine residency at Kings County Hospital in Brooklyn. After two years in the Army, he was briefly at the VA Hospital in Northport, N.Y. In 1952, he joined the Long Beach VA Hospital as Chief of Gastroenterology.

In their two decades together (1952–1972), Stempien and Dagradi were the leading U.S. proponents of endoscopy in gastroenterology, co-authoring 44 articles together, with Rudolph Schindler as co-author of five of them.[127-130] During his VA experience (1954–1989), Dagradi also published 52 papers without Stempien. Stempien published 27 papers without Dagradi. The output of these colleagues and their co-authors addressed a broad range of subjects, including gastric ulcer,[131] duodenal ulcer,[132] acute gastrointestinal hemorrhage,[133] bleeding varices,[134] the Mallory-Weiss lesion,[135] and hemorrhagic erosive gastritis.[136]

Stempien retired in 1976, and Dagradi left the VA in 1989. During their productive years beginning in 1948, this pair made major contributions to the study of the upper gastrointestinal tract. These were all the more notable since their enthusiasm for endoscopy was not at that time universally shared by gastroenterologists. Many did not foresee its importance, nor its lucrative potential, but instead focused on more basic science research. The VA and the country are in debt to the vision and energy of Drs. Schindler, Stempien and Dagradi.

An important element in the post-WWII surge of interest in gastroenterology was the Duke University School of Medicine. Malcolm P. Tyor received his M.D. from Duke in 1945. After post-graduate training at the University of Wisconsin and Bowman-Gray School of Medicine, he spent a year at Oak Ridge and then, in 1953, joined the faculty at Duke. By then, Tyor had published ten significant papers in excellent journals and he expected to continue his research at Duke. But when Duke's chief of Gastroenterology, Dr. Julian Ruffin, informed Tyor that "he could do his research on Friday afternoon" after all patients were cared for, Tyor spoke to Dr. Eugene Stead, Chair of Medicine and notable in U.S. medicine for promoting research and developing young scientists. Stead immediately called all parties together with the result that Tyor was promptly reassigned to the VA. There, his research thrived.

While at the Durham VA Hospital, from 1955 until he returned to Duke in 1963, Tyor published 21 papers in very good peer-reviewed journals which made substantial contributions to our knowledge of hepatic coma[137-139] and lipid metabolism and absorption.[140-142]

While at Duke, Tyor recruited and mentored two young researchers who became substantial contributors to the VA and to the understanding of gastroenterology. They were Paul Webster, M.D. and Charles Mansbach, M.D.

Paul Webster received his M.D. at Bowman-Gray School of Medicine in 1956. After an internship at the Boston City Hospital, he served in the Army for two years. Upon returning to civilian life, Webster trained with Leslie Zieve at the Minnesota VA Medical Center for three years. In 1963, he joined the faculty at Duke University. Almost unbelievably, the same thing happened to him as had happened to Mal Tyor. When

Webster spoke to his Division Chief, Dr. Julian Ruffin, about time to conduct basic research, he was told "he could do his research on Friday afternoons." Webster also appealed to the Chairman, Dr. Eugene Stead, as had Tyor nine years earlier. According to Webster, Stead spoke to his secretary, saying "call Malcolm (Tyor) and Julian (Ruffin). I want both of them in my office tomorrow morning at 9:00 a.m.[143] The result was the same. Webster moved to the Durham VA Medical Center and with Tyor worked for five years very productively on basic research that included fundamental work on the synthesis of protein in the pancreas[144] and the control of protein synthesis.[145, 146] In 1968, Webster relocated to the Augusta, Georgia VA Hospital where for a decade, continuing his research as a VA Medical Investigator and publishing 38 papers in peer-reviewed journals, he made major contributions to pancreatic physiology, demonstrating in both the pigeon and rat pancreas that feeding stimulates and fasting inhibits protein production and cell growth.[147-149] He was also able to show that pancreozymin stimulates pancreatic growth[150] and to induce pancreatic cancer in rats.[151] While at the Augusta VA Medical Center, Webster recruited Dr. Manjit Singh, who continued as an independent investigator. In 1978, Webster left the VA Hospital for the Medical College of Georgia.

Manjit Singh received his M.B. B.S. in 1959 from the Glancy Medical College in Amritsar, Punjab. From 1960 to 1968, he undertook post-graduate training in internal medicine and gastroenterology at his parent university and received his M.D. in 1964. From 1968–70, he was a Fellow at the University of Rochester, New York and from 1971-73 a research Fellow at the Medical College of Georgia. In 1973, he joined Paul Webster on the staff at the VA Hospital in Augusta. By 1978, when Webster moved to the Medical College of Georgia, Singh and his colleagues had published 36 articles in peer-reviewed journals. Singh's important contributions center on the long-term effects of ethanol on the pancreas[152, 153] and the effect of deficiency of zinc, folate and thiamine[154, 155] on the pancreas. These studies are important because alcohol is an important cause of chronic pancreatitis, and folate and thiamine may also be important factors in this disease. Singh's extensive training in India and in the United States has paid handsome dividends to the VA and to science.

Shortly after Paul Webster moved from Durham to Augusta, Malcolm Tyor recruited another talented investigator, Charles M. Mansbach, M.D. Mansbach received his M.D. from New York University in 1963, trained in internal medicine at Duke from 1964 to 1966, and then completed an N.I.H. fellowship in gastroenterology at Duke. In 1970, he joined the Durham VA, where he spent thirteen very productive years. The focus of his research was fat digestion in man[156, 157] and fat-related intestinal enzymes.[158, 159] In 1986, he moved to the University of Tennessee, where he continued his research at the Memphis VA Medical Center. Mansbach's achievements are impressive, especially his continued study of lipid mobilization in the intestine[160] and his reexamination of phospholipases[161] and alkaline lipase.[162] His current work on intracellular lipid metabolism[163, 164] testifies to the centrality of the Department of Veterans Affairs to the best research in this country.

In 1955, Morton I. Grossman, M.D., moved to the Wadsworth Veterans Hospital. This was a major event for U.S. gastroenterology and for the VA owing to the prodigious amount of research accomplished by Grossman and his colleagues in Los Angeles and the numerous investigators he trained or influenced.

Figure 23.1 Morton Grossman

Mort Grossman received his M.D. from Northwestern University in 1944. After a one-year internship at Cook County Hospital in Chicago he spent six years working with the eminent physiologist Dr. Andrew Ivy. In 1946, the Ivy-Grossman physiological unit decamped to the University of Illinois, where productivity increased. In 1951, Grossman became Chief of the Physiology Division of the U.S. Army Medical Nutrition Laboratory, first in Chicago and then Denver. During these years before joining the VA, Grossman influenced two younger physicians who would assume important roles in the story of VA research, Doctors Armand Littman and Lionel Bernstein.

Armand Littman received his M.D. degree from the University of Illinois in 1943 and took his residency at Cook County Hospital. From 1946 to 1950, he was a Fellow in the Physiology Department of the University of Illinois with Doctors Ivy and Grossman. In 1959, Littman joined the Hines VA Hospital as Chief of Medicine and held that post until his retirement in 1995. During his tenure, he was a key role model as both clinician and clinical investigator. He and his colleagues were probably the first to explain that intolerance to milk was caused by lactase deficiency.[165, 166] In 1971, Littman was Chair of the large VA-wide cooperative study on gastric ulcer.[167, 168] Finally, Littman was responsible for the rigorous design of a double-blind controlled study of antacids for peptic ulcer.[169] During his tenure, he published fifty studies in peer-reviewed journals.

Lionel Bernstein received his M.D. at the University of Illinois in 1945. After an internship at Cook County Hospital, he spent 1946-1948 in military service, completed a residency in medicine at Cook County from 1949 to 1951, and for the next four years worked in physiology with Mort Grossman at the University of Illinois and in Denver, Colorado. Bernstein joined the Hines VA in 1956 as Chief of the Gastroenterology section and between 1962 and 1966 served as Chief of Medicine at the Chicago Westside VA. An energetic and stimulating investigator, Bernstein's major achievement during this period was establishing a clinical test for esophagitis by perfusing acid into the esophagus[170, 171] and conducting other clinical evaluations of esophagitis.[172] The perfusion of acid into the esophagus causes pain when the patient has esophagitis. This was the first objective test for esophagitis. In the period 1966 to 1970, Lionel Bernstein was the Director of the Research Service in VA Central Office, where he served with distinction.

Returning to the career and contributions of Mort Grossman, it should be noted that his most important single contribution was made in 1948 while he was at the University of Illinois and before he moved to the Wadsworth VA Hospital in Los Angeles. This was establishing direct evidence that a hormone was released in response to distention of the antral pouch in dogs.[173] This was the first hint in mammals, including man, that gastrin released from the antrum of the stomach would stimulate secretion. This is important in understanding peptic ulcer in man as well as the pathogenesis of Zollinger Ellison syndrome.

In 1955, Grossman was considering an academic position in physiology when, despite his limited formal clinical training,[174] he was enticed by Bill Bachrach, a gastroenterologist and friend and Dr. Roger Egeberg, Chief of Medicine at Wadsworth, to become Wadsworth's Chief of Gastroenterology. The reader may recall that five years earlier Egeberg had attracted James Halsted to Wadsworth to the same position. Egeberg's shrewd judgment of people surely contributed to his later ascension to the position of Secretary of the Department of Health, Education and Welfare. In 1962, Grossman was appointed a Senior Medical Investigator. In 1973, he and his colleagues applied for and were awarded an NIH grant to create a Center for Ulcer Research and Education (CURE), which was jointly funded by the NIH, the VA and UCLA.

From 1955 until his untimely death in 1981, Grossman made a unique contribution to gastroenterology and physiology by his own scientific achievements and his record as a superb trainer of young people. His own words express it best: "My most important contribution is providing a place and atmosphere in which fledgling scientists can develop and grow to independence."[175] During his twenty-six years at Wadsworth VA, Mort Grossman inspired a large number of research fellows. According to one source[176] Grossman supervised a total of 96 Fellows during his career, of whom 57 subsequently served at the Wadsworth VA Hospital. In their memorial to Grossman in 1982, Jon Isenberg and John Walsh listed the thirty Fellows who "continued in academic careers." In chronological order from the start of their fellowship, they were: Stewart Tuttle, Augostino Bettarello, Ian Gillespie, Edward Passaro, Kenneth Wormsley, Roy Preshaw, Sven Andersson, Stanley Konturek, Allan Cooke, Eugene Jacobson, Michael Eisenberg, David Nahrworld, Sverre Emas, Monique Vagne, Leonard Johnson, Scott Jones, Lawrence Way, James Meyer, Gil Barbezat, John Walsh, Jon Isenberg, Attila Csendes, Haile Debas, Graham Dockray, Jorge Valenzuela, Richard Sturdevant, Hermod Peteren, Andrew Soll, David Carter, Gordon Kauffman, Ian Taylor, Tachi Yamada and Travis Solomon.

During his tenure at Wadsworth VA Hospital, Grossman published 318 papers, the majority, often written with Fellows, related to his interest in physiology of the stomach and pancreas, the gastrointestinal hormones, the drugs which impact these organs and diseases such as ulcer. Although a review of these papers is impossible within the confines of this chapter, their impact has been incalculable. While most of this prodigious output occurred at the Wadsworth VA, several notable studies on gastrin were conducted by transatlantic cooperation with Gregory and Tracy.[177, 178]

Further evidence of the unusual and felicitous nature of CURE and its Head, Mort Grossman, is that Dr. Charles Code, an outstanding senior physiologist investigator and teacher, spent five years (1975–1980) at CURE after retiring from the Mayo Clinic. Code was one of the leaders of the gastroenterological profession during the mid-20th century and president of the AGA in 1964. His interests lay in physiology, particularly gastric, and motility of the gut. While at Wadsworth, he continued his work on the interdigestive myoelectric complex[179] and studied the ability of the gastric mucosa to protect itself from gastric acid.[180, 181] Code's five years with Grossman were certainly productive, but equally important was that sojourn's testimony to intellectual curiosity and collegiality.

A key figure in Mort Grossman's career who was vital to CURE was another outstanding physician investigator, Dr. John Walsh. Walsh received his M.D. from Vanderbilt University in 1963. After an internship and residency in internal medicine (1963–1967) at the New York Hospital (Cornell), Walsh spent three years (1967–1970) as a Research Associate at the Bronx VA Hospital where he published nine articles in very good journals, many on post-transfusion hepatitis.[182, 183] While at the Bronx VA, Walsh worked with Doctors Solomon Berson and Rosalyn Yalow (future Nobel Prize winner in 1977) on the radioimmunoassay of Australia antigen.[184] In 1970, Walsh became a Fellow with Grossman at Wadsworth and in 1971 was named a VA Clinical Investigator. When Grossman died in 1981, Walsh shared the responsibilities of directing CURE. In 1993, Walsh became Director of CURE, a position he held until his death in 2000. During his thirty years at Wadsworth VA, Walsh published 405 scientific papers in excellent journals on a wide range of subjects, 300 after Grossman's death.

Walsh continued in the CURE tradition of collaborating with a wide range of investigators, both at Wadsworth and elsewhere, and he also observed the tradition of the institution by focusing on physiology and on the stomach and pancreas. His research from 1981 to 2000 was often on the secretion and release of hormones and peptides such as gastrin, somatostatin, vasoactive intestinal peptide, bombesin, substance P; their effects on secretion in the stomach and pancreas; and their effects on intestinal smooth muscle. In the 1990s, Walsh published many excellent studies on Helicobacter pylori and its role in causing some peptic ulcers.

As CURE's leader after Mort Grossman's death, Walsh faced a formidable challenge. All reports are that he met it extremely well. He was eclectic, collaborative, very energetic and collegial and maintained the high standards that Grossman had established. The achievements of this VA unit from 1955 to 2000 would be rewarding material for a detailed biographical study of the participants.

Another distinguished member of the CURE team was Dr. Jon Isenberg. He received his MD from the University of Illinois in 1963. After an internship at Jackson Memorial in Miami, he completed a residency at the University of Illinois. From 1966 to 1968, he was a Fellow at Wadsworth VA, where, after two years in the Army, he returned in 1970 as a VA Clinical Investigator and key staff member of CURE. He remained there, playing an important role in advancing its success as a research enterprise until he moved to U.C. San Diego in 1979. During his CURE sojourn, Isenberg published more than 100 articles in excellent peer-reviewed journals. A number of his contributions deserve mention: He and his colleagues made the initial observation that secretin produces a paradoxical increase in serum gastrin in patients with the Zollinger-Ellison (ZE) syndrome.[185] This observation is now a diagnostic test. Isenberg, Walsh and Grossman published an important review of ZE syndrome.[186]

Isenberg and Maxwell demonstrated that intravenous amino acids significantly increased gastric acid secretion.[187] He and colleagues made one of the earliest studies on the histamine H_2 receptor antagonists on human gastric secretion in patients with duodenal ulcer and demonstrated their efficacy.[188, 189] These studies were important in establishing these agents as effective treatments for ulcer. Since 10% of the population have peptic ulcer at some time in their lives, the value of effective therapy for ulcer is obvious.

The research of one other trainee/fellow at CURE, Allan Cooke, will be documented, because of his subsequent productivity at the Iowa City VAMC. In 1959, Cooke received his MB, BS from Sydney University in Australia where he also received the M.D. in 1970. After a residency in medicine at the Royal Prince Alfred Hospital from 1959-64, he worked at CURE from 1964 to 1967 as a Fellow, publishing twenty articles in excellent journals[190-194] of which he was first author of fifteen. After leaving CURE in 1967, Cooke spent six months with Dr. J.N. Hunt in England and two years as a Research Fellow in Australia before being recruited in 1970 by Dr. James Christensen to the VA Hospital in Iowa City, Iowa.

The saga of research at the Iowa City VA Hospital is fascinating. The hospital was built in 1952 near the medical school, but its relationship with the school was poor, in striking contrast to other affiliations between VA hospitals and medical schools. In the 1966-68 period, hospital stays were 3-1/2 to 4 weeks, with waits for admission commonly exceeding 160 days. Virtually no research was being conducted. In 1968, Dr. James Clifton, Chair of Medicine, with others from the Medical School went to the VA Central Office and requested that Doctors Tom Chalmers and Lionel Bernstein take steps to improve the affiliation. As a result, "integration was accomplished," all VA staff also became medical school faculty and research projects were speedily initiated in many fields of medicine.[195]

This change at the Iowa VA Hospital came at a propitious time for gastroenterological research in the VA. In 1966, Dr. James Christensen had been recruited to the University of Iowa. After receiving his M.D. from the University of Nebraska in 1957, Christensen completed an internship in California, a three-year residency at Iowa, a two-year

530

fellowship in the Indian Health Service and a fellowship year in Edmonton, Alberta, with Dr. Ed Daniel, an important leader in research in gastrointestinal physiology. In 1966, Christensen joined the faculty at Iowa and two years later set up his motility laboratory at the VA Hospital. From 1968 to 1974, Christensen published 19 excellent papers from the VA during a period when he was becoming one of the few experts in the country on gastrointestinal motility. The research included the responses of the esophagus to distention and electrical stimulation,[196, 197] the pharmacologic identification of the lower esophageal sphincter,[198] an explication of characteristics of the electrical activity of the colon of the cat[199-202] and a study of the esophagogastric junction in various species.[203]

In 1970, Christensen recruited Allan Cooke to the Iowa City VA Hospital—a brilliant move. Over the next six years, Cooke published 19 papers in excellent peer-reviewed journals. His focus was often physiologic, reflecting his rich background with Grossman, Hunt and Christensen. The subjects of his papers included gastric emptying,[204-207] the gastric mucosa and its response to various agents[208, 209] and the identification of a tryptophan receptor controlling gastric emptying in the dog.[210]

In summary, an almost absent affiliation of the Iowa City VA with the University of Iowa was suddenly improved, just in time to allow Christensen and, later, Cooke to do important research.

While the prodigious research program at Wadsworth VA Hospital is understandably focused on Mort Grossman and CURE, another talented investigator, concerned primarily with the liver, deserves consideration. Neil Kaplowitz received his M.D. from New York University School of Medicine in 1967. After PG1 and PG2 years at Bellevue Hospital, he was a Senior Assistant Resident at Albert Einstein, an Assistant Resident at Rockefeller University Hospital (1970-71), and a Gastroenterology Fellow at Cornell - N.Y. Hospital with Dr. Norman Javitt. After two years at the Clinical Investigation Center with the Navy in Oakland, California, Kaplowitz joined Wadsworth as Chief of Gastroenterology in 1975, a position he held until he moved to USC in 1990. During his fifteen years at Wadsworth, Kaplowitz was very productive, publishing ninety-two research papers in peer-reviewed journals. In addition, he was preceptor for a number of research associates who were co-authors of the papers published. For instance, Tadataka Yamada was a co-author on nine papers between 1980 and 1984 although Yamada is listed as a Fellow with Grossman. The collegiality, size and resources of the Wadsworth VA made possible such openness.

The particular interests and expertise of Neil Kaplowitz during his VA tenure include studies of the kinetics of glutathione metabolism in the liver and its efflux from hepatocytes[211-213] and the metabolism of bile acids in the liver.[214, 215] This talented investigator has won national acclaim as an expert in the liver; his years in the VA were mutually rewarding for Kaplowitz and the VA.

The final investigator of the so-called second "wave" who joined the VA during the 1954–55 period was Marcus Rothschild. Receiving his M.D. from the New York University School of Medicine in 1949, he then completed an internship at Beth Israel Hospital in New York and residencies at Mt. Sinai in New York, Beth Israel in Boston and Beth Israel

Hospital in New York. In 1953, he took a two-year Fellowship with Dr. Solomon Berson at the Bronx VA Hospital.

While at the Bronx VA Hospital, Rothschild and his colleagues published five papers on the metabolism of albumin,[216, 217] blood volume determinations[218] and transcapillary circulation.[219] When Rothschild's fellowship was completed, Sol Berson asked him to stay on at the Bronx but Rothschild declined, explaining that he needed to be "his own person."[220] whereupon Berson urged him to consider other VA Hospitals. Initially, Rothschild took the position of Chief of Gastroenterology at the New York VA Hospital but within weeks was named Chief of the Radioisotope Service where he was soon joined by two future long-time collaborators, Doctors Murray Oratz and Sidney Schreiber. Between 1955 and 1992, Mark Rothschild published 118 papers in peer-reviewed journals, with both Oratz and Schreiber co-authors in 88 and one of the two co-authors in 14 others. What a team!

The research of Rothschild and his co-workers was very focused. Their most notable contributions were in albumin metabolism and distribution,[221-223] various studies on acute cardiac overload[224, 225] and the effect of ethanol on various functions of the liver.[226-228] That their research output in the radioisotope laboratory was of very high quality was made possible by the excellent attitude of the local staff and VA Central Office, the support of New York University and, of course, the stellar talent of the investigators themselves.

The impact of two leaders in Gastroenterology (1950s–1960s): Dr. Franz J. Ingelfinger and Dr. Thomas P. Almy.
Let us shift focus to that of trainees of these two outstanding leaders.

While at Boston University, Franz J. Ingelfinger supervised fifty-seven trainees in gastroenterology between 1942 and 1967. (In 1967, Ingelfinger became Editor of the *New England Journal of Medicine*). Of these trainees coming from all parts of the world, six made substantial contributions to research in the VA and several were strongly influenced by Ingelfinger to accept VA career positions. The following trainees contributed to VA research for the years indicated, in order of their joining the VA: John T. Farrar (1955–1963 and 1970–1990); Robert M. Donaldson (1959–1964 and 1973–1985); Charles Pope (1964– present); Edwin Englert (1967–1985); Ward Olsen (1968–2000); Michael Levitt (1978–present.) (Dr. Levitt's contributions have already been covered under the Minneapolis VA Medical Center.)

John T. Farrar, M.D., (*the author of this chapter*), received his M.D. degree from Washington University School of Medicine in 1945. After completing an internship and two years of service in the Army, he had a year of pathology at the Mallory Institute of Pathology at the Boston City Hospital, training in internal medicine at Boston University, a three-year Fellowship in gastroenterology with Franz Ingelfinger and one year on the Boston University faculty.

In 1955, he was recruited by Thomas P. Almy, M.D., to be Chief of Gastroenterology at the recently completed VA Hospital in New York City. When he arrived in the fall, the clinical services were well organized but only Dr. Marcus Rothschild was conducting any research, as previously described. The three medical schools with services at nearby Bellevue Hospital—New York University, Cornell University Medical College and Columbia University—were responsible for selecting VA faculty. These medical schools were completely supportive of research, as will become apparent.

Within eight months of arriving, Farrar became the Assistant Director of Professional Services for Research, a title that several years later was changed nationwide to Associate Chief of Staff for Research. Since both hospital management and staff were very supportive of research, he was charged with designing and supervising the construction of a large research laboratory in one wing of the hospital in what had originally been intended to be a 40-bed unit. This construction and the purchase of lab benches and equipment were extremely rapid and, simultaneously, a formal Research Committee was formed of service chiefs and representatives from Cornell, New York University and Columbia Medical Schools. The Columbia representative was Dr. Dickinson Richards, a Nobel Laureate in Medicine in 1956. At the time, the prominence of the Research Committee members did not seem surprising to Farrar and his colleagues, rather was what was expected in the highly important enterprise of research that was the outgrowth of enlightened academic medicine. One other indication of the felicitous staffing of the VA was the prominence, excellence and apparent availability of the leaders in the VA Central Office. Dr. William Middleton, a distinguished leader in American medicine and former Dean of Medicine at Wisconsin, was Chief Medical Director from 1955 to 1963. He visited the New York VA on several occasions. Farrar visited the VA Central Office at least twice in eight years and received personal letters from Middleton. All in all, it was a very stimulating atmosphere. During the eight years Farrar served at the New York VA Hospital, he and his colleagues published eighteen papers, ten in peer-reviewed journals.

Their interests were primarily gastrointestinal motility as recorded by a telemetering capsule[229-231] and intestinal absorption.[232, 233] In 1963, Farrar left the New York VA Hospital for an academic post in Richmond, Virginia at the Medical College of Virginia. This medical school had a strong affiliation with the Hunter Holmes McGuire VA Hospital, but research in gastroenterology was scant, at best. Nevertheless, within a few years, a very productive team was formed there which would make important contributions to the science of lipids and gallstones in man. This team was Leon Swell, Ph.D.; Z. Reno Vlahcevic, M.D.; and Daniel Gregory, M.D.

Leon Swell received his Ph.D. in biochemistry at George Washington University in 1952, but the previous year he had been recruited as a basic scientist to the Martinsburg VA Hospital, which had an affiliation with that university. Between 1953 and 1964 when Swell moved to the Richmond VA Hospital, he and his colleagues published thirty-five papers in peer-reviewed journals, primarily biochemical in emphasis. In almost all of these articles, Professor Carleton Treadwell, Chair of Biochemistry at George Washington University, was a co-author. Such productivity emanating from a small VA Hospital that is geographically very distant from any academic center is very unusual. The quality and number of papers reflect very favorably on Leon Swell and his drive and talent. The work during those 11 years was almost all on lipids and focused on several areas: the mechanisms of cholesterol absorption[234, 235] and the effect of dietary fat on blood cholesterol.[236, 237] When Swell moved his laboratory from the Martinsburg VA Hospital to the Richmond VA Hospital in 1964 he was "already nationally recognized as a distinguished lipid biochemist."[238] Swell continued to publish excellent articles on lipids until 1968, when he and colleagues used an isolated perfused dog liver model to demonstrate that cholesterol precipitation in bile was prevented by perfusing the liver with primary bile acids.[239] At about the same time, William Admirand and Donald Small reported that the solubility of cholesterol in bile was dependent on a critical concentration of bile acids.[240] These two observations came at a time shortly after John Farrar, as Chair of Gastroenterology at the Medical College of Virginia, had recruited the second member of the Richmond VA Hospital research team, Z. Reno Vlahcevic, M.D..

Reno Vlahcevic was a native of Yugoslavia and received his M.D. in 1956 at the Medical School of the University of Zagreb, Croatia. After several years of post-graduate training in Zagreb, he emigrated to the United States for an internship at the Salem Hospital. This was followed by a residency and fellowship at the Lemuel Shattuck Hospital in Boston with Dr. Thomas Chalmers. Then he took another fellowship in gastroenterology at Western Reserve University. He came to Richmond, Virginia in 1966 as the Chief of Gastroenterology at the VA Hospital.

The presence of Leon Swell, a lipid biochemist, and Reno Vlahcevic, a clinician, at the same hospital at the time of the observations of Admirand and Small provided an exceptional opportunity. The two investigators bonded immediately and launched a collaborative effort that continued until Swell retired in 1983. From 1970 to1983, Vlahcevic and Swell were co-authors, with others, on 45 articles in excellent journals. The first collaborative study demonstrated that patients with gallstones have a diminished bile acid pool in comparison to patients without gallstones.[241] This study led Vlahcevic and colleagues to contemplate a study of the Navajo Indians in New Mexico who were known to have a high incidence of gallstones. Contact was made with Dr. Daniel Gregory, whose career was initially discussed when he was with Leslie Zieve at the Minneapolis VA Hospital. Gregory was Chief of Gastroenterology at the Albuquerque VA Hospital and a consultant to the Indian Public Health Hospital in Gallup, N.M., where gallstones and their complications were of epidemic proportion. Gregory had already published eight publications in peer-reviewed journals between 1966 and 1972, so he was receptive to collaboration with the Richmond team of Swell, Vlahcevic and colleagues who wished to study bile acid kinetics in the Indians. It seems likely that the study of the Indians would not have occurred had Gregory not had a very good relationship with a young Indian Chief whose mother suffered from gallstone complications. The Navajo Tribal Council reviewed and approved a protocol in which Indian subjects were used in clinical research that demonstrated that all Indians, male and female, had diminished bile acid pools and the bile was lithogenic.[242, 243]

The team of Swell, Vlahcevic and Gregory was so felicitous that Gregory moved to the Richmond VA in 1972 and soon became Associate Chief of Staff for Research. From 1972 until his departure in 1979, Gregory published twenty articles in peer-reviewed journals, most with Vlahcevic. From 1966 to 2000, Vlahcevic published 96 articles in peer-reviewed journals. Each of the three co-investigators, Swell, Vlahcevic and Gregory, made special contributions to the esprit de corps that rendered the collaboration very productive.

The importance of the studies on bile acids derive from the fact that, in humans, gallstones form in the biliary tree when bile acid concentrations are low in the bile. These experiments have led to the administration of bile acids in man to dissolve existing gallstones.

The second investigator whose VA research career was very much affected by Franz Ingelfinger's leadership is Robert M. Donaldson, M.D. Donaldson received his M.D. from Boston University in 1952. After an internship at Montreal General Hospital, he spent two years in the U.S. Navy. In 1955, he returned for a two-year medical residency at the Boston VA Hospital with Dr. Maurice Strauss, which was followed by a two-year fellowship in gastroenterology with Dr. Seymour Gray. In 1959, Donaldson returned to the Boston VA Hospital for a five-year Clinical Investigatorship with Ingelfinger as his mentor. During his five years at the Boston VA Hospital, Donaldson made substantial contributions, particularly to the understanding of the pathogenesis of steatorrhea in the blind loop syndrome[244, 245] and published nine peer-reviewed research papers. In 1964-7, he spent three years in Madison, Wisconsin with Robert Schilling, then headed the Gastroenterology section at Boston University for six years. In 1973, Donaldson moved to the West Haven VA Hospital where he spent twelve productive years before moving to the Dean's Office at Yale. While at the West Haven VA, his particular research interests were intrinsic factor and its secretion[246, 247] and absorption of cobalamin.[248] In addition, he published twelve other peer-reviewed articles and many editorials and other advisory papers.

The third fellow of Franz Ingelfinger to make major contributions to research in the VA is Dr. Charles E. Pope. He received his M.D. at Western Reserve University in 1957, spent two years in training at Strong Memorial Hospital in Rochester, NY and then completed a two-year medical residency at University of Washington, Seattle. After a one-year fellowship with Dame Sheila Sherlock at the Royal Free Hospital in London, he had a two-year fellowship with Franz Ingelfinger. Upon completing it, Ingelfinger "encouraged him" to consider the VA as a next step. Wade Volwiler was Head of Gastroenterology at the University of Washington and he recruited Pope to the VA, where he became a Clinical Investigator in 1965 and Chief of Gastroenterology in 1967. Working full-time at the VA and maintaining strong university connections for thirty years, Pope is at the time of writing arguably the foremost U.S. expert on esophageal motility. During his VA career, he has published 55 original papers in peer-reviewed journals and many editorials and reviews, which is, of course, to be expected from a highly respected clinical investigator. His particular interests were several: mechanics of the lower esophageal stricture,[249, 250] measuring the force of esophageal peristalsis,[251] histologic changes in the esophageal mucosa in reflux[252, 253] and electromyography of human esophageal muscle.[254] Pope's studies have helped very much in the diagnosis of disturbances of motility of the esophagus in patients as well as the understanding and treatment of acid reflux from the stomach into the esophagus. This talented investigator has been a valuable asset to the VA, both because of his outstanding work and the high esteem in which he is held in his profession.

The fourth member of the Ingelfinger coterie to join the VA was Ward A. Olsen. After receiving his M.D. in 1959 from the University of Wisconsin Medical School and completing an internship and residency at the Boston City Hospital, he spent two years in the military, and then took a chief residency. From 1965 to 1967, he had a fellowship with Ingelfinger, joining the VA in Madison, Wisconsin in 1968. During the next thirty years at the VA, he compiled an excellent clinical and research record, publishing forty-two papers in excellent peer-reviewed journals. His principal subjects of study were intestinal absorption,[255, 256] the effect of ricinoleic acid and other surfactants on small intestinal structure and function,[257, 258] and intestinal sucrase activity.[259, 260] More recently, Olsen and his colleagues have studied lactase deficiency in man.[261, 262] Ward Olsen's research productivity at the Madison, Wisconsin VA Hospital has been consistently of very high quality.

The final physician to be discussed as an Ingelfinger acolyte is Dr. Edwin J. Englert. He received his M.D. from the Columbia University College of Physicians and Surgeons in 1951 and after house-staff training at Columbia and completion of a two- year fellowship with Ingelfinger (1957-1958), was recruited by Dr. Maxwell Wintrobe, Chair of Medicine of University of Utah, to be the first Chief of Gastroenterology at the University. Based at the VA, he published all of his research from the VA until his untimely death in 1985. Englert's interests were in gallstones in dogs and man[263-266] and participation in multi-center controlled trials.[267, 268] He published 25 articles in peer-reviewed journals during his tenure in Salt Lake City, and his leadership also paved the way for the innovative research of Dr. John G. Moore.

John Moore received his M.D. from the University of Utah in 1961. After an internship and residency at the St. Louis City Hospital, he took a fellowship with Englert at the University of Utah, which was followed in 1965 by a Chief Residency in medicine at Utah. He spent two years (1966-1968) in Vietnam with the U.S. Army and in 1968 joined the staff of the university-affiliated Salt Lake City VA Hospital. Between 1968 and 1995, he published 75 original research articles in peer-reviewed journals. His special contributions were observations on the circadian rhythm of gastric acid secretion in man,[269, 270] the circadian rhythm of the emptying of the stomach[271, 272] and other studies of gastric emptying.[273, 274] In addition, he conducted very interesting studies on the odor of modern and ancient (10,000 year old) stools.[275, 276] As with many other careers summarized in this chapter, the Salt Lake VA hospital was a congenial and stimulating place for research to thrive, and John Moore's research thrived in Utah.

The second major senior figure to influence younger colleagues in VA careers was Dr. Thomas P. Almy. He received his M.D. from Cornell University Medical College in 1939 and from 1943 to 1968 served on the Cornell faculty where he was responsible for training the next generation of gastroenterologists, a number of whom went on to conduct their own significant research in the VA. Almy influenced them profoundly. In a recent interview about the VA in the early 1950s, he said "the VA was a marvelous resource suddenly made available" and a "tremendous boon to academic medicine" because up to then, "most teaching of residents and fellows had been on patients who were part of a private practice system."[277] Researchers in the VA were not distracted by the financial aspects of private practice. In addition, the veteran patient typically supported VA research and was willing to participate.

In 1955, Tom Almy became Chief of the Cornell Division at Bellevue Hospital in New York City, a post that involved supervision of Cornell's academic activities at both Bellevue Hospital and the nearby VA. Similar academic posts at Bellevue existed for New York and Columbia Universities. The section devoted to Franz Ingelfinger's influence on VA research mentioned that Tom Almy had recruited the author of this chapter (John Farrar) to the VA Hospital in New York in 1955. Almy was also active in other activities at the VA including the selection of several Chiefs of Medicine.

Among Almy's most outstanding recruits to Bellevue and the VA system was Dr. Charles S. Lieber. Lieber received his M.D. in 1955 from the University of Brussels in Belgium. After an internship, residency and fellowship at the University Hospital in Brussels, in 1958 he came to the United States to work with Charles Davidson at the Thorndyke Memorial Lab (Harvard Services) at Boston City Hospital. In 1963, he moved to Almy's service at Bellevue, where he spent five years.   In 1967, when Bellevue Hospital's University services were all taken over by New York University, Lieber was recruited to the Veterans Hospital in the Bronx by the new chair of Medicine at Mt. Sinai Medical School, Dr. Solomon Berson, of radioimmunoassay fame. The Bronx VA extended an extremely warm welcome to Lieber and his entire unit, which moved with him.

In the course of more than thirty years at the VA, Charles Lieber established himself as one of the outstanding investigators in the country in the field of liver disease. Before Lieber's studies, the prevailing thinking was that alcoholic liver disease, from an acute fatty liver to cirrhosis, was probably caused by concomitant malnutrition rather than a direct effect of alcohol. In fact, Dr. Charles Davidson of the Thorndyke Lab in Boston, a mentor of Charles Lieber, was a strong proponent of the malnutrition theory of liver damage occurring with high alcohol intake. Lieber first established that alcohol itself is hepatotoxic, showing in volunteers given diets enriched with vitamins and protein on a metabolic ward that alcohol produced a fatty liver.[278] He also showed that in baboons even with adequate diets, alcohol caused both fatty liver and cirrhosis[279] and that these effects were associated with significant hematological changes even in the absence of poor nutrition.[280]   These studies are important because, up to then, many physicians had speculated for decades that damage to the liver in the alcoholic patient was caused more by poor nutrition than by alcohol itself.

Lieber and his group then undertook very important studies on the role of alcohol dehydrogenase in the metabolism of ethanol and the effect of drugs on that metabolism.[281-284] The striking hepatic changes observed in their human and animal studies led to the discovery of a new pathway of ethanol metabolism, the microsomal ethanol oxidizing system (MEOS) involving a unique form of cytochrome P-450, now called CYP2F1.[285-287] One of the very important aspects of this new metabolic pathway was that in addition to catalyzing ethanol oxidation, this system activates other compounds to highly toxic metabolites, explaining many alcohol-drug interactions as well as the increased vulnerability of heavy drinkers to analgesics, including acetaminophen.[288] Lieber and his team continued to pursue the effects of the increased blood acetaldehyde seen in alcoholics[289] on liver mitochondria,[290] myofibroblasts[291] and stellate cells[292] in primates. These findings suggest that acetaldehyde contributes to hepatic fibrogenesis.[293] In addition to the studies covered here, Lieber published in excess of 650 papers in peer-reviewed journals between 1968 and 2001. The VA system gave Charles Lieber the best of opportunities and he made the most of them, rewarding the VA and countless men and women with his imaginative and important research.

Marvin Sleisenger, M.D., was a close colleague of Almy and also made major contributions to the VA. Sleisenger received his M.D. from Harvard University in 1947. After three years of training in medicine at the Beth Israel Hospital in Boston, he took a two-year fellowship at the University of Pennsylvania with Dr. Tom Machella. At the end of his fellowship, he was recruited by Almy to the Gastroenterology Division at Cornell. In 1955, when Almy became Chief of the Cornell Division at Bellevue Hospital, Sleisenger was named as Chief of Gastroenterology at New York Hospital-Cornell University. After twelve very successful years at Cornell, Sleisenger was recruited as Chief of Medicine to the San Francisco VA Hospital, which had a very close affiliation with the University of California at San Francisco (UCSF). When Sleisenger moved to the San Francisco VA Hospital in 1967, it was to a medical complex that was attracting other prominent physicians from the East, most likely in response to UCSF and the VA Hospital administration's conscious effort to become an outstanding clinical and investigative center. Their effort was successful, with Sleisenger playing an important role in its success. From 1967 to 2001, he published 31 original articles in peer-reviewed journals and many other editorials and invited articles.

Sleisenger conducted important studies on peptide absorption[294, 295] and human colon cancer[296, 297] and genetic testing for colorectal cancer.[298] His most important research contributions at the VA, however, were recruiting and increasing the strength of the VA-Medical School bond. In 1968, he recruited Young S. Kim, M.D., to be Director of the Gastrointestinal Research Laboratory at the VA Medical Center. Kim received his M.D. from Cornell University Medical College in 1960. After an internship and assistant residency at Kings County-Downstate Medical Center, he had an N.I.H. Clinical Traineeship in gastroenterology at the Cornell Division of Bellevue Hospital with Almy from 1963 to 1965. After one year in the pathology department at Stanford University, Kim spent two years in biochemistry at New York Medical College. When he was recruited to the San Francisco VA Medical Center, he had already completed eight years of training that left him superbly equipped for a career in investigation.

At the San Francisco VA Medical Center, Kim and his colleagues have published more than 280 original articles in peer-reviewed journals. He is acknowledged to be an outstanding investigator. The areas of his particular interest are three: 1. Mucin glycoprotiens: elucidation of molecular biology, regulation and their role in biology, pathogenesis, diagnosis and therapy of colorectal and pancreatic cancer[299-301] 2. Intestinal brush border membrane peptidase and its role in protein digestion and peptide transport[302,]

[303] and 3. A molecular genetic study of familial colorectal cancer with emphasis on the epigenetic mechanism of gene regulation such as methylation of gene promoters.[304, 305]

Figure 23.2 Young Kim

One of Kim's important achievements is the training of research fellows. By 2002, he had trained 120 research fellows, including   Denis McCarthy, Hugh Freeman, C. Richard Boland, Peter Lance, Stephen Itzkowitz, Robert Bresalier, Neil Toribara and Samuel Ho. His contributions to science and the VA are very great owing to his individual ability, training of fellows and his support system, which was led by Marvin Sleisenger.

One other physician who was a product of the Almy-Sleisenger mentoring is Dr. David H. Law, IV. After receiving his M.D. in 1954 at Cornell University Medical College, Law remained at Cornell-New York Hospital for internship, residency and fellowship training. After spending 1958 to 1969 at Vanderbilt, he joined the VA in Albuquerque as Chief of the Medical Service, where he stayed for sixteen years before moving in 1985 to VA Central Office as the Director of Medical Services and then as Deputy Assistant Chief Medical Director for Hospital Based Services. During his twenty-seven years with the VA, David Law was an articulate supporter of excellence in clinical research. His own research interests were in Crohn's disease,[306, 307] total parenteral nutrition[308, 309] and medical ethics.[310]

The next wave" of gastroenterological investigators (1956–1969)

The next group of investigators joining the VA system included Julius Wenger in 1956 at the Atlanta VA Hospital, Harold Roth in 1957 at the Cleveland VAMC, Harold Conn in 1957 at the West Haven VAMC, Arvey Rogers in 1964 at the Miami VAMC, Raymond Koff in 1969 at the Boston VAMC, Gerald Salen in 1969 at the East Orange VAMC and Eugene Schiff in 1969 at the Miami VAMC.

Harold P. Roth earned his M.D. from Western Reserve University in 1939. After an internship at the Cincinnati General Hospital, he was a house officer at the Boston City Hospital and subsequently an Assistant Resident at Barnes Hospital in St. Louis. He then served in the Army from 1943 to 1946 and then returned to Cleveland, where he joined the VA Hospital in 1947. Primarily a clinical investigator, in mid-century Harold Roth earned great respect in the profession by publishing very insightful papers. From the mid-1950s until he took a senior position at the National Institutes of Health in 1974, he published thirty-three articles in peer-reviewed journals. Subjects for which he became well known are the treatment of peptic ulcer, the degree of patient compliance[311-314] and functional esophageal diseases.[315, 316] A very thoughtful and modest investigator, Harold Roth made substantial contributions to our knowledge while working at the Cleveland VAMC.

Julius Wenger received his M.D. from Northwestern University in 1949. After an internship at Michael Reese Hospital in Chicago, he had residencies in internal medicine at Goldwater Hospital and Montefiore Hospital, both in New York City. After a three-year fellowship with Drs. Joseph Kirsner and Walter Palmer at the University of Chicago, Wenger joined the staff of the Atlanta VA Hospital, which was closely affiliated with Emory University Medical School. He spent twenty-seven productive years (1956–1983) at the VA, publishing more than 50 articles in peer-reviewed journals. Of particular interest are his studies on the use and misuse of aspirin,[317] the use of magnet-tipped tubes for studies of the stomach and duodenum,[318] the finding of bile and trypsin in the stomach following a test meal,[319] absorption of bile by aluminum hydroxide,[320] studies of gastric acid secretion in pernicious anemia[321] and exfoliative cytology in the stomach.[322] In addition to these original articles, Julius Wenger played an important role in VA cooperative studies of gastric ulcer.[267, 323]

Harold Conn received his M.D. from the University of Michigan School of Medicine in 1950. After an internship at The Johns Hopkins Hospital, he took his residency and fellowship training at Yale University School of Medicine which included crucial time with the eminent hepatic pathologist, Gerald Klatskin. In 1957, Conn joined the staff of the West Haven VA Hospital, which was closely affiliated with Yale. During the years 1957–2001, Harold Conn published 220 original articles and many chapters and editorials on a very wide range of important subjects. Hepatic encephalopathy was a focus of many papers by Conn, specifically its treatment by lactulose[324-326] and innovative methods of assessing encephalopathy.[327] Other subjects to which Conn has made important contributions are the treatment of variceal hemorrhage with propranolol,[328, 329] the relation of corticosteroids to peptic ulcers[330, 331] and spontaneous bacterial peritonitis in patients with cirrhosis of the liver.[332, 333] He also produced valuable insights regarding observer variation in liver scans[334] and judging the value of submitted abstracts. In summary, Harold Conn played an important role in clinical research, particularly concerning the liver, in the U.S. during the later half of the 20th century. This role was due to his own talents, the excellence of Yale and the unstinting support of the VA where the work was done.

Arvey I. Rogers received his M.D. degree from the University of Texas in Galveston in 1958. After an internship at the Philadelphia General Hospital, he completed a residency in internal medicine at Jackson Memorial Hospital in Miami followed by fellowships in infectious diseases and gastroenterology. In 1964, he became Chief of the Gastrointestinal section at the VA Medical Center in Miami, remaining in this position until 1999. During this tenure, he published more than 75 clinical articles in peer-reviewed journals with many more editorials chapters and reviews. Of particular interest are his original contributions to enhancing the understanding of the mechanisms for neomycin-induced malabsorption,[335-337] his publications on Crohn's disease[338,339] and some original and innovative ways of teaching clinical cases.[340,341] Arvey Rogers was a stimulating clinical researcher who contributed substantially to the Miami VAMC during the last third of the twentieth century.

Raymond S. Koff received his M.D. from Albert Einstein College of Medicine in 1962. After an internship and residency in internal medicine at Barnes Hospital in St. Louis, he spent two years with the National Communicable Disease Commission in Boston and then completed a fellowship in gastroenterology at Massachusetts General Hospital from 1966 to 1969. In 1969, he joined the Boston VA Hospital as a Clinical Investigator and remained there for seventeen years. During that time, he published 65 original articles, almost all in peer-reviewed journals. His particular interests were in the mechanisms of liver injury,[342-344] the epidemiology of viral hepatitis[345-347] and hepatic amyloidosis.[348,349] This talented clinical investigator worked well with others and benefited from the tradition of excellence developed at the Boston VA Hospital by Drs. Maurice Strauss, Ingelfinger, Donaldson and others.

Gerald Salen received his M.D. from Jefferson University Medical College in 1961. After internship and residencies in internal medicine and training in gastroenterology at Jefferson, he spent two years under E. H. Ahrens at Rockefeller University. In 1969, in part because Dr. Norton Spritz had just become Chief of Medicine, he moved to the New York VA Hospital, where he spent four productive research years (1969–1973). In 1973, he moved to the East Orange VA Hospital, where he became one of the outstanding clinical and laboratory researchers in the country. While with the VA, by 2000 Salen and his colleagues had published 242 papers in peer-reviewed journals with a preponderance in journals of highest quality. Salen's contributions are substantial and can be divided into three groups: inherited disorders, treatment of gallstones and primary biliary cirrhosis with bile acids and regulation of bile acid synthesis. The inherited disorders they studied include: cerebrotendinous xanthomatosis and its treatment with chenodeoxycholic acid,[350] sitosterolemia, a syndrome of premature atherosclerosis caused by accumulation of plant sterols,[351] and Smith-Lemli-Opitz sydrome, in which people cannot manufacture cholesterol[352,353] and mutation in cholesterol 7 O hydroxylase is associated with a hypercholesterolemic phenotype.[354] Salen and his associates demonstrated the importance of treating primary biliary cirrhosis with ursodeoxycholic acid[355] and greatly increased our understanding of the regulation of bile acid synthesis.[356]

In an interview in October 2002, Gerald Salen deflected comment on his distinguished achievements by saying, "The VA has been marvelous to me. The leadership both locally and nationally has recognized the importance of science." Salen's success, although probably primarily a result of innate intelligence and drive, was also helped by influences from Jefferson, Rockefeller University and the New York VA Medical Center with its Cornell and NYU affiliations.[357]

Eugene R. Schiff received his M.D. from Columbia University College of Physicians and Surgeons in New York in 1962. After an internship and first-year residency at Cincinnati

General Hospital, he spent two years in the Public Health Service in San Francisco as an epidemic intelligence officer. In 1966-7, he had a second-year residency at Parkland Memorial Hospital, which was followed at the same institution by a two-year fellowship with Drs. John Dietschy and John Fordtran. In 1969, he was recruited by the University of Miami School of Medicine to be based at the Miami VA Hospital. Within a single year, Gene Schiff established the first stand-alone Hepatology section in the VA system, and he continued to lead this very productive section until 1985, when he moved to the Medical School. During his sixteen years at the Miami VAMC, he published approximately 80 original articles in peer-reviewed journals plus many book chapters and editorials. During his VA career, Gene Schiff earned a reputation for important research that helped him to become one of the nation's outstanding hepatologists. His particular interests while in the VA were studies of viral hepatitis, including hepatitis A and its sequelae,[358] hepatitis B,[359-361] including its prevalence in dentists,[362] and hepatitis C.[363] Another productive interest of his was cooperating with surgeons on important diagnostic[364] and therapeutic procedures in patients with liver disease.[365-368] His far-reaching cooperation with both surgeons and other prominent hepatologists were key to Gene Schiff's important record of achievement at the Miami VA Hospital.

The last wave of early VA investigators (1970–1975).

Of the early VA investigators, the last wave included Jay Donald Ostrow in 1970 at the Philadelphia VA Hospital; Steven Schenker in 1970 at the Nashville VAMC; Michael Sorrell in 1971 at the Omaha VAMC; Will Linscheer in 1972 at the Syracuse VAMC and Philip Toskes in 1973 at the Gainesville VAMC.

Jay Donald Ostrow received his M.D. from Harvard Medical School in 1954. After an internship at Johns Hopkins, he took a residency and fellowship at the Peter Bent Brigham Hospital and then embarked on a three-year research fellowship at the Thorndike Memorial Lab at the Boston City Hospital with Dr. Rudi Schmid. In 1962, Ostrow joined the faculty at Case Western Reserve; in 1970 he was recruited by Frank Brooks to the University of Pennsylvania, where he began his twenty-five-year-long career with the VA as Chief of Gastroenterology at the Philadelphia VA Hospital. His combination of native ability and superb training yielded an investigator who brought distinction to VA research programs. During his tenure in Philadelphia (1970–78) and the Chicago Lakeside VAMC (1978-1995), Ostrow published 55 original papers in excellent peer-reviewed journals plus many editorials, reviews and chapters. His interests centered on the chemistry of gallstone formation[369-373] and studies of bilirubin and its photoisomers[374-377] After his retirement, Ostrow continued working and publishing at the Seattle VAMC on bilirubin levels in Gilberts syndrome[378] and the interaction of human serum albumin and bilirubin.[379] In summary, he had a most productive and innovative research career.

Steven Schenker received his M.D. in 1955 from Cornell University Medical College. He took his internship and residencies in Internal Medicine at the Harvard Medical Services of the Boston City Hospital. After a fellowship in Gastroenterology at the University of Cincinnati College of Medicine, he spent two years as a Clinical Associate at the N.I.H. (1959-1961). Then he returned to Boston City Hospital - Thorndike Memorial Lab where he spent two years with Dr. Rudi Schmid. Next, Schenker spent another year in Cincinnati and six years on the faculty at the University of Texas, Southwestern Medical School in Dallas. While in Dallas, he worked with Dr. Burton Combes with whom he collaborated on twelve original papers. In 1970, Schenker was recruited by Vanderbilt University School of Medicine as a Professor of Medicine and Head, Division of Gastroenterology, a full-time position at the VA Hospital in Nashville. This extensive recounting of Schenker's training is important because of its length and extraordinarily high quality. Admittedly, his time in Dallas was not, strictly speaking, training since he was an Assistant and then Associate Professor. In addition, before he arrived at the VA in Nashville, he had already published 56 original articles. Still, it is an important lesson for those interested in serious research. A splendid fifteen years of "training" with such mentors as Drs. Leon Schiff, Rudi Schmid and Burton Combes is a hard record to beat! Steve Schenker's devotion to high quality certainly paid off in excellent research productivity in his twelve years at the Nashville VA Hospital and thirteen years at the Audie L. Murphy Memorial Veterans Hospital in San Antonio, Texas. While associated with these two hospitals, he published 141 original papers in very good peer-reviewed journals on a wide variety of subjects primarily related to the liver, ethanol, nutrition and the metabolism of drugs.

Several advancements made by Steven Schenker and his colleagues are particularly notable. They demonstrated that analgesics and sedatives that are detoxified by oxidation in the liver (i.e. meperidine, chlordiazepoxide , diazepam) are under-metabolized by the diseased liver, whereas similar agents conjugated by glucuronidation (i.e. oxazepam, lorazepam and morphine) are relatively spared in the setting of mild to moderate liver disease.[380-387] These concepts have stood the test of time and are clinically useful because the dosage of many drugs will depend on the presence of normal or impaired metabolism in the liver. Another major contribution made by Schenker and his colleagues was the demonstration that fat accumulation in the liver caused by tetracycline toxicity is the result, at least in part, of impaired exit of fat via VLDL from the liver.[388, 389] Schenker compiled a superb record as an innovative and talented investigator, mostly within the VA system.

Michael F. Sorrell received his M.D. from the University of Nebraska School of Medicine in 1959. After an internship at Nebraska, he spent six years in the private practice of medicine, then in 1966 returned to Nebraska for his residency and gastroenterology fellowship. In 1969, he took another fellowship with Dr. Carroll Leevy in New Jersey. He joined the Omaha VA Hospital in 1971 as a Director of the Alcohol Center and remained in the VA until 2000 for a highly productive and innovative career of research, primarily on the liver. During Sorrell's twenty-nine VA years, he published 156 original articles in peer-reviewed journals and became one of the leaders among hepatologists and liver transplantation experts. His particular interests were the effects of ethanol and acetaldehyde on the metabolism of proteins in the liver cells,[390-396] the role of immunology in alcoholic liver disease,[397, 398] and the role of liver transplantation.[399, 400] Sorrell distinguished himself as an energetic and important research scientist.

Willem G. Linscheer received his M.D. from the University of Leiden in Belgium in 1951. After a decade's training in medicine and gastroenterology in Belgium, in 1962 he was recruited by Dr. Thomas Chalmers at the Lemuel Shattack Hospital in Boston. He remained there ten years, publishing eighteen original papers with Edward Moore, Frank Iber and Chalmers, a very talented group. In 1972, Linscheer joined the Syracuse VAMC, where he had a productive research career until his retirement in 1999. During these twenty-seven years, he published 39 original articles in peer-reviewed journals. His particular contributions were on the mechanisms of the protective effect of propylthiouracil on acetaminophen toxicity[401-405] and on cholesterol and oleic acid absorption and metabolism.[406-408] This modest, productive scientist, trained abroad, made substantial contributions in this country and to its veterans.

Philip P. Toskes received his M.D. from the University of Maryland School of Medicine in 1965. After a medical internship and two-year residency at the University of Maryland Hospital, he completed a two-year fellowship at the University of Pennsylvania with Dr. Frank Brooks, which was followed by three years as a Research Internist at the Walter Reed Army Institute of Research. In 1973, Toskes was recruited by the University of Florida College of Medicine in Gainesville to be a Research and Education Associate, later a Clinical Investigator and Chief of Gastroenterology at the Gainesville VA Medical Center, where he remained until 1985 when he moved full-time to the Medical School. Toskes's VA tenure yielded excellent research, including the publication of 43 articles in peer-reviewed journals and many other editorials and chapters. During his VA years (1973–1985) Toskes became one of the country's acknowledged experts on the pancreas and pancreatic dysfunction.[409-411] Another particular interest of Toskes was small intestinal bacterial overgrowth,[412, 413] its detection by the d-(14C)-xylose breath test[414, 415] and altered myoelectric activity in experimental blind loop syndrome.[416] With Toskes's contributions to pancreatic physiology and blind loop syndrome, it is not surprising that other studies of impaired absorption and maldigestion were published.[417-419] The VA provided this talented investigator with the time and resources that allowed him to make significant scientific advances.

Summary

This review of the major early figures involved in research in gastroenterology within the VA system demonstrates the important role they played after WWII as part of the burgeoning research in this country. The protected time they enjoyed by working within the VA, the availability of patients and absence of the demands of private practice made the VA an ideal partner to the universities. Rarely, however, did research in gastroenterology in the VA flourish without a close university affiliation.

It would be marvelous to be able to document how the contributions of VA investigators have affected the diagnosis and treatment of disease as well as the effect on the cost of health care. Unfortunately, this cannot be easily accomplished because there is rarely a single advance that can be credited with these changes and the task of assigning credit would be divisive and daunting. Suffice it to say that the output of the 56 investigators discussed in this chapter and their role in research in gastroenterology is very impressive.

References

1. Smith, D.C., *The American Gastroenterological Association 1897-1997. A Century of Service to the Profession and the Public.* Bethesda, MD: AGA, 1999, 56.

2. Kirsner, J.B., *The Development of American Gastroenterology.* New York: Raven Press, 1990, 242-243.

3. Smith, *American Gastroenterological Service.* 1999a, 58.

4. White, B.V., "Thomas Angel Warthin, 1909-1997." *Trans Am Clin Climatol Assn*, 2001. **112**: xlix.

5. *Who's Who in America.* Marquis, 1998, 4517.

6. Drake, E.H. and Warthin, T.A., "Amebic Abscess of the Liver: Therapeutic Problems in Various Types of Late Hepatic Amebiasis." *N Engl J Med*, 1948. **239**: 45-49.

7. Warthin, T.A., Warren, R. and Wissing, E.G., "Combined Medical and Surgical Management of Upper Gastrointestinal Hemorrhage." *N Engl J Med*, 1949. **241**: 473-478.

8. Warthin, T.A., Ross, F.P., Bake, D.V. and Wissing, E.G., "Management of Upper Gastrointestinal Hemorrhage." *Ann Intern Med*, 1953. **139**: 241-253.

9. Warthin, T.A., Peterson, E.W. and Barr, J.H., Jr., "Treatment of Idiopathic Hemochromatosis by Repeated Phlebotomy." *Ann Intern Med*, 1953. **38**: 1066-1069.

10. Zimmerman, H.J., MacMurray, F.G., Rappaport, H. and Alpert, L.K., "Studies of the Liver in Diabetes Mellitus. I. Structural and Functional Abnormalities." *J Lab Clin Med*, 1950. **36**: 912-921.

11. Zimmerman, H.J., "Studies of the Liver in Diabetes Mellitus. Ii. The Significance of Fatty Metamorphosis and Its Correlation with Insulin Sensitivity." *J Lab Clin Med*, 1950. **36**: 922-928.

12. Zimmerman, H.J., Alpert, L.K. and Howe, J.S., "The Effect of Nitrogen Mustard on Liver Function and Structure in Patients with Neoplastic Disease." *J Lab Clin Med*, 1952. **40**: 387-389.

13. Thomas, L.J. and Zimmerman, H.J., "The Pattern of Liver Abnormality in Metastatic Carcinoma." *J Lab Clin Med*, 1952. **39**: 882-887.

14. Humoller, F. and Zimmerman, H., "Relation of Choline Oxidase Activity to Dietary Fatty Livers." *Am J Physiol*, 1953. **174**: 199-202.

15. Telephone interview with Leonard Seeff, M.D., February 15, 2002.

16. Finkelstein, J.D., "Methionine Metabolism in Mammals: Effects of Age, Diet, and Hormones on Three Enzymes of the Pathway in Rat Tissues." *Arch Biochem Biophys*, 1967. **122**: 583-590.

17. Finkelstein, J.D. and Martin, J.J., "Methionine Metabolism in Mammals. Distribution of Homocysteine between Competing Pathways." *J Biol Chem*, 1984. **259**: 9508-9513.

18. Finkelstein, J.D., "Transmethylation in Liver Diseases." in *Cholestasis*, Gentilini, P. and others, Editors. 1994, Elsevier Science Chapter 26.

19. Finkelstein, J.D., Martin, J.J. and Harris, B.J., "Methionine Metabolism in Mammals. The Methionine-Sparing Effect of Cystine." *J Biol Chem*, 1988. **263**: 11750-11754.

20. Finkelstein, J.D., Kyle, W.E. and Martin, J.J., "Abnormal Methionine Adenosyltransferase in Hypermethioninemia." *Biochem Biophys Res Commun*, 1975. **66**: 1491-1497.

21. Finkelstein, J.D., Harris, B.J., Martin, J.J. and Kyle, W.E., "Regulation of Hepatic Betaine-Homocysteine Methyltransferase by Dietary Methionine." *Biochem Biophys Res Commun*, 1982. **108**: 344-348.

22. Tabor, E., Gerety, R.J., Drucker, J.A., Seeff, L.B., Hoofnagle, J.H., Jackson, D.R., April, M., Barker, L.F. and Pineda-Tamondong, G., "Transmission of Non-a, Non-B Hepatitis from Man to Chimpanzee." *Lancet*, 1978. **1**: 463-466.

23. Hoofnagle, J.H., Seeff, L.B., Bales, Z.B. and Zimmerman, H.J., "Type B Hepatitis after Transfusion with Blood Containing Antibody to Hepatitis Core Antigen." *N Engl J Med*, 1978. **298**: 1379-1383.

24. Hoofnagle, J.H., Seeff, L.B., Bales, Z.B., Wright, E.C. and Zimmerman, H.J., "Passive-Active Immunity from Hepatitis B Immune Globulin. Reanalysis of a Veterans Administration Cooperative Study of Needle-Stick Hepatitis. The Veterans Administration Cooperative Study Group." *Ann Intern Med*, 1979. **91**: 813-818.

25. Seeff, L.B. and others, "Type B Hepatitis after Needle-Stick Exposure: Prevention with Hepatitis B Immune Globulin - Final Report of the Veterans Administration Cooperative Study." *Ann Intern Med*, 1978. **88**: 285-293.

26. Seeff, L.B., Zimmerman, H.J., Wright, E.C., Finkelstein, J.D., Garcia-Pont, P., Greenlee, H.B., Dietz, A.A., Leevy, C.M., Tamburro, C.H., Schiff, E.R., Schimmel, E.M., Zemel, R., Zimmon, D.S. and McCollum, R.W., "A Randomized, Double Blind Controlled Trial of the Efficacy of Immune Serum Globulin for the Prevention of Post-Transfusion Hepatitis. A Veterans Administration Cooperative Study." *Gastroenterology*, 1977. **72**: 111-121.

27. Seeff, L.B., Cuccherini, B.A., Zimmerman, H.J., Adler, E. and Benjamin, S.B., "Acetaminophen Hepatotoxicity in Alcoholics. A Therapeutic Misadventure." *Ann Intern Med*, 1986. **104**: 399-404.

28. Seeff, L.B., Hollinger, F.B., Alter, H.J., Wright, E.C., Cain, C.M., Buskell, Z.J., Ishak, K.G., Iber, F.L., Toro, D., Samanta, A., Koretz, R.L., Perrillo, R.P., Goodman, Z.D., Knodell, R.G., Gitnick, G., Morgan, T.R., Schiff, E.R., Lasky, S., Stevens, C., Vlahcevic, R.Z., Weinshel, E., Tanwandee, T., Lin, H.J. and Barbosa, L., "Long-Term Mortality and Morbidity of Transfusion-Associated Non-a, Non- B, and Type C Hepatitis: A National Heart, Lung, and Blood Institute Collaborative Study." *Hepatology*, 2001. **33**: 455-463.

29. Alter, H.J. and Seeff, L.B., "Recovery, Persistence, and Sequelae in Hepatitis C Virus Infection: A Perspective on Long-Term Outcome." *Semin Liver Dis*, 2000. **20**: 17-35.

30. Seeff, L.B., Miller, R.N., Rabkin, C.S., Buskell-Bales, Z., Straley-Eason, K.D., Smoak, B.L., Johnson, L.D., Lee, S.R. and Kaplan, E.L., "45-Year Follow-up of Hepatitis C Virus Infection in Healthy Young Adults." *Ann Intern Med*, 2000. **132**: 105-111.

31. Halsted, J., Adams, W., Sloan, S., Walters, R. and Bassett, S., "Clinical Effects of Acth in Ulcerative Colitis." *Gastroenterol*, 1951. **19**: 698-721.

32. Sloan, S., Briggs, J. and Halsted, J., "Acth Therapy for Ulcerative Colitis Complicated by Perforation of Coexisting Peptic Ulcer." *Gastroenterol*, 1951. **18**: 438-442.

33. Halsted, J., Yuhl, E., Stirrett, L. and Barker, W., "Association of Peptic Ulcer with Chronic Ulcerative Colitis." *Gastroenterology*, 1954. **26**: 65-69.

34.   Swendseid, M., Halsted, J. and Libby, R., "Excretion of Cobalt 60-Labeled Vitamin B12 after Total Gastrectomy." *Proc Soc Exper Biol and Med*, 1953. **83**: 226-228.

35.   Halsted, J., Gasster, M. and Drenick, E., "Absorption of Radioactive Vitamin B12 after Total Gastrectomy; Relation to Microcytic Anemia and to Site of Origin of Castle's Intrinsic Factor." *N Eng J Med*, 1954. **251**: 161-168.

36.   Swenseid, M., Gasster, M. and Halsted, J., "Limits of Absorption of Orally Administered Vitamin B12: Effect of Intrinsic Factor Source." *Proc Soc Exper Biol Med*, 1954. **86**: 834-836.

37.   Halsted, J., Swenseid, M., Gasster, M. and Lewis, P., "Absorption of Radioactive Vitamin B12 in Patients with Disease of Small Intestine: Relation to Macrocytic Anemia." *Trans Amer Clin Climat Assn*, 1955. **66**: 18-36.

38.   Halsted, J., Swenseid, M., Lewis, P. and Gasster, M., "Mechanisms Involved in Development of Vitamin B12 Deficiency." *Gastroenterology*, 1956. **30**: 21-36.

39.   Citrin, Y., Sterling, K. and Halsted, J., "The Mechanism of Hypoproteinemia Associated with Giant Hypertrophy of the Gastric Mucosa." *N Eng J Med*, 1957. **257**: 906-912.

40.   Halsted, J.A., "Geophagia in Man: Its Nature and Nutritional Effects." *Am J Clin Nutr*, 1968. **21**: 1384-1393.

41.   Halsted, J.A., Hackley, B.M. and Smith, J.C., "Plasma-Zinc and Copper in Pregnancy and after Oral Contraceptives." *Lancet*, 1968. **2**: 278-279.

42.   Halsted, J.A., "Nutrition Research in Developing Nations." *Am J Clin Nutr*, 1969. **22**: 823-827.

43.   Halsted, J.A. and Smith, J.C., "Plasma-Zinc in Health and Disease." *Lancet*, 1970. **1**: 322-324.

44.   Halsted, J.A. and Zimmerman, H.J., "Gastrointestinal and Liver Disease: Veterans Administration Hospitals." *Med Clinics N America*, 1968. **52**: 1265-1501.

45.   Telephone interview with John Balint, M.D., March 13, 2002.

46.   D.H. Gregory, personal communication with author, May 30, 2002.

47.   Zieve, L., Hill, E. and Nesbitt, S., "Studies of Liver Function Tests; Combined Intravenous Bromsulfalein-Hippuric Acid-Galactose Test." *J Lab Clin Med*, 1950. **36**: 705-709.

48.   Zieve, L., Hanson, M. and Hill, E., "Studies of Liver Function Tests; Derivation of Correlation Allowing Use of Bromsulfalein Test in Jaundiced Patients." *J Lab Clin Med*, 1951. **37**: 40-51.

49.   Zieve, L. and Hanson, M., "Studies of Liver Function Tests; Effect of Repeated Injections of Sodium Benzoate on Formation of Hippuric Acid in Patients with Liver Disease." *J Lab Clin Med*, 1953. **42**: 872-876.

50.   Zieve, L., "Studies of Liver Function Tests; Dependence of Percentage Cholesterol Esters Upon Degree of Jaundice.." *J Lab Clin Med*, 1953. **42**: 134-139.

51.   Zieve, L. and Hill, E., "Influence of Alcohol Consumption on Hepatic Function in Healthy, Gainfully Employed Men." *J Lab Clin Med*, 1953. **42**: 705-712.

52.   Zieve, L., Hill, E., Nesbitt, S. and Zieve, B., "Incidence of Residuals of Viral Hepatitis." *Gastroenterology*, 1953. **25**: 495-531.

53. Zieve, L. and Hill, E., "Note on Hepatic Function 1 to 3 Decades after Episode of Jaundice During Childhood." *Gastroenterology*, 1955. **28**: 418-423.

54. Zieve, L., "Pathogenesis of Hepatic Coma." *Arch Intern Med*, 1966. **118**: 211-223.

55. Derr, R.F. and Zieve, L., "Decreased Cerebral Uptake of Oxygen in Coma--a Consequence of Decreased Utilization of Atp." *J Neurochem*, 1973. **21**: 1555-1557.

56. Zieve, L., Doizaki, W.M. and Zieve, J., "Synergism between Mercaptans and Ammonia or Fatty Acids in the Production of Coma: A Possible Role for Mercaptans in the Pathogenesis of Hepatic Coma." *J Lab Clin Med*, 1974. **83**: 16-28.

57. Zieve, L., "Amino Acids in Liver Failure." *Gastroenterol*, 1979. **76**: 219-221.

58. Webster, P.D. and Zieve, L., "Clinical Significance of the Urine Amylase Excretion Rate." *Postgrad Med*, 1962. **31**: A18-A24.

59. Webster, P.D. and Zieve, L., "Alterations in Serum Content of Pancreatic Enzymes." *N Engl J Med*, 1962. **267**: 654-658.

60. Webster, P.D. and Zieve, L., "Alterations in Serum Content of Pancreatic Enzymes." *N Engl J Med*, 1962. **267**: 604-607.

61. Gregory, D.H. and Messner, R.P., "Studies on the Reliability of the Isotopic Calcium Absorption Test in Patients with Chronic Renal Disease." *J Lab Clin Med*, 1969. **74**: 464-471.

62. Shafer, R.B. and Gregory, D.H., "Calcium Malabsorption in Hyperthyroidism." *Gastroenterol*, 1979. **63**: 235-239.

63. Gregory, D.H. and Van Uelft, R., "Calcium Absorption Following Gastric Resection." *Am J Gastroenterol*, 1972. **57**: 34-40.

64. Vennes, J.A. and Silvis, S.E., "Endoscopic Visualization of Bile and Pancreatic Ducts." *Gastrointest Endosc*, 1972. **18**: 149-152.

65. Silvis, S.E., Rohrmann, C.A. and Vennes, J.A., "Diagnostic Criteria for the Evaluation of the Endoscopic Pancreatogram." *Gastrointest Endosc*, 1973. **20**: 51-55.

66. Rohrmann, C.A., Silvis, S.E. and Vennes, J.A., "Evaluation of the Endoscopic Pancreatogram." *Radiology*, 1974. **113**: 297-304.

67. Vennes, J.A., Jacobson, J.R. and Silvis, S.E., "Endoscopic Cholangiography for Biliary System Diagnosis." *Ann Intern Med*, 1974. **80**: 61-64.

68. Silvis, S.E., "Final Report on the United States Multicenter Trial Comparing Ranitidine to Cimetidine as Maintenance Therapy Following Healing of Duodenal Ulcer." *J Clin Gastroenterol*, 1985. **7**: 482-487.

69. Peura, D.A., Johnson, L.F., Burkhalter, E.L., Hogan, W.J., LoGuidice, J.A., Schapiro, M., Klasky, I., Belsito, A.A., Butler, M.L. and Silvis, S.E., "Use of Trifluoroisopropyl Cyanoacrylate Polymer (Mbr 4197) in Patients with Bleeding Peptic Ulcers of the Stomach and Duodenum: A Randomized Controlled Study." *J Clin Gastroenterol*, 1982. **4**: 325-328.

70. Silvis, S.E., "Presidential Address, 1982. Research in Gastrointestinal Endoscopy." *Gastrointest Endosc*, 1982. **28**: 231-232.

71. Duane, W.C., "The Intermicellar Bile Salt Concentration in Equilibrium with the Mixed- Micelles of Human Bile." *Biochim Biophys Acta*, 1975. **398**: 275-286.

72. Duane, W.C., Ginsberg, R.L. and Bennion, L.J., "Effects of Fasting on Bile Acid Metabolism and Biliary Lipid Composition in Man." *J Lipid Res*, 1976. **17**: 211-219.

73. Duane, W.C. and Hanson, K.C., "Role of Gallbladder Emptying and Small Bowel Transit in Regulation of Bile Acid Pool Size in Man." *J Lab Clin Med*, 1978. **92**: 858-872.

74. Duane, W.C., "Simulation of the Defect of Bile Acid Metabolism Associated with Cholesterol Cholelithiasis by Sorbitol Ingestion in Man." *J Lab Clin Med*, 1978. **91**: 969-978.

75. Duane, W.C. and Wiegand, D.M., "Mechanism by Which Bile Salt Disrupts the Gastric Mucosal Barrier in the Dog." *J Clin Invest*, 1980. **66**: 1044-1049.

76. Duane, W.C., Levitt, D.G., Mueller, S.M. and Behrens, J.C., "Regulation of Bile Acid Synthesis in Man. Presence of a Diurnal Rhythm." *J Clin Invest*, 1983. **72**: 1930-1936.

77. Mitchell, J.C., Logan, G.M., Stone, B.G. and Duane, W.C., "Effects of Lovastatin on Biliary Lipid Secretion and Bile Acid Metabolism in Humans." *J Lipid Res*, 1991. **32**: 71-78.

78. Duane, W.C., Levitt, M.D. and Elson, M.K., "Facilitated Method for Measurement of Biliary Secretion Rates in Healthy Humans." *J Lipid Res*, 1993. **34**: 859-863.

79. Bond, J.H. and Levitt, M.D., "Use of Breath Hydrogen (H2) to Quantitate Small Bowel Transit Time Following Partial Gastrectomy." *J Lab Clin Med*, 1977. **90**: 30-36.

80. Bond, J.H., Levitt, D.G. and Levitt, M.D., "Quantitation of Countercurrent Exchange During Passive Absorption from the Dog Small Intestine: Evidence for Marked Species Differences in the Efficiency of Exchange." *J Clin Invest*, 1977. **59**: 308-318.

81. Levitt, M.D., Aufderheide, T., Fetzer, C.A., Bond, J.H. and Levitt, D.G., "Use of Carbon Monoxide to Measure Luminal Stirring in the Rat Gut." *J Clin Invest*, 1984. **74**: 2056-2064.

82. Vennes, J.A. and Bond, J.H., "Approach to the Jaundiced Patient." *Gastroenterology*, 1983. **84**: 1615-1618.

83. Bond, J.H., "Endoscopy and the Evolution of the Gi Specialties: Asge Presidential Address--1993." *Gastrointest Endosc*, 1993. **39**: 725-728.

84. Bond, J.H., "Control of the Volume of Gastrointestinal Endoscopy." *Gastrointest Endosc*, 1993. **39**: 102-103.

85. Bond, J.H., "Studies Show That It Is Now Time to Vigorously Promote Screening for Colorectal Cancer." *Am J Med*, 1997. **102**: 329-330.

86. Bond, J.H., "Colorectal Cancer and Polyps: Clinical Decisions for Screening, Early Diagnosis, and Surveillance of High-Risk Groups." *Compr Ther*, 1996. **22**: 100-106.

87. Levin, B. and Bond, J.H., "Colorectal Cancer Screening: Recommendations of the U.S. Preventive Services Task Force. American Gastroenterological Association." *Gastroenterology*, 1996. **111**: 1381-1384.

88. Bond, J.H., "Polyp Guideline: Diagnosis, Treatment, and Surveillance for Patients with Colorectal Polyps. Practice Parameters Committee of the American College of Gastroenterology." *Am J Gastroenterol*, 2000. **95**: 3053-3063.

89.   Levitt, M.D., "Intestinal Gas Production--Recent Advances in Flatology." *N Engl J Med*, 1980. **302**: 1474-1475.

90.   Levitt, M.D. and Bond, J.H., "Flatulence." *Annu Rev Med*, 1980. **31**: 127-137.

91.   Strocchi, A., Furne, J.K., Ellis, C.J. and Levitt, M.D., "Competition for Hydrogen by Human Faecal Bacteria: Evidence for the Predominance of Methane Producing Bacteria." *Gut*, 1991. **32**: 1498-1501.

92.   Levitt, M.D. and Ellis, C., "Serum Isoamylase Measurements in Pancreatitis Complicating Chronic Renal Failure." *J Lab Clin Med*, 1978. **93**: 71-77.

93.   Levitt, M.D., Ellis, C.J. and Meier, P.B., "Extrapancreatic Origin of Chronic Unexplained Hyperamylasemia." *N Engl J Med*, 1980. **302**: 670-671.

94.   Levitt, M.D. and Ellis, C., "A Rapid and Simple Assay to Determine If Macroamylase Is the Cause of Hyperamylasemia." *Gastroenterology*, 1982. **83**: 378-382.

95.   Levitt, M.D., Levitt, D.G., Furne, J. and DeMaster, E.G., "Can the Liver Account for First-Pass Metabolism of Ethanol in the Rat?" *Am J Physiol*, 1994. **267**: G452-457.

96.   Levitt, M.D., Fine, C., Furne, J.K. and Levitt, D.G., "Use of Maltose Hydrolysis Measurements to Characterize the Interaction between the Aqueous Diffusion Barrier and the Epithelium in the Rat Jejunum." *J Clin Invest*, 1996. **97**: 2308-2315.

97.   Eiseman, B., Van Wyk, J. and Griffen, W.O., Jr., "Methods for Extracorporeal Hepatic Assist." *Surg Gynecol Obstet*, 1966. **123**: 522-530.

98.   Eiseman, B., Lindeman, G.M. and Johnson, J., "Method for Determining Patency of Portocaval Shunt." *Surg Forum*, 1955. **5**: 200-204.

99.   Eiseman, B., Bakewell, w. and Clark, G.M., "Studies in Ammonia Metabolism; I. Ammonia Metabolism and Glutamate Therapy in Hepatic Coma." *Am J Med*, 1956. **20**: 890-895.

100.   Eiseman, B., Fowler, W.G. and White, P.J., "The Role of Ammonia in the Production of Hepatic Coma." *Surg Forum*, 1956. **6**: 369.

101.   Clark, G.M. and Eiseman, B., "Studies in Ammonia Metabolism. Iv. Biochemical Changes in Brain Tissue of Dogs During Ammonia Induced Coma." *N Eng J Med*, 1958. **259**: 178-180.

102.   Eiseman, B. and others, "Prolonged Hypothermia in Experimental Pneumococcal Peritonitis." *J Clin Invest*, 1956. **35**: 940-946.

103.   Wotkyns, R.S., Hirose, H. and Eiseman, B., "Prolonged Hypothermia in Experimental Pneumococcal Peritonitis. Ii. Survival of Hypothermic Animals and Effect of Combined Hypothermia and Antibiotics." *Surg Gynecol Obstet*, 1958. **107**: 363-369.

104.   Eiseman, B., Wotkyns, R.S. and Hirose, H., "Hypothermia and Infection: Three Mechanisms of Host Protection in Type 3 Pneumococcal Peritonitis." *Ann Surg*, 1964. **160**: 994-1006.

105.   Silen, W., Eiseman, B. and Brown, W., "Peptic Ulcer and Pulmonary Emphysema." *Am Rev Resp Dis*, 1959. **80**: 155-157.

106.   Silen, W. and Eiseman, B., "The Nature and Cause of Gastric Hypersecretion Following Portacaval Shunts." *Surgery*, 1959. **46**: 38-47.

107.   Brown, W.H., Earley, T. and Eiseman, B., "Common Duct Pressures Following Spincterotomy." *Surg Forum*, 1957. **7**: 419.

108.   Eiseman, B., Brown, W., Virabutr, S. and Gottesfeld, S., "Sphincterectomy: An Evaluation of Its Physiological Rationale." *Arch Surg*, 1959. **79**: 294-303.

109.   Eiseman, B., Knipe, P., McColl, H.A. and Orloff, M.J., "Isolated Liver Perfusion for Reducing Blood Ammonia." *Arch Surg*, 1961. **83**: 356-363.

110.   Eiseman, B., Liem, D.S. and Raffucci, F., "Heterologous Liver Perfusion in Treatment of Hepatic Failure." *Ann Surg*, 1965. **162**: 329-345.

111.   Kern, F., Jr., Eiseman, B. and Normell, L., "Lipid Metabolism in the Ex Vivo Perfused Liver." *Am J Clin Nutr*, 1965. **16**: 116-122.

112.   Liem, D.S., Waltuch, T.L. and Eiseman, B., "Function of the Ex Vivo Pig Liver Perfused with Human Blood." *Surg Forum*, 1964. **15**: 90.

113.   Moore, T.C., Normel, L. and Eiseman, B., "Effect of Seritonin Loading on Histamine Release and Blood Flow of Isolated Perfused Liver and Lung." *Arch Surg*, 1963. **87**: 42.

114.   Telephone interview with Thomas Starzl, M.D., March 2002.

115.   Starzl, T.E., Kaupp, H.A., Jr., Brock, D.R., Lazarus, R.E. and Johnson, R.V., "Reconstructive Problems in Canine Liver Homotransplantation with Special Reference to the Postoperative Role of Hepatic Venous Flow." *Surg Gynecol Obstet*, 1960. **111**: 733-743.

116.   Starzl, T.E., Kaupp, H.A., Jr., Brock, D.R. and Linman, J.W., "Studies on the Rejection of the Transplanted Homologous Dog Liver." *Surg Gynecol Obstet*, 1961. **112**: 135-144.

117.   Starzl, T.E., Marchioro, T.L., von Kaulla, K.N., Hermann, G., Brittain, R.S. and Waddell, W.R., "Homotransplantation of the Liver in Humans." *Surg Gynecol Obstet*, 1963. **117**: 659-676.

118.   Marchioro, T.L., Axtell, H.K., LaVia, M.F., Waddell, W.R. and Starzl, T.E., "The Role of Adrenocortical Steroids in Reversing Established Homograft Rejection." *Surgery*, 1964. **55**: 412-417.

119.   Starzl, T.E. and Marchioro, T.L., "The Reversal of Rejection in Human Renal Homografts with Subsequent Development of Homograft Tolerance." *Surg Gynecol Obstet*, 1963. **117**: 385-395.

120.   Brettschneider, L., Daloze, P.M., Huguet, C., Porter, K.A., Groth, D.G., Kashiwagi, N., Hutchison, D.E. and Starzl, T.E., "The Use of Combined Preservation Techniques for Extended Storage of Orthoptic Liver Homografts." *Surg Gynecol Obstet*, 1968. **126**: 263-274.

121.   Starzl, T.E., Weil, R., 3rd, Iwatsuki, S., Klintmalm, G., Schroter, G.P., Koep, L.J., Iwaki, Y., Terasaki, P.I. and Porter, K.A., "The Use of Cyclosporin a and Prednisone in Cadaver Kidney Transplantation." *Surg Gynecol Obstet*, 1980. **151**: 17-26.

122.   Starzl, T.E., Groth, C.G., Brettschneider, L., Penn, I., Fulginiti, V.A., Moon, J.B., Blanchard, H., Martin, A.J., Jr. and Porter, K.A., "Orthotopic Homotransplantation of the Human Liver." *Ann Surg*, 1968. **168**: 392-415.

123.   Francavilla, A., Hagiya, M., Porter, K.A., Polimeno, L., Ihara, I. and Starzl, T.E., "Augmenter of Liver Regeneration: Its Place in the Universe of Hepatic Growth Factors." *Hepatology*, 1994. **20**: 747-757.

124. Starzl, T.E., *The Puzzle People: Memoirs of a Transplant Surgeon.* Pittsburgh and London: University of Pittsburgh Press, 1992

125. Haubrick, W.S., "Gastrointestinal Endoscopy", in *The Growth of Gastroenterologic Knowledge During the 20th Century*, Joseph B. Kirsner, Editor. 1944, Lea and Febiger: Baltimore Chapter 30.

126. Stempien, S.J. and Greene, W.W., "Gastroscopy under Pentathol-Curare Anesthesia." *Gastroenterol*, 1958. **10**: 978-981.

127. Schindler, R. and Dagradi, A.E., "Gastroscopic Observations Following Various Types of Surgery for Gastroduodenal Ulcer." *Surg Gynec Obst*, 1955. **100**: 78-82.

128. Stempian, S.J., Dagradi, A.E., Sanders, D.M. and Schindler, R., "Clinical and Radiological Correlations with Optical Esophagoscopy." *Jama*, 1955. **159**: 22-23.

129. Dagradi, A.E., Killeen, R.N. and Schindler, R., "Esophageal Hiatus Sliding Hernia; an Endoscopic Study." *Gastroenterology*, 1958. **35**: 54-61.

130. Dagradi, A.E., Graves, J.G., Stempian, S.J. and Schindler, R., "The Value and Limitations of Gastroscopy in the Diagnosis of Antral Lesions." *Amer J Dig Dis*, 1962. **7**: 993-1000.

131. Dagradi, A.E. and Johnson, D.E., "An Evaluation of Radiology and Gastroscopy in the Differential Diagnosis of Gastric Ulcer." *Gastroenterology*, 1957. **33**: 703-713.

132. Stempian, S.J., Dagradi, A.E. and Steinspir, L.J., "Intractable Duodenal Ulcer: Objective Evaluation as a Basis for Surgical Selection." *Am J Dig Dis*, 1963. **8**: 484-491.

133. Dagradi, A.E., Stempien, S.J. and Lee, E.R., "The Indication for Endoscopy in Acute Gastrointestinal Hemorrhage." *Gastrointest Endosc*, 1966. **13**: 22-24.

134. Dagradi, A.E., Stempien, S.J. and Owens, L.K., "Bleeding Esophagogastric Varices. An Endoscopic Study of 50 Cases." *Arch Surg*, 1966. **92**: 944-947.

135. Dagradi, A.E., Stempien, S.J., Juler, G., Broderick, J. and Wolinski, S., "The Mallory-Weiss Lesion: An Endoscopic Study of Thirty Cases." *Gastrointest Endosc*, 1967. **13**: 18-19.

136. Dagradi, A.E., Lee, E.R., Bosco, D.L. and Stempien, S.J., "The Clinical Spectrum of Hemorrhagic Erosive Gastritis." *Am J Gastroenterol*, 1973. **60**: 30-46.

137. Tyor, M.P. and Sieker, H.O., "Biochemical, Blood Gas and Peripheral Circulatory Alterations in Hepatic Coma." *Am J Med*, 1959. **27**: 50-59.

138. Owen, E.E., Tyor, M.P., Flanagan, J.F. and Berry, J.N., "The Kidney as a Source of Blood Ammonia in Patients with Liver Disease: The Effect of Acetazolamide." *J Clin Invest*, 1960. **39**: 288-294.

139. Owen, E.E., Tyor, M.P. and Giordano, D., "The Effect of Acute Alkalosis on Renal Metabolism of Ammonia in Cirrhotics." *J Clin Invest*, 1962. **41**: 1139-1144.

140. Janssen, B., Jr., Tyor, M.P., Owen, E.E. and Ruffin, J.M., "Absorption of I 131-Labeled Lipids after Introduodenal Administration; Effect of Lipid Prefeeding." *Gastroenterology*, 1960. **38**: 211-216.

141. Tyor, M.P. and Ruffin, J.M., "Effect of Prefeeding of Fat on I 131 Triolein Absorption in Subtotal Gastrectomy Patients." *Proc Soc Exp Biol Med*, 1958. **99**: 51-64.

552

142. Johnson, J.H., Horswell, R.R., Tyor, M.P., Owen, E.E. and Ruffin, J.M., "Effect of Intestinal Hormones on I-131-Triolein Absorption in Subtotal Gastrectomy Patients and Intubated Normal Persons." *Gastroenterology*, 1961. **41**: 215-219.

143. Paul Webster, M.D., personal communication with author, April 2002.

144. Webster, P.D., Gunn, L.D. and Tyor, M.P., "Effect of in Vivo Pancreozymin and Methacholine on Pancreatic Lipid Metabolism." *Am J Physiol*, 1966. **211**: 781-785.

145. Webster, P.D. and Tyor, M.P., "Effects of Fasting and Feeding on Uridine-3-H Incorporation into Rna by Pancreas Slices." *Am J Physiol*, 1967. **212**: 203-206.

146. Webster, P.D. and Tyor, M.P., "Effect of Fasting and Feeding on Lipid Metabolism of Pigeon Pancreas." *Am J Physiol*, 1966. **210**: 1076-1079.

147. Morisset, J.A. and Webster, P.D., "Effects of Fasting and Feeding on Protein Synthesis by the Rat Pancreas." *J Clin Invest*, 1972. **51**: 1-8.

148. Webster, P.D., Singh, M., Tucker, P.C. and Black, O., "Effects of Fasting and Feeding on the Pancreas." *Gastroenterology*, 1972. **62**: 600-605.

149. Black, O., Jr. and Webster, P.D., "Protein Synthesis in Pancreas of Fasted Pigeons." *J Cell Biol*, 1973. **57**: 1-8.

150. Mainz, D.L., Black, O. and Webster, P.D., "Hormonal Control of Pancreatic Growth." *J Clin Invest*, 1973. **52**: 2300-2304.

151. Dissin, J., Mills, L.R., Mains, D.L., Black, O., Jr. and Webster, P.D., 3rd, "Experimental Induction of Pancreatic Adenocarcinoma in Rats." *J Natl Cancer Inst*, 1975. **55**: 857-864.

152. Singh, M., LaSure, M.M. and Bockman, D.E., "Pancreatic Acinar Cell Function and Morphology in Rats Chronically Fed and Ethanol Diet." *Gastroenterol*, 1982. **82**: 425-434.

153. Singh, M., "Effect of Chronic Ethanol Feeding on Pancreatic Enzyme Secretion in Rats in Vitro." *Dig Dis Sci*, 1983. **28**: 117-123.

154. Perez-Jimenez, F., Bockman, D.E. and Singh, M., "Pancreatic Acinar Cell Function and Morphology in Rats Fed Zinc-Deficient and Marginal Zinc-Deficient Diets." *Gastroenterol*, 1986. **90**: 946-957.

155. Singh, M., "Effect of Thiamine Deficiency on Pancreatic Enzyme Secretion in Rats in Vitro." *Am J Clin Nutr*, 1982. **36**: 500-504.

156. Mansbach, C.M., 2nd, Cohen, R.S. and Leff, P.B., "Isolation and Properties of the Mixed Lipid Micelles Present in Intestinal Content During Fat Digestion in Man." *J Clin Invest*, 1975. **56**: 781-791.

157. Mansbach, C.M., 2nd, "The Origin of Chylomicron Phosphatidylcholine in the Rat." *J Clin Invest*, 1977. **60**: 411-420.

158. Mansbach, C.M., 2nd and Parthasarathy, S., "Regulation of De Novo Phosphatidylcholine Synthesis in Rat Intestine." *J Biol Chem*, 1979. **254**: 9688-9694.

159. Mansbach, C.M., 2nd, Pieroni, G. and Verger, R., "Intestinal Phospholipase, a Novel Enzyme." *J Clin Invest*, 1982. **69**: 368-376.

160. Halpern, J., Tso, P. and Mansbach, C.M., 2nd, "Mechanism of Lipid Mobilization by the Small Intestine after Transport Blockade." *J Clin Invest*, 1988. **82**: 74-81.

161. Mansbach, C.M., 2nd, "Phospholipases: Old Enzymes with New Meaning." *Gastroenterology*, 1990. **98**: 1369-1382.

162. Rao, R.H. and Mansbach, C.M., 2nd, "Alkaline Lipase in Rat Intestinal Mucosa: Physiological Parameters." *Arch Biochem Biophys*, 1993. **304**: 483-489.

163. Kumar, N.S. and Mansbach, C.M., 2nd, "Prechylomicron Transport Vesicle: Isolation and Partial Characterization." *Am J Physiol*, 1999. **276**: G378-386.

164. Mansbach, C.M. and Dowell, R., "Effect of Increasing Lipid Loads on the Ability of the Endoplasmic Reticulum to Transport Lipid to the Golgi." *J Lipid Res*, 2000. **41**: 605-612.

165. Dahlqvist, A., Hammond, J.B., Crane, R.K., Dunphy, J.V. and Littman, A., "Intestinal Lactase Deficiency and Lactose Intolerance in Adults. Preliminary Report." *Gastroenterology*, 1963. **45**: 488-491.

166. Littman, A. and Hammond, J.B., "Diarrhea in Adults Caused by Deficiency in Intestinal Disaccharidases." *Gastroenterology*, 1965. **48**: 237-249.

167. Littman, A., "The Veterans Administration Cooperative Study on Gastric Ulcer: Healing, Recurrence, Cancer." *Proc Inst Med Chic*, 1970. **28**: 67-68.

168. Littman, A., "The Veterans Administration Cooperative Study on Gastric Ulcer. 1. Goals and Design." *Gastroenterology*, 1971. **61**: Suppl 2:567-569.

169. Littman, A., Welch, R., Fruin, R.C. and Aronson, A.R., "Controlled Trials of Aluminum Hydroxide Gels for Peptic Ulcer." *Gastroenterology*, 1977. **73**: 6-10.

170. Bernstein, L.M. and Baker, L.A., "A Clinical Test for Esophagitis." *Gastroenterology*, 1958. **34**: 760-781.

171. Bernstein, L.M., Pacini, R., Fruin, R.C. and Gorvett, E., "Esophagitis as a Cause of Upper Abdominal Pain." *Jama*, 1958. **168**: 27-33.

172. Bernstein, L.M., Fruin, R.C. and Pacini, R., "Differentiation of Esophageal Pain from Angina Pectoris: Role of the Esophageal Acid Perfusion Test." *Medicine*, 1962. **41**: 143-162.

173. Grossman, M.I., Robertson, C.R. and Ivy, A.C., "Proof of a Hormonal Mechanism for Gastric Secretion - the Humoral Transmission of the Distension Stimulus." *Am J Physiol*, 1948. **153**: 1-9.

174. Walsh, J.H. and Isenberg, J.I., "Morton I. Grossman, the Man." *Gastroenterology*, 1982. **83**: 325-328.

175. Soll, A.H. "Morton I. Grossman." *Memorial service for Morton Grossman at UCLA, June 7, 1981*, 1981,

176. Todisco, A. and Yamada, T., "The History of Gastrointestinal Hormones." in *The Growth of Gastrointestinal Knowledge During the 20th Century*, Kirsner, J.B., Editor. 1994, Lea and Febiger: Philadelphia.

177. Grossman, M.I., Tracy, H.J. and Gregory, R.A., "Zollinger-Ellison Syndrome in a Bantu Woman, with Isolation of a Gastrin-Like Substance from the Primary and Secondary Tumors. Ii. Extraction of Gastrin-Like Activity from Tumors." *Gastroenterology*, 1961. **41**: 87-91.

178. Gregory, R.A., Tracy, H.J. and Grossman, M.I., "Isolation of Two Gastrins from Human Antral Mucosa." *Nature*, 1966. **209**: 583.

179. Poitras, P., Steinbach, J.H., VanDeventer, G., Code, C.F. and Walsh, J.H., "Motilin-Independent Ectopic Fronts of the Interdigestive Myoelectric Complex in Dogs." *Am J Physiol*, 1980. **239**: G215-220.

180. Kelly, D.G., Code, C.F., Lechago, J., Bugajski, J. and Schlegel, J.F., "Physiological and Morphological Characteristics of Progressive Disruption of the Canine Gastric Mucosal Barrier." *Dig Dis Sci*, 1979. **24**: 424-441.

181. Dayton, M.T., Schlegel, J.F. and Code, C.F., "The Effect of Celiac and Superior Mesenteric Ganglionectomy on the Canine Gastric Mucosal Barrier." *Surg Gastroenterol*, 1984. **3**: 63-67.

182. Holland, P.V., Walsh, J.H., Morrow, A.G. and Purcell, R.H., "Failure of Australia Antibody to Prevent Post-Transfusion Hepatitis." *Lancet*, 1969. **2**: 553-555.

183. Walsh, J.H., Purcell, R.H., Morrow, A.G., Chanock, R.M. and Schmidt, P.J., "Posttransfusion Hepatitis after Open-Heart Operations. Incidence after the Administration of Blood from Commercial and Volunteer Donor Populations." *Jama*, 1970. **211**: 261-265.

184. Walsh, J.H., Yalow, R. and Berson, S.A., "Detection of Australia Antigen and Antibody by Means of Radioimmunoassay Techniques." *J Infect Dis*, 1970. **121**: 550-554.

185. Isenberg, J.I., Walsh, J.H., Passaro, E., Jr., Moore, E.W. and Grossman, M.I., "Unusual Effect of Secretin on Serum Gastrin, Serum Calcium, and Gastric Acid Secretion in a Patient with Suspected Zollinger-Ellison Syndrome." *Gastroenterology*, 1972. **62**: 626-631.

186. Isenberg, J.I., Walsh, J.H. and Grossman, M.I., "Zollinger-Ellison Syndrome." *Gastroenterology*, 1973. **65**: 140-165.

187. Isenberg, J.I. and Maxwell, V., "Intravenous Infusion of Amino Acids Stimulates Gastric Acid Secretion in Man." *N Eng J Med*, 1978. **298**: 27-29.

188. Mainardi, M., Maxwell, V., Sturdevant, R.A. and Isenberg, J.I., "Metiamide, an H2-Receptor Blocker, as Inhibitor of Basal and Meal- Stimulated Gastric Acid Secretion in Patients with Duodenal Ulcer." *N Engl J Med*, 1974. **291**: 373-376.

189. Ippoliti, A.F., Sturdevant, R.A., Isenberg, J.I., Binder, M., Camacho, R., Cano, R., Cooney, C., Kline, M.M., Koretz, R.L., Meyer, J.H., Samloff, I.M., Schwabe, A.D., Strom, E.A., Valenzuela, J.E. and Wintroub, R.H., "Cimetidine Versus Intensive Antacid Therapy for Duodenal Ulcer: A Multicenter Trial." *Gastroenterology*, 1978. **74**: 393-395.

190. Cooke, A.R. and Grossman, M.I., "Studies on the Secretion and Motility of Brunner's Gland Pouches." *Gastroenterology*, 1966. **51**: 506-514.

191. Preshaw, R.M., Cooke, A.R. and Grossman, M.I., "Quantitative Aspects of Response of Canine Pancreas to Duodenal Acidification." *Am J Physiol*, 1966. **210**: 629-634.

192. Cooke, A.R., Nahrwold, D.L., Preshaw, R.M. and Grossman, M.I., "Comparison of Endogenous and Exogenous Gastrin in Stimulation of Acid and Pepsin Secretion." *Am J Physiol*, 1967. **213**: 432-436.

193. Cooke, A.R., Nahrwold, D.L. and Grossman, M.I., "Effect of Bilateral Adrenalectomy on Gastric Acid and Pepsin Secretion from Gastric Fistulas and Heidenhain Pouches in Dogs." *Gastroenterology*, 1967. **52**: 488-493.

194. Cooke, A.R. and Grossman, M.I., "Comparison of Stimulants of Antral Release of Gastrin." *Am J Physiol*, 1968. **215**: 314-317.

195. Telephone interview with James Clifton, M.D., January 29, 2002.

196. Christensen, J. and Lund, G.F., "Esophageal Responses to Distension and Electrical Stimulation." *J Clin Invest*, 1969. **48**: 408-419.

197. Christensen, J., "Patterns and Origin of Some Esophageal Responses to Stretch and Electrical Stimulation." *Gastroenterology*, 1970. **59**: 909-916.

198. Christensen, J., "Pharmacologic Identification of the Lower Esophageal Sphincter." *J Clin Invest*, 1970. **49**: 681-691.

199. Christensen, J. and Hauser, R.L., "Longitudinal Axial Coupling of Slow Waves in Proximal Cat Colon." *Am J Physiol*, 1971. **221**: 246-250.

200. Wienbeck, M. and Christensen, J., "Effects of Some Drugs on Electrical Activity of the Isolated Colon of the Cat." *Gastroenterology*, 1971. **61**: 470-478.

201. Christensen, J. and Rasmus, S.C., "Colon Slow Waves: Size of Oscillators and Rates of Spread." *Am J Physiol*, 1972. **223**: 1330-1333.

202. Christensen, J., Weisbrodt, N.W. and Hauser, R.L., "Electrical Slow Wave of the Proximal Colon of the Cat in Diarrhea." *Gastroenterology*, 1972. **62**: 1167-1173.

203. Christensen, J., Conklin, J.L. and Freeman, B.W., "Physiologic Specialization at Esophagogastric Junction in Three Species." *Am J Physiol*, 1973. **225**: 1265-1270.

204. Cooke, A.R., Chvasta, T.E. and Weisbrodt, N.W., "Effect of Pentagastrin on Emptying and Electrical and Motor Activity of the Dog Stomach." *Am J Physiol*, 1972. **223**: 934-938.

205. Anuras, S., Cooke, A.R. and Christensen, J., "An Inhibitory Innervation at the Gastroduodenal Junction." *J Clin Invest*, 1974. **54**: 529-535.

206. Cooke, A.R., "Duodenal Acidification: Role of First Part of Duodenum in Gastric Emptying and Secretion in Dogs." *Gastroenterology*, 1974. **67**: 85-92.

207. Cooke, A.R., "Control of Gastric Emptying and Motility." *Gastroenterology*, 1975. **68**: 804-816.

208. Cooke, A.R., "The Role of Acid in the Pathogenesis of Aspirin-Induced Gastrointestinal Erosions and Hemorrhage." *Am J Dig Dis*, 1973. **18**: 225-237.

209. Cooke, A.R. and Kienzle, M.G., "Studies of Anti-Inflammatory Drugs and Aliphatic Alcohols on Antral Mucosa." *Gastroenterology*, 1974. **66**: 56-62.

210. Stephens, J.R., Woolson, R.F. and Cooke, A.R., "Osmoltye and Tryptophan Receptors Controlling Gastric Emptying in the Dog." *Am J Physiol*, 1976. **231**: 848-853.

211. Ookhtens, M., Hobdy, K., Corvasce, M.C., Aw, T.Y. and Kaplowitz, N., "Sinusoidal Efflux of Glutathione in the Perfused Rat Liver. Evidence for a Carrier-Mediated Process." *J Clin Invest*, 1985. **75**: 258-265.

212. Fernandez-Checa, J.C., Ookhtens, M. and Kaplowitz, N., "Effect of Chronic Ethanol Feeding on Rat Hepatocytic Glutathione. Compartmentation, Efflux, and Response to Incubation with Ethanol." *J Clin Invest*, 1987. **80**: 57-62.

213. Ookhtens, M., Lyon, I., Fernandez-Checa, J. and Kaplowitz, N., "Inhibition of Glutathione Efflux in the Perfused Rat Liver and Isolated Hepatocytes by Organic Anions and Bilirubin. Kinetics, Sidedness, and Molecular Forms." *J Clin Invest*, 1988. **82**: 608-616.

214. Takikawa, H. and Kaplowitz, N., "Binding of Bile Acids, Oleic Acid, and Organic Anions by Rat and Human Hepatic Z Protein." *Arch Biochem Biophys*, 1986. **251**: 385-392.

215. Takikawa, H., Ookhtens, M., Stolz, A. and Kaplowitz, N., "Cyclical Oxidation-Reduction of the C3 Position on Bile Acids Catalyzed by 3 Alpha-Hydroxysteroid Dehydrogenase. Ii. Studies in the Prograde and Retrograde Single-Pass, Perfused Rat Liver and Inhibition by Indomethacin." *J Clin Invest*, 1987. **80**: 861-866.

216. Rothschild, M.A., Bauman, A., Yalow, R. and Berson, S.A., "Tissue Distribution of I131 Labelled Human Serum Albumin Following Intravenous Administration." *J Clin Invest*, 1955. **34**: 1354-1358.

217. Bauman, A. and Rothschild, M.A., "Rate of Intravascular Equilibration of Intravenously Administered I-131 Labeled Albumin in Various Body Sites." *J Lab Clin Med*, 1956. **48**: 20-25.

218. Rothschild, M.A., Bauman, A., Yalow, R.S. and Berson, S.A., "Effect of Splenomegaly on Blood Volume." *J Appl Physiol*, 1954. **6**: 701-706.

219. Bauman, A., Rothschild, M.A., Yalow, R. and Berson, S.A., "Pulmonary Circulation and Transcapillary Exchange of Electrolytes." *J Appl Physiol*, 1957. **11**: 353-361.

220. Interview with Marcus Rothschild, M.D., February 13, 1992 at Dr. Rothschild's home.

221. Rothschild, M.A., Schreiber, S.S., Oratz, M. and McGee, H.L., "The Effects of Adrenocortical Hormones on Albumin Metabolism Studied with Albumin-I-131." *J Clin Invest*, 1958. **37**: 1229-1235.

222. Rothschild, M.A., Oratz, M., Franklin, E.C. and Schreiber, S.S., "The Effect of Hypergammaglobulinemia on Albumin Metabolism in Hyperimmunized Rabbits Studied with Albumin-I-131." *J Clin Invest*, 1962. **41**: 1564-1571.

223. Rothschild, M.A., Oratz, M., Evans, C. and Schreiber, S.S., "Alterations in Albumin Metabolism after Serum and Albumin Infusions." *J Clin Invest*, 1964. **43**: 1874-1880.

224. Schreiber, S.S., Oratz, M., Evans, C., Reff, F., Klein, I. and Rothschild, M.A., "Cardiac Protein Degradation in Acute Overload in Vitro: Reutilization of Amino Acids." *Am J Physiol*, 1973. **224**: 338-345.

225. Schreiber, S.S., Oratz, M., Evans, C.D., Gueyikian, I. and Rothschild, M.A., "Myosin, Myoglobin, and Collagen Synthesis in Acute Cardiac Overload." *Am J Physiol*, 1970. **219**: 481-486.

226. Oratz, M., Rothschild, M.A. and Schreiber, S.S., "Alcohol, Amino Acids, and Albumin Synthesis. Ii. Alcohol Inhibition of Albumin Synthesis Reversed by Arginine and Spermine." *Gastroenterology*, 1976. **71**: 123-127.

227.   Kreek, M.J., Rothschild, M.A., Oratz, M., Mongelli, J. and Handley, A.C., "Acute Effects of Ethanol on Hepatic Uptake and Distribution of Narcotics in the Isolated Perfused Rabbit Liver." *Hepatology*, 1981. **1**: 419-423.

228.   Rothschild, M.A., Oratz, M. and Schreiber, S.S., "Effects of Ethanol on Protein Synthesis." *Ann N Y Acad Sci*, 1987. **492**: 233-244.

229.   Farrar, J.T., Zworykin, V.K. and Baum, J., "Pressure-Sensitive Telemetering Capsule for Study of Gastrointestinal Motility." *Science*, 1957. **126**: 975-976.

230.   Farrar, J.T. and Bernstein, J.S., "Recording of Intraluminal Gastrointestinal Pressures by a Radiotelemetering Capsule." *Gastroenterology*, 1958. **35**: 603-612.

231.   Horowitz, L. and Farrar, J.T., "Intraluminal Small Intestinal Pressures in Normal Patients and in Patients with Functional Gastrointestinal Disorders." *Gastroenterology*, 1962. **42**: 455-464.

232.   Grossier, V.W. and Farrar, J.T., "Absorption of Radioactive Sodium from the Intestinal Tract of Man. I Effect of Intestinal Motility. Ii. Effect of and Organomercurial." *J Clin Invest*, 1960. **39**: 1607-1618.

233.   Grossier, V.W. and Farrar, J.T., "Effect of Intestinal Motility on the Absorption of Sodium in Man." *Am J Dig Dis*, 1962. **7**: 57-68.

234.   Swell, L., Trout, E.C., Jr., Hopper, J.R., Field, H., Jr. and Treadwell, C.R., "Mechanism of Cholesterol Absorption. Ii. Changes in Free and Esterified Cholesterol Pools of Mucosa after Feeding Cholesterol-4-C14." *J Biol Chem*, 1958. **233**: 49-53.

235.   Swell, L., Trout, E.C., Jr., Hopper, J.R., Field, H., Jr. and Treadwell, C.R., "Mechanism of Cholesterol Absorption. I. Endogenous Dilution and Esterification of Fed Cholesterol-4-C14." *J Biol Chem*, 1958. **232**: 1-8.

236.   Swell, L., Law, D.H., Field, H., Jr. and Treadwell, C.R., "Composition of Lymph Cholesterol Ester Fatty Acids Feeding of Cholesterol and Oleic Acid." *Proc Soc Exp Biol Med*, 1960. **104**: 7-8.

237.   Swell, L., Field, H., Jr., Schools, P.E., Jr. and Treadwell, C.R., "Fatty Acid Composition of Tissue Cholesterol Esters in Elderly Humans with Atherosclerosis." *Proc Sac Exp Biol Med*, 1960. **1960**: 651-655.

238.   Gregory, D.H., personal communication with author,

239.   Swell, L., Bell, C.C.J. and Entenman, C., "Bile Acids and Lipid Metabolism. 3. Influence of Bile Acids on Phospholipids in Liver and Bile of the Isolated Perfused Dog Liver." *Biochim Biophys Acta*, 1968. **164**: 278-284.

240.   Admirand, W. and Small, D., "The Physiochemical Basis of Cholesterol Gallstone Formation in Man." *J Clin Invest*, 1968. **47**: 1043.

241.   Vlahcevic, Z.R., Bell, C.C., Buhac, I., Farrar, J.T. and Swell, L., "Diminished Bile Acid Pool Size in Patients with Gallstones." *Gastroenterology*, 1970. **59**: 165-173.

242.   Bell, C.C., McCormick, W.C., Gregory, D.H., Law, D.H., Vlahcevic, Z.R. and Swell, L., "Relationship of Bile Acid Pool Size to the Formation of Lithogenous Bile in Male Indians of the Southwest." *Surg Gynecol Obstet*, 1972. **134**: 473-478.

243. Vlahcevic, Z.R., Bell, C.C., Gregory, D.H., Buker, G., Juttijudata, P. and Swell, L., "Relationship of Bile Acid Pool Size to the Formation of Lithogenic Bile in Female Indians of the Southwest." *Gastroenterology*, 1972. **62**: 73-83.

244. Donaldson, R.M., Jr., "Studies on the Pathogenesis of Steatorrhea in the Blind Loop Syndrome." *J Clin Invest*, 1965. **44**: 1815-1825.

245. Donaldson, R.M.J., "Microbial Populations of the Human Intestine." *Gastroenterology*, 1967. **53**: 1003-1005.

246. Kapadia, C.R. and Donaldson, R.M.J., "Macromolecular Secretion by Isolated Gastric Mucosa: Fundamental Differences in Pepsinogen and Intrinsic Factor Secretion." *Gastroenterology*, 1978. **74**: 535-539.

247. Kapadia, C.R., Schafer, D.E., Donaldson, R.M.J. and Ebersole, E.R., "Evidence for Involvement of Cyclic Nucleotides in Intrinsic Factor Secretion by Isolated Rabbit Gastric Mucosa." *J Clin Invest*, 1979. **64**: 1044-1049.

248. Kapadia, C.R., Serfilippi, D., Voloshin, K. and Donaldson, R.M.J., "Intrinsic Factor-Mediated Absorption of Cobalamin by Guinea Pig Ileal Cells." *J Clin Invest*, 1983. **71**: 440-448.

249. Pope, C.E., 2nd, "A Dynamic Test of Sphincter Strength: Its Application to the Lower Esophageal Sphincter." *Gastroenterology*, 1967. **52**: 779-786.

250. Pope, C.E., 2nd, "Effect of Infusion on Force of Closure Measurements in the Human Esophagus." *Gastroenterology*, 1970. **58**: 616-624.

251. Pope, C.E., 2nd and Horton, P.F., "Intraluminal Force Transducer Measurements of Human Oesophageal Peristalsis." *Gut*, 1972. **13**: 464-470.

252. Pope, C.E., 2nd, "Mucosal Response to Esophageal Motor Disorders." *Arch Intern Med*, 1976. **136**: 549-555.

253. Brand, D.L., Eastwood, I.R., Martin, D., Carter, W.B. and Pope, C.E.n., "Esophageal Symptoms, Manometry, and Histology before and after Antireflux Surgery; a Long-Term Follow-up Study." *Gastroenterology*, 1979. **76**: 1393-1401.

254. Tibbling, L., Ask, P. and Pope, C.E.n., "Electromyography of Human Oesophageal Smooth Muscle." *Scand J Gastroenterology*, 1986. **21**: 559-567.

255. Olsen, W.A. and Rogers, L., "Intestinal Absorption in Diabetes: Binding of D-Glucose to Brush Borders." *Endocrinology*, 1971. **89**: 1329-1330.

256. Olsen, W.A. and Rosenberg, I.H., "Intestinal Transport of Sugars and Amino Acids in Diabetic Rats." *J Clin Invest*, 1970. **49**: 96-105.

257. Gaginella, T.S., Stewart, J.J., Gullikson, G.W., Olsen, W.A. and Bass, P., "Inhibition of Small Intestinal Mucosal and Smooth Muscle Cell Function by Ricinoleic Acid and Other Surfactants." *Life Sci*, 1975. **16**: 1595-1605.

258. Cline, W.S., Lorenzsonn, V., Benz, L., Bass, P. and Olsen, W.A., "The Effects of Sodium Ricinoleate on Small Intestinal Function and Structure." *J Clin Invest*, 1976. **58**: 380-390.

259. Olsen, W.A. and Korsmo, H., "The Intestinal Brush Border Membrane in Diabetes. Studies of Sucrase-Isomaltase Metabolism in Rats with Streptozotocin Diabetes." *J Clin Invest*, 1977. **60**: 181-188.

260.   Kaufman, M.A., Korsmo, H.A. and Olsen, W.A., "Circadian Rhythm of Intestinal Sucrase Activity in Rats. Mechanism of Enzyme Change." *J Clin Invest*, 1980. **65**: 1174-1181.

261.   Witte, J., Lloyd, M.L., Lorenzsohn, V., Korsmo, H. and Olsen, W.A., "Biosynthetic Basis of Adult Lactase Deficiency." *J Clin Invest*, 1990. **86**: 1138-1142.

262.   Lloyd, M., Fischer, M., Mevissen, G., Goodspeed, R., Olsen, W.A. and Montei, N., "Regulation of Intestinal Lactase in Adult Hypolactasia." *J Clin Invest*, 1992. **89**: 524-529.

263.   Englert, E.J., Harman, C.G. and Wales, E.E.J., "Gallstones Induced by Normal Foodstuffs in Dogs." *Nature*, 1969. **224**: 280-281.

264.   Cheung, L.V., Englert, E.J., Moody, F.G. and Wales, E.E., "Dissolution of Gallstones with Bile Salts, Lecithin, and Heparin." *Surgery*, 1974. **76**: 500-503.

265.   Englert, E.J., Harman, C.G., Freston, J.W., Straight, R.C. and Wales, E.E.J., "Studies on the Pathogenesis of Diet-Induced Dog Gallstones." *Am J Dig Dis*, 1977. **22**: 305-314.

266.   Wales, E.E., Englert, E., Peric-Golia, L. and Straight, R.C., "The Spontaneous Amorphous Black Pigment Gallstone of the Domestic Dog." *J Comp Pathol*, 1982. **92**: 381-385.

267.   Englert, E.J., Freston, J.W., Graham, D.Y., Finkelstein, W., Kruss, D.M., Priest, R.J., Raskin, J.B., Rhodes, J.B., Rogers, A.I., Wenger, J., Wilcox, L.L. and Crossley, R.J., "Cimetidine, Antacid, and Hospitalization in the Treatment of Benign Gastric Ulcer: A Multicenter Double Blind Study." *Gastroenterology*, 1978. **74**: 416-425.

268.   Graham, D.V., Akdamar, K., Dyck, W.P., Englert, E., Jr., Strickland, R.G., Achord, J.L., Belsito, A.A., Vlahcvevic, Z.R., Komfield, R.N. and Long, W.B., "Healing of Benign Gastric Ulcer: Comparison of Cimetidine and Placebo in the United States." *Ann Intern Med*, 1985. **102**: 573-576.

269.   Moore, J.G. and Englert, E., Jr., "Circadian Rhythm of Gastric Acid Secretion in Man." *Nature*, 1970. **226**: 1261-1262.

270.   Moore, J.G. and Halberg, F., "Circadian Rhythm of Gastric Acid Secretion in Men with Active Duodenal Ulcer." *Dig Dis Sci*, 1986. **31**: 1185-1191.

271.   Goo, R.H., Moore, J.G., Greenberg, E. and Alazraki, N.P., "Circadian Variation in Gastric Emptying of Meals in Humans." *Gastroenterology*, 1987. **93**: 515-518.

272.   Larsen, K.R., Moore, J.G. and Dayton, M.T., "Circadian Rhythms of Acid and Bicarbonate Efflux in Fasting Rat Stomach." *Am J Physiol*, 1991. **260**: G610-614.

273.   Moore, J.G., Christian, P.E., Datz, F.L. and Coleman, R.E., "Effect of Wine on Gastric Emptying in Humans." *Gastroenterology*, 1981. **81**: 1072-1075.

274.   Christian, P.E., Moore, J.G. and Datz, F.L., "Comparison of Tc-99m Labeled Liver and Liver Pate as Markers for Solid-Phase Gastric Emptying." *J Nucl Med*, 1984. **25**: 364-366.

275.   Moore, J.G., Krotoszynski, B.K. and O'Neill, H.J., "Fecal Odorgrams. A Method for Partial Reconstruction of Ancient and Modern Diets." *Dig Dis Sci*, 1984. **29**: 907-911.

276.   Moore, J.G., Straight, R.C., Osborne, D.N. and Wayne, A.W., "Olfactory, Gas Chromatographic and Mass-Spectral Analyses of Fecal Volatiles Traced to Ingested Licorice and Apple." *Biochem Biophys Res Commun*, 1985. **131**: 339-346.

277.   Almy, T.P., "Personal Interview with John Farrar, M.D." Dec. 1, 2001.

278.   Lieber, C.S. and Rubin, E., "Alcoholic Fatty Liver in Man on a High Protein and Low Fat Diet." *Am J Med*, 1968. **44**: 200-206.

279.   Lieber, C.S. and DeCarli, L.M., "An Experimental Model of Alcohol Feeding and Liver Injury in the Baboon." *J Med Primato*, 1974. **3**: 153-163.

280.   Lindenbawn, J. and Lieber, C.S., "Hematologic Effect of Alcohol in Man in the Absence of Nutritional Deficiency." *N Eng J Med*, 1969. **281**: 333-338.

281.   Di Padova, C., Roine, R., Frezza, M., Gentry, R.T., Baraona, E. and Lieber, C.S., "Effects of Ranitidine on Blood Alcohol Levels after Ethanol Ingestion: Comparison with Other H2-Receptor Antagonists." *JAMA*, 1992. **267**: 83-86.

282.   Dohmen, K., Baraona, E., Ishibashi, H., Pozzato, G., Moretti, M., Matsunaga, C., Fujimoto, K. and Lieber, C.S., "Ethnic Differences in Gastric O-Alcohol Dehydrogenase Activity and Ethanol First-Pass Metabolism." *Alcohol: Clin Exp Res*, 1996. **20**: 1569-1576.

283.   Frezza, M., Di Padova, C., Pozzato, G., Terpin, M., Baraona, E. and Lieber, C.S., "High Alcohol Levels in Women: Role of Decreased Gastric Alcohol Dehydrogenase Activity and First Pass Metabolism." *N Engl J Med*, 1990. **322**: 95-99.

284.   Yokoynma, H., Baraona, E. and Lieber, C.S., "Molecular Cloning and Chromosomal Localization of the Adh7 Gene Encoding Human Class Iv (O) Adh." *Genomics*, 1996. **31**: 243-245.

285.   Lieber, C.S. and DeCarli, L.M., "Ethanol Oxidation by Hepatic Microsomes: Adaptive Increase after Ethanol Feeding." *Science*, 1968. **162**: 917-918.

286.   Obnishi, K. and Lieber, C.S., "Reconstitution of the Microsomal Ethanol Oxidizing System (Meos): Qualitative and Quantitative Changes of Cytochrome P-450 after Chronic Ethanol Consumption." *J Biol Chem*, 1977. **252**: 7124-7131.

287.   Takahashi, T., Lasker, J.M., Rosman, A.S. and Lieber, C.S., "Induction of Cytochrome P4502e1 in Human Liver by Ethanol Is Caused by a Corresponding Increase in Encoding Messenger Rna." *Hepatology*, 1993. **17**: 236-245.

288.   Sato, C., Matsuda, Y. and Lieber, C.S., "Increased Hepatotoxicity of Acetaminophen after Chronic Ethanol Consumption in the Rat." *Gastroenterology*, 1981. **80**: 140-148.

289.   Korsten, M.A., Matsuzaki, S., Feinman, L. and Lieber, C.S., "High Blood Acetaldehyde Levels after Ethanol Administration: Differences between Alcoholic and Non-Alcoholic Subjects." *N Engl J Med*, 1975. **292**: 386-389.

290.   Lieber, C.S., Baraona, E., Hernandez-Munoz, R., Kubota, S., Sato, N., Kawano, S., Matsumura, T. and Inatomi, N., "Impaired Oxygen Utilization: A New Mechanism for the Hepatotoxicity of Ethanol in Sub-Human Primates." *J Clin Invest*, 1989. **83**: 1682-1690.

291.   Savolainen, E.R., Leo, M.A., Timpl, R. and Lieber, C.S., "Acetaldehyde and Lactate Stimulate Collagen Synthesis of Cultured Baboon Liver Myofibroblam." *Gastroenterology*, 1984. **87**: 777-787.

292.   Moshage, H., Casini, A. and Lieber, C.S., "Acetaldehyde Selectively Stimulates Collagen Production in Cultured Rat Liver Fat-Storing Cells but Not in Hepatocytes." *Hepatology*, 1990. **12**: 511-518.

293. Mak, K.M., Leo, M.A. and Lieber, C.S., "Alcoholic Liver Injury in Baboons: Transformation of Lipocytes to Transitional Cells." *Gastroenterology*, 1984. **81**: 188-200.

294. Addison, J.M., Burston, D., Dalrymple, J.A., Mathews, D.M., Payne, J.W., Sleisenger, M.H. and Wilkinson, S., "A Common Mechanism for Transport of Di- and Tri-Peptides by Hamster Jejunum in Vitro." *Clin Sci Mol Med*, 1975. **49**: 313-332.

295. Sleisenger, M.H., Burston, D., Dalrymple, J.A., Wilkinson, S. and Mathews, D.M., "Evidence for a Single Common Carrier for Uptake of a Dipeptide and a Tripeptide by Hamster Jejunum in Vitro." *Gastroenterologoy*, 1976. **71**: 76-81.

296. Toribara, N.W. and Sleisenger, M.H., "Screening for Colorectal Cancer." *N Engl J Med*, 1995. **332**: 861-867.

297. Bresalier, R.S., Ho, S.B., Schoeppner, H.L., Kim, Y.S., Sleisenger, M.H., Brodt, P. and Byrd, J.C., "Enhanced Sialylation of Mucin-Associated Carhobydrate Structures in Human Colon Cancer Metastasis." *Gastroenterology*, 1996. **110**: 1354-1367.

298. Terdiman, J.P., Conrad, P.G. and Sleisenger, M.H., "Genetic Testing in Hereditary Colorectal Cancer: Indications and Procedures." *Am J Gastroenterology*, 1999. **94**: 2344-2356.

299. Gum, J.R., Byrd, J.C., Hicks, J.W., Torlbara, N.W., Lamport, D.T.A. and Kim, Y.S., "Molecular Cloning of Human Intestinal Mucin Cdnas: Sequence Analysis and Evidence for Genetic Polymorphism." *J Biol Chem*, 1989. **264**: 6480-6487.

300. Lee, H.W., Ahn, O.H., Crawley, S.C., Li, J.D., Gum, J.R., Basbaum, C.B., Fan, N.O., Szymkowski, D.E., Han, S.V., Lee, B.H., Sleisenger, M.H. and Kim, Y.S., "Phorbol 12-Myristate 13-Acetate up-Regulates the Transcription of Muc2 Intestinal Mucin Via Ras Erk and Nj-Kb." *J Biol Chem*, 2002. **277**: 32624-32631.

301. Kim, G.E., Bae, H.I., Park, H.U., Kuan, S.F., Crawley, S.C., Ho, J.J.L. and Kim, Y.S., "Aberrant Expression of Muc5ac and Muc6 Gastric Mucins and Sialyl-Tn Antigen in Intraepithelial Neoplasms of the Pancreas." *Gastroenterology*, 2002. **123**: 1052-1060.

302. Kim, Y.S., Birthwistle, W. and Kim, Y.W., "Peptide Hydrolases in the Brush Border and Soluble Fractions of Small Intestinal Mucosa of Rat and Man." *J Clin Invest*, 1972. **51**: 1419-1430.

303. Erickson, R.H., Yoon, B.C., Koh, D.Y., Kim, D.H. and Kim, Y.S., "Dietary Induction of Angiotensin-Converting Enzyme in Proximal and Distal Rat Small Intesting." *Am J Physiol*, 2001. **281**: G1221-G1227.

304. Deng, G., Chen, A., Hong, J., Chae, H.S. and Kim, Y.S., "Methylation of Cpg in a Small Region of the Hmlh1 Promoter Invariably Correlates with the Absence of Gene Expression." *Cancer Res*, 1999. **59**: 2029-2033.

305. Terdiman, J.P., Gum, J.R., Conrad, P.G., Miller, G.A., Weinberg, V., Crawley, S.C., Levin, T.R., Reeves, C., Schmitt, A., Hepburn, M., Sleisenger, M.H. and Kim, Y.S., "Efficient Detection of Hereditary Nonpolyposis Colorectal Cancer Gene Carriers by Screening for Tumor Microsatellite Instability before Germline Genetic Testing." *Gastroenterology*, 2001. **120**: 21-30.

306. Cufley, G.A., Gregory, H.H., Danemann, H. and Law, D.H., "Crohn's Disease, 1961-1971: An Epidemiologic Study in Albuquerque, New Mexico." *Amer J Digestive Dis*, 1972. **17**: 954.

307. Singleton, J.W., Law, D.H. and Kelley, M.I., "National Cooperative Crohn's Disease Study: Adverse Reaction to Study Drugs." *Gastroenterology*, 1979. **77**: 870 (part 872 of 872 parts).

308. Law, D.H., "Total Parenteral Nutrition." *Advances in Internal Med*, 1972. **18**: 389-410.

309. Law, D.H., "Current Concepts in Nutrition. Total Parenteral Nutrition." *New Engl J Med*, 1977. **297**: 1104.

310. Nelson, W.A. and Law, D.H., "Clinical Ethics Education in the Department of Veterans Affairs." *Cambridge Quarterly of Healthcare Ethics*, 1994. **3**: 143-148.

311. Roth, H.P. and Berger, D.J., "Studies in Patient Cooperation in Ulcer Treatment. I. Observation of Actual as Compared to Prescribed Antacid Intake on a Hospital Ward." *Gastroenterology*, 1960. **38**: 630-633.

312. Roth, H.P., Caron, H.S., Ort, R.S., Berger, D.J., Merrill, R.S., Albee, G.W. and Streeter, G.A., "Patients' Belief About Peptic Ulcer and Its Treatment." *Ann Intern Med*, 1962. **56**: 72-80.

313. Roth, H.P., Caron, H.S. and Hsi, B.P., "Estimating a Patient's Cooperation with His Regimen." *Am J Med Sci*, 1971. **262**: 269-273.

314. Caron, H.S. and Roth, H.P., "Patients' Cooperation with a Medical Regimen. Difficulties in Identifying the Noncooperator." *JAMA*, 1968. **203**: 922-926.

315. Roth, H.P. and Fleshler, B., "Diffuse Esophageal Spasm; Clinical, Radiological, and Manometric Observations." *Ann Intern Med*, 1964. **61**: 914-923.

316. Kopald, H.H., Roth, H.P., Fleshier, B. and Pritchard, W.H., "Vagovagal Syncope; Report of a Case Associated with Diffuse Esophageal Spasm." *N Engl J Med*, 1964. **271**: 1238-1241.

317. Wenger, J. and Einstein, S., "The Use and Misuse of Aspirin: A Contemporary Problem." *Int J Addict*, 1970. **5**: 757-775.

318. Wenger, J., Allee, J.G. and Landy, M.S., "Magnet-Tipped Tubes for Studies of the Stomach and Duodenum." *Am J Dig Dis*, 1970. **15**: 383-393.

319. Wenger, J. and Trowbridge, C.G., "Bile and Trypsin in the Stomach Following a Test Meal." *South Med J*, 1971. **64**: 1063-1064.

320. Wenger, J. and Heymsfield, S., "Absorption of Bile by Aluminum Hydroxide." *J Clin Pharmacol*, 1974. **14**: 163-165.

321. Wenger, J., Backerman, I., Steinberg, J. and Gendel, B.R., "Studies of Gastric Hydrocholoric Acid Secretion in Pernicious Anemia: The Value of near-Maximal Stimulation Techniques." *Am J Med Sci*, 1967. **253**: 539-548.

322. Wenger, J. and Penfold, E., "An Improved Compressed Air Apparatus for Exfoliative Cytology of the Stomach." *Gastroenterology*, 1970. **59**: 358-363.

323. Wenger, J., Brandborg, L.L. and Spellman, F.A., "The Veterans Administration Cooperative Study on Gastric Ulcer. 6. Cancer I. Clinical Aspects." *Gastroenterology*, 1971. **61**: Suppl 2: 598-560.

324. Conn, H.O., Leevy, C.M., Vlahcevic, Z.R., Rodgers, J.B., Maddrey, W.C., Seeff, L. and Levy, L.L., "Comparison of Lactulose and Neomycin in the Treatment of Chronic Portal-Systemic Encephalopathy. A Double Blind Controlled Trial." *Gastroenterology*, 1977. **72**: 573-583.

325. Atterbury, C.E., Maddrey, W.C. and Conn, H.O., "Neomycin-Sorbitol and Lactulose in the Treatment of Acute Portal-Systemic Encephalopathy. A Controlled, Double-Blind Clinical Trial." *Am J Dig Dis*, 1978. **23**: 398-406.

326. Fessel, J.M. and Conn, H.O., "Lactulose in the Treatment of Acute Hepatic Encephalopathy." *Am J Med Sci*, 1973. **266**: 103-110.

327. Conn, H.O., "Trailmaking and Number-Connection Tests in the Assessment of Mental State in Portal Systemic Encephalopathy." *Am J Dlg Dis*, 1977. **22**: 541-550.

328. Conn, H.O., Grace, N.D., Bosch, J., Groszman, R.J., Rodes, J., Wright, S.C., Matloff, D.S., Garcia-Tsao, G., Fisher, R.L. and Navasa, M., "Propranolol in the Prevention of the First Hemorrhage from Esophagogastric Varices: A Multicenter Randomized Clinical Trial. The Boston-New Haven-Barcelona Portal Hypertension Study Group." *Hepatology*, 1991. **13**: 902-912.

329. Conn, H.O., "Prophylactic Propranolol: The First Big Step." *Hepatology*, 1994. **236**: 619-632.

330. Conn, H.O. and Poynard, T., "Corticosteroids and Peptic Ulcer: Meta-Analysis of Adverse Events During Steroid Therapy." *J Intern Med*, 1994. **236**: 619-632.

331. Conn, H.O. and Poynard, T., "Adrenocorticosteroid Administration and Peptic Ulcer: A Critical Analysis." *J Chronic Dis*, 1985. **38**: 457-468.

332. Conn, H.O., "Spontaneous Peritonitis and Bacteremia in Laennec's Cirrhosis Caused by Enteric Organisms. A Relatively Common but Rarely Recognized Syndrome." *Ann Intern Med*, 1964. **60**: 568-580.

333. Garcia-Tsao, G., Conn, H.O. and Lerner, E., "The Diagnosis of Bacterial Peritonitis: Comparison of Ph, Lactate Concentration and Leukocyte Count." *Hepatology*, 1985. **5**: 91-96.

334. Conn, H.O. and Spencer, R.P., "Observer Error in Liver Scans." *Gastroenterology*, 1972. **62**: 1085-1090.

335. Rogers, A.I., Vloedman, D.A., Bloom, E.C. and Kaiser, M.H., "Neomycin-Induced Steatorrhea." *JAMA*, 1966. **197**: 185-190.

336. Rogers, A.L. and Bachorik, P.S., "Neomycin Effects on Glucose Transport in Rat Small Intestine." *Digestion*, 1969. **1**: 159-164.

337. Rogers, I.A., "Malabsportion Due to Prolonged Administration of Neomycin." *Excerpta Medical Foundation, Drug Induced Diseases*, 1969. **3**: 141-155.

338. Harary, A., Gluck, C.A. and Rogers, A.I., "Gastric Retention of Enteric Coated Azulfidine Tablets: A Complication of Gastroduodenal Crohn's Disease." *Digestive Diseases and Sciences*, 1974. **29**: 1063-1065.

339. Harary, A. and Rogers, A.I., "Gastroduodenal Crohn's Disease." *Postgraduate Medicine*, 1983. **74**: 129-137.

340. Barkin, J.S. and Rogers, A.I., "A Hypothetical Case of Gastrointestinal Bleeding." *Postgraduate Medicine*, 1975. **57**: 107-122.

341. Reisman, T., Morton, R. and Rogers, A.I., "A Hypothetical Case of Chronic Diarrhea." *Postgraduate Medicine*, 1976. **59**: 203-209.

342. Koff, R.S., Fitts, J.J. and Satesin, S.M., "D-Galactosamine Hepatotoxicity. Ii. Mechanism of Fatty Liver Production." *Proc Soc Exp Biol Med*, 1971. **138**: 89-92.

343. Koff, R.S., Gordon, G. and Sabesin, S.M., "D-Galactosamine Hepatitis, I. Hepatocellular Injury and Fatty Liver Following a Single Dose." *Proc Soc Exp Biol Med*, 1971. **137**: 695.

344. Sabesin, S.M. and Koff, R.S., "D-Galactosamine Hepatotoxicity. Iv. Further Studies of the Pathogenesis of Fatty Liver." *Exp Mole Pathol*, 1976. **24**: 424-434.

345. Koff, R.S., "Epidemiology of Viral Hepatitis." *Crit Rev in Environmental Control*, 1970. **1**: 383.

346. Koff, R.S., Slavin, M.M., Connelly, L.J.D. and Rosen, D.R., "Contagiousness of Acute Hepatitis B." *Gastroenterology*, 1977. **72**: 297-300.

347. Hansson, B.G., Calhoun, J.K., Wong, D.C., Feinstone, S.M., Purcell, R.H., Pannuti, C.S., Pereira, J.L., Koff, R.S., Dienstag, J.L. and Iwarson, S., "Serodiagnosis of Viral Hepatitis a by a Solid-Phase Radioimmunoassay Specific for Igm Antibodies." *Scand J Infect Dis*, 1981. **13**: 5-9.

348. Chopra, S., Rubinow, A., Koff, R.S. and Cohen, A.S., "Hepatic Amyloidosis: A Histological Analysis of Primary (Al) and Secondary (Aa) Forms." *Am J Path*, 1984. **115**: 106.

349. Rubinow, A., Koff, R.S. and Cohen, A.S., "Severe Intrahepatic Cholestasis in Primary Amyloidosis. A Report on Four Cases and a Review on the Literature." *Am J Med*, 1978. **64**: 937.

350. Berginer, V.M., Salen, G. and Shefer, S., "Long-Term Treatment of Cerebrotendinous Xanthomatosis with Chenodeoxycholic Acid." *N Engl J Med*, 1984. **311**: 1649-1652.

351. Salen, G., Shefer, S., Nguyen, L., Ness, G.C., Tint, G.S. and Shore, V., "Sitosterolemia." *J Lipid Res*, 1992. **33**: 945-955.

352. Irons, M., Elias, E.R., Salen, G., Tint, G.S. and Batta, A.K., "Detective Cholesterol Biosynthesis in Smith-Lemli-Opitz Syndrome." *Lancet*, 1993. **341**: 1414.

353. Tint, G.S., Irons, M., Elias, E.R., Batta, A.K., Frieden, R., Chen, T.S. and Salen, G., "Defective Cholesterol Biosynthesis Associated with the Smith-Lemli-Opitz Syndrome." *N Engl J Med*, 1994. **330**: 107-113.

354. Pullinger, Salen, G. and Kane, "Mutation in Cholesterol 7 O Hydroxlase Is Associated with Hypercholesterolemia Phenotype." *J Clin Invest*, 2002. **110**: 109-117.

355. Batta, A.K., Arora, R., Salen, G., Tint, G.S., Eskreis, D. and Katz, S., "Characterization of Serum and Urinary Bile Acids in Patients with Primary Bilary Cirrhosis by Gas-Liquid Chromatography-Mass Spectrometry: Effect of Ursodeoxycholic Acid Treatment." *J Lipid Res*, 1989. **30**: 1953-1962.

356. Shefer, S., Nguyen, L., Salen, G., Batta, A.K., Brooker, D., Zaki, F.G., Rani, I. and Tint, G.S., "Feedback Regulation of Bile-Acid Synthesis in the Rat. Differing Effects of Tautocholate and Tauroursocholate." *J Clin Invest*, 1990. **85**: 1191-1198.

357. Salen, G., Pesonal communication with the author.

358. Gordon, S.C., Reddy, K.R., Schiff, L. and Schiff, E.R., "Prolonged Intrahepatic Cholestasis Secondary to Acute Hepatitis A." *Ann Intern Med*, 1984. **101(5)**: 635-637.

359. Gordon, S.C., Jeffers, L.J., DeMedina, M.D., Reddy, K.R. and Schiff, E.R., "Immunoglobulin M Antibody to Hepatitis B Core Antigen and Fulminant Hepatitis B." *Ann Intern Med*, 1985. **102**: 415-416.

360.   Cancio-Bello, T.P., de Medina, M., Shorey, J., Valledor, M.D. and Schiff, E.R., "An Institutional Outbreak of Hepatitis B Related to a Human Biting Carrier." *J Infect Dis*, 1982. **146**: 652-656.

361.   Seeff, L.B., Zimmerman, H.J., Wright, E.C., Finkelstein, J.D., Garcia-Pont, P., Greenlee, H.B., Dietz, A.A., Leevy, C.M., Tamburro, C.H., Schiff, E.R., Schimmel, E.M., Zemel, R., Zimmon, D.S. and McCollum, R.W., "A Randomized, Double Blind Controlled Trial of the Efficacy of Immune Serum Globulin for the Prevention of Post-Transfusion Hepatitis.   A V.A. Cooperative Study." *Gastroenterology*, 1977. **72**: 111-121.

362.   Feldman, R.E. and Schiff, E.R., "Hepatitis in Dental Professionals." *JAMA*, 1975. **232**: 1228-1230.

363.   Davis, G.L., Balart, L.A., Schiff, E.R., Lindsay, K., Bodenheimer, H.C., Jr., Perillo, R.P., Carey, W., Jacobsen, I.M., Payne, J. and Dienstag, J.L., "Treatment of Chronic Hepatitis C with Recombinant Interferon Alfa.   A Multicenter Randomized, Controlled Trial.   Hepatitis Interventional Therapy Group." *N Engl J Med*, 1989. **30:321**: 1501-1506.

364.   Pereiras, R.J., Ruiz, R., Viamonte, M.J. and Schiff, E.R., "Percutaneous Cholangiography with the Chiba University Needle: A New, Safe, and Accurate Method in the Diagnosis of Cholestatic Syndromes." *Rev Interam Radiol*, 1976. **1(2)**: 17-19.

365.   Hutson, D.G., Pereiras, R., Zeppa, R., Levi, J.U., Schiff, E.R. and Fink, P., "The Fate of Esophageal Varices Following Selective Distal Splenorenal Shunt." *Ann Surg*, 1976. **183**: 496-501.

366.   Hutson, D.G., Zeppa, R., Levi, J.U., Schiff, E.R., Livingstone, A.S. and Fink, P., "The Effect of the Distal Splenorenal Shunt on Hypersplenism." *Ann Surg*, 1977. **185**: 605-612.

367.   Zeppa, R., Hensley, G.T., Levi, J.U., Bergstresser, P.R., Hutson, D.G., Sr., Livingstone, A.S., Schiff, E.R. and Fink, P., "The Comparative Survivals of Alcoholics Verson Nonalcoholics after Distal Spleuorenal Shunt." *Ann Surg*, 1978. **187**: 510-514.

368.   Russell, E., Yrizarry, J.M., Huber, J.S., Nunez, D.J., Hutson, D.G., Schiff, E.R., Reddy, K.R., Jeffers, L.J. and Williams, A., "Percutaneous Transjejunal Biliary Dilatation: Alternate Management for Benign Strictures." *Radiology*, 1986. **159**: 209-214.

369.   Trotman, B.W., Morris, T.A., III, Sanchez, H.M., Soloway, R.D. and Ostrow, J.D., "Pigment Vs. Cholesterol Cholelithiasis: Identification and Quantification by Infra-Red Spectroscopy." *Gastroenterology*, 1977. **72**: 495-498.

370.   Black, B.E., Carr, S.H., Ostrow, J.D. and Ohkubo, H., "Equilibrium Swelling of Black Pigment Gallstones: Evidence for Network Polymer Structure." *Biopolymers*, 1982. **21**: 601-610.

371.   Moore, E.W., Celic, L. and Ostrow, J.D., "Interactions between Ionized Calcium and Sodium Taurocholate: Bile Salts Are Important Buffers for Prevention of Calcium-Containing Gallstones." *Gastroenterology*, 1982. **83**: 1079-1089.

372.   Ohkubo, H., Ostrow, J.D., Carr, S.H. and Rege, R.V., "Polymer Networks in Pigment and Cholesterol Gallstones, Assessed by Equilibrium Swelling and Infrared Spectoscopy." *Gastroenterology*, 1984. **87**: 805-814.

373.   Shimizu, S., Sabsay, B., Veis, A., Ostrow, J.D., Rege, R.V. and Dawes, L.O., "Isolation of an Acidic Protein from Cholesterol Gallstones Which Inhibits the Precipitation of Calcium Carbonate in Vitro." *J Clin Invest*, 1989. **84**: 1990-1996.

374.   Stoll, M.S., Zenone, E.A. and Ostrow, J.D., "Excretion of Administered and Endogenous Photobilirubins in the Bile of the Jaundiced Gunn Rat." *J Clin Invest*, 1981. **68**: 134-141.

375.   Stoll, M.S., Zenone, E.A., Ostrow, J.D. and Zarembo, J.E., "Preparation and Properties of Bilirubin Photoisomers." *Biochem J*, 1979. **183**: 139-146.

376.   Rege, R.V., Webster, C.C. and Ostrow, J.D., "Interactions of Unconjugated Bilirubin with Bile Salts." *J Lipid Res*, 1988. **29**: 1289-1296.

377.   Hahm, J.S., Ostrow, J.D., Mukerjee, P. and Celic, L., "Ionization and Self-Association of Unconjugated Bilirubin, Determined by Rapid Solvent Partition from Chloroform, with Further Studies of Bilirubin Solubility." *J Lipid Res*, 1992. **33**: 1123-1137.

378.   Persico, M., Persico, E., Bakker, C.T.M., Rigato, I., Amoroso, A., Torrella, R., Bosma, P.J., Tiribelli, C. and Ostrow, J.D., "Hepatic Uptake of Organic Anions Affects the Plasma Bilirubin Level in Subjects with Gilbert's Syndrome Mutations in Ugtiai." *Hepatology*, 2001. **33**: 627-632.

379.   Weisiger, R.A., Ostrow, J.D., Koehler, R.K., Webster, C.C., Mukerjee, P., Pascolo, L. and Tiribelli, C., "Affinity of Human Serum Albumin for Bilirubin Varies with Albumin Concentration and Buffer Composition: Results of a Novel Ultrafiltration Method." *J Biol Chem*, 2001. **7**: 7.

380.   Klotz, U., Avant, G.R., Hoyumpa, A., Schenker, S. and Wilkinson, G.R., "The Effects of Age and Liver Disease on the Disposition and Elimination of Diazepam in Adult Man." *J Clin Invest*, 1975. **55**: 347-359.

381.   Klotz, U., McHorse, T.S., Wilkinson, G.R. and Schenker, S., "The Effect of Cirrhosis on the Disposition and Elimination of Meperidine in Man." *Clin Pharmacol Ther*, 1974. **16**: 667.

382.   McHorse, T.S., Wilkinson, G.R., Johnson, R.F. and Schenker, S., "The Effect of Acute Viral Hepatitis in Man on the Disposition and Elimination of Meperidine." *Gastroenterology*, 1975. **68**: 775-780.

383.   Shull, H.J., Jr., Wilkinson, G.R., Johnson, R.F. and Schenker, S., "Normal Disposition of Oxazepam in Acute Viral Hepatitis and Cirrhosis." *Ann Intern Med*, 1976. **84**: 420-425.

384.   Kraus, J.W., Desmond, P.V., Marshall, J.P., Johnson, R.F., Schenker, S. and Wilkinson, G.R., "Effects of Aging and Liver Disease on Disposition of Lorezapam." *Clin Pharmacol Ther*, 1978. **24**: 411-419.

385.   Roberts, R.K., Wilkinson, G.R., Branch, R.A. and Schenker, S., "Effect of Age and Parenchymal Liver Disease on the Disposition and Elimination of Chlordiazepoxide (Librium)." *Gastroenterology*, 1978. **75**: 479-485.

386.   Desmond, P.V., James, R., Schenker, S., Gerkens, J.F. and Branch, R.A., "Preservation of Glucuronidation in Carbon Tetrachloride-Induced Acute Liver Injury in the Rat." *Biochem Pharmacol*, 1981. **30**: 993-999.

387.   Gerkens, J., Desmond, P.V., Schenker, S. and Branch, R.A., "Hepatic and Extrahepatic Grlucuronidation of Lorazepam in the Dog." *Hepatology*, 1981. **1**: 329-335.

388.   Breen, K.J., Schenker, S. and Heimberg, M., "Fatty Liver Induced by Tetracycline in the Rat: Dose-Response Relationships and Effect of Sex." *Gastroenterology*, 1975. **68**: 714-723.

389.   Breen, K.J., Schenker, S. and Heimberg, M., "Effect of Tetracycline on the Metabolism of [1-[14]c]Oleate by the Liver." *Biochem Pharmacol*, 1979. **28**: 197-200.

390.   Sorrell, M.F., Tuma, D.J., Schafer, E.C. and Barak, A.J., "Role of Acetaldehyde in the Ethanol-Induced Impairment of Glycoprotein Metabolism in Rat Liver Slices." *Gastroenterology*, 1977. **73**: 137-144.

391. Sorrell, M.F. and Tuma, D.J., "Selective Impairment of Glycoprotein Metabolism by Ethanol and Acetaldehyde in Rat Liver Slices." *Gastroenterology*, 1978. **75**: 200-205.

392. Sorrell, M.R., Nauss, J.M., Donohue, T.M.J. and Tuma, D.J., "Effects of Chronic Ethanol Administration on Hepatic Glycoprotein Secretion in the Rat." *Gastroenterology*, 1983. **84**: 580-586.

393. Tuma, D.J., Jennett, R.B. and Sorrell, M.F., "Effect of Ethanol on the Synthesis and Secretion of Hepatic Secretory Glycoproteins and Albumin." *Hepatology*, 1981. **1**: 590-598.

394. Donohue, T.M.J., Tuma, D.J. and Sorrell, M.F., "Acetaldehyde Adducts with Proteins: Binding [14c]Acetaldehyde to Serum Albumin." *Arch Biochem Biophys*, 1983. **220**: 239-246.

395. Volentine, G.D., Ogden, K.A., Kortje, D.K., Tuma, D.J. and Sorrell, M.F., "Role of Acetaldehyde in the Ethanol-Induced Impairment of Hepatic Glycoprotein Secretion in the Rat in Vivo." *Hepatology*, 1987. **7**: 490-495.

396. Smith, S.L., Jennett, R.B., Sorrell, M.F. and Tuma, D.J., "Acetaldehyde Substoichiometrically Inhibits Bovine Neurotubulin Polymerization." *J Clin Invest*, 1989. **84**: 337-341.

397. Zetterman, R.K. and Sorrell, M.F., "Immunologic Aspects of Alcoholic Liver Disease." *Gastroenterology*, 1981. **81**: 616-624.

398. Klassen, L.W., Tuma, D. and Sorrell, M.F., "Immune Mechanisms of Alcohol-Induced Liver Disease." *Hepatology*, 1995. **22**: 355-357.

399. Hoofnagle, J.H., Kresina, T., Fuller, R.K., Lake, J.R., Lucey, M.R., Sorrell, M.F. and Beresford, T.P., "Liver Transplantation for Alcoholic Liver Disease: Executive Statement and Recommendations. Summary of a National Institutes of Health Workshop Held December 6-7, 1996, Bethesda, Md." *Liver Transpl Surg*, 1997. **3**: 347-350.

400. Heffron, T.G., Langnas, A.N., Matamoros, A.J., Anderson, J.C., Mack, D.R., McCashland, T.M., Dhawan, A., Kaufman, S., Zetterman, R.K., Pillen, T.J., Sudan, D., Jerius, J., Donovan, J.P., Sorrell, M.F., Vanderhoof, J.A. and Shawl, B.W.J., "Preoperative Estimation in Living Related Donor Transplantation: Clinical Correlation and Donor/Recipient Ratio." *Transplant Proc*, 1996. **28**: 2370.

401. Linscheer, W.G., Raheja, K.L., Cho, C. and Smith, N.J., "Mechanism of the Protective Effect of Propylthiouracil against Acetaminophen (Tylenol) Toxicity in the Rat." *Gastroenterology*, 1980. **78**: 100-107.

402. Raheja, K.L., Linscheer, W.G. and Cho, C., "Hepatotoxicity and Metabolism of Acetaminophen in Male and Female Rats." *J Toxicol Environ Health*, 1983. **12**: 143-158.

403. Raheja, K.L., Linscheer, W.G., Cho, C. and Mahany, D., "Protective Effect of Propylthiouracil Independent of Its Hypothyroid Effect on Acetaminophen Toxicity in the Rat." *J Pharmacal Exp Ther*, 1982. **220**: 427-432.

404. Raheja, K.L., Linscheer, W.G., Cho, C. and Coulson, R., "Failure of Exogenous Prostaglandin to Afford Complete Protection against Acetaminophen-Induced Hepatotoxicity in the Rat." *J Toxicol Environ Health*, 1985. **15**: 477-484.

405. Banerjee, A., Linscheer, W.G., Chiji, H., Murthy, U.K., Cho, C., Nandi, J. and Chan, S.H., "Induction of an Atpase Inhibitor Protein by Propylthiouracil and Protection against Paracetamol (Acetaminophen) Hepatotoxicity in the Rat." *Br J Pharmacol*, 1998. **124**: 1041-1047.

406. Chijiiwa, K. and Linscheer, W.G., "Effect of Intraluminal Ph on Cholesterol and Oleic Acid Absorption from Micellar Solutions in the Rat." *Am J Physiol*, 1984. **246**: G492-499.

407. Chijiiwa, K. and Linscheer, W.G., "Distribution and Monomer Activity of Cholesterol in Micellar Bile Salt: Effect of Cholesterol Activity." *Am J Physiol*, 1987. **252**: G309-314.

408. Linscheer, W.G., Atreyee, B., Uma, K.M., John, W., Sandor, N. and Jyotirmoy, N., "Lovastatin Induces Synthesis of Cholesterol, Which Acts as a Secretogogue of Biliary Phospholipids in Rats." *Am J Physiol*, 1995. **268**: G242-250.

409. Toskes, P.P., Deren, J.J. and Conrad, M.E., "Trypsin-Like Nature of the Pancreatic Factor That Corrects Vitamin B12 Malabsorption Associated with Pancreatic Dysfunction." *J Clin Invest*, 1973. **52**: 1660-1664.

410. Toskes, P.P., Dawson, W., Curington, C., Levy, N.S. and Fitzgerald, C., "Non-Diabetic Retinal Abnormalities in Chronic Pancreatitis." *N Eng J Med*, 1979. **300**: 942-946.

411. Toskes, P.P., "Does a Negative Feedback System for the Control of Pancreatic Exocrine Secretion Exist and Is It of Any Clinical Significance?" *J Lab Clin Med*, 1980. **95**: 11-12.

412. King, C.E. and Toskes, P.P., "Small Intestinal Bacterial Overgrowth." *Gastroenterol*, 1979. **76**: 1035-1055.

413. Toskes, P.P., Giannella, R.A., Jervis, H.R., Rout, W.R. and Takeuchi, A., "Small Intestinal Mucosal Injury in the Experimental Blind Loop Syndrome. Light-and Electron-Microscopic and Histochemical Studies." *Gastroenterol*, 1975. **68**: 193-203.

414. Toskes, P.P., King, C.E., Spivey, J.C. and Lorenz, E., "Xylose Catabolism in the Experimental Rat Blind Loop Syndrome: Studies, Including Use of a Newly Developed D-(14c)Xylose Breath Test." *Gastroenterol*, 1978. **74**: 691-697.

415. King, C.E., Toskes, P.P., Spivey, J.C., Lorenz, E. and Welkos, S., "Detection of Small Intestinal Bacterial Overgrowth by Means of a 14c-D-Xylose Breath Test." *Gastroenterol*, 1979. **77**: 75-82.

416. Justus, P.G., Fernandez, A., Martin, J.L., King, C.E., Toskes, P.P. and Mathias, J.R., "Altered Myoelectric Activity in the Experimental Blind Loop Syndrome." *J Clin Invest*, 1983. **72**: 1964-1071.

417. Jacobson, D.G., Curington, C., Connery, K. and Toskes, P.P., "Trypsin-Like Immunoreactivity as a Test for Pancreatic Insufficiency." *N Eng J Med*, 1984. **310**: 1307-1309.

418. Steinberg, W.M., King, C.E. and Toskes, P.P., "Malabsorption of Protein-Bound Cobalamin but Not Unbound Cobalamin During Cimetidine Administration." *Dig Dis Sci*, 1980. **25**: 188-191.

419. King, C.E. and Toskes, P.P., "Nutrient Malabsorption in the Zollinger-Ellison Syndrome. Normalization During Long-Term Cimetidine Therapy." *Arch Intern Med*, 1983. **143**: 349-351.

<u>Chapter 24. VA Research in Nephrology</u>
<u>Richard P. Wedeen</u>

The impact of VA research on nephrology in the twentieth century is evident when the contributions of VA nephrologists are examined in light of the history of understanding the kidney in health and disease. In the nineteenth century, major advances were made by physicians seeking anatomic-physiologic correlations that revealed the structural basis of kidney disease. Understanding renal disease in modern terms began in 1827 with Richard Bright's pathophysiologic correlations between renal pathology and albuminuria. In 1842, William Bowman described the microscopic components of the nephron and began to discern the physiologic functions of the kidney. The contributions of the German physiologists Karl Ludwig in 1844, and Rudolf Heidenhain in 1876, clarified the functions of the glomerulus and tubule in the production of urine. At the same time, Volard and Fahr refined the histologic description of the diseased kidney, "Bright's Disease," as it was then called, and introduced a classification of renal disease that remains in use today. Primacy in unraveling the secrets of the kidney shifted to the United States in the early part of the twentieth century as the ideas of Ludwig and Heidenhain were applied in the clinic by Arthur Cushny in 1917, and by Thomas Addis and Jean Oliver in 1931. Micropuncture studies by Alfred N. Richards in 1929 and physiologic studies by Homer Smith and his colleagues through the 1960s characterized glomerular filtration and tubular transport as we understand them today. The role of the counter-current multiplier system in driving the concentrating and diluting process of the kidney unfolded before the probing observations of Wirtz, Hargitay and Kuhn in 1951. Description of the fine structure of the diseased kidney was led by Jack Chrurg and Conrad Pirani in the 1950s and 1960s using percutaneous needle biopsy and electron microscopy.

The emergence of nephrology as a distinct clinical science and subspecialty of Internal Medicine provides the context in which the contributions of VA researchers can be understood. As the descriptions of the structure and function of the kidney in health and disease progressed, post-World War II VA research focused on physiology, renal biopsy, and on dramatic new treatments - antibiotics and the renal replacement therapies, dialysis and transplantation.

In the United States, clinical scientists concerned with the kidney defined themselves as nephrologists and created the American Society of Nephrology (ASN) in 1967. Nephrology was officially recognized as a distinct subspecialty in 1971 when the American Board of Internal Medicine offered the first certifying examinations. The fledgling society convened the leading international gathering of nephrologists, attracting over 5000 attendees to its annual congress.

VA clinical scientists were among the movers and shakers who created nephrology as a subspecialty. The expansion of medical research in the VA after World War II corresponded to the growth of the subspecialty dedicated to the diagnosis and treatment of renal diseases. VA investigators were among the founders of nephrology. They pioneered the development of innovative research techniques such as micropuncture. They developed and perfected the clinical therapies, hemodialysis and renal transplantation, that revolutionized medical practice in the twentieth century. VA research and nephrology came to maturity at the same time, in the same place.

This survey of renal researchers funded by the VA through 1980 is by no means complete. Rather, it represents a "convenience sample" of leaders in nephrology who have been supported by VA research. While the whole of the VA contribution is greater than the sum of its parts, some outstanding parts will be described here. Since most medical scientists receive research support from multiple sources, it is often difficult to separate VA- from non-VA-supported research. Consequently, this chapter gives investigators the opportunity to express in their own words, the contribution that the VA made to their work and their careers. When investigators did not avail themselves of this opportunity, key contributions of some of the most distinguished investigators have been captured from available sources.

In describing the VA's role in nephrological research in the twentieth century, it is fitting to begin with a recent winner of the prestigious Albert Lasker Award for Clinical Medical Research, Belding H. Scribner.[1] Dr. Scribner shared the award with Willem J. Kolff for the development of the artificial kidney. In the words of Joseph L. Goldstein, Chairman of the Lasker Awards Jury, and Nobel laureate:[2]

> "In 1960, the impossible became possible. The psychological and technical barriers to chronic dialysis came crashing down through the research of Belding Scribner, a young professor of medicine at the University of Washington in Seattle. Like Kolff, Scribner was a dedicated physician whose imagination was triggered by a patient who was slowly dying of end stage renal disease. After a sleepless night agonizing over the fate of his patient, Scribner got out of bed at 4:00AM and in a sudden flash jotted down an idea about how to solve the problem of circulatory access. His idea was elegant in its simplicity: sew plastic tubes into an artery and vein in the patient's arm for connection to the artificial kidney…the Scribner shunt…."

In 2002, approximately 520,000 patients received hemodialysis in the United States at a cost of over $28 billion. In addition to the seminal advance that made repetitive hemodialysis feasible, Dr. Scribner played major roles in the development of medical ethics committees in the United States and in providing funding for dialysis by Medicare. The research to develop the Scribner shunt was funded by the VA as early as 1956. Since 1995, the American Society of Nephrology has awarded the Belding H. Scribner Award annually to nephrologists who made major contributions to the care of kidney patients. Tragically, on June 19, 2003, Dr. Scribner died in a drowning accident near his houseboat in Portage Bay, Washington.

In 1971, Edward D. Freis (Chapter 9), received the Albert Lasker Foundation Clinical Research Award. Dr. Freis, who served in the VA from 1949 to 1987, led the VA cooperative studies that established the importance of reducing blood pressure to prevent the complications of hypertension.[3] Dr. Fries was Chairman of the High Blood Pressure Research Council of the American Heart Association, winner of the Middleton Award, and Senior Medical Investigator for the Veterans Administration. He published the "first successful use of antihypertensive drugs to reverse several signs and symptoms of malignant hypertension," and the "first report of the use of thiazide diuretics in the treatment of hypertension."[4]

Dr. Freis noted that VA cooperative studies "proved for the first time that reduction of blood pressure with antihypertensive drugs reduced morbidity and mortality. Prior accepted medical opinion was that antihypertensive treatment was of no therapeutic benefit." In recognition of Freis's work, since 1985 the American Heart Association Council on High Blood Pressure has presented the Edward D. Freis Award to researchers who have made major contributions to the care of hypertensive patients .

Thomas E. Starzl was a prime mover in developing renal transplantation. His achievements include reports in the 1960s on the addition of monoclonal anti-lymphocyte serum to standard antirejection therapies.[5, 6] He was also responsible for the earliest descriptions of hyperimmune rejection and the use of HLA matching.[7] Dr. Starzl, whose research had an immeasurable impact on the clinical management of transplant patients, recognizes the VA's pioneering and "determined" support for his work:

"My involvement in transplantation began at the VA Research Hospital (now the 'Lakeside VA'). There, in the summer of 1958, I performed on dogs the first liver transplantations ever done in any species. This work continued in Chicago until late 1961, and expanded to the kidney.

"In 1961, I moved from Northwestern University to the University of Colorado as Chief of Surgery at the Denver Veteran's Administration Hospital. There, the first kidney transplantation series compiled west of the Atlantic Coast was begun at the Denver VA in March 1962. One year later, the first liver transplantations were done in the same operating room. The VA central office provided research and clinical funding for our work at the Denver VA from 1962 until the time of my departure for the University of Pittsburgh in 1980. VA research support continued for another 15 years at the Pittsburgh VA Hospital (Oakland), which is affiliated with the University of Pittsburgh....

"The Denver VA hospital became the first designated end-stage renal disease center in the United States. This was a crucial step in establishing the national ESRD (End-stage Renal Disease) system two years later by the development of the national ESRD system that was written into law by an amendment to the Social Security Act....

"You may be shocked at the magnitude of the VA's role in the development of transplantation of all organs. In my opinion, kidney transplantation as it presently exists in the United States could never have gone airborne had it not been for the continuous and determined support of the VA throughout the lean 1960's and 1970's. In 1968, I was given the William S. Middleton award for 'Outstanding Research in the Veterans Administration System.' I was employed by the VA continuously from 1961 through 1998, the last 3 years as a Distinguished Physician appointee."

The 1965 winners of the VA's Middleton Award were Lucien B. Guze and George M. Kalmanson of the VA Medical Center in Los Angeles. While not nephrologists, their work was on the mechanisms of bacterial infections of the kidneys (pyelonephritis) and associated infections of the urinary tract. These investigators isolated from the kidneys of animals pleuro-pneumoinia-like organisms that indicated that sequestered forms of bacteria with high resistance to antibiotics could account for the resistance to treatment of urinary tract infections.[8, 9]

Calvin M. Kunin was also an infectious disease specialist, not a nephrologist, but his contributions to the understanding of urinary tract infections warrants his inclusion in this history of VA nephrology research. Dr. Kunin was Professor and Chairman of Preventive Medicine, University of Virginia School of Medicine, and became Chief of Medical Service at William S. Middleton Memorial VA Hospital, Madison, Wisconsin and Professor and Chairman, Department of Internal Medicine, Ohio State University College of Medicine. Among his many honors were visiting professorships at West Virginia University; Makerere University Medical School, Kampala, Uganda; Vanderbilt University; Boston City Hospital; and the Brockton & West Roxbury VA Medical Center. Dr. Kunin's research centered around antibiotic therapy of urinary tract infections, particularly in children.[10, 11]

Belton A. Burrows was another VA investigator whose work was primarily in another field but whose contributions significantly advanced the field of nephrology.[12, 13] He served as Chief of the Radioisotope units at the Boston VA Hospital, the Boston University Medical Center, and the Veterans Administration Central Office. Dr. Burrows was a member of the ASCI and Editor of the *Journal of Nuclear Medicine*. Writing on behalf of his father, Warren Burrows described Belton Burrows's accomplishments:

> "... construction of an 'iron room' made of 12" thick nickel-steel armor plates from the battleship *USS Illinois*. By performing isotope counting in the 'iron room,' one was able to significantly reduce all background radiation.... In 1950, Burrows described a dilution technique utilizing K-42 to measure 'exchangeable K' as well as total body K. These studies were expanded in 1952-1953 to demonstrate that 'exchangeable K' corresponded to metabolically active K, and could be measured by subtracting total K-42 from total urine specific activity of K-42 and K-39.... The Boston VA lab was instrumental in perfecting the renogram. Initially the tracer isotope I-131 Diodrast was utilized to measure tubular renal function. Liver uptake of this material was a background problem and use of a protein carrier eliminated the hepatic effect on excretion and made renal measurement more accurate. Later I-131 Hippuran replaced Diodrast as a Tracer. Burrows's lab addressed several issues related to renovascular hypertension. In addition to identifying unilateral renal disease with the renogram, it demonstrated that parenchymal renal disease could be differentiated from renal artery stenosis by differential response to mannitol loading..."[12,13]

Gerald DiBona was Professor of Physiology at the University of Iowa, College of Medicine, and Chief of the Iowa City VAMC Medical Service until 1997 when he became

Professor at the Karolinska Institute, Stockholm, Sweden. A member of the ASCI and the AAP, Dr. DiBona described receiving VA support for more than three decades:

"I have worked continuously at the Iowa City VAMC since July 1, 1969 to the present and have received VA research funding continuously from July 1, 1969...The VA-supported research concerns the physiology and pathophysiology of the mechanisms whereby renal sympathetic nerve activity controls renal function.[14, 15] This has involved studies performed under normal physiological conditions and under pathophysiological conditions, focusing on the experimental models of salt-sensitive hypertension and the edema-forming conditions of congestive heart failure, nephrotic syndrome and cirrhosis of the liver. This body of work has been recognized for its establishment of an important role for the renal sympathetic neural control of the kidney. Perhaps the citation that accompanied the William S. Middleton Award for Outstanding Achievement in Medical Research that I received from the VA in 1995 is most descriptive: 'for his internationally recognized contributions in the study of the neural regulation of renal function in normal physiologic conditions and in edema forming states such as hypertension, nephrosis, cirrhosis and congestive heart failure.... Dr. DiBona has single-handedly elevated our understanding of the interactions between the central nervous system and the kidney from one of complete ignorance to a topic of widely appreciated importance in the regulation of overall cardiovascular function.'"

The influence of VA-supported renal research on nephrology is also demonstrated by four VA investigators who were elected president of the ASN; Barry M. Brenner (1987), Thomas E. Andrioli (1993), William M. Bennett (2000), and Roland Blantz (2002). Dr. Brenner, Samuel A. Levine Professor of Medicine at Harvard Medical School, has been awarded honorary degrees from Harvard, Long Island University, Universite de Paris and the Royal College of Physicians. In 1969 after leaving the NIH where he was a Senior Investigator, Dr. Brenner was appointed Chief of Nephrology at the VA Hospital in San Francisco, remaining in that post until 1976 when he moved to Harvard. His awards, too numerous to list in their entirety, include the Homer Smith Award in Renal Physiology of the American Heart Association and ASN, the Richard Bright Award of the American Society of Hypertension, the Donald Seldin Award of the National Kidney Foundation, and the John Peters Award of the ASN.

Dr. Brenner stated:

"Our most important contribution related to our success in obtaining the first measurements of mammalian glomerular capillary pressure.[16, 17] . . . Although the pressure-measuring device was constructed at the NIH, the measurements in glomerular capillaries of the rat were made at the Fort Miley VA Hospital. My VA years were indeed important and productive and allowed me to grow in confidence and stature as a physician-scientist.... Support, both financial and personal, was always generous and nurturing. I am thus indebted to the VA system which served me extremely well in the early years of my independent career."

Dr. William Bennett, who served as ASN president from 2000 to 2001, recognizes the importance of VA support: "I had VA Merit Review funding from 1974–1986. The grant was my first real substantial funding and enabled me to develop the experimental model and make some early insights into the pathogenesis of aminoglycoside nephrotoxicity using the Fisher 344 rat strain."[18,19] He went on to point out:

"The support by the VA was pivotal in establishing a nephrotoxicity laboratory at Oregon Health Sciences University and doing the first experiments developing an experimental model of aminoglycoside nephrotoxicity. This led to numerous publications and indeed the laboratory at one point was considered one of the best in the descriptive features of this model and starting to unravel the pathophysiologic events that take place. As mentioned above, the observation that the height of the serum level could be dissociated from nephrotoxicity was novel at its time and now has been accepted into clinical practice. A description of acquired resistance to nephrotoxins such as gentamicin although earlier described in the 1920s and 1930s was resurrected by observations in our laboratory as indicated above."

Roland Blantz elected to the presidency of the ASN for 2002–2003, described the VA contributions to his research as follows:

"I have worked at the VA since 1972, when after Fellowship I soon became Chief of Nephrology at the VA (San Diego). I was initially funded by a VA Merit Review at that time, and have been continuously funded by the VA since 1972. The current title of the VA Merit Review (research grant) is, 'Angiotensin-adrenergic interactions in the kidney', but I also held a component of a VA/JDF (Juvenile Diabetes Foundation) diabetes program project grant in conjunction with Jerry Olefsky. While I was Chief of Nephrology I was also a Research Associate and later a Clinical Investigator, both career development awards, during the 1970's. I was appointed Professor of Medicine at UCSD in 1980, and went part time in the VA somewhere during the mid 1980's, and have held an FTE at UCSD since that time. I was ACOS for Research in 1987-88....

"Research that was funded by both the VA and continuously funded by NIH was conducted in VA space, and therefore VA supported. In the 1970s, the studies that were conducted were primarily micro-puncture physiology studies, which examined the mechanisms of acute renal failure, glomerular immune injury, hormonal effects, and were focused on glomerular hemodynamics. Early studies in the 1970's, (we) designated for the first time the glomerular hemodynamic effects of angiotensin II.[20] Angiotensin, in addition to producing vaso-constriction, also decreased the glomerular ultra-filtration coefficient (KF or LpA), and studies designated certain states such as chronic salt depletion which manifested these same hemodynamic changes. Early studies in the late 1970s demonstrated that tubuloglomerular feedback (TGF) systems were important to the regulation of glomerular filtration and that administration of the carbonic anhydrase inhibitor, benzolamide, reduced GFR by TGF mechanisms.[21] This was the first practical demonstration of a role for TGF. In the 1970s and 1980s, there were a variety of studies which determined the mechanism of glomerular hemodynamic effects of immune injury in a variety of models, including anti-glomerular basement membrane disease, a model of membranous nephropathy, and mesangio-capillary, or membrano-proliferative nephritis. A variety of studies in the 1980's and early 1990's examined the mechanism of glomerular hemodynamics alterations in elevated angiotensin II and adrenergic conditions and interaction among these systems."

VA support for nephrology had an indirect effect as well as a direct effect: VA-funded investigators formed the backbone of nephrology in American medical schools and so can be considered to have produced more academic nephrologists than any single medical school. VA-trained nephrologists contributed substantially to the evolution of understanding of the etiology, pathophysiology, and treatment of renal disease in the twentieth century. Research honed their clinical skills and those of their colleagues, and their innovative contributions received world-wide recognition. Charles R. Kleeman, distinguished for his research on the role of aldosterone in modulating renal function,[22] trained as a medical resident at the West Haven VA Hospital from 1953 to 1956 and subsequently served as Director of the Division of Nephrology at the West Los Angeles VAMC and Professor of Medicine at UCLA. He is a member of the Association of American Physicians (AAP) and the ASCI. Solomon Papper published some of the earliest papers on the pathophysiologic mechanisms of edema and diuresis.[23] Dr. Papper was appointed Distinguished Physician by the VA in 1986.

Jack W. Coburn, who worked with Charles Kleeman in Los Angeles, reported,

"I was supported by VA research funds from the time that I returned as a Clinical Investigator to Wadsworth VA Hospital (as it was known then) from my Military Service at Walter Reed Army Medical Center. The VA Research support continued until 1992 (although I became part time at the VA in 1984). What became the Nephrology Section was known as the Metabolism Section from the time Charles Kleeman became Chief here in 1955 until the Nephrology and Endocrine Sections were separated in 1970 when I became Chief of Nephrology.... There are a number of nephrologists who were here as Research Associates, Clinical Investigators, and Medical Investigators who left Wadsworth to become active investigators in other institutions ... these include: Allan Arieff, Joel Kopple, David B.N. Lee, Frederick Singer, Francisco Llach and Arnold Brickman.... (to name a few)."

Dr. Coburn's work focused on unraveling the mysteries of uremic bone disease, in particular the role of vitamin D and aluminum in the etiology and treatment of osteomalacia. While bone disease remains a major problem for patients with end-stage renal disease, the identification of aluminum as an important underlying cause has modified the management of all such patients by reducing the intake of aluminum-containing antacids.

"We published data providing strong evidence that aluminum accumulation (in part from the Al-gels given to control phosphate retention) was the cause of this osteomalacia.[24,25] (We) showed that one could induce a similar disease by administering parenteral aluminum to dogs,....(and) that the histologic features of aluminum bone disease could be reversed by aluminum chelation with deferoxamine.

(We further) showed that the conversion from aluminum gels to calcium carbonate led to gradual reduction of plasma aluminum and to improvement of the abnormal bone formation observed due to aluminum."

H. Earl Ginn did his earliest research in kidney diseases as a medical resident at the VA Hospital in Oklahoma City in 1960. After completing his fellowship in renal disease, he returned to the VA in Oklahoma City where he was a Clinical Investigator from 1961 to 1974. Dr. Ginn reported:

"I suspect (the paper entitled) 'Human renal transplantation: an investigation of the functional status of the denervated kidney after successful homotransplantation in identical twins,' ...was my most important contribution to Nephrology. ....[26] This was the third or fourth successful kidney transplant in identical twins. The function parameters we measured were more extensive than any previously or subsequently published. This investigation was accomplished while I was still a Resident in the Oklahoma City VA & Oklahoma University Medical Center (Univ. Med. Cntr). The transplant recipient was a navy veteran who was service connected for chronic glomerulonephritis, and his donor brother was a pilot in the USAF Strategic Air Command. (The) VAH provided me with bench space and lab equipment and supplies. General Curtis E. LeMay, Commander of SAC, provided us with a SAC air transport from Oklahoma City to Richmond, VA, where Dr. David Hume at the Medical College of Virginia, Richmond, VA, and our Oklahoma University Medical Center Chairman of Surgery, Dr. John Schilling, as first assistant, performed the transplant. I had responsibilities to hemodialyze him prior to surgery, to manage his hypertension and to control his fluid and electrolyte balance after surgery until his blood pressure returned to normal range. This experience convinced me that I should commit my professional life to "Renal Medicine," i.e., what we eventually labeled "Nephrology"....

"My clinical research during July 1961–June 1964...(included)...the effect of ethanol administration on urinary excretion of magnesium ...postural hypertension ... nephrotoxicity...consequent to bismuth...removal of bromide by hemodialysis... phosphaturia in magnesium deficient rats....

"I was Head of Nephrology and Medical Director of the 10-bed Hemodialysis Center at the Nashville VAH that was built during my early tenure. ...VAH provided office space and research laboratory space, equipment, and supplies through 1971, when I moved office space to Vanderbilt. This was the first VAH that was provided funding for the Hemodialysis Center and Renal Transplant program.[27]

"Between 1965 and 1971 I was salaried by an NIH Career Research Development Award. Dr. John 'Bud' Peters was the VAH Central Office Medical Director for all VAH Dialysis and Transplant Projects. I had known Bud since I was a medical student at Emory University, Ga., and he gave us extraordinarily strong support."

Several major contributions to many areas of nephrology were made by Manuel Martinez-Maldonado, now Vice-Provost for Research, Oregon Health Sciences University, and his group. Dr. Martinez-Maldonado began his nephrological career under the tutelage of Donald Seldin. He and his group performed studies of the mechanisms of urine concentration and dilution, tubular sodium reabsorption, the treatment of acute hypercalcemia, polycystic kidney disease, hypertension, and the intrarenal renin-angiotensin system.[28,29] In addition, Dr. Martinez-Maldonado reported that he "converted the Atlanta VA Medical Center into one of the premier teaching hospitals in the National VA Medical system and into the best clinical teaching experience at Emory University."

Another distinguished nephrologist whose research was been funded by the VA is James P. Knochel, Chair of Internal Medicine at Presbyterian Hospital of Dallas, and Clinical Professor of Internal Medicine, Southwestern Medical Center. Dr. Knochel is editor of *Kidney International* and on the editorial board of many journals including the *American Journal of Kidney Diseases, Seminars in Renal Diseases*, and *Mineral and Electrolyte Metabolism*. In Dr. Knochel's own words:

"The scope of my research activities that were funded by the VA included biochemical and physiological disorders of skeletal muscle leading to myopathy, rhabdomyolysis, myoglobinuria and acute renal failure. These particular disorders included derangements of potassium metabolism, environmental heat exposure, uremia, hypophosphatemia and phosphorous deficiency and alcoholism....[30,31] In 1971, the VA generously funded development of a combined hemodialysis/metabolic unit for the purposes of studying metabolism in uremia. We were able to show that uremic toxicity was associated with electrical depolorization of muscle cells and the development of a 'sick cell' characterized by a depressed content of potassium, and accumulation of sodium, chloride, water and calcium. Dialysis therapy was shown to reverse these changes back to normal....

"One cannot work at a VA hospital and avoid becoming interested in the metabolic effects of alcoholism. With the availability of the auto analyzer at that time, it was noted that virtually all severe alcoholics become hypophosphatemic, within 1-3 days following admission to the hospital. This observation led to a number of studies showing that skeletal muscle was the dominant site of phosphorous deficiency in these patients, amounting to deficits as much as 1800 millimoles of total body phosphorous. Chronic alcoholics were studied by the techniques we had at hand. We showed that their muscle cells were electrically depolarized and in terms of muscle composition commonly showed potassium deficiency, and always showed accumulations of salt, water and calcium and a reduction in magnesium. Every patient showed a severe phosphorous deficit in skeletal muscle. Our next studies involved experimental animals. Dogs were trained to ingest alcohol daily in an amount equivalent to one-fifth of hard liquor per day in a 70 kg man. After weeks of this preparation, it was shown that dogs develop severe phosphorous deficiency in skeletal muscle and during refeeding, become hypophosphatemic and develop acute rhabdomyolysis. We then proceeded to intentionally deplete dogs of phosphorous to a level observed in patients with chronic alcoholism. During re-feeding, administration of calories in the absence of adequate phosphorous led to the rapid appearance of hypophosphatemia. This was associated with a sharp elevation of creatine phosphokinase activity and the histologic appearance of rhabdomyolysis....

"I worked at the Dallas VA from July 1969 until July 1988, when I left to become the Chairman of Internal Medicine at Presbyterian Hospital of Dallas. Frankly, I believe the VA is unfortunately given inadequate recognition for the enormous amount of support they contribute to research, particularly by young investigators."

John D. Conger worked in the VA from 1973 until he retired in 2000. Over this period, he was Director of the Hemodialysis Unit, Associate Chief of Staff for R&D, and Chief of Staff at the VA Medical Center in Denver, Colorado. He also served as Assistant Dean and Director of the Renal Fellowship Program at the University of Colorado School of Medicine. Dr. Conger is a member of the ASN, ASCI and the AAP. He wrote:

"My research interests have been in the mechanisms and functional consequences of the aberrant vascular reactivity of the ischemically injured kidney.[32] The stimulus for this interest was an observed prolongation of acute renal failure in patients with vigorous dialysis where there were untoward hemodynamic effects including minimal to moderate hypotension. At the time, I was running an acute dialysis program aboard the *USS Sanctuary* in Viet Nam (1969–70). The subsequent research efforts over some 28 years were performed both in animal models and humans. The former was supported in large part by the VA. The findings seemed to indicate that the ischemic kidney has a striking hypersensitivity to hemodynamic perturbations resulting in recurrent and prolonged ischemic injury. While the mechanisms of this aberrant vascular reactivity are of considerable pathobiologic interest, the clinically important contributions of these observations have included the need to develop continuous-mode dialysis techniques that provide better hemodynamic stability and care in the use of pharmacologic agents that may have intense vasoconstrictive effects in the post-ischemic kidney."

Lawrence G. Raisz worked in the VA system from 1952 to 1960. Dr. Raisz reported:

"Following my internship on the Harvard service at the Boston City Hospital, I elected to go to New York University where Homer Smith had established a pioneer unit in renal physiology. After two years, I decided to return to Boston to complete my residency and contacted my old teachers, Charlie Davidson at Boston City Hospital, and Maurice Strauss, who was then the Head of Medicine at the Cushing VA Hospital in Framingham. The choice was not difficult. Maury offered the opportunity to continue to do some research during my residency as well as the far pleasanter environment in Framingham. I started my residency in October of 1950, but it was extremely short-lived. A week after I arrived, I received a notice that I was being recalled to the military service. Nevertheless, during that brief month, I learned that the VA could be a wonderful environment in which to develop an academic career. The next two years were spent happily at San Antonio doing research in the burn unit of the Brook Army Hospital. By the time I had completed my tour of duty, the Cushing VA in

Framingham had become the Boston VA, in a magnificent new building in Jamaica Plain. The new building not only had superb clinical facilities but a large laboratory to which even lowly residents like myself could have access. Maury Strauss was our leader and our inspiration. I had the good fortune to work with him on a review of the treatment of acute renal shutdown and a monograph 'Clinical Management of Renal Failure.' In the research arena, my mentor was Jack Rosenbaum. Before his untimely death in 1957 of metastastic cancer, Jack inspired a generation of young clinical investigators to carry out precise studies of renal function and particularly of effects of hormones in humans. There were many bright and productive investigators at the Boston VA who created an exciting atmosphere, including Solomon Papper, Franklin Williams, Irwin Arias and many others who went on to distinguished academic careers. Perhaps my most important VA-supported research publication was the study on 'The effects of cortisone and hydrocortisone on water diuresis and renal function in man,' published with Jack Rosenbaum in the *Journal of Clinical Investigation* in 1957.[33]

"My initial research efforts in calcium were supported by Dr. Strauss in Boston and by the Chiefs of Medicine at the Syracuse VA Hospital. However, the opportunity to switch fields and begin the new adventure of calcium studies was dependent on direct research funding as a VA clinical investigator.

"Having left nephrology so many years ago, it is difficult for me to put the accomplishments of the Boston VA group and my own small group at Syracuse in context, but we certainly were able to flourish and be productive by virtue of support from the VA system. These were great times for young investigator! At Syracuse, I was fortunate to work with a number of outstanding fellows including Bill Au, Bob Siber, Bob Lindeman and Cannes Van Buren, all of whom went on to successful academic careers."

Richard P. Wedeen *(the author of this chapter)* joined the VA Medical Center in East Orange, New Jersey in 1978 as Associate Chief of Staff for Research and Development and Professor of Medicine at the University of Medicine and Dentistry of New Jersey-the New Jersey Medical School. A member of the ASCI, Dr. Wedeen had also served as a Visiting Lecturer at Harvard Medical School with Sam Their and as Visiting Professor of Medicine at the University of Antwerp with Marc DeBroe. Owing to his interest in integrating Occupational Medicine and Nephrology, he was appointed Professor of Preventive Medicine and Community Health at the New Jersey Medical School. As former Chief of Medicine at the Jersey City Medical Center, Dr. Wedeen brought to the East Orange VAMC two other nephrologists, John Maesaka and Vecihi Batuman, from Jersey City, who both developed distinguished academic careers in nephrology. These New Jersey VA nephrologists published clinical research on lead nephropathy and basic research on concentrative transport of organic acids using a technique of section-freeze-dry autoradiography developed in Dr. Wedeen's laboratory.[34,35] While at the VA, Dr. Wedeen pioneered a new area in nephrology with the publication in 1983 of a paper, "Occupational Renal Diseases" in the *American Journal of Kidney Diseases* at the request of the editor, George Porter.[36] At the VA, Dr. Wedeen published a history of lead poisoning *Poison in the Pot: The Legacy of Lead*, which chronicled the ancient sagas of this heavy metal as well as the history of lead nephropathy.[37] While working at the VA, Dr. Wedeen was able to contribute to the history of nephrology by pioneering the concept of occupational renal disease, delve into the history of medicine, and help mold public policy on lead poisoning in adults.

Dr. John Maesaka's first work at the VA addressed the mechanism of tubular backleak in acute tubular necrosis induced by maleic acid.[38] His later VA-supported research

"...dealt with hyponatremic, hypouricemic patients that allowed us to differentiate SIADH from renal salt wasting syndrome.[39] This was the insight paper that was expanded at LIJ (Long Island Jewish Hospital) and here at Winthrop where we demonstrated natriuretic activity in plasma from candidates with renal salt wasting in neurosurgical patients and Alzheimer's disease. We are in the process of trying to isolate and identify the salt wasting protein. As an offshoot of these studies, we got into apoptosis in Alzheimer's disease, isolated prostaglandin D2 synthase and identified it as the apoptotic factor. We are the first to demonstrate apoptosis by PGD2S...."

Dr. Batuman noted:

"The VA has funded our research exploring mechanisms of renal handling and toxicity of filtered myeloma light chains. This work has resulted in significant insight into mechanisms of renal disease seen in patients with multiple myeloma. More important, it has revealed that filtered small proteins are endocytosed by a receptor-mediated process, and that myeloma light chains are ligands for the endocytic receptors cubilin and megalin. Most recent work, currently supported by the VA (2002), shows that excessive endocytosis of light chains by proximal tubule cells results in the induction of inflammatory cytokines that may be responsible for the chronic tubulointerstitial disease. This research shows that excessive protein endocytosis can cause tubulointerstitial inflammation not only in multiple myeloma, but also in other proteinuric diseases associated with increased filtration of low-molecular weight proteins, including immunoglobulin light chains."[40,41]

Our understanding of nutrition in renal failure was improved by the major contributions of Joel D. Kopple. He served as president of the National Kidney Foundation in 1986 and his numerous honors include the Louis Pasteur Medal and Award of the University of Strasbourg, France, the David M. Hume Award of the National Kidney Foundation, the E.V. McCollum Award of the American Society of Clinical Nutrition, the Thomas Addis Medal of the International Society of Renal Nutrition and Metabolism and the Malpighi Medal of the University of Messina, Italy. The Council on Renal Nutrition of the National Kidney Foundation established a lectureship in his honor in 2001. Dr. Kopple recorded:

"I worked at the Wadsworth VA Medical Center for 18 years, from July 1963 until January 1982. That time included three years of medical residency, one or two years fellowship training in Nephrology and Metabolism (as our training program was called at the time), and then a number of staff appointments, usually in research positions. It was a period of tremendous growth and personal and academic enrichment. Probably the most important pieces of research that I participated in at Wadsworth involved the following: 1. Studies of lead metabolism and the contribution of respiratory lead intake to body lead burden in normal individuals. 2. The demonstration that histidine is an essential amino acid in normal and uremic individuals. 3. Evidence that in individuals receiving total parenteral nutrition, taurine is an essential (indispensable) amino acid. 4. The dietary protein and energy requirements in patients with chronic renal failure and those undergoing maintenance hemodialysis and dietary protein requirements in patients undergoing continuous ambulatory peritoneal dialysis.[42] 5. Dietary requirements for other nutrients in acute or chronic renal failure.[43] 6. Growth hormone and insulin-like growth factor-1 increase renal blood flow and glomerular filtration rate."

Carlos A. Vaamonde received his medical degree in Argentina and his post-doctoral training under the tutelage of Sol Papper at the Medical College of Virginia. From 1971 to 2001 Dr. Vaamonde was Chief of the Nephrology Section at the VA Hospital in Miami and was Professor of Medicine at the University of Miami School of Medicine in 1975 until his retirement in 2001. He was made Honorary Professor at the University of Buenos Aires in 1992 and received the first Victor Raúl Maitallo Award of the Latin American Society of Nephrology and Hypertension in 1996. His VA-supported research included studies of the renal effects of hypothyroidism, acid-base balance, and nephrotoxicity. His work on hypothyroidism helped to:

"unravel the pathogenetic mechanisms involved in the abnormalities of renal function in human hypothyroidism...The research work became involved with experimental animals. [It]demonstrated that the decreased GFR (regularly observed in hypothyroidism) was not caused by a decreased number of functioning nephrons (like in chronic renal disease) but rather by a diminished GFR per single nephron and was not the consequence of redistribution of filtrate from deep juxtamedullary glomeruli to superficial glomeruli;[44] the fractional excretion of bicarbonate in these rats was higher than in normal rats, and closely related to the impaired Na reabsorption characteristic of experimental hypothyroidism.[45]"

Some of the research performed decades ago, while cutting edge at the time, has receded into history thanks to further advances. The innovative research of Paul R. Schloerb falls into this category.

In 1956, Dr. Schloerb reported on:

"...the use of isolated jejunal perfusion to remove toxic uremic metabolites. After presentation at the American College of Surgeons meeting in San Francisco, I was deluged with phone calls, worldwide, with requests for information and treatment. This was prior to general use of chronic hemodialysis and renal transplantation...we identified rapid jejunal and gastric transfers of water, urea, hydrogen, sodium, potassium, chloride, and HCO_3, but not phosphate, creatinine or probably many other larger unmeasured molecular weight substances. Although promising at the time, with the early subsequent development of renal homotransplantation and availability of chronic hemodialysis and peritoneal dialysis, further application of intestinal dialysis was not appropriate."[46]

Edward J. Weinman has been a Professor of Medicine at the University of Texas, Houston, Texas, at the UCLA School of Medicine, West Virginia School of Medicine and the University of Maryland. Of his VA-supported work, he wrote:

"I have been supported by research funds from the Department of Veterans Affairs since 1971 except for a brief period that I was out of the VA system. Initial funds from the VA established our renal micropuncture laboratories in Houston, Texas and supported detailed studies on the renal transport of organic anions. We focused initially on the absorption and secretion of uric acid and the effect of drugs and simulated clinical conditions on these transport processes.[47] In the rat, uric acid was filtered at the glomerulus. In the proximal tubule, uric acid was reabsorbed and secreted; the dominant direction being tubular reabsorption. Uric acid transport was influenced by the state of hydration of the animal but was not directly linked to sodium transport. In other studies, we established that oxalate was filtered at the glomerulus and secreted in the proximal tubule.[48] There was a small absorptive flux but net secretion was the prevailing direction. Neither uric acid nor oxalate was transported to a significant degree at nephron segments other than the proximal tubule. These experiments examining two important constituents of renal stones established the basic physiology of these two anions and provided the base for subsequent molecular and biochemical studies of others.

"In recent years, VA research funds have supported studies that identified the Na+/H+ Exchanger Regulatory Factor (NHERF) family of proteins. In the course of study of the inhibition of sodium-hydrogen exchange transport in the brush border membrane of the proximal tubule of the kidney by cAMP dependent protein kinase (PKA), we demonstrated that an additional co-factor was required. These experiments ultimately lead to the isolation and cloning of a new family of PDZ (PSD-95/Dig-1, Drosophilae disc large/ZO-1) motif proteins now containing two members (NHERF and NHERF2). Subsequent experiments defined an expanding role for these proteins in systems other than the kidney including the effect of estrogen in estrogen-receptor positive breast cancer cell lines, testicular differentiation, and cell cycle regulation....

"Having defined the physiologic role of NHERF in the regulation of NHE3 and defined the biochemistry of the NHE3/NHERF interactions, we have expanded our research efforts to include development of a knock-out mouse, and to determine the role of NHERF in renal glomerular injury and in the maintenance of the glomerular barrier to albumin. These efforts have also been supported by VA research funds."

Dr. Weinman's research exemplifies the serendipity of physiology transformed by modern techniques into molecular biology and genetic engineering. Having started on a quest for the mechanisms whereby organic materials are transferred across cell membranes in order to be conserved or excreted by the kidneys, decades later this work not only identifies the membrane protein responsible for the transport process, but identifies the gene responsible for the protein. And then the gene turns out also to be responsible for modulating calcium transport in bone with implications for osteoporosis in humans. The fruits of basic research are often unexpected.

Irwin Singer served as Chief of the VA Medical Service at the University of Pennsylvania Division of Medicine, Philadelphia and Chief of Staff at the VA Lakeside Medical Center, Chicago. His research was at both the basic science level, which centered on studying cellular functions in the toad bladder, and at the clinical level, which included studying the actions of lithium in humans.[51,52]

John T. Daugirdas, Chicago Westside VA Medical Center and Professor of Medicine, University of Illinois at Chicago School of Medicine, served as editor of the Rapid Communications Section, *International Journal of Artificial Organs* and as editor of *Hypertension, Dialysis and Clinical Nephrology*. He is a member of the editorial boards of *Kidney International, ASAIO Journal, Dialysis and Transplantation, Journal of Blood Purification,* and the *American Journal of Kidney Disease.* Dr. Daugirdas's VA-supported research has been concerned with metabolic aspects of uremia and renal replacement therapy.[53,54]

Many other VA-funded investigators applied the critical skills learned while conducting VA-supported research to the practice of nephrology within the community, bringing the twentieth century's remarkable advances in treatment of kidney disease from the bench to the bedside. Practicing in communities around the world are dozens of nephrologists who trained in VA nephrology programs in an environment dedicated to the acquisition of new knowledge. Their contribution to the practice of modern nephrology cannot be overestimated.

Conclusion

This survey of investigators supported by VA funding for renal research reflects the impact of the Department of Veterans Affairs on nephrology in the mid twentieth century. The recipients of VA funding for kidney research became leaders in American medicine. The focus of VA-funded research has remained on clinical medicine driven by the needs of the veteran population. While many investigators within the VA made seminal contributions to the basic sciences, all have made contributions to the practice of medicine. Peer-reviewed competition for research grants in the VA Merit Review system has assured veterans that the physicians serving them are not only excellent clinicians but also at the cutting edge of medical science.

References

1. Hegstrom, R., Quinton, W.E., Dillard, D.H., Cole, J. and Scribner, B.H., "One Year's Experience with the Use of Indwelling Teflon Cannulas and Bypass." *Trans Am Soc Artif Intern Organs*, 1961. **7**: 47-56.

2. Goldstein, J.L., Http://Laskerfoundation.Org/Awards/Library/2002-Gold-Intro.Shtlm.

3. Freis, E.D. for VA Cooperative Study on Antihypertensive Agents, "Effects of Treatment on Morbidity in Hypertension." *JAMA*, 1970. **213**: 1143-1152.

4. Freis, E.D. and Wilson, I.M., "Potentiating Effect of Chlorothiazide (Diuril) in Combination with Antihypertensive Agents." *Med Ann DC*, 1957. **9**: 468.

5. Starzl, T.E., Groth, C.G., Terasaki, P.I., Putnam, C.W., Brettschneider, L. and Marchioro, T.L., "Heterologous Antilymphocyte Globulin, Histoincompatiblity Matching, and Human Renal Homotransplantation." *Surg Gynecol Obstet*, 1968. **126**: 1023-1035.

6. Starzl, T.E., Todo, S., Fung, J., Demetris, A.J., Venkataramman, R. and Jain, A., "FK 506 for Liver, Kidney, and Pancreas Transplantation." *Lancet*, 1989. **2**: 1000-1004.

7. Starzl, T.E. and Marchioro, T.L., "The Reversal of Rejection in Human Renal Homografts with Subsequent Development of Homograft Tolerance." *Surg Gynecol Obstet*, 1963. **117**: 385-395.

8. Gonick, H.C., Goldberg, G., Rubini, M.E. and Guze, L.B., "Functional Abnormalities in Experimental Pyelonephritis. I. Studies of Concentrating Ability." *Nephron*, 1965. **2**: 193-206.

9. Guze, L.B., Hubert, E.G., Montgomerie, J.Z. and Kalmanson, G.M., "Observations on the Killing of Microbial Protoplasts by Serum." *Nature*, 1967. **214**: 1343-1344.

10. Kunin, C.M., "The Natural History of Recurrent Bacteriuria in Schoolgirls." *N Engl J Med*, 1970. **282**: 1443-1448.

11. Kunin, C.M., "Long-Term Therapy of Urinary Tract Infections." *Ann Intern Med*, 1975. **83**: 273-274.

12. Relman, A.S., Lambie, A.T., Burrows, B.A. and Roy, A.M., "Cation Accumulation by Muscle Tissue; the Displacement of Potassium by Rubidium and Cesium in the Living Animal." *J Clin Invest*, 1957. **36**: 1249-1256.

13. Block, J.B. and Burrows, B.A., "Diagnostic Use of I131-Diodrast in Hypertension Due to Unilateral Renal Disease." *Circulation*, 1959. **18**: 696-.

14. Slick, G.L., Aguilera, A.J., Zambraski, E.J., DiBona, G.F. and Kaloyanides, G.J., "Renal Neuroadrenergic Transmission." *Am J Physiol*, 1975. **229**: 60-65.

15. DiBona, G.F. and Sawin, L.L., "Effect of Renal Nerve Stimulation on NaCl and H2O Transport in Henle's Loop of the Rat." *Am J Physiol*, 1982. **243**: F576-580.

16. Brenner, B.M., Troy, J.L. and Daugharty, T.M., "The Dynamics of Glomerular Ultrafiltration in the Rat." *J Clin Invest*, 1971. **50**: 1776-1780.

17. Brenner, B.M., Troy, J.L., Daugharty, T.M. and MacInnes, R.M., "Quantitative Importance of Changes in Postglomerular Colloid Osmotic Pressure in Mediating Glomerulotubular Balance in the Rat." *J Clin Invest*, 1973. **52**: 190-197.

18. Gilbert, D.N., Houghton, D.C., Bennett, W.M., Plamp, C.E., Reger, K. and Porter, G.A., "Reversibility of Gentamicin Nephrotoxicity in Rats: Recovery During Continuous Drug Administration." *Proc Soc Exp Biol Med*, 1979. **160**: 99-103.

19. Bennett, W.M., Plamp, C.E., Gilbert, D.N., Parker, R.A. and Porter, G.A., "The Influence of Dosage Regimen on Experimental Gentamicin Nephrotoxicity: Dissociation of Peak Serum Levels from Renal Failure." *J Infect Dis*, 1979. **140**: 576-580.

20. Blantz, R.C., Konnen, K.S. and Tucker, B.J., "Angiotensin II Effects Upon the Glomerular Microcirculation and Ultrafiltration Coefficient of the Rat." *J Clin Invest*, 1976. **57**: 419-434.

21. Tucker, B.J., Steiner, R.W., Gushwa, L.C. and Blantz, R.C., "Studies on the Tubulo-Glomerular Feedback System in the Rat. The Mechanism of Reduction in Filtration Rate with Benzolamide." *J Clin Invest*, 1978. **62**: 993-1004.

22. Kleeman, C.R. and Maxwell, M.H., "Contributory Role of Extrarenal Factors in the Polyuria of Potassium Depletion." *N Engl J Med*, 1959. **260**: 268-271.

23. Papper, S., Saxon, L., Rosenbaum, J. and Cohen, H., "Effects of Isotonic and Hypotonic Salt Solutions on Renal Excretion of Sodium." *J Lab Clin Med*, 1956. **47**: 776-782.

24. Hodsman, A.B., Sherrard, D.J., Alfrey, A.C., Brickman, A.S., Miller, N.L., Maloney, N.A. and Coburn, J.W., "Bone Aluminum and Histomorphometric Features of Renal Osteodystrophy." *J Clin Endocrinol Metab*, 1982. **54**: 539-546.

25. Ott, S.M., Maloney, N.A., Klein, G.L., Alfrey, A.C., Ament, A.C., Coburn, J.W. and Sherrard, D.J., "Aluminum Is Associated with Low Bone Formation in Patients on Chronic Parenteral Nutrition." *Ann Intern Med*, 1983. **98**: 910-914.

26. Ginn, H.E., Unger, H.E., Hume, D.E. and Shilling, J.A., "Human Renal Transplantation. An Investigation of the Functional Status of the Denervated Kidney after Successful Homotransplantation in Identical Twins." *J Lab Clin Med*, 1960. **56**: 1-13.

27. Ginn, H.E., Frost, A. and Lacy, W.W., "Nitrogen Balance in Hemodialysis Patients." *Am J Clin Nutr*, 1968. **21**: 385-393.

28. Martinez-Maldonado, M., Eknoyan, G. and Suki, W., "Effects of Cyanide on Renal Concentration and Dilution." *Am J Physiol*, 1969. **217**: 451-458.

29. Suki, W., Yuim, J.J., Von Minden, M., Saker-Hebert, C., Eknoyan, G. and Martinez-Maldonado, M., "Acute Treatment of Hypercalcemia with Furosemide." *N Engl J Med*, 1970. **283**: 933-937.

30. Knochel, J.P. and Schlein, E.M., "On the Mechanism of Rhabdomyolysis in Potassium Depletion." *J Clin Invest*, 1972. **51**: 1750-1758.

31. Knochel, J.P., Barcenas, C., Cotton, J.R., Fuller, T.J., Haller, R. and Carter, N.W., "Hypophosphatemia and Rhabdomyolysis." *Trans Assoc Am Physicians*, 1978. **91**: 156-168.

32. Conger, J.D., Robinette, J.B. and Hammond, W.S., "Differences in Vascular Reactivity in Models of Ischemic Acute Renal Failure." *Kidney Int*, 1991. **39**: 1087-1097.

33. Raisz, L.G., McNeely, W.S., Saxon, L. and Rosenbaum, J.D., "The Effects of Cortisone and Hydrocortisone on Water Diuresis and Renal Function in Man." *J Clin Invest*, 1957. **36**: 767-779.

34. Batuman, V., Landy, E., Maesaka, J.K. and Wedeen, R.P., "Contribution of Lead to Hypertension with Renal Impairment." *N Engl J Med*, 1983. **309**: 17-21.

35.   Wedeen, R.P. and Weiner, B., "The Distribution of p-Aminohippuric Acid in Rat Kidney Slices. I. Tubular Localization." *Kidney Int*, 1973. **3**: 205-213.

36.   Wedeen, R.P., "Occupational Renal Disease." *Am J Kidney Dis*, 1984. **3**: 241-257.

37.   Wedeen, R.P., *Poison in the Pot: The Legacy of Lead.* Carbondale, IL: Southern Illinois University Press, 1983

38.   Maesaka, J.K. and McCaffery, M., "Evidence for Renal Tubular Leakage in Maleic Acid-Induced Fanconi Syndrome." *Am J Physiol*, 1980. **239**: F507-513.

39.   Maesaka, J.K., Batuman, V., Yudd, M., Salem, M., Sved, A.F. and Venkatesan, J., "Hyponatremia and Hypouricemia: Differentiation from the syndrome of inappropriate secretion of antidiuretic hormone." *Clin Nephrol*, 1990. **33**: 174-178.

40.   Batuman, V., Sastrasinh, M. and Sastrasinh, S., "Light Chain Effects on Alanine and Glucose Uptake by Renal Brush Border Membranes." *Kidney Int*, 1986. **30**: 662-665.

41.   Batuman, V. and Guan, S., "Receptor-Mediated Endocytosis of Immunoglobulin Light Chains in Cultured Proximal Tubule Cells." *Am J Physiol*, 1997. **272 (Renal Physiol 41)**: F521-530.

42.   Kopple, J.D., Sorensen, M.K., Coburn, J.W., Gordon, S. and Rubini, M.E., "Controlled Comparison of 20-g and 40-g Protein Diets in the Treatment of Chronic Uremia." *Am J Clin Nutr*, 1968. **21**: 553-564.

43.   Kopple, J.D. and Coburn, J.W., "Metabolic Studies of Low Protein Diets in Uremia. I. Nitrogen and Potassium." *Medicine (Baltimore)*, 1973. **52**: 583-595.

44.   Michael, U.F., Barenberg, R.I., Chavez, R., Vaamonde, C.A., and Papper, S. "Renal handling of sodium and water in hypothyroid rat." *JU Clini Invest*, 1972. **51**:1405-1412.

45.   Michael, U.F., Kelley, J., and Vaamonde, C.A. "Impaired renal bicarbonate reabsorption in the hypothyroid rat." *Am J Physiol*, 1979. **236**: F536-F540.

46.   Schloerb, P.R., "Enterodialysis: An Approach to the Problem of Renal Substitution." *Surg Forum*, 1956. **7**: 58-62.

47.   Weinman, E.J., Steplock, D., Suki, W.N. and Eknoyan, G., "Urate Reabsorption in Proximal Convoluted Tubule of the Rat Kidney." *Am J Physiol*, 1976. **231**: 509-515.

48.   Weinman, E.J., Frankfurt, S.J., Ince, A. and Sansom, S., "Renal Tubular Transport of Organic Acids: Studies with Oxalate and PAH in the Rat." *J Clin Invest*, 1976. **61**: 801-806.

49.   Cunarro, J.A., Schultz, S.E., Johnson, W.A. and Weiner, M.W., "Effects of Ischemia on Metabolite Concentrations in Dog Renal Cortex." *Ren Physiol*, 1982. **5**: 143-155.

50.   Koretsky, A.P., Wang, S., Murphy-Boesch, J., Klein, M.P., James, T.L. and Weiner, M.W., "31P NMR Spectroscopy of Rat Organs, in Situ, Using Chronically Implanted Radiofrequency Coils." *Proc Natl Acad Sci U S A*, 1983. **80**: 7491-7495.

51.   Singer, I., Rotenberg, D. and Puschett, J.B., "Lithium-Induced Nephrogenic Diabetes Insipidus: In Vivo and in Vitro Studies." *J Clin Invest*, 1972. **51**: 1081-1091.

52.   Singer, I., "Lithium and the Kidney." *Kidney Int*, 1981. **19**: 374-387.

53.   Daugirdas, J.T. and Nawab, Z.M., "Acetate Relaxation of Vascular Smooth Muscle." *Kidney Int,* 1987. **32**: 39-46.

54.   Yu, A.W., Ing, T.S., Zabaneh, R.I. and Daugirdas, J.T., "Effect of Dialysate Temperature on Hemodynamics and Urea Removal." *Kidney Int,* 1995. **48**: 237-243.

Chapter 25. VA Contributions to Rheumatology
Thomas Benedek, M.D.

Musculo-skeletal (rheumatic) complaints and diseases have become the most prevalent category of medical problems in the United States. "Arthritis and rheumatic conditions" in 1985 were estimated to affect 35 million people.[1] The prevalence estimate had increased to 42.7 million in 1992.[2] According to a 1991-92 survey of adults who stated that they suffered from a medical or psychiatric disability the disability was attributed to "arthritis or rheumatism" by 17.1% and to "back or spine problems" by an additional 13.5%.[3] Diagnostically, the vast majority are osteoarthritis. The cost of musculo-skeletal conditions (medical and traumatic) was estimated in 1992 to have been $149.4 billion, of which 48.4% was for medical expenses. Only 5.6% of expenditures was related to treatment of trauma. $77.1 billion was attributed to lost income. In the 18-44 year age group, lost income accounted for 58.9%; for those 45-64 years old, 73.7% and 26.2% for those above age 65.[4]

Interest in addressing musculo-skeletal ailments as a medical specialty was slow to develop. The first organization of physicians with an interest in rheumatic diseases, the forerunner of the American College of Rheumatology, was founded in 1933. As of 1946, it had 285 members. This slow expansion may, in part, be attributed to the deficiency of rheumatologic training programs – at that time there were still only five.[5] In 1949, the annual national expenditure for rheumatologic research was $300,000![6] Then, coincidentally, three events occurred that stimulated interest in rheumatology, both as a clinical specialty and an area for basic research. These were the discovery of rheumatoid factor and of the L.E. (lupus erythematosus) cell in 1948 and of the therapeutic effect of cortisone in 1949. By 1950, the membership of the American Rheumatism Association (ARA) had increased to 600 and by 1956 to 1169, a quadrupling within a decade. Membership passed 3,000 in 1978. The National Institute for Arthritis and Metabolic Diseases (NIAMD) was established in 1950, and the subspecialty examining board for rheumatology gave its first examination in 1960.[5] These few data, to which must be added the low funding for research in the VA budget, explain the paucity of rheumatologic research within the VA prior to 1960 and its slow development over the next decade. Few trained rheumatologists were employed by the VA and effective collaboration with the slowly increasing number of medical school faculty rheumatologists and basic scientists still was minimal, although this began to be encouraged after 1946.

Most VA investigators spend only a portion of their careers with the VA. For many individuals their rheumatologic contributions were incidental to a variety of other interests, while a few are clearly associated with the clinical and/or laboratory investigation of a particular subject. It was common for authors to indicate only their academic affiliation, making it difficult to determine whether their projects were partially or entirely based at the VA. A few case reports and small clinical investigations began to be published in the late 1940s, while basic research that required specialized laboratories and training began about a decade later. The first VA author on rheumatologic topics may have been John C. Nunemaker, M.D., Chief of Medicine at the Salt Lake City VA Hospital. He co-authored a case report on psoriatic arthritis in 1948 and another on anklylosing spondylitis in identical twins in 1950.[7, 8]

Thomas M. Brown, M.D., was at the Rockefeller Institute in 1939 when he participated in some animal experiments with cultures of "pleuropneumonia-like organisms" (PPLO, later called mycoplasma).[9] In 1948, Dienes et al. (Boston) reported a possibly pathogenetic association between PPLO and Reiter's disease (an arthritic syndrome now called reactive arthritis).[10] At the same time Brown, who was by then Chief of Medicine at the Washington, D.C. VA Hospital, was studying the antibiotic sensitivity of human PPLO. He found that Myochrysine (gold sodium thiomalate), then a standard treatment for rheumatoid arthritis (RA), did not affect PPLO, while they were sensitive to Aureomycin (chlor-tetracycline). Clinical improvement occurred on Aureomycin therapy in several patients with various rheumatologic diagnoses, whether or not prostatic or cervical cultures had grown PPLO.[11]

Subsequently, Brown speculated that "rheumatic diseases" result from an immunologic reaction of which PPLO are an important antigen. He compared the sensitivity of PPLO to several antibiotics and found Terramycin (oxy-tetracycline) to be the most effective.[12] Neither Brown's hypothesis of a pathogenetic role of PPLO in rheumatic diseases nor his advocacy of tetracycline therapy for RA gained wide acceptance however, and they have largely been forgotten.

Almost simultaneously with the introduction of cortisone as an anti-rheumatic drug, several British reports claimed that another adrenal hormone, desoxycorticosterone (DOCA), was effective against RA. However, in 1950 several papers had already appeared that contradicted this claim. One of them came from the Cleveland VA Hospital. The authors included Norman P. Shumway, the Chief of Medicine, but the lead author was W.E. James, a medical resident. According to their literature review, improvement of RA from DOCA had been claimed in about 80% of cases, but lacked adequate documentation. They performed a double-blind study, a type of study that was then still quite unusual. The injections were IM DOCA + IV saline, IM cholesterol + IV saline, IM cholesterol and IV ascorbic acid, IM DOCA + IV ascorbic acid. Although treatments were changed weekly, there was no benefit from DOCA in any of five men with RA.[13] This paper was important especially because of the methodology it employed.

Among the early studies, the one that was most broadly relevant to both rheumatology and orthopedics, and in the VA to compensation issues, was published in 1950 by John D. Southworth and Solomon R. Bersack, radiologists at the Washington, DC VA Hospital. It pertained to the question whether complaints of low back pain are attributable to congenital anomalies of the lumbo-sacral vertebrae. Since gastrointestinal x-ray examinations include the skeletal area of interest, such films of 550 patients who had *not* been examined for skeletal complaints, and therefore were assumed not to have low back symptoms, were reviewed. The most frequent anomalies were spina bifida occulta (18.2%), and a range of enlargements of the last lumbar and/or first sacral vertebrae, potentially resulting in a fusion of the two (8.4%). Of the patients over 40 years of age, 25.4% had some degree of osteoarthritis. However, there was no relationship between this and the presence of an anomaly. Thus, lumbo-sacral skeletal anomalies should not be considered either a cause of low back pain or predisposing to the development of osteoarthritis.[14]

It should not be surprising that the first VA scientists to publish rheumatologically relevant research were not rheumatologists. Studies pertaining to the elucidation of the diagnostic specificity of the L.E. cell were begun by John R. Walsh and Hyman J. Zimmerman from the Omaha, NB VA Hospital in 1953. They found an association between the occurrence of L.E. cells and allergic reactions to penicillin.[15] In 1955, Zimmerman, now Chief of Medicine at Chicago West Side VA Hospital, with two residents reported a study of hepatic function in systemic lupus erythematosus (SLE). They concluded that abnormal hepatic test results usually reflected plasma protein abnormalities, presumably attributable to SLE, rather than concurrent parenchymal liver disease.[16] In two cases of severe non-fatal hepatic failure without any evidence of SLE, however, "false-positive" L.E. cells were found.[17] An oft-cited paper co-authored with Paul Heller, a hematologist on Zimmerman's service, pertained to criteria for differentiating the L.E. cell from other phagocytic blood cells.[18]

As it turned out, the importance of recognizing L.E. cells was about to diminish, owing particularly to the work of another VA physician. George J. Friou at West Haven, CT, VA Hospital devised a method for the detection of the L.E. cell phenomenon by fluorescence microscopy (published 1958).[19] The cell nuclei, which did not have to be human, were treated with the patient's serum, followed by anti-human rabbit gamma globulin conjugated with a fluorescent dye that bound itself to the nuclei. The addition of the patient's serum causes fluorescence under ultraviolet light if the serum contains anti-nuclear antibodies. The reacting factor in LE serum was shown to react with nucleohistone (DNA).[20] The fluorescence test is more sensitive and less labor intensive than that required to recognize the L.E. cell. This technique proved to be an extremely important discovery. Its sensitivity led to its application with various refinements in subsets of SLE and other connective tissue diseases.[21] For example, staining of cell nucleoli rather than nuclei is associated not with SLE but with scleroderma.[22]

William R. Merchant, an internist, participated with Thomas Brown in the PPLO studies in Washington. After 1954, when he became ACOS/R&E at the Pittsburgh University Drive VA Hospital, he for several years participated in entirely different investigations. He joined a team led by Sidney Cobb, M.D., at the University of Pittsburgh School of Public Health, which performed pioneering studies on the epidemiology of rheumatoid arthritis (RA) and osteoarthritis, published during 1955-57,[23-26] These were the first U.S. community-based studies of the prevalence of rheumatoid arthritis. Interview and examination results were correlated and indicated that positive answers to a mere three questions— "Do you have morning stiffness, joint tenderness, pain on motion?"—provided a practical index for the identification of this disease. (This work also is an early example of the contribution of VA personnel to non-VA research.)

David S. Howell, M.D., became affiliated with the Miami, Florida VA Hospital in 1955 and spent his entire career there, in conjunction with a faculty appointment at the University of Miami Medical School, where he became Professor of Medicine. He may be considered the first full-time VA rheumatologic investigator. Dr. Howell's first studies of lasting importance (1960-1961) pertained to the rheumatoid factor. He was the lead author in demonstrating that "false positive" test results occur most frequently in hepatic diseases and that non-hepatic false positive rheumatoid factor reactions may be minimized by testing the euglobulin (less soluble in ammonium sulfate than "pseudoglobulin") fraction of the serum rather than the whole serum.[27]

Howell's international reputation, however, is based on his decades of investigation of cartilage. These studies, with numerous collaborators, focused mainly on the biochemical factors that mediate the deterioration of articular cartilage, both in experimental models of osteoarthritis and in human specimens. The former mainly used rat and calf cartilage, while human specimens were obtained at arthrotomy or arthroscopy. The first of these reports was published in 1960: "A profile of electrolytes in the cartilaginous growth plate of growing ribs."[28] This report not only identifies all of the major electrolytes in growing bovine rib cartilage, but notes the differences in their concentration related to developmental zones.

Much of the work on cartilage metabolism required the development of innovative micro-analytical methods. This phase of the investigations was carried out particularly in collaboration with Howell's colleague, Julio C. Pita, Ph.D. For example, Howell demonstrated that calcium is stored on proteoglycan, and that hydrolytic enzymes release phosphate from nucleotides at the sites of calcium storage.[29]. This work was made possible by Pita's development of an ultramicro-spectrophotometric method and a newly designed micropuncture pipette. An x-ray analytic technic was used to detect sulfur as a marker for mucopolysaccharide in growing cartilage. This technic demonstrated defective organization of immature cartilage in rachitic (vitamin D-deficient) calves, and that this microstructural abnormality inhibited normal calcification.[30] Basic studies such as these have added to the understanding of the growth and maintenance requirements of articular cartilage, and therefore to the understanding of diseases that affect that tissue, such as rickets and osteoarthritis.

Cartilage degeneration is the primary process of osteoarthritis and an important secondary process even in rheumatoid arthritis. Its pathophysiology was a major research interest of Howell's and a little later also of Kang's group (see below) of investigators. Review of this research demonstrates how bits of information gradually accumulate to form a comprehensible, if yet incomplete picture. This work was begun in 1973 by Howell and Roy D. Altman, one of Howell's former (1967-1969) fellows (see below). An early study pertained to intra-articular pyrophosphate. While this substance was known to be increased in "pseudo-gout," a new micro-assay demonstrated excess concentrations also in some cases of gout and most cases of osteoarthritis.[31] Whether pyrophosphate has a more general pathogenetic effect in articular disease than was formerly suspected has still not been ascertained.

The main focus of Howell and Altman was on the effect of several enzymes on proteoglycans. These are large hydrated protein-polysaccharide complexes to which collagen fibers are attached in articular cartilage. Initially, the experiments used rabbits in which osteoarthritis had been induced by an operation on a knee and employed Pita's analytic methods. It was found that more proteoglycan could be extracted from osteoarthritic cartilage than from normal cartilage. This indicated that either the size of the proteoglycan polymers had been reduced and/or the association of proteoglycans with collagen fibers had diminished. An ultramicroassay of proteoglycans obtained results that differentiated normal cartilage from discolored cartilage. This chemical approach indicated that the degraded proteoglycan may indicate the earliest phase of osteoarthritis.[32] A clinically applicable method to demonstrate the osteoarthritic process before there is gross cartilage damage was an important goal toward which the above research is a beginning.

In 1976, Asher I. Sapolsky and others including Howell, showed that enzymes called metalloproteases are capable of digesting proteoglycan. These enzymes are present in articular cartilage and are probably secreted by chondrocytes (cartilage cells). Three enzymes were detected by these investigators, one of which is active at physiologic rather than acid pH.[33] These are called collagenase, gelatinase and stromolysin. In 1983, Howell with two of his former (1979-1981) fellows, J.-P. Pelletier and J. Martel-Pelletier, then in Montreal, showed that collagenase, a collagen digesting enzyme, also exhibits activity in human osteoarthritic cartilage.[34] Subsequently, they found that the increased activity of collagenase in osteoarthritic cartilage was approximately of the same magnitude as the increase of neutral metalloprotease.[35] Although additional chondrolytic enzymes can be demonstrated in rheumatoid arthritis, the same investigators (1985) found that the neutral metalloprotease activity in the cartilage of rheumatoid patients increases about eight-fold from normal, as it does in osteoarthritis.[36]

Roy D. Altman, early in his career at the Miami VA Hospital, participated with Howell in the studies of cartilage cited with Howell's work. Altman began clinical studies of the symptoms and treatment of Paget's disease of bone in 1973 and became a leading authority on this disease.[40] In 1977 he published data on up to 24 months of etidronate therapy. Most important were the findings that all biochemical signs of improvement occur in the first six months of therapy, that skeletal pain may increase during therapy, and that doses larger than 5 mg/kg/day are more likely to be associated with temporarily increased pain, but with no greater improvement.[41] In 1980, Altman reviewed rheumatologic findings in 290 cases, of whom 97% were seen because of some symptom, with Paget's disease an incidental finding. Degenerative joint disease of the spine or interphalangeal joints was the most frequent diagnosis.[42] He pointed out the frequent difficulty of distinguishing the pain of osteoarthritis or less frequent rheumatologic symptoms from that of Paget's disease.[41]

Subsequently, Altman supported the foregoing conclusion with a study of just the lumbar spine, one of the most frequent areas of involvement in Paget's disease. Of 25 patients with low back pain and multifocal involvement, including at least some lumbar vertebrae, the authors concluded that the pain was attributable to Paget's disease in only three cases and in all the others was more plausibly owing to osteoarthritis. The mean age of these three Paget's patients was 12 years less than that of the osteoarthritics. Furthermore, these three obtained symptomatic benefit from etidronate, while this was true of only 22% of the others; biochemical markers of Pagetic activity improved in all.[43]

Armin E. Good, a rheumatologist at Ann Arbor, Michigan VA Hospital, and eventually professor of medicine at the University of Michigan, beginning in 1962 published numerous observations of unusual manifestations of rheumatic diseases. Most pertained to Reiter's disease, ankylosing spondylitis and rheumatoid arthritis. Some examples are:

1. Popliteal cysts can extend into the calf in cases of rheumatoid arthritis and may be confused with thrombophlebitis.[44]

2. Stemming from a suggestion that gout predisposes to the calcification of articular cartilages, knee roentgenograms of patients with definite diagnoses of gout and of rheumatoid arthritis were examined for evidence of chondrocalcinosis. This was detected in only 5% of cases of gout and 8% of cases of rheumatoid arthritis of similar ages, indicating that gout and chondrocalcinosis do not seem to be associated.[45]

3. Good (1977) described three people with HLA-B$_{27}$ positive ankylosing spondylitis in whom rheumatoid factor positive rheumatoid arthritis with subcutaneous nodules developed, an extremely rare finding. He concluded that the presence of the HLA antigen that is highly associated with ankylosing spondylitis does not modify the development of rheumatoid arthritis.[46]

4. In a follow-up study of 97 men with Reiter's disease, 92% of whom initially suffered from low back pain, this persisted in 62% of them two or more years after its onset. During the period of observation ankylosing spondylitis developed in 14% of the patients who carried HLA-B$_{27}$. Good suggested that Reiter's disease in its early phase may manifest two initially indistinguishable types of sacroiliitis: one that is virtually limited to carriers of HLA-B$_{27,}$ that is aggressive and develops into ankylosing spondylitis, and an indolent variety in which minor radiographic sacroiliac changes develop.[47]

Morris Reichlin, M.D., is a distinguished immunologist who spent a highly productive period (1973–1981) at the Buffalo, NY VA Hospital. His rheumatologic studies began in 1968 and pertained mainly to the identification and characterization of antibodies in SLE and later also in polymyositis. In 1969 he reported on a previously unidentified soluble cytoplasmic antigen which he called "Ro" that reacted with serum from cases of SLE.[48] In 1971 he described an SLE antigen of nuclear ribonucleoprotein, designated "Mo,"[49] and in 1974 described another cytoplasmic antigen, designated "La." [50] The following year, Margaret Alspaugh and Eng Tan independently discovered Ro and La, which they designated SS-A and SS-B, respectively, owing to their frequent association with Sjogren's syndrome.[51] Of particular interest in Reichlin's discovery was that anti-Ro and less frequently anti-La occurred in typical cases of SLE even in the absence of detectable ANA.[52] In 1979, Reichlin and Peter J. Maddison demonstrated the deposition of anti-Ro in the kidneys of patients dying of lupus nephritis who had a diminution of this antibody in serum, suggesting a direct pathogenetic role for this antibody. [53]

Reichlin's research on the serologic abnormalities of polymyositis overlapped with the SLE studies. He and his colleague Martha Mattioli in 1976 discovered a distinct antigen in calf thymus cell nuclei which reacts with antibody from sera of cases of polymyositis (PM) and, rarely, with cases of dermatomyositis (DM).[54] This was the first finding of an antibody associated specifically with this myopathy. In the following year, Masahiko Nishikai and Reichlin showed that a radioimmunoassay of serum myoglobin is a particularly sensitive method for following the course of PM, but less so for DM, in which the abnormalities are smaller.[55] Soon thereafter, the same investigators showed that the antibody they had discovered is actually a group of antibodies. As in the SLE studies, they identified each antibody by the first two letters of the name of the first patient in which it was detected. "Jo-1" occurred most frequently.[56] They then purified this antigen and partially identified its chemical properties. Other laboratories subsequently showed that these substances are tRNA synthetases, enzymes that attach one specific amino acid to their transfer-RNA. Jo-1 technically is histidyl tRNA synthetase. In 1981, Reichlin's group showed antibodies to Jo-1 to be highly associated with two MHC class II antigens, HLA-DR3 and HLA-DRW6.[57] The detection of the Jo-1 antigen has proven to be helpful in diagnosing polymyositis.

Ference Gyorkey, a Hungarian immigrant, in 1965 became Chief of Pathology at the Houston, TX VA Hospital, where he spent the remainder of his career. A productive investigator, he has been particularly noted for applying electron microscopy to various clinical problems. His principal rheumatological contribution was the description and clinical correlation of "microtubular structures." These are aggregates of filamentous material in cytoplasm consisting of a network of individual tubules 200-220 Å wide and 1000 Å long. In 1969, Gyorkey detected these structures in glomerular capillary cells in all of five cases of lupus nephritis, suggesting a causal relationship.[58] The existence and renal site of these structures was soon confirmed by other investigators, but attempts to prove that they are viruses have failed.[59] By 1972, Gyorkey had found the microtubular structures in all of 52 cases of systemic lupus erythematosus (SLE) but in no case of drug-induced lupus or other renal diseases. These structures were present in smaller numbers in a few cases of other connective tissue diseases.[60] Their significance has not been elucidated. In 1978 Gyorkey also detected them in squamous cells in SLE and discoid LE.[61] The lack of renal specificity was first shown in 1970 by another VA investigator, Ralph Schumacher, who detected the structures in the epithelium of synovial venules.[62] In 1973, Norman Talal and his collaborators detected structures with the same appearance in peripheral lymphocytes, most frequently in cases of DLE (13/22), but also in SLE (10/19), and in one case of Sjogren's syndrome, but in none of 15 other individuals.[63] Talal's team made the same finding in labial salivary gland cells from 6/20 patients with Sjogren's syndrome.[64] In 1982, Gyorkey also detected them in Kaposi's sarcoma.[65]

H. Ralph Schumacher, Jr., upon completion of his fellowship in 1967, joined the Philadelphia VA Hospital as chief of rheumatology, with a faculty appointment in the University of Pennsylvania Department of Medicine. Promoted to Professor of Medicine in 1979, he maintained a very active research program at the VA Hospital throughout his career. His training included electron microscopy, and his first publication as a VA investigator (1969) pertained to the electron microscopic study of the vasculature of normal monkey synovium "as a preliminary to consideration of the role of the small blood vessels in the pathogenesis of the joint inflammation in the rheumatic diseases."[66] And, indeed, the ultrastructure of synovium and the cytology of synovial fluid have been major aspects of

Schumacher's research. Schumacher was the first to use electron microscopy in investigating the ultrastructure of synovium in a wide variety of clinical and experimental conditions. These included systemic lupus erythematosus,[67] hemochromatosis,[68] scleroderma,[69] early rheumatoid arthritis,[70] hypertrophic osteoarthropathy,[71] ochronosis,[72] chondrocalcinosis,[73] sickle cell disease,[74] thalassemia trait,[75] acute leukemia,[76] secondary syphilis,[77] experimentally injected carbon particles,[78] and clinically injected corticosteroid,[79] as well as the cartilage of relapsing polychondritis.[80]

Schumacher also undertook a lengthy series of investigations into the morphology of crystals of mono-sodium urate and calcium pyrophosphate. These began in 1970 and continued into the 1990s. Their overall goal was to elucidate the pathophysiology of crystal-inducedinflammation, mainly by the application of various electron microscopic techniques. Schumacher first demonstrated in vitro the rapidity with which phagocytosed mono-sodium urate crystals kill their phagocytes.[81] Then, in a comparative study, he found that mono-sodium urate crystals are both phagocytosed and more rapidly lethal to their phagocytes than calcium pyrophosphate crystals.[82] The latter crystals were also detected in the synovium of patients who clinically did not have pseudo-gout, the disease associated with the intra-articular deposition of such crystals: hemochromatosis,[68] ochronosis[72] and osteoarthritis.[83]

The demonstration of mono-sodium urate crystals in a synovial effusion has been accepted as proof of the diagnosis of gout. Schumacher showed this to be a not entirely reliable criterion. He found both that mono-sodium urate crystals may be at least temporarily undetectable in an acutely inflamed gouty joint[84] and that these crystals may be present in an asymptomatic joint of someone with a history of gout.[85]

In 1977 Schumacher was the first to report that a third type of crystal, hydroxyapatite, may be present intracellularly in both acute and chronic inflammatory synovial effusions.[86] Owing to the small size of these crystals, electron microscopy is required to visualize them. Their rate of phagocytosis is similar to that of mono-sodium urate crystals.[87] Schumacher found that injection of hydroxy-apatite crystals into dogs' knees elicits acute inflammation, suggesting that these crystals, like mono-sodium urate and calcium pyrophosphate, probably initiate clinical synovitis.[86] Evidence for this is that hydroxy-apatite crystals sometimes are associated with an erosive arthritis.[88]

An important addition to the understanding of the mechanism of gouty inflammation took place in 1978 when Schumacher demonstrated that the major classes of immunoglobulins (IgG, IgA, IgM) all adhere to mono-sodium urate crystals, prompting his surmise that "the protein-crystal interaction is sufficient to involve the crystal in immunologic reactions."[89] Subsequently he showed that Fc fragments, the immunologically active part of the IgG molecule, are detectable on mono-sodium urate crystals.[90] Soon thereafter, a potentially important equilibrium was discovered. Coating mono-sodium urate crystals with IgG prior to their phagocytosis stimulated the release of superoxide (HO_2), which is believed to be an inducer of inflammation. However, pre-incubating such crystals with the lysate (content) of killed phagocytic cells blocked superoxide production.[91] And three years later it was shown that engulfed IgG-coated mono-sodium urate crystals produce more superoxide than

IgG-coated crystals of calcium pyrophosphate.[92] In 1993 Schumacher compared mono-sodium urate crystals that were aspirated during an acute gouty attack with crystals obtained from the same joint when the inflammation was subsiding He found that during the acute phase the crystals were predominantly coated with IgG, while during convalescence the IgG nearly disappeared and was replaced by apolipoprotein. Schumacher suggested that this protein substitution may at least partially explain the mechanism whereby gouty inflammation resolves, but this has yet to be proved.[93]

 James R. Klinenberg, who served as president of the American Rheumatism Association (1983–84) was a physician at the Los Angeles VAH, with a faculty appointment at the University of California, Los Angeles from 1966 to 1972. His research focused on the metabolism of uric acid[94] and the action of various drugs on the binding of urate to plasma proteins. The goal of these investigations was to determine whether the effect of drugs on dissociating the protein binding correlated with and might be predictive of the drugs' uricosuric action.

Klinenberg measured protein binding quantitatively by an equilibrium dialysis method he devised.[95] He first tested the effect of several drugs on urate-protein binding in normal adults and found that aspirin exerted the strongest dissociative effect. While the effect of phenylbutazone was nearly as strong as that of aspirin, sulfinpyrazone, an analogue of phenylbutazone and a stronger uricosuric agent, did not affect protein binding.[96] Nevertheless, in vitro studies of the binding of urate to serum albumin did not substantiate the lack of effect of sulfinpyrazone and showed a good correlation with the results of clinical experiments.[97, 98] While Klinenberg and his colleagues were unable to determine how the dissociation of urate from protein affects urate excretion, they concluded that in vitro testing for urate displacing activity is a valid method for screening drugs to identify potential clinical uricosuric agents.[99]

The parenteral injection of one of several gold compounds became the favored treatment of rheumatoid arthritis in the 1930s and remained so for half a century. It was administered at arbitrary intervals in an arbitrary dosage, irrespective of the patient's size or other parameters. First at the Sepulveda, California VA Hospital and then at the Long Beach VA Hospital, also in California, Arthur Lorber focused his research on the premise that gold therapy might give more predictable results if serum gold concentrations were maintained at a quantitated serum level and correlated with biochemical criteria. In 1968 he adapted atomic absorption spectrophotometry, a simpler method than previously available, to measure serum gold concentrations.[100] By occasionally adjusting the dosage of the injected medication, based on the serum gold concentration maintained above 0.3 mg%, he obtained symptomatic improvement that was somewhat more rapid than with the standard gold treatment, without increasing toxicity.[101] Lorber and his team found that, during five years of gold therapy, serum albumin tended to increase while gamma globulin decreased, with IgM and rheumatoid factor showing the greatest decreases.[102, 103]

In 1979 Lorber and his colleagues described "carbon rod atomic absorption analysis" (CRA), which permitted the detection of picogram concentrations of gold.[104]. They anticipated that "some prognostic value may be realized through monitoring lymphocyte gold binding as an aid in predicting good from poor responding patients for chrysotherapy."[105] They continued their investigations until 1982, when the therapeutic use of gold compounds began to be replaced by immunosuppressants such as methotrexate.

Not long after Lorber began his gold investigations, Herbert M. Rubinstein began working on the same topic at the Hines, IL VA Hospital. In 1972, comparing Lorber's spectrophotometric analysis to neutron activation analysis, he confirmed Lorber's conclusion of their similar sensitivity and the former's greater simplicity, [106] By putting patients on a standard dosage he essentially confirmed that neither toxic reactions nor therapeutic response correlated with the variable serum gold concentration.[107]

Hildegard R. Maricq, while on the staff of the Lyons, NJ VA Hospital in 1963, began investigating the configuration of the nailfold capillaries in vivo under the magnification of a wide field stereo-microscope. Initially she compared the capillary patterns of healthy and schizophrenic individuals.[108] By1972, shortly before leaving the VA to assume a faculty position at the University of South Carolina School of Medicine, she began to investigate nailfold capillary patterns in patients with connective tissue diseases. Her most diagnostic finding was the presence of enlarged, deformed capillary loops in cases of scleroderma and dermatomyositis.[109] These preliminary observations were subsequently confirmed by her and others, and capillary loop abnormalities have become accepted as having diagnostic importance in rheumatology.

Richard S. Panush began his VA career at VAH Gainesville, Florida, in 1973. His research interest at that time was focused on possible immunologic mechanisms of action of anti-rheumatic drugs. The experimental system he used involved stimulating human lymphocytes to incorporate tritiated thymidine (one of the nucleosides of DNA) by in vitro exposure to various mitogenic and antigenic biologic substances to determine whether various drugs used in rheumatologic therapy interfere with these effects. His first study (1975), which pertained to the effect of aspirin on this system, showed that in therapeutic concentrations aspirin inhibits lymphocyte responsiveness, both in cells exposed in vitro and in healthy persons who have taken aspirin.[110] C.R. Anthony and Parish also studied the interaction with normal leukocytes of aspirin labeled with radioactive carbon. They found that aspirin binds reversibly to these cells, with the binding quantitatively related to their relative concentrations.[111]

A number of structurally unrelated drugs were then tested and were found to have similar suppressive effects on lymphocyte binding. The diminished binding could partially be attributed to cell death, but the non-lethal injuries to the lymphocytes remained unidentified.[112] In 1977 an examination of lymphocytes from unmedicated rheumatoid arthritis patients yielded seemingly paradoxical results. Reactivity of lymphocytes to stimulants was subnormal, but unstimulated lymphocytes exhibited increased thymidine uptake.[113]

Panush and S.J. Ossakow found the response to the analgesic, acetaminophen, to differ from that of the other drugs that had been tested. In vitro, acetaminophen increased the responsiveness of lymphocytes but only when added soon after exposure to the stimulant.

Cells obtained from healthy persons who had taken acetaminophen did not exhibit the stimulant effect.[114] By 1978, Panush concluded that his evidence suggested that drug-induced lymphocyte inhibition might predict more effective response to that drug in rheumatoid arthritis.[115]

Subsequently Panush and his colleagues studied immunoglobulin production by mononuclear peripheral blood cells, differentiating IgG, IgA and IgM. Comparing healthy donors with cases of rheumatoid arthritis, they found that the production of both IgG and IgM was diminished in rheumatoid arthritis (IgG –57%, IgM –71%) and that the differences persisted after stimulation of the cells with a mitogen (IgG -37%, IgM -50%). These abnormalities could not be related to age, clinical features, or medication, suggesting a selective impairment of IgG and IgM secretion by peripheral blood monocytes associated with rheumatoid arthritis.[116]

These investigators then examined the secretion of IgM rheumatoid factor by mononuclear cells obtained from peripheral blood, marrow, and synovial fluid from seropositive cases of rheumatoid arthritis. Their findings showed that only 15 ng/ml was produced by peripheral blood cells, 71 ng/ml by marrow cells, but 6652 ng/ml by synovial fluid monocytes, indicating that IgM rheumatoid factor is primarily produced in synovial fluid.[117]

In 1981 Panush and Ossakow began an effort to elucidate the validity of the commonly held belief that rheumatoid arthritis could be caused or ameliorated by dietary factors. In their first study, some patients with RA followed a general diet that was somewhat restricted in calories, while others received a diet without dairy products, fruits, certain vegetables, additives or preservatives. Both patient groups received supplementary vitamins. The authors say that they were able to make the two diets indistinguishable in their view. After ten weeks, a similar minority of subjects on each diet showed some improvement, mainly in stiffness. These results were considered to make dietary effects unlikely to influence the symptomatology.[118] Whether any adjustments in medications resulted was not stated.

A further study, however, was stimulated by a patient with chronic mild RA who claimed to experience exacerbations of her disease when she consumed meat, milk or beans. For one month she was placed on a synthetic diet to which encapsulated lyophilized foods or placebo were periodically added. Her symptomatic responses were consistent with exacerbations being associated with dairy products. This was supported by immunologic findings.[119] An additional 18 patients subsequently participated in these food-challenge experiments. Two similar patient groups were identified, one whose exacerbations were limited to the consumption of shrimp, the other to nitrates. Neither group had rheumatoid factor. Panush concluded conservatively that food allergy may play a role in rheumatic disease (his term) on an immunologic basis and is amenable to study by the techniques used in these experiments.[120]

Panush and his colleagues were able to induce synovitis in some strains of rabbits by having them drink cow's milk instead of water for several months. The milk-fed rabbits developed high titers of anti-milk, anti-casein, and anti-bovine serum albumin antibodies.

Unfortunately the authors did not comment whether this resulted in a difference in titers related to the presence or absence of synovitis.[121]

The effect of exclusion diets on clinical and laboratory aspects of rheumatoid arthritis has been the subject of several European studies since Panush's publications. They agree that there is a subset of patients who improve both symptomatically and in laboratory indices on diets. Darlington found that the addition of corn or wheat products to a hypoallergenic diet was more likely to be adverse than the addition of milk products.[122, 123] Kjeldsen-Kragh and associates in Oslo employed a vegetarian diet. They found that patients who were responsive to the diet improved in the first month and their improvement persisted for a year. Laboratory parameters tended to worsen among the 56% of the diet non-responders compared to the control group that remained on their usual diets.[124, 125]

The first experiments with isotopic tracer scanning of joints were conducted by T.E. Weiss and associates in New Orleans in 1965 using iodine-labeled serum albumin.[126] The greatest question in evolving this approach lay in determining which isotope and which compound most sensitively detected inflammation. In 1969, Floyd A. Green, M.D., chief of rheumatology at the Buffalo, NY VA hospital, with several nuclear medicine collaborators, beginning with Marguerite T. Hays, M.D., initiated studies to address this problem.[127] They first used technetium ^{99m}pertechnetate and found that, after intravenous injection, the isotope entered and left an inflamed joint more rapidly than a normal joint. This was shown both in dogs with urate induced acute synovitis and in patients with clinical arthropathy.[128, 129] This finding contradicted that of Cohen and Lorber (Sepulveda VA Hospital,), who concluded in 1971 that albumin labeled with either iodine or technetium better identified joint inflammation than pertechnetate.[130] Around 1974, technetium pyrophosphate scans began to replace pertechnetate scans in experiments, particularly for evaluating bone metabolism rather than joint inflammation. Still, in 1979 Green viewed the results up to that time pessimistically because "in individual cases it is very difficult to draw definite conclusions from a 'positive' scan independent of the clinical and radiological findings."[131] Nevertheless, Green's investigations, now led by Karen C. Rosenspire, continued. Rosenspire, Green and associates found Tc pyrophosphate to be insufficiently sensitive to distinguish a rheumatoid joint from a normal joint.[132] In cases of rheumatoid arthritis, however, bone usually retained both Tc pyrophosphate and Tc methylene diphosphate more avidly than did bone of healthy individuals, indicating accelerated metabolism.[133] The initial question of an optimal joint scanning technic remained unsettled.

Donald Resnick, chief of radiology at San Diego, CA VA Hospital, is best known for his comprehensive text, with Gen Niweyama, a pathologist, *Diagnosis of Bone and Joint Disorders*, which was first published in 1981.[134-136] Much of its contents result from the experience of the authors, which is documented in numerous publications, mainly in radiologic journals, beginning in 1970. The text discusses most aspects of diagnostic radiology pertaining to rheumatic diseases, with some emphasis on normal variants and diseases of the axial skeleton.[137-141] Resnick also carried out comparative studies to determine optimal imaging technique, including a comparison of tomography and magnetic resonance imaging of the shoulder that demonstrated the latter's greater sensitivity.[142-144]

In the 1970s the Memphis, TN VA Hospital acquired a particularly productive group of basic immunologists, beginning in 1973 with Andrew H. Kang. Arnold E. Postlethwaite and Alexander S. Townes were added in 1974 and 1975, respectively. Two areas of their interest at that time were chemotaxis, the response of cells to chemical stimuli as occurs in wound repair, and experimental arthritis.

Postlethwaite and Kang showed in 1976 that in an *in vitro* system whole type I chick collagen as well as its fragments attract human monocytes.[145] Potential clinical relevance of this observation was that when leukocytes from scleroderma patients were cultured with type I collagen they secreted a factor that attracted human monocytes, a response differing significantly from control subjects.[146] These investigators also showed that after stimulation with a mitogen or an antigen, human lymphocytes produce a substance that attracts human fibroblasts[147] and that these cells have receptor sites to which a chain of the collagen molecule specifically binds.[148] A second factor chemotactic for fibroblasts was found to be generated by activation of serum complement.[148]

In 1976, Kang and Townes with David E. Trentham, a colleague at Harvard University, developed a new experimental arthritis in rats,[149, 150] to which mice subsequently were also found to be susceptible.[151] The principal experimental polyarthritis, called "adjuvant arthritis," previously had been produced in rodents by the injection of a reagent consisting primarily of dead Mycobacterium tuberculosis in paraffin oil (Freund's adjuvant). The new experimental model was elicited by the intradermal injection of type II collagen (C-II) in paraffin oil.[152, 153] C-II, which constitutes at least 80% of the collagen of articular cartilage, is absent from synovium. At first, the collagen was extracted from the articular cartilage of rats, humans and chickens, but later bovine vitreous humor was found to be a more convenient source.[152]

The development and severity of the arthritis was related to the dosage injected and to the age but not the sex of the animal. Clinical response was less consistent than that following adjuvant administration, although immunologic responses could be detected in virtually all C-II-treated animals.[153] The syndrome begins as a synovitis and progresses to joint destruction, and occasionally to auricular chondritis, which suggests an analogy with human relapsing polychondritis.[154] In 1982 the Memphis investigators found that C-II disease could be transferred to healthy rats by intravenous injection of a serum fraction from arthritic animals. Inflammation usually began within 4-6 hours and lasted 4-6 days. The inflammation-inducing activity was isolated to an IgG anti-collagen antibody.[155]

Kang and Townes also showed that pre-treatment of rats with homologous (i.e., rat) C-II diminished development of the arthritis and other immunologic responses following the injection of heterologous C-II.[156] In 1990 Michael A. Cremer, Townes and Kang found that development of adjuvant arthritis could not be blocked by pre-treatment with C-II and that antibodies to C-II could not be detected in sera from adjuvant arthritis, proving that adjuvant arthritis and C-II arthritis are different immunologic disease models.[157] In 1988 Kang and his Japanese coworkers showed that arthritis could be induced in two species of female monkeys by immunization with C-II.[158] Subsequently, Cremer and other Japanese coworkers found that female monkeys are much more susceptible to C-II disease than males, therein differing from rodents and resembling human sufferers of rheumatoid arthritis.[159] The Kang team was able to detect anti-collagen antibodies in rheumatoid arthritis sera. However, these antibodies are not specific for a type of collagen, nor for rheumatoid arthritis.[160]

Kang and his colleagues used their collagen-II induced arthritic rats to obtain important information complementary to data Howell's group was gathering. They showed in 1989 that chemical indications of potential cartilage injury begin by the third day of inflammation. Three metal-containing enzymes, "metallo-proteases" discovered in the preceding decade, participate in the destruction of articular cartilage. The investigators found that destructive enzymes and their effect, loss of proteoglycan from the cartilage matrix, can be detected simultaneously. Collagenase appears at the margins of the cartilage, while stromolysin is found in cells of the synovium and in chondrocytes. Thus, apparently cartilage cells are stimulated to produce an enzyme that degrades the matrix in which they are situated.[161]

Upon joining the Seattle VAH in 1971, William P. Arend began collaborative immunologic research with Mart Mannik, a rheumatologist at the University of Washington. This association continued until 1974, while Arend's studies continued beyond 1980. Their focus was on elucidating the characteristics of antigen-antibody ("immune") complexes. Immune complexes were developed in rabbits and various sensitive analytical technics were employed in investigating them. Findings included the following: 1. Immune complexes that contain more than two antibody molecules per antigen molecule fix complement (a serum protein complex that participates in various immune reactions) and are eliminated from circulation more rapidly than smaller complexes.[162] Large immune complexes preferentially adhere to macrophages, and this reaction does not require complement.[163] 2. The number of receptor sites for IgG on alveolar macrophages was increased by repeated antigenic stimulation of the animal. However, adherence of IgG to the receptor sites was found to be related to a quality of the sites ("affinity"), rather than to their number.[164] 3. The interaction of human serum albumin and antibody obtained from rabbits immunized with human serum albumin was investigated. The composition of the complexes they formed depended within a range on the magnitude of antigen (human serum albumin) excess that reacted with the rabbit antibody serum. The immune complex was not altered further by increasing the excess antigen from 100 to 500 times.[165] 4. In later work variations in the specificity of anti-IgG antibodies were studied in relation to the relative contributions of IgG antigen to the structure and functions of the immune complexes.[166] These aggregations may be relevant to rheumatoid arthritis, because some rheumatoid patients have large amounts of these complexes in the circulation. 5. Carol G. Ragsdale, M.D. and Arend studied the effect that adherence of immune complexes to the surface of human monocytes has on these cells' secretion of plasminogen activator. The alternative activation was mainly attributed to elastase.[167] 6. Another alteration in monocyte (macrophage) activity upon exposure to surface-bound immune complexes was found to be loss of their ability to phagocytose IgG-sensitized sheep erythrocytes, but not latex particles. This altered activity appeared to be modulated by cyclic nucleotides.[168]

More directly related to clinical medicine were studies of possible immunologic causes of neutropenia in systemic lupus erythematosus (SLE) and Felty's syndrome.

In 1978 one of Arend's fellows, Gordon Starkebaum, M.D., and associates sought to determine the cause of leukopenia in a patient with SLE. They found that an excess of IgG was bound to his neutrophils and the capacity of his serum to bind IgG to neutrophils was increased. The investigators concluded that anti-neutrophile antibodies accounted for the neutropenia, although the stimulus for the production of these antibodies was unknown.[169] This case led to a systematic investigation of neutrophile binding in SLE. Examination of one half of the SLE patients' sera showed excess IgG bound to neutrophils and 58% of the sera showed increased binding activity. This was attributed both to immune complexes and neutrophile-reactive antibodies. However, these abnormal immunologic abnormalities were not found to correlate with abnormal leukocyte counts.[170]

Next, Starkebaum and his colleagues undertook similar studies in patients with Felty's Syndrome. The prevalence of abnormalities was similar to that found in SLE: 47% of the patients had increased binding of IgG to neutrophils and 62% if the sera had increased binding activity in comparison to both normals and cases of uncomplicated rheumatoid arthritis.[171] The concentration of immune complexes, which tends to be elevated in uncomplicated rheumatoid arthritis, also was greater in cases of Felty's syndrome. A strong correlation between the presence of IgG neutrophile-binding activity and levels of immune complexes was considered evidence for the presence of such complexes.[172] Regrettably, none of these reports included leukocyte counts. Comparisons of tests for immune complexes have shown large inconsistencies; in rheumatoid arthritis their presence correlated best with coexistent vasculitis. Dutch investigators reported in 1988 that they could not detect anti-leukocyte antibodies in cases of Felty's syndrome.[173] Thus, the cause or causes of neutropenia in SLE and Felty's syndrome remain uncertain. This probably impedes the development of more specific therapy.

Norman Talal began his career at the NIAMD. A career-orienting event occurred in 1964 when he co-authored with J.J. Bunim, the Director of the Institute, a paper on the development of malignant lymphoma during the course of Sjogren's syndrome.[174] This stimulated a permanent interest in Sjogren's syndrome, particularly its association with neoplasia. A parallel phase of Talal's researches began in 1969 with the study of the NZB mouse model of systemic lupus erythematosus (SLE). Talal joined the VA at the San Francisco, CA VA Hospital in 1971.

In 1973 Talal and colleagues investigated the relative proportions of B and T lymphocytes in the peripheral blood and salivary gland biopsies of patients with Sjogren's syndrome. B cells (mediators of humoral immunity) tended to be diminished and T cells (mediators of cellular immunity) increased in the blood, and while salivary gland infiltrates showed focal increases of both cell types, T cell infiltrates predominated.[175]

Then they investigated the concentration of beta$_2$ microglobulin in saliva and found a five-fold increase in cases of Sjogren's syndrome compared to normal controls. They also analyzed synovial fluid for this protein and found its concentration to be elevated, particularly in rheumatoid arthritis. Both abnormalities appeared to be correlated with the severity of the inflammation, normalizing with beneficial response to therapy[176].

In 1978 Talal and his associates serially studied the development of malignant lymphomas in nine cases of Sjogren's syndrome.[177] They confirmed the 1964 observation of Talal and Bunim that a decline in immunoglobulins and auto-antibodies in Sjogren's syndrome indicates conversion of benign lymphadenopathy to malignant lymphoma. Lymphomas had various histologic patterns, but characteristics of monoclonal B-cells.

In 1974 and 1975, at the Albuquerque VA Medical Center, Raphael J. DeHoratius and Ronald P. Messner investigated the occurrence of anti-lymphocyte antibodies in families in which a member suffered from SLE. Such antibodies were found in 82% of the patients, 16% of their relatives and only 3% of control subjects.[178] However, anti-lymphocyte antibodies occurred with increased frequency both among consanguinous relatives and non-consanguinous household contacts.[179]

In 1973, R.A. Sylvester and Talal had devised a radioimmunoassay for anti-RNA antibodies. In their first studies, this class of antibody was detected in 76% of mice with experimental lupus, 70% of cases of clinical SLE, 42% of cases of DLE, 19% of Sjogren's syndrome, and 14% of RA, versus 4% of control subjects.[179] At the same time, an electron microscopic study of lymphocytes from patients with SLE and with DLE was performed. The structures Gyorkey had described in renal tubular cells in SLE were found in 34% of cases of SLE and 59% of DLE. The presence of these structures was not found to be correlated with the presence of anti-RNA antibodies. The authors speculated that these findings were additional evidence that DLE and SLE represent manifestations of the same disease spectrum.[180]

In a comparative clinical study of cell-mediated cytotoxicity, Talal, with six collaborators, assessed the cytotoxic activity of killer (K)-lymphocytes, now called NK. These cells are not adherent like other lymphocytes and they kill some viruses and tumor cells without phagocytosis. Lysis requires binding to a receptor on the NK cells of a specific antibody that is attached to the susceptible cells. The test system used chicken erythrocytes coated with antibody. It was found that lymphocytes from cases of active SLE had a diminished cytotoxic capacity, while cells from controlled SLE, Sjogren's syndrome, and rheumatoid arthritis behaved normally.[181] The authors suggested that testing for inhibition of cytotoxicity may provide a guide for following the activity of certain immune-mediated diseases.[182] However, no clinically practical test using NK cells has as yet been devised.

Another group of experiments on NZB/NZW mice pertained to the effect of sex hormones on their antibody responses and survival. Pre-pubertal castration of males, but not of females, caused premature death. Castrated females given androgen had better survival rates than those given estrogen. Auto-antibody responses also differed between the sexes. Females developed IgG antibodies to DNA while males developed IgM antibodies. Titers in both sexes increase with age. The age-related increase was smaller in castrated females than in normal females, and the antibody titer of castrated males was the same as in castrated females.[183] Over all, the lupus-like disease is suppressed by androgens and accelerated by estrogens.[184] Androgen administration begun after the onset of the disease still reduced the severity of renal disease and prolonged survival, despite persistence of anti-DNA antibodies, suggesting that androgens modulate auto-immunity through more than one mechanism. These findings suggest that hormone modulation of auto-immunity might be beneficial for patients with SLE.[185] Clinical testing of this hypothesis has given equivocal results. A double-blind study of women with mild to moderately severe SLE using dehydroepiandrosterone (DHEA) showed some improvement,[186] while Lahita and colleagues using 19-nor testosterone obtained no effect in women and worsening in men.[187]

After Talal moved to the San Antonio, TX VA Medical Center in 1981 he continued research on Sjogren's syndrome and the role of NK cells in autoimmunity. In 1983 Talal's team found that in Sjogren's syndrome (SS-1, no concurrent autoimmune diseases) there is diminished NK activity in the blood and that this activity is diminished even more in Sjogren's syndrome (SS-2, with another autoimmune disease, usually rheumatoid arthritis.) Patients had higher concentrations of circulating immune complexes than controls, but this was discounted as a mechanism depressing NK activity because the two factors were not correlated in individual subjects. Since NK cells have anti-neoplastic activity, the authors speculated that the diminished NK activity may be a facilitating factor in the development of lymphoma in Sjogren's disease.[188] Diminished NK activity in SLE and in SS-1 and SS-2 has been confirmed.[189]

Talal and associates found in 1984 that there is reduced NK cell activity both in the blood and synovial fluid in rheumatoid arthritis. NK cells were already known to suppress immunoglobulin (Ig) production. They studied the effect on Ig production in blood and synovial fluid that had been depleted of NK cells. Before removal of NK cells Ig production in rheumatoid blood was 2.5 times greater and in synovial fluid 4.3 times greater than in the blood of control subjects. Depletion of NK cells from control blood did not alter Ig production, while the depleting effect from blood and from synovial fluid was greatest in specimens with the highest Ig content These findings indicate that this effect of NK cells depends on prior damage to Ig producing cells.[190]

Normal human monocytes and macrophages inhibit NK activity. Therefore incubation experiments were performed with macrophage-supplemented cell suspensions from rheumatoid blood and synovial fluid. Results showed that monocytic cells from rheumatoid synovial fluid, but not from peripheral blood of the same patient, inhibited NK function.[191]

B lymphocytes secrete immunoglobulins and this activity in part is controlled by T lymphocytes. The differentiating characteristics of lymphocytes include surface features. Michael J. Dauphinée, Talal and associates found CD5 B lymphocytes to be quantitatively normal in SLE, but to be similarly increased in Sjogren's syndrome and rheumatoid arthritis.[192] Subsequently they found that CD5 T lymphocytes are decreased in SS-1, but are quantitatively normal in SS-2 and in rheumatoid arthritis.[193] The importance of these findings remains to be determined.

Xerostomia (dry mouth) and parotid gland swelling are diagnostic symptoms of Sjogren's syndrome, but also occur in AIDS. In AIDS, as in Sjogren's syndrome, there is an increase of CD + B lymphocytes, and infection in vitro of human T lymphocytes with AIDS virus (HIV-1) induces similar functional abnormalities as are found in T lymphocytes of Sjogren's syndrome. Of Sjogren's syndrome patients who did not have AIDS, 30% were found to have antibodies against the AIDS virus. These patients also lacked the SS-A and SS-B antigens that are typically detected in the blood of Sjogren's syndrome patients. While the AIDS virus certainly does not cause Sjogren's syndrome, these immunologic findings are evidence of a possible pathogenetic role of a retrovirus in an autoimmune disease.[194]

Thomas G. Benedek in 1956 became Chief of Rheumatology at the Pittsburgh, PA VA Hospital, where he remained throughout his career, with a faculty appointment in the University of Pittsburgh School of Medicine and later also in its History Department. During the period under review, he pursued several clinical research projects, particularly regarding the involvement of the lungs in scleroderma[195] and rheumatoid arthritis, and began research in the history of the rheumatic diseases[196-199] in which he became an authority. His principal clinical observation was that men who had had long exposure to silica dust but normal chest roentgenograms may without additional silica exposure abruptly develop gross pulmonary nodules upon the onset of rheumatoid arthritis. He suggested that the nodular fibrosis should be attributed to the rheumatoid disease facilitated by the coincidental presence of silica.[200, 201]

Epilogue

The research by VA clinicians and basic scientists in rheumatology and relevant basic immunology during the three decades from 1950 through 1980 is representative of research in non-federal academic institutions. Research topics were not administratively mandated, and VA research, at least in rheumatology, was not skewed toward problems that were particularly prevalent among VA beneficiaries. For example, while osteoarthritis in an aging population and gout in a predominantly male population certainly are problems in which the VA might well exhibit greater interest than in a disease of young women, such as subacute lupus erythematosus, research in osteoarthritis and in gout resulted from the interest of individual investigators, as did research in subacute lupus erythematosus. As cooperation with medical school investigators increased and VA physicians increasingly held medical school faculty appointments, VA and academic research interests became virtually indistinguishable. One result has been a continued increase in both research diversity and productivity.

The publications alluded to in this chapter were identified by the investigators as being among their most important contributions or selected for their importance by the author. "Importance" must be considered within the scientific environment of the time, however, rather than retrospectively from the present. While some work continues to be viewed as important to this day, as providing enduring validity or as a foundation for subsequent research, other efforts, though important when they were undertaken, have become obsolete. One must also distinguish between the accrual of experimental data and the development of analytic techniques. Even when results of experiments lose their importance, techniques devised or adapted to achieve them may continue to be useful in other applications. For example, when gold salts were a primary treatment for rheumatoid arthritis, studies of their metabolism were highly relevant. This application of atomic absorption spectrometry disappeared when these medications became obsolete, but until recently the important trace metal selenium has been detected by a modification of this method.[202]

References

1.   "Arthritis Prevalence and Activity Limitations - United States, 1990." *MMWR*, 1994. **43**: 433-438.

2.   "Prevalence and Impact of Chronic Joint Symptoms - Seven States, 1996." *MMWR*, 1998. **47**: 345-351.

3.   "Prevalence of Disabilities and Associated Health Conditions - United States, 1991-1992." *MMWR*, 1994. **43**: 730-739.

4.   Yelin, E. and Callahan, L.F., "The Economic Cost and Social and Psychological Impact of Musculoskeletal Conditions." *Arthritis Rheum*, 1995. **38**: 1351-1362.

5.   Benedek, T.G., "A Century of American Rheumatology." *Ann Intern Med*, 1987. **106**: 304-312.

6.   Robinson, W.D., Boland, E.W., Bunim, J.J., Crain, D.C., Engleman, E.P., Graham, W., Lockie, L.M., Montgomery, M.M., Ragan, C., Ropes, M.W., Rosenberg, E.F. and Smyth, C.J., "Rheumatism and Arthritis. Tenth Rheumatism Review." *Ann Intern Med*, 1953. **39**: 497-618, 758-915, p814.

7.   Nunemaker, J.C. and Hartman, S.A., "Psoriatic Arthritis." *Ann Intern Med*, 1950. **33**: 1016-1023.

8.   Stephens, F.E. and Nunemaker, J.C., "Spondylitis in Identical Twins Reared Apart." *J Heredity*, 1950. **41**: 283-286.

9.   Swift, H.F. and Brown, T.M., "Pathogenic Pleuropneumonia-Like Microorganisms from Acute Rheumatic Exudates and Tissues." *Science*, 1939. **89**: 271-272.

10.   Dienes, L., Ropes, M.W., Smith, W.E., Madoff, S. and Bauer, W., "The Role of Pleuropneumonia-Like Organisms Associated with Various Rheumatic Diseases." *N Eng J Med*, 1948. **238**: 509-515, 563-567.

11.   Brown, T.M., Wichelhausen, R.H. and Merchant, W.R., "The in Vivo Action of Aureomycin on Pleuropneumonia-Like Organisms Associated with Various Rheumatic Diseases." *J Lab Clin Med*, 1949. **34**: 1404-1410.

12.   Brown, T.M., Wichelhausen, R.H. and Merchant, W.R., "A Study of the Antigen-Antibody Mechanism in Rheumatic Diseases." *Am J Med Sci*, 1951. **221**: 618-625.

13.   James, W.E., Little, R.C. and Shumway, N.P., "Effect of Desoxycorticosterone and Ascorbic Acid on Rheumatoid Arthritis." *Am J Med Sci*, 1950. **220**: 490-495.

14.   Southworth, J.D. and Bersack, S.R., "Anomalies of the Lumbo-Sacral Vertebrae in Five Hundred and Fifty Individuals without Symptoms Referrable to the Low Back." *Radiology*, 1950. **64**: 624-634.

15.   Walsh, J.R. and Zimmerman, H., "The Demonstration of the 'L.E.' Phenomenon in Patients with Penicillin Hypersensitivity." *Blood*, 1953. **8**: 65-71.

16.   Kofman, S., Johnson, G. and Zimmerman, H., "Apparent Hepatic Dysfunction in Lupus Erythematosus." *Arch Int Med*, 1955. **95**: 669-676.

17.   Heller, P., Zimmerman, H., Rozengvaig, S. and Singer, K., "The L.E. - Cell Phenomenon in Chronic Hepatic Disease." *N Eng J Med*, 1956. **254**: 1160-1165.

18.   Heller, P. and Zimmerman, H., "Nucleophagocytosis; Studies of 336 Patients." *Arch Int Med*, 1956. **97**: 208-224.

19.   Friou, G.J., Finch, S.C. and Detre, K.D., "Interaction of Nuclei and Globulin from Lupus Erythematosus Serum Demonstrated with Fluorescent Antibody." *J Immunol*, 1958. **80**: 324-329.

20.   Friou, G.J., "Identification of the Nuclear Component of the Interaction of Lupus Erythematosus Globulin and Nuclei." *J Immunol*, 1958. **80**: 476-481.

21.   Friou, G.J., "The Significance of the Lupus Globulin-Nucleoprotein Reaction." *Ann Intern Med*, 1958. **49**: 866-875.

22.   Ritchie, R.F., "Antinuclear Antibodies." *N Eng J Med*, 1970. **282**: 1174-1178.

23.   Cobb, S., Merchant, W.R. and Warren, J.E., "An Epidemiologic Look at the Problem of Classification in the Field of Arthritis." *J Chron Dis*, 1955. **2**: 50-54.

24.   Cobb, S., Thompson, D.J. and Merchant, W.R., "On the Measurement of the Prevalence of Arthritis and Rheumatism from Interview Data." *J Chron Dis*, 1956. **3**: 134-139.

25.   Cobb, S., Merchant, W.R. and Rubin, T., "The Relation of Symptoms to Osteoarthritis." *J Chron Dis*, 1957. **5**: 197-204.

26.   Cobb, S., Warren, J., Merchant, W.R. and others, "An Estimate of the Prevalence of Rheumatoid Arthritis." *J Chron Dis*, 1957. **5**: 636-643.

27.   Howell, D.S., Malcolm, J.M. and Pike, R., "The F-II Agglutinating Factors in Serums of Patients with Non-Rheumatic Diseases." *Amer J Med*, 1960. **29**: 662-671.

28.   Howell, D.S., Delchamps, E., Riemer, W. and Kiem, I., "A Profile of Electrolytes in the Cartilaginous Plate of Growing Ribs." *J Clin Invest*, 1960. **39**: 919-929.

29.   Howell, D.S., Pita, J.C. and Marquez, J.F., "Ultramicro Spectrophotometric Determination of Calcium in Biologic Fluids." *Anal Chem*, 1966. **38**: 434-438.

30.   Howell, D.S., "Histologic Observations and Biochemical Composition of Rachitic Cartilage with Special Reference to Mucopolysaccharides." *Arthritis Rheum*, 1965. **19**: 337-354.

31.   Altman, R.D., Muniz, O.E., Pita, J.C. and Howell, D.S., "Articular Chondrocalcinosis. Microanalysis of Pyrophosphate (Ppi) in Synovial Fluid and Plasma." *Arthritis Rheum*, 1973. **16**: 171-178.

32.   Moskowitz, R.W., Howell, D.S., Goldberg, V.M., Muniz, O. and Pita, J.C., "Cartilage Proteoglycan Alterations in an Experimentally Induced Model of Rabbit Osteoarthritis." *Arthritis Rheum*, 1979. **22**: 155-163.

33.   Sapolsky, A.I., Keiser, H., Howell, D.S. and Woessner, J.F., "Metalloproteases of Human Articular Cartilage That Digest Cartilage Proteoglycan at Neutral and Acid pH." *J Clin Invest*, 1976. **58**: 1030-1041.

34.   Pelletier, J.-P., Martel-Pelletier, J., Howell, D.S., Ghandur-Mnaymneh, L., Enis, J.E. and Woessner, J.F., "Collagenase and Collagenolytic Activity in Human Osteoarthritic Cartilage." *Arthritis Rheum*, 1983. **26**: 63-68.

35.   Martel-Pelletier, J., Pelletier, J.-P., Cloutier, J.M., Howell, D.S., Ghandur-Mnaymneh, L. and Woessner, J.F., "Neutral Proteases Capable of Proteoglycan Digesting Activity in Osteoarthritic and Normal Human Articular Cartilage." *Arthritis Rheum*, 1984. **27**: 305-312.

36. Martel-Pelletier, J., Cloutier, J.M., Howell, D.S. and Pelletier, J.-P., "Human Rheumatoid Arthritic Cartilage and its Neutral Proteoglycan-Degrading Proteases. The Effect of Anti-Rheumatic Drugs." *Arthritis Rheum*, 1985. **28**: 405-412.

37. Dean, D.D. and Woessner, J.F., "Extracts of Human Articular Cartilage Contain an Inhibitor of Tissue Metalloproteases." *Biochem J*, 1984. **218**: 277-280.

38. Dean, D.D., Martel-Pelletier, J., Pelletier, J.-P., Howell, D.S. and Woessner, J.F., "Evidence for Metalloprotease Inhibitor Imbalance in Human Osteoarthritic Cartilage." *J Clin Invest*, 1989. **84**: 678-685.

39. Dean, D.D., Schwartz, Z., Muniz, O.E., Swain, L.D., Howell, D.S. and Boyan, B.D., "Matrix Vesicles are Enriched in Metalloproteases that Degrade Proteoglycans." *Calcif Tis Internat*, 1992. **50**: 342-349.

40. Altman, R.D., Johnston, C.C., Khairi, M.R., Wellman, H., Serafini, A.N. and Sankey, R.R., "Influence of Sodium Etidronate on Clinical and Laboratory Manifestations of Paget's Disease of Bone (Osteitis Deformans)." *N Eng J Med*, 1973. **289**: 1379-1384.

41. Khairi, M.R., Altman, R.D., DeRosa, G.P., Zimmerman, J., Schenk, R.K. and Johnston, C.C., "Sodium Etidronate in the Treatment of Paget's Disease of Bone. A Study of Long-Term Results." *Ann Intern Med*, 1977. **87**: 656-663.

42. Altman, R.D., "Musculoskeletal Manifestations of Paget's Disease of Bone." *Arthritis Rheum*, 1980. **23**: 1121-1127.

43. Altman, R.D., Brown, M. and Gargano, F., "Low Back Pain in Paget's Disease of Bone." *Clin Orthop*, 1987. **217**: 152-161.

44. Good, A.E., "Rheumatoid Arthritis, Baker's Cyst and Thrombophlebitis." *Arthritis Rheum*, 1964. **7**: 56-64.

45. Good, A.E. and Rapp, R., "Chondrocalcinosis of the Knee with Gout and Rheumatoid Arthritis." *N Eng J Med*, 1967. **277**: 286-290.

46. Good, A.E., Hyla, J.F. and Rapp, R., "Ankylosing Spondylitis with Rheumatoid Arthritis and Subcutaneous Nodules." *Arthritis Rheum*, 1977. **20**: 1434-1437.

47. Good, A.E., "Reiter's Syndrome: Long-Term Follow-up in Relation to Development of Ankylosing Spondylitis." *Ann Rheum Dis*, 1979. **38: sup**: 39-45.

48. Clark, G., Reichlin, M. and Tomasi, T.B., Jr., "Characterization of a Soluble Cytoplasmic Antigen Reactive with Sera from Patients with Systemic Lupus Erythmatosus." *J Immunol*, 1969. **102**: 117-122.

49. Mattioli, M. and Reichlin, M., "Characterization of a Soluble Nuclear Ribonucleoprotein Antigen Reactive with SLE Sera." *J Immunol*, 1971. **107**: 1281-1290.

50. Mattioli, M. and Reichlin, M., "Heterogeneity of RNA Protein Antigens Reactive with Sera of Patients with Systemic Lupus Erythematosus. Description of a Cytoplasmic Nonribosomal Antigen." *Arthritis Rheum*, 1974. **17**: 421-429.

51. Alspaugh, M. and Tan, E., "Antibodies to Cellular Antigens in Sjogren's Syndrome." *J Clin Invest*, 1975. **55**: 1067-1073.

612

52. Provost, T.T., Ahmed, A.R., Maddison, P.J. and Reichlin, M., "Antibodies to Cytoplasmic Antigens in Lupus Erythematosus. Serologic Marker for Systemic Disease." *Arthritis Rheum*, 1977. **20**: 1457-1463.

53. Maddison, P.J. and Reichlin, M., "Deposition of Antibodies to a Soluble Cytoplasmic Antigen in the Kidneys of Patients with Systemic Lupus Erythematosus." *Arthritis Rheum*, 1979. **22**: 858-863.

54. Reichlin, M. and Mattioli, M., "Description of a Serological Reaction Characteristic of Polymyositis." *Clin Immunol Immunopathol*, 1976. **5**: 12-20.

55. Nishikai, M. and Reichlin, M., "Radioimmunoassay of Serum Myoglobin in Polymyositis and Other Conditions." *Arthritis Rheum*, 1977. **20**: 1514-1518.

56. Nishikai, M. and Reichlin, M., "Heterogeneity of Precipitating Antibodies in Polymyositis and Dermatomyositis." *Arthritis Rheum*, 1980. **23**: 881-888.

57. Arnett, F.C., Hirsch, T.J., Bias, W.B., Nishikai, M. and Reichlin, M., "The Jo-1 Antibody System in Myositis: Relationships to Clinical Features and HLA." *J Rheum*, 1981. **8**: 925-930.

58. Gyorkey, F., Min, K.W., Sincovics, J.G. and Gyorkey, P., "Systemic Lupus Erythematosus and Myxovirus." *N Engl J Med*, 1969. **280**: 333.

59. Pincus, T., Blacklow, N.R., Grimley, P.M. and Bellanti, J.A., "Glomerular Microtubules of Systemic Lupus Erythematosis." *Lancet*, 1970. **2**: 1058-1061.

60. Gyorkey, F., Sinkovics, J.G., Min, K.W. and Gyorkey, P., "A Morphologic Study on the Occurrence and Distribution of Structures Resembling Viral Nucleocapsids in Collagen Diseases." *Am J Med*, 1972. **53**: 148-158.

61. Gyorkey, F., Gyorkey, P. and Sinkovics, J.G., "Microtubules in the Epidermis in Systemic Lupus." *N Engl J Med*, 1978. **298**: 973-974.

62. Schumacher, H.R., Jr., "Tubular Paramyxovirus-Like Structures in Synovial Vascular Endothelium." *Ann Rheum Dis*, 1970. **29**: 445-447.

63. Goodman, J.R., Sylvester, R.A., Talal, N. and Tuffanelli, D.L., "Virus-Like Structures in Lymphocytes of Patients with Systemic and Discoid Lupus Erythematosus." *Ann Intern Med*, 1973. **79**: 396-402.

64. Daniels, T.E., Sylvester, R.A., Silverman, S., Jr., Polando, V. and Talal, N., "Tubuloreticular Structures within Labial Salivary Glands in Sjogren's Syndrome." *Arthritis Rheum*, 1974. **17**: 593-597.

65. Gyorkey, F., Sinkovics, J.G. and Gyorkey, P., "Tubuloreticular Structures in Kaposi's Sarcoma." *Lancet*, 1982. **2**: 984-985.

66. Schumacher, H.R., "The Microvasculature of the Synovial Membrane of the Monkey: Ultrastructural Studies." *Arthritis Rheum*, 1969. **12**: 387-404.

67. Labowitz, R. and Schumacher, H.R., Jr., "Articular Manifestations of Systemic Lupus Erythematosus." *Ann Intern Med*, 1971. **74**: 911-921.

68. Schumacher, H.R., Jr., "Ultrastructure of the Synovial Membrane in Idiopathic Haemochromatosis." *Ann Rheum Dis*, 1972. **31**: 465-473.

69. Schumacher, H.R., Jr., "Joint Involvement in Progressive Systemic Sclerosis (Scleroderma): A Light and Electron Microscopic Study of Synovial Membrane and Fluid." *Am J Clin Pathol*, 1973. **60**: 593-600.

70. Schumacher, H.R., Jr., "Synovial Membrane and Fluid Morphologic Alterations in Early Rheumatoid Arthritis: Microvascular Injury and Virus-Like Particles." *Ann N Y Acad Sci*, 1975. **256**: 39-64.

71. Schumacher, H.R., Jr., "Articular Manifestations of Hypertrophic Pulmonary Osteoarthropathy in Bronchogenic Carcinoma." *Arthritis Rheum*, 1976. **19**: 629-636.

72. Schumacher, H.R. and Holdsworth, D.E., "Ochronotic Arthropathy. I. Clinicopathologic Studies." *Semin Arthritis Rheum*, 1977. **6**: 207-246.

73. Schumacher, H.R., "Ultrastructural Findings in Chondrocalcinosis and Pseudogout." *Arthritis Rheum*, 1976. **19 Suppl 3**: 413-425.

74. Schumacher, H.R., Andrews, R. and McLaughlin, G., "Arthropathy in Sickle-Cell Disease." *Ann Intern Med*, 1973. **78**: 203-211.

75. Dorwart, B.B. and Schumacher, H.R., "Arthritis in Beta Thalassaemia Trait: Clinical and Pathological Features." *Ann Rheum Dis*, 1981. **40**: 185-189.

76. Weinberger, A., Schumacher, H.R., Schimmer, B.M., Myers, A.R. and Brogadir, S.P., "Arthritis in Acute Leukemia. Clinical and Histopathological Observations." *Arch Intern Med*, 1981. **141**: 1183-1187.

77. Reginato, A.J., Schumacher, H.R., Jimenez, S. and Maurer, K., "Synovitis in Secondary Syphilis. Clinical, Light, and Electron Microscopic Studies." *Arthritis Rheum*, 1979. **22**: 170-176.

78. Schumacher, H.R., "Fate of Particulate Material Arriving at the Synovium via the Circulation. An Ultrastructural Study." *Ann Rheum Dis*, 1973. **32**: 212-218.

79. Gordon, G.V. and Schumacher, H.R., "Electron Microscopic Study of Depot Corticosteroid Crystals with Clinical Studies after Intra-Articular Injection." *J Rheumatol*, 1979. **6**: 7-14.

80. Shaul, S.R. and Schumacher, H.R., "Relapsing Polychondritis. Electron Microscopic Study of Ear Cartilage." *Arthritis Rheum*, 1975. **18**: 617-625.

81. Schumacher, H.R. and Phelps, P., "Sequential Changes in Human Polymorphonuclear Leukocytes after Urate Crystal Phagocytosis. An Electron Microscopic Study." *Arthritis Rheum*, 1971. **14**: 513-526.

82. Schumacher, H.R., "Pathology of the Synovial Membrane in Gout. Light and Electron Microscopic Studies. Interpretation of Crystals in Electron Micrographs." *Arthritis Rheum*, 1975. **18**: 771-782.

83. Gibilisco, P.A., Schumacher, H.R., Hollander, J.L. and Soper, K.A., "Synovial Fluid Crystals in Osteoarthritis." *Arthritis Rheum*, 1985. **28**: 511-515.

84. Schumacher, H.R., Jr., Jimenez, S.A., Gibson, T., Pascual, E., Traycoff, R., Dorwart, B.B. and Reginato, A.J., "Acute Gouty Arthritis without Urate Crystals Identified on Initial Examination of Synovial Fluid. Report of Nine Patients." *Arthritis Rheum*, 1975. **18**: 603-612.

85. Agudelo, C.A., Weinberger, A., Schumacher, H.R., Turner, R. and Molina, J., "Definitive Diagnosis of Gout by Identification of Urate Crystals in Asymptomatic Metatarsophalangeal Joints." *Arthritis Rheum*, 1979. **22**: 559-560.

86. Schumacher, H.R., Smolyo, A.P., Tse, R.L. and Maurer, K., "Arthritis Associated with Apatite Crystals." *Ann Intern Med*, 1977. **87**: 411-416.

87. Maurer, K.H. and Schumacher, H.R., "Hydroxyapatite Phagocytosis by Human Polymorphonuclear Leucocytes." *Ann Rheum Dis*, 1979. **38**: 84-88.

88. Schumacher, H.R., Miller, J.L., Ludivico, C. and Jessar, R.A., "Erosive Arthritis Associated with Apatite Crystal Deposition." *Arthritis Rheum*, 1981. **24**: 31-37.

89. Hasselbacher, P. and Schumacher, H.R., "Immunoglobulin in Tophi and on the Surface of Mono-Sodium Urate Crystals." *Arthritis Rheum*, 1978. **21**: 353-361.

90. Bardin, T., Chernian, P.V. and Schumacher, H.R., "Immunoglobulins on the Surface of Monosodium Urate Crystals: An Immuno-Electron Microscopic Study." *J Rheum*, 1984. **11**: 339-341.

91. Rosen, M.S., Baker, D.G., Schumacher, H.R. and Chernian, P.V., "Products of Polymorphonuclear Cell Injury Inhibit IgG Enhancement of Mono-Sodium Urate-Induced Surperoxide Production." *Arthritis Rheum*, 1986. **29**: 1473-1479.

92. Nagase, M., Baker, D.G. and Schumacher, H.R., "Immunoglobulin G Coating on Crystals and Ceramics Enhances Polymorphonuclear Cell Superoxide Production: Correlation with Immunoglobulin Absorbed." *J Rheum*, 1989. **16**: 971-976.

93. Ortiz-Bravo, E., Sieck, M. and Schumacher, H.R., "Changes in the Protein Coating of Mono-Sodium Urate Crystals During Active and Subsiding Inflammation." *Arthritis Rheum*, 1993. **36**: 1274-1285.

94. Seegmiller, J.E., Klinenberg, J.R., Miller, J. and Watts, R.W., "Suppression of Glycine-^{15}n Incorporation into Urinary Uric Acid by Adenine-8-^{13}C in Normal and Gouty Subjects." *J Clin Invest*, 1968. **47**: 1193-1203.

95. Klinenberg, J.R. and Kippen, I., "The Binding of Urate to Plasma Proteins Determined by Means of Equilibrium Dialysis." *J Lab Clin Med*, 1970. **75**: 503-510.

96. Bluestone, R., Kippen, I. and Klinenberg, J.R., "Effect of Drugs on Urate Binding to Plasma Proteins." *Br Med J*, 1969. **4**: 590-593.

97. Bluestone, R., Kippen, I., Klinenberg, J.R. and Whitehouse, M.W., "Effect of Some Uricosuric and Anti-Inflammatory Drugs on the Binding of Uric Acid to Human Serum Albumin in Vitro." *J Lab Clin Med*, 1970. **76**: 85-91.

98. Schlosstein, L.H., Kippen, I., Whitehouse, M.W., Bluestone, R., Paulus, H.E. and Klinenberg, J.R., "Studies with Some Novel Uricosuric Agents and their Metabolites: Correlation between Clinical Activity and Drug-Induced Displacement of Urate from Its Albumin-Binding Sites." *J Lab Clin Med*, 1971. **82**: 412-418.

99. Campion, D.S., Bluestone, R. and Klinenberg, J.R., "Uric Acid. Characterization of its Interaction with Human Serum Albumin." *J Clin Invest*, 1973. **52**: 2383-2387.

100. Lorber, A., Cohen, R.L., Chang, C.C. and Anderson, H.E., "Gold Determination in Biological Fluids by Atomic Absorption Spectrophotometry: Application to Chrysotherapy in Rheumatoid Arthritis Patients." *Arthritis Rheum*, 1968. **11**: 170-177.

101. Lorber, A., Simon, T.M., Leeb, J. and Carroll, P.E., Jr., "Chrysotherapy: Pharmacological and Clinical Correlates." *J Rheumatol*, 1975. **2**: 401-410.

102. Lorber, A., Simon, T., Leeb, J., Peter, A. and Wilcox, S., "Chrysotherapy. Suppression of Immunoglobulin Synthesis." *Arthritis Rheum*, 1978. **21**: 785-791.

103. Lorber, A., Simon, T.M., Leeb, J., Peter, A. and Wilcox, S.A., "Effect of Chrysotherapy on Parameters of Immune Response." *J Rheumatol Suppl*, 1979. **5**: 82-90.

104. Lorber, A., Wilcox, S.A., Vibert, G.J. and Simon, T.M., "Carbon Rod Atomization Analysis: Application to in Vivo Lymphocyte Gold Quantitation." *J Rheumatol Suppl*, 1979. **5**: 31-39.

105. Lorber, A., Wilcox, S., Leeb, J. and Simon, T., "Quantitation of Gold Lymphocyte Binding during Chrysotherapy." *J Rheumatol*, 1979. **6**: 270-276.

106. Dietz, A.A. and Rubinstein, H.M., "Serum Gold. I. Estimation by Atomic Absorption Spectroscopy." *Ann Rheum Dis*, 1973. **32**: 124-127.

107. Rubinstein, H.M. and Dietz, A.A., "Serum Gold. II. Levels in Rheumatoid Arthritis." *Ann Rheum Dis*, 1973. **32**: 128-132.

108. Maricq, H.R., "Capillary Morphology and the Course of Illness in Schizophrenic Patients." *J Nerv Ment Dis*, 1966. **142**: 63-71.

109. Maricq, H.R. and LeRoy, E.C., "Patterns of Finger Capillary Abnormalities in Connective Tissue Disease by 'Wide-Field' Microscopy." *Arthritis Rheum*, 1973. **16**: 619-628.

110. Panush, R.S. and Anthony, C.R., "Effects of Acetylsalicylic Acid on Normal Human Peripheral Blood Lymphocytes. Inhibition of Mitogen- and Antigen-Stimulated Incorporation of Tritiated Thymidine." *Clin Exp Immunol*, 1976. **23**: 114-125.

111. Anthony, C.R. and Panush, R.S., "Interaction of [^{14}C]Acetylsalicylic Acid with Normal Human Peripheral Blood Lymphocytes." *Clin Exp Immunol*, 1978. **31**: 482-489.

112. Panush, R.S., "Effects of Certain Antirheumatic Drugs on Normal Human Peripheral Blood Lymphocytes. Inhibition of Mitogen- and Antigen-Stimulated Incorporation of Tritiated Thymidine." *Arthritis Rheum*, 1976. **19**: 907-917.

113. Lloyd, T.M. and Panush, R.S., "Cell Mediated Immunity in Rheumatoid Arthritis: Impaired Lymphocyte Responsiveness, Humoral Immunosuppressants, and Correlations with Clinical Status in Patients Off Drug Therapy." *J Rheumatol*, 1977. **4**: 231-244.

114. Panush, R.S. and Ossakow, S.J., "Effects of Acetaminophen on Normal Human Peripheral Blood Lymphocytes: Enhancement of Mitogen- and Antigen-Stimulated Incorporation of Tritiated Thymidine." *Clin Exp Immunol*, 1979. **38**: 539-548.

115. Panush, R.S., "Clinical Drug Efficacy and in Vitro Inhibition of Lymphocyte Responses in Rheumatoid Arthritis." *Arthritis Rheum*, 1978. **21**: 171-173.

116. Panush, R.S., Katz, P. and Longley, S., "In Vitro Immunoglobulin Production by Mononuclear Cells in Rheumatoid Arthritis." *Clin Immunol Immunopathol*, 1983. **28**: 252-264.

117. Panush, R.S., Bittner, A.K., Sullivan, M., Katz, P. and Longley, S., "IgM Rheumatoid Factor Elaboration by Blood, Bone Marrow, and Synovial Mononuclear Cells in Patients with Rheumatoid Arthritis." *Clin Immunol Immunopathol*, 1985. **34**: 387-391.

118. Panush, R.S., Carter, R.L., Katz, P., Kowsari, B., Longley, S. and Finnie, S., "Diet Therapy for Rheumatoid Arthritis." *Arthritis Rheum*, 1983. **26**: 462-471.

119. Panush, R.S., Stroud, R.M. and Webster, E.M., "Food-Induced (Allergic) Arthritis. Inflammatory Arthritis Exacerbated by Milk." *Arthritis Rheum*, 1986. **29**: 220-226.

120. Panush, R.S., "Food Induced ('Allergic') Arthritis: Clinical and Serologic Studies." *J Rheumatol*, 1990. **17**: 291-294.

121. Panush, R.S., Webster, E.M., Endo, L.P., Greer, J.M. and Woodard, J.C., "Food Induced ('Allergic') Arthritis: Inflammatory Synovitis in Rabbits." *J Rheumatol*, 1990. **17**: 285-290.

122. Darlington, L.G., Ramsey, N.W. and Mansfield, J.R., "Placebo-Controlled, Blind Study of Dietary Manipulation Therapy in Rheumatoid Arthritis." *Lancet*, 1986. **1**: 236-238.

123. Darlington, L.G., "Dietary Therapy for Rheumatoid Arthritis." *Clin Exp Rheumat*, 1994. **12**: 235-239.

124. Kjeldsen-Kragh, J., Haugen, M., Borchgrevink, C.F. and Forre, Ø., "Vegetarian Diet for Patients with Rheumatoid Arthritis - Status Two Years after Introduction of the Diet." *Clin Rheumat*, 1994. **13**: 475-482.

125. Kjeldsen-Kragh, J., Mellbye, O.J., Mollnes, T.E., Hammer, H.B., Sioud, M. and Forre, Ø., "Changes in Laboratory Variables in Rheumatoid Arthritis Patients During a Trial of Fasting and One-Year Vegetarian Diet." *Scand J Rheum*, 1995. **24**: 85-93.

126. Weiss, T.E., Maxfield, W.S., Murison, P.J. and Hidalgo, J.U., "Iodinated Human Serum Albumin (I^{131}) Localization Studies of Rheumatoid Arthritis Joints by Scintillation Scanning." *Arthritis Rheum*, 1965. **8**: 976-987.

127. Green, F.A. and Hays, M.T., "Joint Scanning: Mechanism and Application." *Arthritis Rheum*, 1969. **12**: 299 (abstract).

128. Hays, M.T. and Green, F.A., "The Pertechnetate Joint Scan. I. Timing." *Ann Rheum Dis*, 1972. **31**: 272-277.

129. Green, F.A. and Hays, M.T., "The Pertechnetate Joint Scan. II. Clinical Correlations." *Ann Rheum Dis*, 1972. **31**: 278-281.

130. Cohen, M.B. and Lorber, A., "Avoiding False-Positive Joint Scans by the Use of Labeled Albumins." *Arthritis Rheum*, 1971. **14**: 32-40.

131. Green, F.A., "Joint Scintiscans: Present Status." *J Rheumatol*, 1979. **6**: 370-373.

132. Rosenspire, K.C., Kennedy, A.C., Russomanno, L., Steinbach, J., Blau, M. and Green, F.A., "Comparison of Four Methods of Analysis of ^{99m}Tc Pyrophosphate Uptake in Rheumatoid Arthritic Joints." *J Rheumatol*, 1980. **7**: 461-468.

133. Rosenspire, K.C., Kennedy, A.C., Steinbach, J., Blau, M. and Green, F.A., "Investigation of the Metabolic Activity of Bone in Rheumatoid Arthritis." *J Rheumatol*, 1980. **7**: 469-473.

134. Resnick, D. and Niwayama, G., *Diagnosis of Bone and Joint Disorders*. First ed. W.B. Saunders, 1981

135. Resnick, D. and Niwayama, G., *Diagnosis of Bone and Joint Disorders*. Second ed. W.B. Saunders, 1988

136. Resnick, D. and Niwayama, G., *Diagnosis of Bone and Joint Disorders.* Third ed. W.B. Saunders, 1996

137. Resnick, D., "Patterns of Peripheral Joint Disease in Ankylosing Spondylitis." *Radiology*, 1974. **110**: 523-532.

138. Resnick, D., Shaul, S.R. and Robins, J.M., "Diffuse Idiopathic Skeletal Hyperostosis (DISH): Forestier's Disease with Extraspinal Manifestations." *Radiology*, 1975. **115**: 513-524.

139. Resnick, D., Niwayama, G., Goergen, T.G., Utsinger, P.D., Shapiro, R.F., Haselwood, D.H. and Wiesner, K.B., "Clinical, Radiographic and Pathologic Abnormalities in Calcium Pyrophosphate Dihydrate Deposition Disease (CPPD): Pseudogout." *Radiology*, 1977. **122**: 1-15.

140. Resnick, D., Feingold, M.L., Curd, J., Niwayama, G. and Goergen, T.G., "Calcaneal Abnormalities in Articular Disorders. Rheumatoid Arthritis, Ankylosing Spondylitis, Psoriatic Arthritis, and Reiter Syndrome." *Radiology*, 1977. **125**: 355-366.

141. Naides, S.J., Resnick, D. and Zvaifler, N.J., "Idiopathic Regional Osteoporosis: A Clinical Spectrum." *J Rheum*, 1985. **12**: 763-768.

142. Sartoris, D.J. and Resnick, D., "MR Imaging of the Musculoskeletal System: Current and Future Status." *Am J Roent*, 1987. **149**: 457-467.

143. Resnick, D., "Common Disorders of Synovium-Lined Joints: Pathogenesis, Imaging Abnormalities, and Complications." *Am J Roent*, 1988. **151**: 1079-1093.

144. Habibian, A., Stauffer, A., Resnick, D., Reicher, M.A., Rafii, M., Kellerhouse, L., Zlatkin, M.B., Newman, C. and Sartoris, D.J., "Comparison of Conventional and Computed Arthrotomography with MR Imaging in the Evaluation of the Shoulder." *J Comput Assist Tomogr*, 1989. **13**: 968-975.

145. Postlethwaite, A.E. and Kang, A.H., "Collagen-and Collagen Peptide-Induced Chemotaxis of Human Blood Monocytes." *J Exp Med*, 1976. **143**: 1299-1307.

146. Stuart, J.M., Postlethwaite, A.E. and Kang, A.H., "Evidence for Cell-Mediated Immunity to Collagen in Progressive Systemic Sclerosis." *J Lab Clin Med*, 1976. **88**: 601-607.

147. Postlethwaite, A.E., Snyderman, R. and Kang, A.H., "The Chemotactic Attraction of Human Fibroblasts to a Lymphocyte-Derived Factor." *J Exp Med*, 1976. **144**: 1188-1203.

148. Chiang, T.M., Postlethwaite, A.E., Beachey, E.H., Seyer, J.M. and Kang, A.H., "Binding of Chemotactic Collagen-Derived Peptides to Fibroblasts. The Relationship to Fibroblast Chemotaxis." *J Clin Invest*, 1978. **62**: 916-922.

149. Trentham, D.E., Townes, A.S. and Kang, A.H., "Autoimmunity to Type II Collagen: An Experimental Model of Arthritis." *J Exp Med*, 1977. **146**: 857-868.

150. Trentham, D.E., Townes, A.S., Kang, A.H. and David, J.R., "Humoral and Cellular Sensitivity to Collagen in Type II Collagen- Induced Arthritis in Rats." *J Clin Invest*, 1978. **61**: 89-96.

151. Stuart, J.M., Townes, A.S. and Kang, A.H., "Nature and Specificity of the Immune Response to Collagen in Type II Collagen Induced Arthritis in Mice." *J Clin Invest*, 1982. **69**: 673-683.

152. Stuart, J.M., Cremer, M.A., Dixit, S.N., Kang, A.H. and Townes, A.S., "Collagen-Induced Arthritis in Rats. Comparison of Vitreous and Cartilage-Derived Collagens." *Arthritis Rheum*, 1979. **22**: 347-352.

153. Stuart, J.M., Cremer, M.A., Kang, A.H. and Townes, A.S., "Collagen-Induced Arthritis in Rats. Evaluation of Early Immunologic Events." *Arthritis Rheum*, 1979. **22**: 1344-1351.

154. Cremer, M.A., Pitcock, J.A., Stuart, J.M., Kang, A.H. and Townes, A.S., "Auricular Chondritis in Rats. An Experimental Model of Relapsing Polychondritis Induced with Type II Collagen." *J Exp Med*, 1981. **154**: 535-540.

155. Stuart, J.M., Cremer, M.A., Townes, A.S. and Kang, A.H., "Type II Collagen-Induced Arthritis in Rats. Passive Transfer with Serum and Evidence That IgG Anticollagen Antibodies Can Cause Arthritis." *J Exp Med*, 1982. **155**: 1-16.

156. Cremer, M.A., Hernandez, A.D., Townes, A.S., Stuart, J.M. and Kang, A.H., "Collagen-Induced Arthritis in Rats: Antigen-Specific Suppression of Arthritis and Immunity by Intravenously Injected Native Type II Collagen." *J Immunol*, 1983. **131**: 2995-3000.

157. Cremer, M.A., Townes, A.S. and Kang, A.H., "Adjuvant-Induced Arthritis in Rats. Evidence That Autoimmunity to Homologous Types I, II,IX and XI is not Involved in the Pathogenesis of Arthritis." *Clin Exp Immunol*, 1990. **82**: 307-312.

158. Yoo, T.J., Kim, S.Y., Stuart, J.M., Floyd, R.D., Olson, G.A., Cremer, M.A. and Kang, A.H., "Induction of Arthritis in Monkeys by Immunization with Type II Collagen." *J Exp Med*, 1988. **168**: 777-782.

159. Terato, K., Arai, H., Shimozuru, Y., fukuda, T. and Cremer, M.A., "Sex-Linked Difference in Susceptibility of Cynomolgus Monkeys to Type II Collagen-Induced Arthritis." *Arthritis Rheum*, 1989. **32**: 748-758.

160. Stuart, J.M., Huffstutter, E.H., Townes, A.S. and Kang, A.H., "Incidence and Specificity of Antibodies to Types I, II, III, IV and V Collagen in Rheumatoid Arthritis and Other Rheumatic Diseases as Measured by ^{125}I-Radioimmunoassay." *Arthritis Rheum*, 1983. **26**: 832-840.

161. Hasty, K.A., Reife, R.A., Kang, A.H. and Stuart, J.M., "The Role of Stromelysin in the Cartilage Destruction That Accompanies Inflammatory Arthritis." *Arthritis Rheum*, 1990. **33**: 388-397.

162. Mannik, M., Arend, W.P., Hall, A.P. and others, "Studies on Antigen-Antibody Complexes. 1. Elimination of Soluble Complexes from the Circulation." *J Exp Med*, 1971. **133**: 713-739.

163. Arend, W.P. and Mannik, M., "In Vitro Adherence of Soluble Immune Complexes to Macrophages." *J Exp Med*, 1972. **136**: 514-531.

164. Arend, W.P. and Mannik, M., "The Macrophage Receptor for IgG: Number and Affinity of Binding Sites." *J Immunol*, 1973. **110**: 1455-1463.

165. Arend, W.P. and Mannik, M., "Determination of Soluble Immune Complex Molar Composition and Antibody Association Constants by Ammonium Sulfate Precipitation." *J Immunol*, 1974. **112**: 451-461.

166. Arend, W.P. and Sturge, J.C., "Composition and Biologic Properties of Soluble IgG-Anti-IgG Immune Complexes: Effects of Variations in the Specificity of Rabbit Antibodies to Different Structural Components of Human IgG." *J Immunol*, 1979. **123**: 447-454.

167. Ragsdale, C.G. and Arend, W.P., "Neutral Protease Secretion by Human Monocytes. Effect of Surface-Bound Immune Complexes." *J Exp Med*, 1979. **149**: 954-968.

168. Ragsdale, C.G. and Arend, W.P., "Loss of Fc Receptor Activity after Culture of Human Monocytes on Surface-Bound Immune Complexes. Mediation by Cyclic Nucleotides." *J Exp Med*, 1980. **151**: 32-44.

169. Starkebaum, G., Price, T.H., Lee, M.Y. and Arend, W.P., "Autoimmune Neutropenia in Systematic Lupus Erythematosus." *Arthritis Rheum*, 1978. **21**: 504-512.

170. Starkebaum, G. and Arend, W.P., "Neutrophil-Binding Immunoglobulin G in Systemic Lupus Erythematosus." *J Clin Invest*, 1979. **64**: 902-912.

171. Starkebaum, G., Singer, J.W. and Arend, W.P., "Humoral and Cellular Immune Mechanisms of Neutropenia in Patients with Felty's Syndrome." *Clin Exp Immunol*, 1980. **39**: 307-314.

172. Starkebaum, G., Arend, W.P., Nardella, F.A. and Gavin, S.E., "Characterization of Immune Complexes and Immunoglobulin G Antibodies Reactive with Neutrophils in the Sera of Patients with Felty's Syndrome." *J Lab Clin Med*, 1980. **96**: 238-251.

173. Goldschmeding, R., Breedveld, F.C., Engelfriet, C.P. and von dem Borne, A.E., "Lack of Evidence for the Presence of Neutrophil Autoantibodies in the Serum of Patients with Felty's Syndrome." *Brit J Haemat*, 1988. **68**: 37-40.

174. Talal, N. and Bunim, J.J., "The Development of Malignant Lymphoma in the Course of Sjogren's Syndrome." *Am J Med*, 1964. **36**: 529-540.

175. Talal, N., Sylvester, R.A., Daniels, T.E., Greenspan, J.S. and Williams, R.C., Jr., "T and B Lymphocytes in Peripheral Blood and Tissue Lesions in Sjogren's Syndrome." *J Clin Invest*, 1974. **53**: 180-189.

176. Michalski, J.P., Daniels, T.E., Talal, N. and Grey, H.M., "Beta$_2$ Microglobulin and Lymphocytic Infiltration in Sjogren's Syndrome." *N Engl J Med*, 1975. **293**: 1228-1231.

177. Zulman, J., Jaffe, R. and Talal, N., "Evidence that the Malignant Lymphoma of Sjogren's Syndrome is a Monoclonal B-Cell Neoplasm." *N Engl J Med*, 1978. **299**: 1215-1220.

178. DeHoratius, R.J. and Messner, R.P., "Lymphocytotoxic Antibodies in Family Members of Patients with Systemic Lupus Erythematosus." *J Clin Invest*, 1975. **55**: 1254-1258.

179. DeHoratius, R.J., Pillarisetty, R., Messner, R.P. and Talal, N., "Anti-Nucleic Acid Antibodies in Systemic Lupus Erythematosus Patients and Their Families. Incidence and Correlation with Lymphocytotoxic Antibodies." *J Clin Invest*, 1975. **56**: 1149-1154.

180. Attias, M.R., Sylvester, R.A. and Talal, N., "Filter Radioimmunoassay for Antibodies to Reovirus RNA in Systemic Lupus Erythematosus." *Arthritis Rheum*, 1973. **16**: 719-725.

181. Feldmann, J.L., Becker, M.J., Moutsopoulos, H., Fye, K., Blackman, M., Epstein, W.V. and Talal, N., "Antibody-Dependent Cell-Mediated Cytotoxicity in Selected Autoimmune Diseases." *J Clin Invest*, 1976. **58**: 173-179.

182. Goodman, J.R., Sylvester, R.A., Talal, N. and Tuffanelli, D.L., "Virus-Like Structures in Lymphocytes of Patients with Systemic and Discoid Lupus Erythematosus." *Ann Intern Med*, 1973. **79**: 396-402.

183. Roubinian, J.R., Papoian, R. and Talal, N., "Androgenic Hormones Modulate Autoantibody Responses and Improve Survival in Murine Lupus." *J Clin Invest*, 1977. **59**: 1066-1070.

184.   Roubinian, J.R., Talal, N., Greenspan, J.S., Goodman, J.R. and Siiteri, P.K., "Effect of Castration and Sex Hormone Treatment on Survival, Anti- Nucleic Acid Antibodies, and Glomerulonephritis in NZB/NZW F1 Mice." *J Exp Med*, 1978. **147**: 1568-1583.

185.   Roubinian, J.R., Talal, N., Greenspan, J.S., Goodman, J.R. and Siiteri, P.K., "Delayed Androgen Treatment Prolongs Survival in Murine Lupus." *J Clin Invest*, 1979. **63**: 902-911.

186.   Barry, N.N., McGuire, J.L. and Van Vollenhoven, R.F., "Dehydroepiandrosterone in Systemic Lupus Erythematosus: Relationship between Dosage, Serum Levels, and Clinical Response." *J Rheum*, 1998. **25**: 2352-2356.

187.   Lahita, R.G., Cheng, C.Y., Monder, C. and Bardin, C.W., "Experience with 19-Nortestosterone in the Therapy of Systemic Lupus Erythematosus: Worsening Disease after Treatment with 19-Nortestosterone in Men and Lack of Improvement in Women." *J Rheum*, 1992. **19**: 547-555.

188.   Miyasaka, N., Seaman, W., Bakashi, A., Sauvezie, B., Strand, W., Pope, R. and Talal, N., "Natural Killing Activity in Sjogren's Syndrome." *Arthritis Rheum*, 1983. **26**: 954-960.

189.   Struyf, N.J., Snoeck, H.W., Bridts, C.H., DeClerck, L.S. and Stevens, W.J., "Natural Killer Cell Activity in Sjogren's Syndrome and Systemic Lupus Erythematosus: Stimulation with Interferons and Interleukin-2 and Correlation with Immune Complexes." *Ann Rheum Dis*, 1990. **49**: 690-693.

190.   Combe, B., Pope, R., Darnell, B., Kincaid, W. and Talal, N., "Regulation of Natural Killer Cell Activity by Macrophages in the Rheumatoid Joint and Peripheral Blood." *J Immunol*, 1984. **133**: 709-713.

191.   Tovar, Z., Pope, R.M. and Talal, N., "Modulation of Spontaneous Immunoglobulin Production by Natural Killer Cells in Rheumatoid Arthritis." *Arthritis Rheum*, 1986. **29**: 1435-1439.

192.   Dauphinée, M.J., Tovar, Z. and Talal, N., "B Cells Expressing CD5 Are Increased in Sjogren's Syndrome." *Arthritis Rheum*, 1988. **31**: 642-647.

193.   Dauphinée, M.J., Tovar, Z., Ballester, A. and Talal, N., "The Expression and Function of CD3 and CD5 in Patients with Primary Sjogren's Syndrome." *Arthritis Rheum*, 1989. **32**: 420-429.

194.   Talal, N., Dauphinée, M.J., Dang, H., Alexander, S.S., Hart, D.J. and Garry, R.F., "Detection of Serum Antibodies to Retroviral Proteins in Patients with Primary Sjogren's Syndrome (Autoimmune Exocrinopathy)." *Arthritis Rheum*, 1990. **33**: 774-781.

195.   Rodnan, G.P., Benedek, T.G., Medsger, T.A., Jr. and Cammarata, R.J., "The Association of Progressive Systemic Sclerosis (Scleroderma) with Coal Miners' Pneumoconiosis and Other Forms of Silicosis." *Ann Intern Med*, 1967. **66**: 323-334.

196.   Rodnan, G.P. and Benedek, T.G., "An Historical Account of the Study of Progressive Systemic Sclerosis (Diffuse Scleroderma)." *Ann Intern Med*, 1962. **57**: 305-319.

197.   Benedek, T.G. and Rodnan, G.P., "Petrarch on Medicine and the Gout." *Bull Hist Med*, 1963. **37**: 397-416.

198.   Rodnan, G.P., Benedek, T.G. and Panetta, W.C., "The Early History of Synovia (Joint Fluid)." *Ann Intern Med*, 1966. **65**: 821-842.

199.   Rodnan, G.P. and Benedek, T.G., "The Early History of Antirheumatic Drugs." *Arthritis Rheum*, 1970. **13**: 145-165.

621

200.   Benedek, T.G., "Rheumatoid Pneumoconiosis. Documentation of Onset and Pathogenic Considerations." *Am J Med*, 1973. **55**: 515-524.

201.   Benedek, T.G., Zawadzki, Z.A. and Medsger, T.A., Jr., "Serum Immunoglobulins, Rheumatoid Factor, and Pneumoconiosis in Coal Miners with Rheumatoid Arthritis." *Arthritis Rheum*, 1976. **19**: 731-736.

202.   Jacobson, B.E. and Lockitch, G., "Direct Determination of Selenium in Serum by Graphite-Furnace Atomic Absorption Spectrophotometry with Deuterium Background Correction." *Clin Chem*, 1988. **34**: 709-714.

LaVergne, TN USA
08 July 2010
188839LV00001B/1/P